REFERENCE SERIES

The United States Air Force and Humanitarian Airlift Operations 1947–1994

by

Daniel L. Haulman

Air Force Historical Research Agency
Maxwell Air Force Base, Alabama

AIR FORCE HISTORY AND MUSEUMS PROGRAM
Washington, D.C.
1998

Published by Books Express Publishing
Copyright © Books Express, 2011
ISBN 978-1-780394-47-3

Books Express publications are available from all good retail
and online booksellers. For publishing proposals and direct
ordering please contact us at: info@books-express.com

Foreword

This book supplements previous reference works produced by the Air Force Historical Research Agency through the Air Force History Support Office for Air Force and general public use. These works include publications about Air Force organizations, unit lineage and honors histories, air bases, campaigns, chronologies, contingencies, and aerial victory credits. These materials provide data for those who will make decisions about future Air Force structures and operations and for service members who need reference information about the past. The present volume covers an often overlooked category of Air Force operations: humanitarian airlift.

The USAF has participated in hundreds of major humanitarian airlift operations since its birth. These airlifts have saved the lives of thousands of people in the United States and abroad and have served as tools of U.S. diplomacy, demonstrating the versatility of air power not only as a weapon of war but also as an instrument of peace. The future will continue to demand humanitarian airlift operations, and this book will help planners to appreciate, in quantitative and qualitative terms, how these operations were conducted in the past.

Acknowledgments

I am indebted to many individuals and organizations for providing information, advice, and encouragement. I worked under the overall leadership of two commanders of the Air Force Historical Research Agency, Col. Richard S. Rauschkolb and Col. Elliot V. Converse III. The agency's senior historian, Mr. Warren A. Trest; the heads of the Research Division, Dr. Frederick J. Shaw and Mr. R. Cargill Hall; and the Organizational History Branch chief, Dr. A. Timothy Warnock, and fellow historians Mr. Edward T. Russell and Ms. Judy G. Endicott all provided much valuable guidance. I also appreciate very much the support and advice of personnel of the Air Force History Support Office, including Air Force Historian Dr. Richard P. Hallion, Senior Historian Mr. Herman S. Wolk, Mr. Lawrence R. Benson, and Mr. Jacob Neufeld.

Field historians supplied much information. They include, among many others, Dr. Jay H. Smith, Dr. John W. Leland, Dr. Kent M. Beck, Dr. Robert D. Brunkow, and Ms. Margaret J. Nigra of the Military Airlift Command and Air Mobility Command; Mr. Herbert A. Mason, Jr., of the Air Force Special Operations Command; Dr. Timothy R. Keck of the Pacific Air Forces; and Dr. Daniel F. Harrington and Ms. Carol H. Parks of the U.S. Air Forces in Europe. Dr. Charles F. O'Connell, Jr., and Dr. Kenneth C. Kan of the Air Force Reserve history office and SMSgt. Windell R. Mimms, Jr., of the Air National Guard history office also provided significant data on recent airlifts. I am indebted to them all. I also appreciate the editorial advice of Ms. Shelley L. Davis and Dr. Priscilla D. Jones, who reviewed the manuscript and recommended changes that streamlined and improved the book.

Preface

Historians have written extensively about the United States Air Force as an instrument of war, focusing on aerial combat, bombing, strafing, and the transportation of troops and weapons. They have written less about the role of the USAF in supporting disaster relief operations, in helping emerging nations meet the needs of their citizens, and in feeding the hungry anywhere in the world—missions which are cumulatively known as humanitarian airlift. One might even think this is a new role for the U.S. military. This book attempts to fill a historical gap by addressing humanitarian airlift missions as an important part of Air Force heritage.

Rarely acting alone in conducting humanitarian relief efforts, the U.S. Air Force has served with the U.S. Army, Navy, Marine Corps, and Coast Guard. It has worked with other federal agencies such as the Federal Emergency Management Agency, the State Department, and the Agency for International Development. It has also interacted with private charitable organizations.

Air Force humanitarian airlift operations include providing assistance at home and abroad. In the event of a domestic disaster, the federal government follows a procedure first defined by the Federal Disaster Act of 1950. After an emergency, a governor requests federal assistance and the president declares the region a federal disaster area. In recent decades, the Federal Emergency Management Agency has coordinated domestic disaster relief, often requesting the support of the Department of Defense for airlift missions.

In the case of an international disaster, a foreign government requests relief through the U.S. embassy, permitting the State Department's Agency for International Development and its Office of Foreign Disaster Assistance to coordinate the relief effort. Both organizations have used the USAF for airlift when commercial aircraft were not available or could not perform the mission. In recent years, the Department of Defense established its own office of humanitarian assistance to coordinate congressionally-mandated transport of privately donated relief supplies and distribution of excess nonlethal Defense Department cargo.

The Military Airlift Command dominated, but did not monopolize, humanitarian airlifts during the Cold War. Other Air Force commands, such as U.S. Air Forces in Europe, Pacific Air Forces, Tactical Air Command, Alaskan Air Command, Caribbean Air Command, Southern Air Command, and Air Mobility Command took part in significant relief flights. Air Force Reserve and Air National Guard crews and aircraft also participated in many operations, either independently or by complementing active organizations.

Preface

Criteria

Humanitarian airlift as described in this book includes the following types of operations:

1.   Airlift of relief workers, equipment, or supplies to victims of natural disasters, major accidents, civil conflicts, or political emergencies.

2.   Air evacuation from dangerous areas.

3.   Aerial spraying of insecticide or fire-retardant chemicals.

4.   Air rescue from shipwrecks, flooded areas, or other emergency situations.

5.   Airdrops of food to snowbound livestock.

The following types of operations are not included in this book:

1.   Movement of peacekeeping or peacemaking troops, or of former prisoners of war.

2.   Military aeromedical evacuations or air rescues.

3.   Routine supply missions to scientific research stations.

4.   Routine airlifts, such as airdrops of Christmas bundles.

5.   Relief operations not involving airlift, such as land delivery of supplies to storm victims near Air Force installations.

6.   Deliveries of supplies to combat troops.

7.   Hurricane tracking missions.

Categories and Definitions

For each mission, information is arranged in eight categories: the name of the operation, the location of the airlift, the date(s) of the airlift, the nature of the emergency, the Air Force organization(s) involved, the type and amount of cargo airlifted, the type and number of aircraft employed, and a narrative description of operations.

Relatively few relief operations earned official names; the designation of most derived from the disasters or emergencies that engendered them. The location and date of an operation refer not to the disaster or emergency, but to the relief mission that followed. The location refers to the destination of cargo, not its point of origin. The date does not include return flights after cargo deliveries.

The names of many countries changed between 1947 and 1994. To avoid confusion, the category descriptions use the name of the country as it was at the time of the airlift.

In describing damage caused by earthquakes, the text often refers to the Richter scale. Devised by Dr. Charles F. Richter of the California Institute of Technology, this logarithmic scale has graded steps for expressing the magnitude of an earthquake. Each whole number increment represents an enormous increase in magnitude, with a 4.5 earthquake causing slight damage and an 8.5 earthquake causing very devastating damage.

Air Force organizations listed include only those that actually flew airlift missions. The category "Aircraft Employed" includes both the type and the number of aircraft. If one C–130 delivered relief supplies on three separate flights, only one C–130 is listed. In a few cases, available source material provided only the total number of missions per aircraft type. In these cases, the number of missions rather than the number of aircraft is indicated. Civilian aircraft chartered by the Air Force are not listed.

Some entries indicate the amount of financial damage sustained during the emergency. These amounts have not been adjusted for inflation, so the reader should not attempt to compare economic losses for various disasters from the figures provided.

Organization

This book is divided into seven chapters. Each describes humanitarian airlifts in a specific region: North America (United States and Canada); Latin America (including Mexico and Central America); Europe; Africa; southwest Asia; east Asia; and the Pacific (including Australia). In each chapter, humanitarian airlifts are listed chronologically.

Contents

List of Illustrations

After page 374

Introduction

Humanitarian airlift is a U.S. tradition older than the U.S. Air Force. It is almost as old as military aviation itself. Just twelve years after the establishment in 1907 of the Signal Corps' Aeronautical Division, the airplane became an instrument of disaster relief. Humanitarian airlift missions continued through the Roaring Twenties and the Great Depression. Even the vast commitments of World War II did not halt humanitarian airlifts by the U.S. military. The USAF continued the relief airlift tradition during the Cold War and beyond, conducting about 560 relief airlifts in the years between its establishment in 1947 as an independent service and 1994.

Humanitarian Airlift Before 1947

As early as 1919, U.S. Army aircraft from Kelly Field, Texas, dropped food to marooned flood victims along the Rio Grande. Three years later, aircraft from Crissy Field, California, flew rescue workers to a mine where 48 miners were trapped 500 feet underground.[1]

Many early domestic humanitarian flights were flown in response to winter emergencies. In March 1923, Aberdeen Proving Ground in Maryland sent airplanes to bomb an ice jam on the Delaware River. The next month, an aircraft from Chanute Field, Illinois, dropped food to marooned people on South Fox Island in Lake Michigan. In March 1924, aircraft from Chanute Field and Fort Riley, Kansas, saved Union Pacific railroad bridges by bombing an ice jam on the Platte River. Two years later, aircraft from Aberdeen Proving Ground bombed an ice jam on the Susquehanna River in Pennsylvania. When flooding stranded hundreds of people in southern Alabama in March 1929, airplanes from Maxwell Field dropped relief supplies to them.[2]

Humanitarian flights continued in the 1930s, responding to a series of natural disasters. After severe blizzards hit the southwest in 1932, aircraft from the Army's 11th Bombardment Squadron dropped food to snowbound and starving native Americans in Arizona, New Mexico, and Utah.[3] One of the most unusual humanitarian air operations took place in December 1935, when the 5th Bombardment Group bombed Mauna Loa in Hawaii to curb the volcano's lava flow and save the city of Hilo.[4] On February 9, 1936, the 96th Bombardment Squadron flew supplies to marooned residents on islands in the frozen Chesapeake Bay. The next month, the 96th Squadron, the 20th Bombardment Squadron, and the 103d Observation Squadron flew relief supplies to flood victims in Pennsylvania. Another flood in southern Illinois in early 1937 elicited a 9th Airship Squadron relief operation.[5]

Army aircraft also flew humanitarian missions to foreign nations before the establishment of the U.S. Air Force as an independent service in September 1947. In February 1939, the 2d Bombardment Wing delivered medical supplies to earthquake victims in Chile.[6] Four years later, in the midst of World War II, a B–24 from a base in Guatemala dropped a life raft with diphtheria vaccine to a destroyer escorting a British aircraft carrier. The destroyer delivered the vaccine to the carrier, preventing a shipboard epidemic.[7] In September 1944, Army Air Force planes dropped food to starving French citizens; in May 1945, B–17s delivered food to hungry people in the Netherlands in "Operation Chowhound."[8]

Army Air Force aircraft continued flying humanitarian missions after World War II. In February 1947, the Air Rescue Service (Air Rscu Svc) flew relief missions to Bolivia after a flood of the Mamore River.[9] In April 1947, the Tenth Air Force flew equipment, supplies, and workers from Kelly Field to Galveston, Texas, in response to a ship explosion and fire at nearby Texas City.

The Cold War

After the U.S. Air Force was established in 1947, it continued to fly the domestic humanitarian airlift operations conducted by its Army predecessors. U.S. citizens naturally expected the assistance of their armed forces after domestic emergencies, and the end of World War II made that assistance more readily available. Foreign policy developments in the late 1940s, however, expanded humanitarian airlift operations overseas as well.

In 1947, the United States introduced the Marshall Plan, offering to rebuild the war-shattered countries of Europe.[10] The Union of Soviet Socialist Republics (USSR) established puppet states in eastern Europe, precipitating a "Cold War" that lasted four decades and stimulated U.S. humanitarian airlifts. The Cold War compelled the United States to maintain a large peacetime military establishment for the first time in its history and sparked production of military cargo aircraft which, while designed to move troops and equipment to battle, could also deliver food, clothing, tents, and other relief supplies. The Cold War also stimulated the building and maintenance of a worldwide network of air bases that facilitated rapid relief for victims of foreign emergencies, both natural and man-made.

Finally, the Cold War encouraged U.S. political leaders to respond to the needs of developing nations in an effort to keep them from joining the Soviet camp. The fierce competition between the United States and the USSR spawned enormous financial expenditures and the acquisition and development of aircraft, bases, and personnel, which were used to respond to foreign disasters. In this way, preparedness for war saved thousands of lives.

The Utility of Humanitarian Airlift

Obviously, humanitarian airlift operations are of greatest and most direct benefit to the individual victims of disaster or emergency. For them, the rapid movement of cargo or personnel can make a life-or-death difference. But humanitarian airlift operations also benefit as a whole the countries to which they are directed. They allow foreign states to retain economic and political stability in the face of sudden challenge. Relief airlifts have strengthened nations that might be vulnerable to enemies, foreign or domestic. Allowed to fester, emergencies such as natural disasters sometimes fuel civil unrest, mass migrations, or epidemics, which can spill across international borders, threatening regional peace and security. By flying relief supplies to one nation, the United States often indirectly helps other nearby nations.

When the United States airlifts relief supplies to foreign nations, it also benefits itself. Humanitarian airlifts are diplomatic tools in the hands of the president and the State Department. Grateful recipients of relief have extended to the United States not only friendship but also increased trade, access to natural resources, support in international diplomacy, and basing privileges. By hastening another country's recovery from disaster, the United States is acting in its own economic and political interests.

Relief airlifts provide the Air Force with outstanding opportunities for military training, since airlifting refugees, bulldozers, and food is not much different from moving troops, tanks, and the materiel of war. U.S. aircrews who deliver relief supplies to remote disaster sites become familiar with techniques, locations, and conditions they might face in wartime. Nevertheless, in many cases, the United States responds to international emergencies when there is little to expect in return. This policy is rooted in the U.S. humanitarian tradition.

Adaptations for Humanitarian Airlift

From its inception in 1947, the U.S. Air Force has recognized the necessity and importance of airlift and has adapted structurally to achieve this mission. Composed of Air Force and Navy elements under the administrative supervision of the Air Force, the Military Air Transport Service (MATS) was established on June 1, 1948, to serve all branches of the armed forces. For the next decade, MATS consisted of the Continental, Atlantic, and Pacific Divisions. In 1958, the Pacific Division was dissolved, the Continental Division became the Western Transport Air Force, and the Atlantic Division became the Eastern Transport Air Force. In the 1960s, the Navy dropped out of MATS. In 1966, the Military Airlift Command (MAC) replaced MATS. The Western Transport Air Force became the Twenty-second Air Force and the Eastern Transport Air Force became the Twenty-first Air Force.

Humanitarian Airlift Operations

The year 1974 was a watershed for airlift. Air Force Reserve (AF Res) and Air National Guard (ANG) units began using their crews on a volunteer basis in foreign disaster relief operations,[11] and MAC gained command of reserve airlift units.[12] In December, Tactical Air Command (TAC) C–130 airlift assets transferred to MAC,[13] bringing all airlift assets, tactical and strategic, under centralized control for the first time. They remained under MAC until 1992.

In the 1980s, most humanitarian airlift operations were classified as special assignment airlift missions, resulting from a contract between MAC and other federal agencies which reimbursed MAC for each airlift. In 1984, government agencies outside the Department of Defense (DoD) were charged $3,540 per C–130 flying hour, $4,583 per C–141 flying hour, and $12,146 per C–5 flying hour.[14]

Congress passed two important pieces of legislation in 1985 and 1986 that expanded the humanitarian assistance role of the Defense Department. The Denton Amendment to a defense appropriations bill allowed the Air Force to transport privately donated humanitarian cargo on routine or training missions overseas at no charge to donors or recipients. The McCollum Amendment allowed surplus nonlethal DoD supplies to be airlifted to developing nations.[15]

The Goldwater-Nichols Defense Reorganization Act of 1986 changed the process by which DoD reacted to emergencies around the world. The chain of command now ran from the president through the secretary of defense to the theater commander, bypassing the Joint Chiefs of Staff. Airlift assignments no longer went through the chief of staff of the USAF. Joint task forces under theater commanders tapped Air Force elements for humanitarian and other contingency operations.

During the Cold War, the Air Force acquired larger and faster transport aircraft. By the late 1940s, the most common cargo airplanes were twin-engine C–47 Skytrains and four-engine C–54 Skymasters. Other transports of this period included twin-engine C–45 Expediters, C–82 Packets, C–46 Commandos, and four-engine C–74 Globemasters.

By the 1950s, several new transport aircraft had come into service, including the twin-engine C–119 Flying Boxcar—a descendant of the C–82—and the C–123 Provider. The Berlin Airlift had demonstrated the need for larger aircraft. In response, the Air Force acquired the huge, four-engine double-decked C–124 Globemaster II, which served as a strategic airlifter. In the same decade, many transports that had been used through the 1940s, including the C–45, C–46, C–54, C–72, and C–82, went out of service.[16]

The venerable C–130 Hercules, a four-engine turboprop, emerged in the 1950s to become the Air Force's favorite tactical airlifter through the rest of the century. The Hercules could carry large quantities of cargo to relatively small airfields in remote locations and was rugged enough to handle rough landings in combat zones and disaster areas.

4

In the 1960s, several new cargo aircraft entered the Air Force inventory. The most significant was the C–141 Starlifter, a four-engine jet giant designed to replace the C–124 for strategic airlift missions. The C–135 Stratolifter, a variant of the Boeing 707 jet airliner and the KC–135 refueler, was less common. Four-engine propeller aircraft, such as the C–118 Liftmaster and the C–121 Super Constellation, were also used. To move large cargo, the Air Force acquired the gigantic four-engine C–133 Cargomaster. The smaller, twin-engine C–7 Caribou supplemented the C–130 fleet for tactical airlift missions.

During the 1970s, many older cargo types, such as the C–47, C–118, C–119, and C–124, left the inventory of active Air Force units. The C–141s were modified with longer fuselages and air refueling equipment to extend their range and cargo capacity. Culminating the trend toward larger and faster strategic airlifters, the four-engine jet C–5 Galaxy appeared in the early 1980s to replace the C–133. At the time, the Galaxy was the largest aircraft in the world.

Despite the acquisition of larger transport planes during the Cold War, the Air Force never abandoned smaller aircraft, because many airstrips were too small to accommodate the large C–5s and C–141s. In many operations, larger aircraft unloaded relief supplies far from their final destination, shifting the cargo to smaller C–130s or to helicopters, which could move it to smaller airfields in the disaster area. For aeromedical evacuations, the Air Force acquired the twin-engine C–9 Nightingale.

After the Cold War

The Cold War ended not long after Mikhail Gorbachev came to power in the Soviet Union. Gorbachev pursued dramatic internal reforms and established a more cordial relationship with the United States. By the early 1990s, the reforms sparked revolutionary changes in the emerging nations of the former Soviet Union and in eastern Europe. Between 1989 and early 1993, communist governments collapsed in Poland, Hungary, Czechoslovakia, Romania, Yugoslavia, Bulgaria, East Germany, Albania, and the USSR. Gorbachev lost power to Boris Yeltsin, president of Russia. The Berlin Wall was torn down, the Warsaw Pact disintegrated, and Germany reunified. The collapse of communism released a tide of nationalism that split Czechoslovakia, Yugoslavia, and the Soviet Union into at least 21 new republics.

The end of the Cold War multiplied the humanitarian airlifts of the Air Force. The United States assisted its traditional friends, but also expanded its aid to some former adversaries. The Air Force encountered many airfields which had long been off limits to U.S. military aircraft. For the first time, the entire globe became the theater for U.S. relief flights. Between 1947 and 1987, the Air Force flew an average of fewer than 12 humanitarian airlifts per year. In 1991 and 1992, the average jumped to more than 20 airlifts each year.

Humanitarian Airlift Operations

As the demand for U.S. humanitarian airlift was increasing, the end of the Cold War brought a smaller military budget, reducing resources with which the Air Force could perform its traditional relief role. In the early 1990s, the service underwent a massive downsizing and reorganization, inactivating many organizations, including some airlift wings. At the same time, many U.S. military bases around the world prepared to close. In a very real sense, airlifters attempted to do "more with less."

In 1992, the Air Force modernized its airlift organization. For almost 20 years, MAC had had control of all airlift wings. On April 1, intratheater airlift transferred to theater control, and the United States Air Forces in Europe (USAFE) and the Pacific Air Forces (PACAF) each gained a C–130 wing.[17] The Air Force also disestablished the 322d and 834th Airlift Divisions (Alft Divs), which had managed airlift in the European and Pacific theaters.

On June 1, MAC itself was inactivated and was replaced by the Air Mobility Command (AMC).[18] This new command lacked some of the tactical airlift resources of its predecessor but gained some of the tanker assets from the inactivated Strategic Air Command (SAC), allowing it to join tankers and cargo transports under common management. That same year, AMC established a Tanker Airlift Control Center at Scott AFB, Illinois, to streamline use of Air Force airlift resources for theater commanders.[19]

In 1993, the reorganization of airlift assets continued. On October 1, remaining AMC C–130s were transferred to the Air Combat Command.[20] Relinquishing its Air Rscu Svc units to Air Combat Command allowed AMC to concentrate on strategic airlift.[21]

As the Regular Air Force grew smaller in the 1990s, it relied increasingly on AF Res and ANG personnel and resources. By May 1993, more than two-thirds of all airlift wings—44 of 58—belonged to the Guard and Reserve. They served with active duty units as part of an integrated total force.

As the Air Force entered the 1990s, it depended on three primary transport aircraft: the C–130 for tactical airlift and the C–141 and the C–5 for strategic airlift. In the 1990s, the C–17, which combined the large cross section of the C–5 with the short takeoff and landing capabilities of the C–130, entered the inventory. However, it was not produced in sufficient quantities to have much impact on humanitarian airlift operations. The first C–17 squadron became operational in January 1995.

By the early 1990s, the C–141 fleet was approaching the end of its useful life. To employ modern aircraft and to cut costs, AMC contracted with civilian airlines to perform routine missions and humanitarian airlifts. By the end of 1993, commercial aircraft assigned to the Civil Reserve Aircraft Fleet carried more passengers than military aircraft on AMC missions and up to 30 percent of the total cargo.[22]

Both major U.S. political parties recognize the value of humanitarian airlift as an instrument of national policy, and there have been no great fluctuations in the number of relief operations from administration to administration. The rate of natural disasters has had more effect on the frequency of humanitarian operations than have political changes in Washington, D.C.

The Air Force's global network of air bases has encouraged presidents to call on the service for a quick response to emergencies. Disaster strikes suddenly and time is often the most crucial factor in an emergency. While more personnel and cargo can be shipped by land or sea than by air, they cannot be shipped as rapidly. Some places can be reached only by air, particularly when blizzards, floods, or earthquakes cut surface supply routes. Sometimes, as in the Berlin blockade in 1948 and 1949, military forces block surface routes. Airlift allows the United States to reach isolated populations, bringing supplies necessary for survival.

Outstanding Airlifts

Of the more than 560 humanitarian airlift operations the Air Force has conducted since 1947, some stand out as especially significant. In terms of tonnage and aircraft, the Berlin Airlift was the largest in history. It demonstrated the utility of air power as a diplomatic instrument by sustaining two million people in West Berlin isolated by a Soviet blockade. The operation allowed the United States to fulfill a foreign policy objective without war.

Safe Haven in 1956 and 1957 moved more than 10,000 refugees from Europe to the United States after Soviet tanks crushed an anticommunist rebellion in Hungary. It allowed thousands to begin a new life and demonstrated America's commitment to freedom in the face of communism at the height of the Cold War.

Europe was not the only theater for humanitarian airlifts. In 1960, USAF cargo planes delivered over 1,000 tons of relief equipment and supplies to victims of a devastating series of earthquakes in Chile in an operation aptly called Amigos (friends). After terrible floods in South Vietnam in 1964, the Air Force evacuated 1,500 people and delivered more than 2,000 tons of humanitarian supplies.

The Air Force also conducted very large relief operations within the United States. For example, in 1949, USAF cargo planes dropped more than 4,700 tons of food to starving livestock in eight western states after a severe blizzard. After Hurricane Camille, which hit southern Mississippi in 1969, scores of USAF planes delivered more than 5,900 tons of vehicles, electric generators, food, clothing, medicine, and other relief equipment to the Gulf Coast.

Some of the largest humanitarian airlifts in the 1970s were flown to aid millions of famine victims in Africa. In 1973 and 1974, the Air Force flew more than 18,600 tons of food and relief supplies to Mali, Chad, and Mauritania, in operations called Authentic Assistance and King Grain.

Humanitarian Airlift Operations

When the government of South Vietnam fell to communist forces in 1975, the Air Force transported more than 50,000 refugees in four overlapping humanitarian airlift operations. Babylift, New Life, Frequent Wind, and New Arrivals also moved 8,000 tons of cargo, some of it to temporary refugee camps on islands in the Pacific.

Under the leadership of President George Bush, the United States flew several large humanitarian operations in the early 1990s. Provide Comfort, Provide Hope, Provide Promise, and Provide Relief airlifted tons of relief supplies to Kurds in western Turkey and northern Iraq, to the republics of the former Soviet Union, to Bosnia-Herzegovina in the former Yugoslavia, and to Somalian refugees. Provide Promise was the longest sustained humanitarian airlift in U.S. history.

During the Bush administration, the Air Force also flew several large domestic humanitarian airlifts. For example, in 1992, USAF cargo planes moved more than 28,000 tons of supplies and 12,000 passengers to relieve victims of Hurricane Andrew in south Florida and Typhoon Iniki in Hawaii.

President Bill Clinton continued the humanitarian airlift tradition by authorizing an airlift of more than 3,600 tons of relief supplies for thousands of Rwandan refugees in central Africa after an outbreak of ethnic violence forced them from their homes.

These examples are but a few of the largest humanitarian airlifts flown during the first 50 years of the USAF as an independent service. They demonstrate that when needed, the U.S. Air Force stands ready.

Notes

1. Maurer Maurer, *Aviation in the U.S. Army, 1919–1939* (Washington, D.C.: Office of Air Force History, 1987), pp. 143–45.

2. Ibid.; and Jerome Ennels, "Maxwell Flood Relief, 1929," *Air Power History*, Spring 1989, pp. 30–36.

3. Ernest La Rue Jones Collection, 168.6501–48, 1932–1935, and *Air Corps Newsletter*, 167.63, Jan. 25, 1932; both at Air Force Historical Research Agency (hereafter AFHRA), Maxwell AFB, Ala.

4. Maurer Maurer, *Air Force Combat Units of World War II* (Washington, D.C.: Office of Air Force History, 1983), p. 38.

5. Maurer Maurer, *Combat Squadrons of the Air Force, World War II* (Maxwell AFB, Ala.: USAF Historical Division, Air University, 1969), pp. 106, 188, 192, 320.

6. 2d Bomb Wing Supporting Document, WG–2–SU, AFHRA.

7. 40th Bomb Group Association, *Memories*, issue 25, Jan. 1989, p. 5.

8. 2d Air Division, lineage and honors history, attachment 2, AFHRA.

9. Donald D. Little, *Aerospace Rescue and Recovery Service, 1946–1981: An Illustrated Chronology* (Scott AFB, Ill.: Military Airlift Command History Office, 1981).

10. Bruce Nichols and Gil Loescher, eds., *The Moral Nation: Humanitarianism and U.S. Foreign Policy Today* (South Bend, Ind.: University of Notre Dame Press, 1989), p. 71.

11. USAF Southern Command History, July 1974–June 1975, vol. I, p. xxiv, AFHRA.

12. Eastern Air Force Reserve Region History, July–Dec. 1974, vol. I, p. 21, AFHRA.

13. Tactical Air Command History, July 1974–June 1975, vol. I, p. 99, AFHRA.

14. Military Airlift Command History, 1984, vol. I, p. 145, AFHRA.

15. Military Airlift Command History, 1988, vol. I, pp. 231–34, AFHRA.

16. Charles A. Ravenstein, *Air Force Combat Wings* (Washington, D.C.: Office of Air Force History, 1984).

17. United States Air Forces in Europe History, 1992, vol. I, p. 412, AFHRA.

18. Ibid., p. 340.

19. David J. Lynch, "When the Mission is Aid," *Air Force Magazine*, Feb. 1993, p. 63.

20. "C–130s Become ACC-gained," *Citizen Airman*, Jan. 1994, p. 24; and Jay Smith, AMC Command Historian, notes from AMC/HO.

21. "Restructuring: Air Rescue Service Realigns," *Airman*, Feb. 1993, p. 12.

22. Julie Bird, "Welcome to Mogadishu, Pentagon Style," *Air Force Times*, Oct. 25, 1993, p. 8; 438th Airlift Wing History, 1993, vol. I, p. 61, AFHRA.

Chapter 1
North America

North America is the most important region to which the U.S. Air Force has flown humanitarian airlift operations because it includes the United States itself. Communications networks focused immediate attention on emergencies soon after they occurred, and quick, well-executed military responses satisfied public expectations. Air Force bases scattered across the country made such rapid response possible. Air Force Reserve units participated in more domestic relief airlifts than foreign airlifts. Before the USAF designated MAC as the gaining command for reserve airlift crews on temporary active duty in 1974, these units did not normally deploy overseas.

This chapter describes airlifts to the United States and Canada. A few operations in this chapter, such as Hurricane Hugo in 1989, included relief flights to both the United States and Latin America. Airlifts to Mexico and Central America are discussed in Chapter 2. Hawaii is covered in Chapter 7.

Only Latin America and the Pacific compare to North America in the number of airlift operations. From 1947 through 1994, the Air Force flew 112 relief operations in North America, an average of almost 2.4 operations per year, not including minor rescues or aeromedical evacuations. Most humanitarian airlifts were flown in response to natural disasters. Eighteen airlift operations transported more than 1,000 tons of equipment and supplies.

Not all domestic emergencies required airlift. In some cases, military installations were close enough to the scene of a disaster that ground vehicles could transport relief personnel and supplies. These operations are not recorded here.

Statistics: North American Airlifts

Number of humanitarian airlifts: 112.
Most common emergencies: storms (32), floods (31), and forest fires (26).
Most frequent recipients: United States (109), Canada (2), and Greenland (1).
Three largest operations, in chronological order: Operation Hayride, 1949 (more than 4,700 tons); Hurricane Camille, 1969 (over 5,900 tons); and Hurricane Andrew, 1992 (over 21,000 tons).

Humanitarian Airlift Operations

Chronological Listing: North American Airlifts

1. Hurricane Emma	Sept. 1947
2. Florida Flood	Oct. 1947
3. Maine Forest Fire	Oct. 1947
4. Louisiana/Arkansas Tornado	Jan. 1948
5. Makkovik Fire	Jan. 1948
6. Texas Tornado	May 1948
7. Columbia River Flood	May–June 1948
8. Operation Hayride	Jan.–Mar. 1949
9. Operation Flood-Lift	July 1951
10. Missouri River Valley Flood	Apr. 1952
11. Rio Grande Floods	June–July 1954
12. Operation Ice Cube	Sept. 1954
13. Hurricane Diane	Aug.–Sept. 1955
14. Northern California Flood	Dec. 1955
15. Cumberland Flood	Jan. 1957
16. Hurricane Audrey	June–Aug. 1957
17. Ship Fire	Nov. 1959
18. Northwestern Forest Fires	July 1960
19. Hurricane Donna	Sept. 1960
20. Hurricane Carla	Sept.–Oct. 1961
21. Operation Nava-Snow	Dec. 1961
22. Idaho Flood	Feb. 1962
23. Chlorine Barge Emergency	Sept. 1962
24. Kentucky Floods	Mar. 1963
25. Texas Haylift	Feb. 1964
26. Operation Helping Hand	Mar.-Apr. 1964
27. Montana Flood	June 1964
28. Hurricane Hilda	Oct. 1964
29. Operation Haylift	Dec. 1964
30. Operation Biglift	Dec. 1964–Jan. 1965
31. Colorado Flood	June 1965
32. Hurricane Betsy	Sept. 1965
33. Phoenix Area Flood	Dec. 1965–Jan. 1966
34. Northwestern California Flood	Jan. 1966
35. Mississippi Tornadoes	Mar. 1966
36. Midwest Flood	Mar. 1966
37. Texas Encephalitis Epidemic	Aug. 1966
38. Rocky Mountain Fires	Aug.–Sept. 1967
39. Fairbanks Flood	Aug. 1967
40. Hurricane Beulah	Sept.–Oct. 1967
41. Operation Haylift II	Dec. 1967

42. Alaskan Forest Fire   July–Aug. 1968
43. Minot Flood   Apr. 1969
44. Hurricane Camille   Aug.–Sept. 1969
45. Lubbock Tornado   May 1970
46. Hurricane Celia   Aug. 1970
47. Southern Plains Snowstorm   Feb.–Mar. 1971
48. Operation Combat VEE   July–Aug. 1971
49. Arizona Forest Fire   May 1972
50. South Dakota Flash Flood   June 1972
51. Arizona Flash Flood   June 1972
52. Tropical Storm Agnes   June–Aug. 1972
53. Everglades Airliner Crash   Dec. 1972
54. Operation Snowfall   Feb. 1973
55. Mississippi River Valley Flood   Apr.–May 1973
56. Northwest Forest Fires   Aug. 1973
57. Idaho Flood   Jan. 1974
58. Southwestern Forest Fires   June–Aug. 1974
59. Los Angeles Forest Fires   Aug. 1975
60. Angeles National Forest Fire   Sept. 1975
61. Southern California Forest Fires   Nov. 1975
62. Washington State Floods   Dec. 1975
63. Bethel Power Failure   Dec. 1975
64. Kentucky Coal Mine Disaster   Mar. 1976
65. Teton Dam Disaster   June 1976
66. Ontario Forest Fire   June 1976
67. Big Thompson Canyon Flood   Aug. 1976
68. Operation Sno Go   Jan.–Feb. 1977
69. Johnstown Flood   July 1977
70. California Forest Fires   July–Aug. 1977
71. Snow Blow I   Jan. 1978
72. Snow Blow II   Feb. 1978
73. Arizona Flood   Mar. 1978
74. Wyoming Haylift   Feb. 1979
75. Three Mile Island Nuclear Accident   Mar.–Apr. 1979
76. Wichita Falls Tornado   Apr. 1979
77. Red River Flood   Apr. 1979
78. Central Arizona Forest Fires   July 1979
79. Northwest Fires   Aug. 1979
80. Southern California Forest Fires   Sept. 1979
81. Mount St. Helens Eruption   May-June 1980
82. Palm Springs Area Fire   July–Aug. 1980
83. *Prinsendam* Rescue   Oct. 1980
84. San Bernardino Forest Fires   Nov. 1980

Humanitarian Airlift Operations

85. MGM Grand Hotel Fire	Nov. 1980
86. Las Vegas Hilton Fire	Feb. 1981
87. Louisiana Flood	Apr. 1983
88. Minnesota Encephalitis Epidemic	Aug. 1983
89. Maricopa Flood	Oct. 1983
90. Missouri River Flood	June 1984
91. Utah Coal Mine Fire	Dec. 1984
92. North Carolina Forest Fires	Apr. 1985
93. Idaho Pestilence	June–July 1985
94. Western Forest Fires	July 1985
95. Northern California Floods	Feb. 1986
96. North Carolina Forest Fires	May 1986
97. Southeast Haylift	July 1986
98. Ship Fire	Dec. 1986
99. West Coast Forest Fires	Aug.–Sept. 1987
100. Yellowstone Fires	Aug.–Oct. 1988
101. *Exxon Valdez* Oil Spill	Mar.–May 1989
102. Western Forest Fires	July–Aug. 1989
103. Hurricane Hugo	Sept.–Nov. 1989
104. California Earthquake	Oct. 1989
105. Painted Cave Fire	June–July 1990
106. Arctic Crash	Nov. 1991
107. Hurricane Andrew	Aug.–Oct. 1992
108. Winter Storm	Mar. 1993
109. Midwest Flood	July–Aug. 1993
110. Southern California Wildfires	Oct.–Nov. 1993
111. Southern California Earthquake	Jan. 1994
112. Western Forest Fires	June–Sept. 1994

Operations: North American Airlifts

1.
Name: Hurricane Emma.
Location: Florida, Louisiana, and Mississippi.
Date(s): September 17–21, 1947.
Emergency: A hurricane, with winds up to 120 mph, hit southern Florida and the central Gulf coast.
Air Force Organization(s) Involved: 3d Air Transport Group (Air Trpt Gp).
Airlifted: 12.5 tons of tents, blankets, and emergency equipment; and two U.S. Coast Guard helicopters.
Aircraft Employed: C–74 (two).
Operations: On Wednesday, September 17, Hurricane Emma hit southeast Florida between Miami and Palm Beach—including the cities of West Palm Beach, Popano, Fort Lauderdale, and Miami Beach—with 120 mph winds. Torrential rain, tidal surges, and high winds claimed at least 12 lives and caused $20 million in damage. Hundreds of people were injured and thousands were left homeless. About 1,600 refugees crowded Miami's Hialeah racetrack, which served as a relief center. For 12 hours the storm moved across southern Florida before moving into the Gulf of Mexico.

In response to appeals for federal assistance from Florida, President Harry S Truman authorized aid for the disaster areas on September 17.

The 3d Air Trpt Gp at Brookley AFB near Mobile, Alabama, responded that same day, flying a C–74 aircraft to Floyd Bennett AFB, New York, to pick up two Coast Guard helicopters for transport to Florida. On September 18, the C–74 flew the helicopters to MacDill AFB, Florida, to assist in rescue work around West Palm Beach.

Meanwhile, Hurricane Emma had regained strength over the warm waters of the Gulf of Mexico and veered northwest to hit southeast Louisiana and the Mississippi Gulf coast with 90 mph winds on Friday morning, September 19. Gales pounded New Orleans for five hours, causing at least $3 million in damage. Floodwaters from Lake Pontchartrain inundated east Jefferson Parish, transforming the city into an island, leaving 9,000 refugees crowded in the municipal auditorium. Just west of New Orleans, Moisant International Airport lay under several feet of water, cutting off all air transportation except large cargo planes. The mayor of New Orleans, Delesseps Morrison, declared an emergency and appealed for aid.

The 3d Air Trpt Gp C–74 moved the two Coast Guard helicopters to New Orleans, where an emergency disaster headquarters was established on September 20 at the Port of Embarkation under the command of Brig. Gen. Henry S. Hodes, Fourth Army chief of staff. The disaster headquarters included representatives from the Fourth Army, the Tenth Air Force, and the Eighth Naval District and coordinated relief operations in New Orleans. On September 21, an aerial survey conducted by the relief headquarters located three large breaks in the Lake Pontchartrain levee and surveyed flooding in Metairie, a western suburb. Military relief activities in New Orleans ended on September 22.

On September 19, the same day it struck New Orleans, Hurricane Emma hit the Mississippi Gulf coast. Water rose 13 feet above mean Gulf level, and 20-foot waves lashed the shoreline, sweeping away buildings along 25 miles of coastal Highway 90 between Bay St. Louis and Biloxi, Mississippi. A second 3d Air Trpt Gp C–74 moved 12.5 tons of cargo—including tents, blankets, and emergency equipment—from Marietta, Georgia, to Keesler AFB at Biloxi on September 21. Keesler's commander, Brig. Gen. Edward W. Anderson, sent trucks and ambulances loaded with emergency rations and medical supplies from the base to storm victims. Air Force personnel also distributed two tons of food. Over 2,000 Keesler volunteers helped to remove 1,500 truckloads of rubble from Biloxi and Gulfport beaches and roads after the storm. In the 24 hours after it hit shore, Hurricane Emma dissipated as it moved northwest, leaving at least six people dead and 400 injured in Louisiana and Mississippi.

2.

Name: Florida Flood.
Location: Lake Okeechobee region and south Florida.
Date(s): October 12–15, 1947.
Emergency: A hurricane hit southern Florida, dropping torrential rain that threatened to spill Lake Okeechobee over its banks.
Air Force Organization(s) Involved: 3d Air Trpt Gp and 32d Air Transport Squadron (Air Trpt Sq).
Airlifted: 45 tons of burlap bags.
Aircraft Employed: C–74 (one) and C–54 (three).
Operations: A tropical storm brewing in the western Caribbean Sea in early October began a slow northeastward journey across western Cuba and into the Florida Straits, where it intensified into a hurricane on Saturday, October 11. It hovered over the Everglades the next day, dropping record amounts of rain in an area drenched by Hurricane Emma just a month earlier.

The agricultural commissioner of Florida, Nathan Mayo, described the storm as the worst agricultural disaster in more than a generation to hit the farming district around Lake Okeechobee. Crop damage totaled $20 million. Continuing northeast, the tempest sent wind gusts as high as 94 mph down the streets of Miami, where 1.34 inches of rain fell in a 10-minute period. Flooding of 3,000 homes forced the evacuation of 12,000 people in the Miami area. Torrential rain combined with runoff draining eastward from the Everglades to inundate Fort Lauderdale, Hialeah, Miami Springs, and Opalocka under up to six feet of water as the hurricane swept into the Atlantic on October 13.

Southern Florida's Lake Okeechobee, already brimming with rainwater from Hurricane Emma, threatened to burst its dikes. The U.S. Army Corps of

Engineers, denying rumors that the levees had broken, feverishly operated 19 drag lines to extend dikes and contain the overflowing drainage canals south and east of the lake. Florida officials appealed for sandbags to raise and reinforce the levees. The 3d Air Trpt Gp at Brookley AFB, Alabama, flew four aircraft to Marietta, Georgia, between October 12 and 15 to pick up 45 tons of burlap bags for airlift to West Palm Beach, Florida. A 32d Air Trpt Sq C–74 carried over 20 tons of sandbags on an October 15 flight and three C–54 aircraft carried the remainder.

Engineers and volunteers filled the bags with sand and reinforced the Lake Okeechobee dikes during the third week in October, preventing the lake from spilling into surrounding farmlands and Miami and other coastal cities.

3.
Name: Maine Forest Fire.
Location: Southern coast of Maine.
Date(s): October 21–28, 1947.
Emergency: At least 50 forest fires consumed thousands of acres.
Air Force Organization(s) Involved: First Air Force (reserve units), 35th and 137th Air Force Base Units, 5th Rescue Squadron (Rscu Sq), and 14th Fighter Group (Ftr Gp).
Airlifted: 22 miles of fire hose, at least 600 fire extinguishers, three water pump tank trailers, 1,100 folding cots, morphine, fire-fighting equipment, and 1.25 tons of blankets.
Aircraft Employed: C–82 (one) and C–47 (18+).
Operations: Dry Indian summer winds and a prolonged drought sparked dozens of forest fires in New England in late October. The fires hit coastal Maine, sweeping down wooded slopes toward resort communities along the rocky shore. Forest Commissioner Raymond E. Rendall tracked over 50 separate fires affecting nearly 80 communities.

One fire destroyed 26,000 acres and 300 buildings in a five-mile stretch of the Maine coast. On October 21, 200 homes, two hotels, and a school went up in flames at Kennebunkport. Fires razed major portions of Goose Rock Beach, Cape Porpoise, Biddeford, Brownfield, Newfield, Fortune's Rock, and Waterboro. The fires threatened the famous resort town of Bar Harbor on Mount Desert Island, where residents were evacuated to the mainland. When fire blocked the only road off the island, 400 citizens had to be evacuated by boat. Fire consumed 25 percent of Bar Harbor, including 75 homes.

On October 21, 1947, the Bar Harbor Fire Department contacted Dow AFB near Bangor, Maine, to request assistance in fighting the Mount Desert Island fire. The commander of First Air Force, Maj. Gen. Robert M. Webster, detailed over 1,000 Air Force personnel for fire fighting.

Governor Horace Hildreth declared a statewide emergency on October 23. On October 25, President Truman declared Maine a disaster area and ordered mercy flights.

Humanitarian Airlift Operations

The 35th Air Force Base Unit's "B" Squadron at Mitchel AFB, New York, provided aerial transportation to Maine for First Army, Red Cross, and press personnel. Eighteen First Air Force C–47 aircraft flew morphine, pick axes, portable fire extinguishers, and 22 miles of fire hose from Mitchel AFB to the Bangor airport for distribution to firefighters, while the 14th Ftr Gp at Dow AFB flew reconnaissance missions over the fires to help direct evacuations.

On October 24, a 5th Rscu Sq C–82 transported three water pump tank trailers from Westover AFB, Massachusetts, to Portland, Maine. The next day, two C–47s moved 11,000 feet of fire hose from Schenectady, New York, to Presque Isle, Maine. On October 26, a C–82 and a C–47 airlifted 600 fire extinguishers from Schenectady to Augusta, Maine. From October 27 to 28, Flight D of the 5th Rscu Sq, based at Westover, flew more than 1,100 folding cots and over one ton of blankets from New Bedford, Massachusetts, to refugees at Augusta; and a C–47 airlifted more fire-fighting equipment from South Weymouth Airport in Massachusetts to Augusta.

The fires, which began to subside on October 27, left 13 people dead, 110,000 acres burned, and $30 million in damage. By the end of the month, the fires were under control and the emergency was over.

4.
Name: Louisiana/Arkansas Tornado.
Location: Northwestern Louisiana and southern Arkansas.
Date(s): January 1–2, 1948.
Emergency: A tornado swept a 75-mile path of destruction across northwestern Louisiana and southern Arkansas.
Air Force Organization(s) Involved: Eighth and Tenth Air Forces.
Airlifted: 17 tons of relief supplies, including tents, stoves, electric generators, food, and a water purification unit.
Aircraft Employed: C–54 (three) and C–47 (three).
Operations: A winter storm system swept into northwestern Louisiana and southern Arkansas on the afternoon of December 31, 1947, sparking a tornado that devastated five communities along a 75-mile path. The twister formed near Vanceville, Louisiana, just northeast of Shreveport, and followed a generally northeastward course to Cotton Valley, Louisiana, before doubling back to deal a second destructive blow to these communities. At about 4:30 p.m., the storm hit Cotton Valley from the west, and minutes later it struck from the east, leveling more than 100 buildings and leaving 10 people dead. Thirty injured victims were transported to a hospital at nearby Minden, Louisiana.

At about 5:30 p.m., Governor James H. Davis of Louisiana called out the National Guard and requested federal assistance. Meanwhile, the tornado resumed a northeastward track, cutting a 50-foot wide path through Haynesville before it swept into Arkansas, eventually blowing itself out near El Dorado. In two hours, the tornado had killed 16 people, injured 146, and left more than 1,500 homeless.

On the evening of December 31, the Fourth Army, in charge of overall disaster relief, asked the Tenth Air Force at Brooks AFB, Texas, to airlift relief supplies to Louisiana. On New Year's Day, the Tenth Air Force sent a C–54 loaded with 10 tons of relief supplies—including 50 tents, eight field ranges, three auxiliary electrical power units, and nearly two tons of soup—from the Fort Worth quartermaster depot in Texas to Barksdale, Louisiana. A Tenth Air Force C–47 flew survey parties from San Antonio to the disaster scene that day. Lt. Col. Ben S. Brown and Maj. George A. Beere from Tenth Air Force headquarters participated in an aerial reconnaissance of the stricken area. Another C–47 carried a water purification unit and three electrical generators from Brooks AFB to Barksdale AFB.

Fourth Army requested additional Tenth Air Force airlift on the morning of January 2, 1948. That afternoon, two C–47s carried almost three tons of field ranges, stoves, and relief supplies from Brooks AFB and Fort Worth AFB in Texas to Barksdale AFB for delivery to Cotton Valley.

Meanwhile, the Eighth Air Force, then headquartered at Fort Worth, had carried more supplies aboard two C–54s. The freight was transferred to trucks at Barksdale AFB and driven to the ravaged communities. The Tenth and Eighth Air Forces airlifted more than 17 tons of relief supplies and equipment from San Antonio and Fort Worth to Barksdale AFB aboard six aircraft during the first two days of 1948.

5.
Name: Makkovik Fire.
Location: Labrador (Newfoundland).
Date(s): January 31, 1948.
Emergency: A fire destroyed the warehouse of Makkovik and its supply of food, clothing, and medicine.
Air Force Organization(s) Involved: Newfoundland Base Command.
Airlifted: Unknown quantity of food, clothing, medicine, and communications equipment.
Aircraft Employed: C–47 (one).
Operations: Situated in a remote subarctic region about 130 miles northeast of Goose Bay, Labrador, the fishing hamlet of Makkovik depended on supplies stored in its warehouse to sustain it through long six-month winters, when maritime supply routes were blocked by ice. In late January 1948, fire destroyed Makkovik's warehouse and much of the village, consuming most of its food, clothing, and medical supplies, including precious penicillin stocks. The fire also destroyed the shortwave radios that provided Makkovik's 136 inhabitants with communications to the outside world.

A supply ship had most recently visited Makkovik in September 1947, and another was not scheduled to arrive until the ice cleared the next summer. A villager journeyed 65 miles by dogsled to Cape Harrison to relay a shortwave request for emergency relief to the American and Canadian air base at Goose Bay on

January 31, 1948. The commander of the U.S. portion of the Goose Bay facility, Col. Paul A. Zartman, met with Group Capt. Z. Louie Leigh of the Royal Canadian Air Force to plan the response. The men agreed to send a C–64 Norseman equipped with skis and a C–47 to drop emergency supplies by parachute.

Reverend George Harp of the Makkovik Moravian mission met the C–64 when it landed and described the property the village needed. The C–47, operated by Newfoundland Base Command, dropped the emergency cargo by parachute. The joint Canadian-American mercy flights demonstrated international cooperation and provided food, medicine, clothing, and communications equipment to sustain the villagers until the next supply ship arrived.

6.
Name: Texas Tornado.
Location: McKinney and Princeton, Texas.
Date(s): May 3, 1948.
Emergency: A tornado hit McKinney and Princeton, Texas.
Air Force Organization(s) Involved: Tenth Air Force.
Airlifted: Food rations, emergency equipment, and medical supplies.
Aircraft Employed: C–47 (two), C–54 (two), and C–82 (one).
Operations: At mid-afternoon on May 3, a tornado dipped out of the Texas sky to devastate two towns and a 12-mile stretch of farms north of Dallas. At the cotton mill town of McKinney, population 10,000, three people were killed and 53 were injured. A textile mill, school, hospital, and church were either damaged or destroyed. The tornado also killed one person and injured 10 at Princeton, 10 miles east of McKinney. Between the towns, along Texas State Route 24, dozens of farm houses were splintered and cars were tossed as far as 300 yards from the road. The storm damaged or destroyed 400 homes, leaving 1,000 people without shelter.

By dusk, Governor Beauford H. Jester had appealed for emergency assistance. The Fourth Army asked Brig. Gen. Harry A. Johnson, Tenth Air Force commander at Brooks AFB near San Antonio, Texas, to lend airlift support. On the evening of May 3, the Tenth Air Force flew two C–47, two C–54, and one C–82 aircraft loaded with food, emergency equipment, and medical supplies from Brooks AFB to Hensley Field at Dallas. Ground vehicles ferried the cargo to the nearby disaster area.

The five planeloads of emergency supplies delivered within 24 hours of the tornado allowed the American Red Cross disaster relief headquarters at McKinney to provide almost immediate relief. The five-in-one rations airlifted allowed the Red Cross to serve breakfast to victims the morning after the storm.

7.
Name: Columbia River Flood.
Location: Oregon and Washington.
Date(s): May 27–June 13, 1948.

Emergency: Sudden melting of deep snow in the Cascade Mountains coupled with heavy spring rains flooded the Columbia River valley.

Air Force Organization(s) Involved: 62d Troop Carrier Group (Trp Carr Gp).

Airlifted: 100,000 sandbags, six water pumps, and other emergency relief supplies and equipment.

Aircraft Employed: C–82 (13+).

Operations: Unusually heavy spring rains and rapid thawing of snow in the Cascades swelled the Pacific Northwest's Columbia River and its tributaries in late May, flooding communities along the Washington-Oregon border. High water engulfed portions of Woodland and Kalama, forcing evacuation of Vancouver, Kelso, and Longview, Washington. On Sunday afternoon, May 30, the Columbia River dike burst at Vanport, a suburb of Portland, threatening its 18,500 residents. Parts of the city were under 15 feet of water, including a section of the railroad between Portland and Seattle. Many homes floated away. The Willamette River, unable to drain into the Columbia, flooded portions of northern Portland, including its airport.

Floods in Oregon, Washington, and Idaho left 60,000 people homeless and caused property damage estimated at $75 million. The governors of the three states requested federal aid from Federal Works administrator Philip B. Fleming. On May 31, President Truman declared the flooded districts disaster areas. The next day, 20,000 people began to evacuate 120 miles of the Columbia River valley between Portland and the Pacific Ocean.

The 62d Trp Carr Gp, based at McChord AFB near Tacoma, Washington, began emergency relief flights to deliver supplies and equipment to Spokane and Portland even before the dike burst at Vanport. The group flew 16 sorties between May 27 and 30. During the first two weeks of June, the 62d Troop Carrier Group's C–82 aircraft transported supplies to 2d Infantry Division troops working in the Portland flood area, shuttling between McChord and the civil airport at Hillsboro, Oregon, 15 miles west of Portland.

On June 10, 13 of the group's aircraft carried 100,000 sandbags from McChord AFB to Richland, Washington, to help repair and reinforce dikes near the Hanford atomic energy plant. The 62d Trp Carr Gp ended its relief missions on June 13 when it sent two C–82 aircraft to deliver six water pumps from Milwaukee, Wisconsin, to Richland.

8.

Name: Operation Hayride (also Haylift and Snowbound).

Location: Wyoming, Colorado, North Dakota, South Dakota, Kansas, Nebraska, Nevada, and Utah.

Date(s): January 3–March 15, 1949.

Emergency: A series of blizzards endangered eight western and midwestern states and threatened livestock.

Air Force Organization(s) Involved: Tenth Air Force; 2151st Rescue Unit (Rscu

Un), Air Rscu Svc; 62d Troop Carrier Wing (Trp Carr Wg) (Fourth Air Force) and 316th Trp Carr Wg (Ninth Air Force); and 2473d Air Force Reserve Training Center.

Airlifted: 4,778 tons of livestock feed, food, blankets, clothing, fuel, medical supplies, vehicles, and communications equipment; and 1,128 passengers evacuated.

Aircraft Employed: C–47 (85), C–82 (54), H–5 (9), T–6 (9), L–5 (9), RB–26 (9), C–46 (6), YH–13 (5), RF–51 (5), RF–80 (4), F–51 (18), L–4 (4), C–45 (2), B–25 (2), F–82 (2), B–17 (1), and T–11 (1).

Operations: Eighteen snowstorms in 27 days hit the Rocky Mountain and upper Great Plains states during December 1948 and January 1949, dropping temperatures as low as 40 degrees below zero, blocking roads and railways, and covering ranges and ranches with so much snow that hundreds of thousands of sheep and cattle were threatened with starvation.

The 2151st Rscu Un at Lowry AFB, Colorado, began to airdrop food and medicine to stranded travelers and isolated residents on January 3. For the next 10 days, the unit flew C–47, C–82, L–5, and H–5 aircraft over snow-covered portions of Colorado, Wyoming, and Nebraska. For example, on January 4, a 2151st Rscu Un C–47 delivered 115 blankets and 30 cases of C rations to 482 people stranded at Rockport, Colorado. The next day, the unit airdropped food to passengers stranded in trains at Hillsdale and Egbort, Wyoming, and at Dix, Nebraska.

A 2151st Rscu Un C–82 airlifted two snow-terrain vehicles known as weasels from Cheyenne, Wyoming, to Scottsbluff, Nebraska, on January 7 to help deliver emergency supplies. The next day, a C–47 aircraft dropped insulin and penicillin to blizzard-bound medical personnel at Harrison, Nebraska.

On January 11, despite the 2151st Rescue Unit's efforts to answer emergency requests for assistance from local and state government agencies, Governor Val Peterson of Nebraska phoned Gen. Curtis E. LeMay, commander of SAC at Offutt AFB, Nebraska, to request additional emergency assistance. This request was relayed to the Continental Air Command (CONAC), which contacted the Tenth Air Force's Maj. Gen. Harry A. Johnson at Brooks AFB, Texas. General Johnson called a Tenth Air Force domestic emergency relief team into action under Lt. Col. Joe E. McNay, who set up operations at Lincoln, Nebraska, on January 12.

Working with the Fifth Army, the Tenth Air Force team airdropped food, medicine, and livestock feed until January 16, when improved weather eliminated the need for further relief flights. But more snowstorms in the following days forced Governor Peterson to ask for a renewal of the humanitarian flights, which resumed on January 24. The Tenth Air Force coordinated Air Force aerial relief missions in Wyoming, Kansas, Colorado, North Dakota, South Dakota, and Nebraska, in an operation called Hayride.

Meanwhile, on January 24, the Fourth Air Force at Hamilton AFB, California, had begun to send cargo aircraft to Nevada to airdrop livestock feed to starving herds. The Fourth Air Force sent 62d Trp Carr Gp C–82s from McChord AFB, Washington, to a naval airfield at Fallon, Nevada, where they flew with the

Ninth Air Force's 316th Trp Carr Gp to deliver food and provide medical care to isolated blizzard victims and to airdrop bales of hay and livestock feed to starving cattle and sheep.

Thirty C–82 and 12 C–47 cargo aircraft delivered over 2,500 tons of emergency supplies in eastern Nevada and western Utah in 33 days, flying more than 660 sorties. Many of the airplanes shuttled between Fallon and Ely, Nevada, carrying local ranchers who directed the airdrop of hay to the starving herds.

Meanwhile, the Tenth Air Force had continued airlift operations farther east, and the domestic emergency relief team headquarters moved from Lincoln, Nebraska, to Lowry AFB, Colorado, on January 26.

On January 29, because of the large number of snow-blocked railroads and highways, President Truman declared the snow-crippled western states a disaster area and authorized further federal assistance. A "Disaster Force Snowbound" was established in Omaha, Nebraska, on February 3 with combined Army and Air Force staffs.

While the Fifth Army coordinated disaster relief missions, authorizing airlift only when ground supply routes were impassable, a provisional Air Division Hayride directed air activities. The Tenth Air Force domestic emergency relief team continued to operate, but moved its headquarters back to Nebraska from Lowry AFB, this time to Omaha.

Often during February, Air Division Hayride and Disaster Force Snowbound canceled livestock feeding missions to save human lives. For example, on February 9, hundreds of people were stranded on snowbound trains west of Rawlins and in the areas of Hanna, Rock River, and Green River in Wyoming. The Tenth Air Force dropped food, blankets, and medicine to the isolated passengers until the trains could move again.

Air relief operations ended on February 26 in Nevada and on March 15 in Nebraska. The Tenth Air Force flew over 2,100 tons of hay, rations, clothing, blankets, milk, coal, and emergency equipment to stricken areas in five states aboard 143 aircraft between January 12 and March 15. Total Hayride missions involved more than 200 Air Force planes delivering over 4,700 tons of supplies in eight states. These missions were performed as the massive Berlin Airlift was underway in Europe (see Operation Vittles, Chapter 3, June 1948–September 1949).

9.
Name: Operation Flood-Lift.
Location: Kansas and Missouri.
Date(s): July 11–22, 1951.
Emergency: The Kansas, Missouri, and Mississippi Rivers between eastern Kansas and western Illinois flooded.
Air Force Organization(s) Involved: Second, Tenth, and Eighteenth Air Forces; Central Air Defense Force; 21st Air Division (Air Div); 314th, 433d, 434th, and 516th Trp Carr Wgs; 7th and 44th Bombardment Wings; 439th Tactical Training

Humanitarian Airlift Operations

Wing; 62d Trp Carr Gp; 301st, 3310th, 3902d, and 4610th Air Base Groups (AB Gps); 4th and 5th Air Rescue Squadrons (Air Rscu Sqs); 32d, 36th, and 67th Troop Carrier Squadrons (Trp Carr Sqs); 108th and 3528th Maintenance Squadrons; 1080th Bombardment Squadron; 3075th Ferrying Squadron; and 2472d Air Force Reserve Training Center.

Airlifted: 300 tons of food, medicine, bedding, life rafts, boats, canteens, gasoline, rope, helicopters, and sandbags.

Aircraft Employed: C–119 (19), C–47 (14), C–46 (12), SA–16 (7), C–124 (4), SB–29 (4), T–11 (4), H–5 (3), C–82 (2), C–54 (1), C–45 (1), B–25 (1), and T–7 (1).

Operations: Torrential rains over central and eastern Kansas during June and the first half of July flooded the tributaries of the Kansas (Kaw) River, inundating Abilene, Manhattan, Junction City, and Fort Riley. Governor Edward Arn appealed for military assistance, and the Fifth Army assumed command of disaster relief operations on July 11. The Fifth Army immediately asked the Tenth Air Force at Selfridge AFB, Michigan, for airlift support. Col. Donald L. Wilhelm assumed command of the Tenth Air Force domestic emergency team to coordinate Operation Flood-Lift and prepared to launch a relief airlift.

The Tenth Air Force supervised all Air Force flood relief missions in Kansas regardless of the commands and units involved. The 4th Rscu Sq at Lowry AFB, Colorado, inaugurated Air Force flood relief by sending an SA–16 aircraft with three rafts and a boat to Cottonwood Falls, Kansas, on July 11 to rescue flood victims marooned on roofs.

The 21st Air Div at Forbes AFB near Topeka, Kansas, began coordinating further rescue operations on July 12. That day the Tenth Air Force airlifted 30,000 sandbags aboard three C–47 aircraft from Scott AFB, Illinois, to Fort Riley and Junction City, Kansas. On July 12, the Kansas River spilled over its banks, flooding North Topeka and North Lawrence under as much as 12 feet of water. As hundreds of Forbes AFB personnel reinforced levees around Topeka, the Tenth Air Force sent Lt. Col. F. B. Gallagher as liaison officer to work with the Kansas state government. Meanwhile, Air Force troop carrier wings flew thousands of sandbags and hundreds of cots, blankets, and other relief supplies to Forbes from bases around the country.

On July 13, as cargo planes delivered huge quantities of sandbags, boats, and rations to Topeka, the flooding Kansas River poured into the Missouri River at the Kansas-Missouri border, inundating 1,300 blocks of Kansas City and drowning 10,000 animals in its stockyards. Governor Forrest Smith of Missouri declared a state of emergency, and President Truman designated both Kansas and Missouri disaster areas on July 14.

Between July 11 and 17, 73 Air Force planes participated in humanitarian airlift operations from at least 12 Air Force bases across the United States. The Tactical Air Command sent 32 planes, SAC sent 22, and 14 came from the Military Air Transport Service's Air Rscu Svc. Air Force pilots flew 300 tons of emergency supplies into Forbes and Wichita AFBs, including more than 130,000 sandbags from Scott AFB, Illinois; more than 1,500 cots and 4,300 blankets from Bowman AFB, Kentucky; 20 boats from St. Louis, Missouri; 200 cases of rations from Columbus, Ohio; and 1,285 parachutes and containers from Ogden, Utah. They even brought Coast Guard helicopters from as far away as Salem, Massachusetts.

In 556 flights involving almost 1,400 flying hours over seven days, Air Force personnel delivered 66 life rafts; 523 cases of rations; 1,250 mosquito nets; 305 gallons of gasoline; 12,600 feet of rope; 10,500 bottles of typhoid serum; 4,643 bottles of water purification tablets; and many other relief supplies, including canned food, bread, milk, mattresses, and canteens. Fifty tons were airdropped to victims in at least 30 eastern Kansas communities. Helicopters rescued victims stranded on roofs and islands of higher ground. As the Tenth Air Force concluded operations from its liaison office at Topeka on July 17, President Truman flew over the flooded areas.

On July 18, the Missouri River spilled into the streets of Missouri's capital, Jefferson City, flooding 20 blocks. The Missouri River, which empties into the Mississippi River 15 miles north of St. Louis, had inundated lowlands around the confluence of the two rivers by July 19. The swollen Mississippi threatened to submerge communities and farms for 150 miles between Alton, Illinois, and Cape Girardeau, Missouri. More than 800 Air Force personnel from Scott AFB helped to contain the rising water by reinforcing, repairing, and enlarging levees around St. Charles and St. Louis, Missouri, and at Chester and Alton, Illinois.

The 62d Trp Carr Gp flew thousands of sandbags from McClellan AFB, California, to Scott AFB to supply the workers. On July 22, the Mississippi River crested at St. Louis, and the waters began to recede. Scott AFB personnel returned home by the end of the month. The floods killed 41 people, drove 165,000 from their homes, inundated two million acres, and cost more than $1 billion in property damage.

10.
Name: Missouri River Valley Flood.
Location: South Dakota, Iowa, Nebraska, Kansas, and Missouri.
Date(s): April 9–20, 1952.
Emergency: The Missouri River flooded communities between Pierre, South Dakota, and Parkville, Missouri.
Air Force Organization(s) Involved: SAC and Tenth and Eighteenth Air Forces.
Airlifted: 550 tons of cots, blankets, tents, burlap bags, carbide lamps, flares, electric generators, medical supplies, rations, tools, life rafts, and other items; and 12,386 troops to work on levees or perform disaster relief.
Aircraft Employed: C–124 (26), C–119 (24), C–47 (12), C–46 (11), C–82 (7), and helicopter of unspecified type (1).
Operations: From the end of March into early April, heavy snow followed by

rapid thawing and heavy spring rains over the tributaries of the upper Missouri River produced a flood that forced more than 100,000 people from their homes, inundated two million acres, and cost more than $200 million in property damage. The Missouri River flooded communities in succession all the way from Pierre, South Dakota, south to Parkville, Missouri, near Kansas City, which had been flooded less than a year earlier (see Operation Flood-Lift, July 1951). Sections of the river spread 18 miles wide.

During the first week in April, the Missouri River flooded 36 blocks of Pierre, some under as much as 10 feet of water. On April 9, the American Red Cross in Pierre asked the Fifth Army for an emergency airlift of relief supplies. According to the domestic emergency plan, the Fifth Army supervised disaster response in 13 midwestern states, including those of the Missouri River area. The Tenth Air Force coordinated humanitarian airlift operations in support of the Fifth Army in the same area.

On April 9, the Tenth Air Force initiated an airlift of cots and blankets in response to the Red Cross request. Meanwhile, the flood crest continued to move downriver at about nine mph. Dikes began to break around Sioux City, Iowa, on April 10. On April 13, Governor Val Peterson of Nebraska invoked the Civil Defense Act in his state, and a Tenth Air Force liaison team moved to Omaha to work with the Fifth Army and the Corps of Engineers under U.S. Army Brig. Gen. Donald G. Shingler. By April 14, the full flood crest had reached Sioux City, inundating 60 blocks of the business district and forcing 10,000 people from their homes.

The crest moved on to threaten Council Bluffs, Iowa, and Omaha, cities on opposite shores of the Missouri River. The airlift concentrated on transporting flood control workers and supplies to the Omaha area via nearby Offutt AFB because the river was predicted to reach its highest level of five feet above the levee in that area. On April 15, the Tenth Air Force coordinated the largest of a series of airlift missions, moving two engineer battalions of 1,200 troops; rations for two days; and four jeeps from La Crosse, Wisconsin, to Offutt AFB. Seven SAC C–124s, three Eighteenth Air Force C–119s (TAC), and one Tenth Air Force C–47 (CONAC) were used for this mission.

The flood control workers constructed parallel wooden fences atop the levees, filling the space between them with earth to contain the rising water. High water had closed the Omaha airport, forcing planes to land at Offutt AFB. On April 16, President Truman flew to Offutt to survey the flood damage and meet with the governors of the flooded states. He immediately declared Nebraska a disaster area.

Efforts of thousands of flood control workers and the airlift paid off on April 18 and 19, when the Missouri River crested at 30 feet but did not flood Omaha, even though the old levees were designed to handle a crest of only 26 feet. On April 20, the Missouri River flooded Sherman AFB near Fort Leavenworth, Kansas, but soon began to recede.

During the 11 days of airlift operations between April 9 and 20, the Tenth Air

Force transported 550 tons of emergency supplies, including 19,650 cots, 32,800 blankets, 104 tents, 21 water pumps, 978 carbide lamps, 200 carbide drums, 113 tons of rations, 24 tons of sandbags, and 400 life rafts. Air Force planes moved 12,386 flood control workers, mostly Army troops, to the flood-threatened region. The airlift used 81 aircraft from six commands, from bases across the country from Washington to South Carolina. Most planes transported supplies from Port Columbus, Ohio, to Offutt AFB, but some delivered relief cargo to Pierre and Sioux City, as well as other communities along the Missouri River. The Tactical Air Command lent 24 C–119s, 12 C–124s, 11 C–46s, and 7 C–82s—mostly from the Eighteenth Air Force—while SAC contributed 14 C–124s and 1 C–47. Air Materiel Command, Air Training Command, Continental Air Command, and Air Defense Command each supplied C–47s. The airlift ended on April 20, as the flood subsided.

11.
Name: Rio Grande Floods.
Location: Texas and Mexico.
Date(s): June 27–July 1, 1954.
Emergency: Heavy rain produced flash floods in the valleys of the Rio Grande and Pecos and Devil's Rivers, killing at least 25 people and leaving 15,000 homeless.
Air Force Organization(s) Involved: 3585th Pilot Training Wing.
Airlifted: No figures for the Air Force alone.
Aircraft Employed: H–19 (13).
Operations: In late June, heavy rain descended on southern Texas and northern Mexico. In some places, more than eight inches fell in 24 hours, causing flash flooding along tributaries of the Rio Grande, including the Pecos and Devil's Rivers. Johnson's Creek flooded Ozona, Texas, leaving 13 people dead. At Del Rio, Texas, the Rio Grande crested 25 feet above flood stage, inundating much of Ciudad Acuna, Mexico, directly across the river and washing out the international bridge between the cities. In the Comstock, Sanderson, Schumla, Langtry, Pandale, and Juno areas of Texas, high water washed out many highway and railroad bridges, marooning trains and motorists. The floods left at least 25 people dead and 15,000 homeless in border communities of Texas and Mexico.

American Red Cross, Southern Pacific Railroad, and Texas state government officials asked Laughlin AFB at Del Rio for military assistance. Col. Richard C. Bender, acting base commander, requested helicopters from other bases for rescue and relief operations.

U.S. Air Force, Army, and Navy helicopters flew emergency missions to Laughlin AFB from San Marcos, San Antonio, and Corpus Christi, Texas. Between June 27 and July 1, they evacuated 266 passengers from a stranded train near Langtry and transported 200 Americans from Ciudad Acuna to Del Rio. The helicopters also rescued people from the river and delivered food, drinking water, medicine, and clothing to flood victims in both Texas and Mexico. Throughout the rescue and relief operations, 21 helicopters, most from the USAF, evacuated more than 1,000 people and transported over 81 tons of relief supplies in 639 sorties.

The 3585th Pilot Training Wing at Gary AFB near San Marcos provided 13 Air Force H–19 helicopters, 25 pilots, and 17 mechanics for the relief missions, with Maj. William M. Hughes directing their operations. The flooding, destructive as it was, could have been worse. A dam 75 miles below Laredo saved the lower Rio Grande valley.

12.

Name: Operation Ice Cube.

Location: Massachusetts.

Date(s): September 2, 1954.

Emergency: A hurricane hit New England, leaving millions of residents without refrigeration.

Air Force Organization(s) Involved: 18th Air Trpt Sq (Medium).

Airlifted: 20 tons of dry ice.

Aircraft Employed: C–54 (one).

Operations: On the morning of August 31, Hurricane Carol swept northward across eastern Long Island and central New England, leaving 55 people dead and $500 million in property damage in New York, Rhode Island, Connecticut, Massachusetts, New Hampshire, and Maine. President Dwight D. Eisenhower declared 25 New England and Long Island counties disaster areas and ordered federal assistance to storm victims.

Blowing down hundreds of power lines, the storm left two million people without electricity in New England alone. Hurricane Carol passed just west of Boston, where wind gusts in excess of 100 mph toppled the famous Old North Church (Christ Church) steeple.

Governor Christian Herter of Massachusetts declared a state of emergency and ordered the Public Health Department to seize dry ice supplies, as tons of food began to spoil. When the state exhausted its supply of dry ice, it arranged to buy tons of the refrigerant from the Pure Carbonic Company of Newark, New Jersey, in a desperate attempt to save remaining food supplies. Governor Herter then contacted the Atlantic Division of MATS for an emergency airlift of dry ice.

On September 2, the 18th Air Trpt Sq (Medium) at McGuire AFB, New Jersey, flew a C–54 with 10 tons of dry ice from Newark Municipal Airport to Boston's Logan Airport. The cargo plane made two trips in an operation appropriately dubbed "Ice Cube." Officials distributed the refrigerant to food warehouses and grocery stores, limiting the spoilage of food supplies to about a million pounds.

13.
Name: Hurricane Diane.
Location: Pennsylvania, New Jersey, New York, Connecticut, Massachusetts, and Rhode Island.
Date(s): August 18–September 2, 1955.
Emergency: Hurricane Diane dumped torrential rain over mid-Atlantic and New England states, causing severe flooding.
Air Force Organization(s) Involved: 2500th Air Base Wing (AB Wg); 2252d Air Reserve Flying Center; 2605th Air Reserve Center; 302d Reserve Troop Carrier Wing; 1708th Ferry Group; 9543d, 9547th, and 9927th Air Reserve Squadrons; 46, 48th, and 49th Air Rscu Sqs; 3033d Test Flight; and unspecified AF Res units of CONAC.
Airlifted: At least 211 tons of chlorinated lime, dry ice, life rafts, food, medicine, gasoline, flashlights, communications equipment, electric generators, and fresh water.
Aircraft Employed: C–46 (18), SA–16 (4), H–19 (6), H–21 (2), C–97 (2), H–13 (1), H–5 (1), and C–47 (number unknown).
Operations: Hurricane Diane struck North Carolina on August 17, bringing torrential rain to Pennsylvania, New Jersey, New York, Massachusetts, Connecticut, and Rhode Island. President Eisenhower declared all six states disaster areas and ordered federal relief, as swollen rivers engulfed communities along their banks on August 18 and 19. Some of the heaviest rain fell over the Pocono Mountains of northeastern Pennsylvania, which had already absorbed extensive rain from Hurricane Connie a week earlier.

On August 18, the Brodhead Creek at Stroudsburg rose 30 feet in 15 minutes, killing 50 people. Personnel of the 9543d Air Reserve Squadron, based at Stroudsburg, coordinated helicopter rescue and relief operations in their home city for the next three days. Meanwhile, on August 18 and 19, the Lackawanna River flooded Scranton, Pennsylvania, inundating and destroying many homes. A 3303d Test Flight helicopter from Olmsted AFB in Middletown rescued many people stranded on roofs. To forestall epidemics, a 2605th Air Reserve Center C–47 from Wilkes-Barre, Pennsylvania, sprayed insecticide over the disaster area around Scranton.

Between August 18 and September 2, many Air Force units located in and around southern New England responded to emergency flood conditions. The 46th, 48th, and 49th Air Rscu Sqs flew 72 sorties over 15 days, evacuating 54 people stranded on roofs, bridges, and in trees, and delivering food, medicine, and engineering personnel throughout Connecticut and Massachusetts. In the same period, the 2500th AB Wg at Mitchel AFB, New York, flew five emergency flights to deliver survival equipment to storm victims in Connecticut.

At the request of the First Army, the 2252d Air Reserve Flying Center and the 302d Reserve Troop Carrier Wing, both from Clinton County, Pennsylvania, airlifted 182 tons of chlorinated lime for sanitation from Harrisburg, Pennsylvania, to Bradley Field, Connecticut, aboard C–46 aircraft between August 21 and 23. Between August 19 and 31, AF Res units flew 48 missions in the flood area, using 18 aircraft and 215 flying hours. By September 2, floodwaters had receded and Air Force emergency missions ended. Hurricane Diane left 250 people dead and caused $150 million in damage.

14.
Name: Northern California Flood.
Location: California, Nevada, and Oregon.
Date(s): December 22–30, 1955.
Emergency: Days of constant rain melted mountain snow and caused two dozen rivers to flood.
Air Force Organization(s) Involved: 41st, 42d, 43d, and 44th Air Rscu Sqs; and AF Res units of the Fourth Air Force.
Airlifted: More than 77 tons of food, medical supplies, clothing, life rafts, life vests, sandbags, blankets, cots, and radio communications equipment; and 70 passengers.
Aircraft Employed: SA–16 (eight), C–124 (two), C–54 (two), C–119 (number unknown), H–19 (two), C–47 (two), H–34 (one), H–21 (one).
Operations: A series of winter storms swept in from the Pacific Ocean during the second half of December, dumping tremendous amounts of rain on northern California, southwestern Oregon, and northwestern Nevada. Between December 15 and 26, 31 inches of rain fell over the coastal mountains, melting snow and sending out of their banks two dozen rivers, including the Klamath, Russian, Eel, Yuba, Feather, and Truckee. During the last week of December, floods covered a million acres, killing 86 people; leaving 50,000 homeless; and causing over $100 million in damage in California, Nevada, and Oregon. Governor Goodwin Knight of California and Governor Charles Russell of Nevada proclaimed states of emergency. President Eisenhower declared the flooded regions of the two states disaster areas.

Air Force rescue and relief efforts began on December 22 when Maj. William M. McDonald of the 41st Air Rscu Sq at Hamilton AFB, California, assumed command of Air Force, Army, Navy, and Coast Guard helicopter missions in accordance with disaster relief plans of the Sixth Army and the Fourth Air Force. The 42d Air Rscu Sq at March AFB, California; the 43d Air Rscu Sq at McChord AFB, Washington; and the 44th Air Rscu Sq at Lowry AFB, Colorado, contributed men and aircraft, some of which deployed to Travis AFB near Sacramento for the emergency.

That same day, H–19 helicopters, directed by SA–16 amphibious planes, rescued 12 people from the Santa Rosa and Guerneville areas, which were being inundated by the rising Russian River in northern California. Meanwhile, a C–54 from McClellan AFB, California, delivered sandbags to Stead AFB near Reno, which was threatened by the Truckee River.

On Friday, December 23, helicopters rescued 14 more people from the Russian River valley, while planes airlifted 1,500 pounds of milk and 200 pounds of medical supplies to Guerneville. Marysville, at the junction of the swollen Feather and Yuba Rivers, was also evacuated. Volunteers from Beale, McClellan, Mather, and Stead AFBs feverishly worked on levees near the threatened communities, filling and stacking sandbags.

The Feather River broke through its levees at Yuba City, about 120 miles northeast of San Francisco and directly across from Marysville on Saturday, December 24. High water inundated this community of 8,000 in 45 minutes. Cargo aircraft from McClellan AFB began airlifting supplies from the Sacramento Air Materiel Area to shelters throughout northern California.

Air Force, Army, Coast Guard, Navy, Marine Corps, and National Guard helicopters rescued 250 persons from Yuba City, Eureka, Arcata, and Crescent City on Christmas Eve in a series of flights coordinated by the 41st Air Rscu Sq. Air Force planes took 6.5 tons of food, clothing, and medicine to Crescent City and two tons to Eureka, where the supplies were distributed by helicopter. On Christmas Day, helicopters rescued 100 people from the Yuba City-Marysville area, and planes delivered 1.5 tons of food and medicine to Arcata near Eureka. That same day, the Civil Air Patrol, under Lt. Col. F. R. Miramontes at the Presidio in San Francisco, began flood relief operations. He set up an emergency headquarters at Stockton, California, where the San Joaquin River was rising rapidly.

On Monday, December 26, Air Force planes moved 3,000 rations from Travis AFB to Arcata, in response to an appeal from the San Francisco Red Cross. The next day, 23 military transports, including two Air Force C–124 Globemasters, airlifted to McClellan AFB 150 tons of flood relief supplies collected by junior chambers of commerce in southern California. A C–119 airlifted 1,700 food rations from McClellan to Travis for distribution to flood refugees. Other supplies were moved by helicopter or ground vehicles from McClellan to refugee centers.

Supplies distributed from McClellan AFB between December 24 and 28 included 1,431 comforters, 1,693 blankets, 400 cots, 158 life vests, 40 life rafts, 55,200 sandbags, 960 rations, 12,600 cans of meat, and 50,000 cans of evaporated milk. Between December 23 and 30, McClellan AFB planes airlifted 77.6 tons of these supplies plus medicine and radio communications equipment on 66 flights to the Yuba City, Marysville, Chico, Gridley, Orland, Arcata, and Verona areas of northern California. They also moved 70 passengers, including medical, engineering, and communications experts.

By December 28, the 41st Air Rscu Sq at Hamilton AFB had coordinated the rescue of 500 flood victims and the airlift of 10.85 tons of food, medicine, and clothing throughout the flooded districts of northern California and Major McDonald had supervised 107 rescue and relief missions. Waters receded at the end of December and flood victims looked forward to a drier new year.

Humanitarian Airlift Operations

15.
Name: Cumberland Flood.
Location: Kentucky, Tennessee, West Virginia, and Virginia.
Date(s): January 29–30, 1957.
Emergency: Heavy rain over western Virginia and adjacent areas caused flash flooding in the Cumberland River Valley region.
Air Force Organization(s) Involved: 2231st and 2259th Air Reserve Flying Centers and 757th Trp Carr Sq.
Airlifted: 10.4 tons of cots and blankets.
Aircraft Employed: C–46 (five).
Operations: A severe winter storm at the end of January dropped heavy rain over the mountains of eastern Kentucky, southern West Virginia, western Virginia, and northeastern Tennessee. Rivers such as the Cumberland, Kentucky, and Clinch flash flooded at least 19 towns, including 8 in Kentucky and 8 in Virginia. A 16-foot wall of water destroyed 150 homes in Pound, Virginia, and water rose as high as 20 feet at Barbourville, Kentucky. Floodwaters up to 10 feet lingered for 18 hours in Hazard, Kentucky, where 50 homes were swept away. In western Virginia alone, 1,000 people had fled their homes by January 30. At least 14 people died in the four-state flooding. Damage ran into the millions of dollars.

On January 29, the American Red Cross requested bedding from the Virginia Military District, which was involved in emergency relief as part of the U.S. Army's Operation Jupiter. At 8:00 p.m., the Virginia Military District contacted the 2231st Air Reserve Flying Center, under Maj. Carl Lindberg, at Sandston, Virginia, for an airlift of 6.7 tons of cots and blankets to Tri-City Airport near Bristol, Tennessee.

Using two C–46s from the 757th Trp Carr Sq and two other C–46s from the 2259th Air Reserve Flying Center at Andrews AFB, Maryland, Major Lindberg delivered the bedding by noon the next day. Although the cargo was relatively light, four aircraft were needed because of weight limitations at Tri-City Airport. During the noon hour on January 30, the Virginia Military District asked the 2231st Air Reserve Flying Center for another airlift of 3.7 tons of cots and blankets to Kanawha Airport at Charleston, West Virginia. A C–46 flew this mission the same day.

In two days and more than 20 hours of flying time, five C–46s delivered 10.4 tons of cots and blankets to the flooded area. In early February, President Eisenhower declared parts of Kentucky, West Virginia, and Virginia major disaster areas and authorized federal financial assistance. By then, floodwaters had subsided and the devastated communities began recovery operations.

16.
Name: Hurricane Audrey.
Location: Louisiana.
Date(s): June 27–August 27, 1957.

Emergency: A hurricane hit southwestern Louisiana, killing over 500 people and driving thousands from their homes.

Air Force Organization(s) Involved: Fourteenth Air Force.

Airlifted: 109 tons of food, clothing, cots, bedding, communications and water purification equipment, fogging machines, and cattle feed.

Aircraft Employed: C–45, C–46, C–47, C–119, SC–54, KC–97, L–20, H–5, H–19, H–21, B–25, and B–26 (43 total aircraft).

Operations: A tropical disturbance, first detected on June 24 in the Bay of Campeche in the southwestern Gulf of Mexico, quickly became a hurricane, moving north toward the Texas and Louisiana coasts. Hurricane Audrey veered northeastward just before hitting land around 8:00 a.m. on June 27 in the vicinity of Cameron, Louisiana, about 30 miles south of Lake Charles. With winds as high as 105 mph, the storm dumped torrential rain and drove extremely high tides that rose to as much as 12 feet above normal. High waves knocked buildings off their foundations before smashing them to pieces.

Although the residents of southwestern Louisiana had received ample warning before the catastrophe, many refused to evacuate. As many as 534 people drowned when sea water covered all of Cameron and most of Vermilion Parishes. About 40,000 lost their homes and damage estimates in Louisiana and Texas totaled $150 million. Worst hit were the towns of Cameron, Creole, and Grand Chenier. About 20,000 refugees crowded shelters in the Lake Charles area after the storm, and thousands of cattle drowned. Hurricane Audrey lost strength as it moved northeast, and its remnants reached the Ohio Valley and New England by month's end.

The Fourth Army directed relief efforts after the hurricane, enlisting the Fourteenth Air Force to supervise airlift operations that involved five USAF commands and 43 airplanes of 12 types, including C–45s, C–46s, C–47s, C–119s, and helicopters. On June 29, President Eisenhower declared Louisiana's flooded regions a disaster area and authorized federal economic assistance. Over 300 Air Force personnel, including 165 air crew members, participated in relief missions that consumed 1,851 man-days.

Between June 27 and August 27, planes directed by the Fourteenth Air Force airlifted more than 109 tons of emergency supplies—including food, clothing, bedding, and communications and water purification equipment—to the disaster area. The airlift encompassed 527 sorties and 455 flying hours. During the two months of relief missions, the USAF also transported 718 passengers and 300 cattle.

17.
Name: Ship Fire.
Location: Houston, Texas.
Date(s): November 8, 1959.
Emergency: A 12,000-ton oil tanker caught fire at the port of Houston, threatening other ships and port facilities.

Humanitarian Airlift Operations

Air Force Organization(s) Involved: 446th Trp Carr Wg.
Airlifted: 125 tons of foamite, a fire-extinguishing chemical.
Aircraft Employed: C–119 (18).
Operations: A few minutes after midnight on Sunday morning, November 8, a spark ignited gasoline that had spilled from barges in the Houston ship channel in Texas. The fire spread quickly to the *Amoco Virginia*, a 540-foot, 12,000-ton oil tanker that had just loaded 130,000 barrels of high test gasoline and diesel fuel. A series of explosions that could be heard 10 miles away rocked the burning ship, killing seven crew members and injuring eight.

Tied up at the Hess terminal on the north side of the Houston ship channel, the *Amoco Virginia* sank in shallow water, frustrating Coast Guard efforts to tow it away from a nearby 200-acre gasoline tank farm. Flames shot 300 feet into the air above the ruined tanker. Firemen rushed to the scene, shut off the main fuel loading line to the ship, and spread foam over the flaming wreckage. The conflagration threatened to ignite other ships and petrochemical facilities in the thickly populated area along the channel and block shipping at the nation's third busiest port. Local supplies of foamite, a chemical used to extinguish petroleum fires, were quickly exhausted.

At 10:00 a.m. on November 8, Houston civil defense officials asked for assistance from nearby Ellington AFB, Texas, home of the Air Force Reserve's 446th Trp Carr Wg. Seven of the wing's C–119 Flying Boxcar aircraft flew around the United States to pick up foamite, while others transported fire-fighting chemicals and equipment from Ellington to Houston.

Firefighters subsequently contained and then extinguished the fire that night. The airlift helped to prevent a recurrence of a disaster like the 1947 tragedy in Texas City, in which 500 persons died.

18.
Name: Northwestern Forest Fires.
Location: Oregon and Montana.
Date(s): July 24–29, 1960.
Emergency: Forest fires raged out of control in the northwestern states, consuming more than 225,000 acres.
Air Force Organization(s) Involved: 313th Trp Carr Sq (Medium) and 514th Trp Carr Wg.
Airlifted: At least two tons of fire-extinguishing foam and fire-fighting equipment and 30 fire-fighting experts.
Aircraft Employed: C–119 (three).
Operations: Prolonged dry weather in the western United States contributed to the outbreak of hundreds of forest fires in California, Oregon, Washington, Idaho, Montana, Wyoming, Utah, Nevada, and Arizona during the last part of July. By July 24, more than 225,000 acres of timber had burned. Over 100 fires spread in Oregon and Washington alone. The largest fire raged in the Anthony Lakes area

of northeastern Oregon, where more than 25,000 acres burned out of control between July 22 and 26.

The governor of Oregon, Mark Hatfield, asked the AF Res unit at Portland International Airport, the 313th Trp Carr Sq (Medium) under Col. Vernon E. Acker, to assist the Oregon State Forestry Department by airlifting fire-fighting equipment and chemicals from Portland to the disaster area. A C–119 delivered the cargo to Pendleton, Oregon, on July 24, and another C–119 airlifted two tons of fire-extinguishing foam from Portland to Baker, Oregon, on July 26. Late that day, firefighters brought the blaze under control, although the fire was not extinguished for several days. Governor Hatfield thanked Colonel Acker for the "outstanding service" and the "willing manner" in which the airlift was performed.

Containment of the Oregon fire, which the airlift helped make possible, allowed firefighters to concentrate on other areas. On Thursday night, July 28, the U.S. Forest Service's eastern region office asked Col. Campbell Y. Jackson, commander of the 514th Trp Carr Wg at Mitchel AFB, New York, to airlift 30 Forest Service experts from Pennsylvania, Virginia, Kentucky, and Illinois, to Missoula, Montana, to supervise fire-fighting efforts in western Montana. A 514th Trp Carr Wg C–119 Flying Boxcar picked up the firefighters from the various states on its way from Mitchel to Missoula on Friday, July 29. The Forest Service personnel helped to coordinate hundreds of firefighters who brought the fires under control during the next month.

19.
Name: Hurricane Donna.
Location: Florida, Puerto Rico, and Mayaguana Island.
Date(s): September 12–18, 1960.
Emergency: A hurricane hit Puerto Rico, the Bahamas, the Florida Keys, and the eastern coast of the United States.
Air Force Organization(s) Involved: 435th, 445th, and 463d Trp Carr Wgs; 1607th and 1608th Air Transport Wings (Air Trpt Wgs); and 823d Air Div.
Airlifted: At least 148 tons of bridge components, road building equipment, water purification equipment, food, water, clothing, blankets, and cots; and at least 119 passengers, including Army engineering personnel, carpenters, and electricians.
Aircraft Employed: C–130 (24), C–119 (24), C–124 (2+), C–54 (number unknown), and C–123 (number unknown).
Operations: In early September, Hurricane Donna, the fourth tropical storm of the Atlantic hurricane season, approached the West Indies from the southeast. On September 5, it swept across Puerto Rico, killing 102 people. The storm drifted across Mayaguana Island in the Bahamas on September 8. On the night of September 9, it struck the Florida Keys with wind gusts in excess of 160 mph.

Hurricane Donna flattened the resort town of Marathon, destroyed five bridges on the Overseas Highway connecting the Keys, and broke the fresh water aqueduct to Key West. Early on the morning of September 10, the hurricane turned northeast and hammered Fort Myers with 115 mph winds. Gathering strength again in the Atlantic after crossing the Florida peninsula, the storm hit North Carolina on September 11 and proceeded north along the eastern seaboard. On September 12, the storm crossed Long Island into New England before dissipating over the Gulf of St. Lawrence.

The hurricane left 121 people dead in the Antilles and 22 dead in the United States. In Florida alone, it destroyed $1 billion in property. On September 12, President Eisenhower declared parts of Florida disaster areas after Governor Leroy Collins requested federal aid.

Air Force cargo aircraft had evacuated bases along Hurricane Donna's path, but returned soon after the storm passed. Air Force officials quickly prepared to airlift relief supplies, equipment, and personnel to the devastated regions. C–124s from Dover AFB, Delaware, and Charleston AFB, South Carolina, flew 5,000 Army cots to San Juan, Puerto Rico; and C–54s carried 18 tons of food, blankets, clothing, and medicine from Patrick AFB, Florida, to Mayaguana in the Bahamas.

During the second week of September, the 435th Trp Carr Wg at Homestead AFB, Florida, used 24 C–119s to airlift water distillation units, food, clothing, blankets, and water cans to Marathon and Key West Naval Air Station (NAS). On the weekend of September 17 and 18, the wing's 77th Trp Carr Sq, stationed at Donaldson AFB, South Carolina, airlifted a panel bridge of the 101st Airborne Division to south Florida to help rebuild the Overseas Highway between the Florida mainland and Key West.

Meanwhile, 24 Ninth Air Force C–130s—most from the 463d Trp Carr Wg at Sewart AFB, Tennessee—airlifted two Army engineering companies from Fort Campbell, Kentucky, and Fort Bragg, North Carolina, to Homestead AFB and Key West to reconstruct the broken causeways connecting the Keys. Using 130 tons of airlifted bridge components and road-building equipment, the engineer companies worked toward each other from opposite ends of the Overseas Highway.

Planes from the 823d Air Div at Homestead AFB carried 1,800 gallons of fresh water to the Florida Keys and airlifted electrical generators to the area. Between September 12 and 18, the 445th Trp Carr Wg flew food and water to Key West NAS for distribution to civilians.

20.
Name: Hurricane Carla.
Location: Texas.
Date(s): September 11–October 5, 1961.
Emergency: A hurricane hit Matagorda Bay, Texas.
Air Force Organization(s) Involved: 443d and 446th Trp Carr Wgs.
Airlifted: At least 59 tons of emergency equipment and relief supplies, including electric generators, insecticide foggers, and tents; and at least 54 passengers, including reporters and Air Force personnel.
Aircraft Employed: C–119 (13).

Operations: Just after midnight on Monday, September 11, Hurricane Carla came ashore at Matagorda Bay on the Texas coast near Port Lavaca, about 80 miles northeast of Corpus Christi. The storm brought wind gusts as high as 173 mph, tides up to 10 feet above normal, and eight inches of rain. Although 300,000 coastal residents had evacuated, the storm claimed 40 lives and sent 563 people to the hospital. Wind and water destroyed more than 2,000 homes and flooded large sections of Freeport, Texas City, and Galveston. Six Texas towns lost telephone service, and Hurricane Carla subsequently spawned tornadoes in Louisiana.

The Fourth Army at San Antonio took charge of military disaster relief and immediately contacted the Fourth Air Force Reserve Region headquarters at Randolph AFB, Texas, for airlift support. Between September 11 and October 5, the reserve region coordinated 23 sorties of 13 aircraft using more than 100 flying hours to deliver support personnel, emergency equipment, and relief supplies to storm victims along the Texas Gulf coast.

The 446th Trp Carr Wg at Ellington AFB, Texas, used C–119s to transport electrical generators from New Orleans to Houston and Galveston. To prevent an epidemic from following the flooding, the wing hauled turbine insecticide sprayers from Buffalo, New York, to Victoria, Texas, on October 4 and 5.

Ellington AFB also supported Army and Navy helicopter flights from its runways. Helicopters and ground vehicles distributed 59 tons of emergency cargo unloaded from Air Force planes at the base during the emergency. The 433d Trp Carr Wg at Kelly AFB, Texas, also used C–119 aircraft to haul emergency personnel, equipment, and supplies, to the devastated Texas coast. Between October 2 and 5, the wing moved two fogging machines from San Francisco to Corpus Christi; 50 tents from Los Angeles to Victoria, Texas; and 50 Air Force trainees from Lackland AFB, Texas, to Galveston to assist in cleanup operations.

21.
Name: Operation Nava-Snow.
Location: Arizona and New Mexico.
Date(s): December 19–21, 1961.
Emergency: Blizzards blocked roads on a Navajo Indian reservation with deep snow, threatening the people and livestock with starvation.
Air Force Organization(s) Involved: 433d Trp Carr Wg and 4900th AB Gp.
Airlifted: 80 tons of food and livestock feed.
Aircraft Employed: C–47 (two) and C–119 (two).
Operations: Severe winter storms during mid-December covered the Navajo Indian reservation in northeastern Arizona and northwestern New Mexico under deep snow that buried pastures and blocked roads. Snowbound Indians and isolated livestock faced malnutrition and starvation. On December 17, the Fourth Army headquarters called the Fourth Air Force Reserve Region headquarters at Randolph AFB, Texas, for an emergency airlift of food to Navajo families and

feed to their herds in the Window Rock area of Arizona. This was not the first time that U.S. military aircraft had been called to the reservation for food deliveries. In January 1932, Army aircraft had dropped food bundles to snowbound and starving Navajos.

The Fourth Air Force Reserve Region immediately contacted the 4900th AB Gp at Kirtland AFB, New Mexico, for assistance. Bad weather on December 18 forced the cancellation of the first missions of Operation Nava-Snow. On December 19, two Kirtland AFB C–47s joined with two C–119 airplanes of the 433d Trp Carr Wg from Kelly AFB, Texas, to begin the airlift, which continued through December 21.

During the three days, the four cargo aircraft flew 31 sorties, consuming 80 flying hours and dropping 80 tons of food packages and bales of hay. Using Kirtland AFB as a staging area, two 433d Trp Carr Wg planes hauled 58 tons of emergency cargo in 11 sorties to the Window Rock area. By December 21, improved weather allowed surface transportation routes to reopen and the emergency airlift ended.

22.
Name: Idaho Flood.
Location: Idaho.
Date(s): February 1962.
Emergency: Warm weather followed heavy snows in the Rocky Mountains, flooding valleys in Idaho and adjacent states.
Air Force Organization(s) Involved: 1st Air Trpt Sq.
Airlifted: 26 tons of sandbags.
Aircraft Employed: C–133 (one).
Operations: During February, relatively warm weather thawed deep snow that had accumulated in the northern Rocky Mountains, flooding river valleys in six states. In Idaho, 4,000 people were forced from their homes and Governor Robert Smylie asked President John F. Kennedy to declare the southern part of the state a disaster area. The Portneuf River, a tributary of the Snake, swelled over its banks, isolating the towns of Lava Hot Springs and Bancroft and threatening to inundate Pocatello.

The Military Air Transport Service diverted a C–133 Cargomaster of the 1st Air Trpt Sq from Dover AFB, Delaware, from a flight to Travis AFB, California, for the emergency. The airplane transported 100,000 empty sandbags weighing 26 tons from the U.S. Army's Sharp General Depot near Stockton, California, to Pocatello, where the Portneuf River rose more than four feet above flood stage. Relief workers filled and placed the sandbags to prevent further flooding along the river.

23.
Name: Chlorine Barge Emergency.
Location: Mississippi.
Date(s): September 21–22, 1962.
Emergency: Recovery of 1,100 tons of poisonous chlorine from a sunken barge in the Mississippi River near Natchez, Mississippi, called for the possible evacuation of 80,000 people.
Air Force Organization(s) Involved: 65th, 403d, 433d, 435th, 442d, and 446th Trp Carr Wgs; and 69th, 77th, 78th, 305th, 357th, and 706th Trp Carr Sqs.
Airlifted: 190 tons of cargo, including 15,200 cots.
Aircraft Employed: C–119 (36) and C–124 (six).
Operations: A barge loaded with 1,100 tons of pressurized liquid chlorine in four 75-foot-long tanks sank in the Mississippi River on March 23, 1961. In September 1962, the U.S. Army Corps of Engineers discovered the sunken barge in 60 feet of water near Natchez, Mississippi, and prepared to salvage the chlorine. Experts feared that if the tanks ruptured during salvage operations, then deadly chlorine gas might be released into the environment. Authorities prepared, therefore, to evacuate 80,000 people in the Natchez area, including residents of three Mississippi counties and three Louisiana parishes.

The Continental Air Command organized an airlift of supplies and equipment from Texas to Vicksburg, Mississippi, to accommodate potential evacuees. On September 21 and 22, 36 C–119s and six C–124s, belonging to six troop carrier wings and six troop carrier squadrons, flew 190 tons of cargo—including 15,200 cots—from Bergstrom AFB, Texas, to Vicksburg, Mississippi. The 42 cargo planes came from 12 bases in Texas, Oklahoma, Missouri, Florida, Michigan, Louisiana, Alabama, and South Carolina. The airlift ended about dawn on September 22, 16 hours after it began.

Salvage operations to lift the chlorine tanks began on October 1. Although the salvage work proceeded without incident, President Kennedy declared the Natchez vicinity a major disaster area on October 10, in response to an appeal from Governor Ross R. Barnett. On November 5, Army engineers recovered the last of the sunken tanks. The crisis ended without the release of chlorine or an emergency evacuation.

24.
Name: Kentucky Floods.
Location: Eastern Kentucky.
Date(s): Week of March 13, 1963.
Emergency: Torrential rain and melting snow flooded five river valleys in eastern Kentucky, forcing at least 25,000 people from their homes.
Air Force Organization(s) Involved: 302d Trp Carr Wg and 926th and 932d Trp Carr Gps.
Airlifted: 2,000 gallons of gasoline and an unknown number of cots.

Humanitarian Airlift Operations

Aircraft Employed: C–119 (three).

Operations: During March, heavy rain and melting snow in the Appalachian Mountains caused severe flooding in eastern Kentucky as the Ohio, Cumberland, Rockcastle, Big Sandy, and Kentucky Rivers spilled over their banks to flood towns such as Harlan, Pikeville, Hazard, and Lothair. At least 25,000 refugees fled their homes. On March 13, President Kennedy responded to an appeal from Lieutenant Governor Wilson Wyatt by declaring 20 eastern Kentucky counties a major disaster area.

At the same time, CONAC headquarters at Robins AFB, Georgia, organized an airlift of supplies to Kentucky in response to Army requests. On March 13, the 302d Trp Carr Wg of Clinton County AFB, Ohio, and the 926th Trp Carr Gp of New Orleans each flew a C–119 Flying Boxcar to haul a total of 2,000 gallons of gasoline from Wright-Patterson AFB, Ohio, to London, Kentucky, for rescue and evacuation vehicles. During the same week, the 926th C–119 and another Flying Boxcar belonging to the 932d Trp Carr Gp at Scott AFB, Illinois, airlifted cots from Camp Pickett, Virginia, to Fort Knox, Kentucky. The Army moved the cots by ground vehicles to refugee shelters. Floodwaters receded by the end of March.

25.

Name: Texas Haylift.

Location: Texas.

Date(s): February 8–9, 1964.

Emergency: Heavy snowfall stranded thousands of cattle near Pampa, Texas, threatening livestock with starvation.

Air Force Organization(s) Involved: 446th Trp Carr Wg.

Airlifted: More than 1,900 bales of hay.

Aircraft Employed: C–119 (seven).

Operations: An immense blizzard struck the Texas panhandle during the first week of February, when more than two feet of snow fell near the city of Pampa. Thousands of cattle, which had survived prolonged subfreezing temperatures, could not reach grass beneath the snow. High drifts blocked roads, preventing farmers from transporting feed to their isolated herds.

On Thursday night, February 6, Maj. Gen. Selden Simpson of the Texas Army National Guard asked Congressman Walter Rogers for an emergency air-drop of hay to 7,000 starving livestock that had been without feed since February 3. Congressman Rogers contacted the Fourth Army at Fort Sam Houston near San Antonio, Texas, which enlisted the Fourth Air Force Reserve Region at Randolph AFB, Texas, for C–119s previously used in operations like Operation Hayride in January 1949 and Operation Nava-Snow in December 1961.

The Air Force approved the operation, and the Fourth Air Force Reserve Region tapped the 446th Trp Carr Wg at Ellington AFB near Houston, Texas, to send seven C–119 Flying Boxcars to Amarillo AFB in the Texas panhandle. On Friday, February 7, National Guardsmen loaded hay aboard the planes at Amarillo and flew 23 sorties over a five-county area on February 8 and 9. Flying low, the C–119 crews dropped more than 1,900 bales of hay to the hungry herds during two days of emergency missions. Saving many cattle, the 446th Trp Carr Wg helped to protect the regional economy while giving servicemen valuable experience.

26.
Name: Operation Helping Hand.
Location: Alaska.
Date(s): March 28–April 17, 1964.
Emergency: An earthquake measuring 8.4 on the Richter scale struck southern Alaska.
Air Force Organization(s) Involved: 62d, 464th, and 516th Trp Carr Wgs; 1254th, 1501st, 1607th, 1608th, 1611th, and 1707th Air Trpt Wgs; 5017th Operations Squadron (Ops Sq); 41st and 76th Air Rscu Sqs; 146th Air Trpt Wg (ANG); and 144th Air Trpt Sq (ANG).
Airlifted: 1,850 tons of electrical generators, water purification equipment, seismographic apparatus, construction equipment, bedding, and clothing; and 850 passengers, including medical, construction, and communications personnel.
Aircraft Employed: C–124 (55), C–123 (17), C–130 (11), C–97 (8), C–135 (4), C–133 (2), C–121 (2), C–118 (1), VC–137 (1), HU–16 (3), HC–54 (1), and H–21 (number unknown).
Operations: At 5:36 p.m. on Good Friday, March 27, the twentieth century's most intense earthquake to hit North America to date struck south central Alaska, leaving 117 people dead or missing and damages estimated at $750 million. Registering at least 8.4 on the Richter scale, the quake produced tidal waves felt as far away as Japan, Hawaii, and California. The initial earthquake, and a long series of aftershocks, left Anchorage, Alaska's most populous city, in ruins and destroyed large sections of Seward, Valdez, Whittier, Cordova, Kodiak, and Kenai.

Governor William Egan proclaimed an emergency. On March 28, President Lyndon B. Johnson declared Alaska a major disaster area and Lt. Gen. Raymond J. Reeves of the Alaskan Command secured almost immediate restoration of communications between Alaska's military bases and Washington, D.C. Within hours of the first tremor, the U.S. military launched Operation Helping Hand to provide emergency disaster relief to citizens of the forty-ninth state.

Twelve kinds of Air Force aircraft participated in airlift operations, flying to Alaska from at least nine different bases, including McChord AFB, Washington; Travis AFB, California; Dover AFB, Delaware; Pope AFB, North Carolina; Dyess AFB, Texas; McGuire AFB, New Jersey; Andrews AFB, Maryland; Scott AFB, Illinois; and Reese AFB, Texas. Most aircraft discharged their cargo at Elmendorf AFB outside Anchorage or at Eielson AFB near Fairbanks. Many flights stopped at bases around the lower 48 states to pick up equipment and personnel.

The 1,850 tons of supplies airlifted to Alaska in 21 days included 115 beds, 667 mattresses, 250 crates of baby formula, 1.4 tons of charcoal, 2.7 tons of canned soup, and a ton of blankets. Communications, construction, and water purification equipment constituted the heaviest cargo. The Military Air Transport Service alone carried 1,375 tons of airlifted materiel, in missions consuming 1,300 hours of flying time. C–123s from the Alaskan Air Command carried 280 tons in 200 flying hours.

Ten C–130s, eight from the 464th Trp Carr Wg and two from the 516th Trp Carr Wg, represented TAC. Alaska ANG C–123s and California ANG C–97s carried more than 157.5 tons of emergency supplies. Air Rescue Service personnel and aircraft from the 41st Air Rscu Sq at Hamilton AFB, California, and the 76th Air Rscu Sq at Hickam AFB, Hawaii, evacuated citizens, flew reconnaissance missions, and airdropped medical supplies. In 21 days, the USAF transported more than 850 passengers and evacuees, including construction workers, medical personnel, engineers, communications experts, and earthquake victims.

On March 28, Edward A. McDermott, director of the Office of Emergency Preparedness, and 26 other government officials flew from Andrews AFB to Elmendorf AFB on a VC–137 of the 1254th Air Trpt Wg. That same day, a Western Transport Air Force (West Trpt AF) C–135 carried medical personnel from Travis AFB to Anchorage. On March 29, the same plane returned to Travis with 48 patients. From March 29 to 30, C–124s of the 1607th and 63d Air Trpt Wgs flew 30 tons of communications equipment and personnel from McGuire, Scott, McChord, and Hill AFBs to Elmendorf.

Meanwhile, a 1611th Air Trpt Wg C–118 carried seismographic equipment and geologists from Albuquerque and San Francisco to Anchorage. On March 31, the same wing ferried 14 DoD officials aboard a C–135 from Andrews AFB to Elmendorf and a C–133 airlifted a 20-ton electrical generator from Seattle to Kodiak. Between March 29 and April 2, C–124 aircraft moved over 30 tons of vans and electrical generators from McGuire AFB to Anchorage. Twelve C–124s from McChord and Travis AFBs flew 124 tons of water purification equipment to Elmendorf.

By March 31, MATS aircraft had flown 21 missions to Alaska, covering 48,700 statute miles in four days. In that same period, eight C–130s of the Tactical Air Command's 464th Trp Carr Wg from Pope AFB, North Carolina, picked up a 100-bed hospital; two 36-bed infirmaries; and 162 doctors, nurses, and medical technicians from Shaw and Seymour Johnson AFBs and flew them to Anchorage.

Air Force airlift missions to Alaska continued for three weeks. By the end of April, Anchorage and other devastated communities in south central Alaska had begun to recover from the disaster and no longer required emergency airlift missions.

27.
Name: Montana Flood.
Location: Montana.
Date(s): June 8–12, 1964.

Emergency: Rapid thawing and late spring snow in the Rocky Mountains coupled with four-inch rains spilled the Sun River and its tributaries over their banks, flooding a host of communities and washing out numerous bridges.

Air Force Organization(s) Involved: 341st Strategic Missile Wing; 62d Trp Carr Wg; 462d Strategic Aerospace Wing; 78th Fighter Wing (Ftr Wg); 120th Ftr Gp (Montana ANG); and Detachment 8, Western Air Rescue Center (Air Rscu Cen).

Airlifted: 35 tons of food, clothing, medicine, telephone equipment, generators, and mail; 194 rescued passengers; and 87 medical and Red Cross personnel.

Aircraft Employed: C–123 (two), C–124 (two), H–19 (four), HH–43 (two), T–33 (two), C–47 (one), CH–3 (number unknown), and UH–1 (number unknown).

Operations: During 1964, snow fell as late as May on the eastern slopes of Montana's Rocky Mountains. Three days of warm rain, up to four inches in places, melted the snow and spilled the tributaries of the Sun River over their banks in early June. On June 8, dams burst on Birch Creek on the Blackfeet Indian Reservation and on Two Medicine Creek near Glacier National Park.

Floodwaters washed out ten bridges, isolating and inundating Browning, Augusta, Choteau, Dupuyer, Vaughn, Sun River, and a host of other Montana communities. Parts of Great Falls, a city of 70,000 at the confluence of the Sun and Missouri Rivers, were under 11 feet of water. Mayor Marian Erdmann estimated $1 million damage in that city alone. In Montana as a whole, 37 people died and 1,200 were left homeless as the floods engulfed 5,000 square miles by June 9. The U.S. Army Corps of Engineers estimated $9.58 million in damages, and Governor Tim Babcock appealed for federal aid after an aerial survey. On June 10, President Johnson declared seven Montana counties a major disaster area.

The 341st Strategic Missile Wing at Malmstrom AFB, just east of Great Falls, responded to the emergency, setting up a disaster control center under Base Commander Col. George Budway by 2:00 p.m. on June 8, while Lt. Col. Thomas Beavers took charge of the 13 base helicopters for rescue and relief missions.

Air Force airlift operations continued from June 8 to 12. Two HH–43 helicopters from the Western Air Rescue Center's Detachment 8 at Glasgow AFB, Montana, joined rescue efforts, sometimes hoisting stranded flood survivors from the tops of buildings. Larson AFB, Washington, sent four H–19 helicopters from the 462d Strategic Aerospace Wing to deliver relief supplies to isolated areas.

Air Force fixed-wing aircraft also participated. The 62d Trp Carr Wg used two C–124 planes to airlift a pair of Army helicopters from Fort Lewis, Washington, to Malmstrom AFB. The Montana Air National Guard's 120th Ftr Gp flew a C–47 and a pair of T–33 planes to carry cargo and locate victims. Two C–123 Providers from Hamilton AFB, California, and Stewart AFB, New York, carried food, clothing, and supplies to the flooded communities. Army aircraft from Fort Lewis participating in the relief missions operated from Malmstrom AFB.

Humanitarian Airlift Operations

By June 12, as floodwaters subsided, Air Force helicopters and airplanes had delivered 35 tons of cargo, including medicine, telephone equipment, generators, mail, food, and clothing. They rescued 194 persons and helped to transport 87 doctors, nurses, and Red Cross personnel.

28.

Name: Hurricane Hilda.

Location: Louisiana.

Date(s): October 2–3, 1964.

Emergency: A hurricane hit south central Louisiana.

Air Force Organization(s) Involved: 433d Trp Carr Wg and Fourth Air Force Reserve Region (unspecified units).

Airlifted: At least 24 tons of blankets, cots, and mattresses.

Aircraft Employed: C–119 (six), T–29 (three), C–54 (one), C–47 (one), C–97 (one), and C–123 (one).

Operations: On October 1, Hurricane Hilda formed off western Cuba and moved into the Gulf of Mexico, heading toward south central Louisiana. Remembering the devastation of Hurricane Audrey, which had killed more than 500 people in 1957 (see Hurricane Audrey, June–August 1957), 150,000 coastal Louisiana residents fled their homes and sought refuge at emergency shelters.

On the night of October 1, Fourth Army headquarters at Fort Sam Houston, Texas, contacted the Fourth Air Force Reserve Region headquarters at Randolph AFB, Texas, to request an airlift of bedding to central Louisiana. Responding to a call from CONAC, the 433d Trp Carr Wg at Kelly AFB, Texas, airlifted 24 tons of blankets to England AFB near Alexandria, Louisiana, aboard six C–119 aircraft on October 2. Two of the cargo planes flew directly from Kelly AFB, where they had been loaded with blankets from Fort Sam Houston. The others flew to Fort Smith, Arkansas, to pick up blankets for delivery to Alexandria.

The six 433d Trp Carr Wg planes returned to Kelly AFB before dawn on October 3. Other Fourth Air Force Reserve Region aircraft—including one C–54, one C–47, three T–29s, and one C–123 from Texas and one C–97 from Oklahoma—also ferried blankets, cots, and mattresses to Louisiana in preparation for hurricane refugees. These 13 planes flew more than 61 hours. Surface vehicles delivered the blankets, cots, and mattresses to emergency shelters.

Hurricane Hilda hit south central Louisiana near Vermilion Bay on the night of October 3 with 120 mph winds, devastating the sugar cane crop. The hurricane generated tornadoes at Larose, Galliano, and Golden Meadow and left 30 people dead. After conferring with Governor John McKeithan, President Johnson declared southeast Louisiana a major disaster area on October 4. In St. Mary Parish alone, 40,000 fled their homes as towns were left without water, sewage, or electricity.

29.
Name: Operation Haylift.
Location: Montana.
Date(s): December 18–21, 1964.
Emergency: Blizzards isolated cattle and sheep in southeastern Montana, threatening them with starvation.
Air Force Organization(s) Involved: 349th and 452d Trp Carr Wgs; and 938th, 940th, 941st, and 945th Trp Carr Gps.
Airlifted: 65 tons of hay and other livestock feed.
Aircraft Employed: C–119 (nine).
Operations: On December 16 and 17, a blizzard from Canada dropped heavy snow that blocked roads and isolated ranches and livestock in southeastern Montana. Temperatures dropped as low as 40 degrees below zero, killing thousands of cattle and sheep. Thick snow cover threatened to starve hundreds of thousands more.

On Friday, December 18, Governor Tim Babcock appealed for federal and military assistance. That same day President Johnson declared eight southeastern Montana counties a disaster area. Within hours, four AF Res C–119 aircraft—one each from the 938th Trp Carr Gp at Hamilton AFB, California; the 940th Trp Carr Gp at McClellan AFB, California; the 941st Trp Carr Gp at Paine AFB, Washington; and the 945th Trp Carr Gp at Hill AFB, Utah—flew to Malmstrom AFB in Montana for an emergency airlift of hay and livestock feed to the starving herds.

The 349th Trp Carr Wg at Hamilton AFB supervised Operation Haylift along with the Department of Agriculture, which purchased feed from Fairfield and Great Falls in central Montana for distribution by air from Malmstrom. Between December 18 and 20, the four C–119s delivered at least 40 tons of hay in the region centered about 225 miles southeast of Great Falls, dropping most of the feed directly over the stranded herds from an altitude of 50 feet and a speed of about 150 mph. Each C–119 carried an average of 5.5 tons per flight. One C–119 dropped 5 tons of hay over a herd of 800 cattle at a ranch about 30 miles from Miles City on the Tongue River. The cattle had been without feed for four days. Montana ANG L–19 aircraft helped to guide the Flying Boxcars to the ranches most in need.

On Sunday, December 20, another blizzard dropped several inches of new snow on southern Montana, grounding the four cargo planes. The 349th and 452d Trp Carr Wgs dispatched five more C–119s from California to Malmstrom AFB, three from Hamilton AFB and two from March AFB. By December 21, nine C–119s were airdropping livestock feed. Between December 18 and 21, C–119s distributed 65 tons of livestock food in 17 sorties over southeastern Montana. By Tuesday, December 22, highway workers had cleared major roads in the region, allowing ground vehicles to take over feed deliveries.

30.
Name: Operation Biglift.
Location: California and Oregon.
Date(s): December 22, 1964–January 22, 1965.
Emergency: Heavy rain flooded the west coast, cutting surface transportation routes and leaving 48 people dead and 17,000 homeless.
Air Force Organization(s) Involved: 349th, 442d, 446th, and 512th Trp Carr Wgs; 9th Strategic Airlift Wing; 146th Air Training Wing; 3635th Flying Training Wing; 908th, 912th, 914th, 917th, 924th, 925th, and 939th Trp Carr Gps; 129th Air Commando Group; 4560th Combat Support Group; 408th Ftr Gp; 4650th Special Air Mission Squadron; Detachment 9, Western Air Rscu Cen; West Trpt AF (unspecified units); and Air Force Flight Test Center (unspecified units).
Airlifted: 1,598 tons of food, clothing, bedding, fuel, hay, grain, vehicles, pipe, medical supplies, sandbags, and mail; and 522 passengers.
Aircraft Employed: C–119 (172), KC–97 (13), UH–19 (12), C–130 (12), CH–21 (9), C–124 (7), C–123 (6), CH–43 (5), H–43 (2), U–6 (2), H–19 (1), C–47 (1), CH–3 (1), VT–29 (1), and CH–47 (1).
Operations: Pacific storms dropped a heavy, steady rain on Oregon and northern California during the last two weeks of December, producing flooding similar to that which had devastated the area nine years earlier. The Klamath, Eel, Mad, Van Duzen, Salmon, Smith, and Russian Rivers spilled over their banks, inundating homes, farms, forests, and factories in the "Redwood Empire." The downpours caused landslides and washed away at least 26 bridges, isolating communities in Humboldt, Del Norte, Siskiyou, and Mendocino Counties in northern California.

Governors Edmund G. Brown of California and Mark Hatfield of Oregon declared the flooded regions disaster areas. On December 22, civil defense officials asked the Sixth Army for military assistance. Sixth Army headquarters at the Presidio in San Francisco established a joint emergency operations center and called for an airlift of food and relief supplies to areas where surface transportation routes were cut.

On December 23, the Sixth Air Force Reserve Region established an airlift command post at Hamilton AFB, California, under Brig. Gen. Jack A. Gibbs. Air Force Reserve participation was directed by Lt. Gen. Edward J. Timberlake from CONAC headquarters at Robins AFB, Georgia. The 349th Trp Carr Wg (AF Res) at Hamilton AFB conducted the bulk of the airlift, using C–119 aircraft to haul supplies from California bases—to which cargo was delivered by other Air Force organizations—to Humboldt County Airport at Arcata, California, about 215 miles north of San Francisco. Four troop carrier wings and seven troop carrier groups of other wings constituted the bulk of Air Force reserve resources committed to the airlift.

Between December 23 and January 22, more than 200 Air Force cargo planes delivered 522 passengers and 1,598 tons of cargo, including food rations, clothing, fuel, sandbags, blankets, hay, grain, medical supplies, mail, vehicles, and pipe. Fifteen types of aircraft—including C–119s, KC–97s, UH–19s, C–130s, CH–21s, C–124s, and C–123s—from California, Georgia, Louisiana, Texas, Alabama, New York, Oregon, Pennsylvania, Missouri, and Washington participated in Operation Biglift. The aircraft represented CONAC (AF Res and ANG), MATS, SAC, the Air Training Command, and the Air Defense Command.

In one month, the Air Force flew 318 sorties for the emergency, using 996 flying hours. Some relief supplies were airdropped to isolated victims in Oregon. Navy, Marine Corps, and Coast Guard aircraft, especially helicopters, contributed to the overall relief efforts, coordinated by the Sixth Army at the Presidio. Operation Biglift ended on January 22 with the reopening of most surface transportation routes in northern California and western Oregon.

31.
Name: Colorado Flood.
Location: Colorado.
Date(s): June 17, 1965.
Emergency: The South Platte River flooded the Denver area.
Air Force Organization(s) Involved: 945th Trp Carr Gp.
Airlifted: 82 tons of cots, bedding, medical supplies, and other relief cargo.
Aircraft Employed: C–119 (six).
Operations: A severe storm system accompanied by hail and tornadoes drenched the eastern Rocky Mountains in central Colorado in mid-June. The rapidly flowing waters of the South Platte River spilled into valley communities, including Castle Rock, Louviers, and Littleton, between Colorado Springs and Denver, just north of the U.S. Air Force Academy. On June 16, up to 20 feet of water flooded Denver. The rampaging flood destroyed or damaged at least 15 bridges in the Denver area. One witness reported that the South Platte River rose 15 feet in one hour.

On June 16, Governor John Love appealed to the USAF at nearby Lowry AFB for aid. The base donated 1,500 cots, 3,500 blankets, and 300 combat rations to the Red Cross for flood victims. At least 200 refugees found temporary shelter at Lowry. When supplies dwindled, the Red Cross requested an Air Force airlift. The AF Res 945th Trp Carr Gp at Hill AFB, Utah, collected cots, bedding, medical supplies, and other emergency goods at their base from the Ogden defense depot.

On June 17, six of the group's C–119s airlifted 82 tons of the relief cargo from Hill AFB to Denver, where Lowry AFB personnel helped to distribute the supplies. The high water subsided almost as quickly as it had risen, and no further airlift missions were needed. By the end of June, the South Platte had resumed its normal rate of flow from the Rocky Mountains to the Great Plains.

32.
Name: Hurricane Betsy Airlift.
Location: Louisiana.
Date(s): September 11–18, 1965.

Humanitarian Airlift Operations

Emergency: Hurricane Betsy hit southeastern Louisiana, flooding extensive portions of New Orleans.

Air Force Organization(s) Involved: 302d, 403d, 433d, 434th, 435th, 440th, 442d, 445th, 446th, 452d, 459th, 512th, and 514th Trp Carr Wgs.

Airlifted: 638 tons of food, blankets, cots, clothing, and communications and kitchen equipment; and 660 rescue and relief workers.

Aircraft Employed: C–119 (113), C–124 (22), C–123 (5), C–47 (1), T–29 (1), C–54 (1), and C–130 (1).

Operations: At dusk on Thursday, September 9, Hurricane Betsy hit the mouth of the Mississippi River in southeastern Louisiana and followed the river to New Orleans. Before dawn on September 10, the hurricane raked the city with 125 mph winds and high tides, killing over 70 people, forcing 185,000 from their homes, and destroying $1 billion in property. Most damage resulted from flooding, against which residents were not insured. The storm slowly dissipated as it moved past Baton Rouge.

Governor John McKeithan appealed for federal relief. On Friday evening, September 10, President Johnson flew to New Orleans and declared southeastern Louisiana a disaster area. Early the next morning, CONAC at Robins AFB, Georgia, initiated an airlift of emergency supplies and equipment to the disaster area in cooperation with the Fourth Army and the Fourth Air Force Reserve Region. C–119, C–124, C–123, and other aircraft from 13 troop carrier wings in 11 states delivered 660 relief and rescue workers and 638 tons of food, blankets, cots, clothing, telephone repair equipment, and field kitchen components between September 11 and 18.

Most of the 157 missions terminated at the naval air station at Alvin Callender Field near New Orleans, but some of the cargo planes unloaded at New Orleans International Airport or at Baton Rouge. The 926th Trp Carr Gp at Callender Field assumed off–loading duties, sometimes using delivery trucks borrowed from New Orleans area department stores.

On the first day of the airlift, 100 tons of supplies arrived in the disaster area; on Sunday, September 12, 26 C–119s and seven C–124s delivered 95 tons of relief cargo. At the peak of the airlift, a C–119 plane was unloaded every 15 minutes, and a C–124 every 30 minutes. Most C–124s carried telephone repair trucks and equipment to restore communications in New Orleans. After a week-long airlift in which 144 Air Force planes took part, CONAC concluded Hurricane Betsy relief operations on September 18.

33.
Name: Phoenix Area Flood.
Location: Phoenix, Arizona.
Date(s): December 31, 1965–January 1, 1966.
Emergency: The Salt and Gila Rivers flooded the suburbs of Phoenix.
Air Force Organization(s) Involved: 942d Air Trpt Gp (Heavy) and

Detachments 15 and 16, Western Air Rscu Cen.

Airlifted: 44 tons of cots, blankets, and other emergency supplies; and 9 victims rescued.

Aircraft Employed: C–124 (two) and H–43 (five).

Operations: When the Salt and Gila Rivers flooded the southern suburbs of Phoenix at the end of December, the local American Red Cross requested assistance to transport relief supplies to the area. The Continental Air Command, in cooperation with the Army, contacted the 452d Trp Carr Wg at March AFB, California.

On December 31, the 942d Air Trpt Gp (Heavy) flew 44.3 tons of emergency cargo, including hundreds of cots and 600 blankets, from March AFB to Phoenix aboard two C–124 cargo planes. On New Year's Day, the airlifted supplies were available to the Red Cross to relieve flood victims. Meanwhile, three H–43 helicopters from Williams AFB, Arizona, and two H–43s from Luke AFB, Arizona, representing Detachments 15 and 16 of the Western Air Rscu Cen, rescued nine flood victims. During a 24-hour period, 50 Air Force reservists participated in seven rescue and relief missions.

34.

Name: Northwestern California Flood.

Location: California.

Date(s): January 5, 1966.

Emergency: The Eel and Mad Rivers and Redwood Creek, swollen by the rains of winter storms, flooded their valleys.

Air Force Organization(s) Involved: 349th Trp Carr Wg.

Airlifted: 4.5 tons of folding cots and blankets and two passengers.

Aircraft Employed: C–119 (one).

Operations: During the first week of January, almost continuous rain from winter storms flooded the Eel and Mad River valleys in the Pacific Coast Range of northwestern California. The floodwaters inundated rural sections near Eureka and Ferndale, forcing thousands of residents to evacuate their homes. As Redwood Creek overflowed, 1,000 fled the Orick area.

The Sixth Air Force Reserve Region, headquartered at Hamilton AFB just north of San Francisco, responded to local appeals for assistance by tapping the 349th Trp Carr Wg (AF Res), also at Hamilton. On January 5, one of the wing's C–119s, crewed by four reservists, flew 300 folding cots and 300 blankets, weighing 4.5 tons, from Sacramento to Arcata, California, near the flooded valleys where Red Cross officials used the supplies in emergency shelters. Waters receded as the weather cleared later in the month, allowing the evacuees to return home.

Humanitarian Airlift Operations

35.
Name: Mississippi Tornadoes.
Location: Mississippi.
Date(s): March 3–4, 1966.
Emergency: Tornadoes skipped through central Mississippi, killing 52 people, injuring 497, and destroying or damaging $12 million in property.
Air Force Organization(s) Involved: 908th Trp Carr Gp.
Airlifted: Blood and two Red Cross mobile canteens.
Aircraft Employed: C–119 (one).
Operations: At dusk on Thursday, March 3, tornadoes struck the Jackson area of central Mississippi, leaving the city without electrical power for nearly seven hours. The twisters killed 52 people, including 12 at Candlestick Park shopping center in suburban Jackson. In western Rankin County, just across the Pearl River east of Jackson, the storms destroyed the Continental Can Company and Jackson Tile Company industrial plants and damaged the Knox Glass Company factory. High winds overturned six railroad cars and destroyed the modern brick Woodville Heights Baptist Church. The storm system caused $12 million in property losses and injured 497 persons.

At 10:00 p.m. on March 3, before electrical power was restored in parts of Jackson, Ralph A. Holberg, Jr., a member of the American Red Cross national board of governors, called the 908th Trp Carr Gp at Brookley AFB, Alabama, to airlift blood to the Mississippi capital. The 908th, under the command of Col. William A. Willis, flew a C–119 Flying Boxcar laden with Red Cross blood, blood derivatives, and two mobile canteens from Brookley AFB to Jackson. The four-man crew, led by Maj. Harold W. Weekley, accomplished the mission by 2:00 a.m., four hours after the call for help. Red Cross officials in Jackson used the blood supplies to assist injured tornado victims who crowded local hospitals.

36.
Name: Midwest Flood.
Location: North Dakota and Minnesota.
Date(s): March 24, 1966.
Emergency: Blizzards flooded the Red River valley between North Dakota and Minnesota.
Air Force Organization(s) Involved: 434th and 440th Trp Carr Wgs.
Airlifted: 19 tons of water pumps and pipe.
Aircraft Employed: C–119 (four).
Operations: During the first week of March, a blizzard struck the Dakotas and Minnesota with winds in excess of 90 mph and heavy snow, leaving 20 people dead. A mid-March thaw flooded parts of the Red River valley between North Dakota and Minnesota. A second severe snowstorm hit the same area between March 21 and 24, dropping up to 14 inches of snow. The new precipitation com-

pounded the flooding, and President Johnson declared North Dakota a major disaster area on March 23.

On March 24, CONAC headquarters at Robins AFB, Georgia, responded to Fifth Army requests for airlift assistance by directing the 440th Trp Carr Wg at General Billy Mitchell Field in Milwaukee and the 434th Trp Carr Wg at Bakalar AFB, Indiana, to airlift six water pumps and 1.25 tons of pipe from civil defense stocks at Chicago O'Hare International Airport to the flooded disaster area.

The 440th Trp Carr Wg flew three pumps from Chicago to Grand Forks, North Dakota, aboard two C–119 Flying Boxcars while the 434th Trp Carr Wg flew three pumps and pipe from Chicago to the Minneapolis-St. Paul airport aboard two other C–119s. Reservists with the 934th Trp Carr Gp unloaded the planes at Minneapolis and Army trucks hauled the cargo 125 miles to Fort Ripley, Minnesota, where it was used to divert floodwaters. The C–119s completed the airlift missions in one day.

37.
Name: Texas Encephalitis Epidemic.
Location: Texas.
Date(s): August 17–30, 1966.
Emergency: An encephalitis epidemic threatened the Dallas and Corpus Christi areas of Texas, killing 11 people and hospitalizing almost 200.
Air Force Organization(s) Involved: 4500th AB Wg.
Airlifted: 14,210 gallons of insecticide.
Aircraft Employed: C–123 (six).
Operations: An encephalitis epidemic broke out in southern and central Texas at the end of July and gathered momentum into August. Spread by mosquitoes, the St. Louis variety of the neurological disease killed 11 people in the Lone Star State, including seven in Dallas and two in Corpus Christi. Over 100 cases in the two cities alarmed Texas health officials, who contacted the U.S. Public Health Service for help in containing the "sleeping sickness," which had no medical cure.

On August 14, the public health service notified TAC headquarters at Langley AFB, Virginia, of a possible need for the 4500th Air Base Wing's Special Aerial Spray Flight, a unit which specialized in dispersing insecticide over large areas. Three C–123 aircraft flew on August 17 from Langley to Love Field in Dallas to begin what was called Operation Dallas Spray.

Aerial spraying missions began on August 19 over Dallas County after permission was obtained from all affected communities. The planes dispensed mosquito-killing chemicals while flying at slow speeds at an altitude of about 150 feet. High winds and rain canceled missions for the next two days, but on August 21, three more C–123s from Hurlburt Field at Eglin AFB, Florida, joined the flight. On August 22, aerial spraying of Dallas County resumed. The Hurlburt planes returned to Florida on August 25, but the three remaining Langley aircraft continued spraying the next day.

Humanitarian Airlift Operations

By August 26, the Special Aerial Spray Flight had treated 475,400 acres around Dallas with 11,885 gallons of insecticide in 56 flying hours. The three C-123s moved to Corpus Christi, Texas, where they sprayed 93,000 acres around that city with 2,325 gallons of insecticide between August 28 and 30. The Special Aerial Spray Flight treated a total of 568,400 acres in Texas using over 14,000 gallons of mosquito-killing chemicals.

Health officials determined that these spraying operations achieved 90 to 95 percent control of the epidemic. Only six of the 175 encephalitis cases confirmed in the Dallas epidemic were contracted after the spraying.

38.
Name: Rocky Mountain Fires.
Location: Idaho and Montana.
Date(s): August 13–September 12, 1967.
Emergency: Fires ignited by lightning and spread by high winds consumed 93,290 acres of mountain forests.
Air Force Organization(s) Involved: 341st Strategic Missile Wing, 516th Tactical Airlift Wing (Tac Alft Wg), 821st and 862d Combat Support Groups, and 941st Military Airlift Group (Mil Alft Gp).
Airlifted: 368 tons of fire-fighting equipment and vehicles and 500 firefighters.
Aircraft Employed: UH–1 (eight), U–3A (one), C–47 (one), C–124 (one), and C–130 (seven).
Operations: During the second week of August, lightning ignited fires in the drought-stricken mountain forests of Glacier National Park in northwestern Montana and Kaniksu National Forest near Bonners Ferry in northern Idaho. High winds spread the fires over thousands of acres, threatening vast quantities of timber resources, wildlife, and adjacent communities.

On August 13, the National Park Service asked the Sixth Air Force Reserve Region for helicopters to carry firefighters and equipment from base camps to remote sites near the fires along mountain summits where there were no roads. The Sixth Air Force Reserve Region tapped Air Force resources within its area of responsibility, including those of SAC. Eight UH–1 helicopters from the 341st Strategic Missile Wing at Malmstrom AFB, Montana; the 821st Combat Support Group at Ellsworth AFB, South Dakota; and the 862d Combat Support Group at Minot AFB, North Dakota, participated in the operations. The 341st Strategic Missile Wing commander, Col. John W. Carroll, directed the task force, which included a C–47 to fly UH–1 spare parts where they were needed. On August 30, President Johnson declared northern Idaho a major disaster area.

At the Glacier National Park fires, Air Force helicopters flew 484 sorties. On an average morning, the helicopters carried almost 500 firefighters from base camps to mountaintop landing zones, returning them in the evening. Air Force helicopters shuttled firefighters between remote sites in the Bonners Ferry region of Idaho and carried injured workers to hospitals. On September 2, a Malmstrom

UH–1 Huey helicopter crashed and burned on takeoff while on a mission against a fire in the Trappers Peak area. Although both the pilot and copilot survived, one was injured severely.

On September 4, the Sixth Army asked the Sixth Air Force Reserve Region to airlift seven passengers, two 2.5 ton trucks, a 1.5 ton trailer, and fire-fighting supplies from Fort Lewis, Washington, to the Coeur d'Alene area of Idaho. McChord AFB's 941st Mil Alft Gp used a C–124 to haul the cargo via Fairchild AFB near Spokane, in eastern Washington, to Idaho.

During the first week of September, seven C–130s from the 516th Tac Alft Wg at Dyess AFB, Texas, airlifted at least seven tons of water tank trucks and fire-fighting equipment from George AFB, California, to Coeur d'Alene. By September 10, rain and cooler temperatures helped to contain the forest fires. On September 12, Air Force airlift operations ended. By then, the Montana and Idaho fires were under control, having consumed 93,290 acres of forest.

39.
Name: Fairbanks Flood.
Location: Alaska.
Date(s): August 14–31, 1967.
Emergency: Heavy rain caused the Chena River in Alaska to flood the city of Fairbanks.
Air Force Organization(s) Involved: 60th, 62d, 436th, and 437th Military Airlift Wings (Mil Alft Wgs); 916th, 917th, and 937th Mil Alft Gps; 146th Air Trpt Wg; 144th Air Trpt Sq; and 124th Ftr Gp.
Airlifted: 974 tons of generators, trucks, food, water purification equipment, laundry equipment, sandbags, telephone cables, medical supplies, clothing, baby bottles, portable latrines, and charcoal; and at least 2,553 passengers, including 2,371 refugees.
Aircraft Employed: C–124 (12), C–133 (3), C–141 (18), C–123 (2), C–54 (2), and C–97 (1).
Operations: Six inches of rain fell in six days over central Alaska during the second week of August. The Chena River flooded downtown Fairbanks under as much as nine feet of water, drove half of the city's 30,000 residents from their homes, killed at least five persons, and destroyed an estimated $200 million in property. On August 14, Mayor H. A. Boucher and Governor Walter Hickel appealed for federal aid and President Johnson declared the state a disaster area.

From the Alaskan Command, Lt. Gen. Robert A. Breitweiser set up a military airlift to deliver emergency supplies to Eielson AFB, 25 miles southeast of Fairbanks. Military airlift wings participating included the 60th from Travis AFB, California; the 62d from McChord AFB, Washington; the 436th from Dover AFB, Delaware; and the 437th from Charleston AFB, South Carolina.

Before flying to Eielson, many of the planes picked up supplies from bases across the country, including McGuire AFB, New Jersey; Peterson AFB,

Colorado; Davis-Monthan AFB, Arizona; Elmendorf AFB, Alaska; and Sharpe Army Depot, California. Between August 14 and 31, 30 MAC C–124s, C–133s, and C–141s delivered to Alaska almost 800 tons of electrical generators, fire trucks, C rations, water purification equipment, washing machines, sandbags, telephone cables, medical supplies, and other relief cargo. Representing the Twenty-first and Twenty-second Air Forces, the planes flew 47 missions in 18 days.

Air Force Reserve and Air National Guard organizations also flew flood rescue and relief missions during the crisis. Between August 15 and 23, the 144th Air Trpt Sq, stationed at Kulis ANG Base near Anchorage, flew C–123s and a C–54 to evacuate 2,371 flood refugees from Fairbanks to Anchorage. Return flights delivered 152 tons of medical supplies, water, and food to Fairbanks. During the nine days, the 144th flew 138 sorties, consuming 223 flying hours.

The Idaho Air National Guard's 124th Ftr Gp flew a C–54 to deliver three tons of diapers, clothing, milk, and baby bottles from Boise to Alaska. A C–97 of the 146th Air Trpt Wg at Van Nuys, California, carried two tons of fresh fruit to the disaster area. During August, three AF Res Mil Alft Gps—the 916th from Carswell AFB, Texas; the 917th from Barksdale AFB, Louisiana; and the 937th from Tinker AFB, Oklahoma—carried 16.5 tons of relief supplies, including medicine, portable latrines, charcoal, and relief workers to Eielson AFB aboard three C–124s.

As September began, the high water receded, and emergency flights to Eielson ended. Ground vehicles transported the airlifted emergency supplies to Fairbanks, where residents worked to restore normal activities.

40.
Name: Hurricane Beulah.
Location: Texas.
Date(s): September 21–October 28, 1967.
Emergency: Hurricane Beulah, with winds up to 160 mph, hit southern Texas, bringing torrential rain to the Rio Grande valley followed by massive flooding.
Air Force Organization(s) Involved: 1st, 19th, and 39th Military Airlift Squadrons (Mil Alft Sqs); 316th and 516th Tac Alft Wgs; and 4500th Special Aerial Spray Flight (4500th AB Wg).
Airlifted: 299 tons of Army amphibious vehicles, jeeps, trucks, rations, and relief supplies; an unknown tonnage of 200,000 sandbags; 21,000 gallons of insecticide; and 200 passengers.
Aircraft Employed: C–124 (one), C–133 (two), C–123 (three), and C–130 (eight).
Operations: After cutting northwestward across the Yucatán peninsula and the southwestern Gulf of Mexico, Hurricane Beulah struck the Texas coast just north of Brownsville on September 19 with winds up to 160 mph. The huge storm, 140 miles across, spawned a host of tornadoes, destroyed 80 percent of the homes on

South Padre Island, pushed tides 10 feet above normal, and killed 10 people before losing strength over the Rio Grande valley on September 21.

The remnants of Beulah proved even more destructive, dumping 30 inches of rain over southern Texas and northeastern Mexico. The floods which followed the hurricane killed at least 30 more people and left $1 billion in property damage. In Texas and Mexico, water covered an area the size of Kentucky, including thousands of acres of citrus and pepper farms. As many as 300,000 refugees sought high ground and shelter. The Arroyo Colorado, a diversion canal of the Rio Grande just north of the Mexican border, flooded Mercedes and Harlingen, Texas. On September 28, President Johnson flew over the inundated area and declared 24 counties disaster areas.

Military aid had arrived in southern Texas even before the president's survey flight. On September 23, two C–133s from the 1st and 39th Mil Alft Sqs of the 436th Mil Alft Wg at Dover AFB, Delaware, flew to Oceana NAS in Virginia to retrieve Army amphibious vehicles for delivery to Harlingen's airport. One of the C–133s made another trip to Corpus Christi for other Army vehicles destined for Harlingen. Meanwhile, a 19th Mil Alft Sq C–124 from Kelly AFB, Texas, flew to Fort Campbell, Kentucky, to get Army personnel and equipment for aerial delivery to Rio Grande International Airport near Brownsville. By September 28, the three Air Force cargo planes had moved 51.3 tons of cargo—mostly amphibious vehicles and equipment—and 27 passengers to the disaster area for the Fourth Army.

Between September 22 and October 5, the 516th Tac Alft Wg at Dyess AFB, Texas, hauled 248 tons of food rations and 173 passengers from El Paso to Laredo aboard five C–130s, consuming 72 flying hours in response to a Fourth Air Force Reserve Region request. The 316th Tac Alft Wg at Langley AFB, Virginia, used three C–130s to airlift 200,000 sandbags from Richmond to Harlingen between September 26 and 28. Workers around Harlingen used the bags to reinforce levees and control flooding.

In response to a request from Governor John B. Connally, the 4500th Special Aerial Spray Flight, also from Langley AFB, sprayed 21,000 gallons of insecticide over a million acres in south Texas between September 28 and October 28, using three specially equipped C–123s. The aerial spraying limited the mosquito population and, thus, the potential for an epidemic. In five weeks, 14 Air Force cargo planes from six organizations contained the destruction and damage of Hurricane Beulah.

41.
Name: Operation Haylift II (Operation Navajo).
Location: Arizona, New Mexico, and Utah.
Date(s): December 16–29, 1967.
Emergency: Two severe blizzards in eight days left deep snow on Indian reservations in Arizona, New Mexico, and Utah. Blocked roads threatened people and livestock with starvation.

Humanitarian Airlift Operations

Air Force Organization(s) Involved: 60th, 63d, 349th, 452d, and 512th Mil Alft Wgs; 433d, 440th, and 446th Tac Alft Wgs; 153d, 161st, and 937th Mil Alft Gps; 908th, 926th, and 939th Tactical Airlift Groups (Tac Alft Gps); 140th and 162d Tactical Fighter Groups (Tac Ftr Gps); 41st, 54th, 302d, and 303d Aerospace Rescue and Recovery Squadrons (Aerosp RR Sqs); Western Aerospace Rescue and Recovery Center; Air Force Special Weapons Center; and 4900th AB Gp.
Airlifted: 858 tons of hay; 349 tons of food, clothing, and medical supplies; 30 snow vehicles; and 1,361 passengers.
Aircraft Employed: C–119 (26), C–124 (9), C–54 (7), HU–16 (4), C–97 (6), C–47 (3), T–29 (3), C–141 (2), HC–130 (2), CH–3 (2), UH–16 (1), HC–97 (number unknown), and HH–43 (number unknown).
Operations: A series of severe blizzards descended on the Navajo and Hopi Indian reservations in Arizona, New Mexico, and Utah between December 13 and 21. Deep snow and drifts as high as 10 feet blanketed 16,000 square miles and blocked roads, stranding hundreds of people and threatening thousands of cattle and sheep with starvation.

On December 15, Raymond Nakai, chairman of the Navajo tribal council, requested aid from the Bureau of Indian Affairs. The Sixth Army, unable to bring immediate relief without an airlift, contacted the Sixth Air Force Reserve Region at Hamilton AFB, California. The next day, the 452d Mil Alft Wg from March AFB, California, initiated Operation Haylift II under the direction of Col. Merle E. Larson.

From December 16 to 19, eight of the wing's C–119s dropped 80 tons of hay in 16 sorties in the snowbound region, while detachments of the Western Aerospace Rescue and Recovery Center rescued stranded Indians and delivered food, clothing, blankets, and medicine aboard helicopters and HC–130, HU–16, and HC–97 planes. Missions were flown from Luke AFB near Phoenix and at Window Rock, Chinle, and Winslow, Arizona.

On December 20, the Sixth Air Force Reserve Region called upon Air Force reserve units across the country and an armada of C–119s, C–124s, C–97s, C–47s, and C–54s delivered hay, snow vehicles, food, medicine, clothing, and other relief supplies to the snowbound area until roads reopened just after Christmas.

Air Force Reserve C–119s dropped bales of hay while flying as low as 30 feet and at speeds as slow as 140 mph over stranded livestock, delivering 858 tons in 161 sorties by December 27. Indian spotters accompanied the haylift flights to guide the planes to places of greatest need. C–124s moved snow plows, snow weasels, and snow buggies to Arizona via Albuquerque. C–141s from the 60th and 63d Mil Alft Wgs at Travis AFB and Norton AFB delivered helicopter fuel to the staging areas, while local tactical fighter groups sent C–54s to help with cargo deliveries.

The Western Aerospace Rescue and Recovery Service transported 1,361 passengers and dropped almost 350 tons of food, blankets, clothing, and medical supplies between December 16 and 29. The Air Force Special Weapons Center at Kirtland AFB, New Mexico, sent C–54s, C–47s, and other aircraft to assist.

Most airlift activities ended when major roads reopened on December 27, but the operation continued for two more weeks. Operation Haylift II saved many lives and limited livestock losses on the reservations to about five percent.

42.
Name: Alaska Forest Fire.
Location: Alaska.
Date(s): July 24–August 2, 1968.
Emergency: Forest fires swept across more than 500,000 acres of Alaska timberland.
Air Force Organization(s) Involved: 935th and 945th Mil Alft Gps and 7th Mil Alft Sq of the 62d Mil Alft Wg.
Airlifted: Eight U.S. Forest Service helicopters and 15 personnel.
Aircraft Employed: C–124 (three).
Operations: Unusually warm and dry weather over central Alaska during July contributed to an outbreak of forest fires. For more than a week, afternoon temperatures exceeded 90 degrees and humidity levels plummeted in the normally wet and cool region. By July 28, 130 fires had consumed 505,000 acres of Alaska timberland. About 1,300 firefighters tried to control the blazes, one of which was raging five miles from Fairbanks.

On July 24, the Fairbanks Bureau of Land Management office called the U.S. Forest Service in Portland, Oregon, to request an airlift to Alaska of fire-fighting helicopters from Boise, Idaho. The Forest Service relayed the request to Sixth Army headquarters in San Francisco, which contacted the Sixth Air Force Reserve Region at Hamilton AFB, California.

On July 25, the AF Res tasked the 945th Mil Alft Gp at Hill AFB, Utah, to airlift three Forest Service helicopters and six passengers from Boise International Airport to Fort Wainwright, Alaska. One of the group's C–124 Globemasters took off from Hill AFB, refueled at McChord AFB, Washington, and landed at Boise before the day ended. The plane and its load of helicopters and passengers proceeded to Fort Wainwright the next day. On July 25 and 26, the 7th Mil Alft Sq of the 62d Mil Alft Wg at McChord used another C–124 to airlift two more Forest Service helicopters from Boise to Fort Wainwright.

On July 28, Sixth Army headquarters asked the Sixth Air Force Reserve Region for another helicopter airlift from Idaho to Alaska. Air Force Reserve headquarters at Robins AFB, Georgia, assigned the mission to the 935th Mil Alft Gp at Richards-Gebaur AFB, Missouri. Using a C–124, the group flew three Forest Service helicopters, nine personnel, and 1,375 pounds of fire-fighting cargo from Boise to Fort Wainwright between July 29 and 31.

By August 3, all USAF airlift aircraft had returned to their home bases, after transporting eight Forest Service helicopters and associated personnel from Idaho to Alaska within a week of the first request for assistance.

Humanitarian Airlift Operations

43.
Name: Minot Flood.
Location: North Dakota.
Date(s): April 10–21, 1969.
Emergency: Runoff from unusually thick accumulations of snow flooded the Mouse River valley and the city of Minot.
Air Force Organization(s) Involved: 810th Strategic Aerospace Division and ANG C–119 units.
Airlifted: 790 blankets, 790 litters, and other relief supplies.
Aircraft Employed: KC–135 (2), C–119 (2), and helicopters (11).
Operations: By April, up to 47 inches of snow had fallen in northern North Dakota. Warm temperatures in early April rapidly melted the deep snow, swelling the Des Lacs, Mouse, and Souris Rivers. On April 10, the Mouse River flooded Minot, a city of more than 30,000. Local officials appealed for aid to Minot AFB, located on a plateau north of the flooded city, and Brig. Gen. Ralph T. Holland, commander of the 810th Strategic Aerospace Division, established the USAF Assistance Control Center under the base commander, Col. George E. Porter.

The Assistance Control Center worked with Minot's Civic Flood Control Center, which included representatives from the Air Force, Red Cross, Salvation Army, U.S. Army Corps of Engineers, civil defense, National Guard, Coast Guard, and local police. Colonel Porter dispatched base personnel and vehicles to deliver sandbags and relief supplies to the local community between April 10 and 21. They also helped to evacuate 12,000 residents from threatened areas of the city.

Most sandbags and supplies came from Minot AFB stocks, but 790 blankets and 790 litters were flown in by SAC KC–135s. Two ANG C–119s delivered other relief supplies. At least one KC–135 came from Malmstrom AFB and at least one of the C–119s from Wisconsin. Eleven helicopters participated in rescue and relief missions, transporting personnel and cargo.

By the third week in April, floodwaters had receded, and the Assistance Control Center ceased operations on April 21. Minot AFB personnel used thousands of sandbags to save important installations such as the water works, but some areas remained under water until May.

44.
Name: Hurricane Camille.
Location: Mississippi.
Date(s): August 19–September 16, 1969.
Emergency: A powerful hurricane tore into the Mississippi coast.
Air Force Organization(s) Involved: 375th Aeromedical Airlift Wing (Aeromed Alft Wg); 116th, 436th, 437th, 438th, 442d, and 445th Mil Alft Wgs; 316th, 317th, 434th, and 440th Tac Alft Wgs; 116th, 118th, 137th, 146th, 164th, 165th, 170th, 172d, 901st, 904th, 911th, 915th, 916th, 917th, 918th, 921st, 937th, 940th, 942d, and 945th Mil Alft Gps; and 910th, 922d, and 926th Tac Alft Gps.

Airlifted: 5,913 tons of vehicles, telephone repair equipment, clothing, medical supplies, food, electric generators, power saws, drinking water, bedding, and Sheetrock; and 3,909 passengers, including 673 hospital patients.

Aircraft Employed: C–141 (16), C–124 (46+), C–118 (5), C–133 (4), C–121 (1), C–119 (4), C–130 (7), C–123 (1), and C–47 (1).

Operations: Hurricane Camille, the strongest storm ever to hit the United States, struck the Mississippi coast on the night of August 17. Packing wind gusts as high as 200 mph and causing a 30-foot tide and torrential rain, the storm devastated the coastal towns of Waveland, Bay St. Louis, Pass Christian, Long Beach, Gulfport, and Biloxi. Hurricane Camille left over 200 people dead and destroyed or damaged $1 billion in property. Ocean-going freighters ran ashore at Gulfport, and Coastal Highway 90 was cut in many places. The 100 miles of coast between New Orleans, Louisiana, and Mobile, Alabama, were littered with uprooted trees and the ruins of buildings. Governor John Bell Williams immediately appealed for federal relief, and, on August 18, President Richard M. Nixon declared 26 Mississippi counties disaster areas.

Directors of the Gulfport and Biloxi Veterans Administration hospitals asked the surgeon general in Washington, D.C., to help move patients from damaged and powerless facilities. On August 19 and 20, the 375th Aeromed Alft Wg from Scott AFB, Illinois, flew 673 patients from Gulfport and Biloxi to veterans' hospitals in Alabama, Georgia, the Carolinas, and Florida aboard five C–118s. Two C–141s from the 437th Mil Alft Wg at Charleston AFB, South Carolina, airlifted a forklift, 40 pallets of emergency relief supplies, 19.6 tons of trucks and trailers, and 24 personnel from Dobbins AFB, Georgia, to the Gulfport area on August 21.

Between August 20 and 23, eight C–141s of the 438th Mil Alft Wg at McGuire moved 87 tons of cargo and 10 passengers to Gulfport from bases in Kentucky, North Carolina, and South Carolina. Five AF Res C–124s of the 901st, 904th, and 916th Mil Alft Gps airlifted 22 telephone line repair trucks from New Jersey to Gulfport and Biloxi on August 23 to restore communications in the disaster area.

That same day, the New Jersey National Guard's 170th Mil Alft Gp sent a C–121 loaded with 10 tons of clothing and medical supplies to Jackson for delivery to storm victims farther south. The 940th Mil Alft Gp at McClellan AFB, California, sent three C–124s laden with emergency generators and Sheetrock. Three C–124s and four C–119s of the 921st Mil Alft Gp and the 922d Tac Alft Gp at Kelly AFB, Texas, transported 16.6 tons of emergency cargo in 21 sorties to southern Mississippi. Between August 19 and 27, the 918th Mil Alft Gp at Dobbins AFB airlifted 162.5 tons of relief supplies to Gulfport on 12 C–124 missions using 61.9 flying hours.

Other Air Force organizations that carried relief supplies and equipment to Gulfport and Biloxi included the 116th and the 445th Mil Alft Wgs from Dobbins AFB; the 442d Mil Alft Wg from Richards-Gebaur AFB, Missouri; the 434th Tac Alft Wg from Bakalar AFB, Indiana; the 440th Tac Alft Wg from General

Humanitarian Airlift Operations

Mitchell Field, Wisconsin; the 316th Tac Alft Wg from Langley AFB, Virginia; and the 317th Tac Alft Wg from Lockbourne AFB, Ohio. Also included were the 911th, 915th, 942d, and 945th Mil Alft Gps from Pittsburgh, Pennsylvania; Homestead AFB, Florida; March AFB, California; and Hill AFB, Utah, respectively.

A host of ANG military airlift groups also participated in the Hurricane Camille relief airlift: the 116th from Atlanta; the 118th from Nashville; the 137th from Oklahoma City; the 146th from Van Nuys, California; and the 172d from Jackson, Mississippi. Most of these units flew C–124 Cargomasters in response to requests of the Third Air Force Reserve Region, headquartered at Dobbins AFB.

By mid-September, at least 85 Air Force cargo aircraft had participated in Hurricane Camille emergency relief missions, delivering more than 5,900 tons of vehicles, electric generators, clothing, medicine, food, power saws, and other relief supplies to southern Mississippi from at least 15 Air Force bases across the United States. The USAF also airlifted 3,909 passengers, including hospital patients and relief workers.

45.
Name: Lubbock Tornado.
Location: Texas.
Date(s): May 11–15, 1970.
Emergency: A tornado stuck the Lubbock, Texas, area.
Air Force Organization(s) Involved: 137th Mil Alft Gp, 914th and 933d Tac Alft Gps, 188th Tactical Reconnaissance Group, and Twenty-second Air Force C–141 unit.
Airlifted: At least 60 tons of radar vans, electronic equipment, electrical generators, and shoes; and 39 Air Force communications specialists.
Aircraft Employed: C–124 (two), C–119 (two), RF–84 (two), and C–141 (one).
Operations: At 9:30 p.m. on May 11, a tornado dipped out of the northwestern Texas sky and cut a six-mile path across the city of Lubbock, leaving 20 people dead and 500 injured within 10 minutes. The mile-wide storm packed 200 mph winds that blew a freight train off its track and peeled marble from downtown office buildings. The storm was accompanied by golf ball-sized hail.

The next morning, in response to appeals for military assistance, the Central Air Force Reserve Region headquarters at Ellington AFB near Houston activated a disaster command post at Reese AFB, about six miles west of Lubbock, to coordinate AF Res relief operations. The 137th Mil Alft Gp from Oklahoma City flew two C–124 Globemasters laden with 60 tons of electronic equipment, radar vans, and 39 Air Force communications specialists from Tinker AFB, Oklahoma, to restore communications facilities knocked out by the twister.

A C–119 Flying Boxcar from the 914th Tac Alft Gp of Niagara Falls airlifted six generators to Reese AFB, while another C–119 from the 933d Tac Alft Gp at General Billy Mitchell Field, Wisconsin, delivered 3,000 pairs of shoes for homeless storm victims. A Twenty-second Air Force C–141 also airlifted relief supplies to the disaster area.

On May 12, in response to a Red Cross request relayed through the Pentagon in Washington, D.C., the 188th Tactical Reconnaissance Group at Fort Smith, Arkansas, flew two RF–84s to photograph the devastated parts of Lubbock for damage assessment and disaster response. The Red Cross estimated that the twister destroyed 430 homes and damaged 1,200; total losses exceeded $100 million. On May 13, President Nixon declared the Lubbock region of the Texas panhandle a major disaster area, releasing more federal funds for the emergency. In a few days, municipal services and power were restored and citizens began rebuilding their devastated city.

46.
Name: Hurricane Celia.
Location: Texas.
Date(s): August 4–20, 1970.
Emergency: A hurricane hit the southern coast of Texas near Corpus Christi.
Air Force Organization(s) Involved: 442d and 512th Mil Alft Wgs, 446th Tac Alft Wg, 921st Mil Alft Gp, 914th and 922d Tac Alft Gps, and 136th Air Refueling Wing.
Airlifted: 241 tons of vehicles, generators, communications and construction equipment, refrigerators, medical supplies, and food; and 658 passengers.
Aircraft Employed: C–124 (nine), C–130 (six), C–119 (five), and KC–97 (one).
Operations: Hurricane Celia crossed the Gulf of Mexico from Cuba on Monday afternoon, August 3, smashing into downtown Corpus Christi on the south Texas coast. The combination of 160 mph winds, high water, and torrential rain destroyed or damaged 22,800 houses in an area with more than 350,000 residents. Other Texas towns—including Aransas Pass, Rockport, Sinton, Robstown, Taft, and Mathis—suffered severe damage.

The hurricane killed 11 people, injured 1,000, and damaged or destroyed about $750 million in property. Cutting a 250-mile swath through 13 counties from the Gulf of Mexico to Del Rio, Hurricane Celia prompted local authorities to appeal for state and federal assistance. The Fourth Army headquarters at San Antonio directed overall disaster relief. It requested that the Central Air Force Reserve Region, headquartered at Ellington AFB near Houston, organize and coordinate a relief airlift.

Region Commander Brig. Gen. John W. Hoff contacted AF Res units from Texas, Missouri, Louisiana, and Oklahoma; and by Tuesday, August 4, the Hurricane Celia relief airlift was in operation. That day, the 512th Mil Alft Wg from Carswell AFB, Texas, airlifted 73 children from their ruined Corpus Christi school to Austin aboard two C–124 aircraft. Three other wing C–124s from Barksdale AFB, Louisiana, and Tinker AFB, Oklahoma, hauled two 2.5-ton trucks, an auger, roofing materials, rations, and 53 Navy construction workers from Gulfport, Mississippi, to Corpus Christi on August 4 and 5.

Meanwhile, the 922d Tac Alft Gp from San Antonio flew three C–119s to airlift three 4.5-ton electric generators along the same route. A 921st Mil Alft Gp C–124 from Kelly AFB, Texas, flew a six-ton line truck and equipment from Gulfport to Corpus Christi. This same equipment had been used the previous year to restore communications in the wake of Hurricane Camille. The group used two more C–124s to fly 150 members of an Army engineering battalion from Albuquerque to the Texas Gulf coast.

On Wednesday, August 5, the 442d Mil Alft Wg from Richards-Gebaur AFB, Missouri, airlifted an Army truck, a generator, wire, and railroad ties from Fort Hood, Texas, to Corpus Christi on another C–124. Between August 5 and 20, six C–130s from the 446th Tac Alft Wg from Ellington AFB, Texas, and the New Orleans NAS hauled three generators, a computer, refrigerators, compressors, a portable hospital, and trucks to Corpus Christi from Fort Hood, Texas; Fort Smith, Arkansas; El Paso, Texas; and Gulfport, Mississippi.

The 136th Air Refueling Wing (ANG) from Dallas used a KC–97 to airlift five tons of powdered milk from Grand Rapids, Michigan, to the Red Cross at Corpus Christi on August 7. The airlift ended on August 20 after transporting 658 people and 241 tons of relief supplies and equipment.

47.
Name: Southern Plains Snowstorm.
Location: Kansas, Oklahoma, and Texas.
Date(s): February 23–March 2, 1971.
Emergency: A snowstorm dropped up to 30 inches of snow over the southern Great Plains.
Air Force Organization(s) Involved: Sheppard Technical Training Center, 313th Tac Alft Wg, 137th Mil Alft Wg (Oklahoma ANG), 704th Tactical Airlift Squadron (Tac Alft Sq) (AF Res), and 302d Special Operations Wing (Sp Ops Wg) (AF Res).
Airlifted: 1.5 tons of food, 562 tons of hay, and 25 passengers.
Aircraft Employed: C–130 (seven), C–119 (three), CH–3 (two), and C–124 (two+).
Operations: On February 21 and 22, an immense snowstorm dropped 30 inches of snow over southwestern Kansas, western Oklahoma, and northern Texas. Winds up to 50 mph piled the snow into 15-foot drifts, blocking highways and stranding thousands of cattle. On February 23, the Kansas Cattlemen's Association estimated that 100,000 cattle in five counties faced imminent starvation. Governor Robert Docking of Kansas, in Washington, D.C., for a governors' conference, asked President Nixon to declare the region a disaster area.

Civil defense officials in Texas, Oklahoma, and Kansas sought Air Force help to airdrop supplies. On February 23, two CH–3 helicopters from Sheppard

Technical Training Center, Texas, carried 1.5 tons of food—including bread and milk—in six flights to 300 residents stranded along Interstate 40 between Erick, Oklahoma, and Amarillo, Texas. The Jolly Green Giant helicopters also carried 25 persons to safety.

Between February 24 and March 2, the 313th Tac Alft Wg, based at Forbes AFB, Kansas, flew five C–130 Hercules aircraft to drop 350 tons of alfalfa hay to feed at least 70,000 cattle stranded in deep snow in five southwest Kansas counties. The planes flew from the municipal airport at Great Bend, Kansas, where thousands of bales of hay were gathered. Air Force Reserve organizations also assisted the airlift, including the 302d Sp Ops Wg from Clinton County AFB, Ohio, which flew three C–119s and dropped 733 bales, and the 704th Tac Alft Sq from Ellington AFB, Texas, which flew two C–130s and dropped 821 bales. The planes ejected the hay bales, which weighed an average of 80 pounds each, while flying less than 100 feet above the snowdrifts.

The 137th Mil Alft Wg of the Oklahoma ANG dropped 150 tons of hay from C–124 airplanes flying over stranded herds in 16 western Oklahoma counties. Local cattlemen rode aboard the planes to guide the aircrews. By March 2, the snow cover had melted enough for cattle to reach traditional sources of feed and the airlift ended.

48.
Name: Operation Combat VEE.
Location: Texas.
Date(s): July 8–August 8, 1971.
Emergency: A Venezuelan Equine Encephalomyelitis (VEE) epidemic, spread by mosquitoes and threatening horses, broke out in Texas.
Air Force Organization(s) Involved: 4500th AB Wg, 24th and 319th Special Operations Squadrons (Sp Ops Sqs), and 548th Special Operations Training Squadron.
Airlifted: 63,391 gallons of insecticide.
Aircraft Employed: C–123 (nine) and C–47 (nine).
Operations: Venezuelan Equine Encephalomyelitis, a nerve disease sometimes fatal to horses but also dangerous to humans, reached epidemic proportions in Colombia, South America, in December 1967. Carried by mosquitoes, it spread through Central America and Mexico during the next three years. By July 3, 1971, the disease had reached Brownsville, Texas, prompting the Department of Agriculture to request Air Force assistance with aerial spraying of insecticide on July 6.

The 4500th AB Wg from Langley AFB, Virginia, deployed two C–123 spray aircraft to Brownsville on July 8. Between July 9 and 12, the planes sprayed 120,000 acres with 2,400 gallons of insecticide. Despite these efforts, the disease spread, persuading the Department of Agriculture to ask the USAF for a larger operation. More C–123s, this time from the 319th Sp Ops Sq at Hurlburt Field at Eglin AFB, Florida, arrived in Brownsville on July 12.

Humanitarian Airlift Operations

On July 17, Col. Edward F. Borsare of the Tactical Air Command's 1st Sp Ops Wg took command of a Combat VEE task force. By July 20, he had gathered the spray aircraft from Brownsville at his headquarters at Ellington AFB near Houston. That same day, the 548th Special Operations Training Squadron deployed nine C–47s to Ellington to participate in the operation. The 24th Sp Ops Sq at Howard AFB in the Panama Canal Zone sent a C–123 on August 3, becoming the fourth organization involved in the spraying missions.

Between July 8 and August 8, the Combat VEE task force flew 258 sorties in 597 flying hours, spraying over 3.5 million acres from Brownsville to Louisiana with more than 63,000 gallons of insecticide. Eighteen C–123 and C–47 aircraft flew during the operation, primarily in the early morning hours because effective spraying required moderate temperatures. By August 8, the combination of Air Force and civilian aerial spraying had halted the epidemic.

49.
Name: Arizona Forest Fire.
Location: Arizona.
Date(s): May 15–21, 1972.
Emergency: A forest fire raged over 28,000 acres of Arizona's Prescott National Forest, threatening many acres of timber and nearby communities.
Air Force Organization(s) Involved: 146th Tac Alft Wg, 940th Tac Alft Gp, and 138th and 151st Mil Alft Gps.
Airlifted: 24 U.S. Forest Service fire engines.
Aircraft Employed: C–124 (seven+) and C–130 (number unknown).

Operations: A forest fire sparked by an unattended campfire swept through the Prescott National Forest near Goodwin, Arizona, in mid-May. Fanned by winds in excess of 30 mph, the conflagration spread until it destroyed more than 28,000 acres of woodlands, including $30 million in timber. Time was crucial. U.S. Forest Service and Department of Agriculture officials, having committed all available fire-fighting resources in Arizona, asked the Western Air Force Reserve Region, headquartered at Hamilton AFB, California, to coordinate an airlift of fire engines from California and Oregon to Luke AFB, Arizona, about 70 miles south of the fire.

Between May 15 and 21, AF Res and ANG organizations flew 24 fire engines to Luke AFB near Phoenix. The 940th Tac Alft Gp (AF Res) from Hamilton AFB flew 10 fire trucks aboard five C–124 Globemaster airplanes from McClellan AFB, California, to Luke. C–130s of the 146th Tac Alft Wg (ANG) at Van Nuys, California, airlifted 10 more fire engines from Beale AFB, California, and Klamath Falls, Oregon, to Luke. Two other ANG organizations, the 138th Mil Alft Gp of Tulsa, Oklahoma, and the 151st Mil Alft Gp of Salt Lake City, Utah, also carried pumper trucks from California to Luke. Like the 940th Tac Alft Gp, they used C–124 aircraft. The fire was under control by May 21 and was completely extinguished by May 24.

50.
Name: South Dakota Flash Flood.
Location: South Dakota.
Date(s): June 10–18, 1972.
Emergency: Up to 14 inches of rain fell on the Black Hills of South Dakota, flooding Rapid City and neighboring communities.
Air Force Organization(s) Involved: 28th Bombardment Wing, 133d and 442d Tac Alft Wgs, and 945th Mil Alft Gp.
Airlifted: 55 tons of mobile canteens, pipe, pumping equipment, food, and clothing; and 251 passengers.
Aircraft Employed: UH–1 (12), C–130 (5), and C–124 (2).
Operations: Up to 14 inches of rain fell over the Black Hills of South Dakota between dusk on June 9 and dawn on June 10. In some places, six inches of rain fell in just two hours. Rapid City, with 43,000 people, was nestled on the banks of Rapid Creek, which flowed out of the hills across the Great Plains. In a few hours, the creek became a raging river that burst Canyon Lake Dam and scoured the center of Rapid City. Neighboring communities such as Keystone, Black Hawk, and Box Elder were inundated, leaving 5,000 people homeless. The flash flood destroyed 1,200 homes and severely damaged 2,500 more. High water destroyed 5,000 vehicles and caused $31 million in structural damage.

Before midnight on June 9, Governor Richard Kneip appealed for help from Ellsworth AFB, a SAC base located on high ground near Rapid City. On June 10, Col. Henry B. McDaniel, Jr., set up an emergency command post at Ellsworth. Between June 10 and 18, 12 UH–1 helicopters belonging to the 28th Bombardment Wing flew 55 sorties in 80 flying hours over the flood-ravaged area, rescuing 14 persons and airlifting 251, and delivering almost four tons of food, clothing, and medical supplies. President Nixon declared Pennington, Meade, Lawrence, and Custer Counties disaster areas and authorized more federal aid on June 11.

The next day, a 442d Tac Alft Wg C–130 hauled 60 24-foot sections of eight-inch pipe, each weighing 220 pounds, from Richards-Gebaur AFB, Missouri, to Ellsworth AFB. The 133d Tac Alft Wg of the Minnesota ANG hauled six pumps weighing 19.5 tons along the same route aboard three C–130s. The pumps and pipe were used to reduce the water level in a lake behind another dam in the Black Hills area to keep it from bursting and causing further flooding.

On June 13, the 442d Tac Alft Wg used another C–130 to carry a mobile canteen and food from Scott AFB, Illinois, to Ellsworth AFB. Two 945th Mil Alft Gp C–124s flew four more mobile canteens from Chicago's O'Hare International Airport to Ellsworth AFB on Wednesday, June 14. Army, Air Force, and civilian aircraft hauled tons of food, clothing, and other emergency supplies to Ellsworth during June. The base dispatched more than 100 vehicles to transport them to flood victims in the Rapid City area.

As many as 1,500 Ellsworth AFB personnel supported local, state, and federal relief authorities. The base donated two tons of chicken, 8,000 hamburger patties, over half a ton of potatoes, and 100,000 units of typhoid and tetanus vaccine. Ellsworth AFB also provided temporary housing for 200 refugees and laundry services for flood victims and relief workers. Governor Richard Kneip, presidential candidate Senator George McGovern, and First Lady Pat Nixon flew to Ellsworth to inspect area flood damage and recovery efforts.

A week after the flash flood, waters receded to normal levels and airlift operations terminated. Property losses totaled $55 million. Included among the 238 dead were seven Air Force personnel and seven dependents.

51.
Name: Arizona Flash Flood.
Location: Arizona.
Date(s): June 22–23, 1972.
Emergency: Four inches of rain in one week produced flooding in the south central Arizona desert.
Air Force Organization(s) Involved: Detachments 15 and 16, 42d Aerosp RR Sq; and 302d Aerosp RR Sq.
Airlifted: 68 flood refugees.
Aircraft Employed: HH–43 (five).
Operations: Four inches of rain fell over central Arizona within one week during the middle of June, causing flash flooding 10 miles north of Scottsdale, just east of Phoenix. Dry desert washes became raging rivers. On June 22, the Arizona Department of Public Safety asked the 42d Aerosp RR Sq at Hamilton AFB, California, for helicopter support to rescue flood victims.

The squadron alerted Detachment 15 at Luke AFB, Arizona, and Detachment 16 at Williams AFB, Arizona. Both bases were in the flood vicinity, Luke to the southwest and Williams to the southeast of Phoenix. Each detachment dispatched one HH–43 Pedro helicopter for emergency rescue flights. The 302d Aerosp RR Sq, a reserve unit at Williams AFB, also responded to the emergency with three HH–43s.

During two days of rescue operations, the three units used five helicopters to rescue 68 flood victims. Most passengers boarded aircraft where they landed at isolated spots of high ground, but some were hoisted aboard helicopters from the isolated spots of high water. The 42d Aerosp RR Sq was responsible for 49 saved lives among the 68 airlifted. The emergency helicopter flights ended on June 23, but Luke AFB also sent ground vehicles and personnel to the disaster area at the request of local officials. Meanwhile, most of the nation's attention was focused on two other floods during the same month: the Rapid City, South Dakota, flood and floods in the east from Tropical Storm Agnes.

52.
Name: Tropical Storm Agnes.
Location: Virginia, Pennsylvania, and New York.
Date(s): June 24–August 10, 1972.
Emergency: After hitting the Florida panhandle as a minimal hurricane, Tropical Storm Agnes moved north, dropping more than 12 inches of rain in four states. Floods engulfed many cities.
Air Force Organization(s) Involved: 313th, 316th, 317th, 403d, 459th, and 463d Tac Alft Wgs; 109th, 118th, 145th, 900th, 913th, 914th, 921st, and 927th Tac Alft Gps; 945th Mil Alft Gp; 106th Air Refueling Group; 111th Tactical Air Support Group; 122d Tac Ftr Gp; and 171st and 909th Aeromedical Airlift Groups.
Airlifted: At least 164 tons of cargo, including water purification equipment, water pumps, water tanks, drinking water, vehicles, food, medical supplies, helicopter fuel, sandbags, clothing, cots, blankets, and generators; and at least 370 passengers, including medical support personnel.
Aircraft Employed: C–130 (72), C–124 (1), C–54 (1), C–121 (number unknown), and O–2 (number unknown).
Operations: When a minimal hurricane named Agnes came ashore in Florida between Apalachicola and Panama City on Monday, June 19, no one guessed it would become the costliest U.S. storm on record. Winds soon diminished below hurricane strength, but the tropical storm moved slowly northward, dropping over six inches of rain in every state along its course from Florida to New York. In Virginia, Maryland, Pennsylvania, and New York, the storm produced 12 to 18 inches of rain between June 21 and 23.

Flooded rivers included the James, Potomac, Susquehanna, Allegheny, Monongahela, Schuylkill, Genesee, and Ohio. Inundated cities included Richmond, Virginia; Harrisburg and Wilkes-Barre, Pennsylvania; and Elmira and Corning, New York. On June 23, President Nixon declared Florida, Virginia, Maryland, Pennsylvania, and New York disaster areas.

The Office of Emergency Preparedness asked TAC at Langley AFB, Virginia, for airlift assistance, and the first of 72 C–130 aircraft flew equipment and supplies to flood victims on June 24. Air Force bases sending or handling emergency airlift planes between June 24 and August 10 included Langley in Virginia, Pope in North Carolina, Dyess and Kelly in Texas, Forbes in Kansas, Andrews in Maryland, Wright-Patterson in Ohio, and Hill in Utah.

Tactical Air Command, Air Force Reserve, and Air National Guard units used C–130, C–124, C–54, C–121, and O–2 aircraft to haul 164 tons of cargo—including water purification equipment, food, medicine, helicopter fuel, sandbags, clothing, cots, blankets, generators, and vehicles—to cities in Virginia, Pennsylvania, and New York. The emergency equipment and supplies came from Indiana, Kentucky, Georgia, Mississippi, Tennessee, Massachusetts, Ohio, and the District of Columbia.

The C–130 airplanes also moved relief cargo among the flooded states. At least 370 passengers, including medical and communications experts, rode on the cargo planes. Air Force reconnaissance aircraft contributed to relief efforts by photographing inundated areas and surveying damage. Tropical Storm Agnes killed 118 people and caused more than $3 billion in property damage and destruction.

53.
Name: Everglades Airliner Crash.
Location: Florida.
Date(s): December 30, 1972.
Emergency: Eastern Airlines Flight 401, a jumbo jet airliner with 176 persons aboard, crashed in the Everglades swamp.
Air Force Organization(s) Involved: Detachment 1, 44th Aerosp RR Sq; and 301st Aerosp RR Sq.
Airlifted: 22 victims evacuated from the crash site and nine medical personnel airlifted to the crash site.
Aircraft Employed: UH–1 (four) and HH–34 (two).
Operations: Eighteen minutes before midnight on Friday, December 29, an Eastern Airlines Lockheed 1011 TriStar jumbo jet on a flight from New York with 176 persons aboard crashed in the Everglades while attempting to land at Miami International Airport. The 200 mph impact tore off the aircraft's left wing and killed 99 passengers and crew. Local officials immediately appealed for help from Homestead AFB, a few miles south of the disaster scene.

Early Saturday morning, December 30, Detachment 1 of Homestead's 44th Aerosp RR Sq flew four UH–1N Huey helicopters on 14 sorties to lift 22 injured passengers to Miami hospitals. In the predawn darkness, an AC–130 gunship from the 415th Special Operations Training Squadron at Hurlburt Field at Eglin AFB, Florida, circled over the crash site with a powerful searchlight to help emergency rescue personnel locate the victims. At the same time, the 301st Aerosp RR Sq (AF Res) from Homestead used two HH–34 helicopters to airlift seven paramedics and two flight surgeons from the base hospital to the crash site in five sorties.

By shuttling medical personnel from Homestead to the disaster scene and carrying victims from the crash vicinity to Miami area hospitals, the six Air Force helicopters helped 77 survivors receive prompt medical attention. Coast Guard and Army helicopter crews also responded to the emergency with missions similar to those of the Air Force. At least 24 Homestead AFB doctors, nurses, and medical technicians went to Miami hospitals to help treat victims of Eastern Airlines Flight 401. The rapid military response minimized the loss of life in this major air disaster.

54.
Name: Operation Snowfall.
Location: South Carolina.
Date(s): February 10–15, 1973.
Emergency: The worst snowstorm in South Carolina history dumped up to 26 inches of snow, stranding motorists and isolating people living in rural areas.
Air Force Organization(s) Involved: 703d Tactical Air Support Squadron; Detachment 9, 44th Aerosp RR Sq; 1st Helicopter Squadron; and 1st Sp Ops Wg.
Airlifted: 10 tons of food, blankets, and medicine; snow removal equipment; and more than 1,000 passengers.
Aircraft Employed: CH–3 (seven), C–130 (five), and HH–43 (two).
Operations: An unusually severe snowstorm struck the southeastern United States on February 9 and 10. The blizzard dropped up to 26 inches of snow on Sumter and Clarendon Counties near Shaw AFB in South Carolina, an area that rarely received snow. The base itself received 17 inches.

Early on Saturday, February 10, Deputy Sheriff William L. Poulos of the Sumter County Sheriff's Department called Col. Paul P. Hoza, acting Shaw AFB commander, to request emergency four-wheel drive vehicles and operators. Later that day, the Clarendon County Civil Defense Office asked for helicopters to airlift motorists stranded on highways, including Interstate 95 and U.S. Highways 76, 378, 521, and 15.

Maj. Gen. Roger K. Rhodarmer, the commander of the Ninth Air Force, which was headquartered at Shaw AFB, approved the use of the 703d Tactical Air Support Squadron's CH–3 Jolly Green Giant helicopters for the rescue missions. A CH–3 from the 1st Helicopter Squadron at Andrews AFB in Maryland stranded by the storm at Shaw was also pressed into service. Squadron personnel rescued 27 people and delivered antibiotics to a nursing home. Seven CH–3s were used to rescue people shivering in snowbound automobiles and trucks. Detachment 9 of the 44th Aerosp RR Sq used a pair of HH–43 helicopters for similar missions.

Two days later, on February 12, Governor John C. West declared a state of emergency and closed some highways to all but emergency vehicles, such as those from Shaw AFB. On February 12 and 13, the CH–3 and HH–43 helicopters airlifted blankets and 2,400 food packets to emergency shelters, some at motels along the highways.

Between February 10 and 15, Air Force helicopters flew 30 missions, conducted 304 landings, and consumed 80 flying hours. They airlifted more than 1,000 passengers—mostly stranded motorists—and transported more than 10.5 tons of food, clothing, and medicine. Five 1st Sp Ops Wg C–130 Hercules aircraft flew snow removal equipment and operators from Hurlburt Field at Eglin AFB in Florida to Shaw AFB on February 13. The next day, the base resumed normal flying operations. On Thursday, February 15, Shaw AFB rescue and relief activities concluded as snow was cleared from the major highways.

Humanitarian Airlift Operations

55.
Name: Mississippi River Valley Flood.
Location: Missouri, Arkansas, and Mississippi.
Date(s): April 2–May 18, 1973.
Emergency: Heavy spring rains over the Mississippi River Valley region caused the river to rise, flooding communities along its banks.
Air Force Organization(s) Involved: 316th Tac Alft Wg, 927th Tac Alft Gp, and 62d Tac Alft Sq.
Airlifted: 17 water pumps, 10 tons of pipe, and 18 tons of sandbags.
Aircraft Employed: C–130 (four).
Operations: A series of storms and frontal systems dropped unusually heavy rains over the Mississippi River Valley region during the late winter and early spring of 1973. By the end of March, the Mississippi River and its tributaries had flooded 6.35 million acres south of St. Louis. The Yazoo River in northwestern Mississippi, unable to drain into the swollen Mississippi River, flooded the Yazoo basin, and the Tallahatchie River inundated the area around Greenwood, Mississippi.

The flooding led the U.S. Army Corps of Engineers at Vicksburg, Mississippi, to request an airlift of water pumps. On April 2, the 62d Tac Alft Sq flew a C–130 from its home base at Little Rock AFB, Arkansas, to Portland, Oregon, where it picked up five pumps, each 25 feet long and weighing about a ton. The C–130 proceeded to Vicksburg, where the U.S. Army Corps of Engineers prepared the pumps for use in the Greenwood area.

The Mississippi River continued to rise through April. Consequently, President Nixon called up U.S. Coast Guard Reserves to aid flood workers sandbagging levees. Before the end of the month, Nixon declared parts of Illinois, Missouri, Arkansas, Mississippi, and Louisiana major disaster areas. Sandbags were needed at the confluence of the Des Peres and Mississippi Rivers near St. Louis, where waters were expected to crest 13 feet above flood stage. On April 24, the 38th Tac Alft Sq of the 316th Tac Alft Wg at Langley AFB, Virginia, flew a C–130 to Pope AFB, North Carolina, where it picked up more than 200,000 empty sandbags weighing 18 tons. The next day, the C–130 carried its burlap cargo to St. Louis, where it was unloaded by members of the U.S. Army Corps of Engineers, the Missouri National Guard, and the ANG.

By the end of April, floodwaters had covered 10 million acres between Hannibal, Missouri, and the Gulf of Mexico, and 35,000 persons had evacuated their homes. On May 6, the 316th Tac Alft Wg at Langley AFB used another C–130 to airlift plastic pipe from LaCrosse Municipal Airport, Wisconsin, to Blytheville AFB, Arkansas, for flood relief. On May 17 and 18, the 927th Tac Alft Gp at Selfridge ANG Base, Michigan, hauled 12 water pumps and 24 sections of pipe weighing 10 tons on another C–130 from Glendive, Montana, to Greenville, Mississippi.

The airlift helped local municipalities in flood control efforts. As the floodwaters subsided, the Mississippi River Commission estimated that 12 million acres had flooded in seven states, leaving behind $360 million in property damage.

56.
Name: Northwest Forest Fires.
Location: Oregon, Idaho, Montana, and California.
Date(s): August 16–26, 1973.
Emergency: A hot, dry summer turned northwestern forests tinder dry. Fires in five states consumed 195,000 acres of timber and brush.
Air Force Organization(s) Involved: 314th, 316th, 317th, and 463d Tac Alft Wgs; and 442d Tac Alft Gp.
Airlifted: 370 tons of fire-retardant chemicals and 300 firefighters.
Aircraft Employed: C–130 (five).
Operations: In August, 52 major forest fires, nourished by the worst drought in 20 years and sparked by lightning, arson, or carelessness, consumed 195,000 acres in Washington, Oregon, California, Idaho, and Montana. A federal interagency fire control center known as the Boise Interagency Fire Center (BIFC)—established in 1969 at Boise, Idaho, to coordinate efforts in such emergencies—marshaled 10,000 firefighters, 23 airplanes, and 54 helicopters, many from the U.S. Forest Service. The center also tapped five organizations of TAC.

Between August 16 and 18, the 314th Tac Alft Wg at Little Rock AFB, Arkansas; the 316th Tac Alft Wg at Langley AFB, Virginia; the 317th Tac Alft Wg at Pope AFB, North Carolina; and the 442d Tac Alft Gp at Richards-Gebaur AFB, Missouri, each provided a C–130 Hercules cargo plane to airlift 300 firemen from Arkansas, Tennessee, Mississippi, and Georgia to Boise and Portland.

During the same month, the 463d Tac Alft Wg at Dyess AFB, Texas, used another C–130 equipped with the Modular Airborne Fire-Fighting System (MAFFS) to drop a fire-retardant chemical on fires in Montana and California. The Tactical Air Warfare Center at Eglin AFB, Florida, had developed the MAFFS after a disastrous series of fires in southern California in 1970. A C–130 could be fully loaded in 20 minutes with 3,000 gallons of fire-retardant chemical, which doubled as reforestation fertilizer. Once loaded, the aircraft could dispense the liquid in eight seconds while flying at about 140 knots at low altitudes of only 100 to 150 feet.

The C–130 made 20 drops around the fires, each releasing up to 18.5 tons. The specially equipped aircraft dispensed the liquid from the air using pressure hoses. By August 26, all major fires in the Pacific Northwest were under control.

57.
Name: Idaho Flood.
Location: Idaho.
Date(s): January 16–19, 1974.
Emergency: Rain and melted snow combined to flood the Coeur d'Alene River

and the Pine Creek valleys in northern Idaho.

Air Force Organization(s) Involved: 48th Aerosp RR Sq.

Airlifted: An electric generator, medical supplies, and 93 passengers.

Aircraft Employed: UH–1 (three).

Operations: During January, the mountains of the northwestern United States, which had accumulated heavy early winter snow, experienced two weeks of relatively warm weather accompanied by heavy rain. The combination of rain and melted snow drove rivers and creeks over their banks in northern Idaho. Floods from the Coeur d'Alene River and Pine Creek struck the vicinity of Pinehurst, Idaho, a community of about 2,000 some 40 miles east of Spokane.

High water washed out bridges, including a section of Interstate 90, closing off access to food supplies. The floods interrupted electrical power, leaving hundreds of people without heat or communications. On January 16, Governor Cecil Andrus declared the Coeur d'Alene wilderness region around Pinehurst a disaster area and appealed for federal assistance. That same day, the 48th Aerosp RR Sq, based at Fairchild AFB, Washington, began four days of rescue and relief operations in the Pinehurst area.

After setting up a command post at a local bank, the unit marshaled three UH–1 Huey helicopters to evacuate flood victims. In two days, the squadron airlifted 93 refugees, some hoisted from the roofs of their inundated homes. Civilian observers helped helicopter crews locate isolated victims. The airlift saved the lives of two women with heart disease and delivered an emergency electrical generator to restore communications and miscellaneous medical supplies. By the end of January, dry winter weather had returned, allowing the swollen streams to subside and residents to return home.

58.

Name: Southwestern Forest Fires.

Location: New Mexico and California.

Date(s): June 30–July 4 and August 30, 1974.

Emergency: Forest fires consumed 10,000 acres of the Lincoln National Forest in the Guadalupe Mountains of New Mexico and 17,500 acres of the San Bernardino National Forest in the San Jacinto Mountains of southern California.

Air Force Organization(s) Involved: 904th Tac Alft Gp.

Airlifted: 144 tons of fire-retardant chemical.

Aircraft Employed: C–130 (two).

Operations: A forest fire spread across 10,000 acres in the Lincoln National Forest in the Guadalupe Mountains of southeastern New Mexico at the end of June and the beginning of July. The U.S. Forest Service's BIFC had just trained the 904th Tac Alft Gp at Hamilton AFB, California, to use the MAFFS. The center now enlisted the group's assistance to extinguish the New Mexico fire.

On June 30, one of the group's C–130s deployed to the Alamogordo municipal airport. Over the next three days, the C–130 crew flew five sorties, dropping

15,000 gallons of fire-retardant chemical called slurry in the path of the fire while flying at 100 to 150 feet. A Forest Service T–34 airplane guided the Hercules to the drop zones. After five days, in which the 904th Tac Alft Gp flew fifteen missions, dropping 90 tons of fire retardant and reforestation fertilizer, firefighters extinguished the fire on July 4.

The U.S. Forest Service tapped the 904th Tac Alft Gp again after a fire erupted on Tuesday, August 27, on the Sobota Indian Reservation near Palm Springs in southern California. The blaze quickly spread over the San Jacinto Mountains, which contained a portion of the San Bernardino National Forest. By August 30, it had consumed almost 17,500 acres of timber and brush, becoming California's worst forest fire of the year.

The 904th Tac Alft Gp deployed a C–130 equipped with the MAFFS from Hamilton AFB to the Ontario airport northwest of Palm Springs. It flew four aerial spray sorties on August 30, dispensing 54 tons of fire retardant in the path of the mountain fire. Workers on the ground and in the air contained the conflagration by the end of the day, limiting the losses to 10 million board feet of lumber and $7.5 million in watershed and timber damage.

59.
Name: Los Angeles Area Forest Fires.
Location: California.
Date(s): August 8–15, 1975.
Emergency: Forest fires swept through 10,000 acres in the San Bernardino and Angeles National Forests of California.
Air Force Organization(s) Involved: 146th Tac Alft Wg and 153d, 904th, and 940th Tac Alft Gps.
Airlifted: 1,400 tons of fire-retardant chemical.
Aircraft Employed: C–130 (five).
Operations: Children playing with matches accidently ignited a forest fire in the Lake Hemet area of the San Bernardino National Forest northeast of Los Angeles on Friday, August 8. A dry summer had left area trees and brush vulnerable, and the fire soon spread over 4,500 acres.

The U.S. Forest Service called the California National Guard's 146th Tac Alft Wg at Van Nuys on August 8 for assistance to combat the fire. Wing personnel immediately loaded two C–130s with special fire-fighting equipment. On August 9, the two planes began spraying fire-retardant chemical around the fire, helping to bring the Lake Hemet blaze under control by nightfall.

A second fire on August 9 in the adjacent Angeles National Forest near Palmdale persuaded the Forest Service to request further Air Force help. During the weekend of August 9 and 10, the 153d Tac Alft Gp at Cheyenne, Wyoming; the 904th Tac Alft Gp at Hamilton AFB, California; and the 940th Tac Alft Gp at McClellan AFB, California, each sent a C–130 for aerial spraying over unburned trees around the fire in the disaster area. Jim Ruppelt, Forest Service liaison, coordinated C–130 aircraft drops staging from Ontario International Airport, California. Two new fires broke out in the nearby San Bernardino mountains on Monday, August 11.

The C–130s carried the MAFFS, and between August 8 and 15, the five ANG and AF Res aircraft dispensed 1,400 tons of the chemical in 104 sorties. Hundreds of firefighters extinguished the last of the Los Angeles fires on August 15. Southern California lost an estimated $5 million in timber resources as the four fires consumed 8,000 acres of timber and brush. Forest Service officials estimated it would take 10 years for reforestation.

60.
Name: Angeles National Forest Fire.
Location: California.
Date(s): September 23–27, 1975.
Emergency: A forest and brush fire spread through the Angeles National Forest, north of the Los Angeles basin.
Air Force Organization(s) Involved: 146th Tac Alft Wg.
Airlifted: 368 tons of fire-retardant chemical.
Aircraft Employed: C–130 (two).
Operations: For the second time in two months, forest and brush fires ignited and spread in the Angeles National Forest north of Los Angeles. Dry, hot, windy weather contributed to the fire, which broke out during the last week of September. On September 23, the BIFC requested two C–130 aircraft equipped with the MAFFS to airdrop fire-retardant chemical around the new fires to keep them from spreading.

The Western Air Force Reserve Region tapped the 146th Tac Alft Wg at Van Nuys, California, for the job. This California ANG wing, having helped fight the August fires, now flew two C–130 Hercules aircraft to Ontario International Airport, California, which served as a Forest Service staging area. For five days, from September 23 to 27, the planes flew aerial spraying missions, dropping 3,000 gallons of fire retardant on each flight.

The 146th Tac Alft Wg completed its fire-fighting missions on September 27 after releasing 368.5 tons of fire-retardant chemical in the path of the advancing fires. The aerial efforts helped Forest Service firefighters contain the fires by the end of the month.

61.
Name: Southern California Forest Fires.
Location: California.
Date(s): November 24–27, 1975.
Emergency: A massive brush and forest fire burned 60,000 acres in the Angeles and San Bernardino National Forests.
Air Force Organization(s) Involved: 146th Tac Alft Wg, 940th Tac Alft Gp, and

74

336th Tac Alft Sq.
Airlifted: 144 tons of fire-retardant chemical.
Aircraft Employed: C–130 (five).
Operations: Terrible brush and forest fires erupted in the Angeles and San Bernardino National Forests north and northeast of Los Angeles in late November. High winds fanned the flames and spread the blazes. One fire alone consumed over 70 square miles in the Tujunga Canyon. The U.S. Forest Service's BIFC asked the Western Air Force Reserve Region to send C–130 aircraft equipped with the MAFFS, used successfully in August and September against similar fires in the same region.

On Monday, November 24, the 452d Tac Alft Wg sent a C–130 from the 336th Tac Alft Sq from Hamilton AFB, California, and two C–130s of the 940th Tac Alft Gp from McClellan AFB, California, to the Ontario airport east of Los Angeles for fire-fighting missions. One C–130 airlifted three air compressors from Hamilton AFB to Ontario to load the planes equipped with the MAFFS. At the same time, the 146th Tac Alft Wg (ANG) from Van Nuys, California, deployed two C–130s equipped with the fire-fighting system to Ontario.

Between November 25 and 27, the specially equipped planes flew 20 sorties in almost 15 flying hours, dropping 144 tons of fire retardant and reforestation fertilizer around the fires. Guided to the drop zones by Forest Service spotter aircraft, the camouflaged C–130s were painted with special orange tail markings enabling Forest Service pilots to distinguish them from background vegetation. Firefighters controlled the blazes with the aid of late autumn rains. By Thanksgiving Day, November 27, the 130s had returned to their home bases after 60,000 acres of timber and brush had been consumed.

62.
Name: Washington State Floods.
Location: Washington.
Date(s): December 6–7, 1975.
Emergency: Melting snow and heavy rain flooded river valleys in the western part of Washington State.
Air Force Organization(s) Involved: 41st Mil Alft Sq.
Airlifted: 62 tons of sandbags.
Aircraft Employed: C–141 (two).
Operations: Heavy snow fell over the Cascade and Coast Ranges in western Washington State at the end of November. Warmer temperatures in early December melted the snow, filling streams to capacity. Heavy rain during the first four days of December spilled rivers out of their normal channels, causing extensive flooding in seven counties around Puget Sound and along the coast.

The Seattle District, U.S. Army Corps of Engineers, estimated flood damage as high as $21 million and requested Air Force support, through the Western Air Force Reserve Region, to airlift 300,000 empty sandbags from Allan Thompson

Airport in Jackson, Mississippi, to Boeing Field in Seattle.

The Military Airlift Command's Twenty-first Air Force directed the 437th Tac Alft Wg at Charleston AFB, South Carolina, to accomplish the mission. On December 6, the wing's 41st Mil Alft Sq sent two C–141 Starlifters from Charleston to Jackson, where each was loaded with 31 tons of sandbags. The aircrews took off for Seattle, but bad weather diverted them to Fairchild AFB, Washington, that night. The next day, the two C–141s flew to Boeing Field in Seattle, where ground personnel unloaded the sandbags.

Under the supervision of the U.S. Army Corps of Engineers, the bags were filled and placed along the swollen rivers around Puget Sound to help control the flooding. The 41st Mil Alft Sq aircrews flew the Starlifters back to Charleston AFB late on December 7. The two-day operation consumed almost 26 flying hours. On December 13, President Gerald R. Ford declared six flooded Washington State counties major disaster areas.

63.
Name: Bethel Power Failure.
Location: Alaska.
Date(s): December 18–28, 1975.
Emergency: A fire destroyed Bethel's only power plant, leaving this Alaskan town with no electricity at the beginning of a season of subfreezing temperatures.
Air Force Organization(s) Involved: 62d Mil Alft Wg.
Airlifted: 76 tons of electrical generators, cables, heaters, transformers, an equipment shelter, cots, and a truck; and support personnel.
Aircraft Employed: C–141 (three) and C–130 (one).
Operations: On December 2, a fire destroyed the only electrical power plant at Bethel, Alaska, a town of almost 3,000 on the Kuskokwim River about 400 miles west of Anchorage. For two weeks the trading center suffered without electricity in temperatures as low as 45 degrees below zero (Fahrenheit). Mayor Eddie Hoffman appealed to the Alaska Disaster Office, which requested assistance from the Federal Disaster Assistance Administration. On December 17, President Ford declared Bethel a federal disaster area and asked the Alaskan Air Command for aid.

On December 18, Air Force Chief of Staff Gen. David C. Jones ordered MAC to transport generators and support personnel from Holloman AFB, New Mexico, to Bethel. The task was assigned to the 62d Mil Alft Wg at McChord AFB, Washington. For the next two days, the wing flew two C–141 Starlifter aircraft and one C–130 Hercules to airlift two 750-kilowatt solar turbine generators, 21 support personnel from the 4449th Mobility Support Squadron, a truck, cots, cables, heaters, transformers, and an equipment shelter from Holloman to Bethel.

The planes landed at Bethel with 62 tons of cargo on December 20. By Christmas Day, local workers realized they needed more generators and requested another airlift. On December 27 and 28, MAC delivered two more generators weighing 13 tons aboard another C–141. Personnel of the 4449th Mobility

Support Squadron helped to connect the airlifted generators, along with two more contributed by the builders of the Alaskan pipeline. By the end of the month, the citizens of Bethel could face the arctic winter assured of electricity and heat.

64.
Name: Kentucky Coal Mine Disaster.
Location: Kentucky.
Date(s): March 9–12, 1976.
Emergency: Two gas explosions trapped 26 coal miners five miles underground.
Air Force Organization(s) Involved: 32d and 50th Tac Alft Sqs.
Airlifted: Four tons of equipment, two vehicles, and 40 rescue workers.
Aircraft Employed: C–130 (two).
Operations: On Tuesday, March 9, a methane gas explosion trapped 15 miners more than five miles underground in the Scotia Coal Company mine near Partridge, Kentucky. The Mining Enforcement and Safety Administration in Washington, D.C., asked for Air Force assistance to transport rescue workers and equipment to the mine.   The same day, MAC Control Center at Scott AFB, Illinois, diverted a 50th Tac Alft Sq C–130 from the 314th Tac Alft Wg from a training mission over Rhode Island to Pittsburgh International Airport. The plane loaded 18 rescue workers and two emergency vehicles and airlifted them to Tri-City Airport in eastern Tennessee, the nearest airfield to the mountainous disaster site.

Three days later, on March 12, a second explosion trapped 11 more miners who had volunteered to help the rescue team. Within an hour, MAC diverted another 314th Tac Alft Wg C–130 from a navigational training mission over the Gulf of Mexico to pick up 22 more rescue workers and four tons of equipment at the Pittsburgh airport and airlift them to the Tennessee airport, where ground vehicles moved the passengers and cargo to the Kentucky mine site. The mission was completed the same day, but despite the best efforts of the aircrews and 40 rescue personnel, all 26 trapped miners died.

65.
Name: Teton Dam Disaster.
Location: Idaho.
Date(s): June 5–6, 1976.
Emergency: A 310-foot high earthen dam on the Teton River collapsed, flooding three towns and several farms.
Air Force Organization(s) Involved: 37th, 41st, and 48th Aerosp RR Sqs.
Airlifted: Unknown numbers of flood victims, disaster workers, medical personnel, and law enforcement officials.
Aircraft Employed: UH–1 (four) and HC–130 (one).
Operations: Around noon, June 5, the new Teton Dam—a huge earthen structure 310 feet high and 2,500 feet long on the Teton River in southeastern Idaho—col-

lapsed. A 15-foot wall of water, carrying four million cubic yards of dirt and rock from the dam, descended on the towns of Rexburg, Sugar City, and Teton. Seven communities, with a total population of 30,000, evacuated their homes as the flood engulfed 35 miles of the Teton and upper Snake River valleys. Millions of gallons of muddy water swept cars and mobile homes downstream. The disaster left 11 people dead and destroyed $500 million in property.

Governor Cecil Andrus closed roads north of Idaho Falls and declared a state of emergency, and Senator Frank Church wired President Ford for federal assistance on June 5. The president declared the region a major disaster area the next day.

Within hours of the dam's collapse on June 5, the Air Force responded to appeals for helicopter support from the Booneville County Sheriff's Office. Detachment 10 of the 37th Aerosp RR Sq at Hill AFB, Utah, used two UH–1 helicopters to fly 33 search and rescue sorties over the flooded region the same day.

Meanwhile, the 48th Aerosp RR Sq's Detachment 22 from Mountain Home AFB, Idaho, also used two UH–1 helicopters to fly 24 sorties in the disaster area. The four helicopters picked up flood victims stranded on high ground or rooftops and shuttled relief workers, medical personnel, and law enforcement officials along the Teton River valley. On June 5, the 41st Aerosp RR Sq at McClellan AFB, California, sent an HC–130 to fly over the flood area to provide radio communications for rescue workers on the ground and in the helicopters. The aircraft also searched for victims as it circled the inundated valley.

Fortunately, the water receded rapidly, and communities began drying out as early as June 6. Mountain Home AFB's 366th Tactical Fighter Wing (Tac Ftr Wg) collected relief supplies and trucked them to Ricks College in Rexburg the week after the flood for evacuees temporarily sheltered there.

66.
Name: Ontario Forest Fire.
Location: Canada.
Date(s): June 9–10, 1976.
Emergency: A 300,000-acre forest fire raged north of Dryden, Canada.
Air Force Organization(s) Involved: 62d Mil Alft Wg.
Airlifted: 36 tons of fire-fighting equipment, including pumps, hoses, and shovels; and four passengers.
Aircraft Employed: C–141 (two).
Operations: A forest fire broke out in northwestern Ontario province, Canada, in early June. Hot, dry weather coupled with abundant fuel contributed to the rapid spread of the fire. The Ontario Natural Resources Department estimated that 250,000 acres of timber had burned by June 8, and the Canadian government appealed to the United States for help. The BIFC asked the Air Force to airlift fire-fighting equipment and personnel to Dryden, a Canadian city just south of the disaster area.

On June 9 and 10, the Military Airlift Command's 62d Mil Alft Wg at McChord AFB, Washington, sent two C–141 Starlifters to carry the requested cargo from Forest Service storage sites to the Dryden municipal airport. One of the Starlifters carried 23.5 tons of water pumps, fire hoses, shovels, rations, and other supplies from Boise Air Terminal via Winnipeg, Canada, to Dryden. The other C–141 airlifted 12.5 tons of similar cargo from Johnson Bell Field in Missoula, Montana, to Dryden via Minot AFB, North Dakota. Neither plane could fly directly to Ontario because of severe weather in the Dryden area on June 9. The two Starlifters transported four fire experts in addition to 36 tons of fire-fighting equipment.

Before the airlift, Canadian officials predicted that the fire might consume a million acres of valuable timber. With the help of MAC, firefighters limited the destruction to 300,000 acres.

67.
Name: Big Thompson Canyon Flood.
Location: Colorado.
Date(s): August 1–3, 1976.
Emergency: Torrential rain caused a flash flood, killing more than 100 people and stranding hundreds of others.
Air Force Organization(s) Involved: 37th Aerosp RR Sq.
Airlifted: 81 flood victims.
Aircraft Employed: UH–1 (two).
Operations: On July 31, the day Colorado celebrated a century of statehood, nature sent tragedy. Fourteen inches of rain fell in a six-hour period over the head-waters of Colorado's Big Thompson River along the eastern slope of the Rocky Mountains, about 40 miles northwest of Denver. A wall of water, at times 28 feet higher than the average river level, gouged through the 30-mile-long Big Thompson Canyon just west of Loveland.

The flash flood caught an estimated 2,500 residents and vacationers in the canyon and carried away homes, cars, trailers, and more than 15 miles of a U.S. highway that followed the river through the mountains. At least 125 people drowned, some carried eight miles beyond the mouth of the canyon by the raging waters. In an eight-mile section of the gorge known as the narrows, all man-made structures disappeared.

The next day, August 1, 1,500 people remained stranded in the canyon. The communities of Glen Haven and Drake nearly washed away, and officials esti-mated $50 million in damage to the area. Governor Richard Lamm called out the Army and ANG and appealed for federal aid. President Ford immediately declared the Big Thompson Canyon a federal disaster area.

On August 1, the Larimer County Sheriff's Office at Loveland asked the 37th Aerosp RR Sq at Francis E. Warren AFB, Wyoming, for helicopter support. The squadron sent a UH–1 helicopter and crew to airlift 51 stranded flood victims out of the canyon the same day. Another 37th Aerosp RR Sq UH–1 helicopter and crew reached the Big Thompson Canyon on August 2, but had to wait to conduct search and rescue sorties until the next day when the weather improved. On August 3, the second helicopter lifted 30 stranded people to safety.

In three days, the two 37th Aerosp RR Sq UH–1 helicopters helped rescue 81 people, shuttling between the canyon and a staging area at Loveland. Army and Army National Guard helicopters also participated in the disaster relief operation, and the Colorado ANG provided fuel trucks and ground personnel. All Air Force search and rescue operations had ended by August 4.

68.
Name: Operation Sno Go.
Location: New York and Pennsylvania.
Date(s): January 31–February 8, 1977.
Emergency: More than 100 inches of snow fell over western New York and Pennsylvania, temporarily paralyzing Buffalo and Pittsburgh.
Air Force Organization(s) Involved: 436th, 437th, and 438th Mil Alft Wgs; 314th and 459th Tac Alft Wgs; and 927th Tac Alft Gp.
Airlifted: 1,160 tons of snow removal equipment and 430 passengers, including Army engineering personnel, disaster relief workers, and government officials.
Aircraft Employed: C–5 (6), C–141 (8), and C–130 (23).
Operations: Between Christmas 1976 and February 1, 1977, more than 150 inches of snow fell over western New York. Almost as much descended on western Pennsylvania in the same period. In the last few days of January, a blizzard brought winds up to 45 mph and 20-foot snowdrifts, paralyzing Buffalo and Pittsburgh. Governor Hugh Carey of New York and Governor Milton Shapp of Pennsylvania appealed to President Jimmy Carter for federal assistance. The mayor of Buffalo, Stanley Makowski, also requested White House aid.

On Sunday, January 30, President Carter declared parts of the two states to be in a state of emergency, a category just short of major disaster status. Thomas Casey, regional administrator of the Federal Disaster Assistance Administration, requested military support.

Between January 31 and February 8, the 436th Mil Alft Wg from Dover AFB, Delaware, flew six C–5 Galaxy aircraft and one C–141 Starlifter with 209 tons of snow blowers and emergency vehicles along with 36 drivers and support personnel from Cedar Rapids, Iowa; Sawyer AFB, Michigan; John F. Kennedy International Airport, New York; Pope AFB, North Carolina; and Griffith AFB, New York, to Niagara Falls International Airport near Buffalo and Greater Pittsburgh International Airport. Two 437th Mil Alft Wg C–141s carried tractors, scoop loaders, dump trucks, graders, trailers, utility vehicles, snow blowers, and members of the 82d Airborne Division from Pope AFB to Niagara Falls between February 2 and 10. The planes were based at Charleston AFB, South Carolina.

Between February 2 and 4, five other C–141s belonging to the 438th Mil Alft Wg at McGuire AFB, New Jersey, carried 91 tons of snow removal equipment and 59 passengers to Niagara Falls from Pope AFB; Buckley ANG Base, Colorado; and Suffolk County, New York. The 314th Tac Alft Wg at Little Rock AFB, Arkansas, whose 50th Tac Alft Sq was deployed at Pope AFB, used more than 20 C–130 Hercules aircraft to airlift snow removal equipment and members of the 20th U.S. Army Engineer Battalion from Fort Bragg, North Carolina, to Niagara Falls International Airport between February 1 and 7.

On February 2, the 927th Tac Alft Gp at Selfridge ANG Base, Michigan, responded to a Fourteenth Air Force (Reserve) call to haul 12,000 snow shovels from Rickenbacker AFB near Columbus, Ohio, to Buffalo. The Air Force Reserve's 459th Tac Alft Wg at Andrews AFB, Maryland, flew a C–130 with 986 pounds of cots and blankets from Pittsburgh to Buffalo on February 2.

Air Force and Air Force Reserve units airlifted more than 1,000 tons of snow removal equipment and vehicles and over 430 personnel—including engineers, vehicle drivers, relief workers, and government officials—to Buffalo and Pittsburgh in just nine days. By mid-February, as weather improved, the cargo planes began to return snow removal equipment and personnel to their original locations.

69.
Name: Johnstown Flood.
Location: Pennsylvania.
Date(s): July 24–28, 1977.
Emergency: Almost 18 inches of rain in three days spilled the Conemaugh River out of its banks and flooded Johnstown, Pennsylvania.
Air Force Organization(s) Involved: 911th Tac Alft Gp.
Airlifted: 38 tons of food, bedding, medical supplies, and household goods.
Aircraft Employed: C–123 (seven).
Operations: Between Tuesday and Thursday, July 19 to 21, almost 18 inches of rain fell over the Conemaugh River that ran through Johnstown, Pennsylvania. Although flood control projects had been completed since the disastrous 1889 Johnstown flood that killed 2,200 people, another flash flood had struck the town. High water funneling through the mountains carried homes off their foundations, buried streets under inches of mud, drove 50,000 residents from their homes along 70 miles of the Conemaugh River valley, and killed at least 72 people. Damage estimates ranged as high as $200 million.

On July 21, President Carter declared seven Pennsylvania counties around Johnstown a major disaster area in response to state and local official requests. On July 24, the civil defense director of Allegheny County, James Curran, asked the Air Force Reserve's 911th Tac Alft Gp at Greater Pittsburgh International Airport to airlift relief supplies to the Johnstown flood victims.

From July 24 through 28, the group used seven C–123 Provider aircraft to transport almost 38 tons of food, bedding, medicine, and other relief cargo from

Allegheny County Airport to Johnstown-Cambria County Airport. The planes consumed nearly 18 flying hours in nine sorties, with the commander of the 911th Tac Alft Gp, Lt. Col. William J. McQuade, flying one of the twin-engine cargo aircraft. Floodwaters receded before the airlift ended on July 28, but ground relief workers faced a long cleanup and restoration effort.

70.
Name: California Forest Fires.
Location: California.
Date(s): July 30–August 19, 1977.
Emergency: Fires sparked by lightning consumed over 380,000 acres of California's national forests.
Air Force Organization(s) Involved: 146th Tac Alft Gp and 153d and 433d Tac Alft Wgs.
Airlifted: 654,500 gallons of fire suppressant.
Aircraft Employed: C–130 (eight).
Operations: By the end of July, forest fires had broken out all over California. Usually caused by lightning and spread by strong winds, the blazes fed on trees made tinder dry by the summer heat. They consumed hundreds of thousands of acres in the Los Padres National Forest near Santa Barbara on the Pacific coast, in the Sequoia National Forest of the Sierra Nevada, and in the Plumas and Modoc National Forests in the northeastern part of the state.

The Forest Service's BIFC requested aid from the Air Force Reserve's Fourth Air Force. California authorities contacted units of the ANG to airdrop fire-retarding chemicals around the fires. Between July 30 and August 19, eight AF Res and ANG C–130s equipped with the portable MAFFS flew 221 sorties in 308 flying hours, dropping 654,500 gallons of fire suppressant along the edge of the fires. Flying at an altitude of 150 feet, each C–130 dropped about 3,000 gallons of fire retardant in 11 seconds.

Because each specially equipped aircraft could be reloaded in about 20 minutes, they could fly several missions each day. The C–130s operated from four Forest Service staging areas: Ontario, Fresno, Stockton, and Redding. The Air Force Reserve's 433d Tac Alft Wg from Kelly AFB, Texas, sent two C–130 Hercules airplanes against four major fires in the Santa Barbara area. Within 20 days, the two planes had dropped 90,000 gallons of the fire-retardant liquid in 32 missions. The other six Hercules aircraft came from the Air National Guard's 146th Tac Alft Gp at Van Nuys, California, and the 153d Tac Alft Wg at Cheyenne, Wyoming.

By August 19, the Forest Service no longer needed Air Force assistance and the planes returned to their home bases. Firefighters were able to contain the fires only after they had consumed more than 594 square miles of California woodland.

71.
Name: Snow Blow I.
Location: Ohio.
Date(s): January 29–31, 1978.
Emergency: A severe blizzard hit northwestern Ohio, dropping so much snow and bringing so much wind that 15-foot snowdrifts stranded almost 8,000 motorists.
Air Force Organization(s) Involved: 437th and 438th Mil Alft Wgs, 317th and 463d Tac Alft Wgs, and 924th Tac Alft Gp.
Airlifted: 600 tons of snow removal equipment and 516 personnel, mostly Army engineering troops.
Aircraft Employed: C–141 (27) and C–130 (16).
Operations: An immense blizzard hit Michigan, Indiana, and Ohio on Thursday, January 26. The next day, President Carter declared a state of emergency in these states. Governor James Rhodes of Ohio called the storm a "killer blizzard looking for victims" as it stranded 7,700 motorists in his state. About 20,000 Ohioans suffered without electricity through Saturday, January 28. Winds as high as 65 mph piled up 15-foot snowdrifts.

President Carter ordered Army units to help exhausted Ohio National Guard troops rescue stranded motorists. On January 28, the Federal Disaster Assistance Administration through the U.S. Army Forces Command directed the Air Force's MAC to transport troops and snow removal equipment from Fort Campbell, Kentucky, and Fort Bragg, North Carolina, to Toledo, Ohio.

Between January 29 and 31, the 437th Mil Alft Wg at Charleston AFB, South Carolina, and the 438th Mil Alft Wg at McGuire AFB, New Jersey, sent 27 C–141 Starlifter aircraft for the task. Another 16 C–130 Hercules airplanes participated, coming from the 463d Tac Alft Wg at Dyess AFB, Texas; the 317th Tac Alft Wg at Pope AFB, North Carolina; and the 924th Tac Alft Gp at Bergstrom AFB, Texas. The planes airlifted 516 Army personnel from the 101st Air Assault Division at Fort Campbell and the 82d Airborne Division, the 27th Engineer Battalion, and the 20th Engineer Brigade at Fort Bragg to Ohio's snowbound northwest corner.

About 600 tons of snow removal equipment—including front end loaders, trucks, road graders, bulldozers, fuel tankers, and support equipment—rode with the troops. Fort Bragg personnel boarded the planes at neighboring Pope AFB. Military Airlift Command and AF Res cargo aircraft operated under Twenty-first Air Force control for the flights to Toledo. The airlift ended on January 31, as improved weather allowed surface transportation to resume.

72.
Name: Snow Blow II.
Location: Massachusetts, Connecticut, and Rhode Island.
Date(s): February 8–17, 1978.

Humanitarian Airlift Operations

Emergency: A blizzard that struck southern New England dumped up to 27 inches of snow, blocking roads and stranding motorists.

Air Force Organization(s) Involved: 60th, 62d, 63d, and 437th Mil Alft Wgs; 314th, 317th, 433d, 440th, 442d, and 463d Tac Alft Wgs; and 130th, 165th, 167th, and 179th Tac Alft Gps.

Airlifted: 2,339 tons of snow removal equipment, generators, and communications gear; and over 1,000 passengers.

Aircraft Employed: C–130 (80), C–141 (33), and C–5 (16).

Operations: The worst winter snowstorm in New England history dumped up to 27 inches of snow on Massachusetts, Connecticut, and Rhode Island on February 6 and 7. Winds gusted in excess of 90 mph, deep snowdrifts blocked roads and highways, and 50 people died. The governors of the three states appealed to President Carter for aid.

The president responded on February 7 by ordering Army troops flown to Boston, Hartford, and Providence for relief efforts as soon as airports reopened. The Federal Disaster Assistance Administration and the Army requested an Air Force airlift just a week after a similar operation in Ohio, Snow Blow I, at the end of January. The new operation was dubbed Snow Blow II.

On February 8, civilian airports at the three state capitals reopened and Air Force cargo aircraft began flying Army personnel and snow removal equipment to those cities. Between February 8 and 17, MAC C–5s and C–141s and AF Res and ANG C–130s airlifted 1,084 Army personnel and 2,339 tons of snow removal equipment to New England. The cargo included bulldozers, tractors, scoop loaders, road graders, compressors, generators, and communications equipment.

Participating Air Force organizations included four MAC wings from California, Washington, and South Carolina; six tactical airlift wings from Arkansas, North Carolina, Texas, Wisconsin, and Missouri; and four tactical airlift groups from West Virginia, Georgia, and Ohio. Cargo and personnel came from Fort Benning and Fort Stewart, Georgia; Fort Polk, Louisiana; Fort Hood, Texas; Fort Campbell, Kentucky; Fort Bragg, North Carolina; Andrews AFB, Maryland; Harrisburg, Pennsylvania; and Savannah, Georgia. The planes unloaded at Boston's Logan International Airport, Bradley International Airport near Hartford, and Theodore F. Green International Airport at Providence.

Snow Blow II encompassed 129 missions, 80 by C–130s, 33 by C–141s, and 16 by C–5s. Redeployment began on February 15, but some units continued flying men and materiel to the stricken New England area until February 17, when the weather improved and major surface transportation routes reopened.

73.
Name: Arizona Flood.
Location: Arizona.
Date(s): March 2–7, 1978.

Emergency: Torrential rains flooded the Salt and Gila River valleys and many tributary creeks.
Air Force Organization(s) Involved: 302d Sp Ops Sq.
Airlifted: Five tons of food, medicine, and equipment; and 39 passengers.
Aircraft Employed: CH–3 (six).
Operations: The month of March descended on Arizona like a lion, bringing storms and heavy rains that spilled the Salt and Gila Rivers over their banks and turned normally dry creek beds into raging rivers. Many people were stranded by high water, some on islands in the middle of streams, others atop flooded vehicles.

On March 2, the Maricopa County Sheriff's Office called Luke AFB's 302d Sp Ops Sq (AF Res) for helicopter support to rescue flood victims and deliver food to stranded families. Federal Aviation Administration (FAA) officials also asked the squadron to lift radar and generators from an island the Salt River was threatening to wash away.

Between March 2 and 4, the 302d Sp Ops Sq used four CH–3 Jolly Green Giant helicopters to carry 39 persons to safety, 17 of whom were in danger of death without rescue. The squadron also delivered a ton of food and medicine to families cut off from supplies by rising waters and airlifted at least 2.3 tons of FAA equipment. On Monday afternoon, March 6, the Arizona Office of Emergency Preparedness asked the 302d Sp Ops Sq to airlift two more tons of food to the St. Johns area of Apache County in eastern Arizona. The next morning, the squadron flew the food from Papago Army Airfield to the St. Johns airport, where it was distributed to flood victims on two CH–3 helicopters.

The 302d Sp Ops Sq used six Jolly Green Giants in four days to rescue or evacuate at least 39 people, deliver three tons of food and medicine, and save at least 2.3 tons of FAA equipment. Unit flood relief operations ended on March 7, as waters receded.

74.
Name: Wyoming Haylift.
Location: Wyoming.
Date(s): February 10–11, 1979.
Emergency: Heavy snow blocked roads, preventing ranchers from feeding their starving cattle.
Air Force Organization(s) Involved: 153d Tac Alft Gp.
Airlifted: 256 bales of hay.
Aircraft Employed: C–130 (two).
Operations: A series of winter storms swept over the ranges of southeastern Wyoming, dropping thick snow that buried grass and blocked the routes ranchers used to feed their cattle. Starvation threatened the herds, and, with them, the regional economy. The Wyoming legislature voted special funds for emergency operations and State Adjutant General Maj. Gen. James Spence contacted the Wyoming ANG for an airlift of hay.

Humanitarian Airlift Operations

The 153d Tac Alft Wg at Cheyenne flew at least two of its C–130 aircraft for the haylift operation on Saturday and Sunday, February 10 and 11. Each plane loaded about 16 bales of hay per mission at Cheyenne. Following an Army National Guard helicopter carrying a local rancher who knew where the threatened herds were, the C–130s flew at about 150 mph at an altitude of approximately 100 feet. At the right moment, six loadmasters in the rear of each plane, secured with safety harnesses, pushed the bales out open cargo doors.

The 153d Tac Alft Wg aircrews flew 16 sorties in two days over herds northwest of Cheyenne. The airdrops helped crews prepare for more typical missions of the unit, including dropping fire retardant over forest fires. The operation saved hundreds of Wyoming cattle during the harsh winter.

75.
Name: Three Mile Island Nuclear Accident.
Location: Pennsylvania.
Date(s): March 28–April 15, 1979.
Emergency: The Three Mile Island nuclear plant malfunctioned, releasing radioactive gases into the atmosphere.
Air Force Organization(s) Involved: 62d, 63d, 436th, and 438th Mil Alft Wgs; and 1st Helicopter Squadron.
Airlifted: At least 202 tons of radiation testing equipment, lead shielding, potassium iodine, water filtration equipment, and water samples.
Aircraft Employed: C–5 (two), C–141 (nine), C–130 (one), UH–1 (number unknown), and CH–3 (number unknown).
Operations: Before dawn on Wednesday, March 28, a malfunction at Metropolitan Edison's Three Mile Island nuclear power plant on the Susquehanna River, about 10 miles southeast of Harrisburg, Pennsylvania, led to the worst accident in U.S. nuclear power history. A leak in the cooling system sent thousands of gallons of high pressure radioactive hot water onto the floor of the containment building and into an adjacent structure. Some radioactive steam escaped into the atmosphere. A cloud of hydrogen gas grew within the reactor core, threatening to drive away cooling water and produce temperatures high enough for a meltdown, which would have released huge amounts of radiation.

Governor Richard Thornburgh issued evacuation orders and requested federal assistance. Four federal agencies—the Nuclear Regulatory Commission, the National Oceanic and Atmospheric Administration, the Federal Disaster Assistance Administration, and the Department of Energy—asked MAC for airlift support.

Immediately after the malfunction, the 1st Helicopter Squadron of the 76th Mil Alft Wg, based at Andrews AFB, Maryland, began to fly scientists over the accident site to monitor radiation levels. Using UH–1 and CH–3 helicopters, the squadron ferried personnel and samples among Three Mile Island, Pittsburgh, and Washington, D.C.

Three days later, on Saturday, March 31, a C–5 belonging to the 436th Mil Alft Wg at Dover AFB, Delaware, flew a 20-ton mobile atmospheric testing station to measure radiation leakage from McConnell AFB, Kansas, to Harrisburg. That same day, two Twenty-first Air Force C–141s moved 58.7 tons of lead bricks, lead sheets, and other shielding material from Suffolk County and Syracuse, New York; and a MAC C–130 airlifted three tons of potassium iodine (25,000 bottles) from Decatur, Illinois, to Harrisburg.

On April 9, as nuclear specialists cooled the reactor and reduced the hydrogen bubble that had developed inside, one C–5 and five C–141s airlifted 118 tons of water filtration equipment and charcoal filters from Pasco, Washington, to Harrisburg. One C–141 Starlifter then flew to Kirtland AFB, New Mexico, to pick up 2.5 tons of radiological equipment for transport to Harrisburg. Between April 11 and 15, two MAC C–141s also transported three 55-gallon water samples from the reactor site to federal testing facilities at Knoxville, Tennessee; Augusta, Georgia; and Idaho Falls, Idaho.

Military airlift wings participating in the airlift between March 31 and April 15 included the 62d at McChord AFB, Washington; the 63d at Norton AFB, California; the 436th at Dover AFB; and the 438th at McGuire AFB, New Jersey. In 16 days, 12 C–5, C–141, and C–130 planes transported more than 200 tons of cargo to or from Harrisburg.

76.
Name: Wichita Falls Tornado.
Location: Texas.
Date(s): April 11–19, 1979.
Emergency: A tornado that hit Wichita Falls, Texas, destroyed eight square miles of the city and killed 44 people, injured 1,000, and left 20,000 homeless.
Air Force Organization(s) Involved: 774th Tac Alft Sq and 303d and 305th Aerosp RR Sqs.
Airlifted: Seven tons of medical supplies, including x-ray machine batteries, sutures, bandages, and intravenous equipment; an unknown quantity of relief supplies; and two satellite communications jeeps.
Aircraft Employed: C–130s (four).
Operations: A tornado cut a mile-wide, eight-mile-long path across the southern end of Wichita Falls in north Texas on Tuesday, April 10. Winds of 225 mph destroyed or damaged 6,800 homes, leaving 20,000 people homeless out of a population of 100,000. The twister killed 44 people, injured 1,000, and destroyed $500 million dollars in property. The storm crippled electrical and communications facilities. Governor William Clements requested federal aid and President Carter designated Wichita Falls a disaster area.

On April 11, the Texas Department of Public Safety requested Air Force assistance to restore communications between Wichita Falls and the state capital at Austin. The 303d Aerosp RR Sq from March AFB, California, and the 305th

Aerosp RR Sq at Selfridge ANG Base, Michigan, each flew an HC–130 airplane with a satellite communications vehicle aboard. One went to Wichita Falls and the other to Austin to restore contact between the disaster area and the capital.

Also on April 11, the 774th Tac Alft Sq from Dyess AFB, Texas, used a C–130 to airlift seven tons of medical supplies and equipment from Kelly AFB near San Antonio to Sheppard AFB, five miles north of Wichita Falls. The cargo came from Air Training Command's Wilford Hall Medical Center and included X-ray equipment, sutures, bandages, and intravenous devices. With the airlifted items, the Air Force Regional Hospital at Sheppard AFB treated 598 persons. On April 19, the 774th flew another C–130 from Dyess to Sheppard with relief supplies collected by members of the Dyess AFB chapel and the 96th Security Police Squadron. By that time, at least 2,500 Sheppard AFB personnel had participated in disaster relief at nearby Wichita Falls.

77.
Name: Red River Flood.
Location: North Dakota and Minnesota.
Date(s): April 22–25, 1979.
Emergency: Heavy rain and melting snow drove the Red River, between North Dakota and Minnesota, 25 feet above flood stage, inundating almost 700,000 acres.
Air Force Organization(s) Involved: 60th, 437th, and 438th Mil Alft Wgs; and 133d, 145th, and 442d Tac Alft Wgs.
Airlifted: 235 tons of sandbags.
Aircraft Employed: C–141 (five) and C–130 (six).
Operations: During the third week of April, a combination of melting snow and heavy rain swelled the Red River to overflowing as it ran north between eastern North Dakota and northwestern Minnesota. Continued rain broadened the river to 15 miles in some places, flooded 270 homes, and forced 1,400 people to evacuate. The flood threatened the 54,000 residents of Grand Forks, North Dakota, and the 8,400 residents of East Grand Forks, Minnesota. By April 25, about 425,000 acres in North Dakota and 274,000 acres in Minnesota were inundated. President Carter declared the flooded region a major disaster area on April 26.

As early as April 19, the Fourth Air Force responded to a Grand Forks Civil Defense Office request for aid by directing ground assistance. On April 21, the U.S. Army Corps of Engineers requested an airlift of sandbags to Grand Forks from Offutt AFB, Nebraska, and Douglas Airport at Charlotte, North Carolina. The next day, five MAC, AF Res, and ANG aircraft accomplished the task.

The following military airlift wings each flew a C–141 Starlifter: the 60th at Travis AFB, California; the 437th at Charleston AFB, South Carolina; and the 438th at McGuire AFB, New Jersey. The Air National Guard's 145th Tac Alft Wg and the Air Force Reserve's 442d Tac Alft Wg each used a C–130 for the April 22 flights. On that one day, the five units airlifted 910,000 empty burlap bags weighing 143 tons.

The Red River continued to rise. On April 23, the U.S. Army Corps of Engineers asked for an airlift of more sandbags. The next day, two more C–141s from the 437th and 438th Mil Alft Wgs and two C–130s from the 145th Tac Alft Wg flew 72 more tons of sandbags from Charlotte to Grand Forks AFB. The 133d Tac Alft Wg used two C–130s on April 25 to move 20 tons of sandbags to Grand Forks from Moline, Illinois, and Milwaukee, Wisconsin.

The 11 planes airlifted more than 235 tons of sandbags to Grand Forks between April 22 and 25. On April 26, the Red River crested 25 feet above flood stage and 31 feet above normal. The river fell over the following days, eliminating the need for additional sandbags.

78.
Name: Central Arizona Forest Fires.
Location: Arizona.
Date(s): July 1, 1979.
Emergency: Forest fires consumed more than 76,000 acres of grassland, brush, and forests.
Air Force Organization(s) Involved: 62d Mil Alft Wg and 146th Tac Alft Wg.
Airlifted: 403 firefighters.
Aircraft Employed: C–141 (two) and C–130 (four).
Operations: Lightning ignited 19 forest fires across Arizona in late June. Winds of 50 mph and 110-degree heat spread the fires, which consumed 76,200 acres of parched Arizona grassland, brush, and forest in the Tonto and Prescott National Forests by July 2. A fire near Prescott burned 26,000 acres. On June 30, the BIFC requested Air Force assistance to airlift firefighters from the Pacific Northwest to Arizona to contain and control the spreading flames.

The next day, July 1, the California Air National Guard's 146th Tac Alft Wg at Van Nuys flew four C–130s in five sorties to transport 241 firefighters from Oregon and Washington to Phoenix. The same day, the Military Airlift Command's 62d Mil Alft Wg at McChord AFB, Washington, moved 162 firefighters to Phoenix aboard two C–141 Starlifters. The six transport planes airlifted more than 400 firefighters to the disaster area in 38 flying hours and seven sorties. The new firefighters joined hundreds of Forest Service personnel who came from the Navajo Indian reservation and California to battle the blazes. Almost 1,000 fire personnel worked to contain the fires. Between June 30 and July 6, Luke AFB near Phoenix also sent several flight line fuel trucks to deliver aviation gasoline to staging areas in the threatened area to refuel Forest Service aircraft.

79.
Name: Northwest Fires.
Location: Idaho and Montana.
Date(s): August 8–11, 1979.

Humanitarian Airlift Operations

Emergency: Forest fires—most ignited by lightning, but some by arsonists—spread across more than 150,000 acres of the Northwest.
Air Force Organization(s) Involved: 934th Tac Alft Gp.
Airlifted: 19.5 tons of supplies and equipment (11.5 tons dropped) and 28 passengers.
Aircraft Employed: C–130 (one).
Operations: A summer with little rain and intense heat made the forests of the northwestern United States kindling. Lightning set off a host of forest fires in Montana, Idaho, California, Oregon, Washington, and Wyoming. By the second week of August, 150,000 acres were aflame. The BIFC committed over 6,000 personnel and 88 contract aircraft to the task of containing and controlling the blazes.

An aircraft chartered by the Forest Service encountered mechanical problems, which prevented it from delivering food and other supplies to front-line firefighters in the Bitterroot Mountains between Idaho and Montana. On August 7, the BIFC requested a substitute aircraft through the Fourth Air Force.

On August 8, the 934th Tac Alft Gp at Minneapolis-St. Paul Airport sent a C–130 and crew to Missoula, Montana, a Forest Service staging area. That same day, the plane dropped seven tons of supplies to ground personnel fighting the fires in eastern Idaho and western Montana. The plane also carried eight passengers. On August 9, the C–130 dropped 4.5 tons of supplies and carried 11 passengers. Eight tons of fire-fighting equipment and supplies and nine passengers rode the Hercules on August 11.

On August 13, the plane and crew returned to Minneapolis-St. Paul after airlifting 19.5 tons of fire-fighting equipment, supplies, and personnel in three days of sorties, not counting deployment and redeployment flights.

80.
Name: Southern California Forest Fires.
Location: California.
Date(s): September 15–22, 1979.
Emergency: Forest fires consumed 40,000 acres of timber and brush east of Los Angeles between September 12 and 22, 1979.
Air Force Organization(s) Involved: 146th and 433d Tac Alft Wgs and 153d Tac Alft Gp.
Airlifted: 732,000 gallons of fire retardant.
Aircraft Employed: C–130 (eight).
Operations: Heat, low humidity, and strong winds combined to spread lightning-generated fires in California at the end of the summer. At least 16 separate fires consumed 90,000 acres between September 12 and 20, stretching the fire-fighting resources of the BIFC to the limit. The worst fires threatened the Los Angeles area in the Angeles and San Bernardino National Forests, where 40,000 acres of brush, scrub, and forest went up in smoke.

As early as September 14, the BIFC, through the Sixth Army's Emergency Operations Center at the Presidio at San Francisco, requested Air Force C–130s equipped with the MAFFS. The Air Force sent eight specially equipped planes to a staging area at the Van Nuys airport near Los Angeles on September 15 and 16. Three came from the 146th Tac Alft Wg (ANG), which was already at Van Nuys. Two more specially equipped C–130s came from the 433d Tac Alft Wg (AF Res) at Kelly AFB, Texas. The 153d Tac Alft Gp (ANG) at Cheyenne, Wyoming, sent three C–130s.

Between September 15 and 22, the eight C–130s and crews flew 254 sorties in almost 168 flying hours, dropping 732,000 gallons of fire-retardant liquid around the Angeles and San Bernardino fires. Each aircraft flew many sorties each day, reloading at Van Nuys and at Norton AFB, California. The planes supplemented firefighters on the ground who worked feverishly to contain and control the spreading flames, some of which reached residential areas in the Los Angeles area. In one 24-hour period, the planes dropped 168,000 gallons—an average of 21,000 gallons per plane—involving about seven sorties per aircraft. By September 22, most of the Los Angeles fires were under control, and the C–130s returned to their home bases.

81.
Name: Mount St. Helens Eruption.
Location: Washington.
Date(s): May 18–June 5, 1980.
Emergency: Mount St. Helens erupted with a gigantic explosion that produced huge clouds of ash and mudslides that devastated 200 square miles of forest.
Air Force Organization(s) Involved: 303d, 304th, and 305th Aerosp RR Sqs; 62d and 63d Mil Alft Wgs; and 9th Strategic Reconnaissance Wing.
Airlifted: 61 persons.
Aircraft Employed: UH–1 (five), HH–1 (five), C–130 (two), C–141 (one), and SR–71 (two).
Operations: Mount St. Helens erupted with the force of 40 hydrogen bombs just after 8:30 on Sunday morning, May 18. The top and north side of the volcano blew off in a tremendous explosion that turned a cubic mile of rock into a 60,000-foot column of ash and reduced the mountain's peak by 1,400 feet.

At the bottom of the volcano, Spirit Lake disappeared. Large trees in a 150-square-mile area were flattened like thousands of match sticks. Ash as fine as talcum powder darkened the sky and settled in a four-inch layer that stretched for almost 200 square miles. Hot mud 20 feet high flowed at speeds up to 30 mph down the Toutle River valley, destroying everything in its path. More than half of those people in the vicinity of the volcano at the time of the eruption perished. Survivors wandered in a new desert, seeking safety.

Before the eruption, the Forest Service contacted the 304th Aerosp RR Sq (AF Res) at Portland International Airport, about 60 miles south of Mount St.

Helens. Seismic rumblings had warned geologists of the pending explosive eruption, and the squadron was on alert for an emergency call. Consequently, the squadron was ready to respond less than two hours after the eruption.

During the first day, Sunday, May 18, the squadron saved 51 lives. Flying 10 UH–1 and HH–1 helicopters in pairs over the grey wilderness, squadron personnel lifted survivors from the path of mudslides, transported others to food and shelter, and warned still others of impending mud flows. Between May 18 and June 5, the 304th Aerosp RR Sq saved 61 people, including four rescue workers caught by a second Mount St. Helens eruption on May 25. The 303d and 305th Aerosp RR Sqs provided personnel to assist the rescue efforts.

Initially, a C–141 from the 63d Mil Alft Wg, stationed at Norton AFB, California, but in transit at McChord AFB, Washington, on May 18, provided an aerial communications platform for rescue coordination. This aircraft was later replaced by a 62d Mil Alft Wg C–130 from McChord and a 303d Aerosp RR Sq HC–130 from March AFB.

Between May 18 and June 5, the 9th Strategic Reconnaissance Wing at Beale AFB, California, used SR–71s to take aerial photographs of the devastated region to aid rescue and recovery efforts. The Air Force missions were part of a wider multi-service rescue and relief operation which saved 101 lives between May 18 and June 5. The missions were coordinated by the Aerospace Rescue and Recovery Service's Rescue Coordination Center at Scott AFB, Illinois.

82.
Name: Palm Springs Area Fire.
Location: California.
Date(s): July 29–August 1, 1980.
Emergency: Brush fires broke out in southern California, some near Palm Springs in the San Bernardino National Forest.
Air Force Organization(s) Involved: 146th and 433d Tac Alft Wgs.
Airlifted: 10,500 gallons of fire retardant.
Aircraft Employed: C–130 (three).
Operations: Drought, heat, and high winds combined at the end of July to spread lightning-generated brush and forest fires in the mountains of southern California. By July 28, seven brush fires had swept across hillsides east of Los Angeles. Some fires blazed across the mountains of the San Bernardino National Forest near Palm Springs. The Forest Service used hundreds of firefighters to contain the fires, which spread rapidly across desert scrub. In the mountains, ground crews were unable to build fire breaks fast enough, and the Forest Service sought Air Force aircraft to spray fire-retarding chemicals around the fires.

On July 29, MAC tasked the 433d Tac Alft Wg (AF Res) at Kelly AFB, Texas, to send two C–130 Hercules airplanes equipped with the MAFFS to Norton AFB in southern California to help fight the fires. Meanwhile, the California Air National Guard's 146th Tac Alft Wg at Van Nuys supplied another fire-fighting C–130.

Using 63d Mil Alft Wg facilities at Norton AFB as a staging area, the C–130 crews flew seven missions between July 29 and August 1, dropping 10,500 gallons of fire retardant around the flaming areas. By the evening of August 1, the fires were under control, allowing the three ANG and AF Res C–130s to return home.

83.
Name: *Prinsendam* Rescue.
Location: The Gulf of Alaska.
Date(s): October 4–5, 1980.
Emergency: The M.S. *Prinsendam*, a Dutch cruise ship with 519 passengers and crew members aboard, caught fire in the Gulf of Alaska, forcing all to abandon ship.
Air Force Organization(s) Involved: 71st Aerosp RR Sq, 17th and 144th Tac Alft Sqs, and the Alaskan Air Command.
Airlifted: 169 blankets, an undetermined quantity of relief supplies, 61 ship passengers and crew members, four pararescuemen, and one flight surgeon.
Aircraft Employed: HH–3 (one), HC–130 (one), C–130 (two), and C–12 (one).
Operations: The luxury Dutch cruise ship M.S. *Prinsendam* sailed with 519 persons aboard from Vancouver, Canada, on September 30, bound for Singapore. It journeyed north to give its 320 tourist passengers a look at Glacier Bay National Park, Alaska. Just after midnight on October 4, as the 426-foot ocean liner cruised in the Gulf of Alaska, about 370 nautical miles southeast of Anchorage, a fire erupted in the engine room and spread quickly through the middle of the ship. The captain radioed for help and ordered passengers into lifeboats.

The Coast Guard coordinated rescue efforts, sending three cutters and several HH–3 and HC–130 aircraft. It also contacted Canadian military forces and the Alaskan Air Command at Elmendorf AFB for assistance. The Coast Guard called on the 1,000-foot supertanker *Williamsburgh*, a few miles away from the *Prinsendam*, to render aid.

On the morning of October 4, Elmendorf's 71st Aerosp RR Sq sent two aircraft, an HH–3 helicopter and an HC–130 airplane, to the disaster site. The Jolly Green Giant helicopter, piloted by Capt. John J. Walters and Capt. William T. Gillian, picked up 169 blankets at Yakutat, Alaska, and delivered them to the *Williamsburgh*. Captain Walters then piloted the HH–3 on a series of flights to carry passengers from lifeboats to the supertanker. With the aid of two pararescuemen, the helicopter hoisted 61 passengers and crewmen to safety.

Meanwhile, the 71st Aerosp RR Sq's HC–130 carried a flight surgeon and two pararescuemen from Elmendorf AFB to Yakutat where Coast Guard helicopters transferred them to the disaster scene. It refueled the Air Force HH–3 helicopter and helped to locate lifeboats. When a Canadian rescue helicopter suffered an instrument panel fire, the HC–130 guided it to Yakutat, saving 13 more lives. The two 71st Aerosp RR Sq crews rescued 74 persons. Combined efforts of Air

Force, Coast Guard, Canadian, and civilian craft saved all 519 persons aboard the fire-ravaged *Prinsendam*.

The 144th Tac Alft Sq from Kulis ANG Base, Alaska, used a C–130 to take relief supplies to Valdez, Alaska, where the *Williamsburgh* and other rescue ships carried survivors. An Alaskan Air Command C–12 and a 17th Tac Alft Sq C–130 from Elmendorf also provided logistical support for the operation. The empty *Prinsendam* continued to burn in the Gulf of Alaska. On October 11, it sank in 8,830 feet of water.

84.
Name: San Bernardino Forest Fires.
Location: California.
Date(s): November 25–29, 1980.
Emergency: Forest fires burned 125 square miles of southern California.
Air Force Organization(s) Involved: 146th and 433d Tac Alft Wgs and 153d Tac Alft Gp.
Airlifted: 1,305 tons (261,000 gallons) of fire retardant.
Aircraft Employed: C–130 (eight).
Operations: For the second time in four months, AF Res and ANG C–130 aircraft and crews equipped with the MAFFS responded to Forest Service requests for aid to contain and control southern California forest fires. The blazes erupted on Monday, November 24. Hot Santa Ana winds gusting up to 90 mph fanned the flames until 11 major fires had spread across 125 square miles of southern California by the end of the week. Some fires burned the edges of San Bernardino, about 80 miles east of Los Angeles, forcing thousands of residents to evacuate.

In cooperation with Governor Edmund G. Brown, Jr., the Forest Service used 4,000 firefighters in the San Bernardino Mountains where the largest fires consumed 23,600 acres of dry brush and trees. By Friday, November 28, President Carter had designated Los Angeles, Riverside, Orange, and San Bernardino Counties federal disaster areas.

On November 25, the U.S. Air Force Airlift Readiness Center and MAC called out C–130 units equipped with the MAFFS: the 433d Tac Alft Wg (AF Res) from Kelly AFB, Texas, sent two airplanes; the 153d Tac Alft Gp (ANG) from Cheyenne, Wyoming, sent three aircraft; and the 146th Tac Alft Wg (ANG) from Van Nuys, California, sent three planes. The C–130s flew that same day to Norton AFB, east of San Bernardino, to load fire-retardant liquid, but high winds postponed airdrops until the next day.

Between Wednesday and Saturday, November 26 to 29, as winds subsided, the eight C–130s flew 87 sorties in 45 flying hours, dropping 261,000 gallons (1,305 tons) of fire retardant on the fringes of the fires. By November 28, the Forest Service had contained 70 percent of the Panorama fire, the largest blaze. On November 29, Air Force aerial participation terminated as fire suppression efforts controlled the blazes.

85.
Name: MGM Grand Hotel Fire.
Location: Nevada.
Date(s): November 21, 1980.
Emergency: A fire raged for six hours at the huge MGM Grand Hotel in Las Vegas, killing 84 people and driving hundreds onto upper balconies or to the roof of the 26-story building.
Air Force Organization(s) Involved: 20th and 302d Sp Ops Sqs; and Detachment 1, 57th Fighter Weapons Wing (Ftr Wpns Wg).
Airlifted: An unknown quantity of compressed air bottles and packs, 310 passengers (20 lives saved), and 60 bodies.
Aircraft Employed: UH–1 (six) and CH–3 (three).
Operations: Early on Friday morning, November 21, a fire broke out on the ground floor of the $106 million MGM Grand Hotel in Las Vegas, home of what was then the world's largest gambling hall. About 3,500 guests and employees were in the 2,076-room, 26-floor building. Flames short-circuited the centralized fire alarm system and toxic clouds of black smoke climbed open stairwells into upper hallways. For six hours the fire roared through the lower floors of the hotel, killing 84 people, injuring 500, and driving hundreds to upper balconies or the roof.

Within an hour of the fire's start, the Las Vegas Metropolitan Police Department had asked Air Force officials at nearby Nellis AFB for helicopters to hoist persons from balconies and the roof to the ground. Fortunately, Nellis was hosting a Red Flag exercise at the time, and many participating units from other states flew helicopters needed for the emergency. The 302d Sp Ops Sq from Luke AFB, Arizona, sent three CH–3 helicopters and the 20th Sp Ops Sq from Eglin AFB's Hurlburt Field in Florida sent three UH–1 aircraft. Detachment 1 of 57th Ftr Wpns Wg, from Indian Springs Auxiliary Field, Nevada, sent another three UH–1 helicopters.

The Air Force helicopters hoisted 20 survivors from balconies and moved 90 from the roof to a ground-level parking lot. Detachment 1, 57th Ftr Wpns Wg, shuttled 200 rescue workers to and from the smoldering building and carried away more than 60 bodies that had been taken to the hotel roof. The detachment airlifted to the disaster scene an unknown quantity of compressed air bottles and air packs from a Department of Energy facility at Mercury, Nevada. Other helicopters, some private and some operated by the police, helped to rescue hotel guests. A total of 300 people were flown to safety by the helicopters. Air Force participation in the emergency ended on November 21, after local fire officials declared the fire extinguished.

86.
Name: Las Vegas Hilton Fire.
Location: Nevada.
Date(s): February 10, 1981.

Emergency: A series of fires broke out in the 2,782-room Las Vegas Hilton, killing eight people, injuring 198, and driving many guests to the roof of the 30-story building.
Air Force Organization(s) Involved: Detachment 1, 57th Ftr Wpns Wg.
Airlifted: 60 air packs for firemen and 54 passengers.
Aircraft Employed: UH–1 (three).
Operations: Just after 8:00 p.m. on Tuesday, February 10, arsonists set fires on four floors of the 30-story Las Vegas Hilton. The huge building, with more than 2,780 rooms, was hosting four conventions at the time. About 4,000 guests and employees evacuated the hotel, but eight people died and 198 went to hospitals, most suffering from smoke inhalation.

The worst fire began on the eighth floor of the south wing, spreading to the twenty-ninth floor within 15 minutes, exploding windows as it climbed. Thick black smoke drove guests to fire escapes or onto the roof, where they waited to be rescued by helicopter. Within 20 minutes of the start of the blaze, Fire Chief Roy Parrish of the Clark County Fire Department called neighboring Nellis AFB for the same kind of helicopter rescue missions that had saved lives at the MGM Grand Hotel fire three months earlier.

Three UH–1 helicopters from Detachment 1, 57th Ftr Wpns Wg, from Indian Springs Air Force Auxiliary Field responded to carry trapped hotel guests from the roof of the 30-story building. The helicopter crews saved nine lives and shuttled 45 firefighters and rescue personnel between the roof and the ground. They also airlifted 60 air packs to firefighters at the disaster scene. Meanwhile, 53 fire vehicles and 400 firemen, some from Nellis AFB, gathered at the hotel to extinguish the flames. Within two hours, workers had brought the fire under control, and Air Force helicopters returned to Indian Springs late that night.

87.
Name: Louisiana Flood.
Location: Louisiana.
Date(s): April 1983.
Emergency: Up to 20 inches of rain fell over southeastern Louisiana, flooding 40,000 homes and the state penitentiary at Angola.
Air Force Organization(s) Involved: Unspecified.
Airlifted: 83 tons of tents, cots, shower facilities, and field kitchen equipment.
Aircraft Employed: C–141 (four).
Operations: A week of torrential rain that began about April 5 flooded large portions of southeastern Louisiana and other parts of the South. In some areas, 20 inches of rain fell, sometimes at a rate of one inch an hour. On April 8, Governor Dave Treen, estimating that 40,000 homes were flooded, declared a state of emergency in 16 of 64 Louisiana parishes and appealed for federal disaster relief through the Federal Emergency Management Agency (FEMA). He also ordered evacuation of the state penitentiary at Angola because it was located near the

Mississippi River and rising water threatened to flood the prison. State police moved the prisoners to higher ground in the Baton Rouge area.

The Military Airlift Command headquarters at Scott AFB, Illinois, authorized four C–141B Starlifter missions to transport shelters, bedding, and facilities for bathing and cooking to the Baton Rouge area. The Starlifter aircrews flew to Gulfport Municipal Airport on the Mississippi coast, loaded 83 tons of tents, cots, shower facilities, and field kitchen components aboard four cargo planes and proceeded to Ryan Field, a civilian airport near Baton Rouge. The airlift allowed Louisiana officials to shelter, bathe, and feed hundreds of prisoner refugees while avoiding the unpleasant alternatives of keeping prisoners in a flooded institution or scattering them among overcrowded smaller prisons.

88.
Name: Minnesota Encephalitis Epidemic.
Location: Minnesota.
Date(s): August 1983.
Emergency: An outbreak of encephalitis in Minnesota prompted the governor to request mosquito spraying to contain the disease.
Air Force Organization(s) Involved: 907th Tac Alft Gp.
Airlifted: Malathion insecticide.
Aircraft Employed: C–123 (three).
Operations: An epidemic of encephalitis threatened Minnesota during August. Spread by the *Culex traslis* mosquito, the disease affects the brain and can be fatal. Responding to reports of 25 cases, Governor Rudy Perpich declared a state of emergency on August 20 and requested federal assistance to spray insecticide.

The 907th Tac Alft Gp at Rickenbacker ANG Base at Columbus, Ohio, responded by flying three C–123s with spraying equipment to Twin Cities AF Res Base at Minneapolis. Each plane bore two propeller engines for low and slow flight and two supplemental jet engines for rapid climbing after a spraying run, and could carry 1,000 gallons of malathion insecticide.

Minnesota officials asked the 907th Tac Alft Gp to treat towns in 11 northwestern Minnesota counties while other areas were sprayed by six civilian aircraft. The 907th Tac Alft Gp air crews flew their planes from Minneapolis to Fargo, North Dakota, which served as their base of operations. Each day, state health officials assigned targets, and the C–123 aircraft flew over the communities at altitudes of about 125 feet at speeds of approximately 150 mph to spray insecticide in 2,000-foot swaths that covered about 660 acres per minute.

In the first three days, the 907th Tac Alft Gp sprayed 90 towns. In seven days of aerial spraying, the group treated 453,358 acres, including 195 towns, in 19 sorties. Aerial spraying operations by Air Force and civilian aircraft helped to end the encephalitis epidemic by the end of August.

89.
Name: Maricopa Flood.
Location: Arizona.
Date(s): October 4–5, 1983.
Emergency: Several days of heavy rain produced a flash flood of the Santa Rosa Wash near Maricopa, Arizona, stranding and threatening to drown 57 people.
Air Force Organization(s) Involved: 302d Sp Ops Sq.
Airlifted: 57 passengers.
Aircraft Employed: CH–3 (four).
Operations: A series of storms struck Arizona from the end of September into early October. Heavy rain produced flash flooding in the mountains of Yavapi County in the central part of the state, prompting Governor Bruce Babbitt to proclaim an emergency on Saturday, September 24. Rain continued intermittently for two weeks, drenching some areas with seven inches. On Tuesday, October 4, the Santa Rosa Wash, normally a dry creek tributary of the Gila River, flooded the area around Maricopa, about 25 miles south of Phoenix.

Late that night, the Arizona Department of Public Safety requested federal military help to evacuate stranded flood victims. The request was referred just before midnight to the U.S. Air Force Rescue Coordination Center at Scott AFB, Illinois. While flying on a training mission, a CH–3 Jolly Green Giant helicopter from the 302d Sp Ops Sq (AF Res) at Luke AFB near Phoenix located—on ground just a foot above floodwaters—several people, five of whom had climbed into the elevated bucket of a front end loader whose wheels were already under water. The aircraft hoisted the refugees to safety. On October 4 and 5, the 302d Sp Ops Sq used four CH–3 helicopters to airlift 57 Maricopa area residents to higher ground.

90.
Name: Missouri River Flood.
Location: Missouri.
Date(s): June 15, 1984.
Emergency: The Missouri River, swollen by heavy rain, flooded northwestern Missouri and northeastern Kansas north of Kansas City, inundating 400,000 acres.
Air Force Organization(s) Involved: Unspecified.
Airlifted: 4.5 tons of pumping equipment.
Aircraft Employed: C–130 (one).
Operations: The Missouri River, swollen by heavy rains during June, spilled over its banks north of Kansas City, flooding 400,000 acres in northwestern Missouri around St. Joseph. The river also inundated large sections of northeastern Kansas. As water 12 feet deep in places submerged farms and small towns such as Levasy and Bean Lake, 500 families fled their homes. The river reached flood stage at Kansas City on June 11, and President Ronald Reagan declared five Missouri and six Kansas counties federal disaster areas.

Experts predicted that the river at St. Joseph would remain above flood stage for two weeks. The U.S. Army Corps of Engineers office at Kansas City asked the USAF to transport pumping equipment from Texas to Missouri. On June 15, a MAC C–130—probably from the 463d Tac Alft Wg—airlifted four flood pumps and equipment weighing 4.5 tons from Dyess AFB, Texas, to Kansas City International Airport, Missouri. The U.S. Army Corps of Engineers transported the pumps by land from Kansas City to the St. Joseph area, about 50 miles north, to help drain critical areas along the Missouri River. Floodwaters receded at the beginning of July.

91.
Name: Utah Coal Mine Fire.
Location: Utah.
Date(s): December 20, 1984.
Emergency: A fire trapped 27 coal miners a mile beneath the earth's surface.
Air Force Organization(s) Involved: 911th Tac Alft Gp.
Airlifted: 24 tons of cargo, including three emergency vehicles, a generator, and a camper shelter; and seven passengers.
Aircraft Employed: C–130 (two).
Operations: A conveyer machine bearing overheated and caused a fire at about 9:30 p.m. on Wednesday, December 19, in the Emery Mining Company's Wilberg Mine, which supplied fuel for a power and light company plant in central Utah. Heat and smoke in the mine trapped 27 miners, including one woman, a mile beneath the earth's surface. About 100 rescue workers gathered at the Wilberg Mine to drill two air shafts and an evacuation tunnel to free the trapped miners, but heavy snow hindered their efforts.

On Thursday, December 20, the Department of Labor's Mine Safety and Health Administration in Pittsburgh asked the 911th Tac Alft Gp to airlift emergency vehicles and equipment from Pennsylvania to the disaster area. The Military Airlift Command authorized a special assignment airlift mission using two C–130 Hercules cargo aircraft to haul seven passengers and 24 tons of cargo—including two trucks, a four-wheel-drive vehicle, a generator, and a camper shelter—from Greater Pittsburgh International Airport to Huntington, Utah, about nine miles from the mine.

Rescue workers used the vehicles and equipment to reach the trapped fire victims, but recovered only dead bodies. By December 23, 25 corpses had been recovered. Eventually all 27 miners were found, dead from carbon monoxide poisoning or smoke inhalation.

92.
Name: North Carolina Forest Fires.
Location: North Carolina.
Date(s): April 5, 1985.

Humanitarian Airlift Operations

Emergency: Forest fires, feeding on drought and high winds, consumed at least 7,000 acres of timber in six counties in western North Carolina.
Air Force Organization(s) Involved: 145th Tac Alft Gp and an unspecified C–141 unit.
Airlifted: 11 tons of fire-fighting equipment, 21,000 gallons of fire retardant, and 190 firefighters.
Aircraft Employed: C–141 (two) and C–130 (one).
Operations: During the early spring, timber fires fed by drought and strong winds consumed thousands of wooded acres in seven southeastern states. The fires were especially destructive in the mountains of western North Carolina, prompting Governor James Martin to call out the National Guard and state prisoners to help about 300 Forest Service rangers battle the flames. By April 5, 7,000 acres were ablaze in six counties.

The Forest Service needed more personnel and equipment, so the BIFC contacted MAC for an airlift. On Good Friday, April 5, two C–141 Starlifter cargo planes transported 190 firefighters and 11 tons of equipment from Redding Municipal Airport and Ontario International Airport in California to Asheville Regional Airport in western North Carolina. That same day, the 145th Tac Alft Gp (ANG) from Charlotte, North Carolina, used a C–130B equipped with the MAFFS to help contain a 2,500-acre blaze in the mountain forests of Burke County near Morganton, North Carolina.

The group flew seven missions on April 5, each lasting about 40 minutes, dropping 21,000 gallons of fire retardant around the burning area. The C–141 airlift, the C–130 airdrops, and the arrival of rain helped firefighters control the mountain fires during the weekend.

93.
Name: Idaho Pestilence.
Location: Idaho.
Date(s): June 21–July 25, 1985.
Emergency: After hordes of grasshoppers, many from public lands in southern Idaho, descended on western farms, the secretary of agriculture proclaimed a state of emergency.
Air Force Organization(s) Involved: 907th Tac Alft Gp.
Airlifted: Malathion insecticide.
Aircraft Employed: C–123 (three).
Operations: A grasshopper population explosion threatened western croplands during the late spring and early summer. On Tuesday, June 18, Secretary of Agriculture John Block declared a state of emergency in 14 western states as grasshoppers infested 11 million acres. Eight adult grasshoppers per square yard consumed as much grass in a day as a 700-pound steer. Some of the affected regions had more than 150 insects per square yard.

The grasshoppers descended en masse on alfalfa, barley, wheat, sugar beet,

100

and potato fields. Farmers sprayed their crops, but vast stretches of public lands adjacent to the farms also needed treatment, especially in southern Idaho. Governor John Evans asked for federal assistance and Congressman Richard Stallings called Verne Orr, the secretary of the Air Force, to request the use of spray planes.

The 907th Tac Alft Gp, stationed at Rickenbacker ANG Base at Columbus, Ohio, flew three C–123K aircraft to Pocatello, Idaho, from June 21 to 23. There, aircrews flew two weeks of aerial spraying operations over southeastern Idaho under the guidance of the Department of Agriculture. Using Pocatello's airport as a staging base, without access to Air Force maintenance facilities, the three C–123s sprayed about 460,000 acres before moving to Boise for two more weeks of spraying missions over southwestern Idaho in the vicinity of Mountain Home AFB.

Meteorological factors required these flights to proceed only in the early morning, so the 907th Tac Alft Gp crews began before dawn each day. They sprayed at altitudes ranging from 150 to 175 feet, covering 650-foot swaths, following directions from Idaho Army National Guard helicopters. Each C–123 could cover 15,000 acres a day, given proper weather. Using malathion insecticide, the C–123 planes achieved a kill rate of 80 to 96 percent.

Between June 21 and July 25, the 907th Tac Alft Gp sprayed 735,000 acres in 73 sorties. Aerial spraying ended the immediate agricultural threat and reduced the potential of another grasshopper pestilence by killing thousands of insects before they could lay eggs.

94.
Name: Western Forest Fires.
Location: California, Idaho, and Montana.
Date(s): July 2–10, 1985.
Emergency: Forest fires swept across 1.5 million acres in 14 western states.
Air Force Organization(s) Involved: 145th, 153d, and 943d Tac Alft Gps; 146th Tac Alft Wg; 4th Mil Alft Sq; and other unspecified C–141 units.
Airlifted: 461 tons of fire retardant and fire-fighting equipment and 285 firefighters.
Aircraft Employed: C–141 (10) and C–130 (eight).
Operations: Between June 27 and July 15, 4,000 fires burned 1.5 million acres of forests in 14 western states, including California, Nevada, Oregon, Idaho, and Montana. In California, temperatures over 100 degrees and winds of 25 mph spread the flames. Cities from San Diego to San Jose suffered damage as the state lost $50 million in property, including 184 homes. California governor George Deukmejian declared an emergency in seven counties and appealed for federal help. The Forest Service and state agencies marshaled almost 16,000 firefighters from around the country to battle the fires.

At the request of the BIFC in Idaho, MAC launched 10 C–141 missions between July 4 and 10 to transport 285 firefighters and 181 tons of cargo to California, Idaho, and Montana. Six C–141 missions hauled 159 tons of fire retardant and equipment from Wainwright Army Airfield, Alaska, to Palmdale and Stockton, California, and to Boise, Idaho.

The Military Airlift Command moved 185 firefighters from Phoenix, Arizona, to Malmstrom AFB, Montana, in two other missions. Air Force C–141s carried 22 tons of fire-fighting equipment from Holloman AFB, New Mexico, to Santa Barbara, California, and 100 firefighters from Indianapolis, Indiana, to Boise. The 145th Tac Alft Gp at Charlotte, North Carolina; the 153d Tac Alft Gp at Cheyenne, Wyoming; the 146th Tac Alft Wg at Van Nuys, California (all ANG organizations); and the 943d Tac Alft Gp (AF Res) flew eight C–130s equipped with the MAFFS to drop 280 tons of fire retardant around the California fires.

Using the Van Nuys airport as a staging area, the C–130s flew 242 sorties between July 2 and 10. On July 6 alone, AF Res and ANG aircraft dropped 108,000 gallons of retardant in 36 sorties, consuming 51.6 flying hours. Most chemicals were dropped on the Las Pilitas fire near San Luis Obispo, which covered 177,000 acres and forced the evacuation of 4,500 people.

The planes dispensed up to 3,000 gallons of fire retardant at a time while flying at altitudes of 100 to 150 feet and speeds of 130 to 150 knots. Each drop covered about 300,000 square feet. Changing weather patterns, which brought cooler, moister Pacific air to the West, helped firefighters control the flames by the end of July.

95.
Name: Northern California Floods.
Location: California.
Date(s): February 18–22, 1986.
Emergency: Rainstorms produced flooding that killed 15 people, left 50,000 homeless, and caused $375 million in damage.
Air Force Organization(s) Involved: 129th Aerospace Rescue and Recovery Group (Aerosp RR Gp) (ANG) and 41st Aerosp RR Sq.
Airlifted: 3,000 sandbags and at least 528 evacuees.
Aircraft Employed: H–3 (four), HC–130 (three), and HH–53 (two).
Operations: From February 12 to 17, a series of storms dropped torrential rain on northern California. The Russian and Yuba Rivers spilled over their banks; and floods left 15 people dead, 50,000 homeless, and $375 million in damage. Governor George Deukmejian designated 33 counties disaster areas, called on the Army and Air National Guards for emergency missions, and appealed for federal assistance.

The Russian River flood began on February 17 and eventually inundated Guerneville, Rio Nido, Hacienda, Monte Rio, and many other towns in Sutter and Sonoma Counties. Raging river currents hindered rescue operations by boat as Lt. Col. Ted Schindler, operations officer of the California Air National Guard's 129th Aerosp RR Gp, assumed command of a joint task force involving airplanes and helicopters from Army and ANG units.

From February 18 to 22, the 129th Aerosp RR Sq flew four H–3 helicopters and two HC–130 cargo planes on 95 emergency sorties. The helicopters evacuated 520 flood victims, saving 33 lives. Most passengers boarded the helicopters from high ground, but some evacuees were hoisted aboard from flooded buildings. The HC–130s provided communications to coordinate rescue flights and air refueling support.

During the Russian River flood, a levee broke on the Yuba River on February 20, producing a temporary 30-square-mile lake that flooded the Marysville suburbs of Linda and Olivehurst about 50 miles north of Sacramento. Up to 10 feet of water inundated the communities, which were evacuated when the levee broke, forcing 24,000 people from their homes. About 4,500 were sheltered and fed at nearby Beale AFB.

Lieutenant Colonel Schindler sent two HH–3 helicopters and one HC–130 from the 129th Aerosp RR Sq. The 41st Aerosp RR Sq flew two HH–53 Jolly Green Giant helicopters and one HC–130 in the Linda and Olivehurst region to rescue at least nine flood victims, including a mother in childbirth; provide communications; and deliver supplies to the disaster area, including 3,000 sandbags from Castle AFB near Merced. Air Force personnel from Beale and Mather AFBs in California launched relief drives for the flood victims.

96.
Name: North Carolina Forest Fires.
Location: North Carolina.
Date(s): Late May 1986.
Emergency: Forest fires consumed more than 70,000 acres and drove 5,000 people from their homes.
Air Force Organization(s) Involved: 145th Tac Alft Gp.
Airlifted: Almost 1,500 tons of liquid fire retardant.
Aircraft Employed: C–130 (two).
Operations: On May 5, a drought-sparked forest fire erupted in Pender County in southeastern North Carolina. Nourished by maritime winds in excess of 20 mph, the fire spread quickly. By May 12, it had consumed more than 70,000 acres and forced 5,000 people to evacuate their homes.

The Forest Service used C–54 airplanes to drop fire-retardant chemicals around the fire, but the inability of these aircraft to turn sharply and the gravity-dispensing systems hindered their effectiveness. The fire continued to rage out of control. Aware that the North Carolina ANG had aircraft with fire-fighting capability at Charlotte, the Forest Service asked the 145th Tac Alft Gp for assistance.

During late May, the 145th Tac Alft Gp flew two C–130 airplanes equipped with the MAFFS against the North Carolina forest fires. Flying 119 sorties in seven days, the planes dispensed almost 1,500 tons of liquid fire retardant around the blazes. Crews landed and took off within 15 minutes for another run. By the end of May, with cooperation from the weather, the Forest Service and ANG had contained the fires.

97.
Name: Southeast Haylift.
Location: North Carolina, South Carolina, Georgia, and Alabama.
Date(s): July 19–28, 1986.
Emergency: A four-month drought threatened livestock on southeastern farms with starvation and caused $1 billion in agricultural losses.
Air Force Organization(s) Involved: 63d, 437th, and 438th Mil Alft Wgs; and AF Res and ANG units.
Airlifted: 536 tons of hay (more than 19,000 bales).
Aircraft Employed: C–141 (24) and C–130 (eight).
Operations: The southeastern United States experienced a prolonged drought during the late spring and early summer. By mid-July, the drought had lasted four months in some areas and a heat wave compounded the problem. An area encompassing 200 southern counties was declared a drought disaster area and farmers drastically cut livestock herds because of a shortage of feed. The Alabama hay crop reached only a quarter of its normal level, and agriculture in the region suffered losses of almost $1 billion.

In mid-July, Governor James Thompson of Illinois urged midwestern farmers to send hay to cattle ranchers in the southeast, and President Reagan authorized an airlift. Between July 19 and 28, 24 MAC C–141 missions and eight AF Res C–130 missions transported 536 tons of hay—more than 19,000 bales—from Illinois, Iowa, Kansas, Missouri, Wisconsin, New York, and Colorado to South Carolina, North Carolina, Georgia, and Alabama. Military airlift wings from Norton AFB, California; Charleston AFB, South Carolina; and McGuire AFB, New Jersey, flew the C–141s, each carrying 800 bales at a time.

President Reagan observed the unloading of a C–141 at Columbia, South Carolina, on July 24. On July 24 and 25, eight AF Res or ANG C–130s hauled about 2,880 bales of hay from Wisconsin and New York to Georgia and North Carolina. The 32 haylift missions in 10 days, along with hay deliveries by train and truck, helped to save hundreds of cattle and the livelihood of many southern livestock farmers.

98.
Name: Ship Fire.
Location: 30 nautical miles off the Florida coast.
Date(s): December 10, 1986.
Emergency: A ship caught fire in the Gulf of Mexico.
Air Force Organization(s) Involved: 55th Aerosp RR Sq; Detachment 5, 39th Aerospace Rescue and Recovery Wing (Aerosp RR Wg); and 20th Sp Ops Sq.
Airlifted: 19 survivors.

Aircraft Employed: HC–130 (one), UH–60 (one), CH–3 (one), and MH–53 (one).

Operations: In early December, the Norwegian ship *Geco Alpha*, a 300-foot seismographic research vessel sailing under the Panamanian flag, caught fire in the Gulf of Mexico about 30 nautical miles south of Destin, Florida. The fire threatened 34 passengers and crew, many of whom donned life vests and boarded life rafts as the ship broadcast distress signals.

On December 10, F–15 fighter aircraft from the 33d Tac Ftr Wg at Eglin AFB, Florida, spotted the burning ship and radioed the 55th Aerosp RR Sq, also based at Eglin, for help. The squadron sent an HC–130 Hercules to serve as an airborne command post and to drop survival equipment to the disaster victims.

Members of the 55th Aerosp RR Sq also flew a UH–60 Blackhawk helicopter to the scene, where it lowered a pararescueman to four survivors, airlifting them to Hurlburt Field. A CH–3 Jolly Green Giant helicopter from Detachment 5, 39th Aerosp RR Wg, at Tyndall AFB, joined the rescue mission. Landing in the water several times, the helicopter picked up 15 victims and carried them to the Eglin AFB hospital. Eventually, the survivors at Hurlburt joined their comrades at the Eglin hospital.

Fifteen of the ship's crew remained with the crippled vessel, eight on board and seven in a nearby raft. As a Coast Guard cutter from New Orleans towed the smoldering ship to a port and 19 victims recovered at the Eglin hospital, one MH–53 helicopter from Hurlburt Field's 20th Sp Ops Sq returned the pararescueman to Eglin AFB.

99.
Name: West Coast Forest Fires.
Location: California and Oregon.
Date(s): August 31–September 9, 1987.
Emergency: Forest fires devastated 970 square miles in several western states, including 491,000 acres of trees and brush in California.
Air Force Organization(s) Involved: 145th, 153d, and 943d Tac Alft Gps; 146th Tac Alft Wg; and 349th Mil Alft Wg.
Airlifted: 2,511 tons of fire retardant and an unknown number of firefighters.
Aircraft Employed: C–130 (eight) and C–141 (number unknown).
Operations: Lightning, heat, low humidity, and gusting winds fed forest fires in the western United States at the end of August and early September, blackening 970 square miles. The Forest Service and state agencies marshaled 19,000 firefighters to create firebreaks and backfires. In California, 1,250 fires consumed 475,000 acres of trees and brush between August 28 and September 6. The worst fire burned 100,000 acres in Tuolumne County, California, just west of Yosemite National Park. Governor George Deukmejian declared a state of emergency in 22 counties.

Humanitarian Airlift Operations

In response to Forest Service requests for C–130s to help drop fire retardant around the worst fires using the MAFFS, AF Res and ANG units deployed on August 31. Eight specially equipped C–130s came from tactical airlift organizations at Charlotte, North Carolina; Cheyenne, Wyoming; March AFB, California; and Van Nuys, California.

Operating out of Van Nuys ANG Base and from Fresno, in southern and central California respectively, the eight C–130s flew 193 sorties between August 31 and September 8. In 211 flying hours, the aircrews dropped 2,511 tons of fire retardant—a total of 558,000 gallons—to slow the spread of the worst fires.

During the same period, the 349th Mil Alft Wg (AF Res) of Travis AFB, California, transported Forest Service firefighters to burning areas in California and Oregon aboard C–141 aircraft. Cooler, wetter weather helped firefighters bring many fires under control by September 8. The next day, AF Res and ANG aircraft began returning to their home bases.

100.
Name: Yellowstone Fires.
Location: Wyoming and Montana.
Date(s): August 22–October 6, 1988.
Emergency: Fires consumed more than half of Yellowstone National Park, threatening lives and property.
Air Force Organization(s) Involved: 60th, 62d, 63d, and 436th Mil Alft Wgs; 349th, 433d, 445th, 446th, and 459th Mil Alft Wgs (AF Res); 94th and 302d Tac Alft Wgs (AF Res); 146th Tac Alft Wg (ANG); 314th Tac Alft Wg; 145th and 153d Tac Alft Gps (ANG); and 943d Tac Alft Gp (AF Res).
Airlifted: More than 4,000 Army and Marine Corps firefighters and 2,498 tons of fire-fighting equipment and supplies.
Aircraft Employed: C–5 (11), C–141 (7), and C–130 (11).
Operations: The summer of 1988 brought dry heat and wind to Yellowstone National Park, turning it and adjacent forest areas in Wyoming and Montana into a giant tinder box. In early August, 10 fires burned more than 580,000 acres, but the Forest Service, following a policy adopted in 1972, allowed the fires to burn naturally. Later in the month, as the fires continued to spread and threaten some of Yellowstone's prime attractions, the Forest Service organized a fire-fighting campaign. On August 19, the Forest Service requested military assistance. The Department of Defense authorized an airlift of Army and Marine Corps troops to fight the fires.

Between August 22 and October 6, at least 29 USAF, AF Res, and ANG aircraft transported more than 4,000 Army and Marine Corps troops and over 2,400 tons of equipment, vehicles, and supplies for the Forest Service. The soldiers constructed firelines to surround and contain the fires. At least 18 C–5 and C–141 aircraft and crews from eight military airlift wings of the Regular Air Force and the AF Res participated in the massive operation, transporting thousands of fire-fighting Army troops from the 9th Infantry Division at Fort Lewis, Washington, to Bozeman and Billings, Montana, and hundreds of marines from Camp Pendleton, California, to West Yellowstone, Montana.

In August, the airlifters transported more than 2,400 troops and, in September, almost 1,800 more. By the end of September, over 60 percent of the firefighters working in the disaster area were military. Cargo airlifted with the soldiers included a fleet of Army jeeps and two Marine Corps Blackhawk helicopters.

A fleet of USAF, AF Res, and ANG C–130s from four tactical airlift wings and three tactical airlift groups supported the C–5s and C–141s, moving firefighters and their equipment from airfields that could accommodate larger planes to small airstrips closer to the fires.

Six C–130s, each equipped with a Forest Service MAFFS, flew low over and around the fires to spray fire retardant. The Air National Guard's 153d Tac Alft Gp and 146th Tac Alft Wg each flew two C–130s, while the Air Force Reserve's 943d Tac Alft Gp flew another two, using the municipal airport at Helena, Montana, as a forward base.

With the help of cooler, wetter weather, the armies of firefighters and their ground and air weapons were able to control the fires by early October. By that time, more than half of Yellowstone's 2.2 million acres had burned, but airlift helped to prevent more extensive destruction. As the ashes cooled, Maj. Gen. John M. Shalikashvili, commander of the 9th Infantry Division, praised the airlift organizations for delivering his troops where they were needed most.

101.
Name: *Exxon Valdez* Oil Spill.
Location: Alaska.
Date(s): March 27–early May 1989.
Emergency: A supertanker ran aground off Alaska, spilling more than 10 million gallons of crude oil.
Air Force Organization(s) Involved: 60th, 63d, 436th, and 438th Mil Alft Wgs; and 176th Tac Alft Gp.
Airlifted: More than 1,000 tons of oil spill cleanup equipment, including oil skimmers, helicopters, landing craft, tow rigs, rubber boats, oil booms, and buoys.
Aircraft Employed: C–5 (17), C–141 (4), and C–130 (4).
Operations: Before dawn on March 24, the 987-foot-long oil tanker *Exxon Valdez* ran aground in Prince William Sound about 25 miles from Valdez, Alaska. Submerged rocks ruptured eight of the giant ship's 11 cargo tanks, spilling more than 10 million of the vessel's 53 million gallons of crude oil. Within days, an oil slick covered hundreds of square miles in Prince William Sound and the Gulf of Alaska, creating an environmental disaster as wind blew the oil onto beaches.

Responding to a request for help from the Exxon Corporation to ship to Alaska heavy cleanup equipment from California, Texas, and Virginia, the Department of Transportation sought help from MAC. Exxon agreed to pay MAC for a massive airlift, which eventually cost almost $4 million. The airlift began on March 27, when a 60th Mil Alft Wg C–5 transported two Navy oil skimmers from Travis AFB, California, to Elmendorf AFB near Anchorage, Alaska.

In early April, President George Bush directed DoD to help contain the environmental disaster, and Lt. Gen. Thomas G. McInerney of the Alaskan Air Command headed an Alaska oil spill joint task force that included elements of the Army, Navy, Air Force, and Marine Corps. McInerney continued to rely on MAC airlift.

Between March 27 and early May, 17 C–5, four C–141, and four C–130 missions transported more than 1,000 tons of equipment and supplies to Alaska for the cleanup operation. Flown by the 60th, 63d, 436th, and 438th Mil Alft Wgs and by the 176th Tac Alft Gp, the cargo aircraft moved items such as helicopters, landing craft, rubber boats, tow rigs, oil booms, oil skimmers, and buoys from Portland, Oregon; Houston, Texas; Norfolk, Virginia; and Air Force bases in California, Delaware, and New Jersey. Some equipment came from Exxon Corporation facilities in the continental U.S. and some from DoD. One of the bulkiest items to be transported on a C–5 was a 16-foot-long buoy that weighed eight tons.

Maj. John Sutton and his crew from the 709th Mil Alft Sq flew the most unusual mission in a 436th Mil Alft Wg C–5 Galaxy when they transported 19 pallets of oil spill cleanup equipment from Billund, Denmark, and Helsinki, Finland, to Alaska, using a polar route that required refueling in Iceland. The Scandinavian-based equipment was on hand for oil spills in the North Sea.

Most of the 25 C–5, C–141, and C–130 airlift flights landed at Elmendorf AFB, where they were unloaded by the 616th Aerial Port Squadron. Trucks transported the cargo to Valdez, headquarters of the cleanup operation.

Airlift was only one facet of the military disaster relief resulting from the *Exxon Valdez* spill. Many Navy ships also played an important role in General McInerney's joint task force. Although the MAC effort ended in early May after about six weeks, the cleanup continued until mid-September. Even then, southern Alaska would require years to recover from the worst oil spill in North American history.

102.
Name: Western Forest Fires.
Location: Idaho and California.
Date(s): Late July–August 7, 1989.
Emergency: Forest fires swept over thousands of acres in southern and western Idaho, eastern Oregon, and California.
Air Force Organization(s) Involved: 60th, 62d, 63d, and 436th Mil Alft Wgs; 146th Tac Alft Wg; and 145th, 153d, and 943d Tac Alft Gps.
Airlifted: More than 990 fire-fighting soldiers and 850 tons of equipment, including six helicopters, heavy equipment, fuel, medical vehicles, trucks, and maintenance supplies; and 3,350 tons of chemical fire retardant.

Aircraft Employed: C–5 (16), C–141 (8), and C–130 (8).
Operations: During late July and early August, forest fires swept across many western states. They were especially severe in western and southern Idaho, eastern Oregon, and California. At the end of July, the Forest Service asked DoD for hundreds of Army firefighters to assist its weary personnel. To transport the Army troops and equipment to the BIFC, where fire-fighting efforts were centralized, DoD relied on MAC.

Four military airlift wings from California, Washington, and Delaware responded to the emergency. Between the end of July and August 7, they flew 16 C–5 and eight C–141 missions to airlift more than 990 Army firefighters and 850 tons of equipment and supplies to Boise. The cargo included six helicopters, medical vehicles, trucks, fuel, and maintenance supplies for the fire-fighting Army units. The troops came from Fort Riley, Kansas; Fort Polk, Louisiana; Fort Campbell, Kentucky; and Fort Carson, Colorado. In most cases, MAC C–5s and C–141s transported the Army firefighters from Air Force bases near the Army forts, including Forbes AFB, Kansas; England AFB, Louisiana; and Peterson AFB, Colorado. Because there was no Air Force base in Kentucky, the USAF used the Army airfield at Fort Campbell to load troops.

Army Col. Anthony C. Trifiletti, who commanded the fire-fighting task force, took charge of the airlifted troops and equipment after they arrived at Boise. Hundreds of soldiers had already received special fire-fighting training. Military Airlift Command-gained ANG and AF Res units also participated in the western forest fire emergency, flying eight C–130s equipped with MAFFSs to drop 3,350 tons of chemical fire retardant on the California fires.

The units included the 146th Tac Alft Wg of the California ANG; the 145th Tac Alft Gp of the North Carolina ANG; the 153d Tac Alft Gp of the Wyoming ANG; and the 943d Tac Alft Gp of the AF Res, based in California. Each unit flew two specially equipped C–130s from Van Nuys, California.

The emergency airlift ended after August 7. By then, MAC, the ANG, and the AF Res had flown more than 280 missions, using 32 aircraft.

103.
Name: Hurricane Hugo.
Location: West Indies and South Carolina.
Date(s): September 19–November 1989.
Emergency: Hurricane Hugo brought winds in excess of 125 mph, high seas, and torrential rain that left thousands of people homeless and without adequate water, food, and electricity.
Air Force Organization(s) Involved: 60th, 63d, 433d, 436th, 437th, 438th, 439th, and 459th Mil Alft Wgs; 105th and 172d Mil Alft Gps; 118th, 133d, 136th, 137th, 302d, 314th, 317th, and 403d Tac Alft Wgs; 109th, 130th, 135th, 139th, 165th, 166th, 167th, 176th, 189th, 907th, and 927th Tac Alft Gps; and Eighth Air Force.

Humanitarian Airlift Operations

Airlifted: More than 2,000 passengers and 4,330 tons of relief equipment and supplies.

Aircraft Employed: C–5 (51), C–141 (53), C–130 (23), and KC–10 (1).

Operations: On September 17, Hurricane Hugo struck the Lesser Antilles in the West Indies, bringing winds in excess of 125 mph, high seas, and torrential rain to the Virgin Islands, Puerto Rico, and their neighbors. Hurricane Hugo left as many as 150,000 people in the islands homeless. In St. Croix alone, 45,000 of 53,000 residents lost their homes. The storm left thousands without running water and electricity, creating food shortages due to lack of refrigeration.

After its destructive sweep through the West Indies, Hurricane Hugo continued to move northwest, striking South Carolina near Charleston on the night of September 21. Packing winds greater than 125 mph, the hurricane brought a 17-foot tidal surge to Charleston. Winds destroyed hundreds of buildings and flooding threatened residents. Hugo was the worst hurricane to hit the United States since Camille in 1969.

Reacting to damage in the Virgin Islands, Puerto Rico, and South Carolina, President Bush declared them federal disaster areas. The Federal Emergency Management Agency coordinated relief efforts, which involved one of the most massive humanitarian airlifts in history.

For Hurricane Hugo relief missions, MAC employed at least 127 aircraft—including 51 C–5s, 53 C–141s, and 23 C–130s—from 29 different Air Force organizations, including 15 ANG units and seven AF Res units. Only seven Air Force units participating in Hurricane Hugo relief efforts were regular active duty MAC organizations. A SAC KC–10 from the Eighth Air Force also assisted.

Flying from 33 locations across the continental United States to the disaster areas, the aircraft transported more than 2,000 passengers and over 4,330 tons of humanitarian cargo to Roosevelt Roads NAS and San Juan International Airport, Puerto Rico; St. Thomas and St. Croix in the U.S. Virgin Islands; and Charleston, South Carolina. The passengers included civil engineers, electricians, heavy equipment operators, medical personnel, air traffic controllers, and hundreds of evacuees. Canned food, bottled water, electrical cable, electrical generators, communications vans, utility vehicles, water purification units, vehicles, tents, water containers, plastic sheeting, and helicopters comprised most of the relief cargo.

Air Force aircraft began flying evacuation missions before the hurricane struck. Using C–130s, the 314th and 317th Tac Alft Wgs evacuated 600 U.S. citizens—including naval personnel, civilian contractors, and their families—from Andros Town in the Bahamas. The 437th Mil Alft Wg at Charleston AFB evacuated its C–141s to other bases before the storm hit, preserving them for use after the emergency. The 53d Weather Squadron and 18th Weather Observation Flight, using WC–130s, tracked the storm, allowing people to receive ample warning.

Examples of some of the missions reflect the magnitude of the airlift operation. Between September 21 and 26, three C–5s of the Air National Guard's 105th Mil Alft Gp airlifted 10 vehicles, two UH–1 helicopters, 32 medical personnel, spare parts, and 70 tons of food and clothing to the Virgin Islands and Puerto Rico. Other C–5s from the 433d and 439th Mil Alft Wgs transported tons of generators, cots, batteries, tents, and mobile air traffic control towers to St. Croix and Puerto Rico.

Starlifters also flew many relief missions. The 63d and 438th Mil Alft Wgs' C–141s transported mobile communications equipment to St. Croix and Puerto Rico. The 459th Mil Alft Wg flew five disaster relief missions in as many days, delivering 71 tons of relief supplies to St. Croix.

In addition to the C–5s and C–141s, C–130s flew many humanitarian missions. A 302d Tac Alft Wg C–130 flown by a 731st Tac Alft Sq crew flew relief supplies to the islands of Antigua and Montserrat from Howard AFB in Panama, where it was on rotation duty. Its cargo included chain saws, water containers, and five tons of plastic sheeting. One 403d Tac Alft Wg C–130 carried civil engineers and dry ice to Charleston after Hurricane Hugo struck.

Besides airlifting relief personnel and supplies to the disaster area, the Air Force conducted aerial spraying flights in the Charleston area to control the mosquito population, which the hurricane's flooding promised to multiply. The 907th Tac Alft Gp sprayed 800,000 acres using a C–130E aircraft specially equipped with spray apparatus. The flights eliminated thousands of mosquitoes that were both a nuisance and potential disease carriers.

When Hurricane Hugo relief flights ended in November, they comprised the largest MAC humanitarian airlift of the year. The effort demonstrated the ability of the Regular Air Force, the AF Res, and the ANG to join together in a common campaign and provided valuable experience for even greater demands overseas in the near future.

104.
Name: California Earthquake.
Location: San Francisco.
Date(s): October 1989.
Emergency: An earthquake measuring 7.1 on the Richter scale devastated the San Francisco Bay area.
Air Force Organization(s) Involved: 60th, 315th, 436th, and 437th Mil Alft Wgs; 512th Mil Alft Wg (Associate); 146th Tac Alft Wg; 913th and 928th Tac Alft Gps; 106th, 129th, and 939th Aerosp RR Gps; 3d and 709th Mil Alft Sqs; and 304th Aerosp RR Sq.
Airlifted: More than 250 tons of relief equipment and supplies and over 100 passengers.
Aircraft Employed: C–5 (three), C–141 (two), C–130 (eight), HC–130 (three), H–3 (three), and UH–1 (one).
Operations: As darkness fell on October 17, the worst earthquake to hit California since 1906 struck the San Francisco Bay region. Registering 7.1 on the Richter scale, with an epicenter near Santa Cruz, the quake killed more than 60

people, injured 1,700, and deprived more than one million of electrical power. The next day, President Bush declared the region a federal disaster area and FEMA took charge of relief efforts.

The Military Airlift Command and airlift units of the AF Res and ANG responded to the call for federal assistance. They employed 20 aircraft—including C–5s, C–141s, C–130s, HC–130s, H–3s, and a UH–1—in the relief operation. During October, the 16 airplanes and four helicopters transported more than 250 tons of equipment and supplies to earthquake victims and moved more than 100 passengers, including medical personnel, construction workers, and pararescuemen.

The airlift began on October 19, when a 60th Mil Alft Wg C–5 Galaxy airlifted a fire truck, heavy rescue vehicles, and paramedics from Los Alamitos NAS to Monterey, where a shopping center roof had collapsed. That same day, the 437th Mil Alft Wg from Charleston AFB, South Carolina, flew a C–141 Starlifter with three tons of relief supplies from Martinsburg, West Virginia, to Moffett Field NAS in the earthquake zone.

On October 24, two 436th Mil Alft Wg C–5s—flown by crews from the 3d and 709th Mil Alft Sqs from the 436th Mil Alft Wg and the 512th Mil Alft Wg (Associate)—transported more than 100 tons of electrical equipment from Tennessee and Pennsylvania to Moffett Field NAS. Maj. Edward F. Briggs and his crew carried two Tennessee Valley Authority 500,000-volt circuit breakers from Nashville, while a crew led by Maj. Dennis O. Vance transported three Westinghouse 230,000-volt circuit breakers and electrical parts from Pittsburgh. The airlifted equipment allowed California utility workers to restore electrical power to hundreds of thousands of people in the San Francisco Bay area.

Air Force Reserve organizations also participated in the earthquake relief operation, transporting 149 tons of cargo and 97 passengers. A 315th Mil Alft Wg C–141 moved tons of excess Hurricane Hugo relief supplies from Charleston AFB to San Francisco. Two C–130s from the 913th and 928th Tac Alft Gps moved Navy Seabees and construction equipment from Fort Hunter Liggett, California, to San Francisco. The 939th Aerospace Rescue and Recovery Group's 304th Aerosp RR Sq flew two HC–130s, a UH–1, and an HH–3 from Portland, Oregon, carrying physicians, pararescuemen, and a communications van to McClellan AFB near Sacramento, for use in the disaster area.

Units of the ANG joined the massive operation. Using one HC–130 and two H–3 helicopters, crews from the 106th and 129th Aerosp RR Gps flew medical evacuation and damage assessment missions from Moffett Field. Six C–130s of the California Air National Guard's 146th Tac Alft Wg ferried medical personnel around the earthquake area. The USAF, AF Res, and ANG personnel and resources played a major role in the overall relief operation and gained valuable experience working as part of a total force.

105.
Name: Painted Cave Fire.
Location: California.
Date(s): June–July 1990.
Emergency: A forest fire burned 4,900 acres and destroyed 450 homes.
Air Force Organization(s) Involved: 146th Tac Alft Wg and 145th, 943d, and 1532d Tac Alft Gps.
Airlifted: Liquid fire suppressant, firefighters, and equipment.
Aircraft Employed: C–130 (10+).
Operations: A forest fire broke out just north of Santa Barbara in late June. It spread quickly, eventually engulfing 4,900 acres and destroying 450 homes. To contain the blaze, the California Department of Forestry and the Forest Service relied on ANG and AF Res units and their C–130 Hercules aircraft.

Eight C–130s, equipped with MAFFSs, sprayed the fire from the air. The California Air National Guard's 146th Tac Alft Wg and the Air Force Reserve's 943d Tac Alft Gp flew the aerial spraying missions, dropping a chemical that served as both a fire suppressant and a fertilizer to encourage new tree growth after the fire.

Other C–130s, flow by crews from the 145th and the 1532d Tac Alft Gps from North Carolina and Wyoming, flew fire-fighting missions, airlifting forestry personnel and equipment. With air support, the Painted Cave Fire was under control by July 2.

106.
Name: Arctic Crash.
Location: Greenland.
Date(s): November 1, 1991.
Emergency: An aircraft with 18 people aboard crashed in a blizzard near the North Pole.
Air Force Organization(s) Involved: 60th Mil Alft Wg and 22d Mil Alft Sq.
Airlifted: Two UH–60G helicopters and a 36-man rescue team.
Aircraft Employed: C–5 (one).
Operations: On October 30, a Canadian C–130 aircraft with 18 crew members aboard crashed in a blizzard about 300 miles from the North Pole. With only about two hours of daylight per day in which to search for survivors, the Canadians asked for help from the United States.

The Twenty-second Air Force diverted a 60th Mil Alft Wg C–5 that was staging at Elmendorf AFB, Alaska, on its way home from Japan to California to assist with the rescue effort. Commanded by Maj. Gregory Doten and a 22d Mil Alft Sq crew, the C–5 loaded a 36-man search and rescue team from the Alaskan National Guard and two UH–60G Pavehawk helicopters with night vision apparatus.

On November 1, the Galaxy discharged its rescue team and the helicopters at Thule, Greenland, to aid the search. The rescuers found 13 survivors of the airplane crash and transported them to a hospital in Thule for treatment. They had endured two days of subfreezing blizzard conditions.

107.
Name: Hurricane Andrew.
Location: Florida.
Date(s): August 25–October 1992.
Emergency: A hurricane with wind gusts as high as 164 mph destroyed thousands of homes in southern Florida, leaving at least 180,000 people homeless.
Air Force Organization(s) Involved: 60th, 62d, 63d, 94th, 118th, 123d, 137th, 302d, 315th, 349th, 403d, 433d, 436th, 437th, 439th, 440th, 445th, 459th, and 512th Airlift Wings (Alft Wgs); 452d Air Refueling Wing; 939th Rescue Wing; 105th, 130th, 135th, 145th, 164th, 165th, 166th, 167th, 172d, 179th, 908th, 911th, 913th, 914th, and 928th Airlift Groups (Alft Gps); 98th Air Refueling Group; 919th Special Operations Group (Sp Ops Gp); 68th, 327th, 328th, 337th, 356th, 357th, 700th, 731st, 756th, 757th, 758th, and 815th Airlift Squadrons (Alft Sqs); and 301st and 304th Rscu Sqs.
Airlifted: In the first 10 days, 14,000 tons of relief cargo, including food, water, generators, tents, refrigerators, stoves, blankets, toilets, diapers, paper products, beverages, fuel, heavy equipment, trucks, bulldozers, ice, batteries, medical supplies, and communications equipment. By September 25, 21,400 tons of cargo, including that airlifted by commercial aircraft on contract; and 13,500 passengers, including Army engineers, marines, returning evacuees, and disaster evaluation teams.
Aircraft Employed: C–130, C–5, C–141, KC–10, KC–135, and HH–60 (numbers unspecified) (724 missions by end of September).
Operations: On August 24, Hurricane Andrew hit southern Florida in the Miami area with sustained winds of 140 mph and gusts up to 164 mph, making it the worst hurricane to hit the United States since Hurricane Camille in 1969. The storm destroyed 63,000 homes and damaged thousands more, leaving at least 180,000 residents homeless. About 750,000 people lost electrical power and running water. Hurricane Andrew also destroyed Homestead AFB.

Hurricane Andrew had not finished its destructive path when it crossed the southern tip of Florida. It intensified over the Gulf of Mexico before hitting Louisiana southwest of New Orleans on August 25. The destruction in Louisiana was a small fraction of that south of Miami. To aid southern Florida, President Bush ordered a massive relief operation to be coordinated by FEMA, and a host of military organizations responded to the emergency.

The largest domestic relief airlift in the history of the U.S. Air Force followed. In the first ten days alone, Air Force aircraft from AMC, the AF Res, and the ANG flew 697 missions to south Florida, averaging almost 70 flights a day. By September 5, the USAF had delivered 14,000 tons of relief cargo, only slightly less than that delivered to Saudi Arabia in the first 10 days of Desert Shield.

The cargo included heavy equipment such as bulldozers, trucks, generators, communications equipment, and water purifiers. Hundreds of aircraft—including C–130s, C–141s, C–5s, KC–135s, KC–10s, and HH–60s—delivered large amounts of fuel, food, water, blankets, medical supplies, tents, refrigerators, propane stoves, toilets, diapers, paper goods, showers, ice, and batteries. Thousands of relief workers rode aboard the Air Force transports, including marines, Army civil engineers, Homestead personnel returning from their pre-storm evacuation, and disaster assessment teams.

The Hurricane Andrew relief airlift demonstrated the Defense Department's "total force" concept by integrating the resources and services of Regular Air Force organizations with those of the AF Res and ANG. By October, at least 20 C–130 wings and groups, nine C–141 wings and groups, and seven C–5 wings and groups flew relief missions to south Florida. Three other wings also employed KC–135 and KC–10 tankers and HH–60 rescue helicopters in the gigantic operation. The AF Res flew at least 191 missions, delivering 2,700 tons of cargo and 2,886 passengers. The ANG used 42 aircraft from 13 organizations to transport 565 tons of cargo and 413 passengers to south Florida in August.

Although the aircrews, aircraft, and relief supplies came from all over the United States, two of the most important staging bases for Hurricane Andrew relief were Charleston AFB in South Carolina, hub of the strategic airlift portion, and Dobbins Air Reserve Base in Georgia, where the 94th Alft Wg coordinated tactical airlift missions. Air Force transports loaded cargo and personnel from as far away as Guantánamo Bay, Cuba; Roosevelt Roads, Puerto Rico; and Howard Air Base in Panama. Most of the equipment, supplies, and personnel came from the continental United States. Airlift terminals in south Florida receiving the cargo included the remnants of Homestead AFB, Miami International Airport, Opa-Locka Coast Guard Air Station, and Kendall-Tamiami Airport.

The Air Mobility Command relied on commercial contract airlift to supplement its fleet of C–130s, C–141s, and C–5s to deliver relief supplies to southern Florida. By September 25, military and commercial aircraft had airlifted over 21,400 tons of relief equipment and supplies to the disaster zone. At least 13,500 workers rode aboard the aircraft. The huge operation laid the foundation for southern Florida's recovery from one of the worst disasters in U.S. history.

108.
Name: Winter Storm.
Location: Florida.
Date(s): March 13–14, 1993.
Emergency: A huge winter storm flooded beachfront areas on Florida's coast.
Air Force Organization(s) Involved: 301st Rscu Sq.
Airlifted: 93 flood victims.
Aircraft Employed: HH–60 (two) and HC–130 (one).
Operations: Between March 12 and 15, a gigantic winter storm swept across the

eastern United States from the Gulf of Mexico to Maine. Packing winds that sometimes exceeded 100 mph and dropping tremendous amounts of snow as far south as Florida, the storm was called the "storm of the century" or a "snow hurricane." The blizzard left 238 people dead, including 50 in Pennsylvania and 44 in Florida, where tornadoes compounded the destruction.

Only seven months earlier, Hurricane Andrew had devastated south Florida. Flooding in Hernando Beach, on Florida's west coast, forced people to flee their homes or to climb up onto rooftops. A 301st Rscu Sq HC–130 from Patrick AFB located some stranded flood victims and reported them to the Coast Guard. Two of the squadron's HH–60 helicopters evacuated survivors to higher ground. The squadron aircraft helped to rescue 93 people.

109.
Name: Midwest Flood.
Location: Iowa, Missouri, and Illinois.
Date(s): July 11–August 1, 1993.
Emergency: A spectacular flood inundated 16,000 square miles in eight midwestern states.
Air Force Organization(s) Involved: 60th, 62d, and 433d Alft Wgs; and other unspecified AMC, AF Res, and ANG airlift wings.
Airlifted: 797 tons of relief equipment and supplies, including one million empty sandbags, 14 water purification systems, water trucks, and five electrical generators; and 141 passengers, including Army troops.
Aircraft Employed: At least 20, including C–5s and C–141s.
Operations: Torrential rain in the midwestern United States flooded the upper Mississippi and lower Missouri Rivers and their tributaries. Water covered about 16,000 square miles in eight states from Minnesota to Kansas. The worst flooding occurred in Iowa, Missouri, and Illinois, where more than 14,000 people filled Red Cross shelters. At Des Moines, Iowa, floodwaters contaminated the main water treatment plant, leaving 250,000 people without clean water.

After President Bill Clinton declared the region a federal disaster area, FEMA and the United States Forces Command requested military airlift support to deliver sandbags, water purification systems, generators, and workers. The subsequent airlift, which lasted from July 11 to August 1, used C–5 Galaxies and C–141 Starlifters on more than 20 missions to Missouri, Illinois, and Iowa. They transported 797 tons of cargo, including 14 water purification systems, water trucks, five electrical generators, and one million empty sandbags. They also moved 141 passengers, mostly Army troops to operate the water systems and fill the sandbags. Aircrews came from the AMC, AF Res, and the ANG.

Between July 12 and 27, Air Force C–5s picked up Army National Guard water purification systems at various locations, including Little Rock and Maxwell AFB, Alabama, and took them to Des Moines International Airport. Some of the systems, which had been used in Saudi Arabia during Desert Storm, weighed 19 tons each, stood 10 feet tall, and could process 3,000 gallons of water an hour. Among the participating C–5 units were the 60th Alft Wg of Travis AFB, California, and the 68th Alft Sq of the 433d Alft Wg, an AF Res organization stationed at Kelly AFB, Texas.

During the same month, C–141 Starlifters from as far away as California, Washington, and South Carolina moved empty sandbags to the disaster region. Air Force personnel from Scott AFB, Illinois, and Whiteman AFB, Missouri, near the flooded areas, volunteered to fill sandbags to shore up surviving levees. Eventually the rain decreased and river levels fell, allowing thousands of people to return home and begin the long process of economic recovery.

110.
Name: Southern California Wildfires.
Location: California.
Date(s): October and November 1993.
Emergency: Fires burned more than 167,000 acres.
Air Force Organization(s) Involved: 146th and 302d Alft Wgs, 153d Alft Gp, and 731st Alft Sq.
Airlifted: At least 1,000 tons of fire retardant.
Aircraft Employed: C–130 (six).
Operations: Wildfires spread across 167,722 acres of southern California, threatening farms and homes around Los Angeles. To help the Forest Service battle the blazes, AF Res and ANG C–130 units employed planes equipped with the MAFFS.

Two C–130s from the Air Force Reserve's 302d Alft Wg from Peterson AFB, Colorado, participated in the operation, with Maj. Luke Coker of the 731st Alft Sq leading the mission. Other Hercules aircraft came from the ANG, including the 146th Alft Wg of Channel Islands ANG Station, California, and the 153d Alft Gp from Cheyenne, Wyoming. By early November, the six C–130s, staging from Channel Islands, had dropped at least 1,000 tons of fire retardant. The Air Force effort, combined with the arrival of cooler, wetter weather, helped the Forest Service ground crews contain the fires, saving many homes.

111.
Name: Southern California Earthquake.
Location: Los Angeles.
Date(s): January 17–25, 1994.
Emergency: An earthquake registering at least 6.6 on the Richter scale struck southern California.
Air Force Organization(s) Involved: 146th, 433d, 439th, 445th, 62d, 436th, 437th, and 438th Alft Wgs; and 144th Ftr Wg.
Airlifted: 170 tons of relief cargo and 270 disaster relief workers.
Aircraft Employed: C–5 (six), C–141 (four), C–123 (two), and C–130 (one).

Humanitarian Airlift Operations

Operations: Early on the morning of January 17, an earthquake registering at least 6.6 on the Richter scale struck Northridge in southern California, just northwest of Los Angeles. The earthquake and thousands of aftershocks left at least 35,000 people homeless and 210,000 homes without utilities. The Federal Emergency Management Agency, supported by DoD, organized relief efforts.

Between January 17 and 25, the AMC, AF Res, and ANG conducted a humanitarian airlift operation for California earthquake victims. Using C–5s, C–141s, C–123s, and a C–130, they transported 170 tons of relief equipment and supplies—including fire trucks, generators, communications vans, first aid supplies, and search and rescue equipment—to the disaster area. They also carried 270 disaster relief workers.

March AFB at Riverside, about 75 miles from the earthquake's epicenter, served as a staging base, and most flights terminated at Los Alamitos in the disaster area. Among the participating airlift wings were the Air National Guard's 146th and the Air Force Reserve's 433d, 439th, and 445th. Aircraft and crews came from California, Texas, Massachusetts, Delaware, South Carolina, Washington, and New Jersey. California's 144th Ftr Wg used a pair of C–123 transports in the emergency.

One C–5, from the 433d Alft Wg, ferried 40 tons of relief cargo—including first aid supplies, search and rescue equipment, and ground-penetrating radar—from Travis AFB in California to Los Alamitos. It also delivered 168 relief workers and six search dogs. Other C–5s from the Massachusetts 439th Alft Wg airlifted relief workers and equipment, including communications vans, from the east to the west coast.

112.
Name: Western Forest Fires.
Location: California, Arizona, Idaho, Nevada, Montana, and Washington.
Date(s): June–September 12, 1994.
Emergency: Fires consumed more than two million acres of forest and brush in six western states.
Air Force Organization(s) Involved: 146th and 302d Alft Wgs and 145th and 153d Alft Gps.
Airlifted: Nearly five million gallons of fire-retardant chemicals.
Aircraft Employed: C–130 (eight+).
Operations: When forest fires in California's San Bernardino and Angeles National Forests threatened homes in June, the Forest Service enlisted the help of the Air Force Reserve's 302d Alft Wg from Peterson AFB, Colorado. Three of the wing's C–130s, equipped with the MAFFS, fought the fire by spraying fire-retardant chemicals from the air.

As fires continued to spread, not only in California but also in neighboring Arizona, additional C–130 units from the ANG joined the Forest Service effort. These included the 145th Alft Gp from Charlotte, North Carolina; the 153d Alft

Gp from Cheyenne, Wyoming; and the 146th Alft Wg from Channel Islands ANG Base, California.

The season proved to be one of the worst in recent memory, with major new fires breaking out in Nevada, Washington, Idaho, and Montana. The same C–130 units participated in fire-fighting operations in those states, the 302d and the 146th operating out of Boise, Idaho, and the 145th and 153d flying out of Spokane, Washington.

By the middle of September, the C–130s had dispensed nearly five million gallons of fire retardant around fires in six western states. The air missions, combined with fire-fighting operations on the ground and the arrival of cooler, wet weather, contained the fires only after they had consumed over two million acres of western forest and brush.

Chapter 2
Latin America

For the purposes of this book, Latin America encompasses the countries, colonies, and territories of the Western Hemisphere excluding Alaska, Canada, and the continental United States. It includes South America, Mexico, Central America, the West Indies, Puerto Rico, and the Virgin Islands.

Humanitarian airlifts to Latin America have been more numerous than to any other region outside the continental United States. They have averaged more than two per year between 1947 and 1994, with a total of 110 airlifts. In that period, the Air Force used more than 700 aircraft to deliver over 22,000 tons of relief cargo to Latin America.

The nations and territories "south of the border" are strategically significant to the United States because of their proximity to and strong economic ties with the United States. This proximity has made airlifts to the region relatively easy, and U.S. bases in Cuba, Puerto Rico, and Panama have also facilitated relief flights. More than half of the Latin American relief operations involved Central America and Mexico.

Natural disasters such as floods, earthquakes, and tropical storms prompted the overwhelming majority of humanitarian airlifts to Latin America. The region has also been politically unstable. Although international wars have been rare, dictatorships, revolutions, and civil wars have been relatively common and some of these political crises generated the need for relief flights. The Denton Amendment to a defense appropriations bill in 1985 allowed DoD to deliver privately donated humanitarian cargo to Central America.

The United States did not limit humanitarian operations to democracies in Latin America. Relief missions were flown to more than 20 countries with a variety of political structures. After Fidel Castro came to power in Cuba in 1959, he aligned his country with the Soviet Union and relied on Moscow for aid and, thus, no U.S. humanitarian airlifts went to Cuba.

During the Cold War, Soviet and Cuban leaders argued that the United States ruthlessly exploited Latin American nations. U.S. humanitarian airlifts to Latin America help to counter that argument, demonstrating the commitment of the United States to the well-being of its southern neighbors.

Humanitarian Airlift Operations

Statistics: Latin American Airlifts

Number of humanitarian airlifts: 110.

Most common emergencies: floods (30), earthquakes (20), and hurricanes and tropical storms (16).

Most frequent recipients: Panama (13), Nicaragua (12), and Colombia (9).

Three largest operations, in chronological order: Amigos Airlift, 1960 (over 1,000 tons); Caribbean Storms, 1979 (2,900 tons); and Haitian Refugees, 1991–1994 (over 6,000 tons).

Chronological Listing: Latin American Airlifts

1. Panamanian Yellow Fever Outbreak	Jan. 1949
2. Ecuadoran Earthquake	Aug. 1940
3. Costa Rican Yellow Fever Epidemic	Sept. 1951
4. Ecuadoran Flood	Mar.–Apr. 1953
5. Operation Salud	Sept.–Oct. 1954
6. Hurricane Hazel	Oct. 1954
7. Tampico Flood	Sept.–Oct. 1955
8. Costa Rican Flood	Oct. 1955
9. Magdalena River Flood	Nov.–Dec. 1955
10. Argentinean Polio Epidemic	Mar. 1956
11. Guatemalan Polio Epidemic	June 1959
12. Arequipa Earthquake	Jan. 1960
13. Brazilian Floods	Mar.–Apr. 1960
14. Amigos Airlift	May–June 1960
15. Hurricane Hattie	Nov. 1961
16. Colombian Flood and Famine	Aug.–Sept. 1962
17. Honduran Medical Airlift	Jan. 1963
18. Alazan Famine	May 1963
19. Parana Fires	Sept. 1963
20. Hurricane Flora	Oct. 1963
21. Panama Canal Zone Evacuation	Jan.–Feb. 1964
22. Bahia Flood	Jan.–Feb. 1964
23. Costa Rican Volcano	Jan. and May–June 1964
24. Nicaraguan Medical Airlift	Feb. 1964
25. Panamanian Forest Fires	Apr. 1964
26. Bolivian Epidemic	June–July 1964
27. Hurricane Cleo	Aug. 1964
28. Bocas del Toro Storm	Sept. 1964
29. Central Chilean Earthquake	Apr. 1965
30. El Salvadoran Earthquake	May 1965
31. Honduran Flood	Sept. 1965
32. Hurricane Inez	Oct. 1966
33. Bold Party	Oct. 1966
34. Peruvian Earthquake	Oct. 1966
35. Quibdó Fire	Oct. 1966
36. Panamanian Flood	Nov. 1966
37. Venezuelan Earthquake	July–Aug. 1967
38. Bonny Date	Sept.–Oct. 1967
39. Savage Fly	Jan.–May 1968
40. Bolivian Floods	Feb. 1968
41. Ecuadoran Drought	Apr. 1968

Humanitarian Airlift Operations

42. Mount Arenal Eruption	July–Aug. 1968
43. Nicaraguan Flood	Aug. 1968
44. Combat Mosquito	May 1969
45. Honduran Refugees	July–Sept. 1969
46. Hurricane Francelia	Sept. 1969
47. Central American Floods	Jan. and Apr. 1970
48. Peruvian Earthquake	June–July 1970
49. Puerto Rican Floods	Oct. 1970
50. Colombian Flood	Nov. 1970
51. Costa Rican Flood	Dec. 1970
52. Ecuadoran Earthquake	Dec. 1970
53. Bolivian Flood	Feb. 1971
54. Project Volcan	Mar. 1971
55. Coronet Roundup	June 1971–May 1975
56. Chilean Double Disaster	July 1971
57. Mexican Flash Flood	July 1971
58. Hurricane Edith	Sept. 1971
59. Tropical Storm Fern	Sept. 1971
60. Peruvian Floods and Earthquake	Mar.–Apr. 1972
61. Managua Earthquake	Dec. 1972–Jan. 1973
62. Nicaraguan Medfly	Apr.–May 1973
63. Guatemalan Flood	June 1973
64. Panamanian Encephalomyelitis Outbreak	July 1973
65. Colombian Flood	Oct. 1973
66. Western Panamanian Flood	Nov. 1973
67. Bolivian Flood	Feb. 1974
68. Chilean Flood	July 1974
69. Colombian Mud Slides	July 1974
70. Hurricane Fifi	Sept.–Oct. 1974
71. Recife Flood	July 1975
72. Kingston Homeless	Jan. 1976
73. Operation Earthquake	Feb.–June 1976
74. Bolivian Airplane Crash	Oct. 1976
75. Hurricane Greta	Sept.–Oct. 1978
76. Costa Rican Flood	Oct. 1978
77. Guyanese Disaster	Nov.–Dec. 1978
78. Saint Vincent Volcano	Apr. 1979
79. Nicaraguan Evacuation	June–July 1979
80. Caribbean Storms	Aug.–Nov. 1979
81. Bolivian Evacuation	Nov. 1979
82. Panamanian Flood	Nov. 1979
83. Colombian Earthquake	Dec. 1979
84. Nicaraguan Flood	Dec. 1979–Mar. 1980

85. Belizean Flood	Dec. 1979
86. Hurricane Allen	Aug. 1980
87. Coco River Flood	Oct. 1980
88. Peruvian Earthquake	July 1981
89. Panamanian Bridge Collapse	May 1982
90. Popayan Earthquake	Apr. 1983
91. Peruvian Flood	June–July 1983
92. Ecuadoran Flood	July–Aug. 1983
93. Argentinean Earthquake	Feb. 1985
94. Chilean Earthquake	Mar. 1985
95. Mexican Earthquakes	Sept. 1985
96. Puerto Rican Mud Slides	Oct. 1985
97. Colombian Volcano	Nov. 1985
98. Jamaican Flood	June 1986
99. El Salvadoran Earthquake	Oct.–Nov. 1986
100. Dupont Plaza Hotel Fire	Jan. 1987
101. Ecuadoran Earthquakes	Mar. 1987
102. Hurricane Gilbert	Sept. 1988–Feb. 1989
103. Peruvian Cholera Epidemic	Apr. 1991
104. Haitian Refugees	Nov. 1991–Sept. 1994
105. Bolivian Epidemic	Apr. 1992
106. Nicaraguan Relief	May 1992
107. Panamanian Orphan Relief	Dec. 1992
108. Nicaraguan Airlift	Late 1993
109. Guatemalan Airlift	Nov. 1993
110. Safe Haven	Aug.–Sept. 1994

Humanitarian Airlift Operations

Operations: Latin American Airlifts

1.
Name: Panamanian Yellow Fever Outbreak.
Location: Republic of Panama.
Date(s): January 16, 1949.
Emergency: The first case of yellow fever in 20 years was reported around Pecora, Panama, raising fears of an epidemic.
Air Force Organization(s) Involved: 98th Bombardment Group (Medium).
Airlifted: 75,000 doses of yellow fever vaccine.
Aircraft Employed: B–29 (one).
Operations: During late December 1948, men clearing jungle near Pacora, Panama, about 15 miles east of Panama City, contracted yellow fever. The Pan American Sanitary Bureau noted this as the first outbreak of the disease in 20 years. By January 1949, eight persons developed yellow fever symptoms and six died. Panama Canal Zone officials planned a vaccination campaign.

The United States Public Health Service stored yellow fever vaccine at its serum laboratory in Hamilton, Montana, just south of Missoula. They asked the Air Force to airlift serum to Panama. On January 16, the Fifteenth Air Force's 92d Bombardment Wing at Spokane AFB, Washington, flew two B–29 Superfortresses to Missoula to pick up the vaccine and carry it to the Canal Zone. Engine trouble forced one plane to land at MacDill AFB, Florida. But the other B–29, belonging to the 98th Bombardment Group (Medium), completed the mission to the Canal Zone on January 16, delivering 75,000 doses of yellow fever vaccine.

The Panama Canal Zone Health Department inoculated U.S. military personnel, Panama Canal employees, and Panamanian citizens. By January 24, more than 30,000 people had been vaccinated against yellow fever, and the epidemic threat faded.

2.
Name: Ecuadoran Earthquake.
Location: Republic of Ecuador.
Date(s): August 10–19, 1949.
Emergency: An earthquake measuring 7.5 on the Richter scale struck central Ecuador.
Air Force Organization(s) Involved: Caribbean Air Command.
Airlifted: 41 tons of food, clothing, tents, medical supplies, and communications equipment.
Aircraft Employed: C–47 (12).
Operations: A severe earthquake registering 7.5 on the Richter scale struck the high valleys of central Ecuador in the Andes on Thursday, August 4, killing 5,000 people and leaving 100,000 homeless. More than half of the 6,000 inhabitants of the town of Pelileo, near the earthquake epicenter, perished. Ambato, a city of

40,000 people 45 miles south of Quito and the capital of agricultural Tungurahua province, lost 80 percent of its buildings, including its cathedral. A priest and 60 children awaiting their first communion were among those who died. Many other towns, including Patate, Pillaro, Guano, Totoras, Montalinos, and Cevallos, suffered severe damage.

President Galo Plaza of Ecuador appealed for relief through the disaster service of the American Red Cross. On Sunday, August 7, Army and American Red Cross disaster teams flew from the Panama Canal Zone to Quito to arrange an airlift. Meanwhile, between August 4 and 10, the joint Caribbean Command collected relief supplies—including food, clothing, tents, medical supplies, and emergency communications equipment—at the Panama Canal Depot in the Canal Zone from stocks at various bases in the Caribbean area. Almost 29 tons were loaded aboard 12 Caribbean Air Command C–47 aircraft on August 10 and flown to Quito on August 11 and 12. The planes continued to shuttle supplies between Howard AFB, Canal Zone, and Quito and Ambato, Ecuador, until August 19.

Between August 11 and 19, Caribbean Air Command aircraft flew 594 emergency support personnel and 41 tons of relief supplies to Ecuador in a series of 74 flights. Air Force planes evacuated 274 earthquake victims from Ambato to Quito for medical treatment. The support personnel and relief supplies furnished by the United States, together with aid from other nations, put Ecuador on the road to recovery by month's end.

3.
Name: Costa Rican Yellow Fever Epidemic.
Location: Republic of Costa Rica.
Date(s): September 7–25, 1951.
Emergency: A yellow fever outbreak in the jungle lowlands of northern Costa Rica killed at least 24 people and threatened to become a major epidemic.
Air Force Organization(s) Involved: Flight B, 4th Air Rscu Sq.
Airlifted: Yellow fever vaccine and Costa Rican medical personnel.
Aircraft Employed: C–82 (one) and H–5 (one).
Operations: During June, a yellow fever epidemic broke out in Alajuela, Heredia, and Limón provinces in the jungle lowlands of northern Costa Rica. For the next three months, Costa Rican public health officials attempted to contain the tropical disease, vaccinating 50,000 people in cooperation with the Pan American Sanitary Bureau and the yellow fever vaccine laboratory at Bogotá, Colombia. By September 10, 17 people had died and 80 others were suspected to have the disease. The Republic of Costa Rica appealed for international assistance to help inoculate persons in remote jungle areas. The State Department referred the request to DoD.

Defense Department officials directed that a helicopter ferry vaccine and medical personnel to the isolated areas. On September 7, a C–82 belonging to Flight B, 4th Air Rscu Sq, at March AFB, California, carried a disassembled H–5 helicopter via Westover AFB, Massachusetts, to the Canal Zone, where it was unloaded and reassembled. The H–5 flew from Panama to Costa Rica on September 11. For the next two weeks, the helicopter, piloted by Capt. John R. Peacock, ferried Costa Rican medical personnel and yellow fever vaccine to 37 remote villages in a 6,000-square-mile area to help inoculate 978 persons. The H–5 operated from a staging base at Altamira, near the Nicaraguan border.

Costa Rican public health officials Dr. Oscar Vargas and Dr. José Cabezas monitored the emergency, along with Dr. Fred L. Soper, director of the Pan American Sanitary Bureau. By the third week in September, they had found no new cases of yellow fever. On September 25, the 4th Air Rscu Sq helicopter concluded emergency medical missions in Costa Rica after helping to end the three-month epidemic, which killed at least 24 people.

4.

Name: Ecuadoran Flood.
Location: Republic of Ecuador.
Date(s): March 28–April 14, 1953.
Emergency: Heavy rain caused flooding that washed out roads and railroad beds between Ecuador's two largest cities, interrupting the movement of food supplies.
Air Force Organization(s) Involved: Caribbean Air Command.
Airlifted: 657 tons of supplies, mostly food.
Aircraft Employed: C–47 (six).
Operations: Heavy spring rain in central Ecuador washed out major roads and railways connecting Ecuador's two largest cities, Guayaquil, a port on the Pacific Ocean coast, and Quito, the country's capital, high in the Andes. Through the U.S. ambassador, Paul Daniels, Ecuador requested assistance to build an air bridge between the cities until ground transportation routes reopened. On March 28, Lt. Col. Hubert Brandon, assistant chief of the Air Force mission to Ecuador, began coordinating a Caribbean Air Command airlift from Albrook AFB in the Panama Canal Zone to Ecuador, and between Quito and Guayaquil.

An aerial survey crew from Albrook photographed the flooded regions of Ecuador, enabling engineers to repair the flood-damaged highways and railroads more rapidly. The Caribbean Air Command hauled two tons of water purification chemicals and large quantities of gasoline from the Canal Zone to Ecuador. Six C–47 aircraft—five from Albrook AFB and one from the Air Force mission to Ecuador—ferried sugar, salt, rice, and gasoline from Guayaquil to Quito, and meat and vegetables on the return leg.

The planes navigated the 150 miles of hazardous air corridors through passes in the cloud-shrouded Andes that provided the only link between the two cities for 17 days, flying 544 hours without an accident. Over 200 members of the Caribbean Air Command participated in the operation, helping transport 657 tons of food and supplies to and within Ecuador between March 28 and April 14.

By mid-April, surface transportation between Guayaquil and Quito was restored, rendering further emergency airlift assistance unnecessary. The

Ecuadoran ministry of economics praised the airlift as a demonstration of solidarity between the peoples of the United States and Ecuador.

5.
Name: Operation Salud (Honduran Flood).
Location: Republic of Honduras.
Date(s): September 29–October 7, 1954.
Emergency: Heavy rain from Hurricane Gilda flooded the Sula Valley of Honduras.
Air Force Organization(s) Involved: 26th Air Rscu Sq and other units of the Caribbean Air Command.
Airlifted: 50 tons of food, medicine, rafts, and water purification equipment.
Aircraft Employed: C–47 (10), H–19 (2), and SA–16 (1).
Operations: Heavy rain from Hurricane Gilda drenched northwestern Honduras at the end of September. The Chamelecon and Ulua Rivers inundated 680 square miles of the Sula Valley. The high water destroyed thousands of acres of banana plantations and left 3,000 people homeless. When the rivers crested on September 27, President Dr. Juan Manuel Galvez of Honduras took charge of relief operations. He appealed for aid to the U.S. ambassador, Whiting Willauer, in the capital city of Tegucigalpa, and President Eisenhower assigned U.S. military relief operations to the Caribbean Command.

On September 29, a Caribbean Command survey team arrived at San Pedro Sula in the stricken area of Honduras with an SA–16 amphibious plane from Albrook AFB in the Panama Canal Zone. The Caribbean Air Command, which was the Air Force component of the Caribbean Command, began sending C–47 aircraft laden with food rations, medical supplies, emergency rafts, and water purification equipment from Albrook to Honduras on September 30. That same day, U.S. military personnel set up emergency communications equipment at San Pedro Sula.

On October 2, a joint task force under Col. W. C. Morse, an Air Force member of the Caribbean Command, took charge of relief operations in Honduras, coordinating Army, Air Force, and Navy missions with Honduran government officials. On October 3, the task force designated the activities Operation Salud. Commander of the Caribbean Command, Maj. Gen. R. C. Hood, arrived in San Pedro Sula on October 4 to review relief efforts firsthand.

Between September 30 and October 7, while Army and Navy boats and helicopters evacuated flood victims and transported medical, engineering, and communications personnel and supplies within Honduras, 10 Caribbean Air Command C–47 aircraft moved food, medicine, and other emergency cargo from the Panama Canal Zone to Honduras. Air Force planes airlifted almost 50 tons of relief supplies, mostly food, to Honduran flood victims.

On October 9, Air Force personnel returned from San Pedro Sula to Albrook AFB. Further U.S. military relief operations in Honduras that month were handled by Navy personnel.

6.

Name: Hurricane Hazel.

Location: Republic of Haiti and the Bahamas.

Date(s): October 1954.

Emergency: Hurricane Hazel hit southwestern Haiti, bringing high winds, tides, and rain. It also hit Eleuthera Island in the Bahamas.

Air Force Organization(s) Involved: Eighteenth Air Force, 456th and 463d Trp Carr Wgs, and 28th Air Rscu Sq.

Airlifted: More than seven tons of food, mostly rice, and medical supplies; and 10 injured victims airlifted to hospitals.

Aircraft Employed: C–119 (four+) and H–19 (one).

Operations: On October 12, Columbus Day, Hurricane Hazel hit a peninsula in southwestern Haiti. Winds of 115 mph brought high tides, leaving 100 people dead, 100,000 homeless, and thousands without food or medical care. The Haitian government appealed for international assistance as the storm continued northward through the Bahamas, ravaging Eleuthera Island.

At the request of the Caribbean Air Command, two C–119 Flying Boxcars from the Eighteenth Air Force's 456th Trp Carr Wg were diverted from a training flight to Panama to fly to San Juan, Puerto Rico, to pick up supplies for hurricane victims in Haiti. The cargo consisted of Red Cross food and medical supplies. Lacking adequate airfields in the disaster area, the airplanes dropped the supplies by parachute over Jeremie, Haiti, which was crowded with hurricane survivors. The airlift complemented Navy efforts in a project called Operation Sante.

On October 17, the 28th Air Rscu Sq at Ramey AFB, Puerto Rico, sent an H–19 helicopter piloted by 1st Lt. William B. Roberts, Jr., to Jeremie. For the next five days, the helicopter flew rescue and relief missions, transporting nine injured hurricane victims to local hospitals and delivering food and medical supplies to Haitians whose surface transportation routes had been cut. On October 23, while flying back to Ramey AFB, Lieutenant Roberts' helicopter was diverted to evacuate an individual with a broken neck from a mountain landslide site about 12 miles south of the Haitian capital of Port-au-Prince. Heavy precipitation contributed to the landslide, which killed 86 people and left 100 missing.

Between October 17 and 24, the 28th Air Rscu Sq H–19 transported at least 10 Haitian storm victims to medical facilities while distributing more than two tons of food and medical supplies. The Republic of Haiti later issued a postage stamp to commemorate the squadron's contribution to Hurricane Hazel relief and recovery efforts.

During the same month, the Eighteenth Air Force relieved other West Indian victims of Hurricane Hazel. The 463d Trp Carr Wg, using C–119 Flying Boxcars, airlifted 10 prefabricated buildings weighing five tons from Hensley Field, Texas, to Eleuthera Island. Each building, when assembled, covered an area 20 by 48 feet. The shelters housed hurricane victims until they could move into more permanent dwellings.

7.
Name: Tampico Flood.
Location: Mexico.
Date(s): September 20–October 28, 1955.
Emergency: A series of hurricanes dumped heavy rain on eastern Mexico, flooding Tampico.
Air Force Organization(s) Involved: Fourteenth Air Force; 6th and 42d Air Divs; 2252d, 2577th, and 2578th Air Reserve Flying Centers; 3510th and 3645th Combat Crew Training Wings; 3585th Flying Training Wing; 3640th Pilot Training Wing; 805th and 806th AB Gps; 47th Air Rscu Sq; San Antonio Air Materiel Area; and 302d and 446th Trp Carr Wgs.
Airlifted: 630 tons of relief supplies, mostly food, clothing, and bedding.
Aircraft Employed: C–46 (12), C–119 (7), C–47 (5), C–45 (5), H–21 (4), SA–16 (2), B–25 (1), YC–124 (1), and H–13 (1).
Operations: Hurricane Hilda hit the Tampico area of eastern Mexico on September 16, inundating the city and swelling the rivers flowing from the Sierra Madre Oriental. Prolonged flooding of Tampico caused Mexican civil authorities to contact Harlingen AFB, Texas, for food relief. On September 20, a week-long Air Training Command airlift began. Cargo aircraft from Harlingen, Brooks, and Randolph AFBs transported food supplies via Brownsville to Tampico until September 28, when the threat of another hurricane suspended missions.

Hurricane Janet struck near Tampico on September 29, dropping more heavy rain and compounding the flooding. Up to 5,000 people died and 80,000 were left temporarily homeless. Only a small portion of the city, including Rihl Airport, escaped high water. Airlift became the chief means of supply. The Continental Air Command directed the Fourteenth Air Force on September 29 to support the Fourth Army in the disaster relief effort. A Fourteenth Air Force operations control center was set up at Harlingen AFB. On October 1, C–46s from Brooks AFB transported operations, communications, and information service teams to Tampico.

Between October 1 and 20, the Fourteenth Air Force supervised Air Force relief efforts, coordinating flights from 15 units, including 38 planes—mostly C–46s, C–119s, C–47s and C–45s—flying 412 sorties. The planes flew to the stricken city from the Texas Air Force bases of Brooks, Harlingen, Randolph, Kelly, and Ellington, transporting 630 tons of food, clothing, bedding, field kitchens, and emergency equipment. C–119s delivered Army amphibious vehicles from Pueblo, Colorado, to Tampico during the first week in October for the Fourth Army to use to reach stranded flood victims.

On October 8, Col. Frank L. Wood assumed command of the temporary Fourteenth Air Force advance headquarters at Harlingen. By October 20, some surface transportation routes to Tampico had reopened, and the airlift began to wind down. All Air Force aircraft had returned to their home bases in Texas by October 28.

8.
Name: Costa Rican Flood.
Location: Republic of Costa Rica.
Date(s): October 15, 1955.
Emergency: 11 inches of rain in 24 hours flooded the Pacific coast of southern Costa Rica, including the towns of Puerto Cortes and Golfito.
Air Force Organization(s) Involved: 26th Air Rscu Sq.
Airlifted: At least one ton of food and medical supplies.
Aircraft Employed: SA–16 and SH–19 (numbers unspecified).
Operations: In the 24 hours between the mornings of October 12 and 13, 11 inches of rain fell over the Pacific coast of southern Costa Rica. Heavy rain fell for two more days, nearly washing away Puerto Cortes, Golfito, and other coastal towns, and the roads connecting them. Robert Woodward, U.S. ambassador to Costa Rica, relayed requests for emergency assistance to the State Department.

On October 15, the 26th Air Rscu Sq at Albrook AFB in the Panama Canal Zone sent aircraft to Golfito to help distribute thousands of pounds of food and medical supplies to Costa Rica's Pacific coast. The prompt relief flights helped to sustain survivors of the disaster until surface transportation routes could be restored. U.S. food donations poured into Costa Rica by land and sea in November to supplement the supplies delivered by air in October.

9.
Name: Magdalena River Flood.
Location: Republic of Colombia.
Date(s): November 30–December 6, 1955.
Emergency: Colombia's Magdalena River crested at its highest level in 50 years, flooding 17 towns and leaving 15,000 people homeless.
Air Force Organization(s) Involved: Caribbean Air Command.
Airlifted: Food and medical supplies.
Aircraft Employed: C–47 (number unspecified).
Operations: At the end of November, Colombia's Magdalena River, swollen by heavy tropical rain, crested at its highest level in 50 years. Cities and towns along the lower part of the 850-mile-long river flooded, forcing more than 15,000 people from their homes. The Republic of Colombia asked the United States for airlift assistance.

On November 30, the Caribbean Air Command headquarters at Albrook AFB in the Panama Canal Zone sent a disaster survey team to Barranquilla, Colombia, a port city at the mouth of the Magdalena River, to prepare for an airlift of food and medical supplies. A C–47 laden with medical supplies completed the first relief shipment from Albrook AFB to Barranquilla on December 2. For four days, C–47s of the Caribbean Air Command delivered American Red Cross food and medicine from the Canal Zone to Colombia.

10.
Name: Argentinean Polio Epidemic.
Location: Republic of Argentina.
Date(s): March 6–17, 1956.
Emergency: Polio infected more than 1,600 Argentineans.
Air Force Organization(s) Involved: 1st Air Trpt Sq and 61st Trp Carr Gp.
Airlifted: 49 iron lungs, six rocking beds, and six respirators.
Aircraft Employed: C–124 (two).
Operations: Between January 1 and March 5, the Buenos Aires area of eastern Argentina suffered 848 cases of polio. In early March, 50 new cases were being reported daily. The government of the provisional president, Pedro Eugenio Aramburu, appealed for international aid to fight the epidemic. On March 5, the U.S. State Department asked the Air Force to arrange an airlift of emergency breathing equipment to Argentina. President Eisenhower's International Cooperation Administration authorized $100,000 to secure scarce iron lungs and other mechanical breathing apparatuses with the cooperation of the National Foundation for Infantile Paralysis.

Between March 6 and 8, a 61st Trp Carr Gp C–124 Globemaster from Donaldson AFB at Greenville, South Carolina, picked up 21 iron lungs in Boston and flew them via Trinidad to Ezeiza International Airport in Buenos Aires. By March 15, the polio epidemic had struck 1,676 men, women, and children, and more than 150 died.

Argentina purchased gamma globulin polio medicine from the United States and asked for additional iron lungs. Between March 15 and 17, the 1st Air Trpt Wg (Heavy), from Dover AFB, Delaware, flew 11 tons of equipment—including 28 iron lungs (in various adult, child, and infant sizes), six rocking beds, and six respirators—from Boston to Buenos Aires aboard another C–124. Argentine military personnel accompanied the cargo.

Between March 6 and 17, two C–124 Globemaster flights transported 49 iron lungs and other mechanical breathing equipment more than 4,000 miles to relieve some of the polio victims. By the end of the month, President Aramburu announced that the plague had subsided with the aid of a vaccination campaign.

11.
Name: Guatemalan Polio Epidemic.
Location: Republic of Guatemala.
Date(s): June 21, 1959.
Emergency: A polio epidemic threatened Guatemala.
Air Force Organization(s) Involved: 29th Air Trpt Sq.
Airlifted: 25,000 units of Salk vaccine.
Aircraft Employed: C–118 (one).
Operations: Alarmed by an outbreak of polio in June 1959, the Guatemalan government asked the United States for supplies of a vaccine serum developed by Dr.

Jonas Salk. The State Department asked MATS to airlift the vaccine to Guatemala.

On June 21, a C–118 Liftmaster from the 29th Air Trpt Sq of the 1611th Air Trpt Wg (Medium), based at McGuire AFB, New Jersey, carried 25,000 units of serum from Bayonne, New Jersey, to Guatemala (city) in a flight of 2,000 miles. Thanks to the airlift, physicians in Guatemala inoculated tens of thousands of people against the paralyzing disease and arrested a dangerous epidemic that might have devastated not only Guatemala but other parts of Central America.

12.
Name: Arequipa Earthquake.
Location: Republic of Peru.
Date(s): January 15–16, 1960.
Emergency: A massive earthquake struck Peru, killing 60 people, injuring 200, and leaving hundreds homeless.
Air Force Organization(s) Involved: Caribbean Air Command.
Airlifted: 15 tons of blankets, tents, and tent-erecting tools.
Aircraft Employed: C–47 (one) and C–54 (two).
Operations: On the morning of January 13, a severe earthquake registering about 7.0 on the Richter scale struck southern Peru around Arequipa, the country's second largest city, about 460 miles southeast of Lima near the active volcano Misti. The area, including towns such as Chuquibamba, Ica, and Palpa, with a combined population of over 200,000, suffered 60 dead and 200 injured. The tremor was felt as far south as Santiago, Chile.

For three days, aftershocks rocked the region, collapsing buildings weakened by the initial quake. Hundreds of people lost their homes, while many more slept outside for fear of being buried alive. Up to 80 percent of the buildings in Arequipa were destroyed.

On January 14, President Manuel Prado and Premier Pedro Beltran of Peru flew to Arequipa to survey the damage and arrange relief efforts. The U.S. ambassador, Theodore E. Achilles, Jr., flew from Lima to Arequipa to offer aid. The Peruvian government promptly accepted the offer and the State Department contacted the Caribbean Command, which included Air Force, Army, and Navy components, to airlift cargo from Panama to Peru.

Between January 15 and 16, the Caribbean Command sent four airplanes laden with 15 tons of supplies, including 1,000 blankets, 50 squad tents, and tent-erecting tools, from Albrook AFB in the Canal Zone to Arequipa. The aircraft included two C–47s—one from the Navy—and two C–54s. The tents and blankets helped to shelter many homeless as the task of rebuilding began.

13.
Name: Brazilian Floods.
Location: Brazil.
Date(s): March 31–April 30, 1960.
Emergency: Two weeks of heavy rain flooded river valleys in five states of northeastern Brazil, leaving 500,000 refugees.
Air Force Organization(s) Involved: 63d Trp Carr Wg and 1608th Air Trpt Wg.
Airlifted: 160 tons of rafts, medical supplies, and food; and two H–34 helicopters and crews.
Aircraft Employed: C–124 (six).
Operations: During the second half of March, heavy rain in northeastern Brazil flooded river valleys and burst dams in five states, forcing 500,000 people from their homes. The São Francisco and Jaguaribe Rivers inundated towns such as Petrolina, Juazeiro, and Oros. On March 29, President Juscelino Kubitschek of Brazil flew from Rio de Janeiro to Fortaleza in the flood-stricken state of Ceara to survey damage and arrange relief. His government requested aid from the United States.

Between March 31 and April 5, six MATS C–124 Globemaster aircraft—three each from the 63d Trp Carr Wg at Donaldson AFB, South Carolina, and the 1608th Air Trpt Wg at Charleston AFB, South Carolina—carried 30 tons of disaster relief supplies and equipment to Fortaleza. Cargo included 20 four-man life rafts, food, medical supplies, and two H–34 helicopters and crews from the Navy. The Globemasters remained in Brazil through April, shuttling an additional 130 tons of emergency supplies from Rio de Janeiro and Natal to Fortaleza.

In addition to saving lives and property, the flood relief airlift demonstrated U.S. support for Latin America at a time when that support was being questioned by the new Cuban government of Fidel Castro.

14.
Name: Amigos Airlift.
Location: Republic of Chile.
Date(s): May 23–June 23, 1960.
Emergency: A series of earthquakes—some registering more than 7.0 on the Richter scale—followed by avalanches, landslides, tidal waves, and volcanic eruptions, devastated southern Chile, leaving 8,000 people dead or missing, 5,500 injured, and at least 248,000 homeless.
Air Force Organization(s) Involved: 63d Trp Carr Wg; 1607th, 1608th, and 1611th Air Trpt Wgs; and Caribbean Air Command.
Airlifted: 1,014 tons of hospital equipment, medical and communications supplies, vehicles, cots, blankets, food, tents, clothing, and water purification equipment; and 2,489 passengers.
Aircraft Employed: C–118 (13), C–124 (66), C–54 (4), C–47 (3), and H–19 (2).
Operations: On Saturday and Sunday, May 21 and 22, a series of immense earth-

quakes struck southern Chile between Concepción and the Gulf of Corcovado. Five tremors registered between 7.25 and 8.5 on the Richter scale and, for 25 miles, the earth's surface sank 1,000 feet. Aftershocks were felt as far away as Buenos Aires on the other side of the continent. The earthquakes spawned the eruption of at least seven volcanoes and set off numerous landslides and avalanches. Tsunamis (tidal waves) devastated the Chilean coast. Towns and cities such as Angol, Puerto Montt, Valdivia, Castro, Concepción, Puerto Saavedra, and Corral were all but destroyed. The multiple disasters left more than 8,000 people dead or missing, 5,500 injured, and 248,000 homeless. Property losses approached $500 million.

On May 23, President Jorge Alessandri Rodríguez of Chile requested U.S. assistance through Ambassador Walter Howe, and the Departments of State and Defense arranged a massive airlift of relief equipment and supplies. On May 26, the Air Force began what became known as the Amigos Airlift.

Between May 23 and June 23, the Eastern Air Transport Air Force of MATS and the Caribbean Air Command airlifted more than 1,014 tons of emergency goods to Chile. Cargo included two 400-bed Army field hospitals, two Army helicopter units (10 helicopters), 64 tons of mobile radar landing approach equipment, 140 tents, 2,000 blankets, radios, trucks, trailers, food, cots, forklifts, medical supplies, water tanks, building materials, and two water purification units.

The 63d Trp Carr Wg from Donaldson AFB, South Carolina; the 1607th Air Trpt Wg from Dover AFB, Delaware; the 1608th Air Trpt Wg from Charleston AFB, South Carolina; the 1611th Air Trpt Wg from McGuire AFB, New Jersey; and the Caribbean Air Command from Albrook AFB in the Panama Canal Zone flew the airlift using 13 C–118, 66 C–124, 4 C–54, 3 C–47, and 2 H–19 missions. The planes carried 2,489 passengers, including refugees, medical personnel, and communications specialists.

Most flights followed a 4,500-mile, 25-hour route from the United States via Tocumen International Airport, Panama, and Limatambo, Peru, to Los Cerrillos International Airport at Santiago and to Puerto Montt in the devastated area. Cargo came from a host of bases and cities, including Lockbourne AFB, Ohio; Tinker AFB, Oklahoma; Pope AFB, North Carolina; Andrews AFB, Maryland; Dover AFB, Delaware; Albrook and Howard AFBs in the Panama Canal Zone; Brookley AFB, Alabama; Cedar Rapids, Iowa; Harrisburg, Pennsylvania; and Atlanta, Georgia. The 7th Army Field Hospital from Fort Belvoir, Virginia, and the 15th Army Field Hospital from Fort Bragg, North Carolina, respectively, set up operations at Puerto Montt and Valdivia, where they were assisted by 10 airlifted helicopters of the U.S. Army's 56th and 57th Helicopter Detachments.

Caribbean Air Command C–54 and C–47 airplanes came from various locations across Latin America. Military Airlift Command C–124s, unable to land safely at U.S. air bases in the Canal Zone because of runway limitations, used Panama's Tocumen International Airport. The United States contributed the largest share of international assistance.

15.
Name: Hurricane Hattie.
Location: British Honduras.
Date(s): November 3–14, 1961.
Emergency: Hurricane Hattie hit British Honduras with 200 mph winds and 15-foot tides, killing 250 people and leaving 15,000 homeless.
Air Force Organization(s) Involved: 63d Trp Carr Wg, 1607th and 1608th Air Trpt Wgs, and 76th Trp Carr Sq.
Airlifted: 98 tons of food, medicine, clothing, communications equipment, and aviation fuel.
Aircraft Employed: C–124s (eight) and C–119 (one).
Operations: On October 31, Hurricane Hattie struck British Honduras with winds up to 200 mph, 15-foot tides, and torrential rain. It left water up to 10 feet deep in the streets of the colonial capital of Belize, a city of 31,000 inhabitants. The hurricane destroyed 40 percent of the city's buildings and heavily damaged 30 percent more. It also devastated Stann Creek, a city of 7,000 people about 33 miles south of Belize, and swamped offshore keys. Hurricane Hattie left 250 people dead, 15,000 homeless, and $150 million in property damage. Sir Colin Thornley, the colonial governor of British Honduras, declared an emergency and appealed for international aid.

Hurricane Hattie practically destroyed Belize's airport, Stanley Field, flattening its control tower and several other buildings. To help put the airfield back into operation for the relief flights, the Eastern Transport Air Force (East Trpt AF) of MATS airlifted communications personnel and cargo for the Air Force Communications Command to British Honduras. On November 3, the 1607th Air Trpt Wg from Dover AFB, Delaware, flew two C–124 Globemasters with eight technicians and 32 tons of communications equipment from Tinker AFB, Oklahoma, to Stanley Field.

Stanley Field also needed fuel supplies for Navy and other helicopters conducting relief operations in British Honduras. Between November 6 and 14, six East Trpt AF C–124s carried 60 tons of aviation fuel from Charleston AFB, South Carolina, to Stanley Field. The planes came from the 63d Trp Carr Wg at Donaldson AFB, South Carolina; the 1607th Air Trpt Wg at Dover AFB; and the 1608th Air Trpt Wg at Charleston AFB.

Mayor Robert King High of Miami asked the people of his city to collect food, clothing, and medicine for the people of British Honduras; and, in early November, six tons of cargo were collected. The 76th Trp Carr Sq at nearby Homestead AFB carried the supplies to Belize aboard a C–119 Flying Boxcar piloted by AF Res Capt. James W. Kehoe.

The Air Force airlift complemented Navy relief operations in the disaster area. Aid from Central American republics and from other parts of the British Empire also helped British Honduras to recover from Hurricane Hattie. By the third week of November, conditions had visibly improved.

16.
Name: Colombian Flood and Famine.
Location: Republic of Colombia.
Date(s): August 20–28 and September 12–15, 1962.
Emergency: A broken dam flooded Florencia, Colombia, leaving 134 people dead or missing, 1,000 dead cattle, and tons of ruined rice. The next month, famine threatened Indians in northern Colombia.
Air Force Organization(s) Involved: Aerial Survey Team Number 2, 1370th Photo-Mapping Wing.
Airlifted: 88 tons of food and emergency supplies.
Aircraft Employed: RC–130 (two+).
Operations: On August 17, a dam burst on the Otequeza River above the city of Florencia, in the Andean mountain jungle, about 350 miles southwest of Bogotá in southwestern Colombia. A flash flood inundated the city, leaving 134 people dead or missing, 1,000 cattle dead, and tons of rice destroyed. The Colombian government and the U.S. embassy in Bogotá contacted the 1370th Photo-Mapping Wing's Aerial Survey Team Number 2, in Colombia conducting aerial photographic missions, to airlift food and other emergency supplies to Florencia.

Operating from Bogotá's El Dorado Airport, the team conducted seven RC–130 flights to the flood-stricken town, airlifting 70 tons of cargo between August 20 and 28. The mercy missions helped to save lives in Florencia and reinforced President Kennedy's efforts with the Peace Corps and the Alliance for Progress to strengthen relations with Colombia.

During the next month, President Guillermo León Valencia of Colombia sought U.S. assistance to fight famine among his country's Indian tribes as part of a campaign to win peasant support against bandits responsible for rural violence in economically distressed areas. That same month, a committee of the Alliance for Progress approved a Colombian government ten-year economic plan, preparing the way for increased U.S. aid in the form of food and Peace Corps volunteers.

Between September 12 and 15, the 1370th Photo-Mapping Wing's Aerial Survey Team Number 2 responded to a Colombian government request to airlift 18 tons of food packages supplied by the Committee for American Relief Everywhere (C.A.R.E.) from Bogotá to the northern Colombian coast. The team delivered the cargo in two flights to Riohacha, where trucks distributed the food.

17.
Name: Honduran Medical Airlift.
Location: Republic of Honduras.
Date(s): January 26–27, 1963.
Emergency: During 1961, 10,000 people flocked to a new medical clinic in the jungles of northwestern Honduras where there had not been a medical doctor in 35 years. Shortages of medical equipment and supplies forced the clinic director to request them from the United States.

Air Force Organization(s) Involved: 403d and 446th Trp Carr Wgs.
Airlifted: Nine tons of medical equipment and supplies.
Aircraft Employed: C–119 (four).
Operations: In 1961, Filipino missionary doctor Filemon Cabansag established a medical clinic in Cuyamel, a town of 3,000 inhabitants in a jungle area of northwestern Honduras where there had not been a medical doctor in 35 years. During its first year, the clinic attracted 10,000 patients from Cuyamel and the surrounding countryside.

Desperate to continue providing medical treatment in the poverty-stricken region, Dr. Cabansag left a doctor and nurse at the clinic while he traveled to the United States to collect medical supplies and equipment. In 1962, he was able to gather nine tons of medical goods—including hypodermic needles, medicine, vitamins, surgical instruments, a refrigerator, an operating table, and two generators—from Detroit and Houston, where he and his brother had received medical training. But Dr. Cabansag had no way to transport his medical cargo to Honduras.

In the fall of 1962, Maj. Sarkis Samarian of the 63d Trp Carr Sq near Detroit read a newspaper article about Dr. Cabansag's problem. Major Samarian suggested that his troop carrier wing, the 403d at Selfridge AFB, Michigan, airlift the medical equipment and supplies to Honduras on cargo aircraft that usually flew empty on AF Res training flights to Panama. Wing Commander Col. Gari F. King liked the idea, and passed the request to CONAC, U.S. Air Force headquarters, the Defense and State Departments, and the government of Honduras, all of which approved the proposal.

On January 26 and 27, 1963, the 403d Trp Carr Wg flew three C–119 Flying Boxcars, one each from the 63d Trp Carr Sq at Selfridge AFB, Michigan; the 64th Trp Carr Sq at O'Hare International Airport at Chicago; and the 65th Trp Carr Sq at Davis Field, Muskogee, Oklahoma. The planes carried eight tons of medical equipment and supplies from Detroit and Houston to Tegucigalpa, Honduras, where there was an airport able to handle the C–119s. The 446th Trp Carr Wg at Ellington AFB, Texas, carried another ton of medical goods from Houston to Tegucigalpa.

Trucks carried the nine tons of airlifted medical cargo from Tegucigalpa northwest to the Cuyamel clinic, where they helped Dr. Cabansag to continue providing emergency medical treatment for the people of northwestern Honduras.

18.
Name: Alazan Famine.
Location: Mexico.
Date(s): May 3, 1963.
Emergency: A prolonged drought and extreme heat wave ruined the crops around Alazan, Mexico.
Air Force Organization(s) Involved: 446th Trp Carr Wg and 923d Trp Carr Gp.

Humanitarian Airlift Operations

Airlifted: 17 tons of food and clothing.

Aircraft Employed: C–119 (three) and C–47 (one).

Operations: The spring brought drought and an extended heat wave to the northeastern Mexican community of Alazan in the state of Tamaulipas, ruining corn, bean, potato, and cotton crops upon which the people depended for food and clothing. By May, the population of about 750 were suffering from malnutrition and related diseases. Some ate their horses, donkeys, and mules after the animals died and starvation threatened. News of the plight of Alazan eventually reached Texas, and radio stations in Dallas, Fort Worth, and Houston appealed for food and clothing donations for the Alazan famine victims. Soon, 17 tons of relief supplies had been collected. Volunteers trucked the cargo to neighboring Air Force bases, where reserve units stood ready to airlift it to Mexico.

On May 3, the 446th Trp Carr Wg at Ellington AFB near Houston and the 923d Trp Carr Gp at Carswell AFB near Fort Worth used three C–119 Flying Boxcars and one C–47 Skytrain to carry the emergency cargo to Miller International Airport at McAllen, Texas, near the Mexican border. From there, the 17 tons of food and clothing were transported by trucks and helicopters to the Alazan area, about 40 miles south of the border. Following the airlift, Praxidis Balboa, the governor of Tamaulipas, and Samuel M. Pereyra, the Mexican consul at Fort Worth, thanked the Texas contributors and AF Res units for their generosity. Heavy rain came to the Alazan area the first week of May, ending the drought.

19.

Name: Parana Fires.

Location: Brazil.

Date(s): September 10–12, 1963.

Emergency: Fires consumed five million acres of forests in southern Brazil's state of Parana, killing 146 people, injuring 406, and leaving at least 1,500 homeless.

Air Force Organization(s) Involved: 345th Trp Carr Sq.

Airlifted: 50.2 tons of food, medicine, and tents; and firefighters and medical personnel.

Aircraft Employed: C–130 (one).

Operations: At the end of August, forest fires, sparked by a seven-month drought, broke out in the state of Parana in southern Brazil southwest of São Paulo. In September, the fires consumed five million acres of trees, including huge reserves for Brazil's paper industry. Destruction ravaged 22 municipalities, including Ipiranga, Curiuva, and Natingui. Eventually the conflagrations killed or injured 552 people, left at least 1,500 homeless, and destroyed $80 million worth of property.

On September 6, Governor Ney Braga of Parana, working with President Joao Goulart of Brazil, requested U.S. aid for the fire victims. U.S. officials in Brazil, including Consul Arthur Feldman at Curitiba, Parana's capital, and

Leonard Wolff, director of the U.S. Food for Peace mission in Brazil, organized a relief effort.

The 345th Trp Carr Sq of the 516th Trp Carr Wg at Dyess AFB, Texas, flew a C–130 Hercules cargo aircraft in Brazil on a routine supply mission to Rio de Janeiro. Between September 10 and 12, Lt. Col. Raymond C. Carleton and his crew flew three trips southwest from Rio to Curitiba and Londrina to deliver 50 tons of food, medicine, and tents, together with firefighters, doctors, and nurses. The mission reinforced President Kennedy's Alliance for Progress and his efforts to bolster the relationship between the United States and Brazil. On September 23, spring rains came to southern Brazil, helping to extinguish the enormous Parana fires.

20.
Name: Hurricane Flora.
Location: Tobago Island, Trinidad and Tobago.
Date(s): October 9, 1963.
Emergency: Hurricane Flora hit Tobago with 110 mph winds, leaving 36 people dead and 17,000 homeless.
Air Force Organization(s) Involved: 3d Air Trpt Sq.
Airlifted: 385 tents and cots.
Aircraft Employed: C–124 (one).
Operations: About noon on September 30, Hurricane Flora hit the island of Tobago just northeast of Trinidad off the northern coast of South America. Winds of 110 mph, high tides, and heavy rain killed 36 people. A major hurricane had not hit Tobago in 30 years, and many of the island's buildings were not constructed to survive high winds. Hurricane Flora damaged or destroyed 90 percent of the dwellings, leaving 17,000 people homeless. The government of Trinidad and Tobago, which had gained independence from Britain the previous year, appealed for international relief. The State Department arranged to airlift relief supplies through DoD.

On October 9, 1st Lt. James P. White and his crew from the 3d Air Trpt Sq of the 1608th Air Trpt Wg at Charleston AFB, South Carolina, flew a C–124 Globemaster cargo aircraft to Tobago. The plane carried 385 tents and cots to provide shelter and bedding for hurricane survivors.

After striking Tobago, Hurricane Flora also devastated Haiti and Cuba. Haiti accepted U.S. aid, which the Navy helped to deliver, but Cuba's Fidel Castro refused all offers of direct aid from the United States and the American Red Cross.

21.
Name: Panama Canal Zone Evacuation.
Location: Canal Zone, Republic of Panama.
Date(s): January 14–February 9, 1964.

Humanitarian Airlift Operations

Emergency: Rioting in Panama endangered the lives of U.S. citizens in the Canal Zone, and many sought to return to the United States for safety.
Air Force Organization(s) Involved: 1608th and 1611th Air Trpt Wgs.
Airlifted: 1,535 passengers.
Aircraft Employed: C–118 (10).
Operations: On January 9, U.S. students at Balboa High School in the Canal Zone raised only the U.S. flag, despite an agreement between the United States and Panama that flags of both nations would fly together if any flags were flown. When Panamanians marching to the school to raise the Panamanian flag were turned away, violence erupted. Riots left 25 people dead and 350 injured. President Roberto Chiari of Panama severed relations with the United States.

Families of U.S. personnel working in the Canal Zone fled to U.S. bases for safety, overcrowding available housing. Many dependents wanted to return to the United States, and the State and Defense Departments arranged for an airlift. Between January 14 and February 9, the East Trpt AF of MATS airlifted 1,535 U.S. nationals—660 adults and 875 children—from Howard AFB in the Canal Zone to Charleston AFB, South Carolina, and Andrews AFB, Maryland. They flew aboard 10 C–118 Liftmasters on 25 missions operated by the 1608th Air Trpt Wg at Charleston AFB and the 1611th Air Trpt Wg at McGuire AFB, New Jersey. About half of the evacuees were children under the age of six. Many fled in haste, leaving most of their belongings in Panama, including winter clothing. Volunteers at Charleston and Andrews AFBs arranged for clothing donations and temporary billeting until the refugees could find homes or return to Panama.

On April 3, the United States and Panama, prodded by the Organization of American States, agreed to resume diplomatic relations and exchange special ambassadors to discuss the conflict, including clauses of the 1903 Panama Canal Treaty. As the dual flag policy returned, the Canal Zone gradually became safe again for U.S. families.

22.
Name: Bahia Flood.
Location: Brazil.
Date(s): January 23 and February 4, 1964.
Emergency: Flooding of the São Francisco and the Jequitinhonha Rivers in eastern Brazil killed 100 people and left 100,000 homeless.
Air Force Organization(s) Involved: 1608th Air Trpt Wg.
Airlifted: 120 tons of food and medical supplies.
Aircraft Employed: C–124 (two).
Operations: During January, torrential rain flooded the Jequitinhonha and São Francisco River valleys of the states of Minas Gerais and Bahia in eastern Brazil. The floods killed 100 people and left 100,000 homeless. Governor Francisco Lomanto, Jr., of Bahia appealed to the United States for food and medicine.

On January 23, the East Trpt AF of MATS diverted a C–124 Globemaster from the 1608th Air Trpt Wg at Charleston AFB, South Carolina, from a routine mission to Rio de Janeiro for use in an emergency airlift to Bahia. The cargo plane flew to Recife on the coast of Brazil, where Brazilian air force personnel helped to load it with food and medical supplies destined for Salvador, capital of Bahia, about 430 miles southwest of Recife. The airplane carried about 100 tons of cargo from Recife to Salvador on three flights. Local religious organizations at Salvador helped to distribute the medical supplies and food, which included corn meal and butter oil.

Another 1608th Air Trpt Wg C–124 carried 20 tons of foodstuffs from Recife to Salvador on February 4. The two Air Force Globemasters provided Brazil with emergency assistance while giving aircrews valuable experience.

23.
Name: Costa Rican Volcano.
Location: Republic of Costa Rica.
Date(s): January 2–9 and May 22–June 5, 1964.
Emergency: A volcano erupted about 30 miles east of San José, Costa Rica. Over the next 15 months, it dumped tons of ash on the city and surrounding country-side.
Air Force Organization(s) Involved: 1607th Air Trpt Wg, 63d Trp Carr Wg, and West Trpt AF.
Airlifted: 289 tons of street sweepers and heavy construction equipment, including trucks, vans, air compressors, stone grapplers, and rock crushers; and 33 U.S. Navy Seabees.
Aircraft Employed: C–133 (nine) and C–124 (three).
Operations: On March 13, 1963, Mount Irazu—an 11,260-foot volcano about 30 miles east of San José, capital of Costa Rica—erupted. Daily eruptions followed for 15 months, but instead of liquid lava flowing down the slopes of the mountain, clouds of blue-black ash rained over a 250-square-mile area, which included San José and its 230,000 inhabitants. By October 1963, 2,000 cattle had died in the vicinity of the volcano. By January 1964, more than 50,000 tons of dust and ash had fallen over the capital.

Costa Rican businessmen purchased three six-ton U.S. street sweepers to clean the streets of San José. President Francisco Orlich of Costa Rica requested U.S. aid to airlift them. Between January 2 and 9, the 1607th Air Trpt Wg from Dover AFB, Delaware, flew three street sweepers from Ontario National Airport near Los Angeles via Kelly AFB, Texas, to El Coco Airport in San José. One C–133 Cargomaster carried 18 tons of equipment.

Mount Irazu continued to erupt during the first half of 1964, dropping 100,000 tons of ash on San José by June and causing $20 million in damage. Ash began to clog the Reventado River at the base of the volcano, threatening to flood the region as the rainy summer season approached. On May 14, Costa Rica and the Agency for International Development (AID) agreed to a flood control project on the Reventado River drainage basin, to be financed in part by a $2 million grant from the Alliance for Progress. The project called for Navy personnel and construction equipment, which MATS agreed to airlift to Costa Rica.

Between May 22 and June 5, the 1607th Air Trpt Wg at Dover AFB, Delaware, and the 63d Trp Carr Wg at Hunter AFB, Georgia, flew two C–133 Cargomasters and three C–124 Globemasters from Quonset Point NAS, Rhode Island, via Brookley AFB, Alabama, to El Coco Airport. Meanwhile, six West Trpt AF C–133s, probably of the 1501st Air Trpt Wg at Travis AFB, California, carried Navy personnel and equipment from the Naval Construction Battalion Center at Gulfport, Mississippi, to San José. The 11 cargo planes carried 271 tons of heavy construction equipment—including dump trucks, vans, air compressors, stone grapplers, and rock crushers—and 33 U.S. Navy Seabees to Costa Rica. The project helped to prevent flooding in the Reventado River valley as the clouds of ash from Costa Rica's Mount Irazu slowly diminished.

24.
Name: Nicaraguan Medical Airlift.
Location: Republic of Nicaragua.
Date(s): February 12–13, 1964.
Emergency: St. Luke's Clinic at Managua, Nicaragua, appealed for medical supplies to continue providing free medical treatment for the needy.
Air Force Organization(s) Involved: 516th Trp Carr Wg and USAF Southern Command (USAF South Comd).
Airlifted: 800 pounds of pharmaceutical and first aid supplies.
Aircraft Employed: C–130 (one).
Operations: Early in 1964, St. Luke's Clinic, the only free medical facility in Managua, capital of Nicaragua, appealed to the United States for donations of medical supplies. Lt. Harold Conway of the 516th Trp Carr Wg at Dyess AFB near Abilene, Texas, became aware of the clinic's need through his church and worked to collect supplies and airlift them to Managua. Doctors, hospitals, and pharmacies in Abilene contributed 800 pounds of drugs, pharmaceutical items, and first aid supplies. The Defense Department, the State Department, and the government of Nicaragua approved an airlift to Nicaragua.

On February 12, a 516th Trp Carr Wg C–130 Hercules cargo aircraft from Dyess AFB carried the medical supplies from Abilene to Howard AFB in the Panama Canal Zone, where they were transferred to a USAF South Comd aircraft.

The airlift helped to save the lives and health of many Nicaraguans, supported the U.S. policy of assistance to Latin America, and provided experience for aircrews.

25.
Name: Panamanian Forest Fires.
Location: Panama.
Date(s): April 4, 1964.
Emergency: Forest fires swept through the mountains of western Panama.
Air Force Organization(s) Involved: USAF South Comd.
Airlifted: Three tons of borax.
Aircraft Employed: C–118 (one).
Operations: Diplomatic relations between the United States and Panama—which had been broken on January 17 during a controversy over which flag or flags should fly over the Canal Zone (see Panama Canal Zone Evacuation, January 1964)—were restored on April 4 through the mediation of the Organization of American States. By then, extensive forest fires were sweeping across dense tropical forests in western Panama near the town of David. The same day, President Roberto F. Chiari of Panama asked the U.S. consulate in Panama (city) to airlift fire-retardant chemicals from the Canal Zone to the David area.

That same day, the USAF South Comd dispatched a C–118 Liftmaster to carry three tons of borax from Howard AFB in the Panama Canal Zone to David. Panamanian firefighters used the chemical to contain the fires, which threatened timber and other agricultural resources. The small but rapid airlift reinforced restored relations between the United States and Panama.

26.
Name: Bolivian Epidemic.
Location: Republic of Bolivia.
Date(s): June–July 1964.
Emergency: In 1959, a hemorrhagic fever epidemic struck Bolivia; by June 1964 it had infected 1,100 people, a quarter of whom died.
Air Force Organization(s) Involved: USAF South Comd.
Airlifted: Medical supplies and personnel.
Aircraft Employed: C–46 (two), C–130 (one), and U–10 (one).
Operations: During 1959, a mysterious disease called hemorrhagic fever, or black typhus, struck the Beni department of central Bolivia. It quickly became an epidemic, infecting 30 new victims each month. By 1964, the hemorrhagic fever epidemic had depopulated several farm villages in the San Joaquín area of Bolivia. Orobayaya was abandoned completely, and San Joaquín's population fell from 2,000 to 900. More than 1,100 people eventually contracted the disease, and a fourth of them died.

By June 1964, doctors had discovered that a mouse-like rodent called the *laucha* carried the virus to humans. That month they launched a campaign in cooperation with the Bolivian government to exterminate *lauchas* in Bolivian dwellings. During the same month, the 605th Air Commando Squadron (Air Comdo Sq) airlifted medical teams from the Panama Canal Zone to Bolivia aboard C–46 aircraft to help in the eradication campaign. During June and July, the squadron flew C–46s to carry medical supplies from Bolivia's administrative capital, La Paz, to San Joaquín.

A USAF South Comd C–130 carried a smaller U–10 plane from La Paz to Santa Cruz, Bolivia, from which the smaller aircraft flew aerial photographic missions to assist in determining the habitat limits of the *lauchas*. Reduction of the rodent population in rural Bolivian residences sharply reduced the spread of hemorrhagic fever, and no new cases were reported after June 28. On July 25, Bolivia dedicated a new hospital in San Joaquín named after American Dr. Henry H. Beye, who died of hemorrhagic fever while researching the disease in Bolivia.

27.
Name: Hurricane Cleo.
Location: West Indies.
Date(s): August 26–27, 1964.
Emergency: Hurricane Cleo hit Guadeloupe, leaving 14 people dead, 100 injured, and $50 million in property damage.
Air Force Organization(s) Involved: 1607th Air Trpt Wg (Heavy).
Airlifted: 7.5 tons of blankets, clothing, and relief supplies.
Aircraft Employed: C–124 (one).
Operations: On August 22, Hurricane Cleo struck Guadeloupe in the Leeward Islands of the West Indies with winds as high as 115 mph. The island group suffered 14 people dead, 100 injured, and $50 million in property damage. Many of the 283,000 residents were left without shelter. Guadeloupe accepted a State Department offer of assistance, and DoD assigned an airlift relief mission to the Military Air Transport Service's East Trpt AF.

On August 26 and 27, the 1607th Air Trpt Wg at Dover AFB, Delaware, flew a C–124 Globemaster laden with 7.5 tons of blankets, clothing, and other relief supplies from New York NAS via Ramey AFB, Puerto Rico, to Guadeloupe. Capt. Robert H. Furr piloted the cargo plane, assisted by five crew members from the 20th and 31st Air Trpt Sqs.

After striking Guadeloupe, Hurricane Cleo went on to hit Haiti, Cuba, and Florida. The Navy responded by ship to Haitian requests for aid during the Guadeloupe airlift.

28.
Name: Bocas del Toro Storm.
Location: Republic of Panama.
Date(s): September 14–15, 1964.
Emergency: A storm with near hurricane-force winds and heavy rain destroyed much of the town of Bocas del Toro on the island of Colón.
Air Force Organization(s) Involved: USAF South Comd.
Airlifted: 1,000 rations, 500 cots and blankets, 200 pounds of medical supplies,

communications equipment, two portable electrical generators, medical person-nel, and patients.

Aircraft Employed: C–47 (two+) and U–10 (two+).

Operations: About midnight, September 13–14, a sudden storm struck Bocas del Toro, a town of 10,000 inhabitants on the island of Colón off the northwest coast of Panama. Winds approaching hurricane force and torrential rain destroyed near-ly eight city blocks, killing one person, injuring at least eight, and leaving 400 homeless. The storm ruined stocks of food and medical supplies and cut commu-nications between the island and the mainland of Panama. The U.S. ambassador in Panama, Jack H. Vaughn, asked the USAF South Comd in the Canal Zone to send a disaster survey team to Bocas del Toro to assess the damage for relief mis-sions.

On September 14, the 605th Air Comdo Sq flew a medical team—led by Maj. Lester H. Keyes, flight surgeon from the 5700th Air Force Dispensary at Albrook AFB in the Canal Zone—and a disaster survey team from Howard AFB to Bocas del Toro. By the afternoon of September 15, the USAF South Comd had conducted nine C–47 and U–10 aircraft flights from the Canal Zone to Bocas del Toro, transporting 1,000 rations, 500 cots and blankets, two portable electrical generators, 200 pounds of medical supplies, and miscellaneous communications equipment. On September 14 and 15, a C–47 circled over Bocas del Toro to pro-vide a radio link between the island and the mainland. The 605th Air Comdo Sq transported injured storm victims to medical facilities in other parts of Panama.

29.

Name: Central Chilean Earthquake.

Location: Republic of Chile.

Date(s): April 2–13, 1965.

Emergency: An earthquake measuring at least 6.5 on the Richter scale struck central Chile. It left 400 people dead and 250,000 homeless and caused $200 mil-lion in damage.

Air Force Organization(s) Involved: 463d Trp Carr Wg and USAF South Comd.

Airlifted: 55 tons of food, tents, medicine, and clothing.

Aircraft Employed: C–130 (four).

Operations: Just after noon on Sunday, March 28, a powerful 90-second earth-quake registering between 6.5 and 7.5 on the Richter scale struck the Santiago, Valparaiso, and Coquimbo provinces of central Chile. Although the epicenter was about 80 miles north of the Chilean capital of Santiago, the quake was felt as far away as Buenos Aires, about 700 miles distant. Between March 28 and 29, 14 major aftershocks shook the Aconcagua Valley.

In Valparaiso, Chile's second largest city, with 300,000 residents, the earth-quake damaged or destroyed 40 percent of the private dwellings. In the town of Llay-Llay, 8,000 people fled their homes to camp in the safer outdoors. At Los

Andes and San Felipe, 80 to 90 percent of homes were destroyed. Mudslides triggered by the tremors killed 300 people in the mining community of El Cobre, about 100 miles north of Santiago. The earthquake killed 400 people, rendered 250,000 homeless, and destroyed $200 million in property.

On April 1, President Johnson approved an aid request from President Eduardo Frei Montalva of Chile, who identified the most urgent needs to the U.S. ambassador, Ralph A. Dungan. On April 2, C–130s belonging to the 463d Trp Carr Wg of Langley AFB, Virginia, on rotational duty with the USAF South Comd at Howard AFB in the Panama Canal Zone, began to airlift relief supplies to Santiago.

Between April 2 and 13, four C–130 Hercules airplanes transported 55 tons of food, tents, medicine, and clothing to Chile. Some cargo was collected at McGuire AFB, New Jersey, from donors in New York and Pennsylvania. The Air Force planes carried a fraction of the relief supplies that poured into Chile from governments and private charities around the world.

30.
Name: El Salvadoran Earthquake.
Location: Republic of El Salvador.
Date(s): May 5–13, 1965.
Emergency: A severe earthquake registering 7.5 on the Richter scale struck El Salvador, killing 125 people, injuring 500, and leaving 7,000 homeless.
Air Force Organization(s) Involved: USAF South Comd, 1608th and 1611th Air Trpt Wgs, 463d Trp Carr Wg, 5700th AB Wg, 29th Trp Carr Sq, and 605th Air Comdo Sq.
Airlifted: 312 tons of bedding, food, medical supplies, tents, and shelters; and at least 207 medical and logistical support personnel.
Aircraft Employed: C–130 (five), C–124 (four), C–118 (two), C–135 (one), C–54 (one), C–46 (one), and C–47 (one).
Operations: Before dawn on May 3, a severe earthquake registering 7.5 on the Richter scale struck central El Salvador. Centered about 10 miles southeast of the capital of San Salvador, the quake killed 125 people, injured 500, and left 7,000 homeless. The government of President Julio Adalberto Rivera requested help from the United States. On May 4, President Johnson announced plans to deliver blankets, cots, emergency rations, vaccine, and field kitchens to El Salvador.

Between May 5 and 13, elements of the 29th Trp Carr Sq of the 313th Trp Carr Wg at Forbes AFB, Kansas, and the 463d Trp Carr Wg from Langley AFB, Virginia—on rotational duty with the USAF South Comd at Howard AFB in the Panama Canal Zone—carried 257 tons of bedding, medical supplies, and food to Ilopango Airport near San Salvador. They flew five C–130 Hercules aircraft on 43 missions, each flight covering a one-way distance of 700 miles. The C–130s also carried 207 medical and logistical support personnel from Army Forces, Southern Command, who set up refugee camps with field kitchens and medical inoculation facilities.

The USAF South Comd also used C–54, C–46, and C–47 aircraft from the 5700th AB Wg and the 605th Air Comdo Sq to airlift medical supplies and support personnel from Howard AFB and Albrook AFB in the Canal Zone to El Salvador.

The East Trpt AF of MATS also airlifted relief supplies to El Salvador between May 5 and 13. Two C–118s, four C–124s, and one C–135 belonging to the 1608th Air Trpt Wg at Charleston AFB, South Carolina, and the 1611th Air Trpt Wg at McGuire AFB, New Jersey, carried 55 tons of medical supplies and shelters from Gulfport, Mississippi; Olmsted AFB, Pennsylvania; and Norfolk, Virginia, to San Salvador via Howard AFB. The cargo included 100 Lister bags, medicine, 60 tents, and four Quonset huts weighing 9.5 tons each.

The 15 cargo planes involved in the airlift carried 312 tons of bedding, food, medical supplies, and shelters from the Canal Zone and the United States to El Salvador in nine days.

31.
Name: Honduran Flood.
Location: Republic of Honduras.
Date(s): September 28, 1965.
Emergency: A flood struck southern Honduras.
Air Force Organization(s) Involved: USAF South Comd and 317th Trp Carr Wg (Medium).
Airlifted: 25 tons of relief supplies.
Aircraft Employed: C–130 (two).
Operations: On September 28, a flood in southern Honduras led the government of President Lopez Arellano to request relief from the United States. Within 12 hours, two C–130s from the 317th Trp Carr Wg (Medium), on rotational duty with the USAF South Comd at Howard AFB in the Panama Canal Zone, airlifted 25 tons of relief supplies to Honduras.

32.
Name: Hurricane Inez.
Location: Dominican Republic.
Date(s): October 10–12, 1966.
Emergency: Hurricane Inez hit the Dominican Republic with 150 mph winds, leaving 200 people dead, 1,000 injured, and 5,000 homeless.
Air Force Organization(s) Involved: USAF South Comd, 317th Trp Carr Wg, and 31st Mil Alft Sq.
Airlifted: 247 tents, 32 tons of rice, blood plasma, and tetanus serum.
Aircraft Employed: C–130 (two) and C–124 (one).
Operations: On Thursday, September 29, Hurricane Inez hit the southern Dominican Republic with 150 mph winds. The storm's powerful gusts, torrential rain, and high tides left about 200 people dead, 1,000 injured, 5,000 homeless, and

$10 million in property losses. The small town of Barahona, with 20,000 people, about 100 miles west of Santo Domingo, suffered extreme damage. The president of the Dominican Republic, Joaquín Belaguer, appealed to the U.S. embassy in Santo Domingo for assistance.

On October 2, the Navy aircraft carrier *Boxer* arrived off the southern coast of the Dominican Republic to fly relief and rescue missions with eight helicopters. The U.S. embassy requested Air Force flights to supplement the naval operations. On October 10, the 31st Mil Alft Sq of the 436th Mil Alft Wg at Dover AFB, Delaware, flew a C–124 Globemaster airplane with 247 tents from Knoxville, Tennessee, to San Isidro Air Base in the Dominican Republic. That same day, a 317th Trp Carr Wg C–130 Hercules aircraft and crew, on rotational duty with the USAF South Comd at Howard AFB in the Panama Canal Zone, flew blood plasma and tetanus serum to Barahona.

Two days later, on October 12, another 317th Trp Carr Wg C–130, under operational control of the USAF South Comd, airlifted 32 tons of rice from Venezuela to the Dominican Republic. The airlifted tents, medicine, and food helped hurricane victims to survive while reconstruction proceeded.

33.
Name: Bold Party.
Location: Mexico.
Date(s): October 14–18, 1966.
Emergency: Hurricane Inez hit northeast Mexico with 135 mph winds and torrential rain, causing extensive flooding in the Tampico area and leaving 251 persons dead and 30,000 homeless.
Air Force Organization(s) Involved: 313th and 516th Trp Carr Wgs.
Airlifted: Unknown quantities of medical supplies, two radio jeeps, fuel bladders, 12 support personnel, and flood victims.
Aircraft Employed: C–130 (two).
Operations: Hurricane Inez, which hit the Dominican Republic in late September (see Hurricane Inez, October 10–12, 1966), moved west over Cuba and into the Gulf of Mexico, where it regenerated in early October. On October 10, it struck northeast Mexico just north of Tampico. Hurricane Inez's 135 mph winds and torrential rains devastated the towns of Manuel, Gonzalez, Aldama, Soto la Marina, Altamira, Ciudad Mante, and Tampico, killing 251 people. Floods left 30,000 homeless as the storm blew itself out over the Sierra Madre Oriental.

The Mexican government accepted U.S. aid, and the United States Strike Command organized a joint task force called Bold Party, composed of elements from all military branches, to conduct relief operations. The Tactical Air Command's 833d Air Div deployed two C–130 Hercules aircraft to support Bold Party.

On October 14, the 313th Trp Carr Wg at Forbes AFB, Kansas, flew one C–130 laden with medical supplies to Tampico. Between October 14 and 18, the cargo plane ferried relief supplies between southern Texas and Tampico and helped to evacuate Mexican refugees from areas isolated by flooding. The 516th Trp Carr Wg at Dyess AFB, Texas, flew another C–130 in support of Bold Party. Between October 14 and 15, the plane carried two radio jeeps, fuel bladders, and 12 support personnel from MacDill AFB, Florida, and Fort Sill, Oklahoma, to Rio Grande Valley International Airport near Harlingen, Texas.

The Bold Party task force flew Army, Navy, Marine Corps, and Air Force aircraft—including cargo planes and helicopters—to airlift 69 tons of food, clothes, blankets, and medical supplies to Tampico and to evacuate 80 flood refugees. Governor Praxedis Balboa of the state of Tamaulipas in northeastern Mexico and Mexican Maj. Gen. Manuel Gómez Ecuevas subsequently expressed their appreciation to the U.S. Strike Command and its elements for their efforts on behalf of the hurricane victims.

34.
Name: Peruvian Earthquake.
Location: Republic of Peru.
Date(s): October 20–21, 1966.
Emergency: An earthquake registering 7.7 to 8.0 on the Richter scale—centered about 150 miles west of Peru on the Pacific Ocean floor—devastated coastal cities, killing 188 people, injuring up to 3,000, and leaving thousands without shelter.
Air Force Organization(s) Involved: USAF South Comd and 317th Trp Carr Wg.
Airlifted: 55 tons of blankets, tents, cots, and other relief supplies.
Aircraft Employed: C–130 (four).
Operations: Late in the afternoon of October 17, a tremendous earthquake registering between 7.7 and 8.0 on the Richter scale struck the eastern Pacific Ocean floor about 150 miles west of Lima, Peru. It was the most intense earthquake since the Alaska earthquake of March 1964 (see Chapter 1, Operation Helping Hand, March–April 1964). The 38-second tremor devastated Lima, Callao, Chorillos, Miraflores, Huacho, Barranco, and other coastal Peruvian cities and towns. Collapsed buildings buried 188 people, injured between 1,500 and 3,000, and left thousands homeless. President Fernando Belaunde Terry of Peru asked the United States for assistance.

Responding to a request from the State Department, the Joint Chiefs of Staff (JCS) directed the United States Southern Command (U.S. South Comd) to airlift Army relief supplies from Panama to Peru aboard Air Force aircraft. On October 20 and 21, four C–130 Hercules aircraft and crews from the 317th Trp Carr Wg at Lockbourne AFB, Ohio, on rotation with the USAF South Comd in the Panama Canal Zone, flew 55 tons of relief supplies from Howard AFB in the Canal Zone to Lima. The cargo included 56 medium tents, 3,000 blankets, and 920 cots. The supplies enabled Peruvian officials to erect temporary shelters while rebuilding efforts were underway.

Humanitarian Airlift Operations

35.
Name: Quibdó Fire.
Location: Republic of Colombia.
Date(s): October 27, 1966.
Emergency: A fire destroyed half of the city of Quibdó, Colombia, leaving 15,000 people homeless.
Air Force Organization(s) Involved: 605th Air Comdo Sq.
Airlifted: 20 tons of food, medical supplies, and eating utensils.
Aircraft Employed: C–47 (eight).
Operations: A fire destroyed half of Quibdó, Colombia, on the night of October 26. Flames consumed 90 percent of the city's businesses and left 15,000 of 80,000 residents homeless. Thirty city blocks burned, including municipal offices, the courthouse, and communications centers. Property losses totaled $10 million.

On October 27, at the request of Reynold E. Carlson, U.S. ambassador to Colombia, the JCS directed the U.S. South Comd to furnish a relief airlift to Colombia. The USAF Southern Command's 605th Air Comdo Sq at Albrook AFB in the Canal Zone flew eight C–47 aircraft laden with 20 tons of food, medical supplies, and eating utensils from Panama to Quibdó that same day. Army Forces, Southern Command, provided the relief supplies. Short runways at Quibdó required use of C–47s rather than the larger cargo planes normally used for airlifts of such magnitude. The operation helped the Colombian government to assist victims while Quibdó was rebuilt.

36.
Name: Panamanian Flood.
Location: Republic of Panama.
Date(s): November 4–6, 1966.
Emergency: Torrential rain flooded the Pacora and Chepo areas of Panama, killing 30 people and leaving more than 800 homeless.
Air Force Organization(s) Involved: USAF South Comd, 5700th AB Wg, and 605th Air Comdo Sq.
Airlifted: Three tons of food, clothing, and medicine; and 105 refugees.
Aircraft Employed: H–19 (two) and U–10 (one).
Operations: On November 3 and 4, torrential rain descended on the wooded mountains of eastern Panama, flooding the Bayano and Pacora River valleys. Rushing waters killed at least 30 people and left more than 800 homeless. In the Pacora and Chepo areas east of the city of Panama, swollen streams washed away houses and drowned hundreds of animals. The president of Panama, Marco A. Robles, requested help from U.S. military units in the Canal Zone while the roads were inundated.

The USAF South Comd conducted rescue and relief operations. Two H–19 helicopters from the 5700th AB Wg at Albrook AFB in the Canal Zone flew more than 50 sorties to carry refugees or shuttle relief supplies from the zone to various parts of Panama east of the canal. A 605th Air Comdo Sq U–10 airplane flew similar missions from Howard AFB in the Canal Zone.

The three aircraft evacuated 105 flood victims and transported more than three tons of food, clothing, and medicine to a relief center in Pacora. When U.S. emergency relief airlift missions entered their third day on November 6, the floodwaters had receded, allowing surface transportation routes to reopen.

37.
Name: Venezuelan Earthquake.
Location: Republic of Venezuela.
Date(s): July 31 and August 4, 1967.
Emergency: An earthquake struck the Caracas area of Venezuela, killing 277 people, injuring 2,000, and leaving 110,000 homeless.
Air Force Organization(s) Involved: USAF South Comd, 47th Tac Alft Sq, and 156th Tac Ftr Gp.
Airlifted: 30 tons of food, medical supplies, clothing, and bedding.
Aircraft Employed: C–130 (one) and C–54 (one).
Operations: On the night of July 29, a major earthquake registering 6.0 on the Richter scale rocked the Caracas area of northern Venezuela. In the Altamira district of eastern Caracas, five high-rise apartment buildings collapsed. Other cities and towns suffering earthquake damage included San Cristóbal, Naiquata, Los Teques, La Guaira, Macuto, Maracay, and Caraballeda. The earthquake left 277 people dead, 2,000 injured, and 110,000 homeless. Property damage totaled $15 million in Caracas alone. President Raul Leoni of Venezuela appealed to the United States for emergency relief.

On July 31, the 47th Tac Alft Sq of the 313th Tac Alft Wg at Forbes AFB, Kansas—serving on rotation with the USAF South Comd—flew a C–130 Hercules aircraft with five tons of medical supplies, bedding, and food, from Howard AFB in the Panama Canal Zone to Caracas. On August 4, the 156th Tac Ftr Gp—an ANG organization stationed in Puerto Rico—flew four C–54 missions to Venezuela to deliver 25 tons of clothing, food, and medicine, including 1,000 gallons of medicinal alcohol. The 30 tons of airlifted relief supplies helped to sustain earthquake survivors while they struggled to rebuild their homes.

38.
Name: Bonny Date.
Location: Mexico.
Date(s): September 29–October 7, 1967.
Emergency: The remnants of Hurricane Beulah produced torrential rain that flooded large sections of Mexico.
Air Force Organization(s) Involved: 516th Tac Alft Wg and 436th and 437th Mil Alft Wgs.
Airlifted: At least 116 tons of relief equipment and supplies, including six UH–1

helicopters, three jeeps and trailers, six 500-gallon fuel bladders, 20 tons of aviation fuel, and communications equipment; and 175 relief workers, including Army personnel to operate the helicopters, jeeps, and communications gear.

Aircraft Employed: C–130 (16), C–141 (2), C–133 (1), and KC–135 (1).

Operations: Hurricane Beulah, which hit southern Texas just north of Brownsville with winds up to 160 mph on September 19 (see Chapter 1, Hurricane Beulah, September–October 1967), generated torrential rain that flooded large parts of Mexico. After inundating portions of Camargo, Reynosa, and Matamoros in the lower Rio Grande valley, the remnants of Beulah moved south. Heavy rain produced floods in the state of Guerrero around the Pacific Ocean port of Acapulco. President Gustavo Díaz Ordaz of Mexico asked President Johnson for U.S. assistance in the flooded areas of northeastern and southwestern Mexico.

On September 28 and 29, the Military Airlift Command's Twenty-first Air Force employed two C–141 Starlifters and one C–133 Cargomaster to airlift six UH–1 helicopters, three jeeps and trailers, six fuel bladders, communications equipment, and 30 support personnel from Fort Campbell, Kentucky, and MacDill AFB, Florida, to Acapulco. The 436th Mil Alft Wg at Dover AFB, Delaware, flew a C–141 and a C–133 on September 28, while the 437th Mil Alft Wg from Charleston AFB, South Carolina, flew another C–141 on September 29. A KC–135 carried 20 tons of aviation fuel to Acapulco for the helicopters.

Between September 29 and October 7, the Tactical Air Command's 516th Tac Alft Wg at Dyess AFB near Abilene, Texas, flew 16 C–130s with 96 tons of relief equipment and supplies and 145 support personnel to Mexico via airfields at Harlingen, Texas, and Acapulco.

The cargo planes participated in relief flights to Mexico under the operation name "Bonny Date." A few weeks after the relief flights ended, President Díaz Ordaz visited President Johnson in Washington, D.C., and thanked him for the relief missions, which helped many of the 500,000 Mexican citizens affected by the flooding.

39.
Name: Savage Fly.
Location: Nicaragua, Costa Rica, and Panama.
Date(s): January 15–May 31, 1968.
Emergency: Mediterranean fruit flies (Medflies) infested citrus groves in Central America.
Air Force Organization(s) Involved: USAF South Comd, Special Air Warfare Center, 1st Air Commando Wing (Air Comdo Wg), and 605th Air Comdo Sq.
Airlifted: Over 600 million sterile Medflies.
Aircraft Employed: C–47, C–123, C–130, and CH–3 (numbers unknown).
Operations: By the late 1960s, the Mediterranean fruit fly had multiplied in Central America to the point that it threatened the citrus fruit industry, with annu-

al losses estimated at $17 million. In 1967, the International Regional Organization for Agricultural Health (Organismo International Regional de Sanidad Agropecuaria or OIRSA) and the International Atomic Energy Agency operated a laboratory at San José, Costa Rica, to produce millions of sterile Medflies to release to reduce fly reproduction. The laboratory operated with funding from the United Nations (UN).

In February 1967, the Nicaraguan air force began to dispense sterile flies in an infested area south of Managua, but the infestation continued and spread to Panama. In November 1967, the two research organizations requested U.S. Air Force assistance. In January 1968, the USAF launched Savage Fly, an operation to develop techniques and equipment to dispense sterile flies to combat pestilence.

The USAF South Comd worked with the Special Air Warfare Center on Savage Fly. Flying C–47, C–123, C–130, and CH–3 aircraft from Howard AFB in the Panama Canal Zone and eventually also from Managua, the 1st Air Comdo Wg and the 605th Air Comdo Sq picked up sterile flies from the laboratory in San José and dispensed them over infested areas south of Managua and in the Boquete area of western Panama. Air crew members released the flies at a rate of up to nine million per flight. The flies were loaded in sealed paper bags that ripped open as they left the planes through specially constructed chutes.

Operation Savage Fly continued from January 15 through May 1968. In less than five months, Air Force planes dispensed a total of 611 million sterile Medflies, 381 million of which were released in Nicaragua and almost 231 million in Panama. At first, the Air Force released the flies in grid patterns to cover all areas, but by March, Air Force pilots concentrated on more heavily infested valleys. At the end of May, a UN scientific research team evaluated the project. Although Savage Fly did not eliminate the Medfly from Central America (see Nicaraguan Medfly, April–May 1973), it reduced the pest's reproduction rate significantly and perfected methods for dispensing sterile flies against insect enemies such as the screwworm fly (see Coronet Roundup, June 1971–May 1975).

40.
Name: Bolivian Floods.
Location: Republic of Bolivia.
Date(s): February 26–29, 1968.
Emergency: Fifteen days of heavy rain flooded large areas in five Bolivian provinces, leaving eight people dead and 10,000 homeless.
Air Force Organization(s) Involved: USAF South Comd and 39th Tac Alft Sq.
Airlifted: 20 tons of tents, blankets, and medical supplies.
Aircraft Employed: C–130 (two).
Operations: During the second half of February, torrential rain generated floods in central Bolivia that killed eight people and left 10,000 homeless. On February 23, the Bolivian government declared a flood emergency in five provinces as the

cities of Santa Cruz, Cochabamba, Sucre, Ororu, and Potosi were inundated. The president of Bolivia, Rene Barrientos Ortuno, declared a national emergency and sought U.S. assistance.

Between February 26 and 29, the USAF South Comd flew 20 tons of tents, blankets, and medical supplies from Howard AFB in the Panama Canal Zone to the Bolivian cities of La Paz, Cochabamba, and Santa Cruz. The command employed C–130 Hercules aircraft and crews of the 39th Tac Alft Sq of the 317th Tac Alft Wg at Lockbourne AFB, Ohio, serving on rotational duty in Panama. The U.S. ambassador to Bolivia, Douglas Henderson, symbolically transferred the cargo to Gen. Alfredo Ovando, chief of the Bolivian armed forces, to distribute to flood victims.

41.
Name: Ecuadoran Drought.
Location: Republic of Ecuador.
Date(s): April 26–27, 1968.
Emergency: A drought parched the agricultural fields of southern Ecuador, threatening the people with starvation.
Air Force Organization(s) Involved: USAF South Comd and 47th Tac Alft Sq.
Airlifted: 46 tons of food.
Aircraft Employed: C–130 (one).
Operations: Drought ravaged the agricultural fields of southern Ecuador during the first part of 1968. Crop failures threatened local peasants with economic ruin, even starvation. At the end of April, President Otto Arosemena Gómez of Ecuador declared an emergency and requested U.S. assistance to airlift food from the port of Guayaquil to the crisis region.

On April 25, the 24th Air Comdo Wg at Howard AFB in the Panama Canal Zone assigned the airlift mission to the 47th Tac Alft Sq of the 313th Tac Alft Wg at Forbes AFB, Kansas, serving on rotational duty. On April 26 and 27, Lt. Col. Robert A. Morrison and an eight-man crew flew one C–130 with 46 tons of food from Guayaquil to La Toma, Ecuador, in a series of four sorties. Maj. Juan Riviera of the Ecuadoran air force accompanied the crew on the first two sorties to guide the C–130 into La Toma, a city surrounded by mountains 8,000 to 10,000 feet high. Trucks carried some of the food, which had been donated by AID, the Cooperative for American Remittances Everywhere (C.A.R.E.), and Ecuadoran welfare agencies, to Macara, Celica, Puyango, Calvas, and other drought-stricken villages.

On April 28, the C–130 and crew returned to Howard AFB, after delivering more food than originally requested by the Ecuadoran government.

42.
Name: Mount Arenal Eruption.
Location: Republic of Costa Rica.
Date(s): July 30–August 1, 1968.

Emergency: Mount Arenal, thought to be an extinct volcano, erupted violently, killing at least 78 people and driving 5,000 from their homes.
Air Force Organization(s) Involved: USAF South Comd and 47th Tac Alft Sq.
Airlifted: 12 tons of blankets, tents, cots, first aid kits, and other disaster relief supplies.
Aircraft Employed: UH–1 (two) and C–130 (one).
Operations: In the morning of July 29, Mount Arenal—a 5,000-foot volcano about 60 miles northwest of San José, Costa Rica—erupted explosively. More violent than the Irazu eruption of 1963–1964 (see Costa Rican Volcano, January and May–June 1964), Mount Arenal threw boulders as far as 30 miles, sent up huge clouds of smoke and noxious gases, and poured smoldering lava over fertile agricultural fields and pastures. Blowing away a large part of its flank, Arenal spewed dust and ash, which accumulated at depths of three feet on the ground. Heavy rain turned the ash to mud that choked roads as 5,000 refugees fled their homes. During the first four days, the volcano killed at least 78 people and left more than 100 missing.

On July 30, Costa Rica's ministry of security asked the USAF South Comd in the Panama Canal Zone to airlift refugees from Pueblo Nuevo and other communities in the volcano's shadow to a relief center 15 miles away. That same day, the 24th Special Operations Wing's 605th Sp Ops Sq flew two UH–1F helicopters with two paramedics and a flight controller from the Canal Zone to Costa Rica. Extensive smoke and ash halted the first evacuation mission, but the helicopters transported Costa Rican officials in two sorties around the disaster area to survey damages and make recovery plans.

On July 31, Costa Rica's president, José Joaquín Trejos Fernández, accepted an offer of further U.S. assistance from President Johnson. A C–130 Hercules cargo aircraft and crew from the 47th Tac Alft Sq of the 313th Tac Alft Wg at Forbes AFB, Kansas, serving rotational duty at Howard AFB, airlifted 12 tons of disaster relief supplies from a stockpile at Corozal, British Honduras, to San José on July 31 and August 1. The plane flew three sorties, transporting 1,500 blankets, 100 tents, 524 cots, and 100 first aid kits.

43.
Name: Nicaraguan Flood.
Location: Republic of Nicaragua.
Date(s): August 21–26, 1968.
Emergency: Torrential rain in north central Nicaragua caused a dam to overflow, flooding the areas of El Salto, Dos Bocas, and the Rosita Mining Camp.
Air Force Organization(s) Involved: USAF South Comd.
Airlifted: 30 parachutes, 26 tons of food and supplies, and 260 refugees.
Aircraft Employed: C–47 (one) and UH–1 (one).
Operations: In the middle of August, a hydroelectric dam in north central Nicaragua overflowed, flooding and isolating three communities and leaving 19

people missing and 2,000 homeless. After a week of struggling to drop food to flood victims by parachute and evacuate those isolated by the high water, Nicaragua requested U.S. assistance.

On August 21, the USAF South Comd flew one C–47 Skytrain airplane and one UH–1 helicopter from the Panama Canal Zone to Nicaragua. The C–47 carried 30 parachutes from an Army stockpile at Fort Kobbe in the Canal Zone to the Nicaraguan air force, which used them to drop 200-pound bundles of relief supplies to flood victims in the El Salto area. From August 21 to 26, the UH–1 flew 30 sorties, evacuating 260 people from El Salto and Dos Bocas to a refugee center at Siuna. The helicopter also delivered 26 tons of food and other relief supplies to those remaining at Dos Bocas and the Rosita Mining Camp.

44.
Name: Combat Mosquito.
Location: Republic of Ecuador.
Date(s): May 14–30, 1969.
Emergency: An encephalitis epidemic in western Ecuador infected 50,000 people and killed 500.
Air Force Organization(s) Involved: 438th Mil Alft Wg and 4500th AB Wg.
Airlifted: 54.4 tons of insecticide.
Aircraft Employed: C–141 (two) and UC–123 (two).
Operations: A major encephalitis epidemic struck western Ecuador during the first five months of 1969. Spread by mosquitoes that bred in coastal marshes, the disease affected 50,000 people. About 500 died, most of them children under the age of five. The Ecuadoran government requested U.S. assistance and, in May, the State and Defense Departments organized Operation Combat Mosquito, an airlift of insecticide to Ecuador.

Trucks took more than 50 tons of malathion insecticide from Wayne, New Jersey, where it was manufactured, to McGuire AFB, New Jersey, home of the 438th Mil Alft Wg. On May 15, and again on May 30, the wing flew a C–141 Starlifter airplane loaded with 90 55-gallon drums of insecticide to Guayaquil, Ecuador.

On May 14, the 4500th AB Wg at Langley AFB, Virginia, flew two UC–123 Provider aircraft to Guayaquil. Between May 15 and 30, the planes sprayed 250,000 acres of Ecuadoran coastal marshes with insecticide delivered by the 438th Mil Alft Wg. Lt. Col. Garrett S. Runey commanded the aerial spray flight, which killed 95 percent of the area's mosquitoes by the end of May. The massive extermination campaign helped to end Ecuador's encephalitis epidemic.

45.
Name: Honduran Refugees.
Location: Republic of Honduras.
Date(s): July 20–September 5, 1969.

Emergency: Heavy rains flooded the Chiquito and Grande Rivers of Honduras, killing at least 50 people and leaving thousands homeless. War broke out between Honduras and El Salvador, adding to the refugee problem.

Air Force Organization(s) Involved: 438th Mil Alft Wg, 118th Mil Alft Gp (ANG), and USAF South Comd.

Airlifted: 26 tons of relief equipment and supplies, including 22 tons of blankets and two UH–1H helicopters.

Aircraft Employed: C–141 (one), C–124 (one), and C–130 (number unknown).

Operations: During the middle of June, torrential rains flooded the Chiquito and Grande River valleys. At least 50 people died and thousands fled their homes. Flood refugees poured into Tegucigalpa, the Honduran capital. That same month, war broke out between Honduras and El Salvador, multiplying the number of displaced persons. After a cease-fire, AID sponsored a series of U.S. Air Force relief airlift missions in response to an appeal from the Honduran government.

On July 29, the 438th Mil Alft Wg of McGuire AFB, New Jersey, flew a C–141 Starlifter aircraft to transport 10 tons of blankets from Brunswick NAS, Maine, to La Mesa International Airport at San Pedro Sula, Honduras. The same C–141 carried 12 more tons of blankets from Maine to La Mesa on August 9.

The 118th Mil Alft Gp (ANG), based at Nashville, Tennessee, airlifted two UH–1H helicopters weighing four tons from Robert Gray Army Airfield, Texas, to Toncontin International Airport at Tegucigalpa on September 5. The group flew a C–124 Globemaster aircraft to ferry the helicopters, which were used to transport refugees and relief supplies within the flood-affected areas of Honduras.

Between July 20 and August 20, USAF South Comd C–130s also carried tents, blankets, cots, plates, mugs, and eating utensils from the Panama Canal Zone to Tegucigalpa. The Air Force carried more than 26 tons of relief cargo to Honduras between July 20 and September 5 for victims of the flooding and the war.

46.

Name: Hurricane Francelia.

Location: Republic of Guatemala.

Date(s): September 10–12, 1969.

Emergency: Hurricane Francelia dropped torrential rain over Guatemala, producing floods that killed 17 people, left 50 missing, and blocked roads.

Air Force Organization(s) Involved: 436th, 437th, and 438th Mil Alft Wgs.

Airlifted: 119.5 tons of rations, medical supplies, blankets, tents, and helicopters.

Aircraft Employed: C–141 (five) and C–133 (one).

Operations: Hurricane Francelia roared from the Gulf of Honduras into the southern coast of British Honduras with 110 mph winds and 10-foot tides on September 2. For the next four days, storm remnants hovered over central and southern Guatemala, dropping torrential rain. Flooding killed 17 people in the Antigua area, left 50 missing in the volcanic highlands, and cut off the roads connecting Guatemala City with its food sources. The Pan American Highway bridges over the Achiguate and Guacalate Rivers washed away. On September 9, the U.S. ambassador to Guatemala, Nathaniel Davis, requested an airlift of helicopters, food, medicine, and other relief supplies to Guatemala.

The Twenty-first Air Force provided relief flights on September 10 and 11. A 436th Mil Alft Wg C–133 Cargomaster aircraft from Dover AFB, Delaware, picked up four UH–1 Army helicopters and crews from Robert Gray Army Airfield in Texas and delivered them to Guatemala City to shuttle refugees and food. The 436th Mil Alft Wg also flew a C–141 Starlifter to Guatemala City laden with food. The 437th Mil Alft Wg of Charleston AFB, South Carolina, used two C–141s to haul tents, blankets, medical supplies, and food from Dobbins AFB, Georgia, to La Aurora Airport at Guatemala City. Two 438th Mil Alft Wg C–141s from McGuire AFB, New Jersey, carried 45 tons of rations from Dobbins to La Aurora Airport.

The C–133 and five C–141 cargo planes hauled more than 119 tons of relief supplies and equipment from the United States to Guatemala to provide refugees with shelter, food, blankets, and medicine until they could return to their homes. The planes also supplied Guatemala City with 100,000 food rations until surface transportation routes were restored.

47.
Name: Central American Floods.
Location: Republic of Costa Rica and Republic of Panama.
Date(s): January 10–11 and April 11–12, 1970.
Emergency: Heavy rains flooded the Sixaola and Changuinola River valleys along the border between Costa Rica and Panama, killing at least 30 people and driving hundreds from their homes.
Air Force Organization(s) Involved: 24th and 605th Sp Ops Sqs and USAF South Comd.
Airlifted: 56 tons of food, drinking water, and medicine; and 576 people rescued.
Aircraft Employed: C–47 (two), C–123 (two), and CH–3 (two).
Operations: Heavy rain in early January flooded the Sixaola and Changuinola River valleys along the Caribbean coast of western Panama and eastern Costa Rica. On January 9, Costa Rica asked the U.S. embassy in San José to help rescue stranded flood victims and airlift relief supplies to emergency shelters. The Panamanian government also requested assistance. The State Department contacted the joint U.S. South Comd in the Panama Canal Zone, which tapped the USAF South Comd for airlift support.

On January 10 and 11, two C–47 Skytrain and two C–123 Provider cargo planes belonging to the 605th Sp Ops Sq at Howard AFB in the Canal Zone airlifted 21 tons of relief supplies to Bocas del Toro, a Panamanian island southeast of the flooded region. During these two days, two CH–3 amphibious helicopters of the 24th Sp Ops Sq transported supplies to refugee centers on the mainland and rescued citizens marooned by floodwaters. One helicopter carried 35 tons of food, drinking water, and other supplies from Bocas del Toro—which also received relief supplies from other sources besides the United States—to Changuinola, Panama, and evacuated 360 persons from the Sixaola River valley to an airstrip aid station at Changuinola. The other CH–3 evacuated 216 persons from the same valley to Puerto Limón, Costa Rica, and dropped fresh water and food to flood victims. The rains stopped on January 10, and floodwaters began receding the next day.

Similar flooding occurred during the first two weeks of April 1970. Thirty people died as the Sixaola and Changuinola Rivers again inundated their valleys near the border of Costa Rica and Panama. The two nations again requested assistance from the State Department, which again contacted the U.S. South Comd for airlift support.

On April 11 and 12, four USAF South Comd transports hauled 21 tons of food, medical supplies, and drinking water from AID and U.S. South Comd emergency stockpiles in the Panama Canal Zone to disaster relief stations in the flooded area. Two amphibious CH–3 helicopters from the 24th Sp Ops Sq helped to distribute supplies and rescue stranded people.

48.
Name: Peruvian Earthquake.
Location: Republic of Peru.
Date(s): June 2–July 3, 1970.
Emergency: An earthquake registering 7.75 on the Richter scale devastated northwestern Peru, killing 70,000 people, injuring 100,000, and leaving 800,000 homeless.
Air Force Organization(s) Involved: USAF South Comd; 24th Sp Ops Wg; 24th Air Trpt Sq; 605th Sp Ops Sq; 39th Tac Alft Sq; and 60th, 89th, 436th, 437th, and 438th Mil Alft Wgs.
Airlifted: At least 732 tons of equipment and supplies, including two CH–47 helicopters, five UH–1 helicopters, one truck, food, clothing, medical supplies, water cans, blankets, tents, cots, sleeping bags, tableware, cooking sets, flashlights, and tools; and 2,827 passengers.
Aircraft Employed: C–130 (six), C–123 (four), C–133 (three), C–141 (two), C–118 (two), and VC–137 (one).
Operations: In the late afternoon of May 31, an earthquake registering 7.75 on the Richter scale struck just west of Peru on the floor of the eastern Pacific Ocean. With an epicenter 211 miles northwest of Lima and 12 miles west of Chimbote, the quake devastated the Callejon de Huaylas valley and towns such as Yungay, Huaras, Caras, and Chimbote between the Andes and the Pacific coast.

An avalanche buried 18,000 of the 25,000 residents of Yungay, and 10,000 of 35,000 people in Huaras perished. Landslides, mudslides, floods from broken dams, and collapsing buildings killed 70,000 people, injured 100,000, and left

800,000 homeless. Broken bridges and buried roadbeds cut highways and railroads in northwestern Peru, isolating earthquake victims. Peru's president, Juan Velasco Alvarado, asked for international assistance. On June 1, the U.S. ambassador to Peru, Taylor Belcher, forwarded a request for helicopters and supplies to the State Department.

The joint U.S. South Comd in the Panama Canal Zone assumed control of U.S. disaster relief operations. In June, six C–130s and crews from the 39th Tac Alft Sq of the 317th Tac Alft Wg at Lockbourne AFB, Ohio, on rotational duty with the USAF Southern Command's 24th Sp Ops Wg, flew 115 tons of relief equipment and supplies from Howard and Albrook AFBs in the Canal Zone to Jorge Chávez Airport in Lima. The cargo included two UH–1 helicopters and crews.

Between June 2 and July 3, while two C–130s continued to bring supplies from Panama, four more shuttled blankets, tents, cots, sleeping bags, and medical supplies from Lima to Chimbote and Anta, Peru, where Army helicopters distributed the cargo throughout the region. Air Force C–130s airdropped about 30 percent of relief supplies directly to villages in the disaster area.

Between June 3 and 19, four 605th Sp Ops Sq C–123 Providers performed similar airlift missions in Lima, Chimbote, and Anta. On June 4, two C–118 aircraft from the 24th Air Trpt Sq moved 9.5 tons of relief supplies from the Canal Zone to Lima.

Between June 2 and July 3, the USAF South Comd airlifted 689 tons of relief supplies aboard 12 cargo planes, evacuated 501 injured persons, and transported 2,827 passengers. The command transported 157 tons of relief cargo from the Canal Zone to Peru on 19 C–130, 4 C–123, and 2 C–118 sorties. The cargo included 615 tents, 5,771 cots, 2,183 sleeping bags, 10,744 blankets, 2,285 flashlights, 732 entrenching tools, 100 cooking sets, 3,000 tableware sets, 500 water cans, 1,856 uniforms, 34 tons of food, and 25 tons of medical supplies.

The Military Airlift Command also participated in the relief effort. On June 5, two C–133s from the 60th Mil Alft Wg at Travis AFB, California, flew two special high-altitude CH–47 Army Chinook helicopters and a 1.5 ton truck from Harrisburg, Pennsylvania, to Lima. They flew via Dover AFB, Delaware, where 436th Mil Alft Wg crews took over, and Howard AFB in the Canal Zone, where the planes refueled. That same day, a C–141 of the 437th Mil Alft Wg at Charleston AFB, South Carolina, carried 25 helicopter crew members and 13 tons of helicopter support equipment from Harrisburg to Lima. On June 11, another C–141, from the 438th Mil Alft Wg at McGuire AFB, New Jersey, loaded five tons of equipment—including fuel bladders and helicopter transmissions—at Harrisburg and flew to Scott AFB, Illinois. There it picked up another 10 tons of cargo, including 300 British Red Cross tents. The Starlifter then proceeded to Lima. A 436th Mil Alft Wg C–133 Cargomaster carried three UH–1 helicopters and 14 tons of equipment from Homestead AFB, Florida, to Lima at the end of the month.

On June 28, Mrs. Richard Nixon, the first lady, flew to Peru aboard an 89th Mil Alft Wg VC–137 aircraft with relief supplies donated by private organizations in the United States. Mrs. Nixon toured the devastated area on an airlifted helicopter.

Between June 5 and 30, six MAC cargo planes hauled more than 43 tons of relief equipment and supplies to the Peruvian capital. USAF Southern Command planes in Peru helped to distribute the cargo. The United States was one of many nations delivering relief supplies to Peru in the wake of the earthquake.

49.
Name: Puerto Rican Floods.
Location: Commonwealth of Puerto Rico.
Date(s): October 1970.
Emergency: Seven days of torrential rainfall flooded Puerto Rico, leaving 60 people dead or missing and 10,000 homeless.
Air Force Organization(s) Involved: 901st and 916th Mil Alft Gps; and Detachment 2, 437th Mil Alft Wg.
Airlifted: More than 16 tons of bedding, including 600 beds and mattresses and 200 blankets.
Aircraft Employed: C–124 (three).
Operations: From October 3 to 9, torrential rain from a stalled tropical depression pelted the island of Puerto Rico. In one 24-hour period, the mountain town of Aibonito received 17 inches of rain, and 33 inches fell on Cavey in three days. Sixteen rivers flooded, inundating towns such as Coamo, Fajardo, Toa Baja, Bauamon, and Barceloneta, and leaving 60 persons dead or missing and 10,000 homeless. On October 6, Governor Luis A. Ferre of Puerto Rico requested that President Nixon declare the island a federal disaster area, as damage estimates climbed to $50 million.

During October, three AF Res C–124 Globemaster airplanes—two from the 901st Mil Alft Gp at L. G. Hanscom Field, Bedford, Massachusetts, and one from the 916th Mil Alft Gp at Carswell AFB, Texas—diverted from routine training flights to Guantánamo Naval Base, Cuba, to Puerto Rico for relief airlift operations. The three planes transported 600 beds and mattresses and 200 blankets—cargo weighing more than 16 tons—from Civil Air Patrol summer camp supplies at Ramey AFB near Mayaguez on the west coast of Puerto Rico to San Juan, 60 miles away on the island's northeast coast, to which most of the flood refugees had fled.

The Globemasters made seven trips between Mayaguez and San Juan. The commander of Detachment 2, 437th Mil Alft Wg at Ramey AFB, Lt. Col. Grover L. Ensley, coordinated the airlift. Army National Guardsmen took the bedding to a Fort Brooks civilian refugee center.

Air Force trucks from Ramey AFB delivered supplies to flooded villages in western Puerto Rico. Navy and Coast Guard helicopters also contributed to the relief effort. On October 10, the rain slowed as the tropical depression moved away from the island. As floodwaters retreated, refugees began to return home.

Humanitarian Airlift Operations

50.
Name: Colombian Flood.
Location: Republic of Colombia.
Date(s): November 16–24, 1970.
Emergency: Torrential rain in northern Colombia flooded the Magdalena River and its tributaries, forcing hundreds of people from their homes.
Air Force Organization(s) Involved: 24th Sp Ops Wg and 40th Tac Alft Sq.
Airlifted: 12 tons of equipment and relief supplies, including three UH–1 helicopters, one U–1A airplane, tents, and medical supplies; and a 36-man disaster relief team, including helicopter crews.
Aircraft Employed: C–130 and CH–3 (numbers unknown).
Operations: During October and the first 10 days of November, torrential rain forced the Magdalena River and its tributaries over their banks, flooding large parts of northern Colombia. The worst flooding in 30 years prompted the president of Colombia, Misael Pastrana Borrero, to ask the U.S. embassy for helicopter support and relief supplies on November 14. The State Department contacted DoD, which assigned relief operations to the joint U.S. South Comd in the Panama Canal Zone.

Between November 16 and 24, C–130 Hercules airplanes and crews of the 40th Tac Alft Sq of the 317th Tac Alft Wg at Lockbourne AFB, Ohio—on rotational duty with the USAF Southern Command's 24th Sp Ops Wg at Howard AFB in the Canal Zone—airlifted a 36-man Army disaster relief team, three UH–1 helicopters, a U–1A airplane, tents, and medical supplies from Panama to Bogotá, Colombia. The Army aircraft flew 201 sorties in northern Colombia, transporting 60 tons of relief supplies—including food, medicine, and drugs—and 192 doctors, nurses, Red Cross personnel, refugees, and relief workers by November 24.

The 24th Sp Ops Wg also flew CH–3 helicopters from Panama to neighboring Colombia with relief cargo. Air Force C–130s and CH–3s airlifted more than 12 tons of emergency equipment and supplies from the Canal Zone to northern Colombia in 10 sorties.

The USAF South Comd aircraft returned from Colombia to the Canal Zone on November 24, carrying Army personnel and helicopters. By then, the Magdalena River and its tributaries had retreated to their usual courses, allowing flood refugees to return home.

51.
Name: Costa Rican Flood Relief.
Location: Republic of Costa Rica.
Date(s): December 5–15, 1970.
Emergency: Extraordinarily heavy rain in Costa Rica flooded three river valleys, forcing hundreds of people from their homes or isolating them from traditional sources of food.

Air Force Organization(s) Involved: 39th Aerosp RR Wg and 24th Sp Ops Wg.
Airlifted: 73 tons of relief supplies, including bedding, food, and medical supplies; and 279 passengers.
Aircraft Employed: C–123 (one) and CH–3 (one).
Operations: During November and December, unusually heavy rain flooded the Rio Estrella, Rio Sixaola, Rio Colorado, and other rivers flowing to the Caribbean Sea from the volcanic highlands around San José in central Costa Rica. Near Limón on the eastern coast, 15 inches of rain fell in a single night. Floodwaters engulfed a host of villages and banana plantations, forcing hundreds of people from their homes, driving them to higher ground, and cutting them off from traditional sources of food. On December 4, the U.S. ambassador to Costa Rica, Walter C. Ploesser, asked the U.S. South Comd in the Panama Canal Zone for aircraft to evacuate refugees and deliver relief supplies.

The next day, a USAF South Comd-directed CH–3 helicopter from the 39th Aerosp RR Wg detachment in the Canal Zone flew to Limón. In the next 10 days, it airlifted 47.7 tons of food, bedding, and medical supplies on shuttle flights between San José and Limón and from those cities to flood victims in the Sixaola and Estrella River valleys. It carried 279 passengers, including relief workers, refugees, and medical personnel. Meanwhile, a USAF South Comd C–123 Provider airplane from the 24th Sp Ops Wg airlifted 25 tons of relief supplies and refugees between San José and Limón.

Air Force airlift operations proceeded despite continued heavy rain until December 15. Army UH–1 helicopters also carried relief supplies and passengers on flood relief operations in Costa Rica between December 5 and 15.

52.
Name: Ecuadoran Earthquake.
Location: Republic of Ecuador.
Date(s): December 11–18, 1970.
Emergency: An earthquake registering 7.6 on the Richter scale struck southern Ecuador near the Peruvian border and was followed by severe aftershocks. The tremors injured hundreds of people and left thousands homeless.
Air Force Organization(s) Involved: 24th Sp Ops Wg and 317th Tac Alft Wg.
Airlifted: 140 tons of relief cargo, including medical supplies, 540 tents, two UH–1 helicopters, food, water, and construction equipment and materiel; and 279 passengers, including disaster survey team personnel.
Aircraft Employed: C–130 (three).
Operations: On December 9, an earthquake registering 7.6 on the Richter scale struck the border of Ecuador and Peru about 275 miles southwest of Quito, Ecuador. Aftershocks in southern Ecuador on December 10 compounded the destruction in cities and villages such as Loja, Cariamango, Celica, and Alamor. The tremors killed 20 people, injured hundreds, and left thousands homeless. President José Maria Velasco Ibarra of Ecuador asked the U.S. ambassador at

Quito, Findley Burns, for airlift support, and Burns contacted the U.S. South Comd in the Panama Canal Zone.

Between December 11 and 18, at least three C–130s from the 317th Tac Alft Wg at Lockbourne AFB, Ohio, on rotational duty with the USAF Southern Command's 24th Sp Ops Wg in the Canal Zone, airlifted 140 tons of relief cargo from Howard AFB in the Canal Zone to and between the Ecuadoran cities of Guayaquil, Quito, and Macara. The cargo included medical supplies, 540 tents, two UH–1 helicopters, food, water, and construction equipment. One C–130 remained in Ecuador for five days, shuttling 50 tons of relief supplies between the port of Guayaquil and Macara in the earthquake region.

The C–130s flew 39 sorties to and within Ecuador, consuming more than 65 flying hours. The cargo planes also transported 279 passengers, including disaster survey team personnel and helicopter crews, with Lt. Col. Victor C. Kelly commanding the USAF South Comd missions in Ecuador. The UH–1 Army helicopters airlifted to Macara helped to distribute relief supplies through the disaster zone.

On December 18, 1970, after eight days of airlift operations to and within Ecuador, the last C–130 returned to the Canal Zone. By then, the worst was over, and many earthquake victims returned to their homes to rebuild.

53.
Name: Bolivian Flood.
Location: Republic of Bolivia.
Date(s): February 13 and 28, 1971.
Emergency: Heavy rain flooded the Beni and Madre de Dios River valleys of northern Bolivia and inundated Riberalta.
Air Force Organization(s) Involved: USAF South Comd, 24th Sp Ops Wg, and 317th Tac Alft Wg.
Airlifted: Seven tons of Red Cross supplies, including food, clothing, and medicine.
Aircraft Employed: C–130 (two+).
Operations: During late January, torrential rain descended on the Beni and Madre de Dios River valleys of northern Bolivia on the edge of the Amazon basin, flooding Riberalta and surrounding areas. The Bolivian government, aware that the USAF South Comd was already flying C–130 aircraft to transport equipment in Bolivia, requested that some of the airplanes carry Red Cross food, clothing, and medicine from La Paz to the flooded region around Riberalta.

On February 13 and 28, at least two 317th Tac Alft Wg C–130s, on rotational duty with the USAF Southern Command's 24th Sp Ops Wg, airlifted seven tons of the Red Cross supplies to the flood victims. As floodwaters in Riberalta receded, the C–130s resumed their civic action missions of hauling rural electrification equipment to underdeveloped areas of Bolivia.

54.
Name: Project Volcan.
Location: Republic of Nicaragua.
Date(s): March 18–28, 1971.
Emergency: The Cerro Negro volcano deposited tons of ash on farmlands around León, Nicaragua, forcing 3,000 people to move.
Air Force Organization(s) Involved: 24th Sp Ops Wg and 40th Tac Alft Sq.
Airlifted: At least 95 tons of food, clothing, bedding, building materials, and personal belongings; and at least 855 passengers.
Aircraft Employed: C–123 (two) and C–130 (two+).
Operations: During the second half of February, the Cerro Negro volcano near León, Nicaragua, discharged great quantities of ash, which settled on nearby farmlands, destroying crops. About 3,000 people faced starvation. A third migrated to León, and the Nicaraguan government planned to resettle the remainder on fertile lands around Nuevo Guinea, 175 miles southeast of the volcano. Nicaraguan leaders concluded that the settlers, given more than 100 acres of free land per family, would soon grow enough food to support themselves. The Nicaraguan government asked the United States to airlift some of the people from León to Nuevo Guinea.

Between March 18 and 28, the USAF South Comd, based in the Panama Canal Zone, conducted Project Volcan. In 10 days, two C–123s from the 24th Sp Ops Wg moved 855 refugees and 58 tons of their personal belongings from León to Nuevo Guinea. The C–123s also carried at least 37 tons of food, clothing, bedding, and building materials from Managua, the Nicaraguan capital, to Nuevo Guinea for the new settlers. C–130 Hercules aircraft from the 40th Tac Alft Sq of the 317th Tac Alft Wg, serving on rotational duty with the USAF South Comd, carried 12 tons of supplies from the Canal Zone to Managua and transported maintenance personnel and equipment for the C–123s in Nicaragua. Project Volcan ended on March 28.

55.
Name: Coronet Roundup.
Location: Commonwealth of Puerto Rico and the Virgin Islands.
Date(s): June 1, 1971–May 10, 1975.
Emergency: A screwworm fly epidemic killed hundreds of livestock in Puerto Rico and the Virgin Islands, reducing food supplies and threatening the regional economy.
Air Force Organization(s) Involved: 1st Sp Ops Wg, 94th and 433d Tac Alft Wgs, and 303d and 305th Aerosp RR Sqs.
Airlifted: More than one billion sterile screwworm flies.
Aircraft Employed: U–10 (two), C–7 (two), C–123 (number unknown), and C–130 (number unknown).
Operations: During the first half of 1971, the parasitic screwworm multiplied in

Humanitarian Airlift Operations

Puerto Rico and the Virgin Islands until it posed a serious threat to livestock herds on which the people depended for meat and milk. Puerto Rico sought help from the U.S. Department of Agriculture, which had developed methods to combat pestilence by releasing sterile insects to reduce reproduction. The department bred millions of screwworm flies at its facility in Mission, Texas, and sterilized them with cobalt radiation. The Air Force transported the sterile flies to Puerto Rico for release in a project called Coronet Roundup.

Between June 1, 1971, and June 30, 1973, the Tactical Air Command's 1st Sp Ops Wg from Hurlburt Field, Florida, conducted Coronet Roundup. The 319th Sp Ops Sq flew C–123 Provider aircraft laden with sterile screwworm flies from Texas via Homestead AFB, Florida, to Ramey AFB, Puerto Rico. From there, the 317th Sp Ops Sq flew two U–10 airplanes over the Virgin Islands and Puerto Rico to distribute up to 2.5 million of the flies per week.

Flying low and slow, the planes dropped boxes of insects, which opened upon impact with the ground. By July 1, 1973, when TAC surrendered responsibility for Coronet Roundup to the AF Res and the C–123s were being phased out of the active Air Force inventory, the 1st Sp Ops Wg had flown 695 C–123 sorties and 1,142 U–10 sorties against the screwworm fly and had eliminated the pest from the Virgin Islands.

On July 1, the Air Force Reserve's Eastern Region assumed operational control of Coronet Roundup. C–130 Hercules aircraft from the 303d and 305th Aerosp RR Sqs and the 433d Tac Alft Wg took turns conducting weekly flights from Mission to Roosevelt Roads NAS, Puerto Rico. Each C–130 could carry 15 million sterile screwworm flies. The 1,980-mile flights also provided AF Res aircrews with navigational training over water.

From Roosevelt Roads, a pair of 94th Tac Alft Wg C–7 Caribou aircraft distributed the flies over Puerto Rico at the rate of up to 8 million per week. The C–7s flew grid patterns at an average altitude of 1,500 feet and a speed of 105 knots. Between June 1971 and May 1975, the Air Force released 1.15 billion sterile screwworm flies in Puerto Rico and the Virgin Islands. By May 10, 1975, when Coronet Roundup ended, the parasitic pest had ceased to be a major threat in that part of the West Indies and the local livestock industry was thriving.

56.
Name: Chilean Double Disaster.
Location: Republic of Chile.
Date(s): July 1, 10, and 21, 1971.
Emergency: A severe winter storm devastated central Chile, killing 15 people. In the same region, an earthquake registering at least 7.0 on the Richter scale killed 82 people and injured 350 others.
Air Force Organization(s) Involved: USAF South Comd and 316th Tac Alft Wg.
Airlifted: 43 tons of blankets, sleeping bags, boots, tents, medical supplies, and heaters.

Aircraft Employed: C–130 (four).

Operations: A severe winter storm struck three provinces of central Chile around the capital of Santiago on June 19. The worst blizzard in 40 years, it killed 15 people and threatened the lives of many isolated by snow. President Salvador Allende Gossens of Chile asked the U.S. embassy for assistance. On June 30, the U.S. South Comd in the Panama Canal Zone directed the USAF South Comd to arrange a relief airlift.

On July 1, Capt. Frederick J. Mueller piloted a C–130 Hercules aircraft laden with 7.45 tons of relief supplies—including 3,350 blankets, 1,000 sleeping bags, portable heaters, and medical supplies—from Howard AFB in the Canal Zone to Santiago. The plane came from the 316th Tac Alft Wg, which had a detachment on rotational duty with the USAF South Comd in the Canal Zone.

Just after 11:00 p.m. on July 8, an earthquake registering at least 7.0 on the Richter scale struck the same region of Chile already suffering from the winter storm. The epicenter was about 50 miles north of Valparaiso, where the cathedral roof collapsed. Illapel, Salamanca, La Ligua, Llay-Llay, and other towns north of Santiago and Valparaiso were devastated. The earthquake killed 82 people and injured 350. Chile again asked for U.S. assistance.

On July 10, two more C–130s flew from Howard AFB to Santiago, carrying 20.5 tons of relief supplies. Another C–130 delivered 15 tons on July 21. The three missions transported almost 43 tons of blankets, sleeping bags, boots, tents, medical supplies, and heaters to the Chilean capital from a U.S. South Comd and AID disaster relief stockpile in the Canal Zone. The four C–130 airplanes flew 16 sorties. U.S. relief supplies, together with aid from other nations, stimulated Chile's recovery from the double disaster.

57.
Name: Mexican Flash Flood.
Location: Mexico.
Date(s): July 1–2, 1971.
Emergency: Torrential rain over northeastern Mexico flooded Nuevo Laredo and neighboring communities along the Rio Grande and its tributaries, cutting roads and isolating communities.
Air Force Organization(s) Involved: Detachments 10 and 11, 43d Aerosp RR Sq.
Airlifted: 19 flood victims and five tons of food and medical supplies.
Aircraft Employed: HH–43 (two).
Operations: Heavy rain descended on northeastern Mexico at the end of June, flooding portions of the Rio Grande and its tributaries in the Nuevo Laredo area. Swollen streams washed out bridges and blocked roads, isolating flood victims from food and medical supplies. The Mexican government sent army units to the area and appealed to the United States for helicopter support.

Humanitarian Airlift Operations

Responding to the emergency were two detachments of the 43d Aerosp RR Sq, Detachment 10 from Laredo AFB and Detachment 11 from Laughlin AFB, Texas. On July 1, Detachment 10 flew an HH–43 Huskie helicopter to Nuevo Laredo and evacuated 19 people stranded by high water. Piloted by Maj. Robert C. Henneman, the helicopter also transported food and medical supplies to Nuevo Laredo and carried Mexican government officials over the area to survey flood damage.

A Detachment 11 helicopter flew similar missions west and southwest of Nuevo Laredo on July 1 and 2. Unable to depend on fuel trucks from its base because of flooded roads, this helicopter received support from Mexican officials at Sabinas and Monclova. While the Detachment 11 helicopter did not rescue flood victims, it did assist in cleanup operations near Nuevo Laredo.

The two 43d Aerosp RR Sq helicopters transported more than five tons of food and medical supplies from southern Texas to the flooded areas of northeast Mexico. Drier weather at the beginning of July allowed waters to recede, and roads reopened.

58.
Name: Hurricane Edith.
Location: Republic of Nicaragua.
Date(s): September 12–17, 1971.
Emergency: Hurricane Edith, with sustained winds of 140 mph, hit northeastern Nicaragua, killing 29 people and leaving thousands homeless.
Air Force Organization(s) Involved: USAF South Comd, 316th Tac Alft Wg, and 24th Sp Ops Sq.
Airlifted: 93 tons of supplies, including tents, blankets, food, medical supplies, water purification tablets, and gasoline; and 83 passengers, including communications experts and medical personnel.
Aircraft Employed: C–130 (three) and C–123 (one).
Operations: Hurricane Edith hit northeastern Nicaragua on September 9 with sustained winds of 140 mph. Gusts of up to 175 mph drove 15-foot waves against the coast. The village of Cabo Gracias a Dios, with 500 residents, suffered almost complete devastation. In the Cape Gracias region, high winds and water left 29 persons dead and thousands homeless. Polluted water posed a disease threat. On September 12, President Anastasio Somoza Debayle of Nicaragua declared a national emergency and asked the U.S. ambassador at Managua for assistance.

From September 12 to 17, the U.S. South Comd directed a joint Army-Air Force relief operation, flying cargo planes and helicopters from Howard AFB in the Panama Canal Zone to Puerto Cabezas on the northeastern coast of Nicaragua. Three C–130 Hercules airplanes from a 316th Tac Alft Wg detachment, on rotational duty with the USAF South Comd, flew almost 80 tons of relief supplies to Nicaragua in 11 sorties. A 24th Sp Ops Sq C–123 Provider aircraft carried other relief cargo to Puerto Cabezas and remained in Nicaragua for five days to ferry supplies and emergency personnel between Managua and small airstrips in the disaster zone.

During the relief operation, Air Force planes carried 93 tons of relief supplies, including 200 tents, 1,000 blankets, 550 cases of food rations, 3,700 water purification tablets, half a ton of medical supplies, and gasoline. The C–130 and C–123 airplanes also transported 83 passengers, including communications experts, medical personnel, and Red Cross workers. Two Army UH–1 helicopters also flew from Panama to Puerto Cabezas for emergency flights within the disaster area. By September 17, all U.S. South Comd aircraft had returned to the Canal Zone.

59.
Name: Tropical Storm Fern.
Location: Mexico.
Date(s): September 15–16, 1971.
Emergency: The remnants of Hurricane Fern dropped torrential rain over northeastern Mexico, flooding the Rio Salado valley about 45 miles south of Nuevo Laredo.
Air Force Organization(s) Involved: Detachment 10, 43d Aerosp RR Sq.
Airlifted: 91 persons.
Aircraft Employed: HH–43 (two).
Operations: After hitting Matagorda, Texas, on September 10, Hurricane Fern drifted southwestward. The storm quickly lost its hurricane-force winds over land, but still generated heavy rain, which caused local flash flooding. By September 14, the storm was over the Nuevo Laredo area of northwestern Mexico, which had flooded earlier in the year (see Mexican Flash Flood, July 1971). When flash floods stranded people in the Rio Salado valley about 45 miles south of Nuevo Laredo, Mexican authorities requested U.S. assistance for search and rescue operations.

On September 15 and 16, Detachment 10 of the 43d Aerosp RR Sq, based at Laredo, Texas, flew two HH–43 helicopters to airlift 91 persons from flooded portions of the Rio Salado valley to a refugee center on high ground north of the river. The helicopters covered a 25-square-mile area, rescuing 54 persons the first day and 37 the second.

60.
Name: Peruvian Floods and Earthquake.
Location: Republic of Peru.
Date(s): March 25–April 3, 1972.
Emergency: Three weeks of heavy rain flooded towns in northwestern Peru. Meanwhile, an earthquake devastated an adjacent region of northern Peru. The two disasters left 60,000 people homeless.
Air Force Organization(s) Involved: USAF South Comd, 24th Sp Ops Wg, and 314th Tac Alft Wg.

Humanitarian Airlift Operations

Airlifted: 135 tons of food, clothing, medical supplies, fuel, and two UH–1N helicopters; and 282 passengers, including Peruvian officials and medical and Red Cross personnel.

Aircraft Employed: C–130 (two).

Operations: During the first three weeks of March, heavy rain descended on the Sechura Desert in northwestern Peru. The Piura River flowing from the Andes to the Pacific Ocean spilled over its banks, flooding the towns of Piura and Catacaos with up to six feet of water for a week. Floodwaters damaged or destroyed more than 8,800 homes in the two communities. Many other towns also experienced major flooding.

Meanwhile, on March 13, a severe earthquake struck an adjacent region of northern Peru. At Juanjui in the state of San Martín, 350 homes suffered damage. Towns across the mountains of north central Peru endured similar destruction.

In Lima, the ministry of housing estimated that the floods and earthquake had left 60,000 people homeless. The Peruvian government asked the U.S. ambassador in Lima for U.S. assistance. On March 25, the U.S. South Comd in the Panama Canal Zone launched a relief airlift.

Between March 25 and April 3, two Air Force C–130 Hercules aircraft flew 29 disaster relief sorties to and within Peru. The planes belonged to the 61st Tac Alft Sq, on rotational duty with the 24th Sp Ops Wg in Panama. The C–130s carried two UH–1 helicopters, relief supplies, and emergency support personnel from Howard AFB in the Canal Zone to Lima.

The C–130s flew relief cargo from Lima to Piura, about 400 miles to the north, and other towns in the flood and earthquake zones, where helicopters distributed it among scattered villages. During 10 days of disaster relief flights, the two airplanes delivered 135 tons of food, clothing, medical supplies, fuel, and other cargo; and 282 passengers, including Peruvian officials, medical personnel, and Red Cross workers.

61.

Name: Managua Earthquake.

Location: Republic of Nicaragua.

Date(s): December 23, 1972–January 30, 1973.

Emergency: An earthquake registering 6.25 on the Richter scale destroyed 60 percent of Managua, Nicaragua, killing 7,000 people and leaving more than 200,000 homeless.

Air Force Organization(s) Involved: 60th, 62d, 63d, 436th, 437th, and 438th Mil Alft Wgs; 317th Tac Alft Wg; 24th Sp Ops Sq; and USAF South Comd.

Airlifted: 1,938 tons of equipment and supplies, including heavy construction vehicles, two field hospitals, water purification plants and kits, blankets, tents, food, water, medical supplies, fuel bladders, fuel, water containers and trucks, communications equipment, generators, and cots; and more than 2,043 passengers, including disaster relief personnel and evacuees.

Aircraft Employed: C–141 (28), C–5 (3), C–130 (8), UH–1 (2), C–118 (1), and C–123 (1).

Operations: Before dawn on December 23, a catastrophic earthquake struck Managua, the capital of Nicaragua, a city of about 300,000 people. Registering 6.25 on the Richter scale, it destroyed 60 percent of the city, killing 7,000 people, injuring at least 10,000, and forcing at least 200,000 from their homes. Broken water mains deprived people of water and made it impossible to fight fires fed by severed natural gas lines. The earthquake damaged or destroyed six hospitals and cut electricity and communications.

Gen. Anastasio Somoza Debayle, Nicaragua's leader, cabled President Nixon for emergency assistance while the U.S. ambassador to Nicaragua, Turner B. Shelton, passed on official requests for aid. The Joint Chiefs of Staff assigned relief response to the Readiness Command, which contacted the U.S. South Comd in the Panama Canal Zone and MAC. United States military forces sent on relief missions to Nicaragua came under command of the U.S. Southern Command's Col. Kenneth E. Murphy (Army), who determined that Managua's Las Mercedes Airport was still usable.

The Air Force conducted airlift operations to Managua from December 23 through January 30, 1973. The USAF South Comd flew the first U.S. military relief planes from Howard AFB to Managua. Six C–130s from the 317th Tac Alft Wg, on rotation to the Canal Zone, flew most of the 256 USAF South Comd-directed relief sorties, carrying 567 tons of medical supplies, generators, cots, communications equipment, food, blankets, and tents from disaster relief stockpiles in the Canal Zone to Managua between December 23 and January 18.

The USAF South Comd flew 10 sorties to distribute supplies, facilitate communications, and transport officials to survey damage. The USAF South Comd UH–1s also scouted landing zones for Army Chinook helicopters from Fort Hood, Texas, which were used to distribute food to refugee centers on the outskirts of Managua. The 317th Tac Alft Wg flew two C–130 airplanes from Pope AFB, North Carolina, to Managua with fuel for the Chinook helicopters.

The 24th Sp Ops Sq provided air traffic control at Las Mercedes Airport during the early stages of the relief airlift. Between December 23 and January 30, the USAF South Comd transported 629 tons of relief equipment and supplies from the Canal Zone to Managua. It also moved 1,343 passengers, including emergency support personnel going to Managua and evacuees leaving the city.

The Military Airlift Command flew three C–5 and 28 C–141 airplanes to Managua for disaster relief between December 24 and January 5. In 43 sorties, the planes moved 1,309 tons of cargo to Managua and 700 passengers either to or from the ruined Nicaraguan capital. The command carried two field hospitals to Nicaragua: one was the 100-bed U.S. Army 21st Evacuation Hospital from Fort Hood, and the other was the U.S. Air Force 1st Tactical Hospital from MacDill AFB in Florida.

Two C–5s and six C–141s took the U.S. Army's 518th Engineer Company and its heavy construction equipment, including bulldozers, trucks, and tractors, from Fort Kobbe in the Canal Zone to Managua. There the equipment was used to demolish half-fallen structures in a 200-square block area. C–5s carried five water purification units and four water trucks from Fort Hood to Managua, while C–141s transported 5,000 five-gallon water containers to the Nicaraguan capital. Most Air Force aircraft came from Twenty-first Air Force wings, but some Twenty-second Air Force planes also participated. The Military Airlift Command also transported mobile communications equipment from Andrews AFB, Maryland, and Atlanta, Georgia, to Nicaragua.

Air Force aircraft flew 299 sorties in the Managua disaster relief airlift, carrying 2,043 passengers and 1,938 tons of cargo. Among the passengers were medical and sanitation personnel, demolition experts, engineers, and communications specialists going to Nicaragua, and almost 900 evacuees, some of whom were taken to the Canal Zone or the United States for medical treatment. The United States was only one of 30 countries that sent aid to Nicaragua.

62.
Name: Nicaraguan Medfly.
Location: Republic of Nicaragua.
Date(s): April 2–May 19, 1973.
Emergency: The Mediterranean fruit fly threatened citrus crops south of Managua, Nicaragua.
Air Force Organization(s) Involved: 24th Sp Ops Gp, 302d Tac Alft Wg, and 704th Tac Alft Sq.
Airlifted: 38 tons of insecticide.
Aircraft Employed: C–123 (three) and C–130 (number unknown).
Operations: During the spring, the Organismo International Regional de Sanidad Agropecuaria (OIRSA) wanted U.S. assistance to fight the Medfly. The insect threatened Nicaragua's citrus crops (see Savage Fly, January–May 1968), and OIRSA requested aerial spraying of infested orchards.

Between April 2 and May 19, the USAF South Comd and the AF Res teamed up to respond to the emergency. The Air Force Reserve's 302d Tac Alft Wg sent volunteer aircrews from its 901st, 906th, 907th, and 911th Tac Alft Gps in Massachusetts, Ohio, and Pennsylvania to the Panama Canal Zone, where they were attached to the 24th Sp Ops Gp.

Air Force Reserve C–130s from various units, including the 704th Tac Alft Sq, flew the 302d Tac Alft Wg aircrews to Panama on a weekly rotational basis beginning on April 6. The C–130s also carried insecticide and equipment to the Canal Zone for aerial spraying operations in Nicaragua.

The AF Res aircrews flew three 907th Tac Alft Gp C–123 Provider airplanes—transferred from the USAF South Comd to the AF Res on April 1—from the Canal Zone to Nicaragua, where they sprayed 18,000 acres of citrus groves about 20 miles southeast of Managua. Each plane carried three 300-gallon tanks of insecticide and a pressurized spray boom under each wing. Pilots guided the planes on 25 low-level flights over the infested orchards, making six applications of insecticide. Adverse weather and the onset of the rainy season in Nicaragua forced the aerial spraying project to end on May 19.

63.
Name: Guatemalan Flood.
Location: Republic of Guatemala.
Date(s): June 29–30, 1973.
Emergency: Heavy rain flooded rivers near Guatemala City, forcing 2,500 people from their homes.
Air Force Organization(s) Involved: USAF South Comd and 316th Tac Alft Wg.
Airlifted: Seven tons of tents.
Aircraft Employed: C–130 (one).
Operations: During May and June, heavy rain flooded river valleys south of Volcan de Fuego, Guatemala, threatening the towns of Singuinala and La Democracia. The Pantaleon River near Guatemala City overflowed, forcing 2,500 people from their homes. On June 29, the Guatemalan government asked the U.S. embassy for assistance to help shelter evacuees. That same day the U.S. South Comd in the Panama Canal Zone launched a joint Army-Air Force disaster relief operation.

On June 29 and 30, a C–130 from the 316th Tac Alft Wg, on rotational duty with the USAF South Comd, airlifted seven tons of tents to Guatemala City from a disaster relief stockpile in the Canal Zone. The cargo consisted of 152 six-man tents. Rain diminished and water receded in southern Guatemala during early July, allowing evacuees to return home.

64.
Name: Panamanian Encephalomyelitis Outbreak.
Location: The Canal Zone and Republic of Panama.
Date(s): July 14–26, 1973.
Emergency: 10 horses and one child in Panama died of encephalomyelitis, a disease spread by mosquitoes.
Air Force Organization(s) Involved: USAF South Comd and 302d and 316th Tac Alft Wgs.
Airlifted: Nine tons of malathion insecticide.
Aircraft Employed: UC–123K (one), UH–1N (one), and C–130 (one).
Operations: During early July, 10 horses and a three-year-old girl died in central Panama from an outbreak of Eastern Equine Encephalomyelitis (EEE), a viral nerve disease spread by mosquitoes from birds and small mammals to horses and humans. No antiviral agent against the disease existed for humans. On July 10, the Panama Canal Company asked the U.S. South Comd for aerial spray missions

against mosquitoes in the Canal Zone. On July 13, the Panamanian foreign ministry asked the U.S. South Comd for the same kind of missions over central Panama adjacent to the canal. On July 14, the U.S. South Comd directed USAF South Comd to coordinate an aerial insecticide campaign against the mosquito population in central Panama.

On July 16, a C–130 from the 316th Tac Alft Wg detachment in the Canal Zone, on rotational duty with the USAF South Comd, airlifted nine tons of malathion insecticide from Langley AFB, Virginia, to Howard AFB in Panama. The USAF South Comd depended on the Air Force Reserve's 302d Tac Alft Wg, which maintained a detachment with three C–123 airplanes at Howard AFB, to distribute the insecticide.

Maj. George S. Rowcliffe commanded the 302d Spray Flight, which sprayed 19,200 acres of the Canal Zone between July 17 and 19, using one UC–123K airplane flying at about 150 feet. On July 23, the plane sprayed an additional 18,400 acres in central Panama, for a total of 37,600 acres. The crew included Maj. William Brimgardner, Capt. Thomas Kumlein, MSgt. Robert A. Potts, MSgt. Bill Anders, and entomologist Lt. Col. Leonard W. Trager, Jr. Five spraying sorties killed more than 90 percent of adult mosquitoes in the treated area, effectively ending the threat of an epidemic. The operation ended on July 26.

65.
Name: Colombian Flood.
Location: Republic of Colombia.
Date(s): October 12, 1973.
Emergency: Heavy rain flooded the Magdalena River valley of northern Colombia, forcing hundreds of people from their homes.
Air Force Organization(s) Involved: USAF South Comd, 463d Tac Alft Wg, and 24th Composite Group (Comp Gp).
Airlifted: 16 tons of tents, cots, mosquito nets, cookware sets, and plastic tableware sets.
Aircraft Employed: C–130 (two).
Operations: During early October, heavy tropical rain in northern Colombia flooded the Magdalena River valley, forcing hundreds of people from their homes. Severe flooding also struck Bogotá in the central mountains and Barranquilla on the northern coast. The Colombian government asked the U.S. ambassador at Bogotá for U.S. assistance to feed and shelter flood refugees. The U.S. South Comd in the Panama Canal Zone directed the disaster relief response.

On October 12, two C–130 Hercules aircraft and crews from the 463d Tac Alft Wg at Dyess AFB, Texas, serving rotational duty with the 24th Comp Gp in the Canal Zone, transported almost 16 tons of disaster relief supplies from Howard AFB in Panama to Barranquilla and Bogotá. The cargo included 300 tents, 500 cots, 500 mosquito nets, 100 cookware sets, and 1,000 plastic tableware sets.

66.
Name: Western Panamanian Flood.
Location: Republic of Panama.
Date(s): November 19–21, 1973.
Emergency: Heavy rain flooded the Bahía Honda area of western Panama, killing six people and leaving 200 families homeless.
Air Force Organization(s) Involved: 24th Comp Gp.
Airlifted: More than one ton of food and 21 passengers.
Aircraft Employed: UH–1 (two).
Operations: On November 17, heavy rain flooded the Bahía Honda area of Veraguas province in western Panama, leaving six persons dead and 200 families homeless. The Panamanian government asked the U.S. ambassador for assistance to evacuate flood victims and transport food.

Between November 19 and 21, the 24th Comp Gp, serving the USAF South Comd in the Canal Zone, flew two UH–1N helicopters to accomplish the mission. The helicopters carried 21 passengers and more than one ton of food on shuttle flights in western Panama during three days of flood relief operations.

67.
Name: Bolivian Flood.
Location: Republic of Bolivia.
Date(s): February 9–10, 1974.
Emergency: Heavy rain flooded the Trinidad area of northern Bolivia along the Mamoré River valley, forcing thousands of people from their homes.
Air Force Organization(s) Involved: USAF South Comd, 24th Comp Gp, 38th Tac Alft Sq, and 316th Tac Alft Wg.
Airlifted: 20 tons of supplies, including 8,500 blankets, 10 field kitchens, food, and 10,000 units of penicillin and vitamins; and seven passengers.
Aircraft Employed: C–130 (two).
Operations: Heavy rain in north central Bolivia at the beginning of February flooded parts of the Mamoré River valley and the area around Trinidad, about 250 miles northeast of La Paz. Thousands of people were forced to abandon their homes and seek shelter at refugee centers. The Bolivian government asked the U.S. ambassador, William P. Stedman, for disaster relief. The USAF South Comd in the Panama Canal Zone organized an airlift in response to the request.

On February 9 and 10, members of the 38th Tac Alft Sq of the 316th Tac Alft Wg, serving rotational duty in Panama under operational control of the 24th Comp Gp, flew two C–130 Hercules airplanes on flood relief missions. On Saturday, February 9, they carried a team of disaster control experts and 20 tons of supplies — including 8,500 blankets, 10,000 units of penicillin and vitamins, 10 field kitchens, and food—from Howard AFB to La Paz. On Sunday, a C–130 flew from La Paz to Cochabamba with the disaster control team and Bolivian officials. Both cargo planes returned to Howard AFB on February 10 after five flood relief sorties.

Humanitarian Airlift Operations

68.

Name: Chilean Flood.

Location: Republic of Chile.

Date(s): July 3–6, 1974.

Emergency: A winter storm system brought torrential rain and flash floods to Chile, leaving thousands of people homeless.

Air Force Organization(s) Involved: 436th and 438th Mil Alft Wgs, 314th Tac Alft Wg, and 24th Comp Gp.

Airlifted: 84 tons of supplies, including 9,940 blankets and 5,076 cots.

Aircraft Employed: C–5 (one), C–141 (one), and C–130 (one).

Operations: At the beginning of July, heavy rain from a winter storm system flooded central Chile, forcing thousands of people from their homes. The Chilean government asked the United States through its ambassador for an airlift of bedding for the refugees.

Between July 3 and 6, Air Force planes airlifted 84 tons of relief supplies to Chile, including 9,940 blankets and 5,076 cots. A C–130 from the 314th Tac Alft Wg, on rotational duty with the 24th Comp Gp in Panama, took nine tons of cargo—including 1,440 blankets and 576 cots—from Howard AFB to Santiago, Chile. A C–141 from the 438th Mil Alft Wg and a C–5 from the 436th Mil Alft Wg transported 75 tons of bedding—including 8,500 blankets and 4,500 cots—from Andrews AFB, Maryland, to Santiago.

69.

Name: Colombian Mud Slides.

Location: Republic of Colombia.

Date(s): July 10–31, 1974.

Emergency: Triggered by heavy rain, massive mud slides in Colombia killed 200 persons and blocked land transportation routes between Bogotá and the agricultural fields around Villavicencio, threatening the country with food shortages.

Air Force Organization(s) Involved: 24th Comp Gp, 32d Tac Alft Sq, and 314th Tac Alft Wg.

Airlifted: 224 tons of farm equipment and grain and 18 passengers.

Aircraft Employed: C–130 (one).

Operations: During early July, heavy rain produced mud slides in central Colombia, killing over 200 people and blocking highways and railroads between Bogotá and the Meta farming region around Villavicencio. Harvesters could not move equipment to their fields and farmers could not deliver products to market in the Colombian capital. Food shortages and economic ruin faced the government of the Colombian president, Misael Pastrana Borrero. After unsuccessfully seeking to charter commercial aircraft for an emergency airlift, Borrero asked the United States for assistance through the ambassador in Bogotá.

The Agency for International Development sponsored an airlift in cooperation with the joint U.S. South Comd in the Panama Canal Zone. Between July 10 and 31, the 24th Comp Gp operated a C–130 airplane within Colombia, using three crews from the 314th Tactical Airlift Wing's 32d Tac Alft Sq, which was serving rotational duty in the Canal Zone. The airplane hauled 224 tons in at least 26 sorties during the 21-day operation, transporting 38 combines, 40 grain dryers, and other Colombian harvesting equipment from Bogotá's El Dorado Airport to Villavicencio, and bagged grain—primarily rice—on the return trips.

The C–130 crews had to grease the wooden floors of the aircraft to load and unload the heavy, bulky cargo. Each flight covered about 70 miles. The plane also carried 18 passengers, including personnel to operate the harvesting equipment. By the end of January, land transportation routes had reopened between Bogotá and Villavicencio, relieving the need for further airlift missions. The C–130 returned to the Canal Zone.

70.
Name: Hurricane Fifi.
Location: Republic of Honduras.
Date(s): September 19–October 15, 1974.
Emergency: Hurricane Fifi struck northern Honduras, producing floods that killed at least 1,000 people and left as many as 100,000 homeless.
Air Force Organization(s) Involved: USAF South Comd; 302d, 314th, and 433d Tac Alft Wgs; 109th, 146th, 172d, 913th, 921st, 924th, 926th, 927th, 934th, and 935th Tac Alft Gps; 156th Tac Ftr Gp; and 24th Comp Gp.
Airlifted: 513 tons of equipment and supplies, including food, clothing, medical supplies, water, water purification and food preparation equipment, generators, blankets, boats, and sandbags; and 985 passengers, including disaster relief personnel and flood evacuees.
Aircraft Employed: C–130 (12+), C–123 (2), UH–1 (2), and C–54 (1).
Operations: On September 18 and 19, Hurricane Fifi struck the northern coast of Honduras with torrential rain and winds as high as 130 mph. As much as 20 inches of rain fell in a 40-hour period, and local rivers flooded cities and towns such as Choloma, San Pedro Sula, La Ceiba, and Tocoa. Flash floods killed at least 1,000 people and forced as many as 100,000 from their homes. High water also engulfed thousands of acres of banana plantations, the foundation of the area's economy.

Honduras asked for U.S. assistance through Ambassador Phillip V. Sanchez. The Air Force participated in disaster relief operations from September 19 through October 15, using C–130, C–123, C–54, and UH–1 aircraft to transport 513 tons of disaster relief cargo from the United States, Puerto Rico, and the Panama Canal Zone to San Pedro Sula, La Ceiba, Tocoa, and Tegucigalpa, the Honduran capital. Cargo included food, clothing, medical supplies, water purification and food preparation equipment, generators, blankets, boats, and sandbags. The planes also carried 985 passengers, including disaster relief personnel and evacuees.

Humanitarian Airlift Operations

Cargo airplanes, including C–130s on rotational duty from the 314th Tac Alft Wg and C–123s from the 302d Tac Alft Wg, transported 180 tons of relief cargo from disaster relief stockpiles in the Canal Zone to Honduras. Two 24th Comp Gp UH–1 helicopters transported another 127 tons of supplies and 781 passengers on 234 sorties in the flooded Aguan River valley in northeastern Honduras.

Tactical Air Command aircraft involved in the relief airlift also included a C–130 from the 433d Tac Alft Wg from Kelly AFB, Texas. Seven AF Res and three ANG C–130 tactical airlift groups from California, New York, Mississippi, Texas, Pennsylvania, Michigan, Missouri, Louisiana, and Minnesota airlifted 206 tons of relief supplies—most donated by private U.S. citizens—to Honduras in late September and early October. The 156th Tac Ftr Gp in Puerto Rico also participated in the relief airlift, flying a C–54. The Hurricane Fifi disaster relief operation was one of the first foreign airlifts in which AF Res and ANG units participated on a voluntary basis.

The Air Force was one of many organizations working to relieve the suffering of the flood victims. Other branches of the U.S. military, private U.S. agencies, and a host of other nations sent aid. Floodwaters receded by mid-October, allowing thousands of people to return home.

71.
Name: Recife Flood.
Location: Republic of Brazil.
Date(s): July 26–29, 1975.
Emergency: Heavy rain in northeastern Brazil flooded Recife and surrounding areas, killing 100 people and leaving 46,000 homeless.
Air Force Organization(s) Involved: 772d Tac Alft Sq, 463d Tac Alft Wg, 24th Comp Gp, and USAF South Comd.
Airlifted: 30 tons of blankets, sheets, and cots.
Aircraft Employed: C–130 (three).
Operations: Beginning about July 17, heavy rain descended on the state of Pernambuco in northeastern Brazil and continued for a week. The Capiberibe and Tapacura Rivers overflowed, flooding the Atlantic coast port of Recife, a city of a million people. As much as 10 feet of water inundated the streets. The floods killed 100 people and left 46,000 homeless.

On July 23, the Brazilian foreign minister announced that assistance would be welcome. The State Department and Joint Chiefs of Staff approved an airlift from the Panama Canal Zone to Brazil as soon as Colombia granted permission for flights over its territory.

On July 26, the 772d Tac Alft Sq of the 463d Tac Alft Wg, serving on rotational duty with USAF Southern Command's 24th Comp Gp in Panama, flew three C–130 Hercules cargo airplanes 3,000 miles from Howard AFB to Recife. The planes carried 30 tons of relief supplies—including more than 12,000 sheets,

10,000 cotton blankets, and 1,300 cots—from AID and U.S. South Comd stockpiles in the Canal Zone.

Two C–130s returned to Panama on July 27 and the last returned on July 29. The airlifted cargo helped Brazilian relief authorities to provide bedding for thousands of flood victims in temporary shelters at Recife.

72.
Name: Kingston Homeless.
Location: Jamaica.
Date(s): January 25, 1976.
Emergency: Civil strife in the slums of Kingston temporarily forced many residents from their homes.
Air Force Organization(s) Involved: 36th Tac Alft Sq and 62d Mil Alft Wg.
Airlifted: 11 tons of tents, field kitchens, drinking water, and cots.
Aircraft Employed: C–130 (one).
Operations: In January, gangs of rival political factions fought in the streets of the western part of Kingston, the capital of Jamaica. They blocked streets, set fires, hurled rocks, and exchanged gunfire, forcing many residents to leave their homes for safety. On January 23, the island government, seeking shelter for the victims, asked the U.S. ambassador for emergency supplies. The State Department and Joint Chiefs of Staff approved an airlift from AID and U.S. South Comd stockpiles in the Panama Canal Zone.

On January 25, a C–130 from the 36th Tac Alft Sq of the 62d Mil Alft Wg, on rotational duty in Panama, flew 11 tons of supplies—including 120 tents, 20 field kitchens, 488 cots, and water cans—from Howard AFB to the international airport at Kingston. It returned to Panama that evening.

73.
Name: Operation Earthquake.
Location: Republic of Guatemala.
Date(s): February 4–June 30, 1976.
Emergency: An earthquake measuring 7.5 on the Richter scale struck Guatemala about 30 miles southwest of Guatemala City.
Air Force Organization(s) Involved: 60th, 62d, 63d, 436th, 437th, 438th, and 443d Mil Alft Wgs; 314th, 317th, and 463d Tac Alft Wgs; and 1300th Mil Alft Sq.
Airlifted: 927 tons of hospital equipment, tents, generators, medical supplies, food, clothing, fresh water, blankets, and construction equipment; and 696 medical, engineering, and communications personnel.
Aircraft Employed: C–5 (2), C–141 (29), and C–130 (33).
Operations: An earthquake registering 7.5 on the Richter scale struck southern Guatemala at 2:50 a.m. on Wednesday, February 4. Although it lasted less than one minute, it left almost 23,000 people dead and over 76,000 injured. One-fourth of Guatemala's population—1.5 million people—were left homeless. The quake

destroyed 300 towns along the Motagua and Mixco faults north and west of Guatemala City. The most severe damage occurred in a 100-mile arc to the north and west of the capital, where many of the country's inhabitants were concentrated. Over 1,000 aftershocks compounded the catastrophe. In the town of Progresso, only two buildings were left standing; and at San Martín, where no house survived, 3,000 people died—10 percent of the population.

President Kjell Laugerud García of Guatemala immediately appealed to the United States for emergency aid. Within 24 hours of the initial tremor, MAC established an airlift from Howard AFB in the Panama Canal Zone to La Aurora Airport in Guatemala City. Led by MSgt. Wayne W. Frankenberger, a 1300th Mil Alft Sq combat control team arrived in La Aurora on February 4 to assess damage and establish air traffic control communications for the airlift. Within 10 days, Air Force cargo aircraft moved over 444 tons of supplies and 230 support personnel to Guatemala, including a 100-bed field hospital, 500 tents, a 15-kilowatt generator, 10,800 penicillin tablets, and 500 pints of blood plasma.

By the end of February, the Twenty-first Air Force had flown 19 strategic airlift missions to Guatemala, carrying communications equipment from Charleston AFB, South Carolina; a mobile hospital from Altus AFB, Oklahoma; dry rations from Memphis, Tennessee, and Fort Smith, Arkansas; helicopter support equipment from Gray Army Air Field, Texas, and Harrisburg, Pennsylvania; water trailers from Howard AFB; a hospital unit from Fort Dix, New Jersey; and an environmental health unit and engineering personnel from Pope AFB, North Carolina.

By March 8, just over a month after the disaster struck, the Air Force had sent more than 60 planeloads of relief supplies and personnel to Guatemala from 10 U.S. bases. The Military Airlift Command transported medicine, water purification systems, blankets, clothing, fresh water, and construction equipment to clear roads and rebuild housing. Nine C–130s also delivered bulk fuel to support Army helicopters that flew mercy flights to remote sites within the country beginning February 10. By the end of Operation Earthquake, MAC had hauled 696 emergency support personnel to Guatemala, including medical doctors, nurses, engineers, and communications experts.

74.
Name: Bolivian Airplane Crash.
Location: Republic of Bolivia.
Date(s): October 15–21, 1976.
Emergency: When a jet airliner crashed on takeoff from Santa Cruz, Bolivia, 75 people died immediately. More than 100 suffered burns and other injuries.
Air Force Organization(s) Involved: 76th Mil Alft Sq.
Airlifted: A burn team and medical supplies.
Aircraft Employed: C–141 (one).
Operations: On October 13, a U.S. Boeing 707 jet airliner crashed on takeoff from Santa Cruz, Bolivia. The accident immediately killed 75 persons, including

3 U.S. citizens, and 40 more died later. More than 100 were injured, most suffering severe burns. The next day, the U.S. ambassador to Bolivia asked the State Department to arrange an airlift of medical experts from the burn center at Brooke Army Medical Center at Fort Sam Houston in Texas to Santa Cruz.

On October 15, a 76th Mil Alft Sq C–141 Starlifter airplane from the 437th Mil Alft Wg at Charleston AFB, South Carolina, flew a burn team and medical supplies from Kelly AFB, Texas, to El Trompillo Airport at Santa Cruz. U.S. medical experts treated burn victims with techniques and equipment not readily available in central Bolivia. The C–141 returned the burn team to the United States on October 21 via Howard AFB in the Panama Canal Zone.

75.
Name: Hurricane Greta.
Location: Republic of Honduras and Belize.
Date(s): September 24–October 5, 1978.
Emergency: Hurricane Greta hit Belize and the northern coast of Honduras, bringing high winds, high tides, and flash floods that left five people dead and hundreds homeless.
Air Force Organization(s) Involved: USAF Southern Air Division (USAF South Air Div) and 24th Composite Wing (Comp Wg).
Airlifted: 50 tons of cots, sheets, tents, water purification equipment, water pumps, generators, food, medicine, and other disaster relief cargo.
Aircraft Employed: C–130 (two).
Operations: Hurricane Greta hit the northern coast of Honduras on September 18, as it moved westward toward Belize. Winds gusting to 100 knots, tidal surges, and floods from torrential rain forced hundreds of people in both countries from their homes. The governments of Honduras and Belize requested U.S. disaster relief. The Joint Chiefs of Staff, reacting to State Department needs, directed the U.S. South Comd in the Panama Canal Zone to prepare an emergency airlift.

Between September 24 and 28, C–130 airplanes from AF Res and ANG units on rotational duty with the USAF South Air Div in the Canal Zone airlifted 50 tons of disaster relief cargo to Puerto Lempira, Honduras, and Stann Creek, Belize. The cargo included 2,000 cots, 3,000 sheets, 500 tents, water purification equipment, water pumps, food, and medicine from Canal Zone stockpiles. The USAF South Air Div, working through its 24th Comp Wg, also airlifted a 13-man disaster area survey team to Honduras. When the team returned to the Canal Zone on October 5, the C–130s had flown eight relief sorties to Honduras and Belize.

76.
Name: Costa Rican Flood.
Location: Republic of Costa Rica.
Date(s): October 23–26, 1978.

Emergency: Heavy rain over southern Costa Rica flooded the Coto Valley, stranding many people.
Air Force Organization(s) Involved: 24th Comp Wg.
Airlifted: 23 flood victims.
Aircraft Employed: UH–1 (two) and O–2 (one).
Operations: Heavy rain produced flash flooding in the Coto Valley of southern Costa Rica near Panama during late October. After Costa Rican officials requested U.S. assistance, the 24th Comp Wg, headquartered at Howard AFB in the Panama Canal Zone, flew two UH–1N helicopters and one O–2A observation plane to the flooded area. In 21 sorties between October 23 and 26, the aircraft evacuated 23 flood victims to safety.

77.
Name: Guyanese Disaster.
Location: Republic of Guyana.
Date(s): November 19–December 22, 1978.
Emergency: When a U.S. congressman visited Jonestown, Guyana, to investigate human rights violations by a U.S. cult, his party was attacked. Five people were killed and 10 were wounded. More than 900 deaths followed as cult members committed mass suicide.
Air Force Organization(s) Involved: USAF South Air Div; 1550th Aircrew Training and Test Wing; 60th, 62d, 63d, 437th, and 438th Mil Alft Wgs; 514th Mil Alft Wg (Associate); and 55th and 305th Aerosp RR Sqs.
Airlifted: 915 bodies; 751 passengers, including graves registration, medical evacuation, communications, and State Department personnel and military; and 708 tons of cargo, including aluminum transfer cases, trucks, jeeps, helicopters, generators, communications equipment, sleeping bags, blankets, and other supplies for airlift personnel.
Aircraft Employed: C–141 (21+), HH–53 (3), HC–130 (2), and C–130 (number unknown).
Operations: During mid-November, reports of U.S. citizens being held against their will led Congressman Leo J. Ryan of California to visit the Peoples' Temple Agricultural Mission at Jonestown in northern South America. Jonestown was a commune organized by Jim Jones about 150 miles northwest of Georgetown, capital of Guyana. When Ryan, a group of reporters, defecting mission members, and relatives prepared to board aircraft at an airstrip at Port Kaituma near Jonestown, Peoples' Temple cult members shot at them, killing Ryan, three reporters, and one defector, and wounding 10 others. Some survivors of the attack flew to Georgetown, where the U.S. ambassador sought military airlift for the dead and wounded. The State Department asked MAC to respond.

As two Guyanese airplanes transported the wounded from Port Kaituma to Georgetown's Timehri Airport, two C–141 cargo planes from the Twenty-first Air Force's 437th and 438th Mil Alft Wgs flew to Guyana. From November 19 to 21, one C–141, with emergency medical personnel, moved the wounded to hospitals at Roosevelt Roads NAS, Puerto Rico, and Andrews AFB, Maryland. On November 20 and 21, the other C–141 carried the bodies of Congressman Ryan and the three reporters to their home states of California and Georgia for burial.

Meanwhile, 914 cult members at Jonestown killed themselves or were killed by their parents, most by drinking a cyanide potion. On November 20, Guyana insisted that the United States remove the bodies because all but three were U.S. nationals. Secretary of State Cyrus Vance authorized an airlift and the Pentagon activated a joint task force composed of elements of the Southern, Readiness, and Military Airlift Commands.

Between November 22 and 29, three HH–53 Jolly Green Giant helicopters from the 55th Aerosp RR Sq from Eglin AFB, Florida, carried 911 bodies from Jonestown to Georgetown, where MAC C–141s loaded them for transport to the United States. Two HC–130 airplanes from the 305th Aerosp RR Sq and the 1550th Aircrew Training and Test Wing refueled the helicopters as they flew 30 shuttle missions between the commune and the capital of Guyana.

In nine missions, the C–141 airplanes carried the 911 bodies from Georgetown to a large mortuary at Dover AFB, Delaware. Because body bags split open, joint task force officials decided to use aluminum transfer cases. Other C–141 Starlifters delivered the cases to Georgetown from Hawaii, California, Utah, Virginia, Tennessee, and the Panama Canal Zone. Some of the planes recycled cases from Dover AFB to Guyana.

Still other C–141s carried graves registration personnel, medical evacuation experts, and joint task force cargo—including jeeps, trucks, generators, and Army helicopters—from bases in the United States to Guyana for the airlift. Southern Air Division C–130s from AF Res and ANG units serving rotational duty in the Canal Zone flew similar missions. Passengers included communications and State Department personnel, and cargo included sleeping bags, blankets, generators, and food for emergency airlift personnel of the joint task force. Between November 21 and 28, the C–130s flew 11 sorties, most from Howard AFB to the Georgetown airport. They also evacuated eight U.S. civilians from Georgetown.

Between November 19 and December 22, MAC C–141s, C–130s, and HH–53s flew more than 59 missions to airlift 915 bodies, 652 passengers, and 648 tons of cargo on the Guyana operation. During the same period, USAF South Air Div C–130s transported 99 passengers and 60 tons of cargo on 11 missions. The Air Force effort, therefore, totaled more than 70 missions carrying 751 passengers, 708 tons of cargo, and 915 bodies. On December 22, two C–141s returned the last joint task force personnel from Georgetown to the United States.

78.
Name: Saint Vincent Volcano.
Location: Saint Vincent.
Date(s): April 14–22, 1979.
Emergency: Mount Soufrière erupted, forcing thousands of people from their homes.
Air Force Organization(s) Involved: USAF South Air Div and 756th Tac Alft Sq.
Airlifted: 30 tons of blankets, cots, tents, medical supplies, cooking kits, and water purification equipment.
Aircraft Employed: C–130 (two+).
Operations: Mount Soufrière, a volcano in the northern part of the Caribbean island of Saint Vincent, erupted on April 13. Knowing that a similar eruption in 1902 had killed 2,000 people, thousands of islanders in 17 villages evacuated their homes. The Pentagon directed the U.S. South Comd to respond to the emergency with an airlift after the State Department received an official request for assistance from the island's British administrators.

The U.S. South Comd directed relief operations to Saint Vincent from April 14 to 22. The 756th Tac Alft Sq of the 459th Tac Alft Wg at Andrews AFB, Maryland, on rotational duty in the Panama Canal Zone with the USAF South Air Div, used C–130s to fly 30 tons of relief supplies and equipment from stockpiles in the Canal Zone to Saint Vincent's Arnos Vale Airport in the southern part of the island. The cargo included 6,937 blankets, 1,165 double cots, 335 single cots, five general purpose tents, 20,000 tetracycline antibiotic capsules, cooking kits, and water purification equipment.

79.
Name: Nicaraguan Evacuation.
Location: Republic of Nicaragua.
Date(s): June 12–July 26, 1979.
Emergency: Civil war in Nicaragua left 15,000 people dead and threatened the lives of many more, including many U.S. civilians.
Air Force Organization(s) Involved: USAF South Air Div; 24th Comp Wg; 118th, 164th, and 442d Tac Alft Wgs; and 437th Mil Alft Wg.
Airlifted: 1,438 passengers and 51 tons of relief supplies, including food and bread.
Aircraft Employed: C–130 (nine) and C–141 (one).
Operations: From May through July, Sandinista guerilla forces in Nicaragua fought to oust Gen. Anastasio Somoza Debayle from power. Somoza and his national guard resisted, bombing and shelling cities and towns taken by the Sandinistas. Intense fighting left 600,000 people homeless, 15,000 dead, and many starving. As the fighting reached the capital city of Managua, civilians trying to leave the country were stranded by an interruption in civil air service. The U.S. embassy requested a military airlift on their behalf.

The Pentagon responded to State Department needs by directing the U.S. South Comd in the Panama Canal Zone to organize the airlift. The command's Air Force component, the USAF South Air Div, used AF Res and ANG resources on rotation to the Canal Zone.

Between June 12 and July 25, the 118th, 164th, and 442d Tac Alft Wgs each supplied three C–130 Hercules cargo aircraft and crews on 24 missions to airlift more than 1,400 refugees—including U.S., Canadian, Japanese, and Nicaraguan civilians—from Managua to Panama. The nine C–130s loaded the passengers at Managua's Las Mercedes International Airport and at Massachapa's Montelimar Airport, about 35 miles southwest of the capital, after Managua's airport closed due to fighting. They flew to Panama's Tocumen International Airport or the Canal Zone. Most embassy personnel left Nicaragua, but the embassy continued to operate at Managua. After Somoza resigned and went into exile on July 17, the United States recognized the Sandinista provisional government.

Besides evacuating civilians, the Air Force flew 51 tons of relief supplies to Nicaragua. C–130s delivered 26 tons of food and blood supplies for the Red Cross. On July 26, a C–141 from the 437th Mil Alft Wg moved 25 tons of vegetable oil from Charleston AFB, South Carolina, to Managua. Many more tons of U.S. food were transported to Nicaragua that summer by non-military means.

80.
Name: Caribbean Storms.
Location: Dominica, Hispaniola, Jamaica, Barbados, Martinique, Guadeloupe, and Puerto Rico.
Date(s): August 31–November 21, 1979.
Emergency: Hurricane David swept across islands in the West Indies with winds up to 150 mph, tides 15 feet above normal, and torrential rain, leaving more than 600 people dead and 210,000 homeless. Tropical Storm Frederic compounded the destruction a few days later.
Air Force Organization(s) Involved: USAF South Air Div; 62d, 436th, 437th, and 438th Mil Alft Wgs; 133d, 314th, 317th, and 463d Tac Alft Wgs; 143d and 166th Tac Alft Gps; and 1300th Mil Alft Sq.
Airlifted: More than 2,900 tons of relief cargo, including tents, plastic sheeting, cots, blankets, C rations, powdered milk, rice, flour, cooking oil, fresh water, water pumps, water purification equipment, medical supplies, clothing, tools, building materials, helicopters, and trucks; and more than 1,400 passengers, including military construction crews and flood evacuees.
Aircraft Employed: C–130 (15+), C–141 (five+), and C–5 (number unknown).
Operations: On August 30, Hurricane David struck the island of Dominica in the West Indies with winds up to 150 mph, tides 15 feet above normal, and torrential rain. The storm left at least 20 people dead and 60,000 homeless on the island. The next day, the hurricane hit the Dominican Republic on the eastern side of Hispaniola, killing more than 600 people and leaving 150,000 homeless. The hur-

ricane also devastated the neighboring islands of Barbados, Guadeloupe, Martinique, Jamaica, and Puerto Rico. A few days later, Tropical Storm Frederick swept across the same islands.

Responding to requests from the State Department, the JCS directed the Atlantic Command and the Military Airlift Command to organize disaster relief operations. The U.S. South Comd and the USAF South Air Div in the Panama Canal Zone supported the effort.

For the following weeks, C–5s and C–141s from the 62d, 436th, 437th, and 438th Mil Alft Wgs transported military construction crews, helicopters, trucks, tents, cots, plastic sheeting, blankets, building materials, clothing, medical supplies, tools, C rations, rice, powdered milk, flour, cooking oil, fresh water, water pumps, and water purification equipment from bases in North Carolina, Mississippi, Kentucky, Delaware, South Carolina, New Jersey, and other parts of the United States to Roosevelt Roads NAS, Puerto Rico.

There, cargo and personnel transferred to smaller C–130 Hercules cargo planes capable of landing at airfields on islands in the Caribbean. Tactical airlift wings and groups flew the C–130s to Dominica, the Dominican Republic, and Jamaica. The Hercules airplanes also helped to evacuate hurricane victims from remote regions of other islands.

By November 21, the Air Force had transported more than 1,400 passengers and over 2,900 tons of disaster relief cargo, much of it from stockpiles in the Canal Zone.

81.
Name: Bolivian Evacuation.
Location: Republic of Bolivia.
Date(s): November 7, 1979.
Emergency: A military coup in Bolivia stranded 133 U.S. tourists and businessmen without civil air transportation in La Paz, where escalating violence threatened their safety.
Air Force Organization(s) Involved: USAF South Air Div, 337th Tac Alft Sq, and 1300th Mil Alft Sq.
Airlifted: 133 U.S. citizens.
Aircraft Employed: C–130 (two).
Operations: At the beginning of November, Col. Alberto Natusch Busch seized power in a military coup d'état against the government of President Walter Guevara Arze in Bolivia. Snipers, barricades, and street fighting erupted in the capital of La Paz, threatening the lives of foreign nationals. France, West Germany, Switzerland, and other countries began evacuating their citizens as commercial air service to and from the capital ceased. On November 6, the U.S. ambassador, Paul H. Boeker, requested a military airlift to evacuate U.S. citizens stranded in La Paz. The Joint Chiefs of Staff, responding to a State Department request, directed the U.S. South Comd in Panama to arrange the airlift.

On November 7, two Air Force C–130 airplanes transported 133 U.S. tourists and businessmen from La Paz's J. F. Kennedy International Airport to Lima, where commercial air service was available. The airplanes belonged to the Air Force Reserve's 337th Tac Alft Sq of the 439th Tac Alft Wg, at Westover AFB, Massachusetts, which was serving the U.S. South Comd on rotation to Panama. The USAF South Air Div and the 1300th Mil Alft Sq supervised the operation.

There were some difficulties. Bolivian military authorities, fearing that planes from other Latin American countries would land with arms for the opposition, blocked the runways at the La Paz airport. A representative of the U.S. military group in Bolivia convinced the Bolivians to allow the Air Force C–130s to land. The C–130s stayed on the ground only 45 minutes to avoid trouble. The airport's 13,000-foot altitude made takeoff by fully loaded cargo planes more difficult than usual. Despite these problems, the airlift was successful.

82.
Name: Panamanian Flood.
Location: Republic of Panama.
Date(s): November 15–16, 1979.
Emergency: A storm system flooded Chiriqui province in western Panama, leaving 1,800 people homeless, with many stranded in high water.
Air Force Organization(s) Involved: 24th Comp Wg.
Airlifted: 27 flood victims and food and fresh water.
Aircraft Employed: UH–1 (two) and O–2 (one).
Operations: A storm struck Chiriqui province in western Panama on November 13 and 14, bringing 50-knot winds and heavy rain that caused flash flooding. About 1,800 people were left homeless, some stranded in waist-deep water. On November 15, the Panamanian government requested U.S. assistance. That day, the 24th Comp Wg at Howard AFB rallied a 14-man team to aid Panamanian and U.S. Army disaster relief personnel.

On November 16, flying two UH–1N helicopters and one O–2A observation airplane, the 24th Comp Wg rescued 27 isolated flood victims—mostly women and children—in the Puerto Armuelles area of southwestern Panama, 30 miles southwest of David. The helicopters carried three people to area hospitals and distributed food and fresh water supplied by Panamanian authorities.

83.
Name: Colombian Earthquake.
Location: Republic of Colombia.
Date(s): December 14–17, 1979.
Emergency: A severe earthquake struck southwestern Colombia, leaving 200 people dead, 500 injured, and thousands homeless.
Air Force Organization(s) Involved: USAF South Air Div, 433d Tac Alft Wg, and 1300th Mil Alft Sq.

Humanitarian Airlift Operations

Airlifted: 87 tons of tents and cots and 118 passengers.

Aircraft Employed: C–130 (four).

Operations: At about 3:00 a.m. on December 12, a severe earthquake registering 7.7 on the Richter scale struck the southwestern coast of Colombia, leaving 200 people dead, 500 injured, and thousands homeless. More than 80 died in Tumaco and El Charco as 10-foot waves devastated other coastal communities and the region suffered 10 aftershocks within an hour after the initial tremor.

Following an official request from the Colombian government for U.S. assistance, the U.S. South Comd in Panama organized an airlift of supplies by cargo planes under operational control of the USAF South Air Div, coordinated by the 1300th Mil Alft Sq.

On December 14, three C–130s from the 433d Tac Alft Wg, on rotational duty with the USAF South Air Div, airlifted 300 large tents and 1,200 double-decker cots from disaster relief stockpiles at Howard AFB to the disaster area. One C–130 remained in Colombia for three more days, shuttling relief supplies and support personnel among the communities of Bogotá, Cali, Tumaco, and Tolemedia. On December 16, a fourth C–130 transported more relief supplies from Howard AFB to Tumaco. By December 17, the four C–130s had carried 87 tons of supplies and 118 passengers in 21 sorties.

84.

Name: Nicaraguan Flood.

Location: Republic of Nicaragua.

Date(s): December 16, 1979–March 12, 1980.

Emergency: Torrential rain in northeastern Nicaragua produced flooding that threatened residents of the area with disease and starvation.

Air Force Organization(s) Involved: USAF South Air Div, 433d Tac Alft Wg, 166th Tac Alft Gp, 1300th Mil Alft Sq, and AF Res and ANG C–130 units.

Airlifted: At least 117 tons of medical supplies, food, and fuel; and 247 passengers, including medical teams.

Aircraft Employed: C–130 (three+).

Operations: During mid-December, heavy rain in northeastern Nicaragua flooded the Coco River valley and 5,000 square kilometers around Puerto Cabezas, Waspan, and Kum. Malnutrition and disease among flood victims persuaded the Nicaraguan government to request an airlift of food and medicine through the U.S. ambassador at Managua. On December 16, the Pentagon directed the U.S. South Comd in Panama to organize relief operations to Nicaragua.

Between December 16 and March 12, AF Res and ANG C–130s and crews on rotational duty with the USAF South Air Div and the 1300th Mil Alft Sq at Howard AFB in Panama—including elements of the 166th Tac Alft Gp and the 433d Tac Alft Wg—airlifted at least 117 tons of medical supplies, food, and fuel from Panama to Nicaragua and from Managua to the disaster area. Some of the 14 C–130 missions transported supplies directly from Howard AFB to Puerto

Cabezas, while others ferried relief cargo from Managua to Puerto Cabezas and Waspam. The cargo planes carried 247 passengers, including medical and survey teams.

U.S. Southern Command medical personnel treated 5,300 flood victims, vaccinating many against disease. They also helped to train local nurses during almost three months of continuous on-site assistance. Army helicopters helped to distribute food and medical supplies and transport doctors and nurses to 10 remote villages in the flooded area.

U.S. Southern Command disaster relief operations to and within Nicaragua concluded on March 12. By then, threats of starvation and disease in northeastern Nicaragua had receded with the floodwaters. The United States carried out the disaster relief operation despite signs of anti-Americanism from the Sandinista government, which had come to power in July 1979.

85.
Name: Belizean Flood.
Location: Belize.
Date(s): December 19, 1979.
Emergency: Heavy rain produced flash flooding, driving many people from their homes and contributing to food shortages.
Air Force Organization(s) Involved: USAF South Air Div, 433d Tac Alft Wg, and 1300th Mil Alft Sq.
Airlifted: 15 tons of rice, flour, and vegetable oil.
Aircraft Employed: C–130 (one).
Operations: During mid-December, heavy rain produced flash flooding in the British colony of Belize, formerly British Honduras. Aware of a food shortage there, the State Department asked DoD to airlift supplies to Belize from Panama and Honduras. On December 18, the Pentagon directed the U.S. South Comd to organize a relief operation.

On December 19, a 433d Tac Alft Wg C–130 and crew—serving under the USAF South Air Div and 1300th Mil Alft Sq while on AF Res rotational duty in Panama—transported 15 tons of food supplies from San Pedro Sula, Honduras, and Howard AFB, Panama, to Belize (city). Much of the cargo came from AID stockpiles and included eight tons of rice, four tons of flour, and three tons of vegetable oil.

86.
Name: Hurricane Allen.
Location: Republic of Haiti and Saint Lucia.
Date(s): August 7–16, 1980.
Emergency: Hurricane Allen, with winds up to 170 mph, struck Haiti and Saint Lucia, killing at least 57 people and leaving hundreds homeless.
Air Force Organization(s) Involved: USAF South Air Div; 436th, 437th, and

Humanitarian Airlift Operations

438th Mil Alft Wgs; 440th Tac Alft Wg; 927th Tac Alft Gp; and 1300th Mil Alft Sq.

Airlifted: 61 tons of helicopters, blankets, tents, water purification units, sump pumps, and vehicles; and 107 passengers.

Aircraft Employed: C–5 (one), C–141 (two), and C–130 (two).

Operations: Between August 3 and 6, Hurricane Allen slashed across islands of the Caribbean Sea with sustained winds of up to 170 mph. It struck Barbados on August 3, Saint Lucia on August 4, Hispaniola (Haiti and the Dominican Republic) on August 5, and Jamaica and Cuba on August 6. The storm left at least 57 people dead and hundreds homeless in Haiti and Saint Lucia, prompting the two nations to seek U.S. assistance. On August 7, responding to a State Department request, DoD directed the Atlantic Command to supervise a disaster relief effort that drew airlift support from the U.S. South Comd in Panama.

That same day, the USAF South Air Div and the 1300th Mil Alft Sq—managing AF Res, ANG, and MAC resources in Latin America—launched two relief flights from Howard AFB, Panama, to Saint Lucia and Haiti. A C–141 Starlifter of the 437th Mil Alft Wg at Charleston AFB, South Carolina, transported a 15-man disaster assistance and survey team, two OH–58 helicopters, a jeep, a trailer, and food from Howard AFB to Port-au-Prince, Haiti.

A C–130 Hercules cargo plane from the 440th Tac Alft Wg—serving the U.S. South Comd on rotational duty in Panama—airlifted more than 2,000 blankets, 100 tents, and cooking equipment from AID stockpiles in Panama to St. Lucia. On August 9, the same C–130 transported 10 tons of food and other relief supplies from Barbados to St. Lucia.

Flying a C–5 from Dover AFB, Delaware, the 436th Mil Alft Wg moved 69 marines and five UH–1N helicopters from Cherry Point, North Carolina, to Port-au-Prince on August 11 to help hurricane victims. The next day, a 438th Mil Alft Wg C–141 transported three water purification units, sump pumps, 800 water containers, and 11 marines to the same destination. The 927th Tac Alft Gp flew more disaster relief equipment and supplies from Panama to Haiti aboard a C–130 on August 16 to complete disaster relief airlift missions to the Caribbean area in the wake of Hurricane Allen.

The C–5, two C–141s, and two C–130s airlifted more than 61 tons of disaster relief equipment and supplies from the United States and Panama to Haiti and St. Lucia between August 7 and 16. The aircraft also transported 107 passengers—mostly workers to clean up storm damage, repair buildings, and distribute supplies—during the same operation. From August 16 to 23, special assignment airlift and routine channel missions returned personnel and equipment, including seven airlifted helicopters, to Panama and the United States.

87.
Name: Coco River Flood.
Location: Republic of Nicaragua.
Date(s): October 20–23, 1980.
Emergency: The Coco River of northeastern Nicaragua flooded the town of Waspam and adjacent areas, creating shortages of food and medicine.
Air Force Organization(s) Involved: USAF South Air Div, 166th Tac Alft Gp, and 1300th Mil Alft Sq.
Airlifted: 40 tons of food, medicine, and latrines.
Aircraft Employed: C–130 (one).
Operations: During mid-October, heavy tropical rain flooded the Coco River valley in the vicinity of Waspam in northeastern Nicaragua, producing shortages of food and medicine. On October 18, the Nicaraguan government, for the second time in less than a year (see Nicaraguan Flood, December 1979–March 1980), asked the U.S. ambassador at Managua for U.S. assistance. Nicaraguan officials wanted U.S. aircraft to haul relief supplies, collected by the Red Cross at Managua, to Waspam. The State Department contacted DoD, which directed the U.S. South Comd in Panama to organize the airlift.

From October 20 to 23, members of the 166th Tac Alft Gp—an ANG unit serving on rotational duty with the USAF South Air Div and 1300th Mil Alft Sq at Howard AFB in Panama—flew a C–130 cargo plane to airlift 40 tons of food, medicine, and latrines on three flights from Managua to Waspam. The cargo included rice, beans, corn, sugar, salt, vegetable oil, soup, juices, and powdered milk. The C–130 crew members transported 10 tons on October 20, 15 tons on October 21, and 15 tons on October 23. Although the crew was ready to airlift more supplies, the Nicaraguan government suspended the operation, claiming lack of storage space at Waspam. On October 23, the C–130 returned to Panama.

88.
Name: Peruvian Earthquake.
Location: Republic of Peru.
Date(s): July 14, 1981.
Emergency: An earthquake south of Ayacucho, Peru, left 10 people dead and thousands homeless.
Air Force Organization(s) Involved: USAF South Air Div, 1300th Mil Alft Sq, and 145th Tac Alft Gp.
Airlifted: 7.7 tons of blankets.
Aircraft Employed: C–130 (one).
Operations: An earthquake struck the Andes just south of Ayacucho in southern Peru on July 7, leaving 10 people dead and thousands homeless. The International Red Cross immediately donated 5,000 blankets from its warehouse in Panama and, with the Peruvian government, requested a U.S. airlift of the cargo to Peru. On July 10, the Pentagon assigned the mission to the U.S. South Comd in Panama.

Humanitarian Airlift Operations

Members of the U.S. Army's 193d Infantry Brigade moved the blankets, packed in 200 cartons, from the Red Cross warehouse in Panama City to Howard AFB, where they were loaded on a C–130 cargo airplane. On July 14, the airplane, flown by a seven-man crew from the Air National Guard's 145th Tac Alft Gp at Charlotte, North Carolina, on rotational duty with the 1300th Mil Alft Sq and the USAF South Air Div, carried the blankets from Howard AFB to Lima. The Peruvian Red Cross accepted the blankets, which weighed almost eight tons, and arranged for their delivery to earthquake victims in the Ayacucho area.

89.
Name: Panamanian Bridge Collapse.
Location: Republic of Panama.
Date(s): May 21–26, 1982.
Emergency: A large suspension bridge over the Chiriqui River collapsed, severing an important highway linking farms of western Panama with cities in the central part of the country.
Air Force Organization(s) Involved: USAF South Air Div, 1300th Mil Alft Sq, and 118th Tac Alft Wg.
Airlifted: 381 tons of food and other cargo and 72 passengers.
Aircraft Employed: C–130 (number unknown).
Operations: On May 3, a large suspension bridge over the Chiriqui River in western Panama collapsed, severing the most important transportation artery between the farms of Chiriqui province with the cities of central Panama and cutting the Pan-American Highway. The Panamanian government asked the U.S. embassy for disaster relief. The request was referred through the State and Defense Departments to the U.S. South Comd in Panama, which prepared to launch a relief airlift.

Between May 21 and 26, C–130 aircraft from the 118th Tac Alft Wg of the Tennessee ANG—on rotational duty with the 1300th Mil Alft Sq and the USAF South Air Div at Howard AFB, Panama—flew 49 sorties to airlift cargo between David, the capital of Chiriqui province, and Panama (city), the national capital. The planes hauled more than 381 tons and 72 passengers, transporting food from David to Panama's Torrijos International Airport and manufactured items back. Panamanian and U.S. Army engineers constructed temporary bridges over the Chiriqui River, rendering the airlift unnecessary after a week of emergency operations.

90.
Name: Popayan Earthquake.
Location: Republic of Colombia.
Date(s): April 1–8, 1983.
Emergency: A Colombian earthquake registering 5.5 on the Richter scale killed 260 people, injured 1,500, and left at least 35,000 homeless.
Air Force Organization(s) Involved: USAF South Air Div, 1300th Mil Alft Sq, and AF Res or ANG units.

Airlifted: At least 34 tons of shelters, medical supplies, electric generators, and floodlights.

Aircraft Employed: C–130 (number unknown).

Operations: On March 31, an earthquake registering 5.5 on the Richter scale struck Popayan and a host of villages in the Andes in southwestern Colombia, leaving at least 260 people dead, 1,500 injured, and 35,000 homeless. The Colombian government, headed by President Belisario Betancur, requested international assistance for the thousands of people who needed shelter. Alerted by the State Department, the JCS assigned disaster relief operations to the U.S. South Comd in Panama on the day of the earthquake. Within 25 hours, U.S. relief supplies were on the way to the devastated region.

Between April 1 and 8, AF Res and ANG C–130s—on rotational duty with the USAF South Air Div and the 1300th Mil Alft Sq in Panama—transported at least 34 tons of tents, plastic sheeting for shelters, medical supplies, electric generators, and floodlights from Office of Foreign Disaster Assistance and AID stockpiles in Panama to Cali, Colombia. They also carried construction and medical personnel to Colombia from the U.S. Army's 193d Infantry Brigade at Fort Kobbe, Panama.

The United States was one of six nations sending supplies and relief workers to Colombia, and U.S. C–130s delivered the first outside relief cargo. By April 8, these C–130s had completed five sorties on behalf of the earthquake victims.

91.
Name: Peruvian Flood.
Location: Republic of Peru.
Date(s): June 26–July 1, 1983.
Emergency: More than 100 inches of rain fell over normally arid northwestern Peru, flooding the Piura region and cutting roads connecting it with other parts of the country.
Air Force Organization(s) Involved: USAF South Air Div, 337th Tac Alft Sq, 118th and 439th Tac Alft Wgs, and 1300th Mil Alft Sq.
Airlifted: 170 tons of food, medicine, and other relief supplies.
Aircraft Employed: C–130 (three).
Operations: During late June, heavy rain produced extensive flooding in the Piura region of northwestern Peru, about 500 miles northwest of Lima, leaving about 40,000 people homeless. More than 100 inches of rain in seven months in the normally arid region flooded roads connecting Piura with other parts of Peru. Food collected at Lima for the flood victims began to spoil. The president of Peru, Fernando Belaunde Terry, requested assistance to airlift disaster relief supplies to the Piura region.

Maj. Gen. William E. Masterson of the USAF South Air Div welcomed the Peruvian relief operation as an opportunity to train AF Res and ANG C–130 crews. Between June 26 and July 1, the 337th Tac Alft Sq of the 439th Tac Alft

Wg and the 118th Tac Alft Wg from the Tennessee ANG—on rotation with the USAF South Air Div and 1300th Mil Alft Sq at Howard AFB in Panama—transported 170 tons of disaster relief supplies, including food and medicine, from Lima to Piura. The 337th Tac Alft Sq flew two C–130s and the 118th Tac Alft Wg flew one C–130 on 13 missions in six days.

One C–130 developed mechanical trouble and required an engine replacement in Lima. The operation provided Peruvian officials and U.S. Air Force personnel an opportunity to cooperate in activities.

92.
Name: Ecuadoran Flood.
Location: Republic of Ecuador.
Date(s): July 24–August 6, 1983.
Emergency: Months of heavy rain isolated 25 remote villages, depriving residents of food, medicine, and medical care.
Air Force Organization(s) Involved: Detachment 1, 2d Air Div.
Airlifted: 10 tons of food and medical supplies and medical personnel.
Aircraft Employed: UH–1 (two).
Operations: From late 1982 through the first half of 1983, unusual weather patterns—caused in part by a change in Pacific Ocean currents (El Niño)—produced persistent, heavy rain in western South America. In Ecuador, 12 feet of rain fell in seven months between November 1982 and June 1983, flooding Guayas province and other parts of the country. High water isolated 25 remote villages, depriving them of food and medicine.

While U.S. military forces conducted a joint training exercise with Ecuadoran forces (Fuerzas Unidas-Ecuador 83) from July 23 to August 6, 1983, U.S. helicopters transported medical personnel, food, and medicine to the flooded region. Detachment 1, 2d Air Div, serving with the 24th Comp Wg in Panama, deployed two UH–1N helicopters to Salinas, Ecuador, on July 24.

During the next two weeks, the helicopter crews, in addition to flying exercise missions, transported 10 tons of rice, powdered milk, and food to the isolated villages. The helicopters airlifted Ecuadoran doctors, nurses, and dentists to the villages to provide medical treatment. The detachment demonstrated that training could be combined with humanitarian airlift and helped to reinforce relations between Ecuador and the United States.

93.
Name: Argentinean Earthquake.
Location: Argentina.
Date(s): February 3, 1985.
Emergency: An earthquake in Argentina left 6 people dead, 238 injured, and 44,000 homeless.
Air Force Organization(s) Involved: 438th Mil Alft Wg.

Airlifted: 500 eight-person tents.

Aircraft Employed: C–141 (one).

Operations: Shortly after midnight on January 26, an earthquake measuring more than 5.0 on the Richter scale struck northern Mendoza province in west central Argentina, leaving 6 people dead, 238 injured, and 44,000 homeless. The quake destroyed 8,600 buildings and damaged more than 30,000 others, causing damage totaling $500 million in towns such as Mendoza, Godoy Cruz, Las Heras, and Guaymallen. On January 28, the acting president, Victor Martínez, declared a state of emergency; two days later, he asked for U.S. assistance. The U.S. embassy in Buenos Aires passed the request to the State Department, which contacted DoD for an emergency airlift on February 2.

On February 3, the 438th Mil Alft Wg at McGuire AFB, New Jersey, flew a C–141 Starlifter cargo plane from Howard AFB, Panama, to Mendoza's El Plumerillo Airport laden with 500 eight-person tents capable of sheltering 4,000 earthquake victims. The vice governor of Mendoza province and Mendoza city officials met the plane when it landed, and Argentinean television, radio, and newspapers covered the relief mission. The airlift improved relations between the United States and Argentina, which had been strained since the Falkland Islands war three years earlier.

94.

Name: Chilean Earthquake.

Location: Republic of Chile.

Date(s): March 15–18, 1985.

Emergency: An earthquake struck central Chile, killing 145 persons, injuring 2,000, and leaving 150,000 homeless.

Air Force Organization(s) Involved: 436th Mil Alft Wg.

Airlifted: 60 tons of plastic sheeting.

Aircraft Employed: C–5 (one).

Operations: On Sunday, March 3, an earthquake registering 7.4 on the Richter scale struck central Chile. The epicenter was 25 miles off the coastal town of Algarrobo, about 200 miles southwest of the quake that had hit Argentina in January (see Argentinean Earthquake, February 1985). Santiago, Algarrobo, San Antonio, Valparaiso, Vina del Mar, and other cities and towns along a strip 800 miles long suffered tremendous damage that killed 145 people, injured 2,000, and left 150,000 homeless. The government of Chile, under President Augusto Pinochet Ugarte, requested U.S. assistance, and the State Department contacted DoD for an emergency airlift.

Between March 15 and 18, Lt. Col. Dan Pruitt and his crew flew a 436th Mil Alft Wg C–5 Galaxy cargo plane with 1,000 rolls of plastic sheeting weighing more than 60 tons from Pease AFB, New Hampshire, via Howard AFB, Panama, to Santiago, Chile. Chilean authorities used the sheeting to construct tents to shelter thousands of homeless earthquake victims.

Humanitarian Airlift Operations

95.
Name: Mexican Earthquakes.
Location: Mexico.
Date(s): September 19–30, 1985.
Emergency: Two earthquakes struck Mexico, killing at least 4,700 people, injuring 30,000, and leaving 40,000 homeless.
Air Force Organization(s) Involved: 60th, 63d, 89th, 349th, 437th, 438th, and 445th Mil Alft Wgs; 136th, 146th, 317th, and 463d Tac Alft Wgs; and USAF South Air Div.
Airlifted: More than 360 tons of cargo and more than 290 passengers.
Aircraft Employed: C–141 (11), C–130 (5), C–5 (4), and C–21 (2).
Operations: On September 19 and 20, two earthquakes, measuring respectively 8.1 and 7.5 on the Richter scale, struck southwestern Mexico. Although the epicenters were 250 miles southwest of Mexico City, the central business section of that metropolitan area of 18 million people suffered severe damage. Collapsing buildings and fires fed by broken natural gas lines killed at least 4,700 people and injured 30,000. The tremors destroyed or damaged 2,500 buildings, leaving at least 40,000 people homeless. The Mexican government, which traditionally had declined offers of outside assistance, agreed to allow an airlift of relief supplies, equipment, and emergency personnel after Secretary of State George Shultz met with the Mexican ambassador, Jorge Espinosa de Los Reyes. The Defense Department assigned relief missions to MAC and the U.S. South Comd when it received the State Department request.

Between September 19 and 30, 22 Air Force cargo planes—including 11 C–141s, 5 C–130s, 4 C–5s, and 2 C–21s—transported more than 360 tons of cargo and 290 passengers from the United States and Panama to Benito Juárez International Airport in Mexico City. Relief equipment and supplies included 16 dogs trained to locate trapped victims, three fire-fighting helicopters, six trucks, 10,000 surgical masks, 1,000 respirator masks, 5,000 body bags, 16 electrical generators, 5,000 blankets, 3,200 cots, 600 sleeping bags, water pumps, hoses, 60 power saws, 200 leather gloves, 600 jackets, communications equipment, plastic sheeting, jack hammers, six vans, oxygen tanks, acetylene bottles, and 74 water tanks.

Among airlifted emergency personnel were firefighters, rescue dog handlers, engineers, mine safety personnel, diplomats, and disaster assessment teams. Seven military airlift wings and four tactical airlift wings participated in the 22 relief missions. They carried cargo and passengers from at least 15 states and 13 Air Force bases in the United States and Panama. On September 23, the 89th Mil Alft Wg carried First Lady Nancy Reagan to Mexico City to express concern and deliver a $1 million check as a promise of additional U.S. assistance.

Air Force emergency airlift operations to Mexico ended on September 30. By then, U.S. and other international assistance had helped Mexican authorities to lay the foundation to reconstruct their devastated capital.

198

96.
Name: Puerto Rican Mud Slides.
Location: Commonwealth of Puerto Rico.
Date(s): October 9–16, 1985.
Emergency: Sixteen inches of rain in 24 hours in southern Puerto Rico produced floods, mud slides, and landslides that killed up to 500 people, injured 3,000, and left 5,000 homeless.
Air Force Organization(s) Involved: 60th, 62d, 63d, 436th, and 437th Mil Alft Wgs; and 314th and 317th Tac Alft Wgs.
Airlifted: 361 tons of cots, tents, water distributing systems, and bridge components; and 66 passengers, including search and rescue teams with dogs.
Aircraft Employed: C–5 (five), C–141 (two), and C–130 (three).
Operations: Torrential rain from a stalled tropical wave that later became Tropical Storm Isabel descended on Puerto Rico during the first week of October. Sixteen inches of rain fell in a 24-hour period from October 6 to 7. Southern Puerto Rico endured flash floods, mud slides, and landslides that killed 500 people, injured 3,000, and left 5,000 homeless. The hillside community of Mamayes, with a population of 1,500, fell victim to a mud slide that buried 250 homes. Floods washed away bridges and polluted water supplies.

Governor Rafael Hernandez Colón of Puerto Rico requested aid from the United States. On October 10, President Reagan declared four parts of southern Puerto Rico a major disaster area. The Federal Emergency Management Agency directed relief operations with DoD participation, and MAC provided 10 airlift support missions.

From October 9 to 16, five C–5s, three C–130s, and two C–141s airlifted 361 tons of relief cargo and 66 passengers from Atlanta and Dobbins AFB, Georgia; Andrews AFB, Maryland; Homestead AFB, Florida; Jackson, Mississippi; and Army depots in Colorado, Kentucky, and Georgia to Mercedita and Roosevelt Roads NAS, Puerto Rico. The cargo included 4,000 cots, 200 tents, 17 water distributing systems, and 218 tons of bridge components; the passengers included search and rescue teams with dogs. Five military airlift wings and two tactical airlift wings provided planes and personnel who joined Army and Navy forces on behalf of the Puerto Rican disaster victims.

97.
Name: Colombian Volcano.
Location: Republic of Colombia.
Date(s): November 15–28, 1985.
Emergency: Nevado del Ruiz volcano erupted, causing mud flows that killed 23,000 people and left 20,000 homeless.
Air Force Organization(s) Involved: USAF South Air Div, 302d Tac Alft Wg, and ANG Units.
Airlifted: More than 100 tons of tents, blankets, cots, medical supplies, helicopter

fuel, and fuel bladders; and 65 passengers.
Aircraft Employed: C–130 (four+).
Operations: On November 13, the Nevado del Ruiz volcano erupted in the Andes northwest of Bogotá, Colombia. The eruption melted snow and ice on the mountain's upper slopes, producing gigantic mud flows that swept into 14 towns, killing 23,000 people and leaving almost that many homeless. A 50-foot wall of mud flowed through the Langunilla River canyon and spread out over 16 square miles, burying the city of Armero under 15 feet of clay and leaving 20,000 of 25,000 residents dead.

The Colombian government requested international assistance, and the State Department asked DoD to arrange an airlift of Office of Foreign Disaster Assistance supplies from Panama to Colombia. The U.S. South Comd was given the assignment.

Between November 15 and 28, the 302d Tac Alft Wg and ANG units, on rotational duty with the USAF South Air Div at Howard AFB in Panama, flew at least 11 missions to Colombia using at least four C–130 Hercules aircraft. The cargo planes carried more than 30 tons of relief supplies to the stricken area of Colombia, about 65 miles northwest of Bogotá. They also carried 71 tons of fuel and support equipment for Army Task Force 210 from the 210th Aviation Battalion from Fort Kobbe, Panama, which employed 12 helicopters within Colombia to deliver tents, blankets, cots, and medical supplies to mud flow survivors. Air Force planes carried much of this cargo from Howard AFB to Palanquero, Colombia, site of a military airfield. Finally, the C–130s transported 65 emergency personnel to rescue victims from one of the worst disasters in South American history.

98.
Name: Jamaican Flood.
Location: Jamaica.
Date(s): June 8–10, 1986.
Emergency: Heavy rains in Jamaica caused flash flooding that left 3,500 people temporarily homeless.
Air Force Organization(s) Involved: USAF South Air Div, 61st Mil Alft Gp, and 146th Tac Alft Wg.
Airlifted: 27 tons of cots.
Aircraft Employed: C–130 (two).
Operations: During early June, torrential rain in Jamaica produced flash floods that left 3,500 people temporarily homeless. The Jamaican government requested assistance through the State Department, which solicited a DoD airlift of Office of Foreign Disaster Assistance supplies from stockpiles at Fort Clayton, Panama.

From June 8 to 10, C–130s flew five missions carrying 27 tons of relief supplies from Panama to Norman Manley International Airport at Kingston, Jamaica. They came from the 146th Tac Alft Wg of Van Nuys ANG Base, California, on rotation with the USAF South Air Div, and the 61st Mil Alft Gp at Howard AFB in Panama. The cargo consisted primarily of 2,000 aluminum folding double cots capable of accommodating 4,000 people.

99.
Name: El Salvadoran Earthquake.
Location: Republic of El Salvador.
Date(s): October 10–November 7, 1986.
Emergency: An earthquake struck San Salvador, El Salvador, killing 1,200 people, injuring 10,000, and leaving as many as 200,000 homeless.
Air Force Organization(s) Involved: USAF South Air Div; 436th, 437th, and 438th Mil Alft Wgs; 118th, 146th, and 463d Tac Alft Wgs; 375th Aeromed Alft Wg; 61st Mil Alft Gp; 166th and 176th Tac Alft Gps; 31st Aeromedical Evacuation Squadron (Aeromed Evac Sq); and 300th Mil Alft Sq.
Airlifted: 393 tons of relief supplies, including blankets, tents, litters, medical supplies, food, communications equipment, plastic sheeting, and water containers; and 254 passengers.
Aircraft Employed: C–5 (3), C–141 (5), and C–130 (10).
Operations: On October 10, El Salvador suffered an earthquake that registered 5.4 on the Richter scale, destroying many buildings in downtown San Salvador. The quake left 1,200 people dead, 10,000 injured, and up to 200,000 homeless. President José Napoleon Duarte of El Salvador immediately requested international emergency assistance, and the Department of State asked DoD to airlift relief supplies from the United States and from stockpiles in Panama to El Salvador.

From October 10 through November 7, MAC and the U.S. South Comd flew relief missions to El Salvador, employing 3 C–5s, 5 C–141s, and 10 C–130s from at least 10 Air Force wings and groups in Delaware, South Carolina, New Jersey, Texas, Tennessee, California, Alaska, Illinois, and Panama. The Air Force cargo planes transported at least 393 tons of relief supplies and emergency equipment, including medical supplies, blankets, tents, litters, plastic sheeting, and water containers; and 254 passengers, including Red Cross workers, construction personnel, and emergency medical and communications teams. Two of the Air Force planes flew cargo and emergency personnel from Switzerland and Costa Rica to El Salvador, but most picked up their cargo in the United States or Panama.

Some of the missions were exceptional. The 463d Tac Alft Wg flew the first U.S. relief mission to El Salvador on October 10, the same day as the earthquake, taking nine tons of medical supplies, food, communications equipment, and paramedics from Homestead AFB, Florida, to Ilopango International Airport in San Salvador aboard a C–130. On October 15 and 16, the 436th Mil Alft Wg flew three C–5 airplanes to San Salvador from Dover AFB, Delaware, and Howard AFB, Panama. They carried more than 195 tons of relief cargo, mostly medical supplies. On November 6 and 7, the 375th Aeromed Alft Wg, the 31st Aeromed

Evac Sq, and the 300th Mil Alft Sq transported 15 injured children to hospitals in Tampa and Boston.

U.S. relief flights aided hundreds of earthquake victims, many of whom had been driven from damaged hospitals, and expressed U.S. support for the regime of popularly elected President José Napoleon Duarte, who was also coping with a civil war.

100.
Name: Dupont Plaza Hotel Fire.
Location: Puerto Rico.
Date(s): January 3–4, 1987.
Emergency: A New Year's Eve fire killed 96 hotel guests and employees and injured 106 others.
Air Force Organization(s) Involved: 62d and 446th Mil Alft Wgs and 313th Mil Alft Sq.
Airlifted: 21 fire victims and families and 25 aeromedical personnel.
Aircraft Employed: C–141 (one).
Operations: On New Year's Eve, a fire broke out in the 22-story Dupont Plaza Hotel in San Juan, Puerto Rico. By dawn, 96 hotel guests and employees were dead and 106 were injured. San Juan hospitals could not treat all of the burn victims.

About the same time as the fire, a 62d Mil Alft Wg C–141, flown by a 446th Mil Alft Wg crew of the AF Res, flew a cross-country aeromedical evacuation training mission from McChord AFB, Washington, to Charleston AFB, South Carolina. When President Reagan learned of the need to transport San Juan fire victims to the United States for medical treatment, he authorized the C–141 aircrew to divert from Charleston to San Juan. Riding on the aircraft were 25 members of the 40th Aeromed Evac Sq.

When the Starlifter landed at San Juan International Airport on January 3, ambulances from area hospitals transported burn victims to the aircraft. Some of the 21 burn patients also had broken bones, requiring them to be carried aboard the aircraft on litters. Patients' families also boarded the C–141 for the flight to the United States. On January 4, the Starlifter flew to New Haven, Connecticut, where some patients were treated at the Yale Burn Center.

101.
Name: Ecuadoran Earthquakes.
Location: Republic of Ecuador.
Date(s): March 8–13, 1987.
Emergency: Earthquakes measuring up to 7.3 on the Richter scale produced landslides and flooding, leaving 300 people dead, 4,000 missing, 20,000 homeless, and 75,000 cut off from traditional sources of food and medical supplies.
Air Force Organization(s) Involved: USAF South Air Div, 315th and 437th Mil Alft Wgs, 317th Tac Alft Wg, and 914th Tac Alft Gp.

Airlifted: 107 tons of relief equipment and supplies, including helicopters, tents, blankets, and plastic sheeting; and 60 passengers.

Aircraft Employed: C–141 (two) and C–130 (four).

Operations: On March 5 and 6, a series of earthquakes registering up to 7.3 on the Richter scale struck Napo province in northeastern Ecuador. The quakes produced landslides and mud slides and flooded the Rio Aguarico valley, leaving 300 people dead, 4,000 missing, and 20,000 homeless. The Ecuadoran government asked the United States for shelters and blankets for the homeless and helicopters to help transport medical personnel, food, and medical supplies from a distribution center at Lago Agrio in the disaster area to 75,000 people in villages whose land arteries were cut. The State Department sought a military airlift of relief supplies from stockpiles in Panama, and MAC and the U.S. South Comd responded.

From March 8 to 13, Air Force cargo planes transported 107 tons of relief equipment and supplies—including two UH–1N Army helicopters, 500 tents, 5,000 blankets, 400 rolls of plastic sheeting for shelters, and five tent repair kits—from Howard AFB, Panama, to Quito, Ecuador, about 50 miles west of the disaster region. The planes also carried 60 passengers, including helicopter crews and engineers. The 437th and 315th Mil Alft Wgs from Charleston AFB, South Carolina, flew two C–141s. The 914th Tac Alft Gp from Niagara Falls, on rotation in Panama, and the 317th Tac Alft Wg from Pope AFB, North Carolina, flew four C–130s.

The airlift of relief supplies from Panama to Ecuador ended March 13, but the Army helicopters remained in Napo province to conduct mercy flights for a month, after which a 437th Mil Alft Wg C–141 returned them to Panama.

102.

Name: Hurricane Gilbert.

Location: Jamaica and Haiti.

Date(s): September 13, 1988–February 7, 1989.

Emergency: A hurricane with 115 mph winds left hundreds of thousands of people in the West Indies homeless and without electricity.

Air Force Organization(s) Involved: 60th, 433d, 436th, and 437th Mil Alft Wgs; 61st Mil Alft Gp; 118th, 314th, and 317th Tac Alft Wgs; and 911th and 928th Tac Alft Gps.

Airlifted: 571 tons of relief cargo, including plastic sheeting, tents, blankets, chain saws, water containers, food, water purification tablets, building materials, clothing, medical supplies, and electrical utility vehicles.

Aircraft Employed: C–5 (six), C–130 (seven+), and C–141 (one).

Operations: Hurricane Gilbert struck the islands of Jamaica and Hispaniola in the West Indies in September with 115 mph winds. In Jamaica, the storm killed at least 26 people, left 500,000 homeless, and deprived the island of electricity. Responding to an appeal from the Jamaican and Haitian governments, the State Department organized a relief operation, coordinated by AID and the Office of

Humanitarian Airlift Operations

Foreign Disaster Assistance. Because commercial airlift of humanitarian relief supplies was not immediately available, the State Department requested a military airlift.

On September 13, a 314th Tac Alft Wg C–130 Hercules aircraft flew a State Department damage assessment team from Homestead AFB, Florida, to Kingston, Jamaica, to determine which supplies were most urgently needed. A day later, four C–130s—one from the 314th Tac Alft Wg and three from the Tennessee Air National Guard's 118th Tac Alft Wg—transported 40 tons of relief equipment and supplies from Howard AFB, Panama, to Kingston. Their cargo included 360 rolls of plastic sheeting for temporary shelters, 200 tents, 9,600 cotton blankets, 10 chain saws, 3,960 five-gallon water containers, and 18 3,000-gallon water storage tanks.

The Military Airlift Command followed up on September 18 and 19 with an airlift of 130 tons of ready-to-eat meals, water purification tablets, tents, blankets, building materials, and other supplies from Howard AFB and from Kelly AFB, Texas. Two C–5s from the 433d and 436th Mil Alft Wgs and a 437th Mil Alft Wg C–141 delivered the cargo to Norman Manley International Airport in Kingston.

More humanitarian relief arrived in Jamaica in October. Among the aircraft transporting 290 tons of electrical utility trucks and equipment to the island were three 436th Mil Alft Wg C–5 Galaxies. Power companies from the United States and Canada loaned vehicles, which were loaded aboard the aircraft in Florida, New York, Texas, and Ontario. By the end of the year, MAC had flown 460 tons of relief cargo to Jamaica.

Jamaica was not the only country in the West Indies devastated by Hurricane Gilbert. Haiti, on the western side of the island of Hispaniola, suffered food shortages. During October, the 928th Tac Alft Gp in Chicago transported 22 tons of food to Port-au-Prince, Haiti's capital, on a C–130 aircraft.

The airlift to Jamaica continued into early 1989. At the end of January and early February, a 911th Tac Alft Gp C–130 carried 21 tons of clothing and hospital equipment to Jamaica for Hurricane Gilbert victims. On February 7, a 60th MAC C–5 closed out the relief operation by transporting 68 tons of cargo, including four prefabricated buildings, from Travis AFB in California to Kingston.

In the five months between September 1988 and February 1989, at least 14 Air Force cargo aircraft delivered 549 tons of relief equipment, vehicles, and supplies to Jamaica and 22 tons of food to Haiti. Other MAC, AF Res, and ANG aircraft flying regular channel missions across the Caribbean Sea also delivered supplies to the West Indies under the terms of the Denton Amendment, which allowed humanitarian cargo to be transported on military flights at no charge to the donors or consignees. The airlift helped Jamaica and Haiti to recover from one of the worst storms of the century.

103.
Name: Peruvian Cholera Epidemic.
Location: Peru.
Date(s): Early April 1991.
Emergency: A severe cholera epidemic struck almost 150,000 people and killed more than 1,000.
Air Force Organization(s) Involved: 436th Mil Alft Wg.
Airlifted: 200 tons of medical supplies.
Aircraft Employed: C–5 (two).
Operations: In January, a cholera epidemic broke out in Peru. It was the first major outbreak of the disease in the Americas since the nineteenth century, and it spread quickly among urban populations lacking clean drinking water and sewage disposal. By April, almost 150,000 Peruvians had contracted the disease, and more than 1,000 had died. The cholera epidemic began to spread beyond the borders of Peru to Ecuador, Colombia, and Brazil, but was especially severe in crowded Lima, Peru's capital and largest city, with a population of seven million.

To help Peru's medical community handle the thousands of disease victims, the United States undertook a medical airlift. During the first week in April, the 436th Mil Alft Wg flew 200 tons of medical supplies to Lima on two C–5 flights. Each flight delivered about 100 tons, which helped to save the lives of hundreds of cholera victims.

104.
Name: Haitian Refugees.
Location: Cuba, Jamaica, and the Bahamas.
Date(s): November 1991–September 1994.
Emergency: A military coup in Haiti and subsequent international economic embargo encouraged thousands of Haitians to flee their country in boats.
Air Force Organization(s) Involved: 60th, 349th, 436th, 437th, and 438th Alft Wgs; 109th Alft Gp; and 301st Alft Sq.
Airlifted: 9,780 passengers and 6,050 tons of cargo, including tents, food rations, and medical supplies.
Aircraft Employed: C–141, C–5, and C–130 (410+ missions).
Operations: At the end of September 1991, Haitian military leaders drove the country's democratically elected president, Jean-Bertrand Aristide, from power. Other countries in the Western Hemisphere responded with an economic embargo. Facing military dictatorship and poverty, thousands of Haitians fled in boats, heading toward Florida.

To stem the mass migration, President Bush ordered Navy and Coast Guard vessels to pick up the refugees and take them to the U.S. naval base at Guantánamo Bay, Cuba, where they could be screened by immigration authorities. Operation GTMO sought to intercept, feed, and shelter the thousands of Haitians while they were being processed either for settlement in the United

States or for return to Haiti. Marine Corps Brig. Gen. George Walls headed the joint operation, which involved establishment of two tent cities on the Guantánamo reservation. Eventually, the tent cities and ships offshore sheltered more than 12,000 Haitian migrants.

Air Force aircraft and crews supported Operation GTMO, transporting Army troops, food rations, tents, and medical supplies from staging bases at Pope AFB and Cherry Point NAS, North Carolina, and Charleston AFB, South Carolina, to refugee camps at Guantánamo. The 60th Alft Wg and several Twenty-first Air Force wings participated in the operation. By the end of 1991, the Air Force had flown 147 missions in support of Operation GTMO: 136 by C–141s, 8 by C–5s, and 3 by C–130s. The aircraft had to fly carefully to Guantánamo Bay to avoid overflying the rest of Cuba, which remained under the hostile control of dictator Fidel Castro.

On January 31, 1992, the United States Supreme Court ruled that Haitians deemed economic rather than political refugees could be repatriated from Guantánamo to Haiti. This process took time, and more Haitians continued to flee their country as others were returned.

The Air Force continued to fly humanitarian supplies to refugee camps in operations variously designated GTMO, GITMO, and Safe Harbor. During the first half of 1992, the 438th Alft Wg flew 26 C–141 missions from Roosevelt Roads NAS, Puerto Rico, to Guantánamo Bay. Each C–141 carried about 15 tons of food and relief supplies to the Haitian refugees. In June, the 349th Airlift Wing's 301st Alft Sq flew two C–5 missions to Guantánamo Bay.

By July 1993, AMC had flown 410 missions in support of Haitian refugee relief operations, transporting 9,780 passengers and more than 6,000 tons of cargo. In 1994, the United States prepared to invade Haiti to restore President Aristide to power and end the mass exodus of refugees. Between June and August, Air Force transports airlifted relief supplies to Guantánamo and to Jamaica and Grand Turk in the Bahamas. Finally, in September, the United States sent military forces to Haiti in a noncombat operation called Uphold Democracy to restore Aristide and stem the flow of refugees.

105.
Name: Bolivian Epidemic.
Location: Bolivia.
Date(s): April 21–24, 1992.
Emergency: A cholera epidemic threatened Bolivia.
Air Force Organization(s) Involved: 349th Alft Wg and 708th and 710th Alft Sqs.
Airlifted: 13 pallets of cots, sleeping bags, and medical supplies.
Aircraft Employed: C–141 (one).
Operations: In April, Bolivia faced the threat of a cholera epidemic. Between April 21 and 24, the United States responded to a diplomatic request for assis-

tance by airlifting 13 pallets of medical supplies and excess DoD cots and sleeping bags to La Paz from Travis AFB, California, and Hill AFB, Utah. Personnel from the 708th and 710th Alft Sqs flew a 349th Alft Wg C–141, landing in the Bolivian capital on April 23. They had to wear oxygen masks when they landed because the airport, high in the Andes, was 13,000 feet above sea level.

106.
Name: Nicaraguan Relief.
Location: Nicaragua.
Date(s): May 21, 1992.
Emergency: Unknown.
Air Force Organization(s) Involved: 60th Alft Wg and 22d Alft Sq.
Airlifted: Relief supplies.
Aircraft Employed: C–5 (one).
Operations: In May, shortly before it was inactivated on June 1, MAC flew one of its last humanitarian airlift missions in response to a State Department request to deliver relief supplies to Nicaragua. A 60th Alft Wg C–5B Galaxy aircraft, flown by a 22d Alft Sq crew, transported relief supplies from Norton AFB, California, to the Nicaraguan capital of Managua on May 21. The State Department reimbursed MAC for the special assignment airlift mission.

107.
Name: Panamanian Orphan Relief.
Location: Panama.
Date(s): December 12, 1992.
Emergency: An orphanage in Panama needed a van for transportation.
Air Force Organization(s) Involved: 914th Alft Gp.
Airlifted: One van.
Aircraft Employed: C–130 (one).
Operations: In late 1992, a missionary named Shirley Watts obtained a van in New York for the Bella Vista Girls Home, an orphanage in Panama. Ms. Watts worked with Maj. James F. Barber, a chaplain from the 914th Alft Gp of the AF Res, to receive permission from DoD to airlift the vehicle on a C–130 scheduled to fly to Panama for rotation duty. On December 12, the aircraft transported the van from Niagara Falls International Airport to Howard AFB in Panama. Bishop James Ottley, head of the orphanage, met the plane and gratefully accepted the vehicle.

108.
Name: Nicaraguan Airlift.
Location: Nicaragua.
Date(s): Late 1993.
Emergency: Nicaraguan schools and hospitals suffered materiel shortages.
Air Force Organization(s) Involved: 433d Alft Wg.

Airlifted: 83 tons of school and hospital supplies.
Aircraft Employed: C–5 (one).
Operations: In late 1993, relief agencies arranged with Capt. Karl McGregor of the 433d Operations Support Squadron for an airlift of privately donated school and medical supplies from the United States to Nicaragua, where schools and hospitals suffered shortages. The airlift was authorized under the Denton Amendment.

A 433d Alft Wg C–5 Galaxy from Kelly AFB, Texas, flown by a 68th Alft Sq crew, transported 83 tons of humanitarian cargo to Sandino Airport at Managua, capital of Nicaragua, late in the year. Among the airlifted school supplies were 60,000 spiral notebooks and pads, 1.5 million pencils, and five million sheets of paper. The AF Res aircraft also carried medical supplies for area hospitals.

109.
Name: Guatemalan Airlift.
Location: Guatemala.
Date(s): November 1993.
Emergency: A town in Guatemala needed medical supplies and fire trucks.
Air Force Organization(s) Involved: 433d Alft Wg and 68th Alft Sq.
Airlifted: Medical supplies and two fire trucks.
Aircraft Employed: C–5 (one).
Operations: The Denton Amendment allowed military aircraft flying to foreign countries to transport privately donated humanitarian cargo on a space-available basis at no charge to the donors or recipients. In November 1993, private relief agencies seeking to deliver medical supplies and fire trucks from the United States to Guatemala obtained permission for a humanitarian airlift from the Defense Department's Office of Humanitarian and Refugee Affairs.

A 68th Alft Sq aircrew of the 433d Alft Wg at Kelly AFB, Texas, performed the mission, flying a C–5 Galaxy aircraft to La Aurora, Guatemala. The airplane carried medical supplies for a new surgical facility at Chocola and two fire trucks for a local fire department.

110.
Name: Safe Haven.
Location: Cuba.
Date(s): August 31–September 10, 1994.
Emergency: Guantánamo Bay was overcrowded with Cuban and Haitian refugees and more were expected.
Air Force Organization(s) Involved: 908th and 934th Alft Gps.
Airlifted: 100 refugees.
Aircraft Employed: C–130 (two).
Operations: During 1994, continuing dictatorships in Cuba and Haiti prompted thousands of refugees to set out in boats for freedom in the United States.

Intercepted by U.S. Coast Guard and Navy vessels, the refugees were taken to Guantánamo Bay, a U.S. military base in Cuba, for shelter, food, and processing for possible immigration.

By August, refugee camps at Guantánamo were filled to capacity with Cuban and Haitian refugees. To make room for more refugees, the United States persuaded the Panamanian government to temporarily shelter up to 10,000 Cuban refugees at four camps set up by U.S. military forces in Panama.

Two AF Res units, the 908th Alft Gp from Maxwell AFB in Alabama and the 934th Alft Gp from Minneapolis-St. Paul, airlifted the first 100 Cuban refugees from Guantánamo to Howard AFB in Panama in early September, using a pair of C–130s. The first, flown by Capt. David Heinlen and a crew from the 908th Alft Gp, carried 53 refugees. Ships moved more refugees from Guantánamo to Panama.

Seasoned by combat experience in World War II, the Air Force was ready to respond to calls for help in fighting forest fires such as those that broke out on the Maine coast in 1947. Aircraft called into service to assist could deliver equipment and personnel to the scene under stressful conditions. (NASM photo.)

A Military Air Transport Service aircraft drops bales of feed to cattle stranded in the snow in Nevada and Utah in February 1949. (NASM photo.)

An Air Force boat is loaded with food supplies for delivery to flood victims inundated by overflowing rivers in the Midwest. (NASM photo.)

A Douglas C–47 is modified with special boom-type spray equipment attached under the wings to more effectively apply insecticide over areas threatened by the devastation of Hurricane Diane in 1955. (NARA photo.)

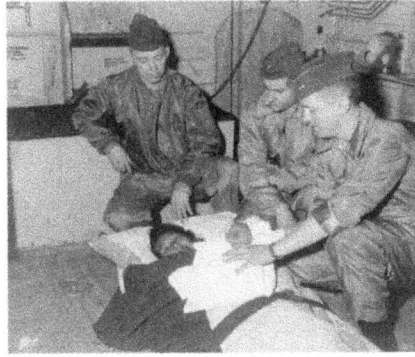

(Above left) A portable water purification unit is unloaded at Elmendorf AFB, Alaska, from a C–124 from the 62d Troop Carrier Wing that flew from McChord AFB, Washington, as part of the rush of equipment to restore normalcy in the aftermath of the 1964 Alaska earthquake. (NARA photo.)

(Above right)The crew of a C–130 of the 5017th Special Operations Squadron of the Alaskan Air Command assists a native Alaskan woman with a newborn en route to the Air Force hospital at Elmendorf AFB, near Anchorage. (NARA photo.)

An Air Force HH–43 airlifts flood victims stranded in the middle of rising waters to safety. (NARA photo.)

Donated materials are transferred from an Air Force plane to a truck provided by Seventh-Day Adventist Disaster Relief at Naval Air Station Chandler in New Orleans to relieve victims of Hurricane Betsy. (NARA photo.)

An airman uses a walkie-talkie to direct work on the construction of a sandbag dike to control rising floodwaters near Grand Forks AFB, North Dakota. (NARA photo.)

Insecticide is loaded on a C–123 at Rio Grande City, Texas, after Hurricane Beulah's violent sweep across southern Texas to help rid flooded areas of mosquitoes. (NARA photo.)

A C–133 belonging to the Georgia Air National Guard airlifted emergency supplies to the hurricane-stricken area of southern Mississippi in August 1969. (NARA photo.)

(Above) Bales of hay are loaded into the cargo hold of an Air Force transport plane for delivery to stranded cattle in Kansas in March 1971. (NARA photo.)

(Below) The Rheingold Brewing Company of New York donated a truckload of portable water packed in 24-can Rheingold beer cases to assist victims of flooding from Tropical Storm Agnes. The Air Force airlifted the water on a C–130 loaded at Wilkes-Barre, Pennsylvania. (NARA photo.)

Stranded citizens are airlifted to safety from a flood-swollen river in Arizona by an HH–43 helicopter belonging to the 302d Aerospace Rescue and Recovery Squadron. (NARA photo.)

A C–130 equipped with the Modular Airborne Fire-Fighting System flies into a fire zone in northern California to drop fire-retardant chemicals to control the blazes. (NARA photo.)

An injured earthquake victim is placed on an Air Force transport plane for evacuation to hospital facilities in Quito, Ecuador. (NASM photo.)

Outboard motors are hoisted into a C–47 for airlift to flood-stricken Honduras in October 1954. (NARA photo.)

American airmen share their in-flight lunches with boys in Haiti during relief efforts for Hurricane Hazel in 1954. (NARA photo.)

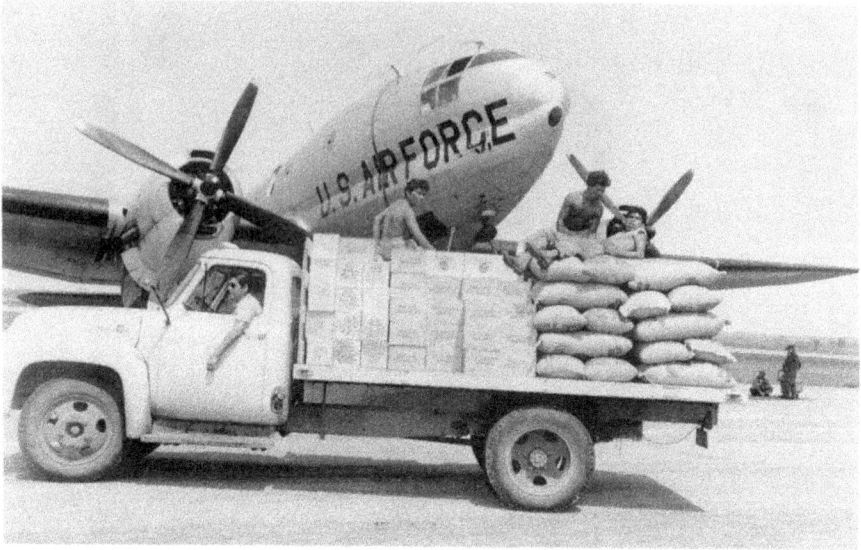

A truck is laden with supplies flown by the Air Force from Harlingen AFB near Houston, Texas, to help Mexico recover from devastating floods left in the wake of several hurricanes. (NARA photo.)

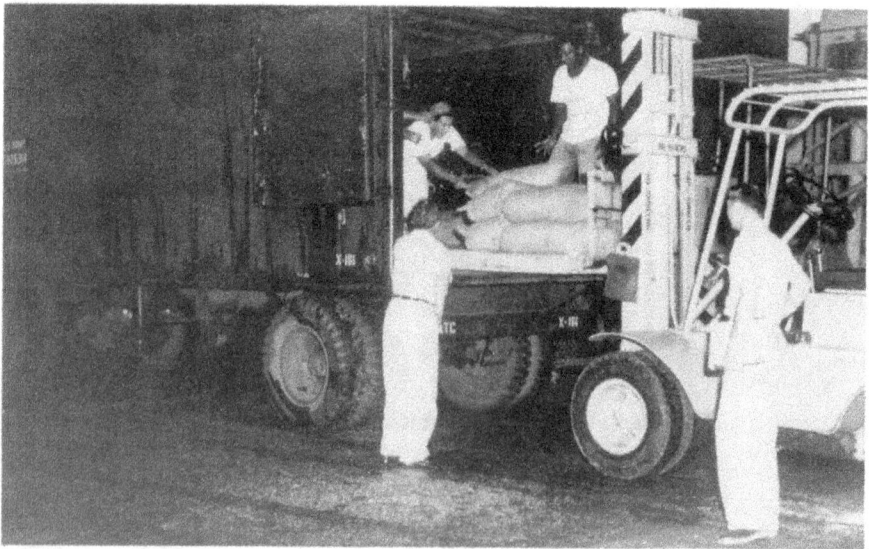

Bags of rice are unloaded at Albrook AFB, Canal Zone, for airlift to Barranquilla, Colombia, by the Caribbean Air Command to help feed stranded flood victims. (NARA photo.)

Citizens are forced from their homes to higher ground as the city streets of Tampico, Mexico, are flooded. (NARA photo.)

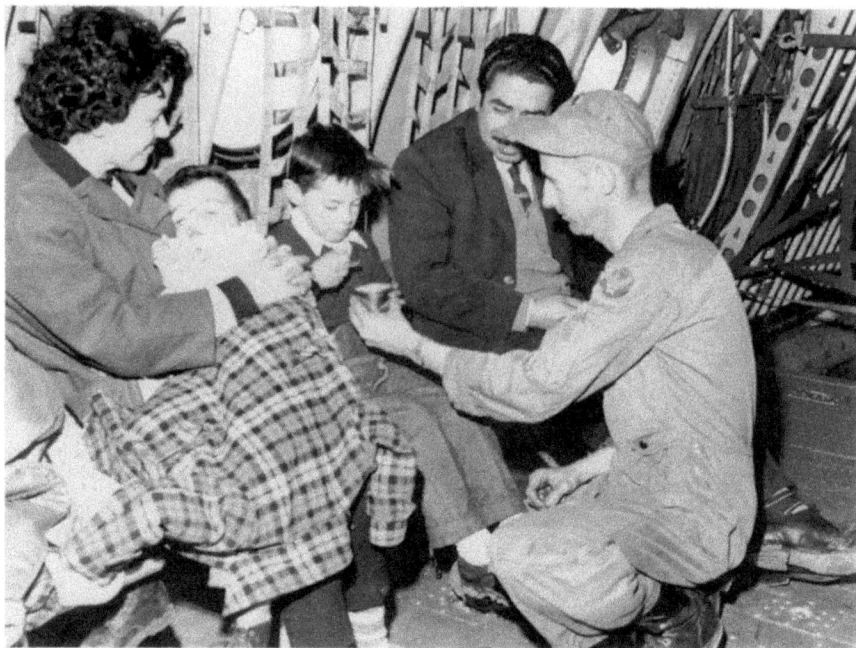

Inside a Military Air Transport Service C–124, a young Chilean refugee accepts food rations from an Air Force sergeant from Dover AFB, Delaware. (NARA photo.)

An Air Force cargo plane takes off from Zihuatanejo, Mexico, which served as a refueling station for U.S. Army helicopters participating with Joint Task Force Bonny Date to relieve the suffering of flood victims. (NARA photo.)

Gen. William K. Skaer talks with earthquake victims at a refugee center in San Salvador on May 6, 1965. (NARA photo.)

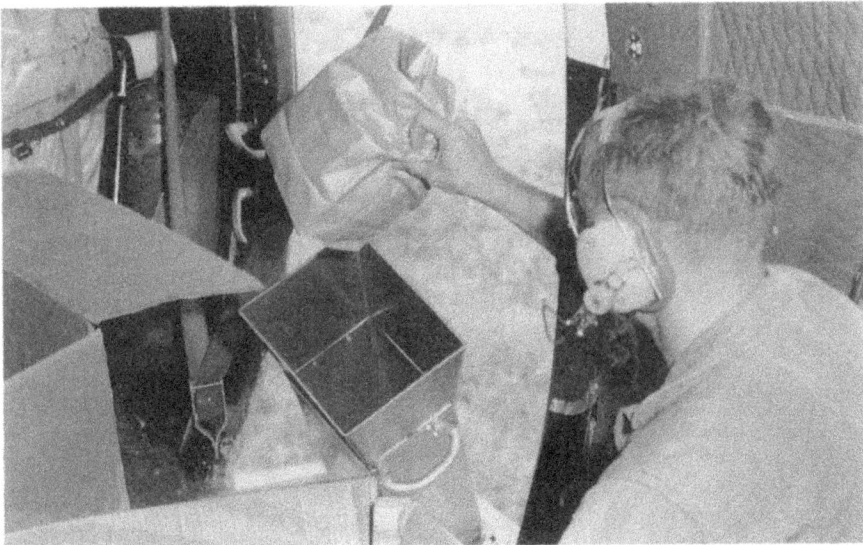

A C–47 loadmaster inserts a bag of sterilized fruit flies into a chute to be dropped over the area infested by the Mediterranean fruit fly. (NARA photo.)

The devastation of the earthquake which hit Peru in 1970 is shown in the rubble left in its aftermath. (NARA photo.)

Supplies are secured to a pallet in preparation for loading onto a C–5 for shipment to Nicaragua. (NARA photo.)

A C–123K sprays insecticide over salt marshes in the Canal Zone to control mosquitoes spreading deadly disease in the area. (NARA photo.)

A member of the medical team sent to assist with the Managua earthquake relief effort takes a break after treating patients in a mobile field hospital shipped to the scene by the Air Force. (NARA photo.)

Victims of floods left in the wake of Hurricane Fifi seek refuge on the roof of a warehouse in Honduras in September 1974. (NARA photo.)

U.S. Army grave registration personnel unload supplies from a UH–1 helicopter to begin the removal of the mass suicide victims in Jonestown, Guyana. (NARA photo.)

American citizens line up to board a C–130 near Las Mercedes Airport in Managua, Nicaragua, for evacuation to the United States on June 16, 1979. (NARA photo.)

A fuel bladder is unloaded from a C–5A in the Dominican Republic to help the Caribbean region recover from the remnants of Hurricane David. (NARA photo.)

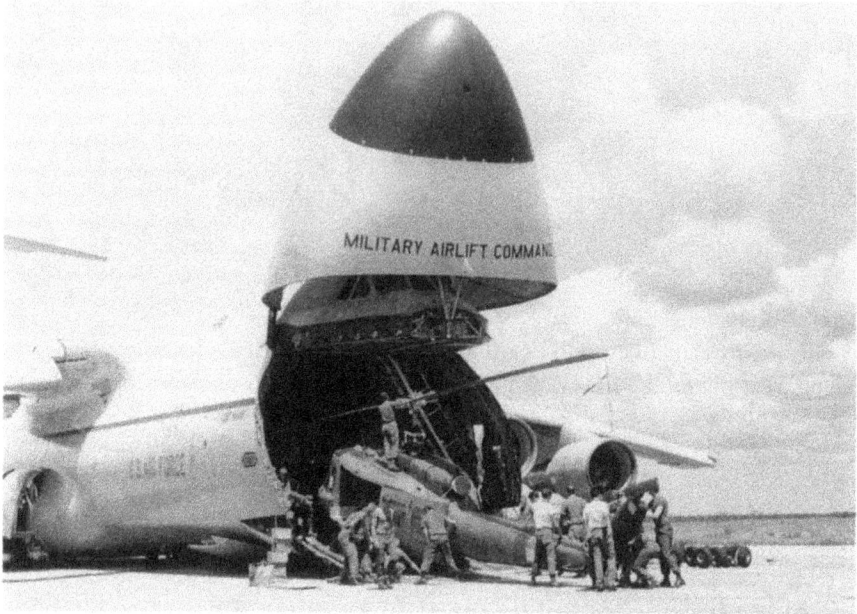

Even helicopters could be airlifted to a disaster area aboard a C–5 cargo plane, such as this U.S. Army UH–1 unloaded in the Dominican Republic on October 7, 1979. (NARA photo.)

Chapter 3
Europe

Europe consists of that part of the Eurasian land mass west of the Ural Mountains and north of the Caucasus Mountains and the Black and Caspian Seas. The USSR is included in this chapter. Several operations were also flown to the former Soviet republics known after the dissolution of the Soviet Union as the Commonwealth of Independent States (CIS). These missions also appear in this chapter, despite the location of some of the republics in Asia.

The United States and Europe have long had close ethnic, cultural, and economic ties. During most of the period covered in this book, the Soviet Union was the only military power capable of threatening the United States with atomic destruction. Its capital and largest cities were in Europe. For all these reasons, Europe has been the most important region for the United States outside of the Western Hemisphere.

The largest humanitarian airlift, Operation Vittles, more commonly known as the Berlin Airlift (1948–1949), took place in Europe. This airlift heralded the beginning of the Cold War, when Eastern Europe fell under the domination of the Soviet Union, and demonstrated the value of humanitarian airlift as an instrument of diplomacy.

In the 40 years between the Berlin Airlift and the fall of the Berlin Wall, the United States conducted relatively few humanitarian airlifts to Europe. Natural disasters, such as hurricanes and earthquakes, occurred less frequently in this area than in other regions. Once Western Europe had recovered from World War II, it could cope economically with its emergencies without much need for outside help. When necessary, a multitude of U.S. bases provided overland relief. Regimes of the Soviet bloc, intent on proving the superiority of communism during the Cold War, usually did not request U.S. assistance, even in an emergency. Only occasionally did a political upheaval, such as the 1956 Hungarian Revolution, provide an opportunity for U.S. airlifters.

The collapse of communism and the dissolution of the Soviet Union and Yugoslavia between 1989 and 1992 produced economic turmoil, civil war, and a need for humanitarian airlifts. With the communists out of power, Eastern Europe welcomed U.S. relief flights. One of the longest sustained airlifts, Provide Promise, began in July 1992 and continued to January 1996 to supply the inhabitants of the former Yugoslavia.

Humanitarian Airlift Operations

Statistics: European Airlifts

Number of humanitarian airlifts: 53.

Most common emergencies: earthquakes (13), floods (11), and collapsed economies (11).

Most frequent recipients: Italy (eight); and the USSR/CIS, Germany, Greece, Romania, and Azores (Portugal) (four each).

Three largest operations, in chronological order: Operation Vittles (Berlin Airlift), 1948–1949 (more than 1.5 million tons); Safe Haven I and II, 1956 and 1957 (over 10,000 passengers); and Provide Promise, 1992–1996 (more than 30,000 tons).

Chronological Listing: European Airlifts

1. Operation Vittles (Berlin Airlift)	June 1948–Sept. 1949
2. Po River Valley Flood	Nov. 1951
3. British Airliner Crash	July 1952
4. Dutch Floods	Feb. 1953
5. Ionian Islands Earthquakes	Aug. 1953
6. Austrian Avalanches	Jan. 1954
7. Juist Island Airlift	Feb. 1954
8. Thessalian Earthquake	May 1954
9. Central European Floods	July 1954
10. Volos Earthquakes	Apr. 1955
11. Lyons Hailstorm	Aug. 1955
12. Operation Snowbound	Feb. 1956
13. Hungarian Refugee Supplies	Nov.–Dec. 1956
14. Safe Haven I and II	Dec. 1956–June 1957
15. Valencia Flood	Oct. 1957
16. *Arnel* Shipwreck Rescue	Sept. 1958
17. French Dam Collapse	Dec. 1959
18. North German Flood	Feb. 1962
19. Spanish Flood	Feb. 1963
20. Santa Maria Island Food Drop	Mar. 1963
21. Blue Boy	July–Aug. 1963
22. *Lakonia* Rescue	Dec. 1963
23. São Jorge Earthquakes	Mar., Apr., and Aug. 1964
24. Yugoslavian Flood	Oct.–Nov. 1964
25. Italian Flood Rescue	Sept. 1965
26. Northern Italian Floods	Nov. 1966
27. Sicilian Earthquakes	Jan. 1968
28. Genoa Flash Flood	Oct. 1970
29. Icelandic Volcano	Jan.–Mar. 1973
30. Romanian Flood	Aug. 1975
31. Italian Earthquake	May 1976
32. Romanian Earthquake	Mar. 1977
33. Yugoslavian Earthquake	Apr. 1979
34. Azores Earthquake	Jan. 1980
35. Italian Earthquake	Nov.–Dec. 1980
36. Greek Earthquakes	Mar. 1981
37. Armenian Earthquake	Dec. 1988–Dec. 1989
38. Soviet Rail Disaster	June 1989
39. Romanian Medical Airlift	Dec. 1989
40. Romanian Relief	Mar., May, Sept., and Dec. 1991
41. Albanian Relief	July–Aug. 1991

Humanitarian Airlift Operations

42. Ukrainian Relief	Oct. 1991
43. Soviet Shortages	Dec. 1991
44. Lithuanian Relief	Feb. 1992
45. Provide Hope (first four phases)	Feb. 1992–Sept. 1994
46. Sarajevo Relief	Apr.–May 1992
47. Provide Promise	July 1992–Jan. 1996
48. Belarus Children	Aug.–Sept. 1992
49. Lithuanian Medical Airlift	Aug. 1992
50. Georgian Medical Relief	Oct. 1992
51. Armenian Flour Airlift	Nov. 1992
52. Albanian Relief	Dec. 1994

Operations: European Airlifts

1.

Name: Operation Vittles (Berlin Airlift).
Location: Germany and Berlin.
Date(s): June 26, 1948–September 30, 1949.
Emergency: The Soviet Union blocked all land routes connecting the noncommunist sectors of western Berlin with western Germany, isolating two million people.
Air Force Organization(s) Involved: Airlift Task Force (Provisional); 1st Airlift Task Force; Combined Airlift Task Force; 7499th Air Div; Alft Wg (Provisional); 60th, 61st, 313th, and 317th Trp Carr Wgs; 7150th Air Force Comp Wg; 7497th Alft Wg (Provisional); 60th, 61st, 313th, 317th, and 513th Trp Carr Gps; 1420th and 1422d Air Trpt Gps (Provisional); 1st, 3d, 8th, 9th, 11th, 12th, 17th, 22d, 23d, 82d, 1250th, 1251st, 1255th, 1256th, 1258th, 1263d, 1267th, 1268th, and 1273d Air Trpt Sqs; 10th, 11th, 12th, 14th, 15th, 19th, 20th, 22d, 29th, 33d, 39th, 40th, 41st, 47th, 48th, 53d, 54th, 330th, 331st, 332d, and 333d Trp Carr Sqs; and 7196th Weather Reconnaissance Squadron.
Airlifted: More than 1.5 million tons of coal, food, and medical and other supplies; and more than 60,000 passengers.
Aircraft Employed: C–47 (108+), C–54 (225), C–82 (5), C–74 (1), and YC–97 (1).
Operations: When Germany surrendered in 1945, the victorious Allies divided the country into four occupation zones according to the terms of the Potsdam agreement. The Soviet Union occupied the eastern portion of Germany and the eastern sector of Berlin, while Britain, France, and the United States took control of the western zones of Germany and the rest of Berlin. The non-Soviet sectors of Berlin lay 110 miles within the Soviet zone, connected to the Anglo-American-French zones of occupied Germany by highway, railroad, and three air corridors.

On June 18, 1948, the United States, Britain, and France announced plans to create a unified West German currency. Objecting to the unified West German state implied by the currency as well as the circulation of the currency in western Berlin, Soviet premier Joseph Stalin cut land routes between western Germany and Berlin on June 24. The blockade separated two million west Berliners from their normal sources of supply.

The Western powers had four options: they could abandon Berlin, cancel the currency reform, force an armored column through the Soviet zone and risk war, or airlift supplies to Berlin until the crisis could be solved diplomatically. They chose the last option. Both the U.S. Air Force and the Royal Air Force (RAF) participated, with the Americans calling the operation "Vittles" and the British calling it "Plain Fare."

Rarely in history had airlift alone saved a large encircled population. Western economic experts estimated that western Berlin would need at least 4,500 tons of coal and food per day to survive the Soviet blockade. Gen. Lucius D. Clay, the military governor of the U.S. zone of Germany, asked the commander of USAFE, Lt. Gen. Curtis E. LeMay, to prepare an airlift. LeMay appointed Brig. Gen. Joseph Smith at Wiesbaden to command a temporary airlift task force.

The airlift began on June 26, 1948. At first, Smith used USAFE C–47s from the 60th and 61st Trp Carr Gps at Rhein-Main and Wiesbaden to transport food and fuel to Tempelhof Airport in western Berlin. He developed flight patterns to avoid collisions and facilitate loading and unloading at regular intervals and initiated one-way operations through the three air corridors. Since the small C–47s could not deliver enough tonnage to sustain the city for a long period of time, Air Force Chief of Staff Gen. Hoyt Vandenberg transferred C–54s from other commands to USAFE for Operation Vittles. He also directed deployment of 90 B–29 bombers to the United Kingdom to signal Allied resolve to sustain the airlift as tensions with the Soviet Union grew.

In late July, a month after the Berlin Airlift began, Maj. Gen. William H. Tunner of MATS, a veteran of the World War II "Hump" airlift from India to China, replaced Smith as task force commander. Working with USAFE's Lt. Gen. John K. Cannon, who replaced LeMay, Tunner increased the daily tonnage to Berlin until it exceeded the 4,500-ton minimum daily requirement. A master of efficiency, Tunner managed the airlift as if the three air corridors were conveyor belts constantly moving to and from Berlin. The northern and southern corridors carried planes from Rhein-Main, Wiesbaden, Fassberg, and Celle in the western zones of Germany to Tempelhof, Gatow, and Tegel Airports in western Berlin, while the middle air corridor carried planes from Berlin back to western Germany. Tunner's organization evolved into a combined airlift task force, which coordinated aircraft from several commands, the U.S. Navy, and the Royal Air Force.

The Berlin airlifters faced several obstacles, natural and artificial, during the massive operation. Storms and fog frequently threatened the flights. Abundant clouds and strict course, altitude, and scheduling prescriptions required pilots to use instruments constantly. Planes failing to land in Berlin as planned had to return to their base of origin to avoid pileups. The Soviet Union harassed the flights with fighter aircraft, antiaircraft artillery, and searchlights. Between August 1948 and August 1949, there were more than 700 such incidents, but none serious enough to interrupt the airlift. The Soviets did not jam radio communications, which might have seriously threatened the flights.

Operation Vittles exceeded expectations. On April 16, 1949, U.S. and British aircraft delivered a record 12,941 tons of coal and food to Berlin. First Lieutenant Gail S. Halvorsen supplemented the regular airlift by dropping candy attached to handkerchief parachutes to the children of Berlin, a practice which was dubbed "Operation Little Vittles." Such success stories reinforced Western support for the airlift and eventually reached beyond the Iron Curtain.

Finally convinced that the Berlin blockade was not achieving its goals, the Soviets reopened land routes between western Germany and Berlin on May 12,

1949. The Allies continued the Berlin Airlift through September to stockpile fuel, food, and medicine in Berlin in case Stalin changed his mind. Operation Vittles transported more than 2.3 million tons of supplies and 227,655 passengers. U.S. aircraft carried more than 1.7 million tons and 62,749 passengers. Contributing 108 C–47s, 225 C–54s, 5 C–82s, 1 C–74, and 1 YC–97, the U.S. Air Force provided most of the aircraft for Operation Vittles. Air Force flights during the 15-month operation totaled 189,963, with only 126 accidents, 70 of them major. The USAF lost 28 airmen in the operation.

The Berlin Airlift, the largest humanitarian airlift operation in history, was militarily and diplomatically significant. Operation Vittles proved above all that airlift could sustain a large population surrounded by hostile forces. The non-Soviet sectors of Berlin escaped absorption by the communist zone, while the western zones of Germany continued moving toward unified democratic statehood. Demonstrating the commitment of the United States to contain Soviet expansion, the Berlin Airlift saved the city without war. It exemplified the ability of the western Allies to work together against a common enemy, and the North Atlantic Treaty Organization (NATO) was born during the airlift.

For the Air Force, Operation Vittles provided abundant lessons about airlift. In addition to yielding a wealth of information about scheduling, loading, air traffic control, and flight patterns, it exposed the need for larger transport aircraft, stimulating development of a new generation of cargo aircraft, including the C–124.

2.
Name: Po River Valley Flood.
Location: Italy.
Date(s): November 1951.
Emergency: A flood inundated 300,000 acres, killing 150 people and leaving 160,000 homeless.
Air Force Organization(s) Involved: 60th Trp Carr Gp and Flight D, 9th Air Rscu Sq.
Airlifted: One helicopter and an unspecified quantity of food and relief supplies.
Aircraft Employed: C–82 (two) and H–5 (one).
Operations: During mid-November, heavy rain flooded the Po River valley in northern Italy, inundating 300,000 acres, killing 150 people and 30,000 cattle, forcing 160,000 people from their homes, and causing damage in the hundreds of millions of dollars. The floods affected 50 villages, including Castelmassa, Rovigo, and Adria. The Italian government, then hosting NATO meetings in Rome, requested international assistance. The State Department's W. Averell Harriman promised U.S. financial support, and Gen. Dwight D. Eisenhower directed NATO military units to join the relief effort.

While U.S. Army trucks transported sandbags from Trieste to the Po River flood region, USAFE prepared airlift operations. When the Italian government requested a U.S. helicopter to transport supplies to Adria, a town surrounded by flood waters, two C–82 cargo planes from the 60th Trp Carr Gp at Rhein-Main Air Base (AB), West Germany, flew to Lyons, France, where the 9th Air Rescue Squadron's Flight D had an H–5H. Air Force personnel disassembled the helicopter and loaded it aboard the C–82s, which carried it and its crew to the flood area. There the helicopter dropped food and emergency relief supplies to flood victims until ground transportation routes reopened.

3.
Name: British Airliner Crash.
Location: Mediterranean Sea.
Date(s): July 27, 1952.
Emergency: A British airliner ditched in the Mediterranean Sea.
Air Force Organization(s) Involved: Flight C, 7th Air Rscu Sq.
Airlifted: 32 passengers rescued.
Aircraft Employed: SA–16 (one).
Operations: On a flight from Malta to Benghazi, Libya, on July 27, a Tropic Airlines Dakota (British DC–3) with 32 passengers and crew aboard lost an engine. When the remaining engine overheated, the plane lost altitude. The pilot ditched the airliner in the Mediterranean Sea about 110 miles northwest of Benghazi after transmitting distress calls. Another British airliner spotted survivors in life rafts and radioed for help as it circled overhead.

A U.S. SA–16 amphibious rescue plane from Flight C, 7th Air Rscu Sq at Wheelus AB, Libya, responded to the emergency. Homing in on the circling aircraft's radio signal, Capt. Kendrick U. Reeves and his six-man crew found the 32 survivors clinging to a pair of sinking life rafts. Although he knew that the rough seas and extra weight would prevent his taking off again, Reeves landed on the sea close to the rafts and took all crash survivors on board to keep them afloat and shelter them until surface vessels could arrive. For this mission, Reeves later won the 1952 Cheney Award. Established in 1927 in memory of 1st Lt. William A. Cheney, the first U.S. casualty in Italy during the First World War, this annual award recognizes acts of valor undertaken in humanitarian interest and performed with aircraft.

British warships soon arrived to complete the rescue. U.S. and British rescuers transferred the crash survivors to a destroyer using U.S. Air Force life rafts and Royal Navy lifeboats, but one of the lifeboats collided with the SA–16. A British frigate towed the damaged aircraft through the rough seas to Benghazi, the nearest port.

4.
Name: Dutch Floods (Operation Humanity).
Location: Kingdom of the Netherlands.
Date(s): February 2–17, 1953.

Emergency: A severe winter storm with winds as high as 100 mph and high tides flooded 700 square miles of the Netherlands.

Air Force Organization(s) Involved: 317th Trp Carr Wg (Medium); 9th and 12th Air Rscu Gps; and 66th, 68th, 69th, 81st, 82d, and 83d Air Rscu Sqs.

Airlifted: 567 tons of food, clothing, blankets, medical supplies, life rafts, boats, shovels, sandbags, and water purification equipment; and more than 160 flood victims evacuated.

Aircraft Employed: C–119 (nine), SA–16 (six), H–19 (three), C–47 (two), and C–82 (one).

Operations: On February 1, a severe winter storm with winds as high as 100 mph swept over the North Sea during high tide, flooding large portions of the southwestern Netherlands. The sea breached dikes in Holland and Zeeland provinces, reclaiming 500,000 acres, one-sixth of the country. Almost 1,400 people died and as many as 100,000 were made homeless in the country's worst flood in 500 years.

After the Dutch government appealed for U.S. assistance, the Army set up the American Military Relief Organization at The Hague to coordinate the U.S. military response. The United States Air Forces in Europe and the Twelfth Air Force lent support.

The 317th Trp Carr Wg (Medium) participated in flood relief operations between February 2 and 17. Nine C–119s flew supplies and equipment to flood victims and dike repair workers. Some planes ferried relief cargo from pickup points in France, West Germany, and Denmark to Dutch airfields at Valkenburg, Gilze-Rijen, and Schipol. From these airfields, other C–119s with Dutch navigators aboard dropped 309 tons of supplies on low flights over the flooded areas. Crews also dropped hay to stranded livestock.

Between February 3 and 12, the 9th Air Rscu Gp, headquartered at Bushy Park in the United Kingdom, employed the 66th, 68th, and 69th Air Rscu Sqs in the relief operations. The 66th Air Rscu Sq, based at Manston RAF Station in the United Kingdom, deployed an H–19 helicopter and crew to Woensdrecht. Piloted by 1st Lt. Richard R. Bragg, who led a four-man crew, it helped to evacuate more than 100 flood victims from the village of Nieuwe-Tonge to high ground southwest of Rotterdam. The helicopter also carried relief supplies to Ochthuizen, Oude-Tonge, and Zierikzee and flew Dutch officials over the disaster area.

A 68th Air Rscu Sq H–19 from Burtonwood in the United Kingdom also evacuated flood victims and flew Dutch officials over the area south of The Hague. The 69th Air Rscu Sq from Fürstenfeldbruck, West Germany, employed another H–19 helicopter to hoist 67 men, women, and children from flooded homes to the vicinity of Zierkzee. The squadron also flew SA–16 amphibious planes to carry flood victims to higher ground and drop food, supplies, and sandbags to workers struggling to rebuild dikes.

Between February 4 and 17, the 12th Air Rscu Gp also employed three squadrons in the flood area: the 81st and 82d Air Rscu Sqs, based at Bordeaux,

France; and the 83d Air Rscu Sq, based at Merignac, France. Led by Col. Robert L. Rizon, the group's SA–16s and C–47s dropped medical supplies, rations, clothes, and sandbags to flood victims and dike repair workers.

Air Force aircraft flew 353 sorties during the flood relief operations, delivering 567 tons of supplies and evacuating 161 people. The U.S. airlift formed only part of an international relief effort, but it saved the lives of many flood victims, demonstrated U.S. good will and flight capabilities, and provided valuable training for future emergencies.

5.

Name: Ionian Islands Earthquakes.

Location: Kingdom of Greece.

Date(s): August 13–17, 1953.

Emergency: A series of earthquakes struck the Ionian Islands of western Greece, leaving 800 people dead, 900 seriously injured, and 100,000 homeless.

Air Force Organization(s) Involved: 60th and 317th Trp Carr Wgs; and 58th, 66th, and 68th Air Rscu Sqs.

Airlifted: More than 135 tons of relief equipment and supplies, including H–13 helicopters, bulldozers, blood plasma, clothing, blankets, cots, food, drinking water, and medical supplies; and an unspecified number of passengers, including earthquake evacuees, medical personnel, disaster relief officials, and reporters.

Aircraft Employed: C–119 (20), SA–16 (3+), and H–5 (1).

Operations: Beginning on August 12, a series of earthquakes struck the Greek islands of Ithaca, Zante, and Cephalonia in the Ionian Sea. The quakes left 800 people dead, 900 seriously injured, and 100,000 homeless, prompting the Greek government to request international emergency assistance. The United States responded, as did Italy, Israel, Britain, France, and Turkey. The State Department, answering an appeal from the U.S. embassy in Athens, enlisted the Defense Department. Supported by Army, Navy, and Air Force assets, the commander of the Sixth Fleet in the Mediterranean directed U.S. relief operations. Between August 13 and 17, USAFE and the Air Rscu Svc performed relief missions for Greek earthquake victims.

Twenty C–119 Flying Boxcars assigned to the 60th and 317th Trp Carr Wgs transported relief equipment and supplies to Araxos and Athens, Greece, from Red Cross headquarters in Geneva, Switzerland, and Air Force bases in the United Kingdom, West Germany, Libya, and French Morocco. The 135 tons of airlifted cargo included Army H–13 helicopters, bulldozers and other earth-moving equipment, blankets, clothing, medical supplies, drinking water, blood plasma, cots, and food.

The 58th Air Rscu Sq at Wheelus AB, Libya, flew SA–16s and one H–5 helicopter to transport medical personnel and supplies to the Ionian Islands and evacuate injured earthquake victims. On August 14, SA–16s of the 9th Air Rescue Group's 66th and 68th Air Rscu Sqs shuttled medical personnel, dropped supplies, and evacuated survivors in the disaster zone. Air Rescue Service aircraft also delivered food and water and transported officials and reporters over the disaster area.

6.
Name: Austrian Avalanches.
Location: Republic of Austria.
Date(s): January 13–16, 1954.
Emergency: Avalanches triggered by blizzards struck the Alpine valleys of western Austria, killing 113 people and leaving hundreds trapped or injured.
Air Force Organization(s) Involved: 81st and 84th Air Rscu Sqs.
Airlifted: 3.5 tons of relief supplies and 128 passengers.
Aircraft Employed: H–19 (five), C–47 (one), and SA–16 (number unknown).
Operations: Alpine blizzards triggered several major avalanches in Vorarlberg province in western Austria on January 12, leaving 113 people dead and hundreds stranded or injured. Two avalanches buried the hamlet of Blons, with a population of 385, and flooded the Lutz River running through town. At the request of the Department of State, the Air Rscu Svc responded to an appeal by the Austrian government for international help.

Between January 13 and 16, the 81st and 84th Air Rscu Sqs—based in West Germany at Sembach AB and Rhein-Main AB, respectively—conducted rescue and relief operations in the Blons area of Austria. Maj. Edward J. Ontko, the commander of the 84th Air Rscu Sq, directed relief flights, which included 99 H–19, 10 SA–16, and 7 CH–47 sorties. Five Air Force helicopters evacuated 69 injured or stranded avalanche survivors to locations where they could transfer to land ambulances.

Air Rescue Service aircraft delivered over three tons of relief supplies and transported 59 passengers, including rescue and medical personnel. One H–19 helicopter made a forced landing near Blons, without serious injury to any personnel. By January 16, surviving avalanche victims had been transported to safety, and U.S. rescue aircraft returned to the West German bases.

7.
Name: Juist Island Airlift.
Location: East Frisian Islands, Federal Republic of Germany.
Date(s): February 12–17, 1954.
Emergency: Ice floes blocking shipping to Juist Island threatened islanders with starvation.
Air Force Organization(s) Involved: 781st Trp Carr Sq.
Airlifted: 13 tons of food.
Aircraft Employed: C–119 (five).
Operations: During January and February, unusually cold weather produced ice floes around the East Frisian Islands in the North Sea just off the West German

mainland. Juist Island, 10 miles off the Ems River estuary near the Netherlands, normally received food supplies by sea, but ice blocked shipping lanes for more than two weeks. Dwindling food stocks threatened residents with starvation. Since the island had no airfield, officials requested an emergency airdrop of food.

The 781st Trp Carr Sq of the 465th Trp Carr Gp responded under Twelfth Air Force direction, flying five C–119 cargo planes to an operations base at Bremen. Between February 12 and 17, the squadron flew six sorties over Juist Island, dropping 63 parachute-equipped bundles of food weighing 13 tons. One bundle burst on landing when its parachute failed to open properly, but the remaining bundles landed undamaged. The food sustained islanders until shipping could resume.

. 8.

Name: Thessalian Earthquake.
Location: Kingdom of Greece.
Date(s): May 14 and 22, 1954.
Emergency: An earthquake struck the Larissa area of Greece, killing 31 people, injuring 160, and leaving more than 10,000 homeless.
Air Force Organization(s) Involved: 60th Trp Carr Wg (Medium).
Airlifted: More than 10 tons of food.
Aircraft Employed: C–119 (three).
Operations: On May 1, an earthquake struck the Thessaly region of Greece northwest of Athens and south of Mount Olympus. In communities around Larissa, including Pharsala and Sophades, more than 4,000 buildings collapsed or were damaged. The earthquake left 31 people dead, 160 injured, and more than 10,000 homeless. The Greek government, though still recovering from the Ionian earthquakes of the previous summer (see Ionian Islands Earthquakes, August 1953), declined offers of foreign assistance, but the Greek Red Cross appealed for relief supplies.

Between May 14 and 22, the 60th Trp Carr Wg (Medium), based at Rhein-Main AB, West Germany, flew three C–119 cargo planes to Athens, delivering more than 10 tons of beef, milk, and other food supplies donated by the German Red Cross for the earthquake victims. Two planes flew seven tons of food from West Germany to Greece on May 14, while a third delivered three tons of beef on May 22. Representatives of the Greek Red Cross met the planes and supervised distribution of their cargo.

9.

Name: Central European Floods.
Location: Federal Republic of Germany and Republic of Austria.
Date(s): July 8–15, 1954.
Emergency: Heavy rain flooded river valleys in central Europe, killing 27 people and leaving 70,000 homeless.
Air Force Organization(s) Involved: 317th Trp Carr Wg and 12th Air Rscu Gp.

Airlifted: 58 tons of relief supplies, including 30 tons of sandbags, and 40 passengers evacuated.

Aircraft Employed: C–119 (seven), C–47 (number unknown), and H–19 (number unknown).

Operations: During early July, nearly continuous rain in central Europe flooded the Danube River and its tributaries, including the Inn, Isar, Enns, and Traun. Floods killed 27 people and left 70,000 homeless in Germany, Austria, Czechoslovakia, and Hungary. The Danube rose 30 feet above normal in some places, flooding cities from Regensburg, West Germany, to Budapest, Hungary, including Passau, Linz, Feldkirchen, Goldwoerth, and Straubing. Soviet troops responded to the emergency in eastern Austria, Czechoslovakia, Hungary, and East Germany. U.S. military units performed relief operations in Bavaria and northwestern Austria.

Between July 8 and 15, Air Force H–19 helicopters from the 12th Air Rscu Gp evacuated 40 people and delivered six tons of supplies to flood victims in Bavaria and Austria. At the same time, 12th Air Rscu Gp C–47s delivered another 22 tons of emergency supplies and equipment. Aircraft from the 81st, 83d, and 84th Air Rscu Sqs of the 12th Air Rscu Gp operated from Erding AB in West Germany under Maj. John C. Ziegler, the commander of the mission. Army helicopters participated in relief activities, lifting victims from the roofs of flooded homes.

Between July 11 and 14, seven C–119 Flying Boxcars from the 317th Trp Carr Wg from Neubiberg AB near Munich dropped 30 tons of sandbags collected at Stuttgart, Rhein-Main AB, and Landstuhl AB, to Army workers reinforcing levees around Straubing, West Germany. Minister President of Bavaria Dr. Hans Ehard thanked the 317th Trp Carr Wg for its flood relief efforts.

By July 15, Air Force aircraft had delivered 58 tons of supplies to Bavarian and Austrian flood victims, supplementing the efforts of the Army in Europe, military forces of other nations, international relief agencies, and local emergency organizations.

10.

Name: Volos Earthquakes.

Location: Kingdom of Greece.

Date(s): April 30, 1955.

Emergency: Earthquakes left 6 people dead, 100 injured, and 45,000 homeless.

Air Force Organization(s) Involved: 60th Trp Carr Wg.

Airlifted: More than a ton of food and medical supplies.

Aircraft Employed: C–47 (one).

Operations: Between April 19 and 21, a series of earthquakes struck Volos, Greece, a port with 55,000 people. The mayor of Volos, George Kartalis, estimated that the tremors left 6 people dead, 100 injured, and 45,000 homeless. Ninety percent of the buildings in Volos, including the main hospital, were severely damaged. Lt. Gen. Fotis Mesinopoulos of the Greek army assumed command of disaster relief operations, and Greek premier Alexander Papagos appealed on April 27 for international emergency assistance.

The U.S.S. *Wood* was in Volos harbor when the earthquakes began on April 19. Its crew was already providing relief when the U.S.S. *Albany* arrived in Volos on April 27 with tents and clothing.

The Air Force also participated in disaster relief operations. On April 30, a C–47, probably from the 60th Trp Carr Wg, airlifted 2,500 pounds of food and medical supplies from Rhein-Main AB, West Germany, to Volos.

11.
Name: Lyons Hailstorm.
Location: France.
Date(s): August 31, 1955.
Emergency: A severe hailstorm destroyed factory roofs in Lyons.
Air Force Organization(s) Involved: 322d Air Div.
Airlifted: 40,000 square feet of canvas tarpaulins.
Aircraft Employed: C–119 (one).
Operations: A severe hailstorm struck Lyons, the second largest city in France, on August 27, destroying factory roofs in the industrial heart of the city. The French government requested U.S. help through the State Department to provide temporary roofing for the factories until they could be repaired. The United States European Command (USEUCOM) in Paris asked USAFE to arrange delivery of canvas.

On August 31, the 322d Air Div flew 40,000 square feet of Army canvas tarpaulins from Bordeaux to Lyons aboard a C–119 Flying Boxcar. The canvas came from the Captieux Ordnance Depot. On the same day, trucks delivered another 60,000 square feet of canvas from Air Force stockpiles at Moulins and Chateauroux. French officials used the canvas as temporary roofing, allowing the factories to continue operations. After the roofs were repaired, the French returned the canvas to U.S. military forces.

12.
Name: Operation Snowbound (Italian Blizzards).
Location: Italian Republic and Kingdom of Greece.
Date(s): February 12–19, 1956.
Emergency: Two weeks of winter storms brought record low temperatures and snows to southern Europe, isolating many towns.
Air Force Organization(s) Involved: 322d Air Div and 60th, 317th, and 465th Trp Carr Wgs.
Airlifted: At least 332 tons of food, blankets, clothing, and medical supplies.
Aircraft Employed: C–119 (40+).
Operations: During the first two weeks of February, winter storms assaulted

western Europe, bringing record low temperatures and snow as far south as Sicily. In Rome, snow accumulated to a depth of eight inches. Twelve straight days of snowfall in the Italian peninsula isolated more than 600 communities as drifts blocked mountain passes and avalanches buried roads. Record-breaking winter weather left 634 persons dead and brought snow to places where it had never before been recorded.

The Italian government requested international assistance, a request which the U.S. ambassador, Clare Boothe Luce, relayed to the State Department. President Eisenhower promised aid to the president of Italy, Giovanni Gronchi. The United States Air Forces in Europe, working with the U.S. Army, organized Operation Snowbound, the largest humanitarian airlift in Europe since the Berlin blockade.

Operation Snowbound lasted from February 12 through 19. The 322d Air Div used at least 40 C–119 Flying Boxcars from the 60th, 317th, and 465th Trp Carr Wgs in France and West Germany. Flying in weather severe enough to ground domestic aircraft, the Boxcars airlifted at least 332 tons of Army relief supplies from Landstuhl AB in West Germany to various locations in Italy, including Rome, Naples, and Pisa, and Catania in Sicily. A few planes also carried relief cargo to isolated communities in northern Greece. Airlifted supplies included 60,000 C rations, 10,500 blankets, overcoats, shirts, pants, overshoes, socks, and medical supplies.

The Italian government awarded the "Star of Solidarity Towards Italy" to more than 400 Air Force personnel who participated in Operation Snowbound. Pope Pius XII held a private audience with about 150 members of the 322d Air Div to express his appreciation.

13.
Name: Hungarian Refugee Supplies.
Location: Central Europe.
Date(s): November–December 1956.
Emergency: Hundreds of thousands of refugees fled Hungary when Soviet troops quelled a revolution there.
Air Force Organization(s) Involved: 322d Air Div and 60th, 317th, and 465th Trp Carr Wgs.
Airlifted: 189 tons of medical supplies, food, blankets, and cots.
Aircraft Employed: C–119 (25).
Operations: During October, thousands of Hungarians rebelled against Communist Party leader Erno Gero in support of Imre Nagy, a former premier who advocated multiple political parties, free elections, removal of Soviet troops, and withdrawal from the Warsaw Pact. Gero, a Stalinist, asked the Soviet Union to intervene on his behalf, but he was forced to step down on October 25 in favor of another Soviet supporter. Nagy won the support of the Hungarian army. By November 1, the revolt appeared to be successful and the Soviet Union agreed to remove its troops from Budapest.

Humanitarian Airlift Operations

The rebels' success was short-lived. On November 4, about 200,000 Soviet troops and 2,500 tanks and armored cars attacked Budapest and drove Nagy from power. Thousands of Hungarians fled to Austria, Switzerland, and West Germany. Responding to a State Department request, USAFE prepared to airlift Red Cross food and medical supplies to the refugees.

During November and December, the 322d Air Div employed 25 C–119 Flying Boxcars of the 60th Trp Carr Wg at Dreux AB, France; the 317th Trp Carr Wg at Neubiberg AB, West Germany; and the 465th Trp Carr Wg at Evreux AB, France, to airlift 189 tons of Red Cross medical supplies, food, blankets, and cots. The cargo was carried from various locations in the United Kingdom, Switzerland, France, and West Germany, to Hungarian refugee centers in Austria, Switzerland, and West Germany. Most of the relief cargo went to Vienna, where most refugees fled, while some was stockpiled at Neubiberg AB, a staging base for Operation Safe Haven, a subsequent airlift of Hungarian refugees to the United States (see Safe Haven I and II, December 1956–June 1957).

14.

Name: Safe Haven I and II (Hungarian Refugee Airlift).
Location: Central Europe.
Date(s): December 11, 1956–June 30, 1957.
Emergency: After Soviet armed forces quelled an anticommunist uprising in Hungary, tens of thousands of refugees fled to Austria and, eventually, to other countries willing to accept them.
Air Force Organization(s) Involved: 1608th and 1611th Air Trpt Wgs.
Airlifted: 10,184 refugees.
Aircraft Employed: C–118, R6D, and C–121 (numbers unknown).
Operations: On December 6, President Eisenhower offered asylum in the United States to 15,000 refugees who escaped to Austria during the Soviet military suppression of the Hungarian uprising (see Hungarian Refugee Supplies, November–December 1956). They traveled by train and bus from Vienna to Munich, where the Intergovernmental Committee for European Migration processed them for flights to the United States. The committee helped refugee families to stay together during the transport process.

The Pentagon directed MATS to prepare an airlift. Between December 11, 1956, and June 30, 1957, the Atlantic Division of MATS conducted two operations, Safe Haven I and II.

Lasting from December 11 to January 3, Safe Haven I involved C–118 and R6D aircraft from the 1611th Air Trpt Wg at McGuire AFB, New Jersey; C–121 Super Constellation aircraft from the 1608th Air Trpt Wg at Charleston AFB, South Carolina; and commercial contract aircraft. President Eisenhower's own airplane, Columbine III, participated in the airlift.

On December 22, Vice President Richard Nixon, accompanied by the commander of USAFE, Lt. Gen. William H. Tunner, observed Safe Haven I operations at Munich Riem Airport. On the busiest day of the operation, December 24, Atlantic Division planes moved 984 refugees from Munich to McGuire AFB. Throughout the airlift, special missions carried women in late stages of pregnancy, infants, and the ill and infirm. During Safe Haven I, 107 flights transported 6,393 passengers to the United States.

In Safe Haven II, which lasted from January 6 through June 30, the 1611th Air Trpt Wg airlifted an additional 3,791 refugees from Neubiberg AB near Munich to McGuire AFB on 66 transatlantic flights.

During Safe Haven I and II, MATS planes airlifted 10,184 Hungarian refugees on 173 flights from West Germany to New Jersey. Commercial contract airliners flew 4,170 refugees on 58 flights. After landing at McGuire AFB, the Hungarians moved to Camp Kilmer, New Jersey, where they were processed for settlement in the United States. Safe Haven was the most significant European humanitarian airlift operation since the Berlin Airlift, transporting more refugees than ever before. In nearly seven months of almost continuous operations, and despite bouts with fog and storms, the 1608th and 1611th Air Trpt Wgs experienced no major accidents and transported all passengers safely.

15.
Name: Valencia Flood.
Location: Spain.
Date(s): October 15–21, 1957.
Emergency: A week of torrential rain flooded the Turia River valley, inundating Valencia. Sixty people were killed and 5,000 were forced from their homes.
Air Force Organization(s) Involved: Sixteenth Air Force and 3970th Ops Sq.
Airlifted: Three tons of food, medical supplies, and clothing; and 12 persons rescued.
Aircraft Employed: H–19 (one).
Operations: During mid-October, a week of heavy rain flooded the Turia River valley of eastern Spain, inundating the country's third largest city, Valencia, with a population of 500,000. The disaster took 60 lives and forced 5,000 people from their homes. The Spanish government requested food and blankets through the U.S. embassy. U.S. military units in Spain responded to the emergency.

On October 15, the 3970th Ops Sq of the 3970th AB Gp flew an H–19 helicopter from Torrejon AB near Madrid to Manises AB near Valencia, where it flew flood relief missions for three days, evacuating 12 injured persons to hospitals and delivering three tons of food and medical supplies. Trucks took more than 4,000 blankets from Air Force facilities at Torrejon AB to Valencia on October 20. The next day, a Sixteenth Air Force plane flew donated clothing to the stricken city.

Humanitarian Airlift Operations

16.
Name: *Arnel* Shipwreck Rescue.
Location: Santa Maria Island, Azores.
Date(s): September 19, 1958.
Emergency: A Portuguese ship with 158 passengers aboard hit rocks and sank.
Air Force Organization(s) Involved: 57th Air Rscu Sq.
Airlifted: 48 shipwreck victims.
Aircraft Employed: SH–19 (one).
Operations: On September 19, the Portuguese ship *Arnel* ran aground on rocks and began to sink off Santa Maria Island in the Azores. While attempting to reach shore by lifeboat, 27 of 158 passengers drowned. The Portuguese air force organized a rescue operation and asked the U.S. Air Force's 57th Air Rscu Sq, based at Lajes Field in the Azores, for assistance. Squadron crew members, using a rescue basket on a cable, hoisted shipwreck victims from the *Arnel* to a hovering SH–19 helicopter and flew them to shore. By the end of the day, the helicopter crew had rescued 48 passengers. Portuguese officials rescued the other shipwreck survivors.

17.
Name: French Dam Collapse.
Location: France.
Date(s): December 1959.
Emergency: The Malpasset Dam on the Reyran River broke, flooding Fréjus and leaving more than 300 people dead and thousands homeless.
Air Force Organization(s) Involved: 322d Air Div.
Airlifted: More than two tons of C rations, 2,000 blankets, 200 pairs of boots, and fresh milk.
Aircraft Employed: C–119 (two+).
Operations: During late November and early December, several days of heavy rain swelled the artificial lake behind the 200-foot-high concrete Malpasset Dam on the Reyran River in southeastern France. The dam collapsed on the night of December 2, releasing millions of gallons of water that descended on Fréjus, a town of 13,500 people. The flood killed at least 323 people, left thousands homeless, and severed highways and railroads along the French Riviera. With the approval of the French government, U.S. military forces in France responded to the emergency.

At least two 322d Air Div C–119s from Dreux AB, France, transported more than 2,000 blankets, 200 pairs of boots, two tons of C rations, and fresh milk to the disaster zone. The airlift complemented relief missions conducted by other branches of the U.S. armed forces and other nations.

18.
Name: North German Flood.
Location: Federal Republic of Germany.
Date(s): February 18–20, 1962.
Emergency: A winter storm with hurricane-force winds flooded Hamburg, leaving more than 300 people dead, 400 injured, and 17,000 homeless.
Air Force Organization(s) Involved: 322d Air Div and Atlantic Air Rscu Cen.
Airlifted: More than 117 tons of blankets, clothing, and food; and nine persons rescued.
Aircraft Employed: C–130 (six) and SH–19 (four).
Operations: On February 16 and 17, a winter storm with hurricane-force winds drove the North Sea over dikes in northern Germany, flooding the Hamburg area at the head of the Elbe River estuary. The flood killed at least 300 people, injured more than 400, and left more than 17,000 homeless. Local and Red Cross officials appealed to the United States for assistance, and U.S. military forces in Europe responded.

Between February 18 and 20, six C–130 Hercules aircraft from the United States Air Forces in Europe's 322d Air Div at Evreux-Fauville AB, France, airlifted 117 tons of relief cargo—including 50,000 blankets and 5,000 sets of winter clothing—from Saint Dizier, France, and Sembach AB, West Germany, to Hamburg. Among the supplies were 30 tons of blankets, clothing, and food collected by American Boy Scouts in West Germany. German and International Red Cross workers distributed the cargo.

During the same three days, four U.S. Air Force SH–19 helicopters from Spangdahlem, West Germany, joined U.S. Army helicopters under operational control of the Atlantic Air Rscu Cen to transport food to the flood victims and evacuate passengers. One Air Force helicopter equipped with a hoist rescued nine persons.

19.
Name: Spanish Flood.
Location: Spain.
Date(s): February 17–18, 1963.
Emergency: The Guadalquivir and Genil Rivers flooded the Ecija, Alcolea del Rio, and Villanueva del Rio areas of Spain.
Air Force Organization(s) Involved: Detachment 9, Atlantic Air Rscu Cen.
Airlifted: Food and 69 passengers evacuated.
Aircraft Employed: HH–19 (four).
Operations: During mid-February, heavy rain flooded the Genil and Guadalquivir River valleys of southern Spain. Spanish authorities requested U.S. military assistance to evacuate or supply stranded flood victims. On February 17 and 18, Detachment 9, Atlantic Air Rscu Cen, based at Moron AB, Spain, flew four HH–19 helicopters on emergency missions. Two helicopters carried food to

those stranded near Ecija on the Genil River on February 17. The helicopter crews also evacuated six flood survivors to higher ground. The next day, two more HH–19 crews evacuated 63 people from flooded areas near Alcolea del Rio and Villanueva del Rio on the Guadalquivir River.

20.
Name: Santa Maria Island Food Drop.
Location: Azores.
Date(s): March 15, 1963.
Emergency: Six weeks of bad weather prevented supply ships from delivering food to Santa Maria Island.
Air Force Organization(s) Involved: 17th Air Trpt Sq.
Airlifted: 4.8 tons of food.
Aircraft Employed: C–124 (one).
Operations: Six weeks of sustained high winds and waves during February and March prevented Portuguese ships from delivering food to Santa Maria Island in the Azores. Recalling that U.S. planes had transported food to the Azores as part of a "People to People" foreign aid policy, island authorities sought U.S. help.

In mid-March, the East Trpt AF diverted a 17th Air Trpt Sq C–124 Globemaster to Lajes AB in the Azores for an emergency airlift. On March 15, the plane airdropped nearly five tons of potatoes, onions, oranges, and other food to Santa Maria islanders, helping them to survive until shipping resumed.

21.
Name: Blue Boy (Yugoslavian Earthquake).
Location: Yugoslavia.
Date(s): July 27–August 8, 1963.
Emergency: A severe earthquake struck Skopje, Yugoslavia, killing more than 2,000 people and leaving more than 100,000 injured or homeless.
Air Force Organization(s) Involved: 1607th and 1611th Air Trpt Wgs, 317th Trp Carr Wg, and 52d Trp Carr Sq.
Airlifted: 455 tons of hospital components, trucks, trailers, jeeps, tents, blankets, and medical supplies; and 410 passengers.
Aircraft Employed: C–130 (26), C–124 (4), and C–135 (3).
Operations: On July 26, a severe earthquake struck Skopje in southern Yugoslavia, killing more than 2,000 people, leaving 100,000 homeless, and destroying or badly damaging 80 percent of the city's buildings. At least 3,000 people were injured. The Yugoslavian government requested U.S. aid through the State Department and agreed to permit emergency military flights into the country.

Within one day, MATS and USAFE organized an airlift, designated "Blue Boy", to fly U.S. Army resources to the Yugoslavian earthquake victims. Relief flights continued from July 27 to August 8. Military Air Transport Service aircraft—three C–135s of the 1611th Air Trpt Wg and one C–124 of the 1607th Air

Trpt Wg—airlifted at least 84 tons of tents, blankets, and medical supplies to Belgrade, Yugoslavia, from Andrews AFB, Maryland, and Chateauroux Air Station, France.

Also, 26 C–130s of the 317th Trp Carr Wg and three C–124s of the 52d Trp Carr Sq, serving the 322d Air Div, transported 371 tons of cargo from Ramstein AB and Rhein-Main AB in West Germany to Belgrade. The cargo included a 120-bed Army mobile field hospital, 24 trucks, 21 trailers, four jeeps, medical supplies, and blankets; and 410 passengers, including medical personnel and drivers. Passing roads lined with cheering Yugoslavs, the Army personnel drove the airlifted vehicles loaded with hospital components and other supplies from Belgrade to Skopje.

Between August 14 and 17, MATS airplanes returned the mobile hospital, vehicles, and Army personnel from Belgrade to Ramstein. Project Blue Boy demonstrated the ability of airlift to fulfill U.S. foreign policy objectives while helping disaster victims. Unlike other Air Force humanitarian airlift operations, Blue Boy assisted a communist country, one that also accepted emergency relief from the Soviet Union.

22.
Name: *Lakonia* Rescue.
Location: Atlantic Ocean, southwest of Portugal.
Date(s): December 23–24, 1963.
Emergency: The Greek luxury liner *Lakonia* caught fire in the Atlantic Ocean, forcing more than 1,000 people to abandon ship.
Air Force Organization(s) Involved: 57th and 58th Air Rscu Sqs.
Airlifted: 42 life rafts, 400 blankets, and survival kits.
Aircraft Employed: HC–54 (six).
Operations: A few days after sailing from Southampton, England, the 609-foot Greek luxury liner *Lakonia* caught fire in the Atlantic Ocean about 180 miles north of Portugal's Madeira Islands. Just after midnight on December 23, the crew broadcast distress signals as more than 1,000 people, including over 600 British tourists, abandoned ship. Since the ship's lifeboats could not accommodate all of the passengers, many passengers wearing life jackets floated in the cold ocean while awaiting rescue.

On December 23 and 24, the 57th and 58th Air Rscu Sqs flew six HC–54 airplanes to the burning ship from Lajes Field in the Azores and Wheelus AB, Libya. The planes dropped 42 life rafts and survival kits to *Lakonia* survivors and circled overhead to locate other victims and direct ships to the scene. They dropped 400 blankets to five ships that arrived by dusk on December 23 to pick up the 896 survivors and 91 bodies.

Humanitarian Airlift Operations

23.
Name: São Jorge Earthquakes.
Location: Azores.
Date(s): March 19, April 3–9, and August 3, 1964.
Emergency: A series of earthquakes struck São Jorge Island, leaving thousands of people homeless.
Air Force Organization(s) Involved: 1605th AB Wg; 1608th Air Trpt Wg; and 1st, 103d, 109th, 133d, and 142d Air Trpt Sqs.
Airlifted: More than 60 tons of clothes, livestock, and Quonset huts.
Aircraft Employed: C–97 (four), C–54 (one), C–133 (one), and C–124 (one).
Operations: For more than a week, beginning February 15, earthquakes associated with a submarine volcanic eruption shook São Jorge Island in the Azores. Almost all of the 2,000 houses in Velos, the island's main town, suffered severe damage. More than 1,000 of São Jorge's 20,000 residents fled by boat to other islands in the archipelago, including Terceira, home of the 1605th AB Wg at Lajes AB.

High winds and rain at first prevented Air Force relief missions from Lajes, but a 1605th AB Wg C–54 flew around São Jorge to take aerial photographs. In the meantime, the wing contributed blankets, mattresses, pillows, and sheets to Terceira's hospitals.

On March 19, the 142d Air Trpt Sq of the Delaware Air National Guard flew a C–97 Stratofreighter loaded with cows, rabbits, turkeys, ducks, and chickens to Lajes for earthquake victims as part of the State Department People to People program.

Between April 3 and 9, the 1st Air Trpt Sq from Dover AFB, Delaware; and the 103d, 109th, and 133d Air Trpt Sqs from the Pennsylvania, Minnesota, and the New Hampshire Air National Guards flew a C–133 and three C–97s to airlift 59 tons of clothes from California to the Azores. Californians donated the clothing in a project called Carpet of Friendship. U.S. Army landing craft carried the cargo from Terceira Island to São Jorge.

In August, the U.S. Army, Navy, and Air Force joined forces to house 200 families on São Jorge. On August 3, the 1608th Air Trpt Wg from Charleston AFB, South Carolina, airlifted four corrugated metal Quonset huts—each 48 feet long when assembled—from the United States to Lajes aboard a C–124 Globemaster. Army landing craft took hut components from Terceira to São Jorge, where Navy Seabees helped Portuguese workers to erect them. The Navy eventually transported 96 more Quonset huts to the Azores by ship.

24.
Name: Yugoslavian Flood.
Location: Yugoslavia.
Date(s): October 29–November 14, 1964.
Emergency: Two weeks of heavy rain flooded five river valleys in northwestern Yugoslavia, inundating Zagreb and forcing 45,000 people from their homes.

Air Force Organization(s) Involved: 322d Air Div and 41st and 52d Trp Carr Sqs.

Airlifted: 169 tons of blankets, sheets, cots, mattresses, medical supplies, children's clothing, and other relief supplies.

Aircraft Employed: C–124 (10) and C–130 (one).

Operations: During late October, heavy rain caused five rivers in northwestern Yugoslavia to overflow. The Sava River rose almost 17 feet above normal, flooding Zagreb, Yugoslavia's second largest city, and forcing 45,000 people from their homes.

Responding to State Department requests, the JCS directed the 322d Air Div at Chateauroux Air Station, France, to arrange an airlift of relief supplies. Between October 29 and November 14, the division organized 11 missions to Yugoslavia: 10 by rotational C–124s of the 52d Trp Carr Sq from Rhein-Main AB, West Germany, and one by a TAC C–130 from the rotational 41st Trp Carr Sq from Evreux-Fauville AB, France.

The 11 cargo planes transported 169 tons of blankets, sheets, cots, mattresses, medical supplies, children's clothing, and other relief supplies from Rhein-Main and Ramstein ABs in West Germany and Toul Rosieres AB, France, to Pleso Airport at Zagreb. Yugoslavian officials distributed the cargo to thousands of homeless flood victims. In the final two days of the operation, November 13 and 14, Air Force planes delivered 19,500 blankets, 10,000 sheets, 2,500 cots, and 2,500 mattresses.

25.

Name: Italian Flood Rescue.

Location: Italy.

Date(s): Early September 1965.

Emergency: Torrential rain produced flooding in central and northern Italy.

Air Force Organization(s) Involved: Detachment 10, Atlantic Air Rscu Cen.

Airlifted: 43 flood victims.

Aircraft Employed: HH–43 (number unknown).

Operations: During the first week of September, heavy rain caused rivers to overflow in central and northern Italy. The flooding, which affected more than one-third of the Italian peninsula, including the area around Rome and also north of Venice, left 55 people dead and thousands homeless.

More than 50 hours of continuous rain in the foothills of the Alps in northeastern Italy prompted local officials to request help from Detachment 10 of the Atlantic Air Rscu Cen at Aviano AB. Flying HH–43B helicopters, the unit evacuated 43 Italian civilians from the flood area. The helicopters also helped rescue officials to locate survivors.

26.
Name: Northern Italian Floods.
Location: Italy.
Date(s): November 11–12, 1966.
Emergency: Heavy rain from a storm system flooded valleys in northern Italy, killing more than 100 people; leaving tens of thousands homeless; and ruining art treasures in Florence, Pisa, and Venice.
Air Force Organization(s) Involved: 322d Air Div, 63d and 436th Mil Alft Wgs, 513th Trp Carr Wg, and 52d Mil Alft Sq.
Airlifted: 205 tons of water purification equipment, generators, rolling stock, and food; and 93 Dutch military relief workers.
Aircraft Employed: C–124 (12) and C–130 (four).
Operations: A powerful storm system with high winds and very heavy rain struck Italy in early November. Rivers such as the Arno and Po and their tributaries overflowed, engulfing 36,000 square miles, killing at least 100 people, and leaving tens of thousands homeless. In Florence, water 20 feet deep flowed at a speed of 35 mph through some streets, destroying priceless Renaissance art and leaving behind tons of mud. After damaging 1,200 paintings at the famous Uffizi in Florence, the Arno River flooded Pisa to the west. Floods also struck Venice, where the Piazza San Marco became a lake. The Italian government appealed for international assistance.

From November 11 to 12, the Military Airlift Command's 322d Air Div airlifted relief equipment, supplies, and personnel from Ypenberg AB in the Netherlands to San Guisto Airport at Pisa for USAFE. The division flew 16 missions: 10 with rotational C–124s of the 52d Mil Alft Sq at Rhein-Main AB, West Germany; two with C–124s of the 63d Mil Alft Wg from Hunter AFB, Georgia, and the 436th Mil Alft Wg from Dover AFB, Delaware; and four with rotational TAC C–130s of the 513th Trp Carr Wg at Mildenhall in the United Kingdom.

Bad weather and poor communications, a change in the load station from Soesterberg to Ypenberg, limited ramp and taxi space, and cargo disorder—which forced some reloading—caused a delay of more than six hours. Nonetheless, the 16 planes transported almost 205 tons of relief cargo and 93 Dutch military relief workers from the Netherlands to Italy in two days. The cargo included water purification equipment, generators, rolling stock, and food.

27.
Name: Sicilian Earthquakes.
Location: Sicily.
Date(s): January 16–27, 1968.
Emergency: Severe earthquakes struck western Sicily, killing more than 200 people and leaving 50,000 homeless.
Air Force Organization(s) Involved: 322d Air Div, 52d Mil Alft Sq, and 62d Tac Alft Sq.

Airlifted: 168 tons of food, tents, kitchen components, blankets, cots, mattresses, medical supplies, trucks, and trailers; and 59 relief personnel, including medical teams, drivers, and cooks.

Aircraft Employed: C–124 (two) and C–130 (one).

Operations: A series of severe earthquakes struck western Sicily beginning on January 15, leaving more than 200 people dead and 50,000 homeless in towns such as Gibellina, Santa Margherita di Belice, Santa Ninfa, and Montevago. The disaster destroyed 9,000 homes in six towns, and losses totaled more than $300 million.

The Italian government requested U.S. aid. The Joint Chiefs of Staff, working with USEUCOM, directed MAC and USAFE to organize an airlift of relief equipment, supplies, and personnel from western Europe to western Sicily.

Between January 16 and 27, three 322d Air Div planes flew 168 tons of relief equipment and supplies on 15 sorties from West Germany, the United Kingdom, and the Italian mainland to Trapani and Palermo, Sicily. The cargo—which included 1,000 cases of C rations, 200 tents, 1,000 blankets, a portable kitchen, medical supplies, cots, mattresses, trucks, and trailers—was collected at Ramstein AB, West Germany; RAF Lakenheath in the United Kingdom; and the Italian cities of Rome, Treviso, and Rimini.

Air Force cargo planes also airlifted 59 relief personnel—including medical teams, drivers, and cooks—to western Sicily. The 52d Mil Alft Sq from Rhein-Main AB, West Germany, flew two rotational C–124s on four sorties, while a rotational 62d Tac Alft Sq C–130E, piloted by Maj. Kenneth E. Perkins, flew 11 more sorties. Through the airlift, the United States provided hundreds of homeless earthquake victims with food, shelter, and medical attention necessary to survive through the first difficult weeks of recovery.

28.

Name: Genoa Flash Flood.

Location: Italy.

Date(s): October 18, 1970.

Emergency: Torrential rain produced flash flooding in northwestern Italy that left 30 people dead around Genoa.

Air Force Organization(s) Involved: 322d Tac Alft Wg and 61st Tac Alft Sq.

Airlifted: 2.5 tons of disinfectant, blankets, medical supplies, and food.

Aircraft Employed: C–130 (one).

Operations: On October 8, heavy rain produced flash flooding in northwestern Italy around the port of Genoa. At least 30 people died. Italian premier Emilio Colombo flew immediately to the disaster area to help direct relief efforts. His government appealed for international assistance as losses mounted beyond $500 million.

The United States Air Forces in Europe directed the 322d Tac Alft Wg to organize an airlift of relief supplies to Genoa. On October 18, the 61st Tac Alft

Sq—on rotational duty as Delta squadron of the 322d Tac Alft Wg—flew 2.5 tons of relief cargo from Rhein-Main AB, West Germany, to Genoa aboard a C–130E piloted by Capt. Fisk Outwater. Supplies included disinfectant, blankets, medical supplies, and food.

29.
Name: Icelandic Volcano.
Location: Iceland.
Date(s): January 23, February 16–March 2, and March 25–27, 1973.
Emergency: A volcano erupted on Heimaey, a tiny island south of the main island of Iceland, forcing all 5,300 residents to evacuate and threatening to bury the fishing village of Vestmannaeyjar and its harbor.
Air Force Organization(s) Involved: Detachment 14, 40th Aerosp RR Wg; 36th Tac Alft Sq; and 9th Mil Alft Sq.
Airlifted: At least 833 tons of industrial equipment, pumps, pipe, and sheep; and at least 477 passengers, including hospital patients, emergency workers, scientists, and reporters.
Aircraft Employed: HH–3 (two), C–130 (two), C–141 (three), and C–5 (one).
Operations: On January 23, a volcano erupted on the small island of Heimaey just south of Iceland's main island. Icelandic authorities ordered the 5,000 residents of the island to evacuate. Most islanders fled by boat, but 33 hospital patients left by air. Lava and cinders temporarily closed Heimaey's one airstrip, so the Icelandic Life Saving Association contacted Detachment 14, 40th Aerosp RR Wg, at Keflavík AB, to request helicopters.

The detachment flew two HH–3E Jolly Green Giant helicopters to Heimaey within hours of the call. In three trips, the helicopters flew the hospital patients from Heimaey to Reykjavík, more than 70 miles away. Helicopter crews also moved 275 stranded island sheep to safety on the main island. Navy aircraft helped to evacuate the rest of Heimaey's sheep.

Heimaey's volcano continued to erupt through February and March, burying homes in the fishing village of Vestmannaeyjar and threatening to close its harbor. U.S. Air Force, Navy, and Marine Corps personnel helped members of the Icelandic Defense Force to move industrial equipment from the village to the airstrip, which was cleared for airlift operations. The 36th Tac Alft Sq of the 316th Tac Alft Wg deployed two C–130E cargo planes to Iceland on February 12. Between February 16 and March 2, the aircrews, under the mission commander, Maj. David Hennessey, airlifted at least 756 tons of cargo—including components of eight fishing factories and hospital equipment—from Heimaey to Keflavík. More than 444 passengers, mostly Icelandic emergency workers, but also scientists and reporters, rode on the planes to and from Heimaey. Operations proceeded despite high winds and cold temperatures.

The Military Airlift Command dispatched three C–141s and one C–5 Galaxy to Keflavík between March 25 and 27. The C–5, from the 436th Military Airlift

Wing's 9th Mil Alft Sq, carried 77 tons of heavy pumps and large pipe from the United States to Iceland and was the first Galaxy ever to land in Iceland. Workers on Heimaey used the airlifted equipment to spray water on the lava to slow its advance on Vestmannaeyjar and its harbor. Although they delayed the lava long enough to remove some of the town's remaining industrial equipment, they were not able to prevent the volcano from burying most of the town.

30.
Name: Romanian Flood.
Location: Romania.
Date(s): August 7, 1975.
Emergency: Heavy rain flooded tributaries of the Danube River, inundating at least 2.5 million acres and leaving thousands of people homeless.
Air Force Organization(s) Involved: 18th Mil Alft Sq.
Airlifted: 60 tons of relief supplies, mostly medicine.
Aircraft Employed: C–141 (two).
Operations: In early July, heavy rain flooded the lower Danube River valley in southern Romania, affecting 24 of 39 provinces. The flood left thousands of people homeless as it turned 2.5 million acres of croplands into lakes. Romanian leader Nicolae Ceausescu proclaimed an emergency and appealed for international aid.

Responding to a State Department request, MAC tapped a unit of the 438th Mil Alft Wg at McGuire AFB, New Jersey, for a relief airlift. On August 7, Capt. Robert Leeds and Capt. Walter Line of the 18th Mil Alft Sq flew two C–141 Starlifter planes loaded with 60 tons of relief cargo—mostly medical supplies—from Ramstein AB, West Germany, to Bucharest, capital of Romania. The U.S. airlift provided one link in a chain of assistance given by the UN to the flood-stricken country. The State Department sent a letter of appreciation to Leeds and Line for their roles in the operation.

31.
Name: Italian Earthquake.
Location: Italy.
Date(s): May 11–13, 1976.
Emergency: A severe earthquake struck northeastern Italy, leaving 900 people dead, 1,800 injured, and 150,000 homeless.
Air Force Organization(s) Involved: 63d Mil Alft Wg.
Airlifted: Emergency communications equipment and medical supplies.
Aircraft Employed: C–141 (one).
Operations: During the night of May 6, a severe earthquake registering more than 6.0 on the Richter scale struck the Friuli region of northeastern Italy. It killed more than 900 people, injured 1,800, and left about 150,000 homeless in towns such as Forgaria, Gemona, Maniago, and Vita D'Asio.

Humanitarian Airlift Operations

On May 8, Italy requested U.S. assistance. Air Force units at Aviano AB in the earthquake area responded with earthmoving equipment, tents, and personnel, but a decision by the Italian air force to temporarily halt air operations at Aviano delayed the airlift. From May 11 to 13, the 63d Mil Alft Wg, based at Norton AFB, California, airlifted emergency communications equipment and medical supplies to Aviano aboard a C–141 Starlifter cargo plane. On May 13, Vice President Nelson Rockefeller arrived at Aviano to express U.S. concern for the earthquake victims.

32.
Name: Romanian Earthquake.
Location: Romania.
Date(s): March 7, 1977.
Emergency: An earthquake struck northeastern Romania, leaving more than 1,300 people dead and 10,000 injured.
Air Force Organization(s) Involved: 32d Tac Alft Sq.
Airlifted: More than six tons of medical supplies.
Aircraft Employed: C–130 (one).
Operations: On March 4, an earthquake registering more than 7.0 on the Richter scale struck Romania north of Bucharest, leaving at least 1,300 people dead and more than 10,000 injured. The quake destroyed 20,000 homes and leveled 32 tall buildings in Bucharest. President Nicolae Ceausescu declared an emergency, and the U.S. embassy asked the State Department to arrange an emergency airlift of medical supplies to the Romanian capital.

On March 7, a C–130 Hercules cargo plane from the 32d Tac Alft Sq of the 314th Tac Alft Wg—which had deployed in February to Rhein-Main AB, West Germany—transported more than six tons of medical supplies to Bucharest from Ramstein AB, West Germany, and Pisa AB, Italy. Capt. Thomas J. Little, Jr., piloted the C–130, and Lt. Col. Roger R. Utley, the squadron commander, rode along. The U.S. ambassador to Romania, Harry G. Barnes, Jr., met the plane at the Bucharest airport and transferred the medical cargo, which came from U.S. Army stocks in West Germany and Italy, to the Romanian Red Cross. The plane returned to Rhein-Main AB the same day.

33.
Name: Yugoslavian Earthquake.
Location: Yugoslavia.
Date(s): April 18–20, 1979.
Emergency: An earthquake struck southern Yugoslavia, leaving 230 people dead, 350 injured, and 80,000 homeless.
Air Force Organization(s) Involved: Twenty-first Air Force, 437th and 438th Mil Alft Wgs, 514th Mil Alft Wg (Associate), and 435th Tac Alft Wg.
Airlifted: 139 tons of tents, cots, generators, blankets, water containers, water

pumps, and a water purification unit; and 25 support personnel.
Aircraft Employed: C–141 (seven) and C–130 (three).
Operations: On Easter Sunday, April 15, a disastrous earthquake struck the Adriatic coast of southern Yugoslavia and Albania, leaving 230 people dead, 350 injured, and 80,000 homeless. The Yugoslavian government requested U.S. assistance for the earthquake victims.

Between April 18 and 20, MAC airlifted more than 130 tons of relief cargo to Titograd, Yugoslavia, on seven C–141s and three C–130s. The 437th Mil Alft Wg, based at Charleston AFB, South Carolina, flew five C–141s to Yugoslavia to deliver 91 tons of equipment and supplies, including 1,250 tents, 654 cots, and a generator. The supplies came from AID and Office of Foreign Disaster Assistance stockpiles in Panama, so the planes loaded at Howard AFB in the Canal Zone. They were unloaded at Titograd International Airport in the disaster area. Two other C–141s, flown by crews of the 438th Mil Alft Wg and 514th Mil Alft Wg (Associate), transported 35 tons of relief cargo, including 2,000 blankets and 5,000 water containers, from McGuire AFB in New Jersey to Titograd.

In the same period, three 435th Tac Alft Wg C–130s from Rhein-Main AB, West Germany, airlifted water pumps, generators, water purification equipment, and other emergency cargo to Titograd from Camp Darby, near Leghorn, Italy. These cargo planes also transported a 25-member airlift control element team from Rhein-Main to Yugoslavia.

34.
Name: Azores Earthquake.
Location: Terceira Island, Azores.
Date(s): January 2–4, 1980.
Emergency: An earthquake devastated Terceira Island in the Azores, leaving 50 people dead, 300 injured, and thousands homeless.
Air Force Organization(s) Involved: 437th Mil Alft Wg.
Airlifted: 700 tents and tent flies and 1,000 blankets.
Aircraft Employed: C–141 (two).
Operations: On January 1, an earthquake registering almost 7.0 on the Richter scale struck the Atlantic Ocean floor about 75 miles northwest of Terceira Island in the Portuguese Azores. Terceira suffered 50 people dead, about 300 injured, and thousands homeless in towns such as Angra and Boscoitos. The Portuguese government requested U.S. assistance for the earthquake victims.

The commander of the 1605th AB Wg at Lajes Field on Terceira Island, Brig. Gen. Richard T. Drury, directed the local U.S. response. Lajes Field, which suffered minor quake damage, provided shelter, food, medical treatment, mattresses, generators, and heavy equipment for earthquake victims, but more tents and blankets were needed for the homeless.

On January 2, the JCS directed MAC to airlift relief supplies to the Azores. The 437th Mil Alft Wg, based at Charleston AFB, South Carolina, launched two

C–141 Starlifters to pick up AID cargo stockpiled at Camp Darby in Italy for delivery to the disaster area. On January 3 and 4, the cargo planes hauled 700 tents and tent flies and 1,000 blankets from Pisa, Italy, to Lajes Field.

35.
Name: Italian Earthquake.
Location: Italy.
Date(s): November 26–December 2, 1980.
Emergency: An earthquake registering 6.8 on the Richter scale struck southern Italy, leaving 3,000 people dead and 310,000 homeless.
Air Force Organization(s) Involved: 322d Alft Div; 438th Mil Alft Wg; and 37th, 39th, and 61st Tac Alft Sqs.
Airlifted: 296 tons of tents, blankets, medical supplies, and other relief cargo; and 112 passengers, including a liaison team, cargo handlers, soldiers for relief work, and power production personnel.
Aircraft Employed: C–130 (11) and C–141 (one).
Operations: On the evening of November 23, the worst earthquake to hit Europe in 65 years struck the mountain villages of southern Italy southeast of Naples. Registering 6.8 on the Richter scale, the initial quake and its subsequent aftershocks left at least 3,000 people dead and 310,000 homeless. After an initial delay, the Italian government requested U.S. aid. On November 26, the Joint Chiefs of Staff directed MAC to support USEUCOM with an airlift.

Normally, U.S. disaster relief supplies for southern Italy would come from AID stockpiles at Camp Darby, near Leghorn, Italy, but these stocks had been depleted in responding to an Algerian earthquake relief operation the previous month. For this reason, most relief cargo for the Italian earthquake victims came from Ramstein AB, West Germany.

Under the management of the 322d Alft Div, the 37th Tac Alft Sq of the 435th Tac Alft Wg, based at Rhein-Main AB in West Germany, launched the first airlift mission. On November 26, a C–130 transported a mobility team with cargo handlers and a K-loader for unloading cargo from other aircraft. Eight 37th Tac Alft Sq C–130s followed, moving 218 tons of tents and blankets from Ramstein to Naples in two days, from November 26 to 27. Other C–130s came from the 39th and 61st Tac Alft Sqs, which were rotating crews to Mildenhall in the United Kingdom. The 438th Mil Alft Wg at McGuire AFB, New Jersey, flew a C–141 to Italy to participate in the emergency airlift, carrying supplies from Rome to Naples.

The airlift involved 28 MAC sorties with at least 11 C–130s and one C–141 and lasted from November 26 through December 2. In eight days, the aircraft transported 296 tons of relief cargo, including tents, blankets, and medical supplies; and 112 passengers, including a liaison team, cargo handlers, soldiers for relief work, and electrical power production personnel. Commercial contract aircraft airlifted additional relief supplies from the United States to Italy. Two DC–8s flew directly to Naples, but a 747 had to land at Rome, where its cargo was transferred to smaller planes for delivery to Capodichino Airport in Naples.

The C–130 and C–141 missions contended with adverse weather that afflicted southern Italy at the end of November. A series of frontal systems brought clouds, rain, hail, and snow to the earthquake area, hampering Army and Navy helicopters participating in the relief efforts.

By December 2, 12 MAC aircraft and three commercial contract planes had delivered 2,000 tents and 20,000 blankets to Naples, helping to shelter the victims of the earthquake as winter approached.

36.
Name: Greek Earthquakes.
Location: Greece.
Date(s): March 6, 1981.
Emergency: A series of earthquakes and aftershocks measuring up to 6.9 on the Richter scale shook central Greece, leaving at least 15 people dead, 53 injured, and thousands homeless.
Air Force Organization(s) Involved: 322d Alft Div.
Airlifted: 225 tents.
Aircraft Employed: C–130 (one).
Operations: From the end of February through early March, a series of earthquakes and aftershocks devastated central Greece near Athens, Corinth, and Thebes. Measuring up to 6.9 on the Richter scale, the tremors left at least 15 people dead, 53 injured, and thousands homeless. At the end of February, the Greek government asked its NATO allies for emergency supplies.

On February 28, the U.S. embassy in Athens asked the 7206th AB Gp at Hellenikon AB, Greece, to provide relief in the local area. The group contributed 169 tents, 39 tarpaulins, 384 wool blankets, and 2,062 folding cots, lent through Greek military channels. The 322d Airlift Division's Detachment 3 at Hellenikon also assisted its host base with local disaster relief.

A second round of tremors in early March convinced the State Department that a military airlift was necessary. On March 6, Secretary of State Alexander Haig requested the airlift. That same day, the 322d Alft Div ordered a C–130 Hercules aircraft and crew, on Bravo Alert at Hellenikon AB, to pick up 225 tents from AID stockpiles at Camp Darby, Italy. On March 6, the C–130 carried the tents from Pisa, Italy, to Athens, where they sheltered some of the homeless. Military Airlift Command-sponsored commercial flights later delivered 2,000 blankets to Athens for earthquake victims.

37.
Name: Armenian Earthquake.
Location: Union of Soviet Socialist Republics.
Date(s): December 9, 1988–February 9, 1989, and December 29, 1989.

Humanitarian Airlift Operations

Emergency: An earthquake killed 25,000 people, injured 130,000, and left 514,000 homeless.

Air Force Organization(s) Involved: 433d, 436th, 437th, 438th, 439th, and 459th Mil Alft Wgs; 512th Mil Alft Wg (Associate); 105th and 172d Mil Alft Gps; and 375th Aeromed Alft Wg.

Airlifted: More than 311 tons of relief cargo, including medical supplies, plastic sheeting, modular shelters, tents, clothing, blankets, cots, food, water bottles, trucks, and boots; and 37 injured Armenian earthquake victims.

Aircraft Employed: C–141 (12), C–5 (5), and C–9 (1).

Operations: On December 7, 1988, the worst earthquake to strike Eurasia in decades ruined 58 towns and villages in northern Armenia, a Soviet republic between the Caspian and Black Seas. The earthquake, which registered 6.9 on the Richter scale, leveled hundreds of large, poorly constructed concrete apartment complexes, leaving an estimated 25,000 people dead, 130,000 injured, and 514,000 homeless.

Soviet leader Mikhail Gorbachev cut short a visit to the United States and returned to inspect the damage and supervise relief efforts. On December 8, his government accepted a U.S. offer of disaster assistance, including a humanitarian airlift to Yerevan, the Armenian capital.

The United States was one of several western nations participating in relief operations to Soviet Armenia. Commercial and military aircraft from many nations—including the United States, Britain, France, West Germany, and Italy— flew so many humanitarian flights to Yerevan's Zvartnots Airport that some of the larger aircraft could not land safely.

The Military Airlift Command, using both its own planes and assets of the AF Res and ANG, flew 20 relief missions for the Armenian earthquake victims. Five C–5s, 12 C–141s, and one C–9 participated in the operation, transporting injured earthquake victims and more than 311 tons of relief cargo, including supplies purchased by the United States or donated by private charities.

Between December 9, 1988, and February 9, 1989, four C–5s from the 433d, 436th, and 439th Mil Alft Wgs and the 105th Mil Alft Gp flew 236 tons of medical supplies, blankets, clothing, and food from AID and Office of Foreign Disaster Assistance stockpiles in the United States and western Europe to Incirlik AB, Turkey, where the cargo was transferred to C–141s for flights to Yerevan. During the same period, 11 C–141s delivered 251 tons of relief cargo to Yerevan from Incirlik and bases in the United States, West Germany, and Italy. The Starlifter crews came from the 438th and 459th Mil Alft Wgs and from the 172d Mil Alft Gp. The cargo included medical supplies, plastic sheeting, modular shelters, clothing, and blankets.

Capt. David Yankovich and his C–5 Galaxy crew from the 436th Mil Alft Wg at Dover AFB, Delaware, initiated the U.S. airlift for the Armenian earthquake victims on December 9. Flying through Ramstein AB, West Germany, he landed at Pisa, Italy, where he took aboard more than 33 tons of medical supplies from stockpiles at nearby Leghorn, Italy. On December 10, Yankovich and his crew delivered the cargo to Incirlik. He could not land his C–5 at Yerevan's Zvartnots Airport because of congestion, so two C–141s from the 438th Mil Alft Wg and the 172d Mil Alft Gp carried the medical cargo from Incirlik on to Yerevan.

The U.S. airlift transported relief supplies to Armenia and carried some seriously injured earthquake victims to the United States for medical treatment. Between February 2 and 9, a 437th Mil Alft Wg C–141, flown by Capt. Glenn R. McGowan and his crew, flew 37 injured Armenians from the Soviet Union through Rhein-Main AB, West Germany, to Andrews AFB, Maryland. First Lady Barbara Bush greeted the aircraft after it landed. A 375th Aeromed Alft Wg C–9 and 12 small commercial airplanes carried the 37 patients to 10 hospitals in the United States for specialized medical treatment that was sponsored by Project Hope, a private charity. Some earthquake victims received prosthetic devices to replace lost limbs.

At the end of December 1989, long after the bulk of the international relief effort was over, the 436th Mil Alft Wg flew the last mission to Armenia, using a C–5 Galaxy to deliver 12 four-wheel drive trucks, 50 field tents, 224 portable heaters, 464 wool blankets, and 120 pairs of insulated boots. No C–5 had landed at Yerevan due to heavy congestion. The cargo came courtesy of the McCollum Amendment to the 1986 Defense Appropriations Act, which authorized the shipment of surplus nonlethal DoD supplies to other nations for humanitarian purposes.

The Armenian earthquake airlift broke new ground. Never before had the Soviet Union allowed direct flights to its cities without Soviet personnel aboard the aircraft. The United States had not airlifted as much cargo to the Soviet Union since World War II. The operation also trained MAC, AF Res, and ANG air crews to operate from a congested facility that lacked mechanized unloading equipment.

Despite the problems, the Armenian airlift validated the improved relationship between the United States and the Soviet Union and warmed relations between the former enemies even further. The airlift also showed Soviet leader Mikhail Gorbachev that U.S. policy toward his country would not change with a change in presidents.

38.
Name: Soviet Rail Disaster.
Location: Union of Soviet Socialist Republics.
Date(s): June 9–11, 1989.
Emergency: A pipeline explosion caused a train wreck and fire.
Air Force Organization(s) Involved: 63d and 438th Mil Alft Wgs; and 6th, 30th, and 53d Mil Alft Sqs.
Airlifted: Burn specialist team and four tons of medical supplies.
Aircraft Employed: C–141 (two).
Operations: On June 4, a pair of trains moving in opposite directions passed each

other near Chelyabinsk, about 750 miles southeast of Moscow on the Trans–Siberian Railroad in the Soviet Union. At the same time, a nearby liquid gas pipeline exploded, derailing one train and crashing it into the other. Flames from the explosion engulfed both trains, killing or injuring more than 850 of the 1,200 passengers. About 100 of the severely burned survivors were children on their way to summer camp in the Crimea. It was one of the worst rail disasters in history.

When President Bush learned of the tragedy, he offered to send U.S. burn specialists and medical supplies to the Soviet Union. Soviet leader Mikhail Gorbachev accepted the offer, and a humanitarian airlift was set in motion.

On June 9, a 63d Mil Alft Wg C–141B Starlifter flown by a 53d Mil Alft Sq crew transported a 17-member burn specialist team and more than four tons of medical equipment from Kelly AFB, Texas, to Andrews AFB, Maryland, on the first leg of the trip to the Soviet Union. Medical personnel and equipment came from the Army Institute of Surgical Research at Brooke Army Medical Center, Fort Sam Houston, near Kelly AFB.

The next day, another C–141B, flown by a seven-man crew from the 438th Military Airlift Wing's 30th Mil Alft Sq, airlifted the burn specialist team and its medical supplies from Andrews AFB to Rhein-Main AB, West Germany. A 6th Mil Alft Sq crew, also from the 438th Mil Alft Wg, took over at Rhein-Main and flew the C–141 on to Moscow, where it landed on June 11. Soviet aircraft transported the burn team and medical supplies from Moscow to Ufa, a city near the disaster area, where local hospitals treated the disaster victims. The airlift demonstrated that the United States and the Soviet Union, which for the past 40 years had been bitter Cold War enemies, could be allies against a common enemy.

39.
Name: Romanian Medical Airlift.
Location: Romania.
Date(s): December 29–31, 1989.
Emergency: A violent revolution produced many wounded civilians in need of medical supplies.
Air Force Organization(s) Involved: 435th Tac Alft Wg and 37th Tac Alft Sq.
Airlifted: 31 tons of medical supplies.
Aircraft Employed: C–130 (two).
Operations: After security forces loyal to President Nicolae Ceausescu opened fire on anticommunist demonstrators in Timisoara, Bucharest, and other Romanian cities in December, a revolution swept across the country. Romanian army units joined the rebellion, allowing it to succeed. On December 25, the new government executed Ceausescu for genocide.

Fierce fighting in the streets of Romanian cities produced hundreds of casualties. In response to a request for medical supplies from the new Romanian government, the United States organized an airlift of 12 pallets to Bucharest.

On December 29, two 435th Tac Alft Wg C–130s, flown by crews of the 37th Tac Alft Sq, took off from Rhein-Main AB in West Germany for Bucharest. Bad winter weather, including low clouds and icy runways, forced the pair of Hercules aircraft to divert temporarily to Aviano AB in Italy. They finally landed in the Romanian capital on December 31 and unloaded more than 31 tons of medical supplies. Two State Department employees and two medical personnel also left the aircraft in Bucharest to supervise distribution of the cargo.

The airlift achieved two purposes. First, it delivered critically needed medical supplies to wounded Romanians, and, second, it laid a foundation for friendly relations between the United States and the new Romanian government.

40.
Name: Romanian Relief.
Location: Romania.
Date(s): March, May, July, September, and December 1991.
Emergency: Poor economic conditions in the wake of the collapse of the communist government fueled violent street demonstrations that threatened free market economic reforms and the movement toward democracy.
Air Force Organization(s) Involved: 436th Mil Alft Wg and 9th and 709th Mil Alft Sqs.
Airlifted: 150 tons of relief supplies, including food, medical supplies, and blankets.
Aircraft Employed: C–5 (five).
Operations: In late 1989, Romanians overthrew the communist government of Nicolae Ceausescu (see Romanian Medical Airlift, December 1989). The National Salvation Front, led by President Ion Iliescu and Prime Minister Petre Roman, organized a new provisional government, promising free market reforms and democracy. Unable to improve economic conditions dramatically in 1990, the government faced increasing protests in the streets of the capital city of Bucharest.

To restore order, the National Salvation Front enlisted miners from other parts of the country, who violently suppressed the demonstrators. But in 1991, the miners led violent antigovernment protests that threatened to bring down the government even as the country moved slowly toward democracy and economic freedom. To help the government to regain stability and satisfy the pressing material needs of the people, the United States airlifted relief supplies to the Romanian capital.

During 1991, the United States airlifted to Bucharest more than 150 tons of relief supplies, including food, blankets, and medical supplies. The 436th Mil Alft Wg from Dover AFB, Delaware, transported the cargo on five flights, one each in March, May, July, September, and December. Some supplies came from excess DoD stocks, with the remainder donated by private agencies such as the Romanian Orphanage Fund of California.

Humanitarian Airlift Operations

The airlift helped the new Romanian government to survive the threat of anarchy or a return to communist dictatorship. In February 1992, Romania held its first free local elections in more than 50 years.

41.
Name: Albanian Relief.
Location: Albania.
Date(s): July and August 1991.
Emergency: The collapse of the communist economy in Albania caused food shortages.
Air Force Organization(s) Involved: 436th and 438th Mil Alft Wgs; 514th Mil Alft Wg (Associate); and 3d, 18th, 30th, and 702d Mil Alft Sqs.
Airlifted: 170 tons of food.
Aircraft Employed: C–5 (one) and C–141 (one).
Operations: Aware of food shortages in Albania growing out of the collapsing communist economy, and of surplus Desert Storm food supplies in Saudi Arabia, Secretary of State James A. Baker III arranged with Albanian officials and DoD for a U.S. humanitarian airlift in July 1991. Dr. Robert K. Wolthuis, the deputy assistant secretary of defense for global affairs, oversaw the relief operation.

Around July 20, a 436th Mil Alft Wg C–5 Galaxy transported 170 tons of food, including "meals ready to eat" and cans of beef stew and salmon, from Dhahran AB in Saudi Arabia to Sigonella NAS in Italy. The cargo filled 36 pallets. From Sigonella, a 438th Mil Alft Wg C–141 Starlifter shuttled the food to Tirana, the Albanian capital, on 10 flights in July and August. Crews from the 18th, 30th, and 702d Mil Alft Sqs of the 438th Mil Alft Wg and 514th Mil Alft Wg (Associate) rotated on the Starlifter shuttle missions, which were dubbed the "Albanian Express."

Famous humanitarian Mother Teresa, perhaps best known for her work among the sick and destitute of Calcutta, India, greeted and thanked one of the crews. Much of the food was distributed by Roman Catholic relief agencies in Tirana, while some was shipped to the families of miners in northern Albania. The airlift allowed U.S. nationals into Albania for the first time since 1946 and encouraged the opening of the country to the West.

42.
Name: Ukrainian Relief.
Location: Union of Soviet Socialist Republics.
Date(s): October 23, 1991.
Emergency: As the Ukraine began to emerge as a republic independent of the Soviet Union, there were shortages of medical supplies in Kiev.
Air Force Organization(s) Involved: 436th Mil Alft Wg and 3d and 709th Mil Alft Sqs.

Airlifted: 146 tons of medical supplies, pharmaceuticals, blankets, and other relief supplies.
Aircraft Employed: C–5 (two).
Operations: In late 1991, the Soviet Union, suffering severe economic problems, began to break up into independent republics. The most important of these, after Russia, was Ukraine. Aware of shortages of medical supplies in the emerging republic, the United States authorized a humanitarian airlift.

Two 436th Mil Alft Wg C–5s, with crews from the 3d and 709th Mil Alft Sqs, flew the airlift on October 23. They carried 60 pallets containing 146 tons of medical supplies, pharmaceuticals, blankets, and other relief supplies from the United States and Germany to Kiev, the Ukrainian capital. The airlift foreshadowed other relief operations to the former Soviet republics in late 1991 and early 1992 (see Provide Hope, February 1992–September 1994).

43.
Name: Soviet Shortages.
Location: Russia, Byelorussia, and Armenia.
Date(s): December 17–22, 1991.
Emergency: As the USSR began to split up into independent countries, some of the larger cities experienced shortages of food and other necessities.
Air Force Organization(s) Involved: 436th and 438th Alft Wgs, 439th Mil Alft Wg, and 31st Alft Sq.
Airlifted: 238 tons of food, medical supplies, cots, blankets, and clothing.
Aircraft Employed: C–5 (three) and C–141 (one).
Operations: December 1991 marked the last month of the existence of the Soviet Union, which was beginning to split up into independent republics. The transition from centralized economic planning toward a free market system left people in the larger cities short of food and other basic necessities. To relieve this situation, the United States donated tons of supplies left over from the Persian Gulf War earlier in the year. Private agencies in the United States also collected medical supplies for the people of the Soviet republics. The Agency for International Development and the Department of Defense Office of Humanitarian Assistance worked together to move supplies to places they were needed.

Between December 17 and 22, the 436th and 438th Alft Wgs airlifted 168 tons of food to three cities in Russia and Byelorussia. Two 436th Alft Wg C–5 Galaxies moved 54 pallets weighing more than 148 tons to St. Petersburg—formerly Leningrad—and Moscow, Russia. One of the Galaxies, flown by a 31st Alft Sq crew, transported 27 pallets of food weighing 75 tons from Pisa AB, Italy, to St. Petersburg on December 20. The other C–5 carried 73 more tons from Pisa to Moscow on December 22. During the same week, a 438th Alft Wg C–141 Starlifter carried 20 more tons of relief supplies from Rhein-Main AB in Germany to Minsk, capital of Byelorussia.

In mid-December, a 439th Mil Alft Wg C–5A from Westover AFB,

Massachusetts, transported 70 tons of cots, blankets, clothing, and medical supplies from Andrews AFB, Maryland, to the crumbling Soviet Union. The cots, blankets, and clothing came from excess DoD supplies, while the medical supplies were donated through Project Hope, a private charitable organization. The Galaxy unloaded about 45 tons of relief supplies at Moscow and delivered the remaining 25 tons to Yerevan, capital of Armenia. Many needy Armenians had fled Azerbaijan, a neighboring republic.

The airlifted supplies helped to ease the republics' transition to independence, but were hardly enough to end the shortages. The December 1991 relief flights were a prelude to Provide Hope, a larger airlift to the former Soviet republics in 1992 (see Provide Hope, February 1992–September 1994).

44.
Name: Lithuanian Relief.
Location: Lithuania.
Date(s): February 6, 1992.
Emergency: Newly independent Lithuania struggled with shortages of food and medicine as it moved toward democracy and a free market economic system.
Air Force Organization(s) Involved: 435th Tac Alft Wg and 37th Tac Alft Sq.
Airlifted: Food and medicine.
Aircraft Employed: C–130 (four).
Operations: During 1990 and early 1991, Lithuania tried but failed to secure its independence from the Soviet Union. After a coup that weakened the Soviet government in August 1991, Lithuania finally broke away, receiving diplomatic recognition from the United States in September. The dissolution of the Soviet Union at the end of 1991 assured Lithuanian sovereignty. Lithuania and the other Baltic states of Estonia and Latvia remained outside the Commonwealth of Independent States, a confederation which most other former Soviet republics joined.

Like many former Soviet republics, Lithuania experienced shortages of food and medical supplies as it struggled to develop permanent democratic institutions and a less centralized economic system. To encourage this and to respond to pressing physical needs in Lithuania, the United States airlifted relief supplies to Vilnius, the Lithuanian capital, in February.

On February 6, four C–130s from the 435th Tac Alft Wg transported food and medical supplies to Vilnius from U.S. bases in Germany. Flown by crews of the 37th Tac Alft Sq, the four cargo aircraft demonstrated the willingness and ability of USAFE to meet diplomatic requirements of the United States in a post–Cold War environment. The Lithuanian relief operation preceded a larger humanitarian airlift to the CIS (see Provide Hope, February 1992–September 1994).

45.

Name: Provide Hope (first four phases).
Location: Commonwealth of Independent States.
Date(s): February 1992–September 1994.
Emergency: With the dissolution of the USSR and the collapse of its centralized economy, the former Soviet republics suffered severe shortages of food and medical supplies.
Air Force Organization(s) Involved: 60th, 62d, 63d, 315th, 349th, 436th, 437th, 438th, 439th, 445th, and 446th Alft Wgs; 512th and 514th Alft Wgs (Associate); 435th Tac Alft Wg; and 105th and 172d Alft Gps.
Airlifted: More than 4,400 tons of food and medical supplies.
Aircraft Employed: C–5, C–141, and C–130 (190 missions by May 1993; 500 by June 1997).
Operations: With the dissolution of the Soviet Union into independent republics at the end of 1991, most of these entities joined a confederation called the Commonwealth of Independent States. As they entered their first year without a centralized economy, the former Soviet republics suffered severe shortages of food and medical supplies. Western nations organized relief efforts.

On January 23, 1992, Secretary of State James Baker announced Provide Hope, an operation to deliver massive amounts of aid to the CIS. Congress appropriated $100 million for relief for the former Soviet republics, and Baker knew that large quantities of food and medicine were available from stockpiles left after the Persian Gulf conflict in 1991.

Richard L. Armitage of the State Department and Dr. Robert Wolthuis of the Defense Department worked together to determine the destinations of the cargo, which would be transported by air to save time. Armitage and Wolthuis wanted most relief supplies to go to hospitals, schools, orphanages, community shelters, and senior citizen centers. The Military Airlift Command's Gen. Hansford T. Johnson placed Col. John B. Sams, Jr., the commander of the 60th Alft Wg, in charge of the first phase of the operation, designated Provide Hope I.

Provide Hope I transported 2,274 tons of food and medical supplies to 24 cities in 10 former Soviet republics. All but 417 tons of the cargo was food, which came from warehouses in Pisa, Italy, and Rotterdam in the Netherlands. The food included beef, ham, pork, chicken, fish, potatoes, rice, vegetables, pasta, bread, and beverages. The remaining supplies were medical, and included bandages, sutures, adhesive tape, cotton, surgical sponges, disposable gloves, patients' clothing, blankets, and sheets. The medical cargo came from the Army Medical Materiel Center at Pirmasens, Germany, and from the United Kingdom. Convoys of trucks transported the food and medical supplies to three aerial ports of embarkation: Rhein-Main AB in Germany and Incirlik AB and Ankara Air Station (AS) in Turkey.

Military Airlift Command aircraft flew 46 C–141 and 19 C–5 flights to the CIS during the 17 days of Provide Hope I. Of these missions, 22 went to Russia;

Humanitarian Airlift Operations

7 each to Armenia and Kazakhstan; 5 to Ukraine; 4 each to Turkmenistan, Azerbaijan, Tajikistan, and Uzbekistan; 3 flights each to Kyrgyzstan and Moldova; and 2 to Belarus. Participating organizations included six regular airlift wings (the 60th, 62d, 63d, 436th, 437th, and 438th); seven AF Res airlift wings (the 315th, 349th, 439th, 445th, 446th, 512th, and 514th); and two ANG airlift groups (the 105th and 172d).

Maj. Robert Gray and a 7th Alft Sq crew flew the first Provide Hope I mission to the CIS in a 60th Alft Wg C–141 to deliver 17 tons of food and medical supplies to Bishkek, Kyrgyzstan, on February 10. Gray commented that he had expected to fly to that part of the world someday, but under combat conditions rather than as part of a humanitarian airlift.

Provide Hope I encountered its share of problems. Some flights covered distances greater than 3,000 miles. One C–141 suffered flat tires in its main landing gear on landing at Moscow on February 21. A C–5 that landed in Kazakhstan could not mechanically "kneel" as it was designed to do for roll-off unloading. The lack of materiel-handling equipment at some locations required some C–141s to carry extra personnel to unload the aircraft, and the C–5 had to carry forklifts. Some remote airfields lacked night navigation facilities, so landings and takeoffs could be scheduled only during daylight. Leaky hoses, the absence of fire-extinguishing equipment, and personnel smoking sometimes threatened refueling on the ground. The lack of deicing equipment in some cities also threatened the safety of the operation. Around some taxiways, people and animals got in the way of the aircraft.

Despite these problems, Provide Hope I proved remarkably successful. It provided immediate temporary relief for some of the needy people in 10 countries and laid the groundwork for Provide Hope II, an even larger relief operation. It demonstrated the commitment of the United States to people who had successfully thrown off a government that for decades had been the chief enemy of the United States. By assisting the people of the former Soviet republics to recover from communism, Provide Hope advanced the interests of the United States.

Provide Hope I was only a stopgap and did not go nearly far enough in meeting the needs of the people in the CIS. Subsequent phases of Provide Hope continued the flow of aid, relying more on the volume of sealift and land transportation than on the speed of airlift.

Using trucks, trains, and ships, USEUCOM supervised Provide Hope II, which delivered more than 19,000 tons of food and medical supplies by land, sea, and air to the CIS in 1992. Despite a greater reliance on surface transportation, Provide Hope II also called for extensive airlift missions, most flown by the Air Force, but some by commercial airlines under contract.

The airlift portion of Provide Hope II involved special assignment airlift missions. The first, flown by a C–5 Galaxy, delivered 75 tons of food and medicine to Moscow on February 29. C–141 Starlifters also participated in Provide Hope II. On April 24, for example, a 437th Alft Wg C–141 transported 12 pallets of medicine and medical supplies weighing 24 tons from Rhein-Main AB in Germany to Minsk, Belarus. Five days later, another C–141 delivered 14 tons of food and medical supplies to Tbilisi, the capital of Georgia, a former Soviet republic where internal unrest had prevented Provide Hope I missions.

Among the airlift wings participating in Provide Hope II were the Twenty-second Air Force's 60th, 62d, and 63d Alft Wgs; the Twenty-first Air Force's 436th and 438th Alft Wgs; the Air Force Reserve's 459th Alft Wg; and the United States Air Forces in Europe's 435th Tac Alft Wg.

Provide Hope III, which copied Provide Hope II, began in October 1992. Of 165 Provide Hope II and III airlift flights between the end of February 1992 and May 1993, Air Force military transports flew 135 missions: 94 by C–141s, 36 by C–5s, and 5 by C–130s. Only 30 Provide Comfort II and III airlift missions in that period were flown commercially.

Provide Hope III airlift missions continued beyond May 1993. By September, Air Force and commercial aircraft had airlifted well over 6,000 tons of cargo to the CIS. Military Airlift Command, Air Mobility Command (which replaced MAC in mid-1992), USAFE, and AF Res aircraft carried more than 4,400 tons of the total. In October 1993, the fourth phase of Provide Hope began and continued through September 1994. More phases followed, as Provide Hope became an ongoing operation. In June 1997, the USAF flew its five hundredth Provide Hope mission.

46.
Name: Sarajevo Relief (before Provide Promise).
Location: Bosnia-Herzegovina.
Date(s): April 16–19 and May 16, 1992.
Emergency: Serbs within Bosnia launched a military campaign against Sarajevo, the Bosnian capital, depriving its people of adequate food, shelter, and medical supplies.
Air Force Organization(s) Involved: 63d and 437th Alft Wgs and 172d Alft Gp.
Airlifted: 131 tons of food, medical supplies, and blankets.
Aircraft Employed: C–141 (seven missions).
Operations: In the summer of 1991, Slovenia and Croatia declared their independence from Serb-dominated Yugoslavia. A few months later, Bosnia-Herzegovina followed suit. Although the United States and the European Community recognized the independence of all three republics in early April 1992, Serbs within Croatia and Bosnia launched military attacks against the new governments. By the middle of the month, the Serbs threatened Sarajevo, the Bosnian capital, cutting the city off from traditional supply sources. To relieve the suffering of the people of Sarajevo, the United States launched a humanitarian airlift.

The Military Airlift Command airlifted 131 tons of food, medical supplies, and blankets to Bosnia and Croatia during April and May. In mid-April, five

Humanitarian Airlift Operations

C–141 missions transported 35 pallets of food rations and 12 pallets each of blankets and medical supplies from stockpiles in Italy to the Bosnian capital.

In May, Serb forces closed the Sarajevo airport, but the United States continued to supply the city through Croatia. On May 16, two more C–141 missions transported 43 tons of food rations from Rhein-Main AB, Germany, to Zagreb, the Croatian capital. From there, trucks delivered the cargo to Sarajevo, 175 miles away. By the end of the month, the United States had airlifted 89 tons of food, 26 tons of medical supplies, and 16 tons of blankets to Bosnia or Croatia. This airlift was a prelude to a larger Bosnian relief operation that began two months later (see Provide Promise, July 1992–January 1996).

47.
Name: Provide Promise.
Location: Bosnia-Herzegovina and Croatia.
Date(s): July 1992–January 1996.
Emergency: Ethnic strife within Bosnia-Herzegovina cut off food supplies to Sarajevo and other cities.
Air Force Organization(s) Involved: 60th, 62d, 94th, 118th, 123d, 133d, 136th, 137th, 146th, 302d, 314th, 315th, 317th, 349th, 403d, 435th, 437th, and 440th Alft Wgs; 23d Wing; 105th, 123d, 130th, 135th, 139th, 143d, 145th, 153d, 165th, 166th, 167th, 179th, 189th, 908th, 910th, 911th, 913th, 914th, 928th, and 934th Alft Gps; 176th Comp Gp; 37th, 40th, 41st, and 312th Alft Sqs; and 2d and 55th Aeromedical Airlift Squadrons (Aeromed Alft Sq).
Airlifted: More than 30,000 tons of food and medical supplies by the end of 1993.
Aircraft Employed: C–130, C–141, C–5, and C–9 (more than 100 total aircraft).
Operations: The collapse of communism in the Soviet Union and Eastern Europe in the late 1980s and early 1990s released a tide of nationalism in Yugoslavia, a federation of Roman Catholic Slovenians and Croats, Eastern Orthodox Serbs, Muslims, Albanians, Macedonians, and people of other ethnic groups. In 1991, Slovenia and Croatia declared their independence from the Serb-dominated Yugoslav federation, and Serbs in Croatia took up arms against the new republic. In early 1992, predominantly Muslim Bosnia-Herzegovina (Bosnia) also declared independence from Yugoslavia. But armed Serbs in Bosnia began seizing territory soon after its declaration of independence and blockaded roads around the Bosnian capital of Sarajevo in the spring.

In April 1992, the United States recognized the independence of Bosnia and began airlifting relief supplies to Sarajevo. In early May, Serb forces took control of the airport, cutting off more than 300,000 people from food and other supplies. After negotiations with the warring parties, the UN organized an international relief effort for Bosnia, with overland truck convoys from Croatia to Sarajevo. The UN took control of the Sarajevo airport at the end of June 1992, reopening it for international relief flights.

To support the UN effort, the United States established a joint task force under USEUCOM for an extended operation called Provide Promise. The vice commander of the 435th Alft Wg at Rhein-Main AB in Germany, Col. Patrick M. Henry, served as Provide Promise's first mobility commander.

U.S. C–130 aircraft began delivering food and medical supplies to Sarajevo on July 3, 1992. Most transports took off from Rhein-Main AB, staging at Zagreb in Croatia or Aviano AB in Italy on the way to Sarajevo, or flew directly to the Bosnian capital. The 435th and 317th Alft Wgs provided the first C–130s, but others began to rotate to Europe for three-week deployments. The Hercules aircraft came from full-time units and from AF Res and ANG units. Before long, about three C–130s were unloading at Sarajevo daily.

While the United States was only one of at least 15 countries airlifting relief supplies to Sarajevo in 1992, by the end of that year U.S. airplanes had delivered over 5,400 tons of food and medical supplies. Despite gunfire around Sarajevo that shot down an Italian cargo airplane in September, no U.S. plane was hit during the year.

Provide Promise expanded dramatically shortly after President Clinton's inauguration in January 1993. In February, Serb mortars hit a market in central Sarajevo, killing 68 people. Two U.S. C–130s evacuated 50 wounded from the Bosnian capital to Ramstein AB in Germany, where they were taken to Landstuhl for medical treatment. During the same month, Bosnian Serbs blockaded Muslim enclaves in eastern Bosnia, preventing the arrival of UN truck convoys.

At the end of February, President Clinton authorized U.S. airdrops of food and medicine to the enclaves, including Tuzla, Srebrenica, Zepa, and Gorazde. C–130s dropped thousands of leaflets explaining the humanitarian nature of the drops and warning people to avoid being hit by falling bundles, as happened in northern Iraq during Provide Comfort. Maj. Gen. James E. Chambers commanded the effort, which began on February 28 with C–130s from the 435th Alft Wg.

To avoid ground fire, the C–130s dropped their cargo at night from altitudes above 10,000 feet. Large parachutes and padded packaging cushioned the fall of the first bundles, which weighed up to a ton. At first, AF Res and ANG C–130s did not participate in airdrops because they lacked the latest navigational equipment to enhance accuracy, but later they flew in formations with Hercules aircraft equipped with this equipment. Provide Promise aircrews used the Global Positioning System, which depended on satellite communications.

To drop food directly over encircled population centers, Provide Promise airlifters experimented with a new tri-wall aerial delivery system, or TRIADS, in which individual meals, each weighing 2.2 pounds, were scattered from boxes ripped open as they departed the aircraft. This method reduced the danger of injury or damage on the ground. By mid-July 1993, Provide Promise had dropped more than 7,000 packages of food and over 500 bundles of medical supplies.

The largest cargo aircraft in the Air Force inventory, C–5s, also participated in the 1993 Provide Promise operation. In April, a C–5 from Travis AFB in

Humanitarian Airlift Operations

California transported relief supplies from Massachusetts to Rhein-Main AB, where they were loaded aboard smaller airplanes for delivery to Bosnia. In August, a 349th Alft Wg C–5, flown by a crew from the 312th Alft Sq, airlifted two water purification systems from Texas to Croatia. Each system weighed over 18 tons. From Croatia, smaller C–130s ferried the water purification components to Sarajevo. In the same month, the Air National Guard's 105th Alft Gp delivered three more water purification systems to Europe for delivery to Sarajevo. Once assembled, the five systems provided Bosnia's capital with a clean water supply, reducing the chances of an epidemic.

Aeromedical evacuation of Bosnian war casualties from Sarajevo continued in the summer, but with a twist. Supplementing C–130 and C–9 flights from Bosnia to Germany, C–141 Starlifters began to airlift the wounded from Europe to the United States for medical treatment. This project was dubbed "Operation Second Chance."

Provide Promise passed a milestone on October 8, 1993, when it surpassed the Berlin Airlift in duration (see Operation Vittles, June 1948–September 1949). By then, U.S. aircraft had transported more than 23,000 tons of relief cargo to Bosnia, with no major injuries or accidents. By the end of the year, Air Force aircraft had delivered more than 30,000 tons of food and medicine to the former Yugoslavia. Unfortunately, fighting in Bosnia continued, claiming as many as 200,000 lives and leaving more than two million people homeless.

Provide Promise airlifters embarked on another secondary operation in December 1993. This mission was designated Provide Santa. Hercules aircraft dropped over Bosnia about 50 tons of toys and children's clothing and shoes donated by U.S. military personnel stationed in Germany and German civilians. Between December and early 1994, Air Force transports from Rhein-Main AB also dropped 30 tons of mattresses, blankets, sleeping bags, candles, and beans over eastern Bosnia, helping people to cope with the winter.

The first damage to a U.S. Provide Promise aircraft occurred in early January 1994 when an exploding artillery shell at the Sarajevo airport hit a C–130. It was the sixth UN relief aircraft to suffer damage since July 1992. While there were no injuries and the damage was minor, Provide Promise flights ended for about a week. To reduce their vulnerability, C–130s landing at Sarajevo approached and departed the airport steeply, keeping their engines running during unloading to allow quicker takeoffs.

In May 1994, five C–141 Starlifters from the 315th and 437th Alft Wgs joined the Provide Promise air fleet under USEUCOM. A recently negotiated UN cease-fire allowed the larger aircraft to participate in the relief operation while the C–130s were transferred from Rhein-Main AB to Ramstein AB. Later in the year, the C–130s resumed Provide Promise missions from the new base, under operational control of the 37th Alft Sq.

Unfortunately, the C–141s did not escape damage. On July 21, a 437th Alft Wg Starlifter, flown by Capt. Craig A. Breker of the 62d Alft Wg, drew ground fire in the vicinity of Sarajevo. Although 25 bullets hit the fuselage and several more struck both wings, damaging the hydraulic and fuel systems, Breker safely returned the aircraft to Rhein-Main AB. The incident forced a temporary suspension of Provide Promise flights.

Between July 1992 and July 1994, nine Air Force planes, including C–130s and C–141s, were hit in or over Bosnia. Flying supplies into Sarajevo meant entering a war zone. Air crews, including women pilots, wore helmets and flak vests for protection against snipers. Provide Promise continued into 1995. By the end of the year, Bosnia's warring factions had signed a peace agreement that finally ended the war, at least temporarily.

48.
Name: Belarus Children.
Location: Belarus.
Date(s): August 31–early September 1992.
Emergency: A nuclear accident at the Chernobyl nuclear power plant in Ukraine in April 1986 caused medical problems among children in neighboring Belarus.
Air Force Organization(s) Involved: Unspecified.
Airlifted: 70 sick children.
Aircraft Employed: C–141 (one).
Operations: In April 1986, a disastrous fire at the Chernobyl nuclear power plant in Ukraine north of Kiev had polluted a large surrounding area, including parts of Belarus, a few miles to the north. Radiation caused cancer among the citizens of Ukraine and Belarus years after the accident. Belarus lacked the medical facilities to provide victims with modern treatment. At the end of August and the beginning of September 1992, an AMC C–141 airlifted 70 children afflicted with cancer as a result of the Chernobyl accident from Minsk, capital of Belarus, to Brussels for specialized medical treatment.

49.
Name: Lithuanian Medical Airlift.
Location: Lithuania.
Date(s): August 26–29, 1992.
Emergency: The Lithuanian ministry of health requested medical equipment and supplies for heart patients.
Air Force Organization(s) Involved: 435th and 438th Alft Wgs and 18th and 37th Alft Sqs.
Airlifted: 15 tons of medical equipment and supplies.
Aircraft Employed: C–141 (one) and C–130 (two).
Operations: When the Lithuanian ministry of health appealed for equipment for young heart patients at hospitals in the Lithuanian capital of Vilnius, an international charitable organization called Children of the World and the Deborah Heart and Lung Center of Brown Mills, New Jersey, responded generously. They donat-

ed over $2.5 million in medical equipment, including heart-lung machines, anesthesiology devices, monitors, gloves, and syringes. Assistant Secretary of Defense for Global Affairs Dr. Robert Wolthuis, who supervised humanitarian assistance operations, agreed to a military airlift of the 15 tons of cargo to Lithuania.

At the end of August, a 438th Alft Wg C–141 Starlifter with an 18th Alft Sq crew took the hospital equipment and supplies from McGuire AFB, New Jersey, to Rhein-Main AB, Germany. A pair of C–130 Hercules transport aircraft from the 435th Airlift Wing's 37th Alft Sq carried the medical cargo on to Vilnius. From there, ground vehicles delivered the equipment and supplies to the hospitals that needed it most.

50.
Name: Georgian Medical Relief.
Location: Georgia.
Date(s): October 26–28, 1992.
Emergency: Hospitals in the Georgian capital of Tbilisi lacked modern medical equipment.
Air Force Organization(s) Involved: 438th Alft Wg and 18th Alft Sq.
Airlifted: 10 tons of medical equipment and supplies and eight U.S. Army medical technicians.
Aircraft Employed: C–141 (one).
Operations: The Republic of Georgia became independent with the dissolution of the Soviet Union at the end of 1991 and quickly suffered a civil war that left thousands of people injured. After the war subsided, Lt. Col. Edward P. Phillips and a U.S. Army medical team associated with the U.S. Provide Hope relief effort for the former Soviet republics determined that hospitals in the Georgian capital of Tbilisi lacked critical medical equipment. Dr. Anthony Gray of the Office of Global Affairs of DoD authorized an airlift of the equipment and a medical team to install it.

On October 26, a 438th Alft Wg C–141 Starlifter took off from McGuire AFB, New Jersey, on the first leg of the mission, with Capt. Derek P. Green serving as aircraft commander. His 18th Alft Sq crew included pilots Capt. Leroy W. Horner and Capt. William B. Miller. Dr. Gray rode along.

The Starlifter stopped at Ramstein AB in Germany on October 27 for crew rest and to load the cargo, which consisted of 10 tons of privately donated and excess DoD medical equipment and supplies. At Ramstein, eight Army medical technicians from Heidelberg also boarded the C–141.

After a flight of about eight hours, the Starlifter landed at Tbilisi International Airport. Georgians unloaded the aircraft and transported the medical cargo to three local hospitals. After helping install the equipment, the Army medical team taught local medical personnel how to use it.

51.
Name: Armenian Flour Airlift.
Location: Armenia.
Date(s): November 1–11, 1992.
Emergency: Bread shortages in Armenia persuaded the country's leaders to appeal to the United States for flour.
Air Force Organization(s) Involved: 60th, 436th, and 439th Alft Wgs; and 22d and 337th Alft Sqs.
Airlifted: 236 tons of flour.
Aircraft Employed: C–5 (four) and C–141 (one).
Operations: When Armenia faced serious food shortages in the autumn of 1992, the government requested U.S. assistance through diplomatic channels. Responding to State Department needs, the Office of Global Affairs of the Defense Department authorized shipments of flour to Armenia, some by airlift.

At the end of October and the beginning of November, trucks transported hundreds of tons of flour from Department of Agriculture stocks at Kansas City, Missouri, to Kelly AFB, Texas. Between November 1 and 11, five Air Force cargo aircraft transported 236 tons of flour from Kelly through Dover AFB, Delaware, and Rhein-Main AB, Germany, to Yerevan, the Armenian capital. Participating organizations included the 60th, 436th, and 439th Alft Wgs; and the 22d and 337th Alft Sqs. The air fleet included four C–5s and one C–141. The airlift helped to sustain Armenians until more flour, some transported by sealift, arrived overland through Turkey.

52.
Name: Albanian Relief.
Location: Albania.
Date(s): December 1994.
Emergency: Orphanages and schools in the Albanian capital needed supplies.
Air Force Organization(s) Involved: 94th Alft Wg.
Airlifted: Four tons of clothing, furniture, schoolbooks, glass, and a refrigerator.
Aircraft Employed: C–130 (one).
Operations: When Hope for the World—a private charitable organization that ran orphanages and vocational schools in foreign countries—needed help transporting supplies to orphanages and schools in Albania, organization officials requested a humanitarian airlift under the terms of the Denton Amendment. The amendment allowed Air Force aircraft on missions to foreign countries to transport privately donated humanitarian supplies on a space-available basis at no charge to the donor or receiver.

Having received permission from DoD for an airlift, a C–130 crew from the 94th Alft Wg, an AF Res organization based at Dobbins Air Reserve Base, Georgia, flew the mission in December. They carried four tons of relief supplies to Tirana, capital of Albania. The supplies, which included beds and other furniture, clothing, books, glass to replace broken windows, and a refrigerator, arrived just before Christmas, appropriate gifts for children in need.

Chapter 4
Africa

Famines, droughts, floods, disease, and pestilence plagued Africa in the half century after World War II. During the same period, nationalism revolutionized the continent, sparking civil and international wars in a region where ethnic and political boundaries did not coincide. Africa benefited from almost 80 Air Force humanitarian airlift operations through 1994.

During the 1950s and early 1960s, Air Force missions operating from bases in Morocco and Libya concentrated on the northern African countries bordering the Mediterranean Sea. When U.S. bases in north Africa closed in the 1960s, relief operations shifted south to tropical Africa, which could be reached by long-range cargo aircraft flying from European bases.

The host of new nations that replaced European colonies suffered from a combination of natural disasters and civil strife induced by tribal rivalries. While these countries possessed an abundance of natural resources important to the United States, the new African regimes often lacked the infrastructure to handle their own emergencies. During the Cold War, U.S. humanitarian airlifts to sub-Saharan Africa encouraged the new nations to view the United States as a friend with whom a mutually beneficial economic relationship could be built.

Drought and famine drew U.S. airlifters to the Sahel region of Africa just south of the Sahara during the 1970s and 1980s. Reports of mass starvation, a long tradition of U.S. humanitarianism, and an abundance of grain from the United States stimulated large humanitarian missions to countries such as Mali, Chad, and Mauritania. In the early 1990s, U.S. humanitarian airlifts extended to Somalia and Rwanda, where political unity disintegrated in the face of ethnic violence.

None of the U.S. relief airlifts to Africa between 1947 and 1994 went to Rhodesia (Zimbabwe) or to South Africa. These countries were better equipped to cope economically with local emergencies, and natural disasters occurred less often than in the tropics or near the Sahara. It is also possible that some ruling white minority governments were reluctant to seek assistance from the U.S. government, which had officially condemned their racial policies.

Humanitarian Airlift Operations

Statistics: African Airlifts

Number of humanitarian airlifts: 79.

Most common emergencies: war and civil strife (18), famine or drought (17), floods (14), and disease (12).

Most frequent recipients: Chad (10), Zaire (8), Morocco (8), and Sudan (6).

Three largest operations, in chronological order: Authentic Assistance, 1973 (over 9,000 tons); King Grain, 1974 (over 9,000 tons); and Provide Relief, 1992–1993 (over 34,000 tons).

Chronological Listing: African Airlifts

1. Egyptian Cholera Epidemic	Sept.–Oct. 1947
2. Mediterranean Airplane Crash	July 1953
3. Casablanca Shipwreck	Apr. 1954
4. Algerian Earthquake	Sept. 1954
5. Tunisian Locust Plague	June 1957
6. Moroccan Locust Plague	Nov. 1957
7. Moroccan Flood	Dec. 1958
8. Moroccan Food Poisoning	Nov. and Dec. 1959
9. Agadir Earthquake	Mar. 1960
10. Congolese Mercy Airlift	July–Oct. 1960
11. Bakwanga Famine Relief	Jan.–Feb. 1961
12. Benghazi Flood	Feb. 1961
13. Egyptian Pestilence	Aug. 1961
14. Elizabethville Refugee Relief	Nov. 1961
15. Kenya Flood and Famine	Nov.–Dec. 1961
16. Somali Flood Relief	Nov. 1961–Jan. 1962
17. Tanganyikan Flood Relief	Apr.–June 1962
18. Congolese Food Airlift	Oct. 1962
19. Tunisian Flood	Dec. 1962
20. Moroccan Flood	Jan. 1963
21. Libyan Earthquake	Feb. 1963
22. Tunisian Bridge Collapse	Nov. 1964
23. Hospital Ship *Hope*	Dec. 1964
24. Somalian Famine Relief	Dec. 1964–Jan. 1965
25. Tunisian Flood	Jan. 1965
26. Moroccan Flood	Dec. 1965
27. Ghanaian Milk Run	Mar. 1966
28. Sudanese Cholera Threat	Apr. 1966
29. Brisk Cargo	Aug.–Sept. 1966
30. Creek Haven	June 1967
31. Ethiopian Flood	May 1968
32. Nigerian Civil War	June 1968
33. Tunisian Flood Relief	Sept.–Nov. 1969
34. Operation Chad	Oct. 1969
35. Moroccan Flooding	Jan. 1970
36. Nigerian Relief Airlift	Jan.–Feb. 1970
37. Chadian Cholera Epidemic	July 1971
38. Authentic Assistance	May–Nov. 1973
39. King Grain	June–Oct. 1974
40. Tenerife Airliner Disaster	Mar. 1977
41. Djibouti Relief	Oct. 1977

42. Zairean Refugee Relief	June 1978
43. Sudanese Flood	Aug. 1978
44. Zairean Famine	Apr. 1979
45. Liberian Riots	Apr. 1979
46. Cyclone Claudette	Jan. 1980
47. Algerian Earthquake Relief	Oct. 1980
48. Gambian Evacuation	Aug. 1981
49. Chadian Food Airlift	July 1982
50. Nigerian Fire	Feb. 1983
51. African Famine Relief	Dec. 1984–Mar. 1985
52. Mozambican Relief	Feb. 1985
53. Project Raft	May 1985
54. Sudanese Famine Relief	Aug. 1985
55. *Achille Lauro* Hostages	Oct. 1985
56. Cameroonian Lake Disaster	Aug. 1986
57. Sudanese Airlift	June 1988
58. Somalian Medical Relief	Aug. 1988
59. São Tomé Medical Airlift	Aug. 1988
60. Nigerois Medical Airlift	Nov. 1988
61. Central African Medical Airlift	Nov. 1988
62. Senegalese Locust Plague	Nov.–Dec. 1988
63. Sudanese Refugee Airlift	Dec. 1988
64. Medflag '89	Jan. 1989
65. Africa I	Apr. 1989
66. Africa II	Sept.–Oct. 1989
67. Medflag Senegal '90	Feb.–Mar. 1990
68. Liberian War Refugees	Feb. 1990
69. Sierra Leonean Airlifts	Feb. and Nov. 1991
70. Ethiopian Drought	June–Sept. 1991
71. Kenyan Food Airlift	June 1991
72. Chadian Relief	July 1991
73. Quick Lift	Sept.–Oct. 1991
74. Angolan Airlift	Oct.–Nov. 1991
75. Sierra Leonean Evacuation	May 1992
76. Provide Relief	Aug. 1992–Feb. 1993
77. Liberian Evacuation	Oct. 1992
78. Rwandan Relief	Apr.–Sept. 1994
79. Egyptian Flood	Nov. 1994

Operations: African Airlifts

1.

Name: Egyptian Cholera Epidemic.
Location: Egypt.
Date(s): September–October 1947.
Emergency: A severe cholera epidemic struck northeastern Egypt, infecting and killing thousands of people.
Air Force Organization(s) Involved: 1st Air Trpt Gp (Provisional), European Air Transport Service, and Far East Air Forces.
Airlifted: More than 28 tons of medical supplies and equipment and at least 1,600 gallons of insecticide.
Aircraft Employed: C–54 (six) and C–47 (two).
Operations: During the last week of September, a cholera epidemic broke out in Egypt north of Cairo. Carried by flies and contaminated water, the digestive tract disease caused dehydration and often death. As the number of cases and deaths climbed into the thousands, the Egyptian government appealed to the World Health Organization of the UN for medical supplies and equipment. Many countries responded.

The United States played a leading role in the international relief effort, relying largely on the newly independent Air Force to deliver emergency cargo. Between September 27 and October 3, the 1st Air Trpt Gp (Provisional) of the Atlantic Division, MATS, flew five cargo planes (probably C–54s) to airlift 26 tons of medical equipment, saline solution, cholera vaccine, blood plasma, and sulfa drugs from Westover AFB, Massachusetts, to Cairo.

Later in October, the European Air Transport Service flew two C–47 Skytrains from Frankfurt in western Germany to Farouk Field in Cairo. The Skytrains, each bearing a pair of 400-gallon insecticide tanks, sprayed the Nile delta area to kill cholera-spreading flies. Spraying and medical treatments reduced the daily death rate from 500 to 100 persons in less than a month.

The Air Force also helped to transport cholera vaccine from China to Egypt. On October 25, a Far East Air Forces C–54, carrying two tons of serum, took off from Shanghai for Cairo.

International emergency efforts helped to end the Egyptian cholera epidemic, which killed more than 4,700 people.

2.

Name: Mediterranean Airplane Crash.
Location: Gulf of Sidra.
Date(s): July 22–23, 1953.
Emergency: A British airplane with 16 people aboard ditched in the Mediterranean Sea north of Libya.
Air Force Organization(s) Involved: 58th Air Rscu Sq.

Humanitarian Airlift Operations

Airlifted: 16 people rescued.
Aircraft Employed: SA–16 (one).
Operations: On July 22, an RAF Hastings aircraft lost two engines over the Gulf of Sidra north of Libya. Radioing for help, it ditched in the Mediterranean Sea about 275 miles east of Wheelus AB, Libya. The 58th Air Rscu Sq of the 7th Air Rscu Gp at Wheelus dispatched three SA–16 amphibious airplanes to search for the British plane.

One of the SA–16s, piloted by Maj. Beverly O. Bush, located the 16 survivors on two life rafts floating on waves running 10 to 12 feet. No surface vessels were in the area. A British destroyer, HMS *Barfluer*, left Malta for the crash site, but could not arrive before dark. Since the 16 survivors were suffering from exposure, Bush landed the SA–16 on the sea and took them aboard, but weight and waves prevented him from taking off. Five hours later, the *Barfluer* arrived to pick up the crash victims. The next morning, the SA–16 took off for Wheelus. Its eight-man crew accomplished the rescue mission with no serious injuries.

3.
Name: Casablanca Shipwreck.
Location: French Morocco.
Date(s): April 3, 1954.
Emergency: A Swedish freighter ran aground and began to break up on rocks. Rough seas hindered assistance by boat.
Air Force Organization(s) Involved: 56th Air Rscu Sq.
Airlifted: 18 persons rescued.
Aircraft Employed: H–19 (one).
Operations: On April 2, the 2,720-ton Swedish cargo ship *Dalsland* ran aground on a reef about 200 yards from shore just northeast of Casablanca, French Morocco. Rough seas prevented tugboats from freeing the vessel, and it began to break up on the rocks. The ship broadcast distress signals, and the 7th Air Rescue Group's Rescue Coordination Center directed the 56th Air Rscu Sq at Sidi Slimane AB, French Morocco, to send a rescue helicopter.

On April 3, an H–19 hoisted 18 passengers and crew by sling and took them to dry land. Fifteen seamen remained aboard for salvage operations, which the helicopter facilitated by stringing a rope to connect the *Dalsland* by cable to the shore.

4.
Name: Algerian Earthquake.
Location: Algeria.
Date(s): September 11–17, 1954.
Emergency: An earthquake left more than 1,300 people dead, 5,000 injured, and 30,000 homeless.
Air Force Organization(s) Involved: 465th Trp Carr Gp and 56th, 57th, and 58th Air Rscu Sqs.

282

Airlifted: 31 tons of tents, food, medical supplies, and blankets; and 88 patients evacuated.

Aircraft Employed: C–119 (six), SA–16 (three), H–19 (three), SB–17 (one), and C–47 (one).

Operations: Before dawn on September 9, a severe earthquake struck the Orleansville area of northern Algeria, about 100 miles southwest of Algiers. The quake killed more than 1,300 people, injured 5,000, and left 30,000 homeless. In Orleansville, population 32,500, almost 95 percent of the buildings collapsed following the initial tremor and 69 aftershocks. Many neighboring communities also suffered heavy damage.

On September 10, the Seventeenth Air Force asked units of the 7th Air Rscu Gp to send aircraft to Algeria for emergency assistance. The 56th, 57th, and 58th Air Rscu Sqs, based at Sidi Slimane AB, French Morocco; Lajes AB in the Azores; and Wheelus AB near Tripoli, Libya, sent a fleet of planes and helicopters that included three SA–16s, three H–19s, one SB–17, and one C–47. They delivered 3.5 tons of relief cargo, including food, medical supplies, and blankets; evacuated 88 patients; and transported doctors and medical technicians. Although the H–19 helicopters were useful in flying medical teams to isolated villages in the destruction zone, they did not evacuate many residents because fearful villagers refused to fly aboard them.

Because France then governed Algeria, the French ministry of the interior contacted the Paris office of USAFE on September 11 to request an airlift of tents from Paris to northern Algeria to shelter some of the homeless. On September 12, the Air Force assigned the mission to the 465th Trp Carr Gp, based at Toul-Rosieres AB, France. Through September 17, the group used six C–119 Flying Boxcars to airlift 28 tons of tents and other equipment from Orly Airport at Paris to Algiers.

At least 14 Air Force airplanes and helicopters delivered more than 31 tons of tents, food, medical supplies, and blankets to Algeria between September 11 and 17. They rescued at least 88 people and ferried medical personnel to earthquake-stricken villages. The French ministry of the interior and the governor-general of Algeria thanked USAFE and the Seventeenth Air Force for the relief missions.

5.
Name: Tunisian Locust Plague (Operation Locust Insecticide I).
Location: Northwestern Africa.
Date(s): June 27–30, 1957.
Emergency: Millions of locusts consumed date and olive crops in southwestern Tunisia, threatening food shortages and economic ruin.
Air Force Organization(s) Involved: 322d Air Div and 465th Trp Carr Wg.
Airlifted: 224 tons of insecticide and spraying equipment.
Aircraft Employed: C–119 (14+) and C–124 (one).

Humanitarian Airlift Operations

Operations: During June, Tunisia suffered the worst locust infestation in its history. Desert winds swept millions of cricket-stage locusts from Algeria—where civil war prevented normal insect spraying operations—into date and olive groves southwest of Tunis, the Tunisian capital. Officials determined that without immediate spraying, the pests would reach full adult stage, when they would become more difficult to eliminate. The prime minister of Tunisia, Habib Bourguiba, asked the U.S. ambassador, G. Lewis Jones, for an airlift to haul large quantities of insecticide donated to his country by Morocco. The State Department enlisted the 322d Air Div of USAFE for the job.

Between June 27 and 30, at least 14 C–119 Flying Boxcars, most from the 465th Trp Carr Wg at Evreux-Fauville AB, France, and one C–124 from Rhein-Main AB, West Germany, airlifted 224 tons of powdered insecticide and spraying equipment from Agadir, Morocco, about 200 miles south of Casablanca, to Tunis. The transport planes staged from Nouasseur AB, about 22 miles east of Casablanca, refueling there and at Algiers, Algeria, on the 1,300-mile flights across northwestern Africa. Trucks took the powdered insecticide and spraying equipment from Al Aouina Airport in Tunis to the locust-plagued area of southwestern Tunisia near Algeria.

Operation Locust Insecticide I, as it was called, involved 27 flights by C–119s and two flights by C–124s. The airlift helped Tunisian authorities to contain the infestation and improved the image of the United States in a region where anti-Western sentiment was on the rise.

6.
Name: Moroccan Locust Plague (Operation Locust Insecticide II).
Location: Morocco.
Date(s): November 22–24, 1957.
Emergency: Millions of locusts threatened to destroy crops in Morocco, and much of the country's insecticide supplies had been depleted fighting a similar infestation in Tunisia earlier in the year.
Air Force Organization(s) Involved: 322d Air Div and 317th Trp Carr Wg.
Airlifted: 61 tons of insecticide.
Aircraft Employed: C–119 (10) and C–130 (one).
Operations: Millions of grasshoppers destroyed crops in Morocco during November. Since Morocco had donated much of its insecticide to Tunisia during a similar infestation (see Tunisian Locust Plague, June 1957), the Moroccan government requested U.S. help to move insecticide from French depots.

In response to a State Department request, USAFE employed the 322d Air Div and the 317th Trp Carr Wg at Evreux-Fauville AB, France. Between November 22 and 24, 11 Air Force cargo planes—10 C–119s and one C–130—airlifted 61 tons of insecticide, some in 55-gallon drums of liquid and some in 55-pound sacks of powder, from Marseille's Marignane Airdrome to Nouasseur AB, Morocco. The airlift helped Morocco to contain the plague before it completely destroyed the harvest.

7.
Name: Moroccan Flood.
Location: Morocco.
Date(s): December 25, 1958.
Emergency: Flash floods struck western Morocco near Marrakech.
Air Force Organization(s) Involved: 56th Air Rscu Sq.
Airlifted: 37 persons rescued.
Aircraft Employed: SH–19 (two).
Operations: Heavy rain in December flooded the Souk El Arba area of western Morocco near Marrakech. Following a Moroccan request for U.S. assistance, U.S. naval and air units stationed in the area began evacuating and feeding flood victims.

On December 25, two SH–19 helicopters from the 56th Air Rscu Sq at Sidi Slimane AB, Morocco, evacuated 37 persons from inundated areas around Tazi to higher, drier ground. The air rescues, in addition to saving lives, cultivated good will among Moroccans, many of whom regarded U.S. military bases as vestiges of French colonial domination.

8.
Name: Moroccan Food Poisoning.
Location: Morocco.
Date(s): November–December 1959.
Emergency: About 10,000 Moroccans suffered partial paralysis after consuming polluted cooking oil.
Air Force Organization(s) Involved: 10th, 14th, and 41st Trp Carr Sqs.
Airlifted: Two 100-bed portable hospitals and six tons of medical supplies.
Aircraft Employed: C–119 (one), C–124 (one), and C–130 (one).
Operations: In March, the U.S. Air Force at Nouasseur AB, Morocco, sold 40 tons of surplus motor oil to a Casablanca dealer. The dealer resold some of the oil to unscrupulous merchants who mixed it with cooking oil. Moroccans who consumed the contaminated oil suffered partial paralysis and nerve damage. First noticed at Meknes, Morocco, in September, the paralysis had crippled 10,000 people by the end of the year.

Once the cause of the mysterious outbreak was determined, the Moroccan government appealed to the Red Cross, the Red Crescent, and the World Health Organization for medical equipment and supplies, such as stretchers, wheelchairs, and crutches. Doctors determined that most victims could be rehabilitated by training healthy nerves and muscles to take over for those lost. Such therapy required treatment tables, sterilizers, and refrigerators. The air forces of the United States, Turkey, and West Germany airlifted 100 tons of medical cargo to Morocco during November and December.

The United States Air Forces in Europe's 322d Air Div shouldered the U.S. share of the airlift. Three of its planes carried Red Cross medical equipment and supplies from Europe to Morocco. A C–119 from the 10th Trp Carr Sq flew a 100-bed portable hospital from Helsinki, Finland, to Port Lyautey, Morocco, on December 9 and 10. A C–124 from the 14th Trp Carr Sq, serving rotational duty with the 322d Air Div in Europe, airlifted supplies for another 100-bed hospital from Vienna to Morocco. The 41st Trp Carr Sq flew a C–130 with six tons of medical supplies from Zurich to Casablanca.

World Health Organization, Red Cross, and Red Crescent officials, working with Moroccan medical personnel, used the airlifted medical cargo to equip rehabilitation hospitals at Meknes and Kenitra in the afflicted area.

9.
Name: Agadir Earthquake.
Location: Morocco.
Date(s): March 1–19, 1960.
Emergency: An earthquake struck Agadir, Morocco, killing more than 10,000 people and leaving thousands injured and homeless.
Air Force Organization(s) Involved: Sixteenth Air Force; 322d Air Div; 10th, 39th, 40th, 41st, and 52d Trp Carr Sqs; and 1454th Aeromed Evac Sq.
Airlifted: More than 575 tons of relief cargo and more than 900 passengers.
Aircraft Employed: C–130 (nine+), C–124 (eight), C–54 (four), C–47 (three), C–119 (five), C–118 (one), and L–20 (one).
Operations: During the night of February 29–March 1, a major earthquake struck Agadir in southwestern Morocco. Aftershocks, fires, and a tidal wave compounded the disaster, which left more than 10,000 people dead and thousands more injured and homeless. King Mohammed V of Morocco ordered survivors to evacuate the city. Many fled to a French naval air station a few miles east of the city, which quickly became a refugee camp and airlift terminal. Ben Simane AB, recently abandoned by the U.S. Air Force, also became a refugee camp.

The Moroccan government appealed for international aid. Many countries responded, including France, Spain, Italy, Switzerland, Canada, Tunisia, West Germany, and the United States. Charles W. Yost, the U.S. ambassador to Morocco, coordinated the U.S. relief effort, working with Crown Prince Moulay Hassan of Morocco. Air Force Maj. Gen. A. G. Hewitt, representing the joint USEUCOM, directed U.S. military relief operations in Morocco.

The United States Air Forces in Europe's 322d Air Div administered an Agadir airlift between March 1 and 19, transporting relief cargo and personnel from Europe and Tunisia to Morocco; airlifting supplies and workers from bases in Morocco to Agadir; and evacuating injured, sick, and homeless earthquake victims from the disaster area. Between March 2 and 4, C–130s of the 39th, 40th, and 41st Trp Carr Sqs transported 262 tons of cargo and 156 passengers from Ramstein AB, West Germany, to Agadir. Between March 2 and 6, C–124s from the 52d Trp Carr Sq, on rotation in Europe, airlifted 134 tons and 83 passengers along the same route. Most cargo and personnel belonged to Company A of the

U.S. Army's 79th Engineer Battalion, which used earthmoving and heavy construction vehicles and equipment to clear rubble and free trapped persons in Agadir. C–119s from the 10th Trp Carr Sq and four C–130s took 74 tons of medical supplies and tents from Manchester, Bovingdon, and Culdrose in the United Kingdom to Morocco. Another C–119 delivered spray disinfectant equipment from Toul, France, and Stuttgart, West Germany. Two 322d Air Div C–119s carried more than 14 tons of tents and medical supplies from Helsinki to Morocco, while one C–130 hauled medical supplies from Tunis, Tunisia. Another C–130 flight took Moroccan troops from Oujda to Agadir to serve as rescue workers.

Air Force cargo airplanes also airlifted personnel and relief cargo from Nouasseur, Ben Guerir, and Sidi Slimane ABs in Morocco to the Agadir disaster area. Several C–130s shuttled between Nouasseur and Agadir, taking in emergency supplies and workers and taking out refugees and medical patients. Seven C–130 sorties transported 69 tons of cargo and 63 passengers from Nouasseur to Agadir. Seven more sorties carried 179 persons and more than nine tons from Agadir back to Nouasseur. By March 19, USAFE had flown 39 C–130, 8 C–124, and 5 C–119 sorties, carrying 575 tons of cargo and 481 persons to and within Morocco for the Agadir emergency.

The Strategic Air Command's Sixteenth Air Force, which operated the air bases at Nouasseur, Ben Guerir, and Sidi Slimane, also participated in the relief effort, transporting supplies and workers to Agadir in 52 C–54 flights, 41 C–47 sorties, and 1 L–20 mission. Col. Arthur L. Tschepl headed a 4310th Air Div disaster control team at Agadir, which coordinated the efforts of ground and air personnel. Planes from the Sixteenth Air Force evacuated almost 500 sick, injured, and homeless people from the disaster area.

The Military Airlift Command supported the Agadir airlift, not only with C–124s on rotation with the 322d Air Div, but also with a C–118 from the 1454th Aeromed Evac Sq. The C–118 carried medical teams and cargo from Rhein-Main AB, West Germany, to Agadir. Between March 2 and 3, it transported patients from Agadir to medical facilities at Tabot and Casablanca, Morocco. Between March 1 and 14, MAC airlifted 185 tons of relief cargo for the Agadir disaster.

Air Force and Navy aircraft transported more than 1,000 tons of matériel to and within Morocco in March. Among the airlifted items were mattresses, cots, stretchers, blankets, trucks, bulldozers, tools, generators, tents, insecticide, food, water, and medicine. Moroccan officials declared that Agadir would rise again.

10.
Name: Congolese Mercy Airlift.
Location: Republic of the Congo.
Date(s): July 15–October 3, 1960.
Emergency: When civil war threatened to destroy the newly independent Republic of the Congo, the leaders of the country appealed to the UN for troops. Food shortages and the need to evacuate refugees required humanitarian airlift missions.

Humanitarian Airlift Operations

Air Force Organization(s) Involved: 322d Air Div, MATS Air Trpt Wg (Provisional) (Europe), and 1602d Air Trpt Wg.
Airlifted: 1,074 tons of food and 2,540 refugees.
Aircraft Employed: C–130 and C–124 (numbers unknown).
Operations: Almost immediately after Belgium granted independence to the Republic of the Congo at the end of June 1960, tribal warfare, provincial secession movements, mutinies among Congolese military units, power struggles among political leaders, and racial violence tore the new nation apart. Belgium sent troops in an attempt to restore order. The prime minister of the Congo, Patrice Lumumba, and the country's president, Joseph Kasavubu, feared reimposition of the colonial regime and appealed to the UN for troops to replace the Belgians. While the United States sent no ground troops, it did join other nations in providing airlift for UN forces.

Lasting from July 1960 through June 30, 1964, Operation New Tape was the largest Air Force airlift since the Berlin blockade of 1948–1949. United States Air Forces in Europe C–130 Hercules and MATS C–124 Globemaster aircraft carried 16,000 of the 20,000 UN troops airlifted, from 16 of the 23 nations that sent troops. The 322d Air Div initially directed the U.S. airlift under the command of Col. Tarleton H. Watkins. The Military Air Transport Service supported the airlift, first with a provisional air transport wing and then with the 1602d Air Trpt Wg, which operated C–124s out of Chateauroux AS, France. In October 1961, MATS took over responsibility for the Congolese operation.

Most of the New Tape flights involved moving combat troops and thus were not strictly humanitarian. Some missions, however, transported refugees and food for civilians. The first set of those missions is included in this airlift.

Initial humanitarian airlift operations in the Congo began in July 1960 after Clare Timberlake, U.S. ambassador at the Congolese capital of Leopoldville, notified the State Department about food shortages in the city. The U.S. ambassador to the UN, Henry Cabot Lodge, on behalf of the Eisenhower administration, promised food deliveries.

Between July 15 and August 10, the 322d Air Div flew 79 C–130 and C–124 sorties to airlift more than 1,000 tons of food to the Republic of the Congo. During this period, 43 C–124 and 29 C–130 sorties delivered 974 tons of food from Chateauroux and Bordeaux, France, and Rhein-Main AB, West Germany, to Leopoldville. On July 17 and 18, seven C–130 sorties airlifted 100 tons of food from Lomé, Togo, to Leopoldville.

The struggle between Congolese and Belgian troops during the crisis led to attacks on whites in the Congo and many sought evacuation. More than 2,500 refugees, including at least 300 U.S. citizens, flew out of the Congo on Air Force C–130s and C–124s between July 15 and October 3. They landed at Brussels, Belgium; U.S. air bases in France and West Germany; and four UN "safe haven" stations in Libya, Ghana, Nigeria, and Senegal. The New Tape operation continued into 1964.

11.
Name: Bakwanga Famine Relief.
Location: Republic of the Congo.
Date(s): January 26–February 9, 1961.
Emergency: Food shortages caused mass starvation.
Air Force Organization(s) Involved: 322d Air Div and 1602d Air Trpt Wg.
Airlifted: 1,000 tons of food, including dried fish, rice, maize, peanuts, and dried beans.
Aircraft Employed: C–130 (16) and C–124 (nine).
Operations: During January, the UN estimated that 200 people were dying of starvation daily in the Bakwanga area in the southern part of the Republic of the Congo. The United Nations' Food and Agriculture Organization asked several member nations in Africa and Europe to donate 1,000 tons of food, while the UN Secretariat asked the United States to airlift the food to a distribution base at Kamina in the famine region. On January 25, President Kennedy pledged support for the Congo famine victims.

The Joint Chiefs of Staff directed USAFE to perform the airlift while continuing to ferry UN troops to and within the Congo (see Congolese Mercy Airlift, July–October 1960). The 322d Air Div used 16 C–130s, while the Military Air Transport Service's 1602d Air Trpt Wg, under operational control of the 322d Air Div, used nine C–124s. Between January 26 and February 9, the 25 cargo planes transported 1,000 tons of dried fish, rice, maize, peanuts, and dried beans from Norway, Egypt, Uganda, Angola, Cameroon, Kenya, and Rhodesia, to the Republic of the Congo.

During the 15-day airlift, Air Force C–130s and C–124s transited a host of African cities and bases, including Cairo, Egypt; Entebbe, Uganda; Luanda, Angola; Garoua, Cameroon; Nairobi, Kenya; Salisbury, Rhodesia; Khartoum, Sudan; Wheelus AB, Libya; and Leopoldville, Kamina, and Luluabourg in the Congo.

12.
Name: Benghazi Flood.
Location: Libya.
Date(s): February 9, 1961.
Emergency: Storms flooded the Benghazi area of Libya, leaving hundreds of people homeless.
Air Force Organization(s) Involved: 7272d AB Wg.
Airlifted: 2.5 tons of blankets and food.
Aircraft Employed: C–54 (one).
Operations: Storms struck the Benghazi area of northeastern Libya in early February, producing floods that left hundreds of people homeless. The U.S. embassy in Tripoli offered aid. On February 9, a C–54 Skymaster from the 7272d AB Wg at Wheelus AB in Libya airlifted 2.5 tons of blankets and food from

Tripoli to Benghazi. The plane joined other aircraft to search for survivors of a Greek fishing vessel, the *Thetis*, which had foundered in the Mediterranean Sea near Benghazi. At least seven of the boat's crewmen were never found.

13.
Name: Egyptian Pestilence.
Location: United Arab Republic.
Date(s): August 12–14, 1961.
Emergency: Insects threatened to destroy the Egyptian cotton crop.
Air Force Organization(s) Involved: 1607th, 1608th, and 1611th Air Trpt Wgs; and 75th and 85th Air Trpt Sqs.
Airlifted: More than 75 tons of insecticide.
Aircraft Employed: C–124 (four), C–118 (four), and C–121 (two).
Operations: Army worms and other insects threatened to destroy Egypt's cotton crop, the country's most valuable agricultural commodity. The United Arab Republic (Egypt) ordered 1,000 tons of Sevin insecticide from Union Carbide in the United States, but commercial aircraft could not deliver it in time to save the crop. President Gamal Abdel Nasser asked the United States to help transport the insecticide.

Between August 12 and 14, 10 MATS airplanes airlifted more than 75 tons of insecticide from the United States to Egypt. Two of the C–124 Globemaster IIs came from the 1607th Air Trpt Wg at Dover AFB, Delaware; the other two came from the 75th and 85th Air Trpt Sqs at Travis AFB, California. Four C–118 Liftmasters also participated, two from the 1611th Air Trpt Wg at McGuire AFB, New Jersey, and two from naval units under MATS control. The 1608th Air Trpt Wg at Charleston AFB, South Carolina, flew two C–121s for the operation.

The 10 planes loaded the insecticide at Dover AFB and at Andrews AFB, Maryland, and flew to Cairo. On the way, they stopped at Ernest Harmon AFB, Newfoundland; Kindley AFB, Bermuda; Lajes Field in the Azores; Torrejon AB, Spain; and Wheelus AB, Libya. With the airlifted insecticide, Egypt salvaged most of the cotton crop.

14.
Name: Elizabethville Refugee Relief.
Location: Republic of the Congo.
Date(s): November 1961.
Emergency: Katanga rebels in the Congo blocked overland food deliveries to about 45,000 Baluba refugees.
Air Force Organization(s) Involved: 1602d Air Trpt Wg.
Airlifted: More than 37 tons of food.
Aircraft Employed: C–124 (two+).
Operations: In 1961, the Air Force continued to airlift UN troops and equipment to the Republic of the Congo (Operation New Tape) because of factional fighting

that threatened the country's security and independence. In September, the JCS approved additional U.S. cargo airlifts within the Congo for humanitarian purposes.

Air Force assistance was required in November when separatist leader Moise Tshombe blocked overland UN food deliveries to about 45,000 Baluba refugees in the Elizabethville area of the Congo. Two MATS C–124s from the 1602d Air Trpt Wg airlifted at least 37 tons of food from Leopoldville to Elizabethville in a three-week period beginning November 8. United Nations aircraft also airlifted food to refugees.

15.
Name: Kenyan Flood and Famine.
Location: Kenya.
Date(s): November 12–17 and December 19, 1961.
Emergency: After a long drought-produced famine, heavy rains caused extensive flooding.
Air Force Organization(s) Involved: 322d Air Div and 39th and 40th Trp Carr Sqs.
Airlifted: 31.5 tons of maize.
Aircraft Employed: C–130 (two).
Operations: After a long drought caused a famine in east Africa, the United States began shipping grain to Mombasa, Kenya. During October and November, very heavy rains caused extensive flooding in the British colony, prompting Governor Sir Patrick Renison to ask the U.S. consulate in Nairobi for an airlift of food to flood victims at Garissa and Ambaseli. The State Department contacted the Pentagon, which asked the United States Air Forces in Europe's 322d Air Div to fulfill the mission.

The 39th and 40th Trp Carr Sqs, based at Evreux-Fauville AB in France, employed C–130 Hercules aircraft—some of which were already in east Africa to track Project Mercury spacecraft—for the task. Between November 12 and 17, a 39th Trp Carr Sq C–130, flown by Capt. Ernest Howell and crew, airdropped 24 tons of maize to Garissa and Ambaseli. Flying low and following ground markers of cloth and smoke, the aircraft discharged 480 sacks of grain, each weighing 100 pounds, to a drop zone only 400 by 600 yards in size. Wood pallets prevented all but eight sacks from rupturing on impact. On December 19, Maj. Frank Sabol and crew flew a 40th Trp Carr Sq C–130 to Garissa, where it dropped 7.5 additional tons of maize to flood victims.

Secretary of State Dean Rusk thanked the 322d Air Div for its role in the disaster relief effort.

16.
Name: Somali Flood Relief.
Location: Somali Republic.
Date(s): November 18, 1961–mid-January 1962.

Humanitarian Airlift Operations

Emergency: Heavy rain flooded the Scebeli and Giuba River valleys, isolating thousands of people from food and medical supplies.
Air Force Organization(s) Involved: 322d Air Div and 40th, 41st, and 53d Trp Carr Sqs.
Airlifted: At least 259 tons of food, medical personnel and supplies, and helicopters.
Aircraft Employed: C–130 (five) and C–124 (number unknown).
Operations: During October and early November, heavy rains in east Africa flooded the Scebeli and Giuba River valleys of the Somali Republic, isolating thousands of people in need of food and medical attention. The U.S. Department of State asked the JCS for a military airlift, and, on November 16, they assigned relief responsibility to USEUCOM.

Between November 18 and mid-January 1962, the 322d Air Div flew at least 259 tons of relief cargo from Europe and Kenya to Somalia. The 40th and 41st Trp Carr Sqs, based at Evreux-Fauville AB, France, flew five C–130s, and the 53d Trp Carr Sq, a MATS unit on rotation to Europe, flew C–124s. The planes carried food, medicine, Army helicopters, and medical personnel to the Mogadishu area on the Indian Ocean coast of the Somali Republic. Relief operations demanded a heavy flight schedule. For example, Capt. Norman Thouvenelle and his crew, flying a 40th Trp Carr Sq C–130, flew 15 sorties in 25 days, most from Mombasa, Kenya, to Mogadishu.

17.
Name: Tanganyikan Flood Relief.
Location: Tanganyika.
Date(s): April 25–June 6, 1962.
Emergency: Heavy rain flooded the Rufiji River valley, cutting overland supply routes and isolating 50,000 people.
Air Force Organization(s) Involved: 63d Trp Carr Wg.
Airlifted: 1,543 tons of corn.
Aircraft Employed: C–124 (two).
Operations: During April, heavy rain flooded the Rufiji River valley of eastern Tanganyika. High water severed overland supply routes, isolating 50,000 people and threatening them with starvation. The Tanganyikan government requested U.S. aid and the State Department's Agency for International Development sponsored an airlift of food, to be delivered by MATS.

The 63d Trp Carr Wg, based at Donaldson AFB, South Carolina, flew the operation between April 25 and June 6. On April 29, one of the wing's C–124s arrived at Dar es Salaam, the Tanganyikan capital, about 100 miles north of the disaster area. Maj. Edward F. McDuffie, Jr., was mission commander at Dar es Salaam.

The plane began to airdrop corn directly to the flood victims on May 2. The crew loaded the grain in 110-pound double bags tied to improvised pallets and dropped them at low altitudes of 100 to 500 feet. Crew members discovered that dropping the corn at about 200 feet minimized the possibility of rupturing the sacks on impact. Each plane carried about 50 bags per flight.

During mid-May, the C–124 developed engine problems and was replaced by another Globemaster II, also from the 63d Trp Carr Wg. The 1602d Air Trpt Wg, involved at the same time in the ongoing UN airlift to the Congo, provided logistical and communications support. By June 2, the two 63d Trp Carr Wg C–124s had dropped 1,543 tons of corn in four drop zones near the towns of Utete, Rusende, Mtanza, and Zombe. Crews from the 9th and 14th Trp Carr Sqs flew 77 airdrop sorties, consuming 138 flying hours.

The airlift helped to feed the 50,000 flood victims until the Rufiji River receded enough to reopen overland supply routes. By June 6, the second C–124 had returned from Dar es Salaam to Donaldson AFB.

18.
Name: Congolese Food Airlift.
Location: Congo.
Date(s): October 11–12, 1962.
Emergency: Secessionist fighting contributed to a food shortage in Kasai province.
Air Force Organization(s) Involved: East Trpt AF and 1602d, 1607th, and 1608th Air Trpt Wgs.
Airlifted: 40 tons of food.
Aircraft Employed: C–124 (two).
Operations: While MATS continued to support UN operations in the Congo in 1962, Albert Kalonji, a Baluba tribal leader, led a brief secession movement in southern Kasai province. The Congolese central government quelled the revolt during early October, occupying Bakwanga, the rebel capital. The fighting contributed to a regional food shortage.

On October 11 and 12, the East Trpt AF—through the 1602d Air Trpt Wg, which had operational control of aircraft supporting the UN in the Congo—airlifted 40 tons of food from Leopoldville to Luluabourg. It employed two C–124s, one each from the 1607th and 1608th Air Trpt Wgs.

19.
Name: Tunisian Flood.
Location: Tunisia.
Date(s): December 11, 1962.
Emergency: A flood struck the Gabes area, forcing thousands of people from their homes.
Air Force Organization(s) Involved: 322d Air Div.
Airlifted: 14,000 blankets.
Aircraft Employed: C–130 (two).

Humanitarian Airlift Operations

Operations: During early December, a flood struck the Mediterranean coastal city of Gabes in eastern Tunisia, forcing thousands of people from their homes. The Tunisian government requested assistance for the flood victims through the U.S. embassy. The State Department contacted USAFE for an airlift of blankets.

On December 11, the 322d Air Div airlifted 14,000 blankets to Tunisia aboard two C–130 Hercules airplanes. One plane carried 12,000 blankets from Rhein-Main AB in West Germany, while the other transported 2,000 blankets from Chateauroux AS, France. The C–130s landed at El Aouina Airport at Tunis. Tunisian authorities unloaded the blankets and moved them overland to Gabes. Despite bad weather over West Germany and delay in securing French diplomatic clearances for the Chateauroux flight, the relief operation concluded successfully, and the Tunisian government thanked the United States for its timely aid.

20.
Name: Moroccan Flood (Clear Lens).
Location: Morocco.
Date(s): January 9–15, 1963.
Emergency: Heavy rain flooded Morocco's Rharb Valley, forcing thousands of people from their homes. Many had to be rescued from roofs and other high points by helicopter.
Air Force Organization(s) Involved: Sixteenth Air Force, 322d Air Div, 1607th Air Trpt Wg, 15th Air Trpt Sq, 52d Trp Carr Sq, 3906th and 3922d Combat Support Groups, and Atlantic Air Rscu Cen.
Airlifted: More than 370 tons of equipment and supplies, including Air Force and Army helicopters, boats, food, field kitchens, tents, blankets, clothing, and medical supplies; and medical, food service, and communications personnel.
Aircraft Employed: C–124 (eight), C–130 (seven), HH–19 (three), C–47 (two), C–54 (number unknown), C–97 (number unknown), T–33 (number unknown), and T–39 (one).
Operations: Torrential rain in December and into the first part of January flooded the Rharb Valley near Rabat in northern Morocco. High water covered nearly 500,000 acres of formerly dry land, including farms and villages, washing out roads, railroads, bridges, and dikes. Thousands of people fled their homes, and disease and starvation threatened the region.

On January 7, local authorities asked Air Force units at Sidi Slimane AB near the disaster area for help. The base commander, Col. Warren D. Johnson, organized a relief task force and contacted the U.S. embassy at Rabat. On January 9, Morocco's King Hassan II asked the U.S. ambassador, John H. Ferguson, for assistance. In cooperation with the U.S. military command in Europe, Ferguson arranged a military relief operation called Clear Lens, involving Army, Navy, and Air Force units. The operation lasted from January 9 to 15. The Air Force airlifted 370 tons of relief equipment and supplies from Europe to Morocco in one week.

Seven C–130 Hercules planes and eight C–124 Globemasters from the 322d Air Div, the 52d Trp Carr Sq, and the 15th Air Trpt Sq, on rotation in Europe from the 1607th Air Trpt Wg, delivered the bulk of the cargo. They flew from Rhein-Main AB, Spangdahlem AB, and Stuttgart Municipal Airport in West Germany, and Chateauroux AS in France to Sidi Slimane AB in Morocco. C–124s carried two Air Rscu Svc HH–19s from West Germany. Other planes carried Army helicopters, food, field kitchens, blankets, tents, boats, clothing, and medical supplies. The C–130s and C–124s also delivered food service, medical, and communications personnel for Moroccan flood victims.

Three HH–19 helicopters of the Atlantic Air Rscu Cen participated in Operation Clear Lens. Two came by C–124 from Spangdahlem AB, but one flew from Moron AB in Spain. The Air Force helicopters evacuated 249 people from rooftops and other high points in the midst of the floodwaters. Army and Navy helicopters made additional rescues.

Strategic Air Command bases at Nouasseur and Sidi Slimane also lent aircraft for disaster relief as part of the contribution of the Sixteenth Air Force. They employed two C–47s and an unknown number of C–54s, C–97s, and T–33s. Some planes helped to spot flood survivors in the inundated area, and some ferried supplies. A T–39 from Wiesbaden AB delivered typhoid vaccine for refugees.

The Clear Lens operation reinforced friendly relations between the United States and Morocco as President Kennedy prepared to discuss the closure of U.S. bases in Morocco.

21.
Name: Libyan Earthquake.
Location: Libya.
Date(s): February 21–28, 1963.
Emergency: An earthquake struck El Marj (Barce), Libya, killing at least 200 people, injuring hundreds, and leaving 10,000 homeless.
Air Force Organization(s) Involved: 322d Air Div, 317th Trp Carr Wg, 7272d AB Wg, 15th Air Trpt Sq, and 58th Air Rscu Sq.
Airlifted: 97 tons of medical equipment and supplies, blankets, clothing, food, and tents; and 205 passengers, including medical and rescue personnel and Libyan officials.
Aircraft Employed: C–130 (two), C–124 (two), C–54 (three), H–16 (two), H–21 (one), H–19 (number unknown), and C–47 (number unknown).
Operations: At sunset, February 21, the worst earthquake in modern Libyan history struck El Marj (Barce), a town of 13,000 about 50 miles northeast of Benghazi. Two more earthquakes the following morning compounded the disaster, which left more than 200 people dead, hundreds injured, and 10,000 homeless. The Libyan government requested assistance through the U.S. embassy. Operating from Wheelus AB near Tripoli, the Air Force played a major role in an international relief effort that also involved U.S. Army and British aircraft.

Humanitarian Airlift Operations

Between February 21 and 28, Air Force airplanes and helicopters flew at least 97 tons of equipment and supplies from Wheelus AB to a relief base at Benghazi, after which they were delivered by truck to El Marj. The cargo included a 36-bed Air Force mobile field hospital, blankets, clothing, food, and tents. The Air Force airlifted 205 personnel during the relief operation, moving medical and rescue personnel and Libyan officials from Wheelus to the disaster area, and evacuating injured earthquake victims by helicopter from El Marj to a hospital at Benghazi.

Among Air Force aircraft participating in the emergency were C–130s from the 317th Trp Carr Wg of the 322d Air Div, C–124s from the 15th Air Trpt Sq, on rotation to Europe under operational control of the 322d Air Div, C–54s and helicopters from the 58th Air Rscu Sq, and C–47s from the 7272d AB Wg at Wheelus. By the end of February, the crisis had abated and Air Force airlift oper-.tions concluded.

22.
Name: Tunisian Bridge Collapse.
Location: Tunisia.
Date(s): November 25–29, 1964.
Emergency: Heavy rain flooded the Miliane River valley, washing out an important railroad bridge.
Air Force Organization(s) Involved: 322d Air Div and 41st and 776th Trp Carr Sqs.
Airlifted: 177 tons of bridge parts and construction equipment and 50 U.S. Army engineers.
Aircraft Employed: C–130 (15).
Operations: During mid-November, heavy rain—falling at a rate of up to five inches in one hour—flooded the Miliane River valley in northern Tunisia. The river washed out an important railroad bridge near Khledia by which Tunisia transported phosphate and iron ore to ports on the Mediterranean Sea. Fearing economic ruin, the Tunisian government appealed for U.S. aid to restore the bridge. The Agency for International Development, working with the JCS, sponsored a relief operation.

Between November 25 and 29, USAFE airlifted 177 tons of Bailey bridge components and construction equipment as well as 50 U.S. Army engineers from the 293d Engineer Battalion, stationed at Baumholder, West Germany, to Tunisia. Fifteen C–130s from the Tactical Air Command's 41st and 776th Trp Carr Sqs, on rotation to Europe under the 322d Air Div, carried the cargo from Ramstein AB, West Germany, to Tunis International Airport. Tunisian army vehicles moved the bridge parts and engineers from the airport to the bridge site.

Within the next month, U.S. Army engineers set up a 135-foot bridge with two support pillars in place of the lost bridge. The restored railroad line permitted the resumption of export shipments vital to the country's economic health.

23.
Name: Hospital Ship *Hope*.
Location: Guinea coast, west Africa.
Date(s): December 3, 1964.
Emergency: The U.S. hospital ship *Hope* suffered a broken generator while on a medical mission to west Africa.
Air Force Organization(s) Involved: 322d Air Div.
Airlifted: One .7 ton generator.
Aircraft Employed: C–130 (one).
Operations: In late 1964, the U.S. hospital ship *Hope* was cruising the western coast of Africa to provide medical care to local populations in underdeveloped areas. Early in December, as the ship anchored off the coast of Guinea, one of its generators broke down. News of the problem reached Air Force Chief of Staff Gen. Curtis E. LeMay, who ordered the airlift of a replacement generator.

On December 3, a TAC C–130, on temporary rotation to Europe and serving the 322d Air Div, airlifted a 1,400-pound generator from Evreux-Fauville AB, France, to Conakry, Guinea. Workers transported the generator to the *Hope* so the ship could continue providing medical care to west Africans.

24.
Name: Somalian Famine Relief.
Location: Somalia.
Date(s): December 31, 1964–January 13, 1965.
Emergency: A severe drought led to crop failure that threatened 700,000 people with starvation.
Air Force Organization(s) Involved: 322d Air Div.
Airlifted: 100 tons of grain sorghum.
Aircraft Employed: C–130 (one).
Operations: A severe drought produced crop failures in Somalia in east Africa, threatening 700,000 people with starvation. The government of Somalia requested aid from the United States. The State Department contacted the Defense Department for food deliveries.

Between December 31 and January 13, an East Trpt AF C–130 airlifted 100 tons of grain sorghum from Food for Peace stocks at Khartoum, Sudan, to Mogadishu, capital of Somalia. The cargo plane, based at Charleston AFB, South Carolina, but on rotation to Europe under operational control of the 322d Air Div, flew the cargo on seven missions. The airlift provided quick relief for Somalian famine victims while they waited for more U.S. grain to be delivered by sea.

25.
Name: Tunisian Flood.
Location: Tunisia.
Date(s): January 7, 1965.

Emergency: Three days of heavy rain flooded nearly 100 square miles, leaving at least seven people dead and more than 16,000 homeless.
Air Force Organization(s) Involved: 322d Air Div and 777th Trp Carr Sq.
Airlifted: 10 tons of bedding, including blankets, comforters, and sleeping bags.
Aircraft Employed: C–130 (one).
Operations: From December 30 through January 1, heavy rain and high winds flooded almost 100 square miles near Zarzis on the coast of southeastern Tunisia. Floodwaters nearly five feet deep left at least seven persons dead and 16,000 homeless. On January 4, the Tunisian National Committee of Social Solidarity, a relief agency, requested bedding from the AID mission in Tunis. The U.S. Army attaché in Tunis notified USEUCOM, which authorized USAFE to undertake a relief airlift of bedding from U.S. military stockpiles in Europe on January 6.

On January 7, the 322d Air Div flew 10 tons of bedding from France to Tunisia aboard a C–130. The plane came from the 777th Trp Carr Sq, on rotation in Europe with the 322d Air Div at Evreux-Fauville AB, France. The plane loaded the bedding at Chateauroux AS, France, and flew to Mellita Airport on the island of Djerba on the Tunisian coast. Tunisian army trucks carried the cargo across a causeway to the mainland and on to Zarzis, about 36 miles away. Included in the airlifted bedding were 3,350 blankets, 208 comforters, and 288 sleeping bags.

26.
Name: Moroccan Flood.
Location: Morocco.
Date(s): December 30, 1965.
Emergency: Heavy rain flooded the Ksar-es-Souk area of Morocco, forcing hundreds of refugees from their homes.
Air Force Organization(s) Involved: 322d Air Div and 48th Trp Carr Sq.
Airlifted: 12.5 tons of Army tents.
Aircraft Employed: C–130 (one).
Operations: At the end of December, a winter storm system dropped unusually heavy amounts of rain on the Ksar-es-Souk area of eastern Morocco, about 225 miles southeast of the capital city of Rabat. Hundreds of refugees fled flooded homes east of the Atlas Mountains. The Moroccan government appealed for aid, and the State Department notified U.S. military forces in Europe.

On December 30, the 322d Air Div airlifted 12.5 tons of Army tents from Rhein-Main AB, West Germany, to Rabat. It employed one C–130 transport plane from the 48th Trp Carr Sq, on rotation in Europe from TAC. Moroccan vehicles transported the tents from Rabat to the disaster area, where they were used to shelter refugees.

27.
Name: Ghanaian Milk Run.
Location: Ghana.
Date(s): March 29–30, 1966.
Emergency: Drought threatened people in northern Ghana with starvation.
Air Force Organization(s) Involved: 322d Air Div.
Airlifted: 25 tons of evaporated milk.
Aircraft Employed: C–130 (two).
Operations: During February, Lt. Gen. Joseph Ankrah replaced Kwame Nkrumah as leader of Ghana, reversing the nation's drift toward the communist bloc. In early March, Ankrah's government appealed to the United States for food supplies to relieve starvation in northern provinces suffering from drought and failure of the nation's transportation system. On March 26, the JCS ordered emergency food deliveries from Army stocks in Europe to Ghana for the Department of State.

On March 29 and 30, the 322d Air Div airlifted 25 tons of evaporated milk from Rhein-Main AB, West Germany, to Accra, capital of Ghana, via Wheelus AB, Libya. Two TAC C–130s, on rotation to Evreux-Fauville AB, France, performed the mission. The AID mission in Accra accepted the milk for the famine victims of northern Ghana. Another 475 tons of U.S. milk was delivered to Ghana by ship.

28.
Name: Sudanese Cholera Threat.
Location: Sudan.
Date(s): April 5–6, 1966.
Emergency: A worldwide cholera epidemic spreading west from India threatened Sudan.
Air Force Organization(s) Involved: 322d Air Div and 347th Trp Carr Sq.
Airlifted: 16 tons of cholera vaccine and other medical supplies.
Aircraft Employed: C–130 (one).
Operations: A cholera epidemic spread west from southern Asia during the early spring. By April, it threatened Sudan in eastern Africa. The Sudanese government requested medical supplies and cholera vaccine from the U.S. embassy at Khartoum, the Sudanese capital, and the State Department notified the Pentagon. The JCS directed U.S. military forces in Europe to respond to the emergency.

On April 5 and 6, the 322d Air Div airlifted 16 tons of cholera vaccine and other medical supplies from Ramstein AB, West Germany, to Khartoum. One C–130 cargo plane and crew, on rotation at Evreux, France, from the 347th Trp Carr Sq, flew the mission. Capt. Robert E. Kindred commanded the flight, which stopped at Wheelus AB, Libya, for refueling and overnight rest en route to Sudan.

Humanitarian Airlift Operations

29.
Name: Brisk Cargo (Chadian Famine Relief).
Location: Chad.
Date(s): August 29–September 21, 1966.
Emergency: A severe drought reduced the millet harvest in Chad, producing a famine that threatened mass starvation.
Air Force Organization(s) Involved: 464th and 516th Trp Carr Wgs.
Airlifted: More than 500 tons of grain sorghum.
Aircraft Employed: C–130 (two).
Operations: Extreme drought in the north central African nation of Chad during the spring drastically reduced the summer millet harvest. By July, food shortages threatened mass starvation. The government of Chad asked Brewster H. Morris, the U.S. ambassador at Fort-Lamy, for food deliveries. In August, over 550 tons of U.S. grain sorghum, a substitute for millet, was delivered by ship to the port of Lagos, Nigeria, on its way to Chad. Railroad cars carried the grain to Maiduguri in northern Nigeria, but there the line ended. Roads to Chad were washed out by heavy summer rains after the drought.

On August 26, the JCS asked the Strike Command to provide an airlift from Maiduguri to Chad for AID. Strike Command established a joint task force at Fort-Lamy. By August 29, they had secured two TAC C–130 airplanes for Operation Brisk Cargo. One cargo plane came from the 516th Trp Carr Wg at Dyess AFB, Texas, and the other from the 464th Trp Carr Wg at Pope AFB, North Carolina. Maj. Gomer Lewis and 1st Lt. John K. Duncan served as aircraft commanders.

Between September 3 and 17, the two C–130s carried more than 10,000 sacks of the sorghum from Maiduguri to the following sites in Chad: Fort-Lamy, Abeche, Am Timan, Faya-Largeau, Ati, and Mongo. The 516th and 464th Trp Carr Wg aircraft carried more than 4,000 sacks to Fort-Lamy; from there, 1,595 sacks were delivered to Abeche, Am Timan, and Ati. The planes logged more than 108 hours of flying time during the two weeks, dropping much of the grain using the low altitude parachute extraction system. Flying into drop zones at about 120 knots at an altitude as low as 15 feet, the C–130 crews used parachutes attached to the loads to help pull palletized grain sacks out of the cargo compartments.

There was a shortage of pallets because the Chadians collected them for wood. But this problem was solved when experiments showed that the grain sacks could be dropped without pallets if placed in larger sacks to absorb the impact of their fall. Lack of radio communications in Chad posed a temporary problem for the joint task force, which was anxious to warn people to clear the area of the drops. Chadian drums, a form of traditional communications, provided a solution. The grain sorghum supplied by the U.S. provided an excellent substitute for the shortage of millet, a staple of the Chadian diet.

30.
Name: Creek Haven.
Location: Libya.
Date(s): June 6–10, 1967.
Emergency: Civil disturbances in Libya after the outbreak of the Arab-Israeli war threatened U.S. citizens in the Tripoli area, who fled to nearby Wheelus AB.
Air Force Organization(s) Involved: 322d Air Div, 438th Mil Alft Wg, 513th Trp Carr Wg, 439th Mil Alft Gp, 36th and 61st Tac Alft Sqs, and 52d Mil Alft Sq.
Airlifted: 6,982 evacuees.
Aircraft Employed: C–130 (13), C–124 (9), C–141 (4), and C–97 or C–118 (3).
Operations: When Israel went to war with Egypt, Syria, and Jordan on June 5, anti-Jewish rioting broke out in Tripoli, capital of Libya. Twenty people were killed, including three Americans. U.S. civilians, including dependents of military personnel, fled to Wheelus AB near Tripoli. The base itself was in danger because of rumors that it was being used to supply Israel.

On June 6, USAFE and the 322d Air Div organized Operation Creek Haven to airlift U.S. nationals from Libya to safer locations in Europe. Between June 6 and 10, the division airlifted 6,982 U.S. citizens, including more than 3,600 military dependents and more than 2,600 other civilians, from Wheelus AB to West Germany, Spain, Italy, the United Kingdom, and Greece. Among the destinations were Bitburg, Hahn, Ramstein, Rhein-Main, Spangdahlem, and Wiesbaden ABs in West Germany; Moron, Torrejon, and Zaragoza ABs in Spain; RAF Bentwaters and Woodbridge in the United Kingdom; Rome, Naples, and Brindisi in Italy; and Athens in Greece. Among the evacuees were 33 patients from the Wheelus AB hospital.

Units lending aircraft and crews under operational control of the 322d Air Div included the 438th Mil Alft Wg; the 513th Trp Carr Wg; the 36th and 61st Tac Alft Sqs, on rotation to the United Kingdom with the 513th Trp Carr Wg; and the 52d Mil Alft Sq, on rotation to West Germany under the 439th Mil Alft Gp. Creek Haven aircraft included 29 cargo planes from MAC, TAC, and USAFE. They flew 87 sorties in five days.

State Department and U.S. military personnel greeted the evacuees on arrival in Europe and made sure they had food, clothing, and medical or financial assistance. Another airlift followed to fly evacuees from Europe to the United States. Safe Haven lasted from June 9 to July 12 and airlifted 2,556 U.S. citizens to Kennedy International Airport in New York or to McGuire AFB in New Jersey, mostly on commercial airliners under contract to MAC.

31.
Name: Ethiopian Flood.
Location: Ethiopia.
Date(s): May 15–17, 1968.
Emergency: Heavy rain flooded the Shebele River valley around the town of

Kelafo, driving hundreds of people from their homes. Starvation and disease threatened the refugees.

Air Force Organization(s) Involved: 9th Mil Alft Sq.

Airlifted: 89 tons of food and medical supplies.

Aircraft Employed: C–141 (one).

Operations: During May, heavy rain flooded the Shebele River valley in the Ogaden province of southeastern Ethiopia, inundating the town of Kelafo and the surrounding region. After the Ethiopian government requested U.S. aid, the Military Airlift Command's Twenty-first Air Force diverted a C–141 Starlifter from a routine mission to Addis Ababa, the Ethiopian capital, for an emergency airlift.

Between May 15 and 17, Maj. Clair Oberdier of the 9th Mil Alft Sq of the 436th Mil Alft Wg and his crew airlifted 89 tons of food and medical supplies from Diredawa to Gode, Ethiopia, a distance of about 250 nautical miles. The plane shuttled the cargo on five sorties. Ethiopian C–47s transported the supplies from Gode to Kelafo because the latter town lacked sufficient runways for the C–141. A USAFE C–124 also flew to Ethiopia to assist. The C–141 missions reduced the time needed to transport relief cargo to flood victims, saving lives.

32.

Name: Nigerian Civil War.

Location: Nigeria.

Date(s): June 7–9, 1968.

Emergency: The Nigerian civil war left as many as one million people dead, mostly from starvation.

Air Force Organization(s) Involved: 9th Mil Alft Sq.

Airlifted: 34 tons of food and medical supplies.

Aircraft Employed: C–141 (one).

Operations: In May 1967, the southeastern part of Nigeria unleashed a three-year civil war by declaring itself independent as the Republic of Biafra. By June 1968, as many as one million people had died, mostly from starvation in the rebellious area. The International Committee of the Red Cross in Geneva, Switzerland, asked the United States to airlift Red Cross food and medical supplies to victims of the civil war.

Between June 7 and 9, a C–141 from the 9th Mil Alft Sq, flown by a seven-man crew led by Maj. Robert C. Kirk, airlifted 34 tons of food and medicine from West Germany to Nigeria. The 439th Aerial Port Squadron at Rhein-Main AB, West Germany, loaded the plane with more than 2,000 boxes of relief supplies. The International Committee of the Red Cross helped to supervise the loading. The plane, diverted from a routine flight to Spain, flew from Rhein-Main AB near Frankfurt via Wheelus AB, Libya, to Lagos, the capital of Nigeria.

The flight brought little relief to starving Biafrans. Nigerian federal government officials, fearing arms smuggling, refused to allow direct airlift to Biafra, and overland deliveries from Lagos were also refused for fear that federal troops would poison the food. Moreover, President Johnson refused to send relief to the Biafrans except through the officially recognized Nigerian government.

33.
Name: Tunisian Flood Relief.
Location: Tunisia.
Date(s): September 30–November 4, 1969.
Emergency: Torrential rain flooded eastern Tunisia, leaving hundreds of people dead and tens of thousands homeless.
Air Force Organization(s) Involved: 7272d Flying Training Wing, 7310th Tac Alft Wg, 47th Tac Alft Sq, and 58th Aerosp RR Sq.
Airlifted: More than 112 tons of food, medicine, clothing, blankets, tents, and clean water; and more than 2,500 persons evacuated.
Aircraft Employed: HH–3 (three), C–130 (four), and C–54 (one).
Operations: Day after day of torrential rain flooded huge sections of Tunisia's low-lying eastern regions during late September and October. As much as 14 inches of rain fell in two hours, leaving hundreds of people dead and tens of thousands homeless as floods swept away villages, roads, bridges, and railroads. Many flood victims were cut off from food supplies.

On September 30, a USAFE HC–130 carried a team of international representatives over the flooded area for an aerial survey. Shortly afterwards, the Tunisian government requested airlift support for stranded flood victims through the U.S. embassy at Tunis and the State Department.

The 47th Tac Alft Sq, on rotation to Europe under the 7310th Tac Alft Wg at Rhein-Main AB, West Germany, began a series of four C–130 missions to North Africa on October 2. The cargo planes airlifted blankets and typhoid serum to Tunis and Bizerte, Tunisia, and to nearby Tripoli, Libya, for the flood victims.

Between October 8 and November 4, the 58th Aerosp RR Sq, based at Wheelus AB, Libya, flew three HH–3E Jolly Green Giant helicopters on rescue and relief missions in Tunisia. Using Tunis, the island of Djerba in the Mediterranean Sea, and Monastir as bases of operation, the three helicopters flew to the Kairouan, Sfax, Gafsa, and Gabes areas, where they rescued more than 2,500 people and delivered 112 tons of food, medicine, clothing, blankets, clean water, and tents. Many people were evacuated from small islands of high ground surrounded by vast expanses of water. Helicopter pilots included Maj. Robert S. Michelson, Maj. Robert W. Davis, and Capt. William M. McGeorge. They conducted their operations in two phases: October 8–15, and, after more rain produced more flooding, October 25–November 4. The three helicopters flew 328 sorties up to 16 hours a day. Most missions were flown in heavy rain with low overcast.

Between October 12 and 31, the 7272d Flying Training Wing, also based at Wheelus AB, flew a C–54 on three missions to Tunisia carrying maintenance personnel and tools for the 58th Aerosp RR Sq helicopters already in Tunisia so that their search, rescue, and relief missions could continue. Two of the three helicopters required engine changes during the operation.

The Air Force was not alone in aiding flood victims in Tunisia. Helicopters from the Sixth Fleet flew mercy missions, as did aircraft from other nations. By November 4, the rains had subsided and many roads had reopened, allowing the U.S. ambassador to release military aircraft committed to the emergency.

34.
Name: Operation Chad.
Location: Chad.
Date(s): October 9–21, 1969.
Emergency: Poor harvests produced famine and heavy rain made roads impassable, blocking overland food deliveries from other areas.
Air Force Organization(s) Involved: 347th Tac Alft Sq.
Airlifted: 164 tons of food and 46 relief workers.
Aircraft Employed: C–130 (two).
Operations: During the second half of 1969, famine resulting from poor harvests struck central and north central Chad. United Nations food was sent to Fort-Lamy in southwestern Chad for overland delivery, but heavy seasonal rain made roads impassable and the government of Chad asked the U.S. embassy at Fort-Lamy for an airlift. The Agency for International Development provided financial sponsorship for Operation Chad.

On October 9, the 347th Tac Alft Sq of the 516th Tac Alft Wg at Dyess AFB, Texas, flew a pair of C–130 Hercules airplanes to Chad for the Strike Command. Between October 13 and 17, the planes airlifted a 46-man relief team and 164 tons of food—including rice, millet, sugar, vegetable oil, and butter—from Fort-Lamy to five scattered locations in the famine area. Some cargo was airdropped in places where landing was not practical. The planes returned to Dyess on October 21.

The French government, which had ruled Chad as a colony, also airlifted food from Fort-Lamy to the needy region. The airlifts helped the people of central and north central Chad to survive until roads reopened.

35.
Name: Moroccan Flooding.
Location: Morocco.
Date(s): January 20, 1970.
Emergency: Heavy rain caused flooding in northern Morocco, forcing hundreds of people from their homes.
Air Force Organization(s) Involved: 436th Mil Alft Wg.
Airlifted: 12 tons of blankets and tents.
Aircraft Employed: C–141 (one).

Operations: Heavy rains returned to northwestern Africa in January, producing the same kind of flooding that had devastated Tunisia a few months earlier (see Tunisian Flood Relief, September–November 1969). This time the rains flooded northern Morocco, and the government requested an airlift of supplies through the U.S. embassy at Rabat.

On January 20, a 436th Mil Alft Wg of the Twenty-first Air Force flew a C–141 Starlifter to airlift 12 tons of blankets and tents from stockpiles in Europe to Sale Airport at Rabat. The plane loaded more than 500 blankets at Nuremberg, West Germany, and 35 tents at Aviano, Italy, before the flight to Morocco. Moroccan ground vehicles transported relief supplies to the disaster area to shelter and comfort the flood victims until they could return to their homes.

36.
Name: Nigerian Relief Airlift.
Location: Nigeria.
Date(s): January 27–February 10, 1970.
Emergency: Civil war in Nigeria resulted in mass starvation among refugees from the rebellious Biafra region.
Air Force Organization(s) Involved: 436th, 437th, and 438th Mil Alft Wgs.
Airlifted: 436.5 tons of trucks, generators, blankets, hospital equipment, kerosene lamps, and other relief cargo.
Aircraft Employed: C–141 (six).
Operations: The Nigerian civil war, resulting from the 1967 rebellion of Biafra, was drawing to a close at the beginning of 1970. Thousands of Biafran refugees were starving because their section of the country was cut off from outside food supplies (see Nigerian Civil War, June 1968). On January 12, President Nixon offered aid to Nigeria for the refugees. The Nigerian government, having already received many food shipments from other countries, requested an airlift of other relief cargo, including hospital equipment, blankets, and trucks to transport food and refugees. They required that the cargo be carried on aircraft from which all military markings were removed. The request was relayed to the State Department through the U.S. embassy at Lagos, the Nigerian capital. The Agency for International Development provided funding, and the JCS authorized the use of six MAC C–141 Starlifter cargo planes, which were repainted for the airlift.

Between January 27 and February 10, the six airplanes airlifted more than 436 tons of relief cargo to Nigeria. All of the planes came from Twenty-first Air Force organizations, including the 436th, 437th, and 438th Mil Alft Wgs. They carried 63 trucks, 70 generators, 10,000 blankets, a 200-bed mobile hospital, kerosene lamps, and other relief cargo on 21 sorties from Charleston AFB, South Carolina, via Ramey AFB, Puerto Rico, and Ascension to Lagos. The Nigerian government used the airlifted supplies for Biafran refugees in camps in southwestern Nigeria.

37.
Name: Chadian Cholera Epidemic.
Location: Chad.
Date(s): July 7–11, 1971.
Emergency: Cholera afflicted Chad, killing hundreds of people and threatening thousands more.
Air Force Organization(s) Involved: 322d Tac Alft Wg and 347th Tac Alft Sq.
Airlifted: Unknown amounts of cholera vaccine and medical supplies and equipment.
Aircraft Employed: C–130 (one).
Operations: A worldwide cholera epidemic spread from Asia to Africa in 1970. During one week in June, more than 400 people in Chad died, and the government appealed for international assistance.

The United States Air Forces in Europe's 322d Tac Alft Wg airlifted cholera vaccine and medical equipment and supplies from Rhein-Main AB, West Germany, to Chad between July 7 and 11. Capt. Bruce C. Bechtel flew the mission in a 347th Tac Alft Sq C–130 Hercules cargo airplane. During July, the 347th Tac Alft Sq served the 322d Tac Alft Wg as Delta Squadron while on rotation to Europe from Dyess AFB, Texas.

38.
Name: Authentic Assistance.
Location: Mali, Chad, and Mauritania.
Date(s): May 15–November 10, 1973.
Emergency: Extreme drought in the Sahel area of Africa just south of the Sahara caused a famine and mass starvation in many countries, including Mali, Chad, and Mauritania.
Air Force Organization(s) Involved: 314th and 317th Tac Alft Wgs and 774th Tac Alft Sq.
Airlifted: 9,250 tons of food, seed grain, medical supplies, and vehicles.
Aircraft Employed: C–130 (nine).
Operations: A severe drought produced famine in the Sahel region of Africa just south of the Sahara in 1973. Crop failures and livestock deaths threatened mass starvation for six million people living in Mali, Chad, and Mauritania. When the governments of these countries appealed for an international airlift of food to remote areas, many nations responded. The Soviet Union, the Federal Republic of Germany, and the United Kingdom provided aircraft. Other nations, including France and the Republic of China, sent food. The United States provided food and airplanes in a six-month airlift called Authentic Assistance.

Funded by the State Department and directed by a joint task force of the Readiness Command, the operation lasted from May 15 to November 10 and used at least nine TAC C–130s. Until late September, 317th Tac Alft Wg planes conducted operations in Mali and Chad. Planes from the 314th Tac Alft Wg took over in late September, flying missions in Mali and Mauritania. The Air Force kept three C–130s at a time in the disaster region until October, when the number increased to four. The planes rotated from the United States about every 45 days.

Staging out of Bamako, Mali; Fort-Lamy, Chad; and Nouakchott, Mauritania, the cargo planes airlifted food, seed grain, medicine, and vehicles to sites at Tombouctou, Goundam, Nara, Gao, and Tassalit in Mali; Abeche, Iriba, Mongo, and Bardai in Chad; and Nema, Kiffa, and Aioun in Mauritania. Among the food items delivered were rice, wheat, flour, and powdered milk. Between May and November 1973, the C–130s carried more than 9,250 tons of relief cargo. A typical planeload was 15 metric tons, and each plane usually flew two sorties a day.

Most crew members stayed at a hotel in Bamako while in Mali, where most of the food was distributed. They typically flew three days for every off day, working up to twelve hours a day. Mission commanders included Maj. Woodie Woodworth and Lt. Col. Arthur P. Guemmer. One 317th Tac Alft Wg loadmaster, SSgt. Willie S. Antley, reenlisted in Toumbouctou.

Problems surfaced during the airlift. Temperatures in the Sahel often reached as high as 114 degrees. Heat prevented the storage of liquid oxygen, so missions were conducted at altitudes below 10,000 feet. Poor fuel, dust, and heat encouraged engine failures. Between July 14 and September 22, six engines were replaced and a few propellers were replaced. Rocky surfaces near short runways damaged airplane tires. Parts were flown in from Europe or the United States, causing delays. Maintenance problems kept the C–130s from flying simultaneously. Sometimes only one plane was flyable. The 774th Tac Alft Sq, on rotation to Europe, flew two C–130s with replacement parts from Europe to Mali. Other C–130s rotating from the United States carried maintenance personnel.

Authentic Assistance provided opportunities for international cooperation, and U.S. forces coordinated airlift flights with forces of other nations. In Mali, Malian officers rode aboard planes to interpret and to supervise loading and unloading by local residents eager to help.

On November 7, the 314th Tac Alft Wg flew its last food delivery mission in Mauritania. Redeployment commenced the next day, and the last plane returned to the continental United States on November 10. After almost six months of sorties, Authentic Assistance concluded, having delivered more than 18.5 million pounds of relief supplies and equipment to African drought victims.

39.
Name: King Grain.
Location: Mali, Mauritania, and Chad.
Date(s): June 13–October 21, 1974.
Emergency: Drought and famine continued to starve thousands of persons in the Sahel region of Africa just south of the Sahara.
Air Force Organization(s) Involved: 463d Tac Alft Wg.

Humanitarian Airlift Operations

Airlifted: 9,424 tons of grain, fuel for grain trucks, and cement for runway repairs.

Aircraft Employed: C–130 (19).

Operations: During late spring, the same drought-plagued Sahel region of Africa to which food airlift missions were flown the previous year (see Authentic Assistance, May–November 1973) required additional relief. The drought and famine, which had lasted six years, had killed as many as 10,000 persons a week. Nations such as Mali, Mauritania, and Chad appealed to the United States and the UN for an airlift of grain to outlying areas when low water in rivers prevented food distribution by boat. Overland deliveries by truck across the Sahara took up to two weeks.

Using AID funding, the Department of State sponsored a new airlift to the Sahel for the UN. The JCS approved an operation called King Grain, and the Readiness Command set up a joint task force under Col. Solomon Harp III, similar to that used for Authentic Assistance in 1973. The task force tapped C–130s from TAC for the operation.

On June 13, the 463d Tac Alft Wg from Dyess AFB, Texas, deployed three C–130s, four aircrews, and 22 maintenance personnel under Maj. Wayne L. Laflamboy to Bamako, Mali, for a grain airlift to six outlying regions. Between June 17 and August 27, the wing flew nine C–130s on 287 missions and 589 sorties to deliver 5,000 metric tons of grain from Bamako to Tombouctou, Nioro, Goundam, Tessalit, and other communities with refugee camps. In early July, the wing began rotate aircraft every 10 days between the United States and Mali. This reduced the type of maintenance problems experienced in 1973, when engines and propellers had to be replaced because of excessive heat and dust storms.

Between August 29 and October 5, five C–130s delivered 3,042 metric tons of relief supplies from Bamako to Nema and Aioun, Mauritania, in 162 missions encompassing 312 sorties. Five 463d Tac Alft Wg C–130s delivered 1,382 metric tons of relief supplies from Maiduguri, Nigeria, and N'Djamena, Chad, to Zouar, Faya Largeau, Fada, Biltine, Abeche, and Mongo in Chad between September 14 and October 21. Chadian operations included 92 missions and 255 sorties.

King Grain lasted from June 13 through October 21 and used 19 C–130s to carry 9,424 metric tons of cargo to and within Mali, Mauritania, and Chad. The cargo was mainly grain, but included fuel for trucks and cement for runway repairs. King Grain involved 541 missions and 1,156 sorties.

40.

Name: Tenerife Airliner Disaster.

Location: Canary Islands.

Date(s): March 27–30, 1977.

Emergency: Two Boeing 747 jumbo jets collided in fog on Tenerife in the Canary Islands, killing at least 580 people and leaving many survivors in need of medical evacuation.

Air Force Organization(s) Involved: 32d Tac Alft Sq and 437th Mil Alft Wg.
Airlifted: 56 patients.
Aircraft Employed: C–141 (one) and C–130 (one).
Operations: On March 27, two Boeing 747 airliners, one belonging to the Dutch KLM Airlines and the other to Pan American, collided in thick fog at Los Rodeos Airport in Santa Cruz de Tenerife in the Canary Islands. Of 643 passengers, at least 580 eventually died from the crash, including all 249 aboard the Dutch plane. The world's worst civil aviation disaster, the accident left many seriously injured survivors, who suffered burns, broken bones, cuts, and bruises.

Aware of the need for immediate emergency medical evacuation, the State Department arranged with the Defense Department for an airlift. On March 27, a 32d Tac Alft Sq C–130 from the 314th Tac Alft Wg, on rotational duty in Europe, flew from Rhein-Main AB in West Germany to the Canary Islands via Rota NAS in Spain. The plane carried medical personnel to Las Palmas. The next day, the C–130 flew to Tenerife, where it picked up 56 crash survivors, including 39 litter and 17 ambulatory patients. It ferried them back to Las Palmas, where a 437th Mil Alft Wg C–141 Starlifter was waiting. Medical personnel transferred the patients from the C–130 to the C–141 during a storm. The Starlifter carried survivors to the United States for medical treatment, unloading them at McGuire AFB, New Jersey; Kelly AFB, Texas; and El Toro NAS and Travis AFB, California. One crash victim died on the transatlantic flight.

Accompanying the injured on the C–130 and C–141 flights were medical personnel from the 2d, 69th, and 72d Aeromed Evac Sqs. Reconfiguration of the C–141 for the patients was not completed in time for its flight to the United States, so medical teams improvised with available equipment and supplies. Pan American airlines transported 326 of the dead Americans on commercial airplanes from the Canary Islands to Dover AFB, Delaware, where the corpses were received in the Air Force mortuary.

41.
Name: Djibouti Relief.
Location: Djibouti.
Date(s): October 14, 1977.
Emergency: Refugees from ethnic fighting in Ethiopia and Djibouti poured into the city of Djibouti, creating a shortage of shelter.
Air Force Organization(s) Involved: 315th and 437th Mil Alft Wgs.
Airlifted: 170 tents and electrical generators.
Aircraft Employed: C–141 (one).
Operations: In 1977, Ethiopia and Somalia quarreled over their borders in eastern Africa. Ethnic Ethiopians (Afars) and Somalis (Issas) fought in eastern Ethiopia and in the small neighboring nation of Djibouti, which became independent from France that year. Refugees poured into Djibouti's major port and capital city, also called Djibouti. The country appealed for U.S. assistance to help shelter evacuees.

Humanitarian Airlift Operations

On October 14, a 437th Mil Alft Wg C–141 Starlifter cargo plane, flown by a 315th Mil Alft Wg (AF Res) crew, transported tents and electrical generators from Ramstein AB, West Germany, to Djibouti. Twenty large and 150 small tents comprised most of the relief cargo, drawn from DoD stocks in Europe.

42.
Name: Zairean Refugee Relief.
Location: Zaire.
Date(s): June 1978.
Emergency: Fighting in Zaire deprived civilians in Shaba province of adequate food and medicine.
Air Force Organization(s) Involved: 438th Mil Alft Wg.
Airlifted: 51 tons of food and medical supplies.
Aircraft Employed: C–141 (two).
Operations: During May, Katangan rebels from sanctuaries in Angola invaded Shaba province (Katanga) in southern Zaire and captured the towns of Kolwezi and Mutshatsa in an important copper and cobalt mining area. The fighting killed more than 260 people and trapped 3,000 engineers and miners, including Europeans and Americans. Zaire appealed for foreign military help to repel the insurgents, and France and Belgium, with logistical support from MAC, sent troops. Belgian and Zairean civil aircraft evacuated refugees. Between May 31 and June 16, MAC redeployed Belgian and French troops to Europe, replacing them with pan-African peacekeeping forces.

While most Air Force flights were not strictly humanitarian, because they involved moving armed troops, the Twenty-first Air Force did perform a mercy airlift related to the emergency. The U.S. ambassador, Walter L. Cutler, declared a disaster in southern Zaire and sought humanitarian assistance for civilians who fled the Kolwezi and Mutshatsa area. On the verge of economic collapse, Zaire could not adequately feed the refugees or provide them with medical care. The Agency for International Development sponsored a relief operation. During June, two 438th Mil Alft Wg C–141 airplanes transported 51 tons of International Red Cross food and medical supplies from Geneva, Switzerland, to Lubumbashi and Kinshasa, Zaire. The planes stopped in the African countries of Senegal and Gabon on the way.

43.
Name: Sudanese Flood.
Location: Sudan.
Date(s): August 2–16, 1978.
Emergency: Heavy rain flooded the upper Nile valley, forcing hundreds of Sudanese from their homes.
Air Force Organization(s) Involved: 60th and 438th Mil Alft Wgs.
Airlifted: 31.5 tons of relief supplies, including 560 tents and refueling equipment for relief helicopters.

Aircraft Employed: C–141 (two).

Operations: Heavy summer rain produced extensive flooding of the upper Nile River valley in Sudan. The government appealed for international assistance, and several countries responded. The Federal Republic of Germany agreed to provide helicopters to deliver food and other relief supplies from Khartoum, the Sudanese capital, to the flooded areas, but the helicopters lacked adequate refueling equipment.

The State Department asked the Air Force to airlift refueling equipment from West Germany to Sudan for the helicopters. On August 2, the Pentagon diverted a 438th Mil Alft Wg C–141 from a cargo mission to Europe. Piloted by Col. Allen G. Myers III, the vice wing commander, the plane carried 5.5 tons of forward area aircraft refueling equipment, including 16 fuel bladders, and six Army technicians, from Rhein-Main AB, West Germany, to Khartoum. Sudanese army personnel helped to unload the airplane. The airlift allowed the German helicopters to distribute more relief supplies to the flood victims.

Later in August, the State Department requested a second airlift to flood-stricken Sudan. A 60th Mil Alft Wg C–141, diverted from a mission to the Pacific, loaded 26 tons of relief supplies, including 560 tents, from the AID stockpile at the Naval Supply Depot in Guam. Between August 14 and 16, the Starlifter carried the relief cargo 10,000 miles to Sudan, stopping at the Indian Ocean island of Diego Garcia on the way. After unloading at Khartoum, the plane took on refueling equipment delivered to Sudan by another C–141 on August 2 and returned it to West Germany. By then, the German helicopters that used the equipment had completed their rescue and relief missions in Sudan.

44.
Name: Zairean Famine.
Location: Zaire.
Date(s): April 9–12, 1979.
Emergency: Drought followed by flood threatened thousands of people in Zaire with malnutrition and starvation.
Air Force Organization(s) Involved: 53d Mil Alft Sq.
Airlifted: 20 tons of vegetable seeds.
Aircraft Employed: C–141 (one).
Operations: During late 1978 and into early 1979, famine struck Zaire in central Africa. Drought produced crop failures, and heavy rains later washed away newly planted seeds. Up to 500,000 people in western Zaire faced malnutrition and starvation and between 25 and 100 children died per week. On January 20, the U.S. ambassador, Walter L. Cutler, declared the situation a disaster.

After Zaire requested U.S. relief, AID and the Office of Foreign Disaster Assistance purchased tons of fast-growing vegetable seeds—including spinach, kale, okra, turnip, lettuce, cabbage, tomato, onion, and collard—for delivery to Zaire. The seeds were developed to grow in poor soil conditions. The Department of State requested a DoD airlift when commercial airlift was not available. On April 3, the JCS notified MAC of the requirement.

The 63d Mil Alft Wg at Norton AFB, California, received the assignment. On April 9, Capt. Mike Moore and his crew flew a 53d Mil Alft Sq C–141 Starlifter from Norton to Yuma Marine Corps Air Station, Arizona, where the seeds awaited delivery.

Between April 10 and 12, the C–141 airlifted nine pallets of the seeds, weighing 20 tons, from Arizona to Zaire. The plane tarried at Charleston AFB, South Carolina, after one of its wings overheated, but proceeded to Africa via Roosevelt Roads NAS, Puerto Rico, and Ascension in the Atlantic Ocean. On April 12, the Starlifter landed at Kinshasa, Zaire, where its cargo was unloaded for planting.

45.
Name: Liberian Riots.
Location: Liberia.
Date(s): April 18, 1979.
Emergency: Rioting erupted in Monrovia after the government proposed an increase in the price of rice. Clashes between citizens and government forces left 28 people dead and hundreds injured.
Air Force Organization(s) Involved: 30th Mil Alft Sq.
Airlifted: Four tons of medical supplies, including bandages, plasma, medicine, sheets, and blankets.
Aircraft Employed: C–141 (one).
Operations: When the Liberian ministry of agriculture proposed a 50 percent increase in the price of rice in April, riots erupted in Monrovia, the nation's capital. Government forces clashed with demonstrators and looters, and the violence left 28 people dead and more than 300 injured. The largest hospital in the city admitted 303 riot casualties, 40 of whom needed major surgery.

The State Department asked DoD for an airlift of emergency medical supplies from the United States to Liberia, with funding from AID and the Office of Foreign Disaster Assistance. On April 15, the JCS directed MAC to perform the operation.

On April 18, a 30th Mil Alft Sq C–141 Starlifter from the 438th Mil Alft Wg at McGuire AFB, New Jersey, airlifted four tons of medical supplies—including bandages, medicine, plasma, blankets, and sheets—to Monrovia. Capt. Paul G. Tucker and his crew flew the Starlifter to Roberts International Airport in the Liberian capital, stopping at Ascension in the Atlantic Ocean for fuel and crew rest on the way. Liberian medical personnel used the airlifted emergency supplies to save those most seriously injured in the civil disturbances.

46.
Name: Cyclone Claudette.
Location: Mauritius.
Date(s): January 10–11, 1980.

Emergency: Cyclone Claudette struck the island of Mauritius, leaving thousands of people homeless.
Air Force Organization(s) Involved: 86th Mil Alft Sq.
Airlifted: 17 tons of emergency supplies, including 300 tents and tent flies.
Aircraft Employed: C–141 (one).
Operations: Cyclone Claudette struck the Indian Ocean island of Mauritius about 500 miles east of Madagascar at the end of December 1979. The storm destroyed or damaged about 7,000 homes, leaving thousands of people homeless and forcing 5,000 to seek shelter in public buildings. At the end of the first week in January 1980, Thomas J. Burke, chargé d'affaires at the U.S. embassy at Port Louis, cabled Washington, D.C., for 300 tents to shelter homeless storm victims. The request was referred to the Military Airlift Command's Twenty-second Air Force, which assigned the mission to a 60th Mil Alft Wg C–141 flying a routine channel mission between Clark AB in the Philippines and the Indian Ocean island of Diego Garcia.

On January 10 and 11, Capt. Michael Mestemaker and his crew from the 86th Mil Alft Sq flew 17 tons of emergency supplies, including 300 tents and tent flies, from Tengah AB in Singapore to Port Louis in Mauritius. When the C–141 landed, it was greeted by Chargé d'Affaires Burke and Sir Harold Watler, the minister of foreign affairs of Mauritius. The mission was accomplished within three days of Burke's cable to Washington.

47.
Name: Algerian Earthquake Relief.
Location: Algeria.
Date(s): October 12–23, 1980.
Emergency: An earthquake measuring 7.2 on the Richter scale left 6,000 people dead and at least 100,000 homeless.
Air Force Organization(s) Involved: 322d Alft Div; 436th, 437th, and 438th Mil Alft Wgs; and 435th Tac Alft Wg.
Airlifted: More than 400 tons of blankets, tents, cots, tent stoves, and water containers; and 87 passengers.
Aircraft Employed: C–141 (14), C–5 (1), and C–130 (1).
Operations: A major earthquake, registering 7.2 on the Richter scale, struck the El Asnam area of northern Algeria, about 120 miles southwest of Algiers, on October 10. The quake left 6,000 people dead and more than 100,000 homeless. It cut roads, railroads, water and gas pipelines, and electric lines.

After the Algerian government requested U.S. disaster assistance, the State Department asked the JCS to transport supplies from AID stockpiles in Italy and Panama to Algiers. The Pentagon assigned the operation to USEUCOM, and MAC provided airlift support.

Between October 12 and 23, the Air Force airlifted over 400 tons of disaster relief supplies to Algiers from Camp Darby near Pisa, Italy, and from Howard AFB, Panama. The cargo included more than 4,700 large tents, 2,900 cots, 42,000 blankets, 1,000 tent stoves, and 1,900 water containers. In the same two weeks, MAC transported 87 passengers to Algeria, including medical personnel, a disaster survey team, and an airlift control element.

Fourteen C–141s, one C–5, and one C–130 performed the operation. Planes and crews came from the 436th, 437th, and 438th Mil Alft Wgs and the 435th Tac Alft Wg. The cargo aircraft originated from Dover, McGuire, and Charleston AFBs in the United States and Rhein-Main AB in West Germany. The 322d Alft Div coordinated the flights for USEUCOM. The planes had to unload their cargo at Algiers because airports in the El Asnam area lacked sufficiently large and strong runways. Algerian ground vehicles carried airlifted supplies to the disaster area.

Despite communications problems, an insufficient number of pallets, and long working hours, the Algerian relief airlift was successful. It saved lives and encouraged the Algerian government to help the United States to negotiate the release of U.S. hostages from Iran.

48.
Name: Gambian Evacuation.
Location: Gambia.
Date(s): August 8, 1981.
Emergency: A rebellion and food shortages in Gambia threatened foreign nationals there.
Air Force Organization(s) Involved: 322d Alft Div and 437th Mil Alft Wg.
Airlifted: 95 U.S. and other foreign nationals.
Aircraft Employed: C–141 (one).
Operations: At the end of July, while President Dawda Kairaba Jawara of Gambia attended the royal wedding of Prince Charles and Lady Diana in London, leftist guerrillas led a rebellion in Gambia. The Gambian government, with military assistance from neighboring Senegal, quelled the rebellion, but continued political instability and food shortages convinced Secretary of State Alexander Haig to reduce the number of U.S. citizens in Gambia. On August 7, he asked DoD to arrange an evacuation airlift.

On August 8, Capt. Robert Zeiner of the 20th Mil Alft Sq flew 95 civilians, including 82 U.S. nationals, from Banjul, Gambia, to Dakar, Senegal, on the west African coast. He used a 437th Mil Alft Wg C–141 in the service of the 322d Alft Div. The flight took about 25 minutes. Australian, Swiss, Sri Lankan, British, Swedish, and Costa Rican citizens joined U.S. evacuees on the airlift.

49.
Name: Chadian Food Airlift.
Location: Chad.
Date(s): July 6–14, 1982.
Emergency: Food shortages brought hunger and starvation to thousands of people in northern and eastern Chad.

Air Force Organization(s) Involved: 37th Tac Alft Sq.
Airlifted: 117.5 tons of sorghum grain and vegetable oil.
Aircraft Employed: C–130 (one).
Operations: A long civil war and a drought produced food shortages in northern and eastern Chad. Chad's new president, Hissene Habre, asked the United States to airlift food from his capital at N'Djamena to the famine areas. On July 2, Secretary of State George P. Schultz asked DoD to organize an airlift for the State Department and AID. The Pentagon used the 322d Alft Div for the operation.

On July 6, a 37th Tac Alft Sq C–130 Hercules cargo airplane from the 435th Tac Alft Wg flew from Rhein-Main AB, West Germany, to Kano in northern Nigeria to set up an operation base for the airlift. The plane carried an airlift control element and two aircrews for rotational duty. Between July 7 and 13, Maj. Charles H. Carter and Capt. Geoffrey W. Jumper alternated to airlift 117.5 tons of food from N'Djamena to Abeche in eastern Chad and Faya Largeau in northern Chad. In seven days, the C–130 delivered 1,570 sacks of sorghum grain in 100-pound sacks and 1,346 boxes containing gallon jugs of vegetable oil.

During seven days of food deliveries, the airlift overcame several obstacles. The plane had to be manually loaded and unloaded in heat as high as 110 degrees. Airports at Abeche and Faya Largeau had only dirt runways, and at one point refugees stormed aboard the plane for evacuation. Radio communications between Kano, N'Djamena, Abeche, and Faya Largeau were almost nonexistent. Poor local food and water supplies forced crews to carry their own rations, and accommodations at Kano were primitive. Despite these difficulties, the C–130 crews fulfilled their mission and returned to Rhein-Main AB on July 14.

50.
Name: Nigerian Fire.
Location: Nigeria.
Date(s): February 1983.
Emergency: A fire destroyed an important telecommunications facility in Lagos, capital of Nigeria, crippling the nation's communications network.
Air Force Organization(s) Involved: Twenty-first Air Force.
Airlifted: 15 tons of communications equipment.
Aircraft Employed: C–141 (one).
Operations: On January 25, a fire destroyed an important telecommunications building in Lagos, capital of Nigeria, threatening that nation's ability to communicate. The State Department, having learned that the Nigerian government needed assistance, contacted the Pentagon for an airlift of telecommunications equipment from the United States to Nigeria.

In early February, the Military Airlift Command's Twenty-first Air Force flew a C–141 laden with 15 tons of communications equipment, including a mobile telex switching system, from Andrews AFB, Maryland, to Lagos. There the Nigerian government used the equipment to restore its crippled communications network.

Humanitarian Airlift Operations

51.

Name: African Famine Relief.

Location: Sudan, Niger, and Mali.

Date(s): December 22, 1984–March 9, 1985.

Emergency: More than 100,000 Ethiopians, fleeing famine, poured into refugee camps in eastern Sudan. Famine also afflicted Niger and Mali in the Sahel region of Africa just south of the Sahara.

Air Force Organization(s) Involved: 437th and 438th Mil Alft Wgs; 514th Mil Alft Wg (Associate); and 6th, 18th, 30th, and 702d Mil Alft Sqs.

Airlifted: More than 212 tons of food, tents, water tanks, blankets, medical supplies, and other relief cargo.

Aircraft Employed: C–141 (eight).

Operations: A prolonged drought killed crops and livestock in the Sahel region of Africa just south of the Sahara during the early 1980s, producing a famine that affected millions of people. By late December 1984, starvation had killed one million in Ethiopia alone. More than 100,000 Ethiopians fled to eastern Sudan, crowding refugee camps around Kassala. United Nations disaster relief officials in Sudan appealed to the United States and other western nations to airlift food and medical supplies to famine victims, some of whom were suffering from diseases related to malnutrition. The State Department and its Agency for International Development asked MAC to airlift relief supplies to Sudan because commercial airlift was inadequate to meet the emergency.

During December, the 6th Mil Alft Sq of the 438th Mil Alft Wg flew two C–141 missions to Sudan. On December 22, Maj. John F. Bauer and his crew flew the first mission, airlifting eight 3,000-gallon water tanks, 3,200 blankets, and six medical tents from Sigonella NAS in Sicily to Kassala. On December 29, the 6th Mil Alft Sq flew a second C–141 mission to Kassala, transporting 22 tons of dried skim milk, five tons of vegetable oil, and a large hospital tent from Rhein-Main AB, West Germany.

In January, President Reagan announced an African hunger relief initiative, promising more aid for famine victims south of the Sahara. Air National Guard units flew relief supplies, many privately donated, to McGuire AFB in New Jersey, to be picked up by MAC C–141s for transport to Africa.

During January, the 438th Mil Alft Wg flew 62 tons of disaster relief supplies from McGuire AFB to Sudan. On January 18 and 19, a 30th Mil Alft Sq C–141 carried nine pallets of medical supplies and a small airplane to Khartoum, capital of Sudan, and another C–141 from the 18th Mil Alft Sq transported medical supplies, corn soya milk, and blankets to Kassala.

The Military Airlift Command flew four additional C–141 relief missions to African famine victims in March. The flights were timed to coincide with visits by Vice President George Bush to Sudan, Niger, and Mali. Between March 3 and 5, a 437th Mil Alft Wg C–141 airlifted medicines and powdered milk from McGuire AFB to Kassala. Between March 4 and 6, a C–141 from the 6th Mil Alft

Sq of the 438th Mil Alft Wg transported medicines and powdered milk from McGuire to Khartoum. At the same time, another C–141 from the 437th Mil Alft Wg carried blankets and canned beans from McGuire to Niamey, capital of Niger. The last C–141, flown by an AF Res crew from the 702d Mil Alft Sq of the 514th Mil Alft Wg (Associate), transported 25 tons of medicine and canned beans from McGuire to Bamako, capital of Mali. The four March famine relief missions delivered 123 tons. Vice President Bush observed three of the deliveries.

Between December 22 and March 9, eight MAC C–141 flights airlifted more than 212 tons of food, tents, blankets, medicine, and other disaster relief supplies from the United States and Europe to Sudan, Niger, and Mali. The airlift supplemented commercial and foreign transport operations aimed at reducing African famine casualties.

52.
Name: Mozambican Relief.
Location: Mozambique.
Date(s): February 1985.
Emergency: While drought caused famine in Mozambique, an insurgency cut supply lines from South Africa. Refugees gathered in camps for relief.
Air Force Organization(s) Involved: Twenty-first Air Force.
Airlifted: 44 tons of blankets.
Aircraft Employed: C–141 (one).
Operations: During the mid-1980s, drought and famine forced many Mozambicans into refugee camps. Despite the presence of a nominally Marxist government in Mozambique, the United States shipped relief cargo. In late January 1985, rebels blew up a bridge in southern Mozambique, severing a railroad by which relief supplies were transported from South Africa to the capital at Maputo.

Responding to a request from Mozambique for additional aid, the State Department arranged for an airlift of blankets. With funding from AID and the Office of Foreign Disaster Assistance, the Military Airlift Command's Twenty-first Air Force organized a special mission. Early in February, a C–141 flew 22 pallets of blankets, weighing 44 tons, from McGuire AFB, New Jersey, to Maputo. The airlifted blankets helped to comfort thousands of refugees in Mozambique who had fled their homes because of famine and insurrection.

53.
Name: Project Raft.
Location: Mali.
Date(s): May 1985.
Emergency: The absence of a ferry to cross the Niger River at Gao prevented truck deliveries of food to famine victims in Mali.
Air Force Organization(s) Involved: Twenty-first Air Force, 322d Alft Div, 435th Tac Alft Wg, and 37th Tac Alft Sq.

Humanitarian Airlift Operations

Airlifted: One M4T6 pontoon bridge and a 15-man detachment from the 565th Engineering Battalion of the U.S. Army Corps of Engineers.
Aircraft Employed: C–141 (three) and C–130 (two).
Operations: After Vice President Bush visited drought-stricken Mali with food supplies in March, famine continued to afflict the country. In May, a ferry used to carry food to Gao on the Niger River required maintenance and was out of operation for several months. The Malian government requested assistance from the United States, and the State Department, working with its Office of Foreign Disaster Assistance, asked USEUCOM to send Army engineers and pontoon bridge components to help construct a raft ferry.

The U.S. European Command organized Project Raft, a five-month operation to transport food across the Niger River to famine victims in eastern Mali. The Military Airlift Command provided airlift, with the 322d Alft Div managing the operation.

In late May, three Twenty-first Air Force C–141s transported pontoon bridge parts and a 15-man detachment from the 565th Engineering Battalion of the U.S. Army Corps of Engineers from Rhein-Main AB, West Germany, to Bamako, capital of Mali. Some bridge parts weighed more than 7.5 tons each. Two 37th Tac Alft Sq C–130s from the 435th Tac Alft Wg shuttled the freight on nine flights from Bamako to Gao. The engineers constructed an M4T6 pontoon bridge with five floats and used it for the next five months to ferry food trucks across the Niger River at Gao.

In November, MAC conducted a reverse airlift to return engineers and bridge components to West Germany. The Pentagon awarded the Humanitarian Service Medal to Army and Air Force personnel participating in Project Raft.

54.
Name: Sudanese Famine Relief.
Location: Sudan.
Date(s): August 12–15, 1985.
Emergency: Heavy rains flooded roads and railroads leading to the famine-stricken western Sudan, cutting off food deliveries to two million persons.
Air Force Organization(s) Involved: 436th Mil Alft Wg.
Airlifted: 35 tons of equipment, including three helicopters, and 22 support personnel.
Aircraft Employed: C–5 (one).
Operations: Heavy summer rains ended a long drought that had produced a famine in Sudan. Starvation and malnutrition threatened two million people in the western part of the country. Floods blocked roads and railroads by which food had been delivered to the famine victims. After the Sudanese government requested U.S. assistance, the State Department asked the Pentagon to airlift helicopters to Sudan so that food distribution could resume. To avoid time-consuming disassembly and reassembly of the helicopters, the State Department asked MAC to

use a C–5, the largest cargo airplane in the free world. The Agency for International Development and the Office of Foreign Disaster Assistance funded the operation.

Between August 12 and 15, the 436th Mil Alft Wg at Dover AFB, Delaware, flew the mission. Using a single C–5, the wing moved 35 tons of cargo, including three Boeing Vertol 107 helicopters owned by Columbia Helicopters, Incorporated, from Portland, Oregon, to Wadi Seidna, Sudan. Airlifted with the freight were 22 support personnel.

Disaster relief officials used the three airlifted helicopters to distribute grain to famine victims in the El Geneina area of western Sudan near the Chad border. In December, a reverse airlift returned the helicopters, support personnel, and equipment to the United States.

55.

Name: *Achille Lauro* Hostages.
Location: Egypt.
Date(s): October 11–12, 1985.
Emergency: Palestinian terrorists hijacked the Italian cruise ship *Achille Lauro* in the Mediterranean Sea north of Egypt and seized 12 U.S. citizens as hostages.
Air Force Organization(s) Involved: 438th Mil Alft Wg.
Airlifted: 11 former hostages.
Aircraft Employed: C–141 (one).
Operations: Palestinian terrorists hijacked the Italian cruise ship *Achille Lauro* in the Mediterranean Sea north of Egypt on October 7. Of the 400 passengers, 12 U.S. nationals were taken hostage. The terrorists killed one hostage, but kept 11 until October 9, when the Palestinians surrendered to Egyptian authorities.

On October 11 and 12, a 438th Mil Alft Wg C–141 airlifted the 11 former hostages from Cairo to Newark, New Jersey, with stops at Sigonella NAS, Italy, and Rhein-Main AB, West Germany. U.S. fighter planes later intercepted an aircraft carrying the terrorists so that they could be brought to trial.

56.

Name: Cameroonian Lake Disaster.
Location: Cameroon.
Date(s): August 27–29, 1986.
Emergency: A gas cloud from Lake Nyos suffocated 1,700 villagers and drove at least 2,000 others from their homes.
Air Force Organization(s) Involved: 50th Tac Alft Sq.
Airlifted: 250 tents.
Aircraft Employed: C–130 (one).
Operations: On August 21, a carbon dioxide cloud bubbled up from the depths of Lake Nyos in a volcanic region of northwestern Cameroon and drifted over the local villages of Lower Nyos, Cha, Subum, and Fang. The gas displaced lighter

air, suffocating 1,700 persons before it dispersed. At least 2,000 people fled their homes, seeking refuge at Wum, Nkambe, and other villages more distant from the lake. Cameroon's president, Paul Biya, requested international assistance.

The State Department's Agency for International Development and Office of Foreign Disaster Assistance asked DoD to airlift tents to Cameroon from a stockpile at Camp Darby near Leghorn, Italy. On August 27, a C–130 Hercules airplane and crew from the 50th Tac Alft Sq of the 314th Tac Alft Wg, on rotation to the United Kingdom, flew from RAF Mildenhall to Leghorn, where it loaded 250 large tents for the refugees. Stopping overnight in Egypt, the C–130 arrived at Douala, Cameroon, on August 29. Lt. Col. Edward Konigsberg, an Air Force Medical Service physician heading a team of U.S. pathologists investigating the disaster, met the plane when it landed. Refugees used the 250 airlifted tents for shelter until scientists could determine when it was safe for them to return to their homes.

57.
Name: Sudanese Airlift.
Location: Sudan.
Date(s): June and August 1988.
Emergency: Civil strife in southern Sudan drove hundreds of thousands of people to refugee camps.
Air Force Organization(s) Involved: 60th and 436th Mil Alft Wgs.
Airlifted: More than 70 tons of plastic sheeting.
Aircraft Employed: C–141 (two) and C–5 (one).
Operations: Continuing civil war between rebels and government troops in southern Sudan drove hundreds of thousands of people to refugee camps in search of food. Unable to shelter all of the refugees, Sudanese officials requested U.S. aid.

On June 2, two C–141s from the 60th Mil Alft Wg at Travis AFB, California, took off on a humanitarian airlift mission to Sudan. They stopped at McGuire AFB, New Jersey, where they loaded 10 pallets of plastic sheeting for shelters. From there, they flew via the United Kingdom, Italy, and Egypt to Khartoum, capital of Sudan, to unload the cargo. Ground vehicles transported the plastic sheeting to the refugee camps.

In August, seasonal flooding worsened refugee conditions in Sudan, prompting another U.S. airlift of plastic sheeting. This time a 436th Mil Alft Wg C–5 carried 858 rolls of the shelter material, weighing 70 tons, from Dover AFB in Delaware to Khartoum. The Galaxy stopped at bases in Spain and Italy for refueling and crew rest. The flight took two days, August 10 and 11.

58.
Name: Somalian Medical Relief.
Location: Somalia.
Date(s): August 25–31, 1988.

Emergency: A civil war in Somalia taxed the medical facilities of Mogadishu.
Air Force Organization(s) Involved: 437th Mil Alft Wg and 41st Mil Alft Sq.
Airlifted: A 200-bed emergency hospital weighing more than 22 tons.
Aircraft Employed: C–141 (one).
Operations: During the summer, fighting between government troops of President Mohammed Siad Barrah and rebel forces led by the northern Isaak clan drove large numbers of wounded into crowded medical facilities of Mogadishu, capital of Somalia, in eastern Africa. In response to a Somalian request for aid, the United States authorized an airlift of a 200-bed mobile emergency hospital.

A C–141 Starlifter from the 437th Mil Alft Wg, flown by Capt. Joseph W. Mancy and a 41st Mil Alft Sq crew, performed the mission between August 25 and 31. Gregory T. Touma, project officer for the secretary of defense's humanitarian affairs office, accompanied the medical cargo, which weighed over 22 tons. Mancy's route from Dover AFB to Mogadishu went through Goose Bay, Labrador; Rhein-Main AB, West Germany; and Cairo.

The airlift did nothing to stem the fighting. The civil war in Somalia was destined to grow until anarchy threatened the country (see Provide Relief, August 1992–February 1993).

59.
Name: São Tomé Medical Airlift.
Location: São Tomé and Principe.
Date(s): August 28–September 3, 1988.
Emergency: São Tomé suffered from shortages of hospital equipment and supplies.
Air Force Organization(s) Involved: 437th Mil Alft Wg and 20th Mil Alft Sq.
Airlifted: 29 tons of hospital equipment and supplies.
Aircraft Employed: C–141 (one).
Operations: When the United States learned of hospital shortages on the island of São Tomé in the nation of São Tomé and Principe, it airlifted excess DoD medical cargo under the humanitarian assistance program. Maj. Steven Avery and a five-man crew from the 20th Mil Alft Sq flew a 437th Mil Alft Wg C–141 Starlifter on the mission, which lasted from August 28 through September 3.

Avery's aircraft was the first MAC airplane to land in São Tomé. It carried 12 pallets of hospital cargo, weighing 29 tons. The shipment included medical supplies, pillows, blankets, bed sheets, hospital equipment, and furniture. Avery's route went from Wright-Patterson AFB in Ohio through Andrews AFB, Maryland; Lajes AB in the Azores; and Monrovia, Liberia. During the same month, MAC also airlifted medical supplies to Somalia (see Somalian Medical Relief, August 1988).

Humanitarian Airlift Operations

60.
Name: Nigerois Medical Airlift.
Location: Niger.
Date(s): November 9, 1988.
Emergency: Niger lacked dental clinics.
Air Force Organization(s) Involved: 436th Mil Alft Wg, 512th Mil Alft Wg (Associate), and 709th Mil Alft Sq.
Airlifted: One mobile dental clinic and two ambulances.
Aircraft Employed: C–5 (one).
Operations: In late 1988, the U.S. government granted $1 million to the developing country of Niger, which lacked adequate medical equipment and facilities. Niger used part of its grant to purchase two ambulances and a mobile dental clinic. The size of the cargo required airlift by C–5, so the Department of State asked MAC for a special mission.

Headed by Lt. Col. James Roberts, a 709th Mil Alft Sq crew from the 512th Mil Alft Wg (Associate) flew the mission, using a 436th Mil Alft Wg C–5. Roberts and his crew left Dover AFB, Delaware, flying through Lajes AB in the Azores for refueling before landing at Niamey, capital of Niger, on November 9. The U.S. ambassador to Niger, Carl Cundiff, met the aircraft and presented the dental clinic and ambulances to Niger in planeside ceremonies. Attendees toured the C–5 after the cargo was unloaded. The airlift demonstrated the commitment of the United States to African countries like Niger.

61.
Name: Central African Medical Airlift.
Location: Cameroon and Chad.
Date(s): November 1988.
Emergency: Medical need.
Air Force Organization(s) Involved: 436th Mil Alft Wg and 9th Mil Alft Sq.
Airlifted: 70 tons of medical cargo, including an ambulance, medical equipment, supplies, and clothing.
Aircraft Employed: C–5 (one).
Operations: During the late 1980s, MAC flew several humanitarian airlift missions to Africa, a continent which was suffering from a series of natural disasters and civil conflicts. Some missions transported direly needed medical equipment and supplies.

At the end of November, a 9th Mil Alft Sq aircrew flew a 436th Mil Alft Wg C–5 Galaxy aircraft from Andrews AFB, Maryland, to central Africa carrying 70 tons of donated medical property. The Galaxy unloaded an ambulance at Douala, capital of Cameroon. The city of Seattle, in Washington State, donated the ambulance to its sister city of Limke, 45 miles from Douala.

The C–5 flew on to N'Djamena, capital of Chad, to unload 31 pallets of medical equipment, supplies, and clothing. The airlift expressed the support of the

United States for Chad, which was combating famine and locust infestation as well as territorial threats from neighboring Libya.

62.
Name: Senegalese Locust Plague.
Location: Northwestern Africa.
Date(s): November 16–30, 1988, and February 1989.
Emergency: Millions of locusts threatened to consume food crops in Senegal.
Air Force Organization(s) Involved: 60th, 63d, 437th, and 438th Mil Alft Wgs.
Airlifted: 442 tons of malathion insecticide, pallets, aircraft fuel, and a forklift.
Aircraft Employed: C–141 (16).
Operations: A locust plague moved from east to west across Africa just south of the Sahara. Millions of insects consumed tons of crops daily. By November, the locusts had moved into Senegal, and the government at Dakar asked the United States to deliver and spray pesticides. The State Department contracted spray aircraft, but could not acquire space on commercial aircraft to deliver the insecticide in time for an effective pest control operation. The Department of Defense's Office of Humanitarian Assistance responded with a MAC airlift.

In mid-November, seven C–141 Starlifters from the 437th and 438th Mil Alft Wgs transported 235 tons of malathion insecticide from McGuire AFB, New Jersey, to Dakar. The cargo consisted of 783 55-gallon, 600-pound drums purchased by AID. A few days later, another Starlifter from the 60th Mil Alft Wg flew 25 additional tons of insecticide from Travis AFB, California, to Dakar.

The Agency for International Development purchased more malathion in Denmark and asked MAC to airlift it to Senegal. At the end of November, four Starlifters transported 152 tons of the insecticide from Billund Airport near Kolding, Denmark, to Dakar. A fifth C–141 delivered pallets to Denmark to help load the aircraft, while a sixth transported an airlift control element team and a 10-ton forklift to the Senegalese capital. Some of the six Starlifters also transported aircraft fuel to Senegal for the contracted spray aircraft.

In early February, the 63d Mil Alft Wg conducted a final airlift to Senegal to fight the locust threat there. Two C–141s from Norton AFB, California, transported 20 more tons of insecticide from McGuire AFB through Bermuda to Dakar. Aircraft under contract with AID sprayed the pesticides in Senegal.

63.
Name: Sudanese Refugee Relief.
Location: Kenya.
Date(s): December 1988.
Emergency: Thousands of starving Sudanese refugees crowded into refugee camps near the border of Kenya.
Air Force Organization(s) Involved: Twenty-first Air Force.
Airlifted: Six tons of parachutes for use as shelters.

Aircraft Employed: C–141 (one).

Operations: In December, the Department of State's Agency for International Development and its Office of Foreign Disaster Assistance asked DoD to airlift excess parachutes from the United States to Africa to shelter Sudanese refugees who had fled their homes seeking food. A Norwegian charitable organization called Norwegian Church Aid was ready to truck the parachutes from the Kenyan capital of Nairobi to southern Sudan, where the refugees crowded into camps.

Near the end of December, a Twenty-first Air Force C–141 flew the mission, transporting six tons of parachutes on six pallets from Lawson Army Airfield at Fort Benning, Georgia, and Harrisburg International Airport, Pennsylvania, to Nairobi's Jomo Kenyatta International Airport. The Norwegian charitable organization trucked the parachutes across the border into southern Sudan to shelter the refugees.

64.
Name: Medflag '89.
Location: Liberia.
Date(s): January 7–20, 1989.
Emergency: Diseases such as malaria, rickets, and scurvy were widespread.
Air Force Organization(s) Involved: 167th Tac Alft Gp.
Airlifted: Medical personnel and medical supplies.
Aircraft Employed: C–130 (two).
Operations: During January, some U.S. military doctors and medical technicians assigned to Europe deployed to Liberia to train medical personnel, inoculate people against diseases, and treat ailments as part of Medflag '89, an eight-day joint-service deployment exercise. Among the medical personnel was Maj. (Dr.) Frederick Foss, a surgeon stationed at Torrejon AB, Spain, who headed a flying ambulance surgical trauma team that worked with Liberian military medics and humanitarian assistance officials.

The Air National Guard's 167th Tac Alft Gp furnished C–130s to transport medical teams in Liberia. Working in 90-degree heat and high humidity, without running water or electricity, U.S. medical personnel immunized 6,000 Liberians against polio, measles, diphtheria, and tetanus. They also treated more than 2,000 people for malaria, rickets, scurvy, malnutrition, parasites, and infections.

Medflag '89 accomplished several purposes. It assisted the people of Liberia in their struggle for better health, demonstrated the U.S. commitment to Africa, provided training for Liberian and U.S. military medical personnel, and provided personnel from different branches of the U.S. armed forces an opportunity to work together in an austere environment.

65.
Name: Africa I.
Location: The Gambia, Equatorial Guinea, and Chad.
Date(s): April 1989.

Emergency: Shortages of medical supplies, food, and electricity.
Air Force Organization(s) Involved: 436th Mil Alft Wg.
Airlifted: 32 pallets of medical supplies, generators, and food.
Aircraft Employed: C–5 (one).
Operations: When they became aware of shortages of medical supplies, food, and electricity in the African countries of The Gambia, Equatorial Guinea, and Chad, the Department of State's African Bureau and the Department of Defense's Office of Humanitarian Assistance organized a humanitarian airlift operation called Africa I. The operation proceeded under the terms of the McCollum Amendment, by which Congress authorized the airlift of surplus nonlethal DoD property to needy nations.

In early April, a 436th Mil Alft Wg crew flew a C–5A Galaxy from Dover AFB, Delaware, to Africa for the airlift. It carried Dr. Robert K. Wolthuis, the DoD director of humanitarian assistance, and 32 pallets of medical supplies, generators, and food.

The C–5 landed first in Banjul, capital of The Gambia, where it unloaded eight pallets of medical supplies on April 10. On hand to meet the aircraft were U.S. ambassador Herbert E. Horowitz, Gambian army officials, British military advisers, and press representatives. Before departing for other parts of Africa, the C–5 crew offered tours of the aircraft.

The next stop was Malabo, capital of Equatorial Guinea, where the Galaxy landed on April 12. There it delivered eight pallets of medical cargo, including the components of a portable hospital and its related supplies. A C–5 had never landed at Malabo, and the 436th Mil Alft Wg crew benefited from an earlier 435th Tac Alft Wg airfield survey. President Obiang Nguema Mbasogo of Equatorial Guinea and Ambassador Charles E. Norris, Jr., of the United States were among the dignitaries who greeted the Galaxy. Again, the delivery of medical supplies generated favorable local publicity.

After refueling at Douala, Cameroon, the Galaxy continued on to N'Djamena, capital of Chad, where it discharged 16 pallets of generators and food. The food consisted of "meals ready to eat," so contamination and spoilage was not a problem. The C–5 returned to the United States via Monrovia, Liberia, in mid-April.

The Africa I operation relieved medical, food, and electrical shortages in The Gambia, Equatorial Guinea, and Chad. It also demonstrated U.S. concern for developing African countries and strengthened ties between them and the United States at a time when natural disasters, disease, and civil strife threatened the region with death, sickness, and starvation.

66.
Name: Africa II.
Location: Sierra Leone, Liberia, Niger, Cameroon, and Chad.
Date(s): September 29–October 15, 1989.

Humanitarian Airlift Operations

Emergency: Several African countries needed medical supplies and food to prevent deaths from disease and malnutrition.
Air Force Organization(s) Involved: 436th and 438th Mil Alft Wgs and 3d Mil Alft Sq.
Airlifted: At least 335 tons of medical supplies, food, cots, and clothing.
Aircraft Employed: C–5 (one).
Operations: Aware that several African countries needed food and medical supplies to fight alarming rates of malnutrition and disease, the Department of Defense's Office of Humanitarian Assistance organized a combined sealift and airlift of excess supplies in the fall of 1989. The operation was called Africa II (see Africa I, April 1989).

On September 30, while a Navy ship cruised toward Douala, Cameroon, with tons of humanitarian cargo, a 436th Mil Alft Wg C–5 Galaxy, flown by a 3d Mil Alft Sq crew, took off from Andrews AFB, Maryland, for its part in Africa II. Its cargo, 65 tons of medical supplies and hospital equipment, filled 35 pallets.

On October 2, the C–5 landed at Lungi Airport in Freetown, Sierra Leone, where it unloaded 11 pallets. Later the same day, the giant aircraft dropped off 12 more pallets of medical supplies at Monrovia, capital of Liberia. The Galaxy unloaded the remaining 12 pallets of medical equipment and supplies at Niamey, Niger, on October 3.

Although temporarily empty, the C–5 was not finished with its Africa II mission. It flew on to Douala, where the Navy had sealifted more cargo. A seven-man airlift control element team, led by Maj. David Cliff, palletized the freight for C–5 airlift to N'Djamena, capital of Chad. Between October 5 and 15, the C–5 shuttled 250 tons of food, 20 tons of clothing, two washing machines, and six refrigerators from Douala to N'Djamena.

The combined sealift and airlift furnished food, clothing, and medical supplies to people in five African nations. Africa II reinforced U.S. foreign policy in Africa and provided the Air Force and the Navy with valuable experience in joint transportation.

67.
Name: Medflag Senegal '90.
Location: Senegal.
Date(s): February 23–March 6, 1990.
Emergency: High rates of disease hampered the development of Senegal.
Air Force Organization(s) Involved: 435th Tac Alft Wg and 37th Tac Alft Sq.
Airlifted: 11 tons of medical equipment and supplies and 60 passengers.
Aircraft Employed: C–130 (one).
Operations: After a successful medical training and humanitarian assistance operation to Liberia in 1989 (see Medflag '89, January 1989), DoD authorized a similar joint operation the following year to the west African country of Senegal.

Like Liberia, Senegal suffered alarming rates of disease and malnutrition. Its medical personnel were eager to learn from their U.S. counterparts.

The resultant operation, called Medflag Senegal '90, took place between February 23 and March 6. The 435th Tac Alft Wg provided airlift for the deploying medical team, launching a C–130 Hercules from Rhein-Main AB in West Germany on February 23. Flown by Capt. Steven L. Hopper and a crew from the 37th Tac Alft Sq, the aircraft first went to Mildenhall in the United Kingdom to load 11 tons of medical equipment and supplies. From there it flew to Lajes AB in the Azores before proceeding on to Dakar, capital of Senegal.

While in Senegal, the medical team trained Senegalese medical personnel, treated diseases and injuries, and inoculated people against epidemics. Hopper and his crew transported the 60-man team to three towns around Senegal: St. Louis, Ziguinchor, and Tambacounda. Although the C–130 crew faced many challenges, such as primitive airfields and runways blocked by livestock, it helped Medflag Senegal '90 to fulfill its objectives. The operation also reinforced U.S. policy toward the developing nations of Africa, encouraging them to regard the United States as a friend.

68.
Name: Liberian War Refugees.
Location: Liberia.
Date(s): February 1990.
Emergency: A civil war in Liberia displaced hundreds of people.
Air Force Organization(s) Involved: 436th Mil Alft Wg and 463d Tac Alft Wg.
Airlifted: 30 tons of relief supplies.
Aircraft Employed: C–5 (one) and C–130 (one).
Operations: In December 1989, Charles Taylor led a rebellion against the government of President Samuel K. Doe of Liberia. The rebellion reflected tribal rivalries in the country and turned into a civil war that lasted into the next year. The United States refused to send troops, but did authorize an airlift to deliver relief supplies to noncombatant Liberians displaced by the fighting.

In February, two MAC airplanes delivered 30 tons of relief supplies to Monrovia, the Liberian capital. A 436th Mil Alft Wg C–5 and a 463d Tac Alft Wg C–130 performed the operation. The airlift relieved some suffering, but the conflict continued. Rebel forces captured and killed President Doe in September and gained control of the country except for the capital city. At the same time, a peacekeeping force from five West African nations attempted to quell the fighting.

69.
Name: Sierra Leonean Airlifts.
Location: Sierra Leone.
Date(s): February 21 and November 14, 1991.

Humanitarian Airlift Operations

Emergency: Like many other African nations, Sierra Leone experienced economic hardships.
Air Force Organization(s) Involved: 436th and 438th Mil Alft Wgs.
Airlifted: 105 tons of medical and other relief supplies.
Aircraft Employed: C–5 (one) and C–141 (one).
Operations: In 1991, the United States conducted humanitarian flights to Ethiopia, Kenya, Chad, Zaire, and Angola to fulfill physical needs created by drought, famine, economic collapse, or civil unrest. The president of Sierra Leone, Joseph Momoh, also requested U.S. humanitarian assistance to relieve his country's poverty, malnutrition, and disease.

Responding to appeals from the State Department, two U.S. military cargo aircraft airlifted 105 tons of medical supplies and other humanitarian cargo to Freetown, the capital of Sierra Leone. The first mission, flown by a 438th Mil Alft Wg C–141 Starlifter aircraft and crew from McGuire AFB, New Jersey, transported 55 tons to Freetown on February 21. On November 14, a 436th Mil Alft Wg C–5 Galaxy and crew from Dover AFB, Delaware, delivered 50 tons of medical and other relief supplies to the same destination.

Besides meeting the physical needs of some of the people of Sierra Leone, the airlifts supported U.S. foreign policy, reinforcing ties between the nations and encouraging the spread of democracy and free market economies in Africa.

70.
Name: Ethiopian Drought.
Location: Ethiopia.
Date(s): June–September 1991.
Emergency: An extended drought created severe food shortages.
Air Force Organization(s) Involved: 436th and 439th Mil Alft Wgs, 512th Mil Alft Wg (Associate), and 3d and 31st Mil Alft Sqs.
Airlifted: More than 1,000 tons of food, blankets, farm equipment, and medical supplies.
Aircraft Employed: C–5 (19+ missions).
Operations: During the summer of 1991, a long drought threatened Ethiopia with malnutrition and starvation. The United States responded to a request from the Ethiopian government for assistance by authorizing shipment of excess DoD rations and other relief supplies from stockpiles in nearby Saudi Arabia, where they had been gathered for a campaign against Iraq earlier in the year.

Military Airlift Command C–5s flown by crews from the 436th Mil Alft Wg and the Air Force Reserve's 439th Mil Alft Wg and 512th Mil Alft Wg (Associate) flew at least 19 airlift missions from Dhahran, Saudi Arabia, to Addis Ababa, capital of Ethiopia, from June through September. The huge aircraft carried more than 1,000 tons of food, farm equipment, medical supplies, and blankets.

71.
Name: Kenyan Food Airlift.
Location: Kenya.
Date(s): June 25, 1991.
Emergency: Kenya suffered drought-induced food shortages.
Air Force Organization(s) Involved: 60th Mil Alft Wg.
Airlifted: 80 tons of food rations.
Aircraft Employed: C–5 (one).
Operations: Like Ethiopia on its northern border, Kenya experienced drought-induced food shortages during the summer of 1991. The Air Force was already flying C–5 Galaxy aircraft laden with food and relief supplies from Saudi Arabia to Ethiopia; thus, when the Kenyan government requested similar assistance through diplomatic channels, relief was quick to come.

On June 25, a 60th Mil Alft Wg C–5 airlifted 80 tons of food rations to Nairobi, capital of Kenya. The 20 pallets of cargo, consisting of "meals ready to eat," were surplus from the Gulf War earlier in the year. The airlift alleviated food shortages while reinforcing friendly ties between Kenya and the United States.

72.
Name: Chadian Relief.
Location: Republic of Chad.
Date(s): July 7, 1991.
Emergency: A drought produced food shortages in Chad, which was recovering from a civil war.
Air Force Organization(s) Involved: 436th Mil Alft Wg.
Airlifted: 70 tons of food and other relief supplies.
Aircraft Employed: C–5 (one).
Operations: During mid-1991, the United States airlifted relief supplies left over from Desert Storm to African countries struggling against drought along the southern edge of the Sahara. In June, C–5 Galaxy cargo aircraft transported food from Saudi Arabia to Ethiopia (see Ethiopian Drought, June–September 1991) and Kenya (see Kenyan Food Airlift, June 1991). In July, it was Chad's turn.

A 436th Mil Alft Wg C–5 delivered 70 tons of food and other relief supplies to N'Djamena, capital of Chad, on July 7. The cargo relieved drought victims and assisted Chad's recovery from a civil war in the 1980s.

73.
Name: Quick Lift.
Location: Central Africa.
Date(s): September 27–October 3, 1991.
Emergency: A mutiny of troops in Zaire touched off rioting and looting across the country, endangering the lives of foreigners.

Humanitarian Airlift Operations

Air Force Organization(s) Involved: Twenty-first Air Force, 322d Alft Div, and 437th and 438th Mil Alft Wgs.
Airlifted: More than 1,000 evacuees.
Aircraft Employed: C–141 (number unknown).
Operations: During the late 1980s and early 1990s, the economy of Zaire suffered hyperinflation fed by economic inefficiency and political corruption. Seething discontent erupted into violence when 3,000 soldiers mutinied over pay and went on a rampage in Kinshasa, the capital, on September 23, 1991. Civilians joined the rebellious soldiers, rioting and looting buildings in the capital and other parts of the country. Five days of disorder left 60 people dead and over 1,000 injured. Thousands of Portuguese, French, Belgian, Greek, and U.S. workers fled for their lives. The State Department notified U.S. nationals to leave Zaire. Some were trapped when violent marauders shut down ferry operations on the Congo River and the international airport at Kinshasa.

With the approval of President Mobutu Sese Seko's government, French and Belgian troops entered Zaire to help the foreigners to escape. U.S. C–141 Starlifter transport aircraft assisted with the evacuation of expatriates in an operation called Quick Lift. After flying French and Belgian troops to Banqui, Central African Republic; Brazzaville, Congo; and Kinshasa, the Starlifters returned to Europe with evacuees. Some of the more than 40 flights, which took about seven hours on a route through Dakar, Senegal, carried as many as 100 passengers. The airlift evacuated more than 1,000 people, including over 600 U.S. citizens, from central Africa to Europe.

74.
Name: Angolan Airlift.
Location: Angola.
Date(s): October and November 1991.
Emergency: Angola struggled to recover from 16 years of civil war.
Air Force Organization(s) Involved: 436th Mil Alft Wg.
Airlifted: 275 tons of relief supplies.
Aircraft Employed: C–5 (four missions).
Operations: At the end of May, and after 16 years of civil war, Angolan president Jose Eduardo dos Santos and UNITA rebel leader Jonas Savimbi agreed to a cease-fire brokered by Portugal, the United States, and the Soviet Union. The war had killed about 300,000 people and had left Angola's economy in ruins. Santos and Savimbi agreed to prepare Angola for free elections the following year.

To encourage Angola's economic recovery and its move toward democracy, the United States offered humanitarian aid. In October and November, the 436th Mil Alft Wg transported at least 260 tons of relief supplies to Luanda, capital of Angola, on four C–5 Galaxy flights. The airlift reinforced U.S. foreign policy, which supported the spread of free markets and democracy in Africa and other parts of the world.

75.
Name: Sierra Leonean Evacuation.
Location: Sierra Leone.
Date(s): May 3–4, 1992.
Emergency: A military coup endangered the lives of U.S. citizens in Sierra Leone, and the State Department advised an evacuation.
Air Force Organization(s) Involved: 10th Ftr Wg; 435th, 437th, and 438th Alft Wgs; and 6th and 76th Alft Sqs.
Airlifted: 438 evacuees.
Aircraft Employed: C–141 (two) and C–130 (two+).
Operations: On April 29, a military coup overthrew the government of President Joseph Momoh in the west African country of Sierra Leone. Political chaos followed, threatening the lives of U.S. nationals in the country, including a 79-member combined services medical team from USEUCOM on a humanitarian training exercise (Medflag), State Department personnel and dependents, and Peace Corps volunteers. On May 2, the State Department ordered the evacuation of its personnel and advised all other U.S. citizens to leave Sierra Leone. At the same time, the State Department asked for military airlift support.

On May 3 and 4, MAC airlifted 438 people, including 42 third-country nationals, from Lungi Airport at Freetown, capital of Sierra Leone. A pair of C–141 Starlifters transported 136 U.S. nationals to Rhein-Main AB, Germany. Each flight took about seven hours. A 437th Alft Wg C–141 flown by a 76th Alft Sq crew carried the Medflag team, while another C–141 flown by a 6th Alft Sq crew of the 438th Alft Wg carried 57 other U.S. citizens, including missionaries and State Department dependents.

Over the same two-day period, C–130s from the 10th Ftr Wg and the 435th Alft Wg evacuated 302 passengers from Freetown to Dakar, Senegal, in nine sorties. At Dakar, the passengers found commercial flights to other destinations or waited until conditions had calmed enough to allow their safe return to Sierra Leone.

76.
Name: Provide Relief.
Location: Somalia and Kenya.
Date(s): August 14, 1992–February 28, 1993.
Emergency: Anarchy and famine threatened the people of Somalia with starvation.
Air Force Organization(s) Involved: 60th, 62d, 63d, 118th, 123d, 133d, 146th, 302d, 314th, 317th, 403d, 437th, 438th, and 463d Alft Wgs; 23d and 176th Comp Wgs; 135th, 143d, 145th, 164th, 172d, 179th, 913th, and 914th Alft Gps; and 8th, 14th, 30th, 50th, 61st, and 327th Alft Sqs.
Airlifted: 23,321 metric tons of relief cargo, including food, water, and medical supplies.

Humanitarian Airlift Operations

Aircraft Employed: C–130 (41) and C–141 (five).

Operations: Years of drought and civil war produced a famine in Somalia that by 1992 had starved an estimated one-quarter of all children under the age of five. The UN announced that 1.5 million people faced imminent starvation unless help was provided quickly. At the same time, gunfire exchanges among rival clans in the capital and port city of Mogadishu prevented safe docking and unloading of food ships.

Ready to join an international effort to aid the Somalian people, President Bush announced a U.S. humanitarian relief operation called Provide Relief on August 14. To respond to the emergency under the guidance of the State Department's Agency for International Development, DoD organized a joint task force under the Central Command. Marine Corps Brig. Gen. Frank Libutti assumed command of the task force and set up headquarters in Kenya, which bordered Somalia on the southwest and maintained refugee camps for Somalis who fled in search of food and peace. Provide Relief was a joint U.S. humanitarian operation involving resources of the Air Force, Navy, Army, and Marine Corps. Col. George N. Williams directed mobility forces at Mombasa, Kenya, the main operation base.

Airlift played a major role in the operation. Before the end of August, eight C–130s from the 314th Alft Wg and five C–141s of the 62d, 437th, and 438th Alft Wgs were in Kenya. Besides Regular Air Force units, the airlift involved volunteers from AF Res and ANG C–130 units, demonstrating the "total force" concept. Eventually, at least 14 airlift wings, two composite wings, and eight airlift groups participated in Provide Relief airlift missions, using 41 C–130 Hercules cargo aircraft and five C–141 Starlifters.

The Starlifters flew from Europe and the continental United States via Egypt to Kenya. Most C–141s came from the 438th Airlift Wing's 30th Alft Sq, already deployed in Europe. Lt. Col. Ron Peck commanded the initial Starlifter package, which arrived in Kenya on August 18. The C–141s transported relief cargo from Mombasa 325 miles to Wajir, a staging base in eastern Kenya near the refugee camps only 20 miles from the Somalian border. Trees had to be cut along the airfield before the large planes could land at Wajir.

Each C–141 carried about 22 tons of food, which was increased to 30 tons after airlift personnel determined the Wajir runways could support the additional weight. The Starlifters could not fly beyond Wajir because most Somalian landing strips were too small to handle them. After stockpiling food at Wajir, the C–141s returned to the United States after August 30. By then, the Starlifters had delivered 1,133 tons of food and relief supplies on 58 flights.

To extend the airlift into Somalia, Provide Relief officials relied on more than 40 smaller C–130 Hercules aircraft. The first C–130s arrived in Kenya on August 20. The 314th Airlift Wing's Col. Nick Williams commanded the first C–130 to land in Somalia, arriving at Belen Huen (Belet Uen) on August 28. Other Somalian towns reached by the C–130s were Baidoa, Bardera, Oddur (Hudor), and Beladweyne. Some airfields were unpaved and only 4,000 feet long, proving a challenge to the C–130s, each of which carried 10 to 15 tons per flight. Crews unloaded the aircraft with engines running to reduce time on the ground. Despite this precaution, snipers fired at a U.S. C–130 airplane at Belet Huen on September 18, temporarily halting the missions.

Despite poor airfields, frequent tire changes, and interruptions of gunfire, Provide Relief flights delivered the equivalent of 28 million meals in the first 42 days. The food included rice, sorghum, wheat, flour, cooking oil, salt, bottled water, beans, and peas. The transports also delivered medical and cooking supplies. Between September 1, 1992, and early January 1993, ANG C–130s transported over 4,000 tons of relief supplies in Kenya and Somalia.

Airlift was only one part of Operation Provide Relief. More tons of food were transported by ship to relief agencies at the ports of Mombasa and Mogadishu. Tragically, marauding armed gangs representing various rival clans stole food in Somalia from relief agencies, which were often forced to make "protection" payments. To insure a more equitable food distribution, President Bush announced a new operation called Restore Hope on December 4, 1992. Armed U.S. military forces would suppress the gangs and help relief agencies to get food to those who needed it most.

Although less strictly humanitarian in its emphasis than Provide Relief, Restore Hope had the same goals, and the two operations proceeded simultaneously until the end of February 1993. By then, almost 2,000 Provide Relief flights had delivered over 23,000 tons of cargo to Kenya and Somalia to feed hundreds of thousands of people. Thousands of tons of relief supplies also arrived by sea or by aircraft from other nations.

U.S. military aircraft played a key role in Provide Relief and Restore Hope, demonstrating the speed and flexibility of air power. By the time Restore Hope ended on May 4, the international Somalian relief effort had become the largest humanitarian operation since the Berlin Airlift.

77.
Name: Liberian Evacuation.
Location: Liberia.
Date(s): October 23–25, 1992.
Emergency: Civil war threatened the safety of U.S. citizens living in the Liberian capital.
Air Force Organization(s) Involved: 179th and 313th Alft Gps.
Airlifted: 96 U.S. evacuees.
Aircraft Employed: C–130 (two).
Operations: The civil war that engulfed Liberia in early 1990 erupted again in mid-October 1992. Three groups—an interim government set up internationally in 1990, the National Patriotic Front of Charles Taylor, and the United Liberation Movement for Democracy in Liberia—fought for control of the capital at

Monrovia, threatening U.S. citizens living there. After the State Department requested military help to evacuate the Americans, USAFE, supporting USEU-COM, organized an airlift.

On October 23, two C–130s, one each from the 179th and 313th Alft Gps, evacuated 62 Americans from Monrovia to Europe. The 179th Alft Gp aircraft was already flying channel missions to west Africa and the 313th Alft Gp C–130 was on rotational duty at RAF Mildenhall in the United Kingdom. On October 25, the 313th Alft Gp C–130 carried out 34 more U.S. nationals. The three C–130 missions in three days evacuated 96 U.S. citizens, including 24 embassy personnel.

78.
Name: Rwandan Relief (Provide Assistance, Support Hope).
Location: Burundi, Tanzania, Zaire, Kenya, and Uganda.
Date(s): April 9–12, 1994, and May 11–late September 1994.
Emergency: Ethnic fighting between the Hutu and Tutsi tribes in Rwanda threatened the lives of U.S. nationals and drove 2.7 million Rwandan refugees into neighboring countries.
Air Force Organization(s) Involved: 60th, 62d, 118th, 123d, 136th, 315th, 349th, 433d, 435th, 436th, 437th, 438th, 439th, 459th, and 621st Alft Wgs; 512th and 514th Alft Wgs (Associate); 452d Air Mobility Wing; and 105th, 139th, 164th, 172d, and 907th Alft Gps.
Airlifted: More than 3,600 tons of relief supplies by August 7.
Aircraft Employed: C–5 (15+), C–141 (28), and C–130 (number unknown).
Operations: When President Juvenal Habyarimana of Rwanda perished in an airplane crash in early April, fighting broke out between the Hutu and Tutsi tribes. Some Hutus attacked Belgians, believing they supported the Tutsis. U.S. nationals mistaken for Belgians became targets for attacks as well. On April 8, the U.S. ambassador, David Rawson, called for all U.S. citizens to evacuate Rwanda and organized an overland convoy from Kigali, the capital, to neighboring Bujumbura, Burundi.

In support of the evacuation, four Air Mobility Command C–141 Starlifter aircraft, some from the 315th Alft Wg, transported 242 U.S. and other foreign nationals from Bujumbura to Nairobi, Kenya, between April 9 and 12. From Nairobi, the evacuees obtained commercial air transportation elsewhere.

The Rwandan crisis did not end with the evacuation of U.S. citizens. As fighting between the Hutu and Tutsi tribes continued, 250,000 refugees fled Rwanda into neighboring Tanzania. To deliver relief supplies to the refugees, four more AMC C–141 Starlifters, flown by crews of the 438th Alft Wg and the 512th Alft Wg (Associate), began a new airlift on May 11. In one week they transported 239 tons of cargo, including 10,000 rolls of plastic sheeting and 100,000 blankets, from Incirlik AB, Turkey, to Mwanza, Tanzania.

The airlift was part of a joint operation called Provide Assistance, coordinated by Patricia L. Irvin, the deputy assistant secretary of defense for humanitarian and refugee affairs. The office responded to requests from the State Department, the UN, and the International Red Cross. Thirteen U.S. C–130s also flew Provide Assistance missions from Nairobi to Bujumbura for Rwandan refugees who fled there. The Air Mobility Command sponsored commercial flights under contract to deliver relief supplies from Pisa, Italy, to refugee camps in Entebbe, Uganda.

The refugee crisis continued through June. After Tutsi military victories within Rwanda, members of the Hutu tribe, fearing retaliation, fled by the millions to Zaire and neighboring countries. More than a million refugees fled to a camp in Goma, Zaire, where a cholera epidemic broke out because of unclean water supplies.

On July 22, President Clinton announced a new Rwandan relief operation called Support Hope. The Air Force supported the operation with a massive airlift. Huge C–5 Galaxies and C–141 Starlifters transported thousands of tons of relief cargo, including water purification and engineering equipment to build up a relief supply infrastructure. Most of the large aircraft flew from Rhein-Main AB, Germany, to Entebbe, Uganda, and Mombasa, Kenya, while smaller C–130s from USAFE transported cargo from those bases to Goma, Bukavu, and Harare in Zaire.

At least 17 airlift wings and five airlift groups participated in the operation, flying at least 57 C–5, C–141, and C–130 aircraft and crews from AMC, USAFE, the AF Res, and the ANG. Unlike the recent Restore Hope operation in Somalia, Support Hope was a humanitarian rather than a peacekeeping operation.

In one of the most notable flights, a 349th Alft Wg C–5 crew flew a water pumping system from Travis AFB, California, nonstop to Goma, Zaire. The 22–hour flight required three aerial refuelings. The pumping system, which could pump 1.7 million gallons of water a day, helped to supply more than a million refugees with fresh water.

By August 7, Air Force transport planes delivered 3,660 tons of relief equipment and supplies and 1,600 relief workers to refugee camps in Zaire and the other countries bordering Rwanda. In early August, Tipper Gore, wife of Vice President Al Gore, visited the Goma refugee camp to show support for the Rwandan relief operation.

Commercial aircraft under AMC contract transported food and medicine from Europe and the United States to central Africa as part of Operation Support Hope. The airlift ended in late September, as Rwandans, no longer fearing for their lives, returned to their homes. Air Force and commercial contract aircraft had transported almost 15,000 tons of relief cargo to the Rwandan refugees.

79.
Name: Egyptian Flood.
Location: Egypt.
Date(s): November 6–8, 1994.
Emergency: Flash floods inundated as many as 70 villages in southern Egypt.

Humanitarian Airlift Operations

Air Force Organization(s) Involved: 437th or 438th Alft Wg.
Airlifted: More than 37 tons of plastic sheeting, blankets, and communications equipment.
Aircraft Employed: C–141 (two).
Operations: At the beginning of November, gales and unusually heavy rain produced flash floods in southern Egypt, inundating 70 villages in three provinces. At Durunka, 200 miles south of Cairo, a bridge collapsed because of a flash flood, causing an explosion and fire at an adjacent military fuel complex. Floodwaters carried blazing fuel into the town, killing over 500 people.

Egyptian requests for aid reached the State Department and the Defense Department's Office of Humanitarian and Refugee Affairs, which approved a humanitarian operation on November 4. Two days later, a pair of AMC C–141s loaded more than 37 tons of relief supplies—including 28 tons of plastic sheeting, nine tons of blankets, and communications equipment—at Dover AFB, Delaware. For two days, the Starlifters airlifted their cargo to Cairo. Egyptians transported the relief supplies overland to the disaster area, where they were used to help flood victims until they could return to their homes.

Chapter 5
Southwest Asia

Southwest Asia consists of that part of Asia west of India and south of the former Soviet Union. This chapter does not include the part of Pakistan that became Bangladesh. Throughout the last half of the twentieth century, Southwest Asia remained vitally important to the United States. To Christians, Jews, and Muslims in the United States, the Middle East was the "Holy Land," a region of special religious significance. Situated between the Soviet Union and the warm water ports of the Mediterranean Sea, the Red Sea, the Persian Gulf, and the Arabian Sea, Southwest Asia was also strategically important during the Cold War. Most importantly, the region possesses more than half the world's known petroleum reserves, the lifeblood of U.S. industry.

Southwest Asia is also an area of great natural and sociological instability. Its people have been victimized by natural disaster, ancient religious antagonisms, and political and social conflict. Through Air Force humanitarian airlifts, the United States assisted victims of these emergencies. Such operations relieved suffering and supported U.S. foreign policy objectives in the region.

There were fewer humanitarian airlifts to the Middle East than to any other region, with an average of less than one mission per year, partly because the area is territorially smaller than other regions and partly because its arid climate does not produce hurricanes.

Since World War II, no region of the world has been more affected by war than Southwest Asia. Between 1947 and 1994, Israel and her Arab neighbors went to war in 1948, 1956, 1967, and 1973; and Israel invaded Lebanon in 1978 and 1982. In 1965, Pakistan and India fought over Kashmir. In 1979, the Soviet Union invaded Afghanistan. Iraq invaded Iran in 1980, precipitating an inconclusive eight-year war. In August 1990, Iraq occupied tiny Kuwait, but was driven out the next year in a short but intense war that involved the forces of twelve nations.

Civil conflict contributed to the volatility of the region, affecting Jordan in 1970, Iran in 1978 and 1979, and Lebanon after 1978. Kurds agitated for a state of their own in western Turkey and northern Iraq. Terrorism, often inspired by schisms within the Islamic world or between Arabs and Israelis, continues to plague the area, despite fragile peace agreements.

Humanitarian Airlift Operations

Statistics: Southwest Asian Airlifts

Number of humanitarian airlifts: 41.
Most common emergencies: earthquakes (10), evacuations (7), floods (7), and war refugees (6).
Most frequent recipients: Turkey (9), Iran (6), Jordan (5), and Pakistan (5).
Three largest operations, in chronological order: Pakistani Flood, 1973 (over 2,400 tons); Afghan Refugees, 1986–1993 (over 1,000 tons and 900 injured passengers); and Provide Comfort I, 1991 (over 7,000 tons).

Chronological Listing: Southwest Asian Airlifts

1. Lebanese Food Airlift	Mar. 1952
2. Operation Hajji Baba	Aug. 1952
3. Turkish Earthquake	Mar. 1953
4. Iraqi and Syrian Floods	Apr. 1954
5. Operation Butterball	Mar. 1956
6. Iranian Floods	Aug. 1956
7. Suez War Evacuation	Oct.–Nov. 1956
8. West Iranian Earthquakes	Dec. 1957
9. Yemeni Fire	Jan. 1961
10. Jordanian Relief	Feb. 1961
11. Mideast Locust Plague	May–June 1962
12. Operation IDA	Sept.–Nov. 1962
13. Turkish Flood	Feb. 1963
14. Pakistani Flood	June–July 1964
15. Nice Way/Elder Blow	Sept. 1965
16. Turkish Earthquake	Aug. 1966
17. Creek Dipper	June 1967
18. Iranian Earthquake	Sept.–Oct. 1968
19. Combat Locust	Feb.–Apr. 1969
20. Fig Hill	Sept.–Oct. 1970
21. Bingol Earthquake	May 1971
22. Pakistani Flood	Aug.–Sept. 1973
23. Cypriot Refugees	Aug.–Sept. 1974
24. Mauritian Cyclone	Feb. 1975
25. Turkish Earthquake	Nov. 1976 and Jan. 1977
26. Evacuation of Iran	Dec. 1978–Feb. 1979
27. Hostage Release	Jan. 1981
28. Lebanese Refugee Relief	Aug. and Oct. 1982
29. Yemeni Earthquake	Dec. 1982
30. Beirut Bombing	Oct.–Dec. 1983
31. Turkish Earthquake	Nov. 1983
32. TWA Hijacking	July 1985
33. Afghan Refugees	Mar. 1986
34. Kuwaiti Invasion Refugees	Sept. 1990
35. Kuwaiti Reconstruction	Mar.–June 1991
36. Provide Comfort I	Apr.–July 1991
37. Snow Eagle	Feb. 1992
38. Turkish Earthquake	Mar.–Apr. 1992
39. Uzbekistan Oil Fires	Apr. 1992
40. Pakistani Flood	Dec. 1992
41. Yemeni Evacuation	May 1994

Humanitarian Airlift Operations

Operations: Southwest Asian Airlifts

1.
Name: Lebanese Food Airlift.
Location: Lebanon.
Date(s): March 1952.
Emergency: In response to a food shortage, the State Department asked the Air Force to airlift 4.5 tons of seed corn to Beirut.
Air Force Organization(s) Involved: 1253d Air Trpt Sq.
Airlifted: 4.5 tons of seed corn.
Aircraft Employed: C–54 (one).
Operations: During March, the State Department asked the Defense Department for a MATS airlift of 4.5 tons of seed corn from the United States to Lebanon because of a food shortage. One C–54 Skymaster cargo plane and crew from the 1600th Air Transport Wing's 1253d Air Trpt Sq performed the mission, flying from Westover AFB, Massachusetts, to Beirut.

2.
Name: Operation Hajji Baba.
Location: Lebanon and Saudi Arabia.
Date(s): August 24–29, 1952.
Emergency: As the end of the Muslim pilgrimage season approached, more than 3,700 pilgrims on their way to Mecca were stranded at Beirut.
Air Force Organization(s) Involved: 1602d and 1603d Air Trpt Wgs, and 41st and 86th Air Trpt Sqs.
Airlifted: 3,763 Muslim pilgrims.
Aircraft Employed: C–54 (13).
Operations: Muslims flocked to Mecca, Saudi Arabia, during August 1952 for the Islamic pilgrimage. Commercial airlines at Beirut International Airport could not handle the huge influx of passengers eager to reach the holy city before the pilgrimage season ended in August. The Lebanese government appealed to the State Department for an airlift of excess passengers from Beirut to Jidda, near Mecca. The Military Air Transport Service's Atlantic Division prepared an operation called Hajji Baba to fulfill the State Department requirement.

Between August 24 and 29, the 1602d and 1603d Air Trpt Wgs conducted the airlift with Brig. Gen. Wentworth Goss serving as the task force commander. Using 13 C–54 Skymaster cargo planes from the 41st Air Trpt Sq from Wheelus AB, Libya, and the 86th Air Trpt Sq from Rhein-Main AB, West Germany, General Goss arranged to take passengers in groups of 50 from the commercial airlines in Beirut. To save time, airport authorities relaxed passport and security restrictions for the Air Force flights. Because of the large number of pilgrims needing rapid transportation, the State Department increased the original goal of moving 1,500 pilgrims by August 27 to 3,500 by August 29. To gather additional passengers, four flights went through Baghdad, Iraq, and Marfaq, Jordan. Because of insufficient aircraft, however, the Air Force was unable to satisfy a request to airlift pilgrims from Tehran, Iran, to Saudi Arabia.

Operation Hajji Baba succeeded, airlifting 3,763 Muslim pilgrims from Beirut to Jidda on 75 trips in six days. Two aircraft aborted for engine changes, but there were no accidents. Muslims throughout the Middle East responded favorably. Ayatollah Kashani, the religious leader of Iran, flew on one of the Air Force flights. A Lebanese religious leader hailed the airlift as a turning point in U.S. relations with the Arab world. Saudi Arabia's King Ibn Saud presented 86 ornate Arab costumes to U.S. airlift participants to express his appreciation. Operation Hajji Baba demonstrated the ability of MATS to serve U.S. humanitarian and diplomatic interests and to improve the image of the United States in the eyes of the Islamic world.

3.
Name: Turkish Earthquake.
Location: Turkey.
Date(s): March 21–22, 1953.
Emergency: An earthquake struck western Turkey south of Istanbul, killing and injuring hundreds of people and leaving thousands homeless.
Air Force Organization(s) Involved: 60th Trp Carr Wg.
Airlifted: 18 tons of blankets and medical supplies.
Aircraft Employed: C–119 (four).
Operations: On March 18, an earthquake strong enough to break a seismograph in Istanbul struck western Turkey south of the Sea of Marmara. The tremor, followed by days of aftershocks, killed or injured more than 500 people and drove thousands from their homes in towns such as Balikesir, Canakkale, Yenice, Gonen, Manyas, and Bursa.

The Turkish government appealed to the International Red Cross in Geneva for medicine and blankets for the injured and homeless. After touring the disaster area, the U.S. ambassador to Turkey, George C. McGhee, offered aid. Turkey, which had joined NATO a year earlier, requested a U.S. airlift of Red Cross supplies. The State Department referred the request to the Pentagon, which directed USAFE to respond.

On March 21, the third day after the initial earthquake, four 60th Trp Carr Wg C–119 Flying Boxcar cargo planes flew from Rhein-Main AB, West Germany, to Geneva, Switzerland, where they picked up 18 tons of Red Cross supplies, including 840 pounds of medicine and 10,000 blankets. The next day, the planes airlifted the relief cargo to Istanbul, about 200 miles north of the disaster site. Turkish ground vehicles moved the medicine and blankets to refugee camps to help the earthquake victims.

4.

Name: Iraqi and Syrian Floods.
Location: Iraq and Syria.
Date(s): April 2–16, 1954.
Emergency: Heavy rain flooded the Tigris River valley of central Iraq, inundating much of Baghdad. Heavy rain also flooded parts of Damascus, Syria.
Air Force Organization(s) Involved: 2d Air Div; 317th Trp Carr Wg; 39th, 40th, and 41st Trp Carr Sqs; and 59th Air Rscu Sq.
Airlifted: More than 54 tons of food, tents, sandbags, clothing, shoes, blankets, and medical supplies.
Aircraft Employed: C–119 (three), C–54 (two), H–19 (two), SA–16 (one), and C–47 (one).
Operations: During late March and early April, heavy rains flooded parts of Iraq and Syria. In Iraq, the Tigris and Euphrates Rivers overflowed, leaving half a million people temporarily homeless. Large parts of Baghdad were inundated. On April 1, the U.S. ambassador to Iraq, Burton Berry, forwarded an Iraqi government request for assistance to the State Department. The International Red Cross also asked for U.S. help for the disaster victims.

Col. James T. Bull, the U.S. air attaché to Iraq, set up an Air Force operations center at Baghdad to handle the airlift of relief supplies. Between April 2 and 8, the 2d Air Div at Dhahran, Saudi Arabia, flew two C–54s and a C–47 to Iraq for disaster relief. After an aerial survey, the three planes delivered 26 tons of tents, sandbags, medical supplies, and other relief cargo from Dhahran and Wheelus AB, Libya, to Baghdad.

The 59th Air Rscu Sq, also based at Dhahran, employed two H–19 helicopters and one SA–16 amphibious airplane for Iraqi flood relief between April 2 and 16. The aircraft dropped more than 15 tons of Iraqi food parcels to flood victims stranded on islands of high ground and evacuated refugees and transported medical personnel. The H–19s and SA–16 flew 82 sorties in central Iraq.

The 317th Trp Carr Wg from Neubiberg AB, West Germany, conducted an additional flood relief airlift to Iraq and Syria between April 9 and 11. Using three C–119 Flying Boxcar cargo airplanes, one each from the 39th, 40th, and 41st Trp Carr Sqs, the wing airlifted 13.5 tons of Red Cross relief supplies from Geneva, Switzerland, and Rome, Italy. Two of the planes landed at Baghdad and one at Damascus, with Capt. Joseph F. Bessler, Maj. Harry E. Shisler, and Maj. Addison Stone serving as aircraft commanders. The cargo included food—such as rice, condensed milk, and jam—clothing, shoes, blankets, and medical supplies.

5.

Name: Operation Butterball.
Location: Turkey.
Date(s): March 11–21, 1956.

342

Emergency: Heavy rain and melting snow flooded parts of northwestern Turkey, forcing hundreds of people from their homes.
Air Force Organization(s) Involved: 322d Air Div; 60th and 465th Trp Carr Wgs; and 11th, 780th, and 782d Trp Carr Sqs.
Airlifted: More than 205 tons of food, tents, blankets, and clothing.
Aircraft Employed: C–119 (six+).
Operations: During early March, heavy rain and melted snow flooded parts of northwestern Turkey, forcing hundreds of refugees from their homes. The Turkish government requested U.S. assistance to feed, shelter, and clothe flood victims. The Defense Department assigned the airlift mission to USAFE and its 322d Air Div.

On March 11, the division launched a relief operation called Operation Butterball to deliver relief supplies to Turkey. Its 465th Trp Carr Wg—based at Evreux-Fauville AB, France—employed C–119 Flying Boxcars from the 780th and 782d Trp Carr Sqs, while the 60th Trp Carr Wg—based at Dreux AB, France—flew an 11th Trp Carr Sq C–119. Lt. Albert J. Soen and his crew landed in Istanbul, Turkey, on March 13; the other planes landed in Istanbul or Ankara. The aircraft would have landed at Athens, Greece, for an overnight stop on the way from western Europe to Turkey, but political unrest in that city prevented such stops during the initial phase of the operation.

When Operation Butterball ended on March 21, at least six C–119s had delivered more than 205 tons of food—mostly butter, cheese, and other dairy products—tents, blankets, and clothing to Turkey. The Turkish Red Crescent, an organization similar to the Red Cross, distributed the relief supplies to flood victims.

6.
Name: Iranian Floods.
Location: Iran.
Date(s): August 1956.
Emergency: Heavy rain caused flash flooding in and around the Iranian capital, driving many people from their homes.
Air Force Organization(s) Involved: 322d Air Div and Detachment 1, 14th Trp Carr Sq.
Airlifted: 27 tons of medical supplies, clothing, rubber boats, and cooking utensils.
Aircraft Employed: C–119 (two) and C–124 (one).
Operations: During August, heavy rain caused flash flooding around Tehran, the capital of Iran. Many persons were driven from their homes, and the Iranian government requested relief supplies from western nations. The United States Air Forces in Europe, alerted by the State Department, responded with an emergency airlift handled by the 322d Air Div.

During mid-August, one C–124 Globemaster II cargo plane, belonging to Detachment 1 of the 14th Trp Carr Sq and piloted by Capt. Friday Henman, flew

20 tons of clothing and medical supplies from London, England, to Tehran, via Rome, Italy; Athens, Greece; and Adana, Turkey. Meanwhile, two 322d Air Div C–119 Flying Boxcars airlifted seven tons of cooking utensils and rubber boats from Geneva, Switzerland, to the Iranian capital.

7.

Name: Suez War Evacuation.

Location: Israel, Syria, and Jordan.

Date(s): October 29–early November 1956.

Emergency: After Egypt closed the Suez Canal to Israeli shipping and threatened the Israeli port of Eilat, Israel invaded Egypt. The war threatened U.S. civilians in the region.

Air Force Organization(s) Involved: 322d Air Div (Task Force 64); 60th, 317th, and 465th Trp Carr Wgs; and Detachment 1, 14th Trp Carr Sq.

Airlifted: 485 U.S. civilian personnel.

Aircraft Employed: C–119, C–124, and C–54 (24 planes total).

Operations: After the Egyptian government closed the Suez Canal to Israeli shipping; nationalized the canal, which had been owned primarily by the British and the French; and threatened ships traveling to the Israeli port of Eilat, Israel invaded Egypt's Sinai peninsula on October 29. British and French forces soon invaded Egypt to seize control of the canal. The war threatened civilians in the area, and the U.S. government decided to evacuate those of its nationals who wished to escape.

ADM Walter F. Boone, commander of Navy forces in the eastern Atlantic Ocean and the Mediterranean Sea, took charge of the overall evacuation. His ships carried 1,700 evacuees from Alexandria, Egypt, and Haifa, Israel, but U.S. aircraft also played a role in the evacuation.

The deputy commander of the 322d Air Div, Col. William S. Barksdale, took command of the airlift portion of the evacuation. His Task Force 64, based at Athenia Airport near Athens, Greece, flew 24 C–119, C–124, and C–54 airplanes from the 322d Air Div. The aircraft flew to Israel, Syria, and Jordan from staging bases near Athens and Adana, Turkey.

Between October 29 and early November, the planes evacuated 485 U.S. civilians, taking 273 of them from Tel Aviv, Israel, to Athens; 186 from Athens on to Rome, Italy; 22 from Damascus, Syria, to Beirut, Lebanon; and 4 from Amman, Jordan, to Beirut. Among those evacuated from Damascus was Mrs. James S. Moose, Jr., the wife of the U.S. ambassador to Syria.

Some cargo planes could not land at Tel Aviv because of fighting in the area. More aircraft were placed on alert than needed because the Navy accomplished most of the evacuation by sea. The 322d Air Division's 465th Trp Carr Wg, for example, prepared 24 C–119s at Adana for the evacuation, but only six flew to Tel Aviv. Only one of these, piloted by Maj. Charles L. Wilson, carried out evacuees.

Most Air Force aircraft participating in the emergency airlift were C–119 Flying Boxcars from the 60th, 317th, and 465th Trp Carr Wgs; but Detachment 1 of the 14th Trp Carr Sq, serving in Europe under the operational control of the 322d Air Div, flew three C–124s for the operation. Some Navy planes also evacuated U.S. nationals from Tel Aviv.

By early November, the evacuation of U.S. civilians was complete. President Eisenhower, reelected on November 6, reaffirmed his opposition to the invasion of Egypt. Israeli, British, and French forces soon withdrew and were replaced by UN peacekeeping troops.

8.
Name: West Iranian Earthquakes.
Location: Iran.
Date(s): December 19, 1957.
Emergency: A series of severe earthquakes struck villages in the Zagros Mountains of western Iran, killing 1,180 people and leaving thousands homeless in freezing weather.
Air Force Organization(s) Involved: 322d Air Div and 9th Trp Carr Sq.
Airlifted: 700 large tents weighing over 20 tons.
Aircraft Employed: C–119 (two) and C–124 (one).
Operations: Between December 13 and 17, a series of earthquakes struck the Zagros Mountains in western Iran. By December 18, the official death toll reached 1,180, and thousands of people were homeless in freezing weather. In the town of Farsan, at least 930 died out of a population of about 1,800. Hundreds died in mountain villages in the Kermanshah area. After the Iranian government requested assistance, Clark S. Gregory, director of U.S. technical aid in Iran, reported casualties and needs to the State Department, which arranged an airlift through USAFE.

To support the airlift, the Air Force used three aircraft that had just returned from delivering Christmas gifts to servicemen in Europe. One of the planes was a C–124 Globemaster II from the 9th Trp Carr Sq, on temporary rotation to Europe under operational control of the 322d Air Div. The other two aircraft were 322d Air Div Flying Boxcars.

On December 19, the relief planes airlifted 700 tents weighing more than 20 tons from Esenboga Field at Ankara, Turkey, to Tehran, capital of Iran. The airlifted tents provided shelter to thousands of homeless earthquake victims facing the beginning of a cold winter.

9.
Name: Yemeni Fire.
Location: Yemen.
Date(s): January 1961.
Emergency: A fire destroyed 600 houses in Hodeida, leaving more than 3,000 persons homeless.

Humanitarian Airlift Operations

Air Force Organization(s) Involved: 322d Air Div.
Airlifted: Food, medicine, and 3,000 blankets.
Aircraft Employed: Unknown.
Operations: During January, a fire destroyed 600 houses in Hodeida, Yemen, near the Red Sea at the southern end of the Arabian peninsula. The inferno left more than 3,000 persons homeless. After the Yemeni government requested U.S. assistance through the State Department, the JCS directed USAFE to conduct an emergency relief operation. By the end of the month, the 322d Air Div had airlifted 3,000 blankets, food, and medical supplies from Europe to fire victims in Hodeida.

10.
Name: Jordanian Relief.
Location: Jordan.
Date(s): February 4–5, 1961.
Emergency: A harsh winter confronted poverty-stricken villagers in southern Jordan with freezing temperatures.
Air Force Organization(s) Involved: 1602d Air Trpt Wg.
Airlifted: 7,000 blankets weighing 14 tons.
Aircraft Employed: C–124 (two).
Operations: After the assassination in 1960 of Jordan's premier, Hazza Majali, King Hussein attempted to develop a closer relationship with his people. He made frequent trips around the country and opened his palace every Monday to hear the concerns of common Jordanians. During the harsh winter of 1961, the suffering of poverty-stricken villagers in southern Jordan came to Hussein's attention, and he purchased 7,000 blankets from the United States and requested that they be airlifted to the Jordanian capital, Amman.

On February 4 and 5, two C–124 Globemaster II cargo aircraft of the 1602d Air Trpt Wg—under the operational control of the United States Air Forces in Europe's 322d Air Div—airlifted 14 tons of blankets from Chateauroux AS, France, to Amman. The planes transported the blankets via Athens, Greece, and Beirut, Lebanon, a route covering 1,750 nautical miles. After delivering the relief cargo, the crews continued on to Singapore, Malaya, to pick up Malayan troops for UN service in Congo.

11.
Name: Mideast Locust Plague.
Location: Iran and Afghanistan.
Date(s): May 10–June 1, 1962.
Emergency: Swarms of locusts descended on Iran and Afghanistan, threatening crops.
Air Force Organization(s) Involved: 464th Trp Carr Wg.
Airlifted: Several thousand gallons of insecticide.
Aircraft Employed: C–123 (one).

Operations: A locust plague threatened crops in Iran and Afghanistan during the late spring. The governments of both countries appealed for U.S. assistance through the State Department's Agency for International Development, which contacted DoD for an aerial insecticide spraying operation.

In early May, a C–123 Provider from the 464th Trp Carr Wg flew to Iran from South Vietnam, where it had participated in defoliation operations. Bearing a 1,000-gallon insecticide tank, the plane sprayed the Istafan and Dezful areas between May 10 and 24. Capt. Charles F. Hagerty served as aircraft commander, and his seven-man crew included pilot Capt. William F. Robinson, Jr., and entomologist Capt. Frank H. Dowell. After spraying about 9,000 acres in Iran, Hagerty's plane flew to Afghanistan, where it sprayed another 8,000 acres from a base at Khandahar between May 25 and June 1.

The aerial spraying brought the regional locust plague under control, and the State Department recognized the crew members for their efforts. Hagerty's plane returned to the United States by way of the Atlantic Ocean, completing what was possibly the first recorded circumnavigation of the earth by a C–123.

12.

Name: Operation IDA.

Location: Iran.

Date(s): September 3–November 12, 1962.

Emergency: A severe earthquake hit northwestern Iran west of Tehran, killing more than 12,000 people and leaving thousands injured and homeless.

Air Force Organization(s) Involved: 322d Air Div; 63d Trp Carr Wg; 1607th Air Trpt Wg; 39th, 40th, 41st, and 52d Trp Carr Sqs; and East Trpt AF.

Airlifted: 901 tons of relief cargo, including a field hospital, tents, blankets, rations, medical supplies, Army helicopters, and trucks.

Aircraft Employed: C–130 (28), C–124 (11), C–133 (7), and C–118 (1).

Operations: On September 1, a massive earthquake struck northwestern Iran, killing more than 12,000 people in over 100 villages and towns west of Tehran, the capital. An estimated 70,000 to 100,000 Iranians lost their homes, and thousands were injured by collapsing buildings. The government of Iran appealed for international emergency assistance, and the International Red Cross purchased thousands of tents for the homeless. To airlift the tents and other relief cargo to Iran, the U.S. ambassador, Julius C. Holmes, requested an emergency operation. In response, the JCS organized Operation IDA (Iranian Disaster Assistance) and assigned airlift responsibilities to USAFE and MATS.

Between September 3 and November 12, 47 U.S. military cargo airplanes airlifted more than 900 tons of relief cargo—including a mobile field hospital, six helicopters, 10,000 blankets, and more than 4,000 tents—from Europe to Iran. The 322d Air Div conducted the first phase of this airlift during the first part of September. Flying 28 C–130 Hercules cargo planes from the 39th, 40th, and 41st Trp Carr Sqs and five C–124 Globemaster II aircraft from the 52d Trp Carr Sq—

then serving under the 322d Air Div on rotational duty in Europe—the division flew 483 tons of relief cargo to Mehrabad Airport at Tehran. From home bases at Evreux, France, and Rhein-Main AB, West Germany, the airplanes picked up their cargo at Chateauroux AS in France and Stuttgart, Ramstein AB, and Landstuhl AB in West Germany. The transports landed at Athens, Greece, or Incirlik AB near Adana, Turkey, for refueling on the 2,500-mile flights.

Relief cargo included 10,000 blankets, 1,000 tents, 659 boxes of food rations, a 100-bed Army field hospital, six UH–1 Army helicopters, three trucks, medical supplies, and water purification equipment. Riding aboard the aircraft were more than 300 U.S. relief workers, mostly medical personnel, a group that included 18 doctors and 22 nurses. Col. Charles W. Howe, commander of the 322d Air Div, flew the lead airplane and served as the task force commander. There were no accidents.

Between September 29 and November 12, the Military Air Transport Service's East Trpt AF conducted the final phases of the airlift. Flying six more C–124s, seven C–133 Cargomasters, and a Navy C–118 under its operational control, the East Trpt AF moved to Tehran 418 tons of additional relief cargo, including more than 3,000 tents from Chateauroux AS and Ramstein AB, and from RAF Mildenhall in the United Kingdom. The 1607th Air Trpt Wg and the 63d Trp Carr Wg participated in the MATS portion of the airlift, which involved 17 missions. In early September, Air Force planes returned cargo from Tehran to Europe, including the Army field hospital and helicopters airlifted by the 322d Air Div. The Cuban missile crisis briefly interrupted the operation during mid-October.

13.
Name: Turkish Flood.
Location: Turkey.
Date(s): February 23–24, 1963.
Emergency: The Ceyhan River flooded an area east of Adana, stranding scores of people.
Air Force Organization(s) Involved: Detachment 11, Atlantic Air Rscu Cen.
Airlifted: 90 flood victims.
Aircraft Employed: HH–19B (two).
Operations: During the last week of February, the Ceyhan River, swollen by heavy rain and melting snow, flooded an area east of Adana in south central Turkey. Around the town of Misis, high water stranded many persons.

The Atlantic Air Rscu Cen, assigned to the Military Air Transport Service's Air Rscu Svc but under the operational control of USAFE, maintained its Detachment 11 at Incirlik AB near Adana. On February 23 and 24, the detachment used a pair of HH–19B helicopters with cable-strung baskets to rescue 90 flood victims, hoisting them from high points in the midst of the rising water to safer locations.

14.
Name: Pakistani Flood.
Location: Pakistan.
Date(s): June 26–July 24, 1964.
Emergency: Floods caused severe food shortages in the towns of Gilgit and Skardu.
Air Force Organization(s) Involved: 322d Air Div and 1608th Air Trpt Wg.
Airlifted: 946 tons of food, mostly grain.
Aircraft Employed: C–130 (seven).
Operations: During June, flooding in Kashmir in the northern part of West Pakistan caused severe food shortages in villages along the Karakoram Range of the Himalayas. When the Pakistani government realized its own airlift of food to the region was inadequate, it asked the United States to airlift grain from stockpiles at Chaklala International Airport at Rawalpindi to the towns of Gilgit and Skardu, about 160 miles to the north. On June 25, Air Force Chief of Staff Gen. Curtis E. LeMay assigned the mission to MATS.

The 322d Air Div conducted the emergency airlift to Pakistan. On June 26–28, the division surveyed the sites and determined what kinds of aircraft and equipment were needed. Seven C–130 Hercules cargo aircraft—five from the 1608th Air Trpt Wg at Charleston AFB, South Carolina, and two from the Naval Air Transport Wing, Atlantic, at McGuire AFB, New Jersey—served the 322d Air Div for the mission. Initially deployed on July 3, the planes flew via France or the Azores, Libya, and Aden—not being permitted to overfly Saudi Arabia or Iran—and landed at Chaklala Airport on July 7 and 8.

Between July 8 and 18, the seven C–130s carried 771 tons of grain from Rawalpindi to Gilgit, which had a small airstrip but no parking ramp. Crews rolled cargo off the planes while their engines continued to run. Between July 11 and 14, C–130s airdropped 175 tons of grain at Skardu, which lacked an airfield. Escarpments and mountains surrounding the small landing zone and unpredictable winds convinced airlifters to let the grain sacks fall freely without parachutes. Triple-bagging prevented the grain from spilling on impact.

The 322d Air Div crews faced many problems during the operation. A lack of electronic navigation aids at Gilgit and Skardu required Pakistani navigators to direct the C–130s. Heat up to 106 degrees Fahrenheit forced crews to limit the number of sorties per day. Airfields at elevations above 5,000 feet limited loads. Runway failure at Chaklala damaged a C–130 landing gear, but it was quickly repaired. Although maintenance crews kept all aircraft operationally ready, other problems hindered operations. Poor local food and water supplies gave more than half of the deployed personnel intestinal ailments. The A–22 containers originally used for grain drops at Skardu broke on impact and had to be abandoned.

Despite these problems, the 322d Air Div delivered most of the food requested by July 18, when the start of the wet monsoon terminated the airlift. The seven

C–130s returned to the United States between July 20 and 24, having delivered more than 946 tons of food to flood victims in 76 sorties.

15.
Name: Nice Way/Elder Blow.
Location: Pakistan.
Date(s): September 15–21, 1965.
Emergency: India and Pakistan went to war over a border dispute in Kashmir. The fighting threatened U.S. citizens in Lahore, Rawalpindi, and Peshawar in West Pakistan and Dacca in East Pakistan.
Air Force Organization(s) Involved: 315th and 322d Air Divs; 6315th Operations Group (Ops Gp); and 29th, 41st, and 76th Air Trpt Sqs.
Airlifted: 1,485 U.S. civilian evacuees.
Aircraft Employed: C–130 (14).
Operations: Unable to agree on their border in Kashmir, India and Pakistan went to war in September. The fighting threatened U.S. citizens in Pakistan, including many women and children. The State Department asked the JCS to arrange an emergency air evacuation. The Pentagon called the operation Nice Way in West Pakistan and Elder Blow in East Pakistan.

The 322d Air Div took charge of Nice Way with Col. Burgess Gradwell serving as the mission commander. The division employed seven C–130s diverted from a NATO training exercise in Turkey: two came from the 29th Air Trpt Sq at McGuire AFB, New Jersey; three from the 41st and 76th Air Trpt Sqs at Charleston AFB, South Carolina; and two from Naval Air Transport Squadron 3 at McGuire AFB, serving MATS.

On September 16, Indian troops suspended their artillery shelling of Lahore, West Pakistan, for two and one-half hours while the seven C–130s attempted to evacuate 599 Americans from there to Tehran. Landing at 15-minute intervals, the cargo planes sometimes took a half hour to load. The last plane, delayed by engine trouble, took off from Lahore after the shelling resumed. One C–130 carried 113 passengers, including many small children seated on parents' laps. The following day, September 17, a C–130 airlifted 29 more U.S. nationals from Rawalpindi, West Pakistan, to Tehran.

In the final phase of Operation Nice Way, on September 21, five C–130 cargo planes airlifted 372 Americans from Kabul, Afghanistan—where they had fled by road from Peshawar, West Pakistan—via Tehran to Turkey, landing at Istanbul's airport at Yesilkoy. About 160 of these evacuees were school children.

The 315th Air Div from PACAF was responsible for Operation Elder Blow, the air evacuation of U.S. nationals from East Pakistan during September. On September 19, seven C–130s from the 6315th Ops Gp airlifted 485 U.S. civilians from Dacca, East Pakistan, to Bangkok, Thailand, and Manila in the Philippines, with Col. John R. Neal serving as the mission commander.

From September 15 to 21, 14 Air Force C–130 cargo planes evacuated 1,485 U.S. civilians from the fighting in Pakistan. The Air Force returned some evacuees to Pakistan in December after fighting ceased.

16.
Name: Turkish Earthquake.
Location: Turkey.
Date(s): August 20–25, 1966.
Emergency: A series of severe earthquakes struck eastern Turkey, killing 2,300 people and leaving thousands injured and homeless.
Air Force Organization(s) Involved: USAFE; 322d Air Div; Detachments 10 and 116, The United States Logistics Group (TUSLOG) headquarters; 41st Mil Alft Sq; Sixteenth Air Force; and 7101st AB Wg.
Airlifted: 48 tons of relief cargo, mostly medical equipment and supplies; and 148 passengers, including 106 medical personnel.
Aircraft Employed: C–130 (two), C–118 (two), C–131 (one), C–54 (one), and T–39 (two).
Operations: On August 19, earthquakes struck eastern Turkey, leaving 2,300 people dead and thousands more injured and homeless in 149 ruined cities and towns, including Erzurum, Varto, and Mus. The Turkish government and the Red Crescent organization, the Muslim equivalent to the Red Cross, appealed for U.S. aid through the U.S. embassy. The United States Air Forces in Europe, assisted by the Military Airlift Command's 322d Air Div, organized an emergency airlift of medical personnel, equipment, and supplies.

Between August 20 and 25, eight Air Force aircraft carried 48 tons of cargo and 148 passengers to forward bases in eastern Turkey. Detachment 10, TUSLOG, airlifted a 36-bed field hospital and medical personnel from Incirlik AB near Adana to Diyarbakir, Turkey, on August 20, using a pair of C–118 cargo planes. On the same day, the 322d Air Div diverted a 41st Mil Alft Sq C–130 from a routine channel mission in Athens, Greece, to airlift four doctors, 40 medical corpsmen, 260 litters and blankets, and other medical supplies and equipment from Ankara to Elazig, Turkey.

Another C–130 from Rhein-Main AB in West Germany flew a forklift and personnel to unload planes at Elazig. Detachment 116, TUSLOG, at Cigli AB, Turkey, airlifted a 5,100-pound water purification unit to Elazig, using a C–131. A C–54 from TUSLOG headquarters at Esenboga, Turkey, flew four doctors, 16 medical technicians, and tons of medical supplies from Ankara to Elazig. In addition to these cargo planes, two T–39s participated in the airlift operation. The Sixteenth Air Force used one to transport tetanus vaccine from Torrejon AB, Spain, to Elazig, while the 7101st AB Wg at Wiesbaden, West Germany, used another to document the airlift with camera crews.

Among the 106 medical personnel airlifted to eastern Turkey were 10 doctors and dentists, 8 nurses, 3 medical corps officers, and 85 medical technicians.

Medical supplies and equipment included litters, cots, blankets, a field generator, and a water filtration unit. Air Force planes also transported communications equipment to the forward bases. The field hospital began operating at Varto, one of the villages in the disaster zone, on August 21. Within a week, the hospital had treated more than 1,000 earthquake victims, mostly Kurds. Turkish army vehicles transported emergency relief cargo and personnel 150 miles from the forward bases at Diyarbakir and Elazig to the disaster area.

The State Department reimbursed the Air Force for the cost of the airlift. In addition to the military airlift, commercial aircraft delivered 2,500 blankets donated to the earthquake victims by Catholic Relief Services.

17.
Name: Creek Dipper.
Location: Jordan.
Date(s): June 10–11, 1967.
Emergency: Israel and her Arab neighbors went to war. Civil disturbances threatened the safety of the international community in Amman, Jordan.
Air Force Organization(s) Involved: USAFE, 322d Air Div, 513th Trp Carr Wg, and 36th and 61st Tac Alft Sqs.
Airlifted: 816 noncombatants, including 252 U.S. citizens and nationals of 29 other countries.
Aircraft Employed: C–130 (10).
Operations: On June 5, Israel and some of her Arab neighbors went to war. In six days of fighting, Israeli armed forces occupied large portions of Egypt, Jordan, and Syria. Citizens of those countries and other Arab states concluded that the United States and other western nations had somehow helped Israel attain this quick and overwhelming victory. Civil disturbances in Libya and Jordan threatened the safety of U.S. citizens there. The State Department arranged to rescue them.

Between June 6 and 10, the 322d Air Div airlifted almost 7,000 U.S. citizens from Libya to safer locations in Europe (see Chapter 4, Creek Haven, June 1967). Meanwhile, as the war raged, the State Department asked USAFE to rescue foreigners in Amman, the Jordanian capital. The 322d Air Div executed Operation Creek Dipper.

Col. Clayton M. Isaacson served as the mission commander for the Amman evacuation, assembling 14 C–130s at Tehran, Iran. Most came from the 36th and 61st Tac Alft Sqs, on rotation to Europe under the 513th Trp Carr Wg but under operational control of the 322d Air Div. To avoid violence, the airlift proceeded under the auspices of the International Red Cross. Large red crosses were painted on each plane and crew members donned white garments with Red Cross markings. The evacuees traveled from their hotels to the Amman airport before dawn to escape public attention.

On June 10 and 11, 13 cargo planes took off for Amman, but three turned back because they were not needed. Col. Gordon E. Mulvey piloted the first

C–130 into Jordan. On June 11, 10 of the aircraft flew 816 evacuees from Amman to Tehran, including 252 U.S. nationals, 261 Britons, and citizens of 28 other nations, including Algeria, Tunisia, Libya, Yugoslavia, Czechoslovakia, and even the Soviet Union. Passengers included embassy officials and workers, businessmen and their families, oil company workers, and members of international organizations. Creek Dipper's C–130s also carried 15 tons of passenger baggage. The State Department arranged for repatriation of evacuees after their arrival in Iran and about 100 U.S. citizens flew to Athens, Greece, the next day.

18.
Name: Iranian Earthquake.
Location: Iran.
Date(s): September 9–October 10, 1968.
Emergency: An earthquake destroyed or damaged 30 villages east of Tehran, leaving almost 10,000 people dead, more than 2,000 injured, and over 90,000 homeless.
Air Force Organization(s) Involved: 436th Mil Alft Wg.
Airlifted: 82 tons of blankets and tents.
Aircraft Employed: C–141 (three) and C–133 (two).
Operations: On August 31, an earthquake measuring 7.8 on the Richter scale struck northeastern Iran east of Tehran. Centered around Kakhk near the Dasht Kavier Desert, the quake destroyed or damaged 30 villages in a 750-square-mile area. Officials estimated almost 10,000 people dead, more than 2,000 seriously injured, and over 90,000 homeless.

After the Iranian government requested U.S. assistance, AID arranged for a humanitarian airlift operation through MAC. On September 9, Maj. Ronald O. Christophori and Capt. Donald D. Hansen and their crews took off on the initial relief mission, flying a pair of C–141s from the 436th Mil Alft Wg at Dover AFB, Delaware. After loading 5,000 blankets at Hill AFB, Utah, and 1,000 tents at Scott AFB, Illinois, they proceeded via Torrejon, Spain; Incirlik, Turkey; and Tehran to Mashhad Airfield in northeastern Iran. Surface vehicles took the relief cargo from Mashhad to the disaster area.

Other missions followed. On September 25, another 436th Mil Alft Wg C–141 took 21.5 tons of tents from Scott AFB to Mashhad. On October 10, two C–133 Cargomaster airplanes, also from the 436th Mil Alft Wg, airlifted 53 tons of tents from Scott AFB to Mashhad. By October 11, five MAC transports had delivered 82 tons of blankets and tents from the United States to northeastern Iran.

19.
Name: Combat Locust.
Location: Saudi Arabia.
Date(s): February 27–April 23, 1969.

Humanitarian Airlift Operations

Emergency: A desert locust plague, spreading eastward from Africa, threatened Red Sea coastal croplands.

Air Force Organization(s) Involved: Special Aerial Spray Flight, 4500th AB Wg; 1st Sp Ops Wg; 319th Sp Ops Sq; 4410th Combat Crew Training Wing; and 4408th Combat Crew Training Squadron.

Airlifted: 16,250 gallons of insecticide.

Aircraft Employed: UC–123 (three).

Operations: A plague of desert locusts threatened to spread from Africa to India during late 1968 and early 1969. By January, the desert locust population in western Saudi Arabia had begun to rise dramatically, threatening irrigated croplands along the Red Sea. The Saudi government requested help from the United States through the State Department and its Agency for International Development, which contacted DoD for an aerial spraying operation. The operation was known as Combat Locust.

During January, Air Force Lt. Col. John D. Mosely, a veterinarian, led a survey team in Saudi Arabia to plan a strategy against the insects. Between February 27 and March 14, three special UC–123 spray-equipped airplanes from the Special Aerial Spray Flight, 4500th AB Wg, deployed from Langley AFB, Virginia, to a forward operating base at Taif Airport, Saudi Arabia. The planes transited Newfoundland, the Azores, Spain, Italy, Turkey, and Iran on their way, delayed by bad weather along the way, including icing, which could damage the delicate spraying equipment.

The mission commander was Lt. Col. Russell J. Folio and Maj. Stanley O. Swanson served as operations officer. Capt. William Dubose, an Air Force entomologist, helped to supervise the insecticide spraying. Operation personnel came from the 4500th AB Wg, the 1st Sp Ops Wg, and the 4410th Combat Crew Training Wing.

The UC–123 operations began on March 16 and continued through April 8. During those three weeks, two of the three planes flew 66 sorties, spraying 975,000 acres with 16,250 gallons of Dieldrin insecticide. The other UC–123 experienced mechanical trouble throughout the operation. The two operational UC–123 Combat Locust planes used 24 nozzles to spray insecticide at a rate of five gallons a minute as they flew 50 to 150 feet above the ground at an average speed of about 150 miles per hour. Lack of navigation aids and midday heat restricted effective spraying to the early morning hours.

Saudi Arabia contributed to the success of Combat Locust by providing insecticide, fuel, ground facilities, and personnel to help load and wash the UC–123s. The U.S. ambassador to Saudi Arabia, Hermann Frederick Eilts, praised the operation and predicted that it would stop the plague and improve relations between the two countries. Combat Locust aircraft and personnel had returned from Saudi Arabia to the United States by April 23.

20.

Name: Fig Hill.

Location: Jordan.

Date(s): September 27–October 28, 1970.

Emergency: A faction of Palestinians fought troops loyal to Jordan's King Hussein in the streets of Amman and other Jordanian cities, with up to 4,000 people killed or wounded.

Air Force Organization(s) Involved: 313th, 316th, 322d, 464th, 513th, and 516th Tac Alft Wgs; 36th, 38th, 47th, 347th, and 779th Tac Alft Sqs; 436th and 437th Mil Alft Wgs; and TUSLOG.

Airlifted: Two mobile military hospitals; more than 186 tons of medical equipment and supplies, water purification equipment, food, tents, and vehicles; and more than 200 medical personnel.

Aircraft Employed: C–130 (23+), C–133 (1), and C–141 (1).

Operations: In September, a Palestinian faction seized civilian airliners in Jordan. In the streets of Amman, the capital, and in other Jordanian cities, fighting erupted between Palestinian guerrillas and troops loyal to King Hussein, leaving up to 4,000 people dead and wounded. The king appealed for international assistance, specifically requesting medical relief and food.

Working with the International Red Cross and the United States Army in Europe, USAFE helped to organize Fig Hill, a medical relief operation for Jordan that included the airlift of two complete mobile military hospitals. From September 27 to 29, 23 C–130s under operational control of the 322d and 513th Tac Alft Wgs flew the 48th Tactical Hospital from RAF Lakenheath in the United Kingdom and the 32d Mobile Army Surgical Hospital from Kitzingen, West Germany, to Amman.

Among the tactical airlift squadrons from the United States that participated in Fig Hill were the 38th and 47th from the 313th Tac Alft Wg, the 36th from the 316th Tac Alft Wg, the 779th from the 464th Tac Alft Wg, and the 347th from the 516th Tac Alft Wg. Daily resupply missions continued between September 30 and October 28, with C–130s flying to Amman from Ramstein AB, West Germany, via Athens, Greece. Some C–130s airlifted more than 82 tons of food, tents, and medical supplies from Turkey to Jordan for TUSLOG between September 27 and October 5.

The Military Airlift Command also supported Fig Hill, flying vehicles and relief supplies to Jordan aboard a 437th Mil Alft Wg C–141 and water purification equipment aboard a 436th Mil Alft Wg C–133.

All Fig Hill planes flew under International Red Cross sponsorship and were painted with large red crosses on white fields. Crews wore civilian clothes and carried no weapons. The two airlifted military hospitals treated both Jordanian and Palestinian victims of the fighting.

Humanitarian Airlift Operations

21.

Name: Bingol Earthquake.

Location: Turkey.

Date(s): May 25, 1971.

Emergency: An earthquake struck the Bingol area of eastern Turkey, leaving 800 people dead and many injured and homeless.

Air Force Organization(s) Involved: USAFE and TUSLOG.

Airlifted: 4.4 tons of medical supplies, tents, and blankets.

Aircraft Employed: C–130 (one).

Operations: On May 23, an earthquake struck the area around Bingol in eastern Turkey. It destroyed 90 percent of the city, where most houses were constructed with sun-dried bricks, and left about 800 people dead. The Turkish Red Crescent agency collected relief cargo at Ankara, the Turkish capital, for shipment to Bingol.

The United States Air Forces in Europe and TUSLOG responded to the disaster after the Turkish government requested assistance. On May 25, a C–130 Hercules cargo plane airlifted 4.4 tons of medical supplies, tents, and blankets, from Incirlik Command Defense Installation to Ankara for the Red Crescent. Turkish vehicles moved the relief supplies to the disaster zone.

22.

Name: Pakistani Flood.

Location: Pakistan.

Date(s): August 20–22 and September 3–22, 1973.

Emergency: The Indus River and its tributaries, swollen by heavy rain, flooded 20,000 square miles in Punjab and Sind provinces in Pakistan, leaving 2,300 people dead and millions homeless.

Air Force Organization(s) Involved: 63d, 436th, 437th, and 438th Mil Alft Wgs; 349th Mil Alft Wg (Associate); and 1st Sp Ops Wg.

Airlifted: More than 2,400 tons of relief equipment and supplies, including helicopters, boats, fuel, pesticides, seed, fertilizer, tents, food, and medical supplies; and at least 61 passengers, including disaster relief teams, helicopter crews, and fuel specialists.

Aircraft Employed: C–5 (two) and C–141 (12).

Operations: The worst flooding ever recorded in Pakistan devastated 20,000 square miles in Punjab and Sind provinces during August and September. The flooding of the rain-swollen Indus River and its tributaries left 2,300 people dead and millions homeless and destroyed five million acres of crops and one million tons of stored grain.

During mid-August, the Pakistani government appealed through the U.S. embassy for assistance. Working with the State Department, the JCS organized a relief operation that included a massive airlift by MAC. Four C–141 and one C–5 aircraft executed the first phase of the airlift between August 20 and 22. Capt.

356

James A. Gault of the 349th Mil Alft Wg (Associate) flew the C–5 Galaxy, transporting six assembled UH–1 rescue helicopters from Osan AB, Republic of Korea, to Karachi, Pakistan. The four C–141 Starlifters carried helicopter crews, disaster relief teams, ten rubber boats with outboard motors, tents, food, medical supplies, and helicopter parts from Kadena AB, Okinawa, Japan, and Osan to Karachi and Lahore, Pakistan. At least 61 disaster relief personnel and 56 tons of relief cargo rode aboard the C–141s. Capt. Michael W. Halloran, Maj. James O'Malley, and Capt. Robert D. Phillips, all of the 63d Mil Alft Wg, were among the pilots.

A second phase of the Pakistani flood relief airlift lasted from September 3 to 19. The Pakistani government again requested U.S. assistance when flooding in northern Pakistan cut routes for fuel distribution. Five C–141s of the 437th Mil Alft Wg, under the mission commander, Lt. Col. Roy Lemley, shuttled fuel and other supplies from Karachi in southern Pakistan to Islamabad and Lahore in the north. Four Starlifters carried fuel bladders enabling them to ferry 9,000 gallons of gasoline per mission, while the other C–141 bore a pair of huge fuel-dispensing systems. The fuel bladders and dispensing equipment, as well as fuel specialists to operate them, came from MacDill AFB in Florida.

In 17 days, the five Starlifters airlifted more than 2,100 tons of fuel and 224 tons of other relief cargo to Lahore and Islamabad in 99 sorties. The giant aircraft weathered Pakistani flying conditions well. Maintenance personnel from the 437th Mil Alft Wg at Karachi easily handled the worst maintenance problems, performing two engine changes.

In the final phase of the flood relief airlift, the Air Force flew three C–141s and a C–5 to rescue surviving food crops in northern Pakistan. The four cargo planes, representing the 436th and 438th Mil Alft Wgs, transported 104 tons of pesticides, seed, fertilizer, and aerial spray equipment from the United States to Karachi and Lahore during September.

The Tactical Air Command participated in the disaster relief, providing 1st Sp Ops Wg crews to fly a pair of Thai C–47s to spray croplands around Lahore. Between September 13 and 22, the crews sprayed 103,000 acres with 21,000 gallons of insecticide in 31 sorties. The aerial spray helped save what remained of Pakistan's rice crop.

Between August 20 and September 22, 14 Air Force cargo planes airlifted more than 2,400 tons of relief cargo for Pakistan flood relief. Six Air Force wings participated, representing the Military Airlift Command, the Tactical Air Command, and the Air Force Reserve.

23.
Name: Cypriot Refugees.
Location: Cyprus.
Date(s): August 7–September 1, 1974.
Emergency: Fighting in Cyprus between Greeks and Turks left thousands of people homeless.

Humanitarian Airlift Operations

Air Force Organization(s) Involved: 60th, 436th, 437th, and 438th Mil Alft Wgs.

Airlifted: 360 tons of relief supplies, including 60,200 blankets, 5,100 tents, water, and cots.

Aircraft Employed: C–5 (five) and C–141 (two).

Operations: During July, Greek military officers on the Mediterranean island of Cyprus drove President Archbishop Makarios III from power. The new president, Nicholas Sampson, threatened to join Cyprus, where the majority of the population were ethnic Greeks, to Greece. Fearing that the loss of Cypriot independence would endanger the Turkish minority and pose a Greek military threat to Turkey, the Turkish government invaded the island.

Fighting between Turkish troops and Greek Cypriots threatened to escalate into a war between Greece and Turkey, both members of NATO. The UN arranged a cease-fire in early August, but by then, the fighting had driven thousands of Cypriots, both Greek and Turkish, from their homes. When Sampson relinquished the Cypriot presidency and the military junta ruling Greece gave up control in Athens, tensions eased, and factions in Cyprus resumed peaceful means to resolve their differences.

Cyprus requested U.S. assistance for persons displaced by the fighting when the cease-fire made international relief efforts practical. The Agency for International Development arranged a relief operation with DoD. The Military Airlift Command provided airlift.

Between August 7 and September 1, seven Air Force cargo planes, including five C–5 Galaxies and two C–141 Starlifters, airlifted 360 tons of relief cargo from the United States to Cyprus. The cargo included 60,200 blankets, 5,100 tents, water, and cots. Military airlift wings participating included the 60th, 436th, 437th, and 438th. The seven planes picked up their loads at Scott AFB, Illinois; Dover AFB, Delaware; and McGuire AFB, New Jersey, and flew via Torrejon AB, Spain, to Akrotiri, Cyprus. Among the pilots was Lt. Col. Howard Geddes of the 75th Mil Alft Sq. Between August 29 and September 1, he flew a C–5 with 72 tons of supplies, including 2,000 tents, from the United States to Cyprus. Some planes also hauled military vehicles from Sweden to Cyprus for UN peacekeeping forces there.

24.

Name: Mauritian Cyclone.

Location: Western Indian Ocean.

Date(s): February 13, 1975.

Emergency: A cyclone hit the island of Mauritius, destroying electrical power and water storage facilities.

Air Force Organization(s) Involved: 63d Mil Alft Wg.

Airlifted: Two tons of electrical generators, water pumps, water storage tanks, and tents.

Aircraft Employed: C–141 (one).

Operations: On February 6, Cyclone Gervaise hit the island nation of Mauritius in the western Indian Ocean east of Madagascar. The storm knocked out the tiny country's electrical power system, destroyed water storage and distribution facilities, and also left many islanders homeless. The government requested U.S. assistance.

On February 13, the 63d Mil Alft Wg rerouted a C–141 Starlifter cargo plane from a routine Pacific mission to Andersen AFB, Guam, where it loaded two tons of electrical generators, water pumps, water storage tanks, and tents. The aircraft carried the cargo from Guam to Mauritius to relieve cyclone victims.

25.

Name: Turkish Earthquake.

Location: Turkey.

Date(s): November 26–29, 1976, and January 20–22, 1977.

Emergency: A major earthquake struck the Van area of eastern Turkey, leaving more than 3,600 people dead and up to 50,000 homeless.

Air Force Organization(s) Involved: Twenty-first Air Force; 436th and 437th Mil Alft Wgs; 39th, 40th, 61st, and 773d Tac Alft Sqs; and 435th Tac Alft Wg.

Airlifted: 606 tons of relief cargo, including tents, heaters, blankets, cots, fuel cans, forklifts, trucks, food, and medical supplies.

Aircraft Employed: C–5 (1), C–130 (22), and C–141 (17).

Operations: A major earthquake struck eastern Turkey near Van and Caldiran on November 24, leaving at least 3,600 people dead and up to 50,000 homeless. The next day, after the Turkish government requested international assistance through the UN, the State Department asked the JCS to arrange a relief operation. The Military Airlift Command and USAFE collaborated on a two-stage airlift. The first part was flown from November 26 to 29, and the second from January 20 to 22.

The first stage involved 30 airplanes: 1 C–5, 14 C–141s, and 15 C–130s carried 486 tons of relief cargo from RAF Mildenhall in the United Kingdom, Ramstein and Rhein-Main ABs in West Germany, Pisa in Italy, and Cigli in Turkey to Incirlik Command Defense Installation in Turkey. Aircraft from other nations also delivered relief supplies. Because the airport near Van in the earthquake zone could not handle large cargo planes such as the C–5 and C–141, their loads were transferred to C–130s, which shuttled relief supplies from Incirlik to Van after making deliveries to Incirlik. Forty C–130 missions delivered 520 tons to Van between November 26 and 29. The cargo included more than 622 tents, 1,320 heaters, 10,000 blankets, 500 cots, 800 fuel cans, forklifts, trucks, food, and medical supplies.

Between January 20 and 22, the Air Force conducted the second phase of the airlift. Three C–141s transported 500 tents and 1,500 tent poles from RAF Mildenhall to Incirlik, and seven C–130 missions moved 86 tons of cargo on to Van in the disaster region.

Humanitarian Airlift Operations

Air Force organizations participating in the two-phase airlift included the 435th Tac Alft Wg, which controlled the 39th, 40th, 61st, and 773d Tac Alft Sqs while they served C–130 rotational duty in Europe, and the 436th and 437th Mil Alft Wgs, which flew the C–5 and C–141s. In addition to the United States, Italy, Pakistan, the United Kingdom, Denmark, Norway, and Iraq also contributed to the Turkish earthquake relief effort.

26.
Name: Evacuation of Iran.
Location: Iran.
Date(s): December 8, 1978–February 17, 1979.
Emergency: A revolution in Iran, accompanied by violent anti-American demonstrations, threatened U.S. workers and their families.
Air Force Organization(s) Involved: 322d Alft Div; 436th, 437th, and 438th Mil Alft Wgs; and 514th Mil Alft Wg (Associate).
Airlifted: More than 5,800 evacuees, 687 tons of cargo, and 169 pets.
Aircraft Employed: C–5 (34) and C–141 (88).
Operations: In August, a revolt of Islamic fundamentalists threatened the regime of Mohammad Reza Pahlavi, the shah of Iran. Since the U.S. government was the shah's principal ally, the anger of the fundamentalists soon turned against the 44,000 U.S. citizens living in Iran, including at least 950 military and civilian DoD employees and about 8,000 defense-related contractor personnel, and there were violent anti-American demonstrations. In December, the JCS directed MAC to evacuate dependents wishing to leave Tehran, the Iranian capital.

From December 8 to 10, 1978, the Twenty-first Air Force accomplished the first phase of the evacuation airlift. Using two C–5 Galaxy and nine C–141 Starlifter airplanes, the Air Force flew 903 passengers from Tehran's Mehrabad Airport to Rhein-Main AB, West Germany; Athens, Greece; Incirlik, Turkey; Dover AFB, Delaware; and McGuire AFB, New Jersey. Detachment 1 of the 322d Alft Div, stationed at Mehrabad under Lt. Col. Robert R. McWilliams, supervised the airlift. Airport restrictions forced the airlift to operate only during daylight.

The Iranian crisis worsened through the end of the year and into early 1979. A general strike in mid-December forced the shah to ask the leader of an opposition party, Shahpur Bakhtiar, to form a new cabinet, which he did on January 6. Ten days later, the shah fled Iran after 37 years in power. The U.S. ambassador to Iran, William H. Sullivan, ordered most U.S. citizens to leave the country. The Military Airlift Command continued the airlift evacuation from Tehran. C–5 and C–141 cargo planes hauled thousands of men, women, and children to safe haven bases in Europe, including Athens and Frankfurt. Most planes came from the 436th, 437th, and 438th Mil Alft Wgs of the Twenty-first Air Force.

On February 1, the Ayatollah Ruholla Khomeini, an Islamic fundamentalist leader, returned to Iran after 15 years in exile. Khomeini appointed a rival government on February 5 and violent demonstrations forced Bakhtiar to resign on

February 11. Iranian radicals seized the Air Force terminal at Mehrabad Airport on February 12, temporarily halting the U.S. airlift evacuation. On February 14, militants took over the U.S. embassy, but the Khomeini regime released the Americans a few days later. The Air Force flew the last evacuation mission from Tehran on February 17.

Between December 8 and February 17, MAC flew 34 C–5 and 88 C–141 missions to transport 5,801 U.S. nationals, 687 tons of their belongings, and 169 pets, from Tehran to safe haven bases in Europe and to the United States. Commercial Boeing 747 airliners chartered by the State Department continued the evacuation from Iran after February 17.

27.
Name: Hostage Release.
Location: Algeria and Rhein-Main AB, West Germany.
Date(s): January 20–25, 1981.
Emergency: Iran released 52 U.S. hostages it had held for 444 days.
Air Force Organization(s) Involved: 55th Aeromed Alft Sq, 435th Tac Alft Wg, and 89th Mil Alft Wg.
Airlifted: 52 former hostages.
Aircraft Employed: C–9 (four) and C–137 (two).
Operations: After seizing the U.S. embassy in Tehran on November 4, 1979, Iranian militants held 52 embassy staff members hostage for 444 days. On January 20, 1981, the day of President Reagan's inauguration, Iran released the hostages and an Algerian airliner transported them to Algiers, Algeria. The Military Airlift Command brought them home.

Two C–9 airplanes from the 55th Aeromed Alft Sq of the 435th Tac Alft Wg, each transporting 26 former hostages, flew from Algeria to Rhein-Main AB, West Germany, on January 21. Former President Carter greeted them when they arrived in West Germany. They spent four days of rest, medical examinations, and debriefing in a military hospital in Wiesbaden.

On January 25, an 89th Mil Alft Wg C–137 airplane, nicknamed Freedom One, airlifted the 52 former hostages from Rhein-Main AB via Shannon Airport, Ireland, to Stewart AFB near West Point, New York. There they were reunited with family members.

A second C–137 and two C–9s of the 89th Mil Alft Wg joined Freedom One a few days later to transport the former hostages and their families to Andrews AFB, Maryland, for a welcome ceremony in Washington, D.C., at the end of the month.

28.
Name: Lebanese Refugee Relief.
Location: Lebanon.
Date(s): August 23–24 and October 17, 1982.

Humanitarian Airlift Operations

Emergency: Fighting around Beirut left thousands of homeless refugees.
Air Force Organization(s) Involved: 435th Tac Alft Wg.
Airlifted: 3,000 air mattresses, 6,000 blankets, and 800 pounds of emergency shelter material.
Aircraft Employed: C–130 (two).
Operations: Retaliating against attacks by Palestinian guerrillas, Israel invaded southern Lebanon in June, ostensibly to wipe out Palestinian bases. Israeli forces penetrated the Beirut area, the site of a raging civil war. Fighting between Israelis and Palestinians, and among Lebanese factions, left thousands of homeless refugees. The Office of Foreign Disaster Assistance, a component of the State Department's Agency for International Development, requested a military airlift of relief supplies to refugees in Lebanon when commercial airlift was not immediately available.

The Military Airlift Command's 435th Tac Alft Wg, based at Rhein-Main AB in West Germany, performed two humanitarian airlifts for the refugees, one in August and one in October. On August 23–24, a 435th Tac Alft Wg C–130 Hercules cargo airplane transported 3,000 air mattresses and 6,000 cotton and wool blankets from a stockpile at Camp Darby near Pisa, Italy, to Cairo, Egypt, and Larnaca, Cyprus. Navy craft took the mattresses and blankets from Egypt and Cyprus on to Lebanon.

On October 17, the 435th Tac Alft Wg flew another C–130 mission for Lebanese refugees, airlifting 10 rolls of plastic shelter material weighing 800 pounds from Pisa to Beirut. Workers used the plastic to construct tents for homeless persons facing the onset of cold weather.

29.
Name: Yemeni Earthquake.
Location: Southern Arabian peninsula.
Date(s): December 17–26, 1982.
Emergency: A major earthquake struck the Yemen Arab Republic, killing hundreds of people and leaving thousands injured and homeless.
Air Force Organization(s) Involved: 322d Alft Div and 437th and 438th Mil Alft Wgs.
Airlifted: 111 tons of tents, blankets, medical supplies and equipment, and diesel generators.
Aircraft Employed: C–141 (four).
Operations: A major earthquake hit Dhamar province of the Yemen Arab Republic north of San'a on December 13. The disaster left hundreds of people dead, thousands injured, and tens of thousands homeless. The U.S. embassy in San'a requested relief supplies from AID and the Office of Foreign Disaster Assistance, which maintained a stockpile at Camp Darby near Pisa, Italy.

The Military Airlift Command's 322d Alft Div organized an airlift. Between December 17 and 26, the division airlifted 111 tons of tents, blankets, medical supplies and equipment, and diesel generators from Pisa to San'a. Four C–141s manned by crews from the 437th and 438th Mil Alft Wgs participated in the operation, which involved six sorties. Among the pilots were Capt. John Bedford of the 6th Mil Alft Sq and 1st Lt. Edward A. Stromski of the 18th Mil Alft Sq, who flew on Christmas Day.

The Military Airlift Command was not alone in responding to the disaster. Commercial airliners delivered 76 tons of U.S. relief cargo to Yemen. Saudi Arabia, France, the Netherlands, Egypt, and the UN also sent aid to the earthquake victims.

30.
Name: Beirut Bombing.
Location: Lebanon.
Date(s): October 23–December 9, 1983.
Emergency: A terrorist drove a bomb-laden truck into a four-story building housing hundreds of U.S. Marines at the international airport in Beirut, Lebanon.
Air Force Organization(s) Involved: 322d Alft Div; 435th Tac Alft Wg; and 315th, 437th, and 438th Mil Alft Wgs.
Airlifted: 218 wounded and 241 dead bombing victims.
Aircraft Employed: C–141 (27), C–9 (7), and C–130 (1).
Operations: In September, President Reagan sent 1,200 U.S. Marines to Beirut as part of a multinational peacekeeping force. Most of the marines were quartered in a four-story building at the city's international airport. On October 23, a terrorist drove a bomb-laden truck into the building. The explosion killed 241 people, including 239 U.S. citizens, and wounded 218 others, 95 seriously.

Within a few hours of the blast, MAC launched an airlift to remove the casualties. Maj. Frederick E. Barton of the 435th Tac Alft Wg flew the first aeromedical airplane into Beirut, a C–9 from Incirlik AB, Turkey, while Capt. John M. Bookas of the 315th Mil Alft Wg (AF Res) followed in a 437th Mil Alft Wg C–141 and loaded both patients and the dead.

Between October 23 and 30, the 322d Alft Div transported 95 seriously wounded U.S. nationals from the bomb site to various locations in Europe for medical treatment. Seven C–9s, seven C–141s, and one C–130 participated. They also airlifted the 241 bodies to Europe for identification. Twenty additional C–141s carried the 239 dead and 218 less seriously wounded U.S. citizens from Europe to the United States between October 23 and December 9. Among the Air Force organizations participating in the airlift were the 322d Alft Div; the 435th Tac Alft Wg; and the 315th, 437th, and 438th Mil Alft Wgs.

31.
Name: Turkish Earthquake.
Location: Turkey.
Date(s): November 1–5, 1983.

Humanitarian Airlift Operations

Emergency: An earthquake measuring 6.0 on the Richter scale left 1,300 people dead and at least 23,000 homeless.
Air Force Organization(s) Involved: 322d Alft Div, 314th and 435th Tac Alft Wgs, 37th and 50th Tac Alft Sqs, and 437th Mil Alft Wg.
Airlifted: 234 tons of relief cargo, including tents, blankets, stoves, plastic sheeting for shelters, food, and clothing.
Aircraft Employed: C–141 (four) and C–130 (six).
Operations: On the morning of October 30, an earthquake registering 6.0 on the Richter scale struck northeastern Turkey near Erzurum. The disaster killed more than 1,300 people and left at least 23,000 homeless. The president of Turkey, Kenon Evren, asked for international emergency assistance, and the U.S. ambassador to Turkey, Robert Strausz-Hupe, promised relief supplies. The State Department's Agency for International Development and Office of Foreign Disaster Assistance maintained stockpiles of such supplies at Camp Darby near Pisa, Italy, and needed to transport them to the Turkish earthquake victims. Airlift provided the quickest solution.

The airlift occurred in two phases because Erzurum runways were too short to handle large cargo planes. In the first phase, C–141s flew relief supplies to Incirlik AB in southern Turkey. In the second phase, C–130s airlifted supplies from Incirlik to a smaller airfield at Erzurum.

Between November 1 and 5, the 322d Alft Div coordinated the airlift operation. Four C–141s of the 437th Mil Alft Wg transported over 200 tons of relief supplies from Italy to Incirlik. The cargo included tents, blankets, stoves, food, clothing, and plastic sheeting for shelters. Capt. James Stewart flew the first C–141, laden with 13 pallets, each measuring 10 feet high by 13 feet wide. The four Starlifters transported 48 pallets to Turkey.

Six C–130 Hercules cargo planes hauled relief cargo from Incirlik to Erzurum in the disaster zone. Three came from the 50th Tac Alft Sq of the 314th Tac Alft Wg, on rotational duty in Europe, and three from the 37th Tact Alft Sq of the 435th Tac Alft Wg, based at Rhein-Main AB, West Germany. Capt. Allan K. Baker flew the first C–130 from Incirlik to Erzurum. One C–130, commanded by Capt. Greg Sveska, flew to Ankara, the Turkish capital, after unloading at Erzurum. It returned with flour and a snow vehicle.

Cargo planes from other nations also airlifted supplies from Ankara to Erzurum. Ten U.S. cargo planes delivered 234 tons of relief supplies to the disaster zone during the first week in November in 17 missions, 4 by C–141s and 13 by C–130s.

32.
Name: TWA Hijacking.
Location: Lebanon, Algeria, and Syria.
Date(s): July 1, 1985.
Emergency: Terrorists hijacked a U.S. airliner, killed one passenger, and held

some of the other passengers hostage for 17 days.
Air Force Organization(s) Involved: 438th Mil Alft Wg.
Airlifted: 39 passengers.
Aircraft Employed: C–141 (one).
Operations: On June 14, two Shiite Muslim terrorists hijacked TWA Flight 847 en route from Athens, Greece, to Rome, Italy. They forced the Boeing 727 airliner, with 104 U.S. nationals and 49 other passengers aboard, to land in Beirut, Lebanon. For the next few days, the hijackers forced the plane to fly twice to Algiers, Algeria, and back to Beirut. After killing Navy seaman Robert Dean Stethem, the terrorists released most of the passengers, including women, children, and the elderly, but held 39 American men for 17 days.

On June 30, the hijackers released the hostages. A Red Cross convoy flew them from Beirut to Damascus, Syria, where a 438th Mil Alft Wg C–141 Starlifter airplane awaited their arrival. Among the seven crew members were Maj. Leroy Edwards, pilot; Capt. Richard S. Wharton, copilot; Sgt. Dennis T. Oehmsen; and Sgt. Leroy A. McKenzie. On July 1, the C–141 carried the former hostages from Damascus to Rhein-Main AB, West Germany, on a six-hour flight. Vice President Bush greeted the liberated passengers after they landed, and TWA returned them to the United States.

33.
Name: Afghan Refugees.
Location: Pakistan.
Date(s): March 1986–July 1993.
Emergency: Soviet intervention in Afghanistan compounded a civil war that forced millions of refugees to flee to Pakistan.
Air Force Organization(s) Involved: 60th, 436th, 437th, and 438th Mil Alft Wgs; and 375th Aeromed Alft Wg.
Airlifted: More than 900 injured war victims and over 1,000 tons of relief cargo, including clothing, medical supplies, food, tents, blankets, sleeping bags, and ambulances.
Aircraft Employed: C–5, C–141, and C–9 (115 total).
Operations: In December 1979, the Soviet Union forcibly installed a puppet regime in Afghanistan. Years of civil war followed, during which hundreds of thousands of people died and millions were left homeless. More than three million people, some with serious injuries, fled to neighboring Pakistan.

In 1986, Congress passed the McCollum Amendment to the Defense Appropriation Act, which authorized federal funds to transport excess nonlethal DoD property and privately donated relief supplies to the Afghan refugees. In cooperation with the Department of State's Agency for International Development, MAC organized an airlift. Overseen by Dr. Robert K. Wolthuis, the Defense Department's director of humanitarian assistance, the airlift had a twofold purpose: first, to airlift relief supplies to the Afghan refugees in Pakistan; and, second, to transport injured Afghans from Pakistan to hospitals in Europe, the United States, and elsewhere for reconstructive surgery and medical treatment not available in Pakistan.

The Military Airlift Command flew the first mission to Islamabad, Pakistan, in early March 1986. A C–5A delivered 69 tons of medical supplies, cold weather clothing, and ambulances and took 16 injured refugees out of the country for medical treatment. A second C–5 mission followed in April, with 66 tons of medical supplies, food, and vehicles. In May, the Air Force began using C–141 planes in addition to C–5s.

The aircraft typically carried food, clothing, medical supplies, and other relief cargo from Andrews AFB in Maryland via Rhein-Main AB, West Germany, and Dhahran, Saudi Arabia, to Chaklala AB near Islamabad. At Chaklala, the airplane exchanged its cargo for aeromedical evacuation patients and took them back via Dhahran and Rhein-Main AB to Andrews AFB.

After C–141s and C–5s delivered patients to Andrews AFB, C–9s of the 375th Aeromed Alft Wg took the refugees to hospitals across the United States. Between May 1986 and December 1987, the 375th Aeromed Alft Wg flew 350 patients on 26 missions. Other patients were treated at facilities in West Germany, England, Egypt, and Canada. After treatment, the Air Force returned the Afghans to Pakistan.

Between March 1986 and the end of 1987, the Air Force flew 41 Afghan refugee relief missions, using 12 C–5s and 29 C–141s from the 436th, 437th, and 438th Mil Alft Wgs. By June 1987, the Air Force had delivered more than 400 tons of relief supplies to Afghan refugees in Pakistan. The cargo included winter clothing, dried food, tents, sleeping bags, blankets, ambulances, and medical supplies. By the end of October, the Air Force had airlifted 416 injured Afghan refugees to the United States, Canada, Europe, and Egypt for medical treatment, with some flights spanning 17,000 miles.

The relief flights continued after 1987. In May 1988, the 60th Mil Alft Wg flew 73 tons of relief supplies on a C–5 from Kadena AB in Japan via the Philippines and Diego Garcia to Islamabad. Between July and December, the 436th Mil Alft Wg flew seven C–5 airlift missions to transport 504 tons of supplies from Andrews AFB to Islamabad via Rhein-Main AB and Dhahran.

By the end of 1988, MAC had airlifted more than 977 tons of humanitarian cargo to the Afghan refugees in Pakistan. Although Soviet forces withdrew from Afghanistan by the end of February 1989, the civil war continued, and homeless and injured refugees continued to seek haven in camps in Pakistan. In November 1991, MAC flew its 100th mission for the Afghan refugees.

In the spring of 1992, with a legitimate government in place in Kabul, Afghan refugees began returning from Pakistan to their native country. The Air Force flew its final patient airlift in July, by which time it had flown over 900 injured Afghans to Europe and the United States for medical treatment. Air Force planes returned 480 of the patients to Pakistan after treatment, while others returned by commercial aircraft. The Air Force delivered its final load of Afghan relief supplies to

Islamabad in July 1993, the 115th airlift mission. The Afghan refugee airlift had lasted more than seven years.

34.
Name: Kuwaiti Invasion Refugees.
Location: Jordan.
Date(s): September 18–28, 1990.
Emergency: When Iraq invaded Kuwait, hundreds of thousands of foreign workers in the two nations fled to neutral Jordan for safety.
Air Force Organization(s) Involved: 436th and 438th Mil Alft Wgs.
Airlifted: 107 pallets of tents, cots, and blankets; and 36 passengers.
Aircraft Employed: C–5 (two) and C–141 (one).
Operations: On August 2, Iraqi president Saddam Hussein sent his army into Kuwait, a small oil-rich nation on Iraq's southeastern border. Within two days, the invaders had control of Kuwait and began to mass on the border of Saudi Arabia. The UN condemned the invasion, and the United States, in an operation called Desert Shield, rushed military forces to Saudi Arabia to discourage further Iraqi aggression.

Fearing large-scale war, thousands of foreign workers from of Egypt, India, Pakistan, Sri Lanka, Bangladesh, and the Philippines fled Kuwait and Iraq and made their way westward to Jordan. By September 6, over 600,000 had fled to Jordan. Most of the refugees were Egyptians, who quickly returned to their native country. But about 100,000 refugees remained in crowded camps in eastern Jordan, taxing that country's ability to shelter and feed them.

Between September 18 and 28, the United States airlifted 107 pallets of relief supplies to refugees in Jordan, using aircraft and crews from MAC. One C–141 from the 438th Mil Alft Wg transported 11 pallets of tents, cots, and blankets to King Abdullah al-Hussein AB. The same aircraft carried 360 refugees to their homes in Sri Lanka, Bangladesh, and the Philippines.

Two C–5 Galaxies from the 436th Mil Alft Wg also participated in the Jordanian refugee relief operation, transporting 96 more pallets of relief supplies from the United States and Islamabad, Pakistan, to Shaheed Mawaffiq Assalti AB in Jordan. From there, trucks moved the cargo overland to the refugee camps.

George Dykes and Robert Wolthuis from the Department of Defense's humanitarian assistance and global affairs offices praised the success of the refugee operation. The airlift relieved the suffering of some of the refugees and reinforced U.S.-Jordanian relations strained by the two countries' divergent policies toward Iraq.

35.
Name: Kuwaiti Reconstruction.
Location: Kuwait.
Date(s): March–July 1991.

Humanitarian Airlift Operations

Emergency: When the Iraqi army retreated from Kuwait in February 1991, they left behind much destruction, including more than 500 burning oil wells.
Air Force Organization(s) Involved: 60th and 436th Mil Alft Wgs.
Airlifted: More than 1,000 tons of fire-fighting equipment and over 100 fire-fighters.
Aircraft Employed: C–5 (42) and C–141 (three).
Operations: Iraq invaded Kuwait in August 1990 and quickly occupied the entire country. An international coalition led by the United States drove out the Iraqis in February 1991, but not before they had set fire to more than 500 of Kuwait's oil wells. Each well burned at a temperature of about 3,000 degrees and sent clouds of thick black smoke as high as 7,000 feet. The smoke merged with that from other fires, blocking sunlight and creating a need for street lights at midday. Intense heat, toxic fumes, and pollution were serious health hazards. For environmental and economic reasons, Kuwait sought to quell the oil well fires as soon as possible.

Most of the world's leading oil fire experts lived in the United States. To transport them and their equipment to Kuwait, the United States undertook a massive airlift, using mostly C–5 Galaxies because of the size and weight of the equipment. Between March 8 and the end of July, 42 C–5 and three C–141 flights delivered more than 1,000 tons of fire-fighting equipment and well over 100 fire-fighters from the United States to Kuwait. The aircraft came from the 60th and 436th Mil Alft Wgs. Many loaded their passengers and cargo at Ellington AFB, near the oil complexes of Houston, Texas, and flew to Kuwait with a stop at Rhein-Main AB, Germany. At least four U.S. oil fire-fighting companies sent personnel and equipment, including bulldozers, for the emergency.

The airlift succeeded. Between March 19 and May 15, the fire-fighting experts capped 100 burning wells. By the end of the year, most of the oil fires in Kuwait had been extinguished.

The Iraqi invaders also left a trail of destruction in Kuwait's capital. In March and June 1991, MAC C–5s delivered relief supplies to Kuwait to help that country to rebuild. The airlifted cargo helped Task Force Freedom, a military organization of the international coalition, to restore the battered infrastructure of Kuwait after the brutal seven-month Iraqi occupation.

36.
Name: Provide Comfort I.
Location: Iraq, Turkey, and Iran.
Date(s): April 5–July 15, 1991.
Emergency: More than a million Kurdish refugees fled their homes in northern Iraq after a failed rebellion against the government of Saddam Hussein.
Air Force Organization(s) Involved: 322d Alft Div; 60th, 349th, 436th, and 437th Mil Alft Wgs; 302d, 306th, 314th, and 435th Tac Alft Wgs; and 37th and 61st Tac Alft Sqs.

368

Airlifted: More than 7,000 tons of relief supplies, including tents, blankets, clothing, food, medical supplies, and clean water; and thousands of passengers, including refugees and medical personnel.

Aircraft Employed: C–130 (22), C–5 (number unknown), and C–141 (number unknown).

Operations: When the Desert Storm international coalition led by the United States attacked Iraq from the air and drove its forces from Kuwait in January and February 1991, it weakened Saddam Hussein's military power. Restive Kurds in northern Iraq, whom the Iraqi dictator had brutally suppressed in 1988, rose in rebellion in early March. When forces loyal to Saddam Hussein quashed the revolt at the end of the month, threatening to repeat the massacres of a few years earlier, hundreds of thousands of Kurds fled their homes. In early April, a million or more crossed the border into western Iran. As many as 450,000 moved into southeastern Turkey. About 400,000 gathered on cold mountain slopes at the Turkish border. The refugees desperately needed food, clean water, clothing, blankets, medical supplies, and shelter, as more than 1,000 died each day from exposure, hunger, or disease.

In response to the emergency, the UN Security Council authorized an international relief effort for the Kurdish refugees. On April 5, the United States and its allies organized an operation called Provide Comfort, which began with airdrops of relief supplies to the Kurds. The Provide Comfort Combined Task Force, including more than 11,000 Americans and thousands of troops from the United Kingdom, France, Italy, the Netherlands, Spain, and Belgium, set up 43 tent camps for the refugees in an 8,000-square-kilometer security zone in northern Iraq. The camps encouraged the Kurds to leave the cold mountain slopes as a first step to returning home. To protect the Kurds from Iraqi military attacks, the task force enforced a no-fly zone, using U.S. and allied fighters and attack aircraft to patrol the region.

U.S. cargo aircraft supported Provide Comfort. A fleet of more than 20 C–130s, most from the 37th and 61st Tac Alft Sqs and the 302d Tac Alft Wg, airdropped about 600 pallets of relief supplies each day to the Kurds in eastern Turkey and northern Iraq during April. The cargo included tents, blankets, food, clothing, and baby care products. Most of the four-engine transports took off from Incirlik AB in Turkey and staged at airfields at Diyarbakir, Silopi, Batman, and Adana. Some C–130s landed and unloaded at Sirsensk in the security zone after a few airdropped pallets accidentally struck refugees. As the Kurds gradually moved down from the mountains to the tent cities and sealifted cargo began arriving in Turkey, C–130 airdrops declined, and more deliveries were made by Army, Navy, and Marine helicopters or trucks.

Other Air Force cargo aircraft, C–5 Galaxies and C–141 Starlifters, moved thousands of tons of relief supplies from Dover AFB, Delaware, and Charleston AFB, South Carolina, through Rhein-Main AB in Germany to Incirlik, Adana, and Diyarbakir. The larger four-jet transports, from military airlift wings such as

369

the 60th, 349th, 436th, and 437th, could not land at the small airstrips in the security zone. For this reason, C–130s, helicopters, and trucks transshipped relief supplies to the Kurds along the border of Turkey and Iraq.

During the first 20 days of Provide Comfort, C–5s and C–141s flew 75 missions from the United States and Europe to Turkey. When Iraqi ground forces approached the camp areas, C–5s transported allied troops from Italy to eastern Turkey. The coalition forces moved overland to Zakhu, just across the border in northern Iraq, to protect the refugees and encourage them to return to their homes.

A 437th Mil Alft Wg C–141, under the command of Lt. Col. Pryor B. Timmons, Jr., delivered Provide Comfort medical supplies and blankets to Tehran for Kurdish refugees who had fled to Iran. This was the first U.S. aircraft to land in that country since the hostage crisis of 1980.

The establishment of a security zone in northern Iraq, with allied air cover and a military presence on the ground, persuaded most Kurdish refugees to leave the crowded camps and return home. By the end of May 1991, only about 41,000 of the hundreds of thousands of refugees originally sheltered in the tent cities remained. Saddam Hussein met with Kurdish leaders in Baghdad, promising them security and some autonomy. On June 7, the UN assumed responsibility for the remaining Kurdish refugees. During the next week, the Provide Comfort Combined Task Force withdrew its ground troops from northern Iraq, ending the first phase of Provide Comfort.

The primary focus of the operation now shifted from delivery of humanitarian relief to deterring Iraqi military forces from attacking Kurds in their home towns. This was accomplished with allied air patrols over northern Iraq and ground forces in eastern Turkey ready to enter Iraq again, if necessary, to protect the Kurds. Provide Comfort airlift missions continued into 1993, but their purpose was no longer primarily to deliver food, clothing, medical supplies, and other humanitarian relief cargo to Kurdish refugees. Sealift played an increasingly important role in supplying Provide Comfort forces and their Kurdish beneficiaries.

The first phase of Provide Comfort involved U.S. commercial aircraft and planes from at least six other nations and embraced missions not strictly humanitarian. Statistics on the contributions of the Air Force to the humanitarian airlift portion of Provide Comfort are, therefore, difficult to determine. It is clear, however, that U.S. aircraft delivered at least 7,000 tons of relief supplies during the first phase of Provide Comfort, which lasted from April 5 through July 15, 1991.

The difficulties encountered during Provide Comfort taught the U.S. military some important lessons. Military planners needed to review airdrop policies in light of the accidental casualties. They needed to select more carefully which cargo to transport. The Kurds refused western clothes and unfamiliar food, such as corn and potatoes. Dehydrated baby food was a poor choice because it had to be mixed with clean water, which was scarce. Provide Comfort also demonstrated the need for better communication between peoples speaking different languages. Despite these problems, the first phase of Provide Comfort achieved many important goals. It sustained the lives of thousands of people, restrained the brutality of Saddam Hussein, and eased population pressure on southeastern Turkey. Humanitarian airlift proved again a most useful instrument of national policy.

37.
Name: Operation Snow Eagle.
Location: Turkey.
Date(s): February 1992.
Emergency: Avalanches buried scores of villages in the mountains of eastern Turkey.
Air Force Organization(s) Involved: Provide Comfort Combined Task Force and 39th Sp Ops Wg.
Airlifted: 115 tons of blankets, food, and medical supplies; and at least 23 passengers, including medical personnel and injured avalanche victims.
Aircraft Employed: MH–60, UH–60, and HC–130 (at least two each).
Operations: At the beginning of February, winter storms dumped tremendous amounts of snow in the mountains of eastern Turkey, causing avalanches that buried scores of villages. At Gormec, an avalanche buried 18 buildings, killing more than 150 people. The Turkish government asked the Provide Comfort Combined Task Force, which had aircraft in the area, for emergency relief. On February 2, the task force launched Operation Snow Eagle.

The 39th Sp Ops Wg and other Air Force units of the Provide Comfort Combined Task Force flew four-engine HC–130 airplanes and MH–60 and UH–60 helicopters in support of Snow Eagle. During February, they delivered 115 metric tons of blankets, medical supplies, food, and other relief supplies to the avalanche victims. They flew medical teams to the disaster sites and conducted aeromedical evacuations, carrying the injured to Sirnak, Cizre, and other cities for medical treatment. By the end of Operation Snow Eagle, task force aircraft had flown 122 missions to 110 villages.

38.
Name: Turkish Earthquake.
Location: Turkey.
Date(s): March and April 1992.
Emergency: An earthquake in eastern Turkey left hundreds of people dead or homeless.
Air Force Organization(s) Involved: 60th, 349th, and 436th Alft Wgs; 314th Ops Gp; and 3d, 22d, 61st, and 312th Alft Sqs.
Airlifted: More than 165 tons of food, medical supplies, clothing, blankets, and other relief supplies.
Aircraft Employed: C–5 (three) and C–130 (two+).

Humanitarian Airlift Operations

Operations: A series of earthquakes struck Erzincan in eastern Turkey on March 13 and 14. The temblors left hundreds of people dead or homeless without adequate food, drinking water, clothing, medical supplies, and other necessities. Fortunately, a U.S. military task force was already in the area providing relief to Kurdish refugees from northern Iraq (see Provide Comfort I, April–July 1991). Task force leaders diverted some Provide Comfort resources to assist the Turkish earthquake victims.

Although most relief supplies arrived in the Erzincan area by land, airlift played a role. Using C–130 Hercules transports, crews from the 314th Operations Group's 61st Alft Sq, on rotational duty with the Provide Comfort task force in eastern Turkey, flew 25 tons of relief equipment and supplies to the disaster area within 48 hours of the emergency. The cargo included food, water, clothing, and blankets.

Larger C–5 Galaxy aircraft delivered more relief supplies to earthquake victims the next month. On April 12 and 13, a 436th Alft Wg C–5 flown by a 3d Alft Sq crew moved 140 tons of food and medical supplies to eastern Turkey in two missions. The next day, a 60th Alft Wg C–5 with a 22d Alft Sq crew flew two more missions from Pisa, Italy, where the United States maintained a supply stockpile, to Ankara, the capital of Turkey. From there, the relief supplies were shipped by ground to the earthquake region. On April 18, still another C–5, flown by a crew from the 349th Airlift Wing's 312th Alft Sq, transported more relief supplies from Pisa to Ankara. In April, three C–5s flew five missions to relieve the earthquake victims.

39.
Name: Uzbekistan Oil Fires.
Location: Uzbekistan.
Date(s): April 1992.
Emergency: Oil well fires raged unchecked for two months, consuming up to 70,000 barrels a day.
Air Force Organization(s) Involved: 60th and 63d Alft Wgs, and 15th and 53d Alft Sqs.
Airlifted: About 95 tons of fire-fighting equipment.
Aircraft Employed: C–141 (five).
Operations: By April 12, 1992, fires in the oil fields of Uzbekistan near Namangan had been burning up to 70,000 barrels of petroleum per day for two months. The government of the new country, a former Soviet republic and a member of the Commonwealth of Independent States, requested U.S. assistance. The United States responded with an airlift of fire-fighting equipment similar to the one flown to Kuwait to fight oil fires in 1991.

During April, MAC airlifted about 95 tons of specialized equipment from Ellington Field, Texas, near Houston, where it was manufactured, to Namangan. Five C–141 Starlifters, three from the 60th Alft Wg at Travis AFB in California and two from the 63d Alft Wg at Norton AFB, also in California, performed the operation. By the time they reached Uzbekistan, they had flown halfway around the world. Each aircraft loaded about 19 tons of fire-fighting devices in Texas and flew to Namangan via McGuire AFB, New Jersey; Rhein-Main AB, Germany; Incirlik AB, Turkey; and Tashkent, Uzbekistan.

The two 63d Alft Wg C–141s bore crews from the 15th and 53d Alft Sqs. The aircraft commanders were 1st Lt. Dwight McArthur and Capt. Adrian Hayes. Hayes flew on from Uzbekistan to Italy, where his aircraft loaded cargo for an air-lift mission to Sarajevo, Bosnia.

Uzbekistan used the airlifted equipment to extinguish the oil fires, saving vast quantities of one of its most valuable resources. The airlift demonstrated the commitment of the United States to the success of the CIS, to which it had already delivered much relief cargo in Operation Provide Hope (see Chapter 3, Provide Hope, February 1992).

40.
Name: Pakistani Flood.
Location: Pakistan.
Date(s): December 6–20, 1992.
Emergency: A flood.
Air Force Organization(s) Involved: 436th Alft Wg (probably).
Airlifted: 415 tons of engineering vehicles and equipment.
Aircraft Employed: C–5 (six missions).
Operations: After a flood in Pakistan in early December, AMC airlifted 415 tons of engineering vehicles and equipment to Islamabad. The cargo was delivered between December 6 and 20 in six C–5 missions, probably flown by the 436th Alft Wg, which was flying relief supplies to Afghan refugees in Pakistan.

41.
Name: Yemeni Evacuation.
Location: Southern Arabian peninsula.
Date(s): May 7–9, 1994.
Emergency: Civil conflict in Yemen threatened the safety of U.S. and other foreign nationals.
Air Force Organization(s) Involved: 4404th Comp Wg (Provisional), 4410th Alft Sq (Provisional), 62d Alft Wg, 23d Ops Gp, and 4th and 41st Alft Sqs.
Airlifted: 623 evacuees, including 448 U.S. citizens.
Aircraft Employed: C–130 (four), C–141 (one), and C–21 (one).
Operations: Civil war in the Yemen Arab Republic during early May threatened the lives of U.S. and other foreign nationals living in San'a, the capital. After the U.S. embassy requested that they be evacuated, the Central Command undertook an airlift, using aircraft from Air Combat Command and AMC.

On May 7 and 9, a C–141 from the 4th Alft Sq, 62d Alft Wg; four C–130s from the 41st Alft Sq of the 23d Ops Gp; and a C–21, temporarily assigned to the 4404th Comp Wg (Provisional) and the 4410th Alft Sq (Provisional), flew the airlift. They evacuated 623 people, including 448 U.S. citizens, from San'a to Riyadh, Saudi Arabia. From Riyadh, the evacuees obtained commercial air transportation elsewhere.

An ambulance is unloaded from an Air Force C–82 at Tempelhof AB in Berlin for use by the public health department of the city's western sector. (NASM photo.)

This plane was the last official aircraft to participate in the Berlin Airlift and flew out of Rhein-Main AB on September 30, 1949, for the final delivery to Berlin. (NASM photo.)

Donations for Austrian avalanche victims are unloaded after delivery from U.S. bases in West Germany. (NARA photo.)

Soldiers unload food and medical supplies provided by the Red Cross from an Air Force cargo plane in Vienna, Austria. From there, the supplies were shipped by truck to the Hungarian border. (NARA photo.)

Hungarian refugees are ready to board a Military Air Transport Service plane at Munich Riem Airport in West Germany en route to the United States as part of the evacuation of over 10,000 people. (NARA photo.)

Tents, blankets, and food are unloaded from a C–130 at Trapani, Sicily, for distribution to homeless earthquake victims. (NARA photo.)

Relief supplies are unloaded from a C–141 in Bucharest, Romania. (NARA photo.)

An airman comforts a grief-stricken resident of the earthquake-shattered village of San Sebastian on the island of Terceira in the Azores. (NARA photo.)

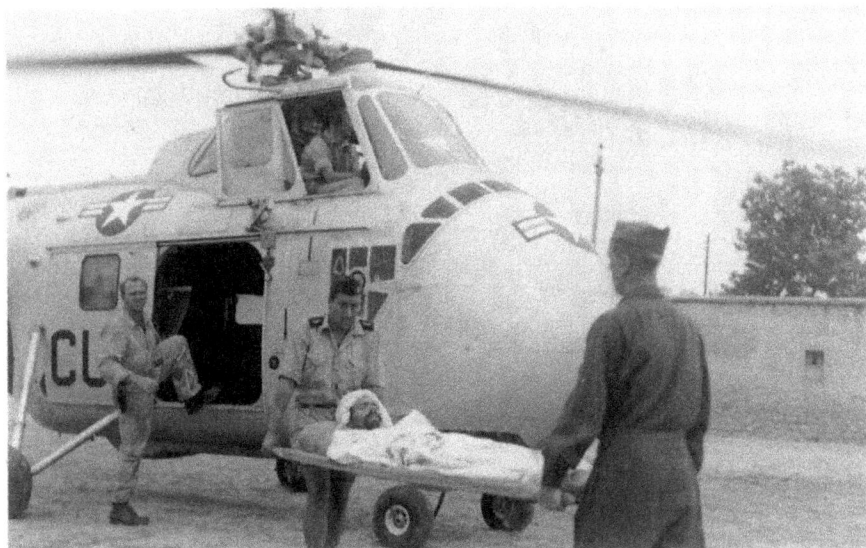

Members of the 58th Air Rescue Squadron help an injured Algerian into an Air Force helicopter after an earthquake struck Orleansville. (NARA photo.)

A U.S. Army helicopter is unloaded from an Air Force C–124 at Mogadishu, Somalia, in November 1961. (NARA photo.)

Moroccan flood refugees crowd onto an Air Force HH–19 helicopter to be flown to the rescue center set up at Sidi Slimane AB communications relay center operated by the Strategic Air Command. (NARA photo.)

Bags of wheat are unloaded from a C–130 in Chad as part of the famine relief effort known as Brisk Cargo. (NARA photo.)

Tunisians help unload food and relief supplies to assist their fellow citizens isolated by floods after severe storms. (NARA photo.)

Local residents gather to look at an Air Force C–130 loaded with grain after it landed on a small desert airstrip near Nema, Mauritania, with supplies to relieve a severe drought. (NARA photo.)

Local children mug for the camera as a captain from the 314th Tactical Airlift Wing takes photos while adults from the community help unload bags of grain from a C–130. (NARA photo.)

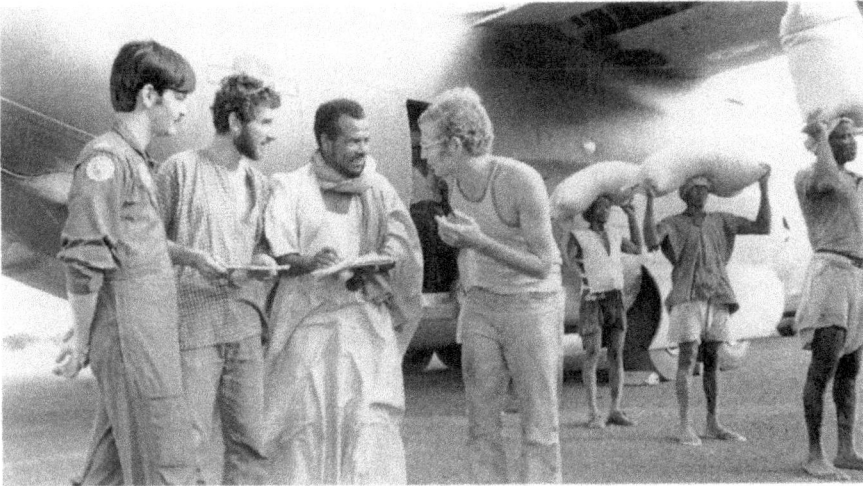

An Air Force pilot, a representative from the U.S. Agency for International Development, a Mauritanian army official, and a Peace Corps volunteer discuss off-loading operations for King Grain, a massive airlift of food to drought-stricken Africa. (NARA photo.)

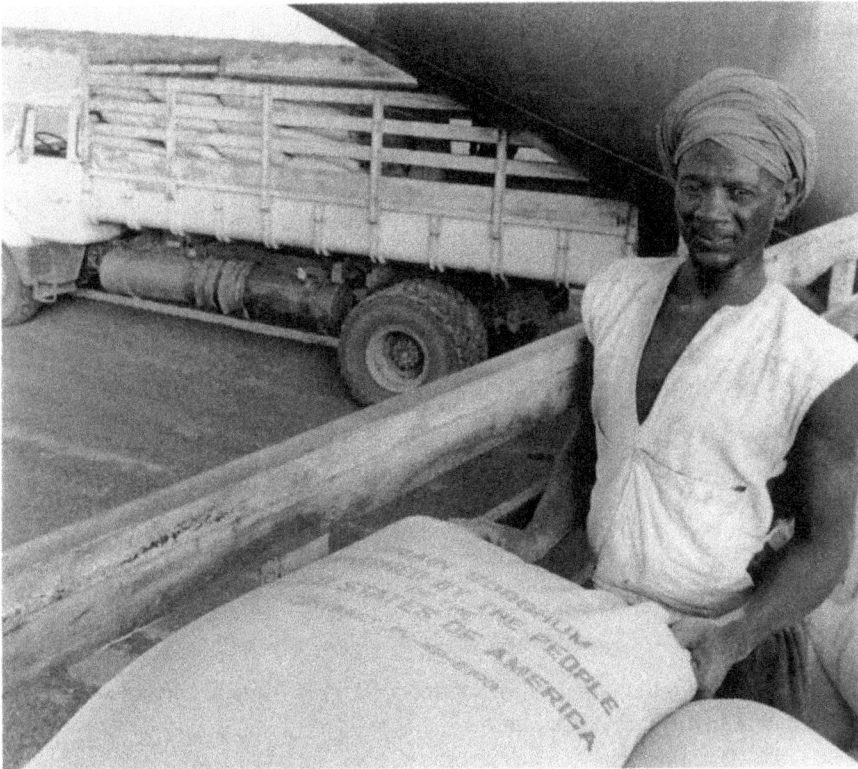

A Mauritanian villager helps unload bags of grain from an Air Force C–130 belonging to the 463d Tactical Airlift Wing. (NARA photo.)

An extending loader is used to load medical and relief supplies onto a commercial contract 747 for airlift to Zaire. (NARA photo.)

A C–130 full of relief supplies for victims of a 1976 Turkish earthquake is unloaded at Incirlik. (NARA photo.)

Pakistani workers load drums of insecticide onto a C–141 at Karachi for shipment to Lahore. (NARA photo.)

Villagers clean up the rubble left in the aftermath of a severe earthquake, as the U.S. military set up tents for temporary shelter in the background. (NARA photo.)

Airmen unload a casket from a C–5 at Charleston AFB, South Carolina, in February 1979, as part of the evacuation of Iran after the Ayatollah Khomeini overthrew the U.S.-supported government of Shah Mohammed Reza Pahlavi. (NARA photo.)

Emergency supplies are placed in a truck as they are unloaded from a C–119 for transport to Indian and Pakistani flood victims. (NARA photo.)

East Pakistani citizens watch the arrival of a C–124 laden with emergency relief supplies. (NARA photo.)

Pakistani laborers unload relief supplies from a C–130 to aid in the nation's recovery from a devastating cyclone. (NARA photo.)

An airman gets a smile from a Korean orphan as he shows her a new dress airlifted by the Air Force in the early 1960s. (NARA photo.)

An Air Force crew member and a young boy unload relief supplies for flood and famine victims from a C–130 at Dacca, Bangladesh. (NARA photo.)

Thai villagers help unload relief supplies from a CH–53 helicopter at Nakhon Phanom AB in January 1975. (NARA photo.)

An Air Force flight nurse straps Vietnamese infants traveling in boxes to the floor of a C–141 in preparation for takeoff from Saigon. (NARA photo.)

Air Force personnel rush Vietnamese refugees onto an awaiting C–130 at Tan Son Nhut AB, near Saigon, in April 1975. (NARA photo.)

Airfield damage on Wake Island was severe in the aftermath of Typhoon Olive. The island rises only 15 feet above sea level. (NASM photo.)

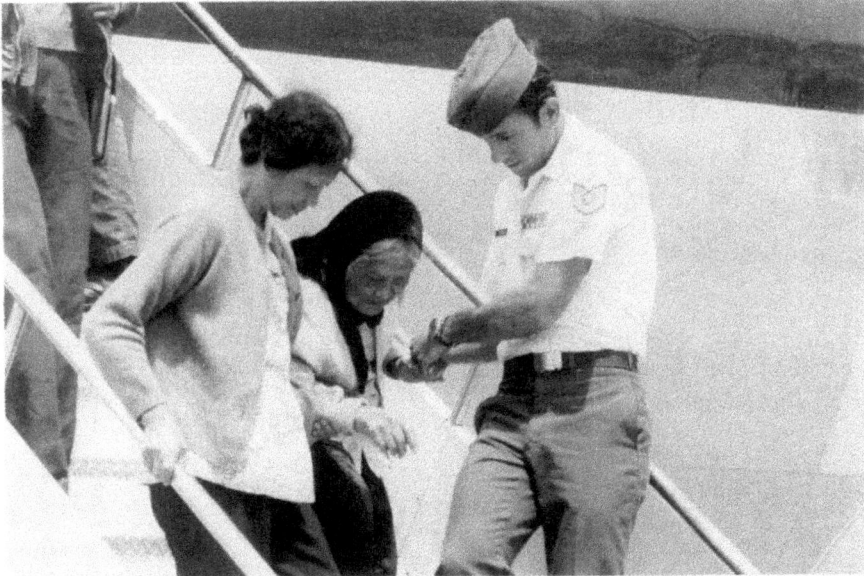

An Air Force sergeant assists an elderly Vietnamese woman as she arrives in the United States in the spring of 1975 after being evacuated from Saigon. (NARA photo.)

An SOS sign marked on the ground (lower right) cries out for help from a flood-stricken valley town in Japan in July 1953. (NASM photo.)

An Air Force C–45 suffered major damage when a roof collapsed on it at Central AB, Iwo Jima, during the onslaught of Typhoon Louise in September 1955. (NARA photo.)

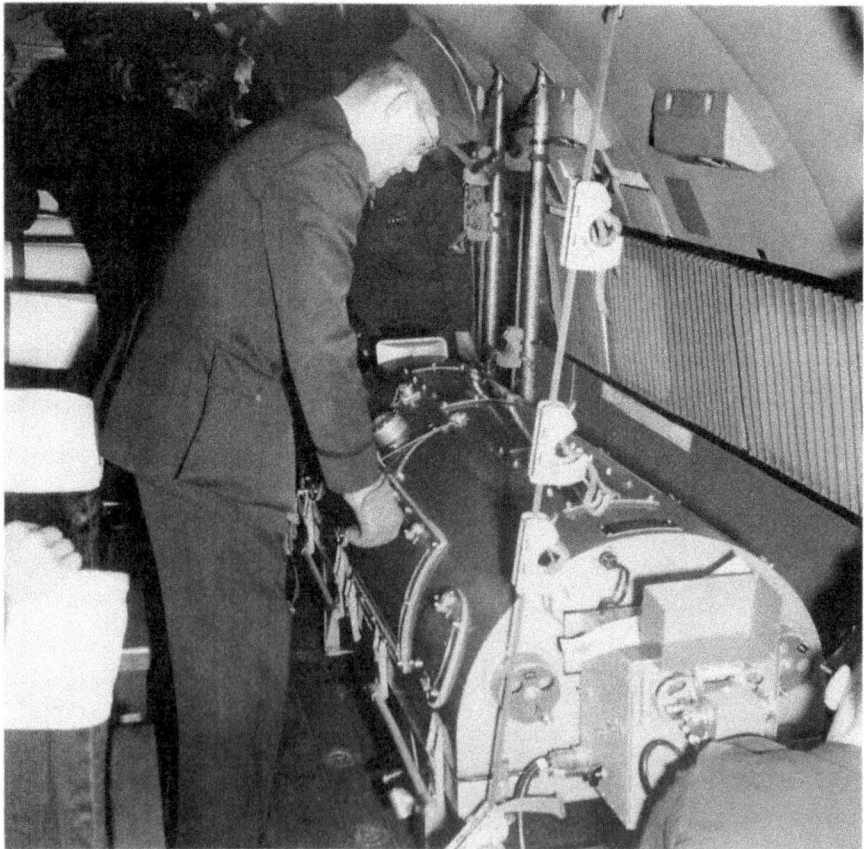

An iron lung is secured for flight on a C–130 cargo plane. (NARA photo.)

Much of Nagoya, Japan, remains under water in the aftermath of Typhoon Vera, the deadliest storm in that nation's history when it hit in early September 1959. (NARA photo.)

U.S. Marines board an Air Force C–118 transport plane at Hickam AFB, Hawaii, for a flight to Guam, and duty as security guards during the recovery from damage left by Typhoon Karen. (NARA photo.)

An Air Force dropmaster gives a final kick to a paradrop container filled with fresh vegetables for snowbound victims of a severe blizzard near Toyama, Japan. (NARA photo.)

A C–130 is loaded with liquid foam and other supplies to help fight fires left by the damage of the Tokachi-Oki earthquake in Japan. (NARA photo.)

A sea of smiling faces surrounds the pilot of a helicopter flown from Clark AB as he distributes a load of relief supplies in a flood-stricken area of the Philippines. (NARA photo.)

Homeless victims of Cyclone Tracy are evacuated on a C–141 after the aircraft unloaded a supply of water purification kits, food, and medical supplies at Darwin Airport in northern Australia. (NARA photo.)

Chapter 6
East Asia

This chapter describes Air Force humanitarian airlifts in the Eurasian mainland east of what is now Pakistan, formerly known as West Pakistan. It does not discuss operations to Japan, Taiwan, the Philippines, and other Pacific Ocean islands, which are covered in Chapter 7. Operations to the Soviet Union or Russia appear in Chapter 3 unless the destination was strictly Siberia.

During the second half of the twentieth century, East Asia has remained important to the United States. It is the most populous region, with China and India having the world's largest populations. An abundance of labor and consumers attracts economic attention from industrialized nations, including the United States. East Asia is also strategically important to the United States because of its proximity to Japan and Taiwan, major U.S. trading partners, and the Philippines, with which the United States has had a historically close relationship.

Nationalism transformed the political landscape of East Asia after World War II. The Allied defeat and expulsion of Japanese forces left a political vacuum in the area, and the United States and the Soviet Union temporarily filled that vacuum in the Korean peninsula, supporting rival regimes. In 1949, the communists in China, with the help of the Soviet Union, came to power in Beijing. Nationalists resisted the return of the French and British to Indochina, Burma, and Malaya. Cultivating new international relationships, the former colonies that became new East Asian nations often turned to the United States, rather than to their old colonial masters, for help in coping with natural disasters.

Korea and Vietnam became the hottest battlefields of the Cold War. Each was divided into two parts, a communist north and a noncommunist south. Between 1950 and 1953, U.S. troops fighting with the UN prevented North Korea from taking over South Korea. U.S. forces fought a protracted war in Vietnam from the early 1960s to 1973, but failed to prevent a communist victory there. The network of U.S. air bases in South Korea and South Vietnam facilitated humanitarian airlifts in East Asia, and the Air Force flew more relief flights in those two countries than in any other part of this region.

Although East Asia is farther from the United States than other regions covered in this book, the Air Force flew more relief operations to this area than to Europe or to Southwest Asia, demonstrating the area's importance to the United States and the ability of air power to extend our national reach. U.S. humanitarian airlifts in this densely populated area relieved victims of natural and man-made disasters. Wars in Korea and Indochina produced refugees, including hundreds of orphans. Only the Middle East compares to East Asia in the percentage of airlifts devoted to war victims.

Humanitarian Airlift Operations

Northeastern Asia—including Siberia, Mongolia, China, and the northern parts of Korea and Vietnam—was off-limits to U.S. airlifters during the Cold War. Until about 1990, the only U.S. humanitarian airlifts to East Asia went to Southeast Asia.

Statistics: East Asian Airlifts

Number of humanitarian airlifts: 63.

Most common emergencies: floods (16), disease or pestilence (14), storms (7), and orphan relief (7).

Most frequent recipients: South Vietnam (16), South Korea (12), India (7), Bangladesh (6), and Thailand (6).

Three largest operations, in chronological order: South Vietnamese Flood, 1964–1965 (1,500 evacuees and over 2,000 tons); Vietnamese Evacuation, 1975 (more than 50,000 refugees and over 8,000 tons); and Sea Angel, 1991 (over 3,000 tons).

Chronological Listing: East Asian Airlifts

1. Himalayan Earthquake	Aug. and Oct. 1950
2. Christmas Kidlift	Dec. 1950
3. Operation Spray Gun	June–Oct. 1951, summer 1952, and Apr. and July–Oct. 1953
4. Indian Pestilence	July 1951
5. Operation Foodlift	July–Aug. 1953
6. Operation Mercy	Aug.–Sept. 1954
7. Indian and Pakistani Flood	Sept. 1955
8. Thai Cholera Epidemic	June 1958
9. East Pakistani Cyclone Relief	Nov. 1960
10. Korean Orphanage Airlift	Early 1961
11. Thai Flood	Sept. 1961
12. Cambodian Flood	Oct. 1961
13. Cheju Do Island Relief	Feb. 1963
14. Operation Lifeline	Apr.–May 1963
15. Saigon Fire	May–July 1963
16. Laotian Medical Airlift	July 1963
17. Locust Infestation	Aug.–Sept. 1963
18. Korean Cholera	Sept. 1963
19. Operation Kunsan	Jan. 1964
20. Thai Medical Airlift	Jan. 1964
21. Vietnamese Cholera Epidemic	Jan.–Feb. 1964
22. South Vietnamese Flood	Nov. 1964–Jan. 1965
23. Operation Warmth	Dec. 1964
24. Dependent Evacuation	Feb.–Mar. 1965
25. South Korean Drought	June–July 1965
26. Vietnamese Orphan Airlift	Aug. 1965
27. Food Airlift	Aug. 1965
28. Elder Blow	Sept. 1965
29. Project Refugee	Oct.–Nov. 1965
30. Operation Paraplegic	Nov. 1965
31. Korat Fire	Late 1965
32. Orphan Evacuation	May 1966
33. Laotian Flood	Sept. 1966
34. Operation Fly Swatter	Oct. 1966–June 1972
35. Bao Loc Milk Run	Nov. 1966
36. Pleiku Orphan Relief	Dec. 1967
37. Refugee and Orphan Aid	Dec. 1967
38. East Pakistani Cyclone	Nov.–Dec. 1970
39. Malaysian Floods	Jan. 1971

Humanitarian Airlift Operations

40. Bonny Jack	June–July 1971
41. Pleiku Evacuation	Apr. 1972
42. Han River Flood	Aug. 1972
43. Cambodian Rice Airlift	Oct.–Dec. 1973
44. Bangladeshi Flood and Famine	Aug. and Dec. 1974
45. Burmese Flood	Aug. 1974
46. Thai Flood	Jan. 1975
47. Singaporean Oil Spill	Jan. 1975
48. Vietnamese Evacuation	Apr.–Sept. 1975
49. Sri Lankan Cyclone	Nov. 1978
50. Cambodian Famine Relief	Dec. 1979
51. Korean Flood	Sept. 1984
52. Korean Shipwreck	Jan. 1985
53. Osan Fire	Apr. 1986
54. Bangladeshi Flood Relief	Sept. 1988
55. Sea Angel	May–June 1991
56. Mongolian Medical Mission	July 1991
57. Chinése Flood Relief	Aug. 1991
58. Mongolian Medical Airlift	Oct. 1991
59. Mongolian Medical Relief	Jan. and Sept. 1992
60. Nepalese Flood	Aug. 1993
61. Indian Earthquake	Oct. 1993
62. Indian Airlift	May 1994
63. Siberian Flood	Oct. 1994

Operations: East Asian Airlifts

1.
Name: Himalayan Earthquake.
Location: India.
Date(s): August and October 23–30, 1950.
Emergency: An earthquake measuring more than 8.0 on the Richter scale struck the Himalayas of northeastern India.
Air Force Organization(s) Involved: 1600th and 1602d Air Trpt Wgs and 1414th AB Gp.
Airlifted: 11 tons of medical supplies.
Aircraft Employed: C–54 (two+).
Operations: An earthquake registering more than 8.0 on the Richter scale, one of the worst in history, struck the Himalayas of northeastern India on August 15. Landslides and flooding compounded the disaster, leaving 1,000 people dead and thousands injured and homeless in India's state of Assam. Prime Minister Jawaharlal Nehru appealed for international emergency aid.

Despite demands resulting from the outbreak of the Korean War, MATS flew two airlifts. In August, a 1414th AB Gp C–54 carried six tons of medical supplies from Dhahran, Saudi Arabia, to Dum Dum Airport in Calcutta, from which they were shipped by other means to Assam. In October, C–54 cargo planes of the 1600th and 1602d Air Trpt Wgs flew five tons of American Red Cross medical supplies to India. The route extended from Westover AFB, Massachusetts; to Frankfurt, West Germany; to Dhahran; to New Delhi, India. Indian vehicles drove the medical supplies from New Delhi to the disaster region.

2.
Name: Christmas Kidlift.
Location: South Korea.
Date(s): December 20–21, 1950.
Emergency: A Communist Chinese military offensive threatened orphanages in the Seoul area.
Air Force Organization(s) Involved: 61st Trp Carr Gp.
Airlifted: About 1,000 children.
Aircraft Employed: C–54 (12).
Operations: In December, Communist Chinese military units driving UN forces from North Korea approached the South Korean capital of Seoul. The directors of several orphanages in the area feared that enemy occupation or combat operations would threaten the lives of their children. For this reason, they moved about 1,000 infants and children up to the age of 12 to Inchon to meet a ship, which, it was expected, would move them to the relatively safe island of Cheju Do. While waiting for the ship, the orphans suffered from inadequate food and shelter and many became ill. When the ship did not arrive, orphanage directors appealed to the Fifth

Air Force chaplain for Air Force assistance. The chaplain relayed the request to the Combat Cargo Command.

The commander of the Combat Cargo Command, Lt. Gen. William H. Tunner, agreed to airlift the orphans from Kimpo Airfield near Seoul to Cheju Do. Flying 12 C–54 Skymasters, the 61st Trp Carr Gp launched Operation Christmas Kidlift from Kimpo on December 20. One aircraft carried as many as 122 passengers. Flight crews gave their own food to the orphans and laid straw mats and blankets on the aircraft floor for the passengers. Ten C–54s arrived at Cheju Do Island the same day, with two landing with radio guidance because the sun had already set. The remaining Skymasters flew to Ashiya and Itazuke ABs in Japan for the night and continued to Cheju Do the next day.

En route to Cheju Do, some children died from malnutrition or overexposure contracted before the airlift, but the majority of the orphans arrived safely on the island, where food and shelter was available at an old school.

The 61st Trp Carr Gp did not forget the airlifted children. In April 1951, group members followed up the exodus with an airlift of six tons of rice for the orphans. In December 1951, one year after the evacuation, the group flew a Santa Claus laden with presents to Cheju Do. The 61st Trp Carr Gp also raised $3,000 for the orphanage.

3.
Name: Operation Spray Gun.
Location: South Korea.
Date(s): June–October 1951, summer 1952, and April and July–October 1953.
Emergency: Large insect populations spread diseases such as malaria and dysentery among South Koreans and UN troops.
Air Force Organization(s) Involved: 315th and 437th Trp Carr Wgs.
Airlifted: DDT insecticide.
Aircraft Employed: C–46 (two) and T–6 (six).
Operations: During the spring of 1951, high rates of insect-borne diseases such as malaria and dysentery alarmed Air Force and Army doctors in South Korea. The 315th Trp Carr Wg responded with an aerial spray operation called Spray Gun. Between June and October, the 437th Trp Carr Wg employed a pair of C–46 airplanes equipped with 850-gallon insecticide tanks and special spray equipment to cover thousands of acres in South Korea with DDT insecticide. Small Army L–5 liaison aircraft assisted the C–46s. The planes flew at low levels ranging from 50 to 100 feet over cities and military installations.

The insecticide sharply reduced swarms of mosquitoes, flies, lice, and ticks. Medical experts reported a decline in the incidence of insect-borne diseases. The onset of cold weather, which temporarily eliminated the insect problem, ended the first phase of Operation Spray Gun in October.

The project resumed in June 1952, with the 315th Trp Carr Wg being replaced by the 437th Trp Carr Wg, which took over its C–46 spray aircraft.

Flying from Brady Field, Japan, the 315th Trp Carr Wg planes sprayed South Korean cities and military installations with insecticide throughout the summer, returning over each target area every week or two. Four Air Force T–6 training aircraft replaced the L–5 Army planes used the previous year to help the two C–46s.

The 315th Trp Carr Wg flew the third phase of the aerial spraying project in April and July to October 1953, using one C–46. During those five months, the plane flew 160 missions and sprayed 588,625 acres in South Korea.

In three years, Operation Spray Gun reduced dangerously high insect numbers and kept disease rates low. Some missions also helped to save forests threatened by pine borers.

4.
Name: Indian Pestilence.
Location: India.
Date(s): July 1951.
Emergency: Swarms of locusts threatened crops in northwestern India as the nation suffered from a drought-induced famine.
Air Force Organization(s) Involved: Twelfth Air Force.
Airlifted: Up to 10 tons of insecticide.
Aircraft Employed: C–47 (two).
Operations: Drought struck northern India in 1951, producing severe food shortages in the second most populous nation in the world. In May, desert locusts invaded the Rajputana region in northwestern India, threatening to destroy thousands of acres of millet, the area's staple food. On June 2, U.S. representatives in New Delhi signed an agreement with the Indian government for a cooperative locust control campaign.

The project enlisted USAFE aircraft assigned to the Twelfth Air Force and U.S. civilian planes that had just completed aerial spraying a locust infestation in Iran. In July, two Air Force C–47s Skytrains and the civilian planes, operating from New Delhi, sprayed 10 tons of aldrin insecticide, diluted with kerosene and diesel fuel, over Rajputana's fields. The pest control campaign reduced the locust population in northwestern India enough to save significant quantities of the millet desperately needed to fight the continuing drought-induced famine.

5.
Name: Operation Foodlift.
Location: South Korea.
Date(s): July–August 1953.
Emergency: The Korean War left thousands of people without adequate food.
Air Force Organization(s) Involved: 315th Air Div and 315th and 483d Trp Carr Wgs.
Airlifted: 429 tons of C rations.
Aircraft Employed: C–46 and C–119 (numbers unknown).

Humanitarian Airlift Operations

Operations: By the time of the Korean War armistice on July 27, 1953, thousands of Korean refugees lacked adequate food. Immediately after the truce, the 315th Air Div airlifted 429 tons of C rations from U.S. military stockpiles in Japan to South Korea. 315th Trp Carr Wg C–46s from Brady AB and 483d Trp Carr Wg C–119s from Ashiya AB participated in the project, dubbed Operation Foodlift.

The United Nations Civil Assistance Command in Korea accepted the food rations for distribution to destitute South Koreans. Each 6-in-1 ration could feed a family of five for one day. The food airlift helped South Koreans survive until more permanent UN and U.S. reconstruction projects could help them recover from the war.

6.
Name: Operation Mercy.
Location: India and Pakistan.
Date(s): August–September 1954.
Emergency: Monsoon rains flooded the Brahmaputra and Ganges Rivers in India and East Pakistan, inundating 36,000 square miles and driving nearly 10 million people from their homes.
Air Force Organization(s) Involved: 315th Air Div; 60th, 317th, 374th, 465th, and 483d Trp Carr Wgs; 60th Trp Carr Gp; and 1600th Air Trpt Gp.
Airlifted: More than 150 tons of relief cargo, including medical supplies, blankets, sheets, food, clothing, and helicopters; and 80 medical personnel.
Aircraft Employed: C–119 (18), C–124 (10), and C–54 (1).
Operations: Heavy summer monsoon rains flooded the Brahmaputra and Ganges River valleys in northeastern India and East Pakistan. Floodwaters inundated 36,000 square miles of land inhabited by nearly 10 million people. The flood caused a food shortage by cutting roads and railways and created a cholera threat by polluting water supplies. After the governments of Pakistan and India requested U.S. assistance to deliver relief supplies to the flood victims, the Air Force organized an airlift called Operation Mercy.

Between early August and early September, at least 27 Air Force cargo planes delivered more than 125 tons of relief cargo and 80 medical personnel to India and Pakistan. The aircraft included 18 C–119 Flying Boxcars, at least 8 C–124 Globemaster IIs, and 1 C–54. Cargo included medical supplies, blankets, sheets, food, clothing, and helicopters. Six wings representing three commands lent aircraft for the operation.

Most of the C–119s belonged to three wings of USAFE. The 60th Trp Carr Gp, assigned to the 60th Trp Carr Wg, flew four C–119 Flying Boxcars to airlift more than 8.5 tons of medical supplies, sheets, blankets, and food from International Red Cross stockpiles in Geneva, Switzerland, to Dacca, East Pakistan. The planes originated from Rhein-Main AB, West Germany, and flew via Greece, Cyprus, Saudi Arabia, and India. From Neubiberg AB in West Germany came six more C–119s of the 317th Trp Carr Wg. They delivered Red

Cross supplies from Geneva to Karachi, West Pakistan; Dacca; and New Delhi, India. Among the aircraft commanders were Maj. Philip N. Currier, Capt. Thomas D. C. McCready, and 1st Lt. Richard D. Noe. The 465th Trp Carr Wg at Toul-Rosiere AB in France used four C–119s to carry 21 tons of Red Cross supplies from Geneva to Karachi and New Delhi. These planes flew via Italy, Cyprus, and Saudi Arabia in flights spanning 6,000 miles.

Wings of the Far East Air Forces' 315th Air Div also participated in Operation Mercy. The 374th Trp Carr Wg, based at Tachikawa AB in Japan, flew eight C–124 Globemaster IIs and one C–54 to airlift two H–19 helicopters; 95 tons of medical supplies, blankets, and clothing; and 80 Army medics from the 37th Medical Preventive Medicine Company in South Korea to Dacca. The planes flew via Clark AB in the Philippines and Calcutta, India. Four C–119s from the 483d Trp Carr Wg airlifted medical supplies and food from Ashiya AB, Japan, to Dacca in early September.

The Military Air Transport Service also lent support to Operation Mercy. Two C–124s, probably from the 1600th Air Trpt Gp, airlifted 27 tons of medical supplies to Dacca from Westover AFB, Massachusetts. Double crews facilitated the long mission, which routed through North Africa.

Operation Mercy ended about September 20. By providing extensive humanitarian aid to flood victims in India and East Pakistan, the United States expressed goodwill. Airlift made this expression practical and prompt.

7.
Name: Indian and Pakistani Flood.
Location: India and East Pakistan.
Date(s): September 1955.
Emergency: Monsoon rains flooded river valleys in south central Asia, inundating thousands of villages and driving at least 16 million people from their homes.
Air Force Organization(s) Involved: 322d Air Div and 317th Trp Carr Wg.
Airlifted: More than 36 tons of medicine, clothing, food, and other relief supplies.
Aircraft Employed: C–119s (9+).
Operations: Especially heavy monsoon rains in September flooded river valleys in some of the most densely populated areas of southern Asia. The Mahanadi, Brahmaputra, Ganges, and other rivers in eastern India and East Pakistan spilled over their banks, flooding thousands of towns and villages and driving at least 16 million people from their homes. As many as 10,000 square miles of land were inundated in East Pakistan and the Indian states of Orissa, West Bengal, Bihar, Assam, and Uttar Pradesh.

Responding to appeals from the International Red Cross and the governments of India and Pakistan, the Air Force launched a humanitarian airlift operation for the flood victims. Between September 5 and 9, at least seven U.S. cargo planes delivered 20 tons of food, medicine, and clothing from International Red

Cross stockpiles in Geneva, Switzerland, to Karachi, West Pakistan, and New Delhi, India. In late September, two C–119 Flying Boxcars from the 317th Trp Carr Wg at Neubiberg AB, West Germany, transported more relief supplies from West Berlin to New Delhi and Karachi. During September, the Air Force airlifted more than 36 tons of relief cargo to flood victims.

The airlift marked the beginning of a larger U.S. relief effort as the State Department organized huge shipments of wheat that reached the subcontinent by sea during October.

8.

Name: Thai Cholera Epidemic.
Location: Thailand.
Date(s): June 1958.
Emergency: A cholera epidemic struck Thailand, killing more than 200 people.
Air Force Organization(s) Involved: 1502d and 1611th Air Trpt Wgs, 483d Trp Carr Wg, and 18th Air Trpt Sq.
Airlifted: More than five tons of medical equipment and supplies, including over 300,000 doses of cholera vaccine.
Aircraft Employed: C–130 (one), C–124 (one), and C–118 (one).
Operations: A cholera epidemic swept across Thailand at the end of May and in June. By June 5, more than 200 people had died from the disease, with more than 1,400 confirmed cases of the disease. Responding to a Thai request for cholera vaccine and medical equipment, Floyd L. Whittington of the State Department coordinated U.S. aid to Thailand, with the Air Force providing airlift support.

On June 10, a C–118 from the 18th Air Trpt Sq of the 1611th Air Trpt Wg flew five tons of medical equipment and cholera vaccine from McGuire AFB, New Jersey, to Travis AFB, California. There the medical cargo was transferred to a 1502d Air Trpt Wg C–124, which airlifted it, along with some medical personnel, across the Pacific Ocean and the South China Sea to Bangkok, capital of Thailand. The commander of the Atlantic Division, Maj. Gen. William S. Stone, accompanied the cargo. A 483d Trp Carr Wg C–130 also participated in the June airlift by flying 300,000 doses of cholera vaccine to Bangkok from reserve military stocks at Manila in the Philippines.

9.

Name: East Pakistani Cyclone Relief.
Location: East Pakistan.
Date(s): November 1960.
Emergency: Two cyclones hit East Pakistan, bringing torrential rains and tidal surges that flooded large areas of the country, killing thousands of people and leaving 100,000 homeless.
Air Force Organization(s) Involved: 322d Air Div and 62d Trp Carr Wg.

Airlifted: 89 tons of blankets, water purification powder, tents, medical supplies, and vitamins.

Aircraft Employed: C–130 (six) and C–124 (one).

Operations: From the warm waters of the Bay of Bengal, two cyclones struck East Pakistan during October. Their torrential rains and tidal surges flooded a host of communities, including Chittagong, Moakhali, Barisal, Noakhali, and Bakergan. Estimates of dead ranged from 4,000 to 15,000, with 100,000 left homeless. President Mohammed Ayub Khan of Pakistan requested U.S. assistance through the State Department, which contacted the JCS for military support. The International Cooperative Assistance Program helped fund the relief, which involved resources from the U.S. Army, Navy, and Air Force.

Between November 3 and 11, the United States Air Forces in Europe's 322d Air Div airlifted more than 77 tons of Army supplies from Europe to East Pakistan. Six C–130s, operated by 40th and 41st Trp Carr Sq aircrews, flew from France to Chittagong and Dacca, stopping en route at Athens, Greece; Tehran, Iran; Karachi, West Pakistan; and Calcutta, India, in an air route that stretched 6,000 miles. Cargo included 25,000 blankets, 20 tons of water purification powder, three tons of sulfa drugs, 39,500 antimalaria tablets, and three tons of vitamins. The planes returned to Evreux-Fauville AB, France, on November 14.

The JCS also directed MATS to airlift relief supplies to the flood victims. In late November, a 62d Trp Carr Wg C–124 transported 35 large Navy hospital tents weighing 12 tons from Point Mugu NAS near Los Angeles, California, to Chittagong, a distance of 10,000 miles. Each tent sheltered an area measuring 50 feet by 16 feet, and the Pakistanis used them to replace school buildings lost in the flood.

After the tents were unloaded, grateful Chittagong residents treated Capt. William L. Butler and his six crew members to an American-style breakfast. On that fourth Thursday in November, it was an appropriate Thanksgiving feast for the Americans.

10.

Name: Korean Orphanage Airlift.

Location: South Korea.

Date(s): Early 1961.

Emergency: A Korean orphanage appealed for children's clothing.

Air Force Organization(s) Involved: 815th Trp Carr Sq.

Airlifted: Two tons of children's clothing.

Aircraft Employed: C–130 (one).

Operations: When U.S. military chaplains in Tokyo, Japan, learned of a need for children's clothing at an orphanage near Osan AB in South Korea, they organized a collection drive. During early 1961, they gathered nearly two tons of clothes. Volunteers from the Tachikawa AB chapel packed the clothes, which filled 55 boxes. An 815th Trp Carr Sq C–130 on a routine training flight airlifted the clothes from Tachikawa to Osan, where they were taken to the orphanage for distribution to the children.

11.
Name: Thai Flood.
Location: Thailand.
Date(s): September 5, 1961.
Emergency: Heavy rain flooded the area around Ban Mae Chiang Hai, isolating 4,000 people.
Air Force Organization(s) Involved: 315th Air Div and 817th Trp Carr Sq.
Airlifted: More than 12 tons of rice and medical supplies.
Aircraft Employed: C–130 (one).
Operations: At the beginning of September, heavy rain flooded the Nam Bae Wang River valley in the Mae Chaem district of northwestern Thailand. High water blocked roads and isolated about 4,000 people in the town of Ban Mae Chiang Hai, depriving them of food supplies. Officials in Chiang Mai, a city about 50 miles east of the flooded town, organized a collection of rice and requested that aircraft drop it to stranded flood victims. The Thai government passed the request to the U.S. air attaché in Bangkok.

On September 4, Capt. James W. Coulter and his crew flew an 817th Trp Carr Sq C–130 Hercules transport plane from the 315th Air Division's Detachment 1 at Naha AB, Okinawa, through Bangkok to Chiang Mai. There the plane was loaded with over 12 tons of rice and medical supplies. On the morning of September 5, Coulter's plane, guided by a Thai C–47, airdropped the grain and medicine in 10 passes to the people of Ban Mae Chiang Hai. Together, the U.S. C–130 and the Thai C–47 delivered more than 300 bags of rice. Thai officials and reporters rode aboard the Hercules to witness the relief effort. On September 6, the C–130 and its crew returned to Okinawa, their mission accomplished.

12.
Name: Cambodian Flood.
Location: Cambodia.
Date(s): October 4–13, 1961.
Emergency: The Mekong River flooded Phnom Penh, capital of Cambodia.
Air Force Organization(s) Involved: 315th Air Div, 815th Trp Carr Sq, and 1503d Air Trpt Wg.
Airlifted: More than 260 tons of water purification and construction equipment and sandbags.
Aircraft Employed: C–130 (two) and C–124 (seven).
Operations: During early October, the Mekong River flooded large parts of Indochina, including Phnom Penh, the capital of Cambodia. The Cambodian government requested water purification and construction equipment, and the U.S.

embassy forwarded the request to the U.S. Pacific Command. The 315th Air Div organized an airlift of Army supplies from Japan to Cambodia, under the direction of Brig. Gen. Theodore G. Kershaw.

The U.S. Army Engineer Agency, Japan, gathered nearly 260 tons of relief equipment, including five water purification units weighing 30 tons each, four 22-ton cranes, and one 20-ton tractor from storehouses in Sagamihara City, Japan. Two C–130s from the 815th Trp Carr Sq at Tachikawa AB, Japan, took the water purification units, while five C–124s from the 1503d Air Trpt Wg at Yokota AB, Japan, stripped of all excess weight, carried the cranes and tractor. The seven transports flew to Phnom Penh on October 4.

Later in October, as the Mekong River flood continued to inundate parts of Phnom Penh, the Cambodian government requested another U.S. airlift, this time to deliver sandbags. On October 13, two 1503d Air Trpt Wg C–124s airlifted 100,000 sandbags from Japan to Cambodia, stopping at Clark AB in the Philippines for refueling. The 315th Air Div supervised the operation, with the cargo coming from the U.S. Army Engineer Agency, Japan.

13.
Name: Cheju Do Island Relief.
Location: Cheju Do Island.
Date(s): February 8, 1963.
Emergency: Heavy snow isolated residents of a South Korean island, depriving them of food and mail.
Air Force Organization(s) Involved: 1503d Air Trpt Wg and 6th Trp Carr Sq.
Airlifted: 3.5 tons of food and mail.
Aircraft Employed: C–124 (one).
Operations: A blizzard isolated inhabitants of Cheju Do Island south of the Korean mainland during early February. With the island's airfield temporarily blocked, residents radioed for food. The 315th Air Div directed the 1503d Air Trpt Wg to drop rations to snowbound islanders. On February 8, Maj. Bernice I. Goode and a crew from the 6th Trp Carr Sq flew a C–124 Globemaster II transport plane over the island. From an altitude of 1,500 feet, the crew airdropped 7,000 pounds of food and mail. Deep snow cushioned the landing of the emergency packages, all of which fell in the target area.

14.
Name: Operation Lifeline.
Location: Republic of Vietnam.
Date(s): April, May, and September 1963.
Emergency: Hundreds of Vietnamese orphans lacked adequate food, clothing, and other supplies.
Air Force Organization(s) Involved: 4440th Aircraft Delivery Group and 817th Trp Carr Sq.

Humanitarian Airlift Operations

Airlifted: More than 14 tons of wheat, clothing, toys, baby food, soap, citrus juice, and other supplies.

Aircraft Employed: C–130 (seven).

Operations: When Air Force Capt. Hiram R. (Rex) Sullivan of Da Nang AB in South Vietnam visited the nearby Sacred Heart Orphanage in June 1962, he was moved by the needs of the 200 children there. He organized an unofficial relief effort he called Operation Lifeline. At first, the operation was limited to Air Force personnel in the Da Nang area willing to lend time and labor, but it grew as Sullivan sent letters of appeal to PACAF. By the time his tour of duty in Vietnam ended in April 1963, Operation Lifeline had grown into an Air Force-wide effort to help more than 700 orphans at seven orphanages across South Vietnam.

Air Force headquarters approved the use of cargo planes to airlift contributions of food, clothing, and other supplies to the South Vietnamese orphanages on a space-available basis. In April, May, and September 1963, seven C–130s—five from the 817th Trp Carr Sq of the 315th Air Div and two from the 4440th Aircraft Delivery Group—airlifted more than 14 tons of wheat, clothing, toys, baby food, soap, and other supplies to Da Nang and Saigon.

Lt. Alfred Schwab piloted the first plane to Da Nang on April 12, delivering half a ton of clothing, food, toys, and soap from the 817th Trp Carr Sq at Naha AB, Okinawa. Robins AFB in Georgia, Amarillo AFB in Texas, and Hickam AFB in Hawaii also contributed goods for the orphan airlift. Most of the wheat came from the Tulia, Texas, area after Lt. Teddy R. Lowe, 315th Air Div air terminal commander at Da Nang AB, wrote to his father in Tulia soliciting food contributions from his community. Volunteers delivered the wheat to Amarillo AFB for the airlift.

Florida citrus growers and canners contributed 760 cases of citrus juice to Operation Lifeline airlift in September. They responded to a request from Capt. E. T. Morgan, an airman from Venice, Florida, stationed in South Vietnam. Morgan's father-in-law, J. Leighton Cornwell, contacted the Venice Chamber of Commerce for support.

At least one of the 4440th Aircraft Delivery Group C–130s flew relief cargo from a modification center at Robins AFB to South Vietnam, stopping at Amarillo and Hickam AFBs to pick up wheat, clothing, baby food, and toys.

15.

Name: Saigon Fire.

Location: Republic of Vietnam.

Date(s): May and July 1963.

Emergency: A fire destroyed part of residential Saigon.

Air Force Organization(s) Involved: 4440th Aircraft Delivery Group and 21st Trp Carr Sq.

Airlifted: More than one ton of clothing.

Aircraft Employed: C–130 (three).

Operations: In late March, a disastrous fire destroyed much of the impoverished Khanh-Hoi suburb of Saigon, capital of the Republic of Vietnam. The conflagration destroyed more than 3,000 dwellings, leaving as many as 25,000 people homeless.

During April, Mrs. David Miller, a former Vietnamese citizen living in Honolulu, organized a collection of clothing for the fire victims. Marine Corps Capt. Tony Russo helped her to contact the Air Force to airlift the clothes to Saigon.

The 4440th Aircraft Delivery Group was already transporting humanitarian contributions to Vietnam aboard cargo planes on a space-available basis in 1963 (see Operation Lifeline, April–May, 1963). Between May 2 and the end of July, the group airlifted more than one ton of the clothing collected by Mrs. Miller from Hickam AFB, Hawaii, to Tan Son Nhut AB in Saigon.

The operation involved three C–130 flights. Lt. R. D. Reneau and a crew from the 21st Trp Carr Sq flew the first plane out of Hickam on May 2 with 800 pounds of clothes. A second C–130 airlifted another shipment on May 10. In July, a third Hercules plane flew from Hawaii to Saigon with a load of 170 parcels, which Maj. Joseph W. Pridgen, an Air Force chaplain, helped to box and distribute to the fire victims in Saigon.

16.
Name: Laotian Medical Airlift.
Location: Laos.
Date(s): July 1963.
Emergency: Shortages of medical supplies and surgical instruments crippled medical services at a hospital at Nam Tha.
Air Force Organization(s) Involved: 315th Air Div and 1501st Air Trpt Wg.
Airlifted: Almost two tons of surgical instruments and medical supplies.
Aircraft Employed: Unspecified.
Operations: Dr. Thomas A. Dooley, known as the "jungle doctor" because of his medical work with refugees in rural areas of Southeast Asia after the 1954 partition of Indochina, founded a small hospital at Nam Tha in northern Laos. After Dr. Dooley died in 1961, Dr. Edgar Buell administered the hospital.

Fighting among various factions within Laos overloaded the hospital at Nam Tha. In July, the Parke-Davis Drug Company donated nearly two tons of medical supplies and surgical instruments to the hospital. A MATS cargo plane from the 1501st Air Trpt Wg at Travis AFB, California, airlifted the cargo across the Pacific Ocean. While in that theater, the 315th Air Div supervised the delivery.

17.
Name: Locust Infestation.
Location: Thailand.
Date(s): August 31–September 16, 1963.

Humanitarian Airlift Operations

Emergency: Locust swarms threatened food crops in central Thailand.
Air Force Organization(s) Involved: Special Aerial Spray Flight, 315th Trp Carr Gp.
Airlifted: Unspecified quantity of insecticide.
Aircraft Employed: C–123 (two).
Operations: Locusts threatened food crops in central Thailand during the summer. In August, the Thai government requested, through the State Department, insecticide spraying by U.S. aircraft. Special C–123s modified to spray chemical defoliants were in use in neighboring South Vietnam in Project Ranch Hand. By replacing herbicide with insecticide and modifying flight patterns, the Air Force could fly the mission.

On August 30, the Special Aerial Spray Flight of the 315th Trp Carr Gp of the 315th Air Div flew a spray-equipped C–123 to Thailand for the project. The next day it flew the first mission against the locusts. On September 8, a second spray-equipped C–123 joined the operation. By September 16, the two planes had flown 17 insecticide missions over 24,000 acres in central Thailand, reducing the locust population and saving many food crops.

18.
Name: Korean Cholera Epidemic.
Location: South Korea.
Date(s): September 28, 1963.
Emergency: A cholera epidemic threatened South Korea.
Air Force Organization(s) Involved: 815th Trp Carr Sq and 315th Air Div.
Airlifted: 504 pounds of cholera vaccine.
Aircraft Employed: C–130 (one).
Operations: A cholera epidemic spread across South Korea from Pusan during September. By September 25, almost 500 people in at least eight communities had been infected, and 19 had died.

On September 28, Capt. Leslie B. Fox and his crew from the 815th Trp Carr Sq, under the operational control of the 315th Air Div, flew a C–130 to airlift 504 pounds of cholera vaccine from Tachikawa AB in Japan to Kimpo AB near Seoul, South Korea. Korean medical authorities used the serum to control the epidemic, which by October 4 had infected 642 persons, with 44 fatalities.

19.
Name: Operation Kunsan.
Location: South Korea.
Date(s): January 1964.
Emergency: Abject poverty affected Koreans near Kunsan AB.
Air Force Organization(s) Involved: 916th Trp Carr Gp.
Airlifted: Almost 30 tons of food, clothing, medical supplies, hand tools, and other items.

Aircraft Employed: C–124 (three).

Operations: When Capt. Jack Heald, Jr., returned to Texas after duty in South Korea in 1963, he organized a relief effort for the needy people in the area around Kunsan AB. Volunteers from Tarrant County in the Fort Worth area supported his project, which was named Operation Kunsan. Contributors included Fort Worth Jaycees, churches, and local fire departments. By early 1964, the benefactors had donated a stockpile of almost 30 tons of food, clothing, medical supplies, agricultural tools and supplies, and sewing machines.

The Air Force approved the airlift of humanitarian supplies to eastern Asia aboard cargo planes on training flights on a space-available basis. The 442d Trp Carr Wg arranged the operation for the Kunsan needy, employing the 916th Trp Carr Gp, based at Carswell AFB, Texas.

During the second half of January 1964, the group used three C–124 Globemaster IIs for the South Korean airlift. The 7,000-mile flights from Carswell AFB to Kunsan AB stopped at Travis AFB, California, and Hickam AFB, Hawaii. Col. Ben J. Mangina, the commander of the 916th Trp Carr Gp, served as aircraft commander of the first plane, which launched on January 18 and landed at Kunsan on the 24th. Another Globemaster II soon followed. Kunsan AB personnel unloaded and distributed supplies to orphanages, schools, and hospitals in Cholla Puk Do province. A third plane delivered medical supplies to Taegu for a civilian hospital.

20.

Name: Thai Medical Airlift.

Location: Thailand.

Date(s): January 1964.

Emergency: High disease rates afflicted the population of Bangkok during the winter of 1964.

Air Force Organization(s) Involved: 137th Air Trpt Wg.

Airlifted: More than 11 tons of medical supplies.

Aircraft Employed: C–97 (two).

Operations: During the early 1960s, Air Force transport planes often flew training missions half empty. Air Force leaders agreed to use available space to airlift humanitarian cargo donated by U.S. communities to needy people in Southeast Asia and other parts of the world.

In 1963, the Loma Linda University Alumni Association in Riverside, California, became aware of medical needs in Bangkok, the capital of Thailand. The association collected more than 11 tons of medical supplies for airlift. In January 1964, two C–97 Stratofreighters from the Oklahoma Air National Guard's 137th Air Trpt Wg, serving MATS, carried the cargo almost halfway around the world to Thailand for a Bangkok hospital.

21.
Name: Vietnamese Cholera Epidemic.
Location: Republic of Vietnam.
Date(s): January 19–February 6, 1964.
Emergency: A cholera epidemic struck South Vietnam.
Air Force Organization(s) Involved: West Trpt AF, 315th Air Div, 1611th Air Trpt Wg, 35th and 817th Trp Carr Sqs, and 44th Air Trpt Sq.
Airlifted: 45 tons of cholera vaccine, saline solution, and other medical supplies; and Navy medical personnel.
Aircraft Employed: C–130 (three) and C–135 (two).
Operations: In early 1964, cholera broke out in Saigon, capital of the Republic of Vietnam, striking over 3,000 people and leaving 300 dead. To save lives, and to protect the health of U.S. military personnel serving in South Vietnam, MATS and the 315th Air Div undertook an airlift of medical supplies and personnel to Saigon.

An 817th Trp Carr Sq C–130 Hercules cargo plane from Naha AB, Okinawa, transported a Navy medical team and vaccine from Taipei, Taiwan, to Saigon on January 19. On January 24, a C–135 from the 44th Air Trpt Sq of the 1501st Air Trpt Wg at Travis AFB, California, airlifted vaccine to South Vietnam for U.S. servicemen. A second C–130 from the 35th Trp Carr Sq at Naha carried 15 tons of medical supplies from Clark AB in the Philippines to Saigon on January 25.

Between January 27 and 29, a C–135 from McGuire AFB's 1611th Air Trpt Wg flew cholera vaccine and saline solution from Almeda NAS, near Travis AFB, to Saigon. The last plane, a Navy C–130 serving the West Trpt AF, took off for Saigon on February 4, also carrying cholera medicine.

The Military Air Transport Service and 315th Air Div had delivered about one million doses of cholera vaccine and saline solution to South Vietnam by early February 1964.

22.
Name: South Vietnamese Flood.
Location: Republic of Vietnam.
Date(s): November 1964–January 1965.
Emergency: Three typhoons generated more than 40 inches of rain in central South Vietnam and caused flooding that left 7,000 people dead and hundreds of thousands homeless.
Air Force Organization(s) Involved: 2d and 315th Air Divs; 315th Trp Carr Gp; 1503d Air Trpt Gp; 35th and 311th Trp Carr Sqs; and Detachment 5, Pacific Air Rscu Cen.
Airlifted: More than 2,000 tons of food, clothing, fuel, boats, and medicine; and more than 1,500 evacuees.
Aircraft Employed: HH–43 (three); and C–123, C–124, and C–130 (numbers unknown).

Operations: Three typhoons struck South Vietnam in November 1964, dropping over 40 inches of rain over the central highlands. Flooding in provinces like Quang Ngai, Quang Tin, and Qui Nhon killed 7,000 people and destroyed more than 50,000 homes. Premier Tran Van Huong requested U.S. aerial relief missions.

Detachment 5, Pacific Air Rscu Cen, flew three HH–43F Huskie rescue helicopters on 63 sorties between November 11 and 15, lifting 80 Vietnamese from roofs and islands of high ground and delivering five tons of food, clothing, and medicine from Da Nang to areas isolated by high water.

During November and December, 315th Air Div C–124s from the 1503d Air Trpt Gp, C–130s from the 35th Trp Carr Sq, and Caribou cargo planes from the Royal Australian Air Force airlifted 1,470 tons of supplies in response to the disaster. The cargo included food and medicine, in addition to fuel for the rescue helicopters. Meanwhile, 2d Air Div units carried more than 1,000 tons of relief supplies and evacuated over 1,500 homeless flood victims in 382 sorties.

The 311th Trp Carr Sq at Da Nang played a leading role in the relief effort. Between November 12 and 30, the squadron airlifted 595 tons of rice, flour, and other supplies to Quang Ngai and 114 tons of similar cargo to Tam Ky. By January 21, 311th Trp Carr Sq C–123s had flown 632 relief sorties, delivering 2,087 tons of food, medicine, clothing, boats, and other supplies, some of which had been delivered to South Vietnam by the C–124s and C–130s. The squadron also moved more than 1,300 passengers, including refugees and medical personnel.

23.
Name: Operation Warmth.
Location: South Korea.
Date(s): December 1964.
Emergency: Seoul area orphanages and hospitals suffered shortages of blankets and medical supplies.
Air Force Organization(s) Involved: 133d Air Trpt Wg.
Airlifted: 3,300 blankets and more than two tons of medical supplies.
Aircraft Employed: C–97 (one).
Operations: Residents of Milwaukee, Wisconsin, launched a collection drive when they learned of the need for blankets for hundreds of orphans in Seoul, the capital of South Korea. By December 1964, they had gathered 3,300 blankets and donated more than two tons of medical supplies for hospitals in the Seoul area.

To airlift the relief cargo to South Korea, the Minnesota Air National Guard's 133d Air Trpt Wg flew a C–97 Stratofreighter airplane. Wing Commander Brig. Gen. John Dolny rode aboard the craft, which landed in Seoul on December 10. Participants in the blanket airlift called it Operation Warmth.

24.
Name: Dependent Evacuation.
Location: Republic of Vietnam.
Date(s): February 9–March 9, 1965.
Emergency: Increasing terrorist attacks against U.S. citizens persuaded President Johnson to order the evacuation of U.S. dependents from South Vietnam.
Air Force Organization(s) Involved: 2d and 315th Air Divs and West Trpt AF.
Airlifted: 376 dependents.
Aircraft Employed: C–130 and C–54 (numbers unknown).
Operations: As military involvement in the Republic of Vietnam escalated, attacks on U.S. military installations increased. In early February 1965, a Viet Cong raid on Pleiku left more than 100 U.S. casualties, prompting President Johnson to order a rapid air evacuation of U.S. dependents, primarily wives and children of personnel of the State and Defense Departments. Johnson also ordered renewed bombing of North Vietnam, which he blamed for the attacks.

The U.S. embassy in Saigon and the Military Assistance Command, Vietnam organized the evacuation airlift, which employed civilian aircraft contracted from Pan American Airways, American Airlines, and United Airlines. Contract carriers, however, could not evacuate the dependents quickly enough, so military transports also participated in the operation. Air Force C–130s from the Military Air Transport Service's West Trpt AF, serving the 315th Air Div, and C–54s from the 2d Air Div carried over 300 of 1,600 U.S. dependents evacuated from South Vietnam between February 9 and March 9, 1965.

Most evacuees left from Saigon, where the 8th Aerial Port Squadron helped load them aboard planes at Tan Son Nhut AB. Hue and Da Nang were other departure points. Civilian contract airliners and the military cargo planes took the dependents either directly to the United States or to safe haven points in the Pacific or Southeast Asian areas. The evacuees landed at San Francisco or Travis AFB, California; Honolulu, Hawaii; Manila in the Philippines; Bangkok, Thailand; or Hong Kong. Most DoD dependents debarked at Travis AFB.

25.
Name: South Korean Drought.
Location: South Korea.
Date(s): June 30 and July 2, 1965.
Emergency: A drought threatened farmlands across South Korea.
Air Force Organization(s) Involved: 815th Trp Carr Sq and 315th Air Div.
Airlifted: 180 irrigation pumps with diesel engines.
Aircraft Employed: C–130 (one).
Operations: In the spring and early summer, drought parched the farmlands of South Korea, threatening farmers with economic ruin and city dwellers with food shortages.

The 315th Air Div, charged with airlift responsibilities in the western Pacific area, prepared to transport 180 irrigation pumps with diesel engines from Osaka, Japan, to three locations in South Korea. A six-man 815th Trp Carr Sq C–130 crew, led by Maj. Romanie Durnin, flew the operation. On June 30, the crew delivered 50 pumps to Pusan and 70 to Kwanju. Two days later, the plane airlifted 60 more pumps to Taegu. In addition to the pumps, the C–130 carried a forklift and a three-man delivery team.

26.
Name: Vietnamese Orphan Airlift.
Location: Republic of Vietnam.
Date(s): August 1965.
Emergency: Hundreds of orphans had to be evacuated from Da Nang because of escalating fighting.
Air Force Organization(s) Involved: 315th Air Div.
Airlifted: More than 400 orphans.
Aircraft Employed: C–130 (two).
Operations: Hundreds of children who had been orphaned by flooding in South Vietnam in 1964 crowded shelters in Da Nang. When escalating fighting in the area threatened their safety in mid-1965, their guardians decided to move them to a new orphanage in Saigon.

In August, the 315th Air Div used a pair of C–130s to airlift more than 400 children, ranging in age from six to 14, from Da Nang to Saigon. The 8th Aerial Port Squadron's Detachment 2 provided refreshments to the children while they awaited airlift at Da Nang.

27.
Name: Food Airlift.
Location: Republic of Vietnam.
Date(s): August 1965.
Emergency: Viet Cong guerrilla troops blocked roads by which food supplies could enter a provincial capital in the central highlands.
Air Force Organization(s) Involved: 309th Air Comdo Sq.
Airlifted: About 45 tons of rice.
Aircraft Employed: C–123 (number unknown).
Operations: In 1965, thousands of South Vietnamese refugees fled guerrilla-controlled areas to the provincial capital of Ban Me Thuot in the central highlands. When the Viet Cong cut roads leading to the town that summer, food shortages quadrupled the price of rice and threatened the people with starvation. The Republic of Vietnam's premier, Nguyen Cao Ky, asked the U.S. Air Force and the South Vietnamese air force to airlift food to the beleaguered town.

In August, the 309th Air Comdo Sq and the Vietnamese 83d Special Air Group collaborated to airlift 90 tons of rice to Ban Me Thuot. The 309th used

C–123 Providers for the humanitarian operation, which helped to feed the refugee-crowded town until a supply highway reopened at the end of the month.

28.
Name: Elder Blow.
Location: East Pakistan.
Date(s): September 19, 1965.
Emergency: Conflict between India and Pakistan endangered U.S. civilians living in Dacca, East Pakistan.
Air Force Organization(s) Involved: 315th Air Div, 464th Trp Carr Wg, and 6315th Ops Gp.
Airlifted: 485 U.S. civilians.
Aircraft Employed: C–130 (seven).
Operations: A territorial dispute between India and Pakistan erupted into military conflict in September 1965. The fighting endangered the lives of U.S. civilians living in Pakistan (see Chapter 5, Nice Way/Elder Blow, September 1965). The State Department asked the JCS to arrange a military airlift of U.S. nationals from Dacca, capital of East Pakistan, to safe haven bases in the Far East. The Pacific Air Forces' 315th Air Div planned the evacuation, which was called Elder Blow.

The commander of the 6315th Ops Gp, Col. John R. Neal, served as the task force commander, using aircrews and planes on rotation in the theater from the 464th Trp Carr Wg. On September 19, seven C–130s loaded 485 U.S. civilians, including government employees and dependents of consulting groups, at Tezgan Airfield at Dacca. They flew to Bangkok for rest and crew changes before continuing on to a safe haven base at Manila in the Philippines. Despite poor communications between Colonel Neal and the U.S. consul at Dacca and delays in obtaining diplomatic and overflight clearances, Operation Elder Blow succeeded in evacuating U.S. civilians from danger in East Pakistan.

29.
Name: Project Refugee.
Location: Republic of Vietnam.
Date(s): October 19–November 25, 1965.
Emergency: Thousands of war refugees crowded cities in South Vietnam.
Air Force Organization(s) Involved: East Trpt AF and 1608th and 1611th Air Trpt Wgs.
Airlifted: 157 tons of clothing material.
Aircraft Employed: C–130 (17).
Operations: As the war in Vietnam intensified, thousands of refugees across South Vietnam fled to the cities for relative safety. Late in the year, the State Department's Agency for International Development requested an airlift of clothing from the United States to South Vietnam as part of Project Refugee.

The Military Air Transport Service's East Trpt AF employed 17 C–130E aircraft for the airlift, which began on October 19 and continued through November 25. Six planes came from the 1608th Air Trpt Wg at Charleston AFB, South Carolina; four from the 1611th Air Trpt Wg at McGuire AFB, New Jersey; and the other seven from naval units assigned to the East Trpt AF. The aircraft loaded 157 tons of clothing at Schenectady, New York, and Olmsted AFB, Pennsylvania. The cargo was unloaded at Da Nang, Nha Trang, and Tan Son Nhut ABs in South Vietnam, where it was given to local Vietnamese refugees.

30.
Name: Operation Paraplegic.
Location: Republic of Vietnam.
Date(s): November 8–9, 1965.
Emergency: South Vietnamese paraplegics needed treatment and rehabilitation.
Air Force Organization(s) Involved: 44th Air Trpt Sq.
Airlifted: 56 South Vietnamese paraplegic medical patients.
Aircraft Employed: C–141 (one).
Operations: By late 1965, the escalating war in Vietnam had produced thousands of casualties. Some of the wounded suffered crippling disabilities. The United States decided to transport some South Vietnamese paraplegic war victims to the United States for treatment and rehabilitation. The move would benefit the patients, symbolize U.S. commitment to South Vietnam, and, possibly, soften U.S. domestic criticism of the conflict.

In November, MATS launched Operation Paraplegic. The 44th Air Trpt Sq flew a C–141 Starlifter cargo aircraft for the operation. On November 8, 56 South Vietnamese paraplegic patients boarded the plane at Tan Son Nhut AB in Saigon and flew via Yokota AB, Japan, and Travis AFB, California, to Stewart AFB, New York, landing less than 24 hours after leaving Saigon. Fourteen South Vietnamese medical technicians accompanied the paraplegics.

At Stewart AFB, Gen. Maxwell Taylor and the Vietnamese ambassador to the United States greeted the patients when they landed on November 9. The patients and medical technicians went to nearby Castle Point Veterans Administration Hospital near Beacon, New York, for treatment, rehabilitation, and training. Eventually, the South Vietnamese returned to their native country, the last reaching South Vietnam in June 1967.

31.
Name: Korat Fire.
Location: Thailand.
Date(s): Late 1965.
Emergency: A fire in Korat left hundreds of people homeless.
Air Force Organization(s) Involved: 18th Tac Ftr Wg and Detachment 4, 38th Air Rscu Sq.

Airlifted: Unspecified quantity of clothing.
Aircraft Employed: HH–43B (one) and C–54 or C–47 (one).
Operations: In late 1965, a large fire gutted 600 buildings in the city of Korat in central Thailand. The eight-hour conflagration left hundreds of people homeless and caused over $1 million dollars in damage. U.S. military organizations such as the 6234th Tac Ftr Wg at Korat Royal Thai AB sent fire-fighting equipment and personnel to help fight the blaze. Detachment 4 of the 38th Air Rscu Sq, based at Korat, flew an HH–43B helicopter to help direct fire fighting from the air.

After the fire, U.S. units at Korat provided relief supplies such as rations and bedding to the homeless. The 18th Tac Ftr Wg at Kadena AB, Okinawa, which periodically rotated aircraft and personnel to Korat, collected clothing and airlifted it to the victims of the fire, flying a C–47 or a C–54 airplane for the mission. Mr. Boonrawd Chotamangsa, the deputy governor of Korat province, thanked U.S. units in Thailand for their assistance during and after the fire.

32.
Name: Orphan Evacuation.
Location: South Vietnam.
Date(s): May 24, 1966.
Emergency: Fighting in Da Nang threatened children at an orphanage.
Air Force Organization(s) Involved: 315th Air Div.
Airlifted: 90 orphans.
Aircraft Employed: C–130 (one).
Operations: In May 1965, fighting broke out between South Vietnamese soldiers loyal to Premier Nguyen Cao Ky and those supporting Buddhist dissidents. Military clashes in Da Nang, where Buddhist rebels fortified some pagodas, threatened the safety of orphaned children at the Sacred Heart Orphanage, a Roman Catholic institution in the city.

On May 24, 1966, a 315th Air Div C–130 Hercules cargo plane airlifted 90 orphans in four sorties from Da Nang to the relative safety of the South Vietnamese cities of Pleiku, Nha Trang, and Saigon. That same week, Ky loyalists took full control of Da Nang.

33.
Name: Laotian Flood.
Location: Laos.
Date(s): September 1, 1966.
Emergency: The Mekong River flooded parts of Laos.
Air Force Organization(s) Involved: 22d Mil Alft Sq.
Airlifted: 11 tons of emergency rations.
Aircraft Employed: C–124 (one).
Operations: In mid-1966, the Mekong River flooded large parts of Laos, including the cities of Luang Prabang and Vientiane. Floodwaters destroyed most of the

nation's rice crop and left thousands of people homeless. King Savang Vatthana called the flood a national disaster and appealed for U.S. help.

The State Department requested a military airlift of food to Laos. On September 1, a C–124 Globemaster II cargo plane from the 22d Mil Alft Sq at Tachikawa AB, Japan, airlifted more than 11 tons of emergency rations from Clark AB in the Philippines via Udorn Royal Thai AB to Vientiane. Officials at the U.S. embassy supervised the distribution of rations to flood victims.

34.
Name: Operation Fly Swatter.
Location: South Vietnam.
Date(s): October 17, 1966–June 1972.
Emergency: Malaria-carrying mosquitoes threatened the health of U.S. troops and South Vietnamese troops and civilians.
Air Force Organization(s) Involved: 12th Air Comdo Sq and 310th Tac Alft Sq.
Airlifted: More than 230,000 gallons of insecticide.
Aircraft Employed: UC–123 (two).
Operations: In October, the 12th Air Comdo Sq, on Ranch Hand defoliation and crop destruction missions in South Vietnam, assumed a secondary mission of destroying malaria-carrying mosquitoes with insecticide. The first UC–123 aircraft diverted for the new mission, nicknamed Patches, was stripped of its camouflage paint and coated with an alodine compound to retard the corrosive effects of the poison. On October 17, it began malaria-control spraying in South Vietnam in an operation called Fly Swatter. Patches originally flew from Tan Son Nhut, but in 1967 it moved to Bien Hoa AB, where the 12th Air Comdo Sq was based.

Insecticide spraying differed greatly from herbicide spraying. Each mosquito-control mission covered more territory because the aircraft delivered only about eight ounces of insecticide per acre, covering 15,000 acres in one sortie. Insecticide spraying also required less precise navigation than defoliation missions.

By mid-1967, the 12th Air Comdo Sq was flying 20 insecticide sorties per month. It delivered 118,985 gallons of insecticide over South Vietnam in 1967 and 111,998 gallons in 1968. The squadron devoted only one of its 19 spray aircraft for the mosquito-control mission.

Questions about the safety, practicality, and morality of herbicide spraying in South Vietnam convinced Ranch Hand administrators to decrease defoliation operations. By July 1970, when the 310th Tac Alft Sq took over spray operations from the inactivated 12th Air Comdo Sq, insecticide sorties outnumbered herbicide sorties. The 310th Tac Alft Sq used two UC–123s against malaria, regularly spraying 15 sites across South Vietnam from its home base in Phan Rang.

The insecticide operation cost several lives. On February 11, 1971, an insecticide plane crashed after going out of control near Phan Rang AB, killing five crew members. On June 1, the second plane suffered minor damage after it was hit with small arms fire.

Humanitarian Airlift Operations

The 310th Tac Alft Sq continued insecticide spraying in South Vietnam after herbicide missions ended in January 1971. In June 1972, the squadron stopped flying the UC–123 spray aircraft, which were transferred to the South Vietnamese air force as part of President Nixon's Vietnamization program. Operation Fly Swatter helped to lower disease rates in populated areas, benefiting both sides of the battlefield.

35.
Name: Bao Loc Milk Run.
Location: South Vietnam.
Date(s): November 17, 1966.
Emergency: Food shortages plagued the people of Bao Loc, a town about 96 miles northeast of Saigon.
Air Force Organization(s) Involved: 19th Air Comdo Sq.
Airlifted: One pallet of powdered milk.
Aircraft Employed: C–123 (one).
Operations: In November, the State Department's Agency for International Development, aware of a food shortage at Bao Loc, a small town about 96 miles northeast of Saigon, requested a military airlift of milk.

Flying a C–123 Provider aircraft from the 19th Air Comdo Sq at Tan Son Nhut AB in Saigon, Capt. Dickie G. Poplin led a five-man crew on the mission on November 17. As the Provider touched down with a pallet of powdered milk on a small airstrip carved from the jungle around Bao Loc, it delivered the one millionth ton of cargo airlifted by the Air Force in Vietnam since January 1, 1964.

36.
Name: Pleiku Orphan Relief.
Location: South Vietnam.
Date(s): December 10, 1967.
Emergency: Orphans in the Pleiku area lacked adequate medical supplies.
Air Force Organization(s) Involved: 315th Air Div.
Airlifted: More than two tons of medical supplies.
Aircraft Employed: C–130 (one).
Operations: In late 1967, orphanages in the Pleiku area of South Vietnam experienced a shortage of medical supplies. Air Force volunteers such as TSgt. Charles A. Malouff of the 633d Combat Support Group, who coordinated assistance at St. Paul's Convent Orphanage in Pleiku, solicited contributions from various sources. Japanese benefactors donated more than two tons of medical supplies for the cause.

To airlift the cargo to Pleiku, the 315th Air Div at Tachikawa AB, Japan, employed one C–130 Hercules cargo aircraft. On December 10, Col. Coleman O. Williams, Jr., the vice commander of the division, piloted the plane from Japan to South Vietnam. At Pleiku, South Vietnamese officials presented crew members with flowers in appreciation of the medical supply airlift.

37.
Name: Refugee and Orphan Aid.
Location: South Vietnam.
Date(s): December 1967.
Emergency: Orphans and refugees in the Saigon area lacked adequate food, clothing, and toys.
Air Force Organization(s) Involved: 824th Combat Support Group.
Airlifted: More than four tons of food, clothing, and toys.
Aircraft Employed: C–54 (one).
Operations: Air Force personnel at Kadena AB in Okinawa launched a collection drive when they learned in late 1967 that Vietnamese refugees and orphans in Saigon needed food, clothing, and toys.

To airlift the cargo to Vietnam, the 824th Combat Support Group used a C–54 Skymaster aircraft. In December, the C–54 flew more than four tons of food, clothing, and toys from Kadena to Tan Son Nhut AB in South Vietnam. Col. Frank E. Marek, commander of Kadena AB and the 824th Combat Support Group, flew the last of three planeloads from Okinawa to Saigon. Vietnamese refugees and orphans and deaf mutes of the Liau Phaiu Orphanage received the donated items.

38.
Name: East Pakistani Cyclone.
Location: East Pakistan.
Date(s): November 18–20 and December 13–16, 1970.
Emergency: A cyclone from the Bay of Bengal struck the Ganges River delta of East Pakistan.
Air Force Organization(s) Involved: 436th, 437th, and 438th Mil Alft Wgs; and 314th and 463d Tac Alft Wgs.
Airlifted: More than 140 tons of equipment and supplies, including eight helicopters, trucks, jeeps, seeds, medical supplies, food, lanterns, cots, generators, radios, and tarpaulins; and at least 57 passengers, mostly technicians to operate the equipment.
Aircraft Employed: C–141 (12) and C–130 (5+).
Operations: On the night of November 13–14, a cyclone with winds of 120 mph moved from the Bay of Bengal into the coastal regions of East Pakistan. A 20-foot wall of water swept across the flatlands of the Ganges River delta and islands offshore. The monster storm, which killed more than 200,000 people and left over two million homeless, ranked among the worst natural catastrophes in history. Floodwaters blocked roads and rail lines, leaving millions of survivors without adequate food, drinking water, clothing, and medical supplies.

Relief supplies poured into Dacca, East Pakistan, from other nations. The Pakistani government requested helicopters to help distribute the supplies among the flood victims. The U.S. ambassador to Pakistan, Joseph S. Farland, arranged for a military airlift, and the State Department's Agency for International Development sponsored the operation.

On November 18–20, six C–141 Starlifter aircraft from the 436th, 437th, and 438th Mil Alft Wgs airlifted eight Army UH–1H helicopters from Pope AFB, North Carolina, to Dacca. Helicopter crews, ground vehicles, and relief workers from the Army's 182d Aviation Company also rode aboard the cargo planes. Between November 20 and December 13, the Army helicopter task force flew 1,259 sorties, distributing one million pounds of food and other relief supplies to isolated inhabitants of coastal East Pakistan. By mid-December, railroads and highways in the region had opened sufficiently to allow the helicopters and their crews to return home.

For the retrieval, MAC again flew six C–141s from the 436th, 437th, and 438th Mil Alft Wgs. Instead of returning to East Pakistan empty, the cargo planes took 109 tons of seeds, medical supplies, and biscuits from U.S. bases between December 13 and 16. At Dacca, loadmasters traded relief supplies for helicopters, vehicles, and personnel of the Army task force for return to the United States.

In addition to the twelve MAC C–141s, TAC C–130s participated in the cyclone relief operation. Three C–130s of the 463d Tac Alft Wg transported food and medical supplies from Clark AB in the Philippines to Dacca in three missions between November 30 and December 18. Among the aircraft commanders were Maj. Keith Ellis, Maj. Steve O'Neill, and Capt. Marcus Shipman.

In late November, the 314th Tac Alft Wg used at least two C–130s to airlift more than 17 tons of medical supplies, trucks, trailers, lanterns, tarpaulins, generators, radios, rations, and other supplies and equipment from a staging base at Tan Son Nhut AB, South Vietnam, to Dacca. Twenty-six technicians rode along to operate the equipment in the disaster zone. The cargo filled 463 pallets.

Between November 18 and December 16, the Air Force airlifted more than 140 tons of relief equipment and supplies and 57 technicians to the disaster zone. Five wings flew at least 17 cargo planes—12 C–141s and 5 C–130s—for the operation, and most flights covered almost 10,000 miles. Despite the assistance, East Pakistanis criticized the Pakistani government in West Pakistan for failing to provide enough disaster relief. Discontent contributed to a secession movement that transformed East Pakistan into the independent state of Bangladesh the following year.

39.
Name: Malaysian Floods.
Location: Malaysia.
Date(s): January 7–11, 1971.
Emergency: After 100 hours of continuous rain, floods inundated communities east of Kuala Lumpur, forcing more than 100,000 people from their homes.
Air Force Organization(s) Involved: 60th and 62d Mil Alft Wgs and 463d Tac Alft Wg.

Airlifted: 35 tons of blankets, medical supplies, boats, outboard motors, and life preservers; six U.S. Army helicopters; helicopter crews; and a five-man medical team.
Aircraft Employed: C–141 (two), C–124 (two), and C–130 (one).
Operations: In early January, the Malay Peninsula suffered the worst floods in 40 years. In one week, 100 hours of continuous rain dropped almost 100 inches of rain at the base of mountains east of Kuala Lumpur, capital of Malaysia. Floods drove more than 100,000 people from their homes, prompting the Malaysian prime minister, Tun Abdul Razak, to declare a national disaster and request international relief. The State Department requested airlift support from DoD, which prepared to transport medical helicopters and crews from South Vietnam and AID boats from the United States.

The 463d Tac Alft Wg at Clark AB in the Philippines used two C–124s and one C–130 in the relief airlift. From January 7 to 9, Lt. Col. Bernard L. Goode and his crew flew three missions in a C–124 from Tan Son Nhut AB near Saigon, South Vietnam, to Kuantan Royal Malaysian AFB, about 60 miles east of Kuala Lumpur, near the flooded area. The Globemaster II aircraft carried four UH–1 Huey medical evacuation helicopters, crews from the U.S. Army's 45th Medical Aviation Company, and 12 tons of blankets. Each trip took three hours. A second C–124 transported two more of the Army helicopters and crews from South Vietnam to Malaysia.

During the same week, the 463d Tac Alft Wg at Clark AB flew a C–130 flood relief mission to Malaysia. Carrying two crews under Capt. Marcus B. Shipman and Capt. Donald J. Godlewski, the Hercules cargo airplane had a two-part mission. First, it transported 12 tons of blankets, one ton of medical supplies, and five medical technicians from Kadena AB in Okinawa via Tan Son Nhut to Kuantan. It then remained at Kuala Lumpur's Surang International Airport, awaiting supplies delivered by MAC C–141 Starlifters. Transfer of the supplies at Kuala Lumpur from the C–141s to the smaller C–130 was necessary because the Starlifters could not land on the short runways at Kuantan.

The two C–141s arrived at the Malaysian capital between January 8 and 11, carrying 50 16-foot boats, 50 outboard motors, and 50 life preservers and flying 10 tons of AID cargo halfway around the world from Scott AFB in Illinois. The Twenty-second Air Force's 60th and 62d Mil Alft Wgs each supplied a Starlifter and crews for the emergency airlift operation.

Using five cargo planes, the Air Force transported 35 tons of relief cargo and supplies, six Army helicopters and crews, and a medical team to Malaysia in January. The airlift helped to save lives and reduce misery in the extensive flood area and strengthened ties between the United States and Malaysia at a time when relations were strained by the war in Vietnam.

40.
Name: Bonny Jack.
Location: India.
Date(s): June 17–July 17, 1971.
Emergency: Thousands of refugees fleeing civil war in East Pakistan crossed into the state of Tripura in India, where overcrowding produced food shortages and a threat of cholera.
Air Force Organization(s) Involved: 464th and 513th Tac Alft Wgs; 436th, 437th, and 438th Mil Alft Wgs; and 58th Mil Alft Sq.
Airlifted: 23,165 refugees and more than 2,000 tons of food, medicine, ambulances, tarpaulins, and other emergency equipment and supplies.
Aircraft Employed: C–130 (seven) and C–141 (six).
Operations: During the spring of 1971, secessionists in East Pakistan rebelled against the government in West Pakistan. Civil war forced hundreds of thousands of refugees into neighboring India. In the state of Tripura in eastern India, overcrowding produced food shortages and the threat of a cholera epidemic. The Indian government appealed for assistance from the United Nations High Commissioner for Refugees, and the U.S. ambassador to India, Kenneth B. Keating, recommended an emergency airlift.

In early June, Col. Charles E. Turnipseed of the Strike Command flew to India and organized Bonny Jack, a U.S. airlift to move Tripura refugees to other parts of India and transport food and medicine to those who remained. He set up a headquarters at Gauhati in the state of Assam in eastern India, where UN and Indian workers collected food and other supplies and where shelters were prepared for the influx of refugees. The airlift began on June 17 and lasted 30 days.

Four C–130s from the 779th Tac Alft Sq of the 464th Tac Alft Wg at Pope AFB, North Carolina, handled the bulk of the airlift. They transported food, medicine, and other supplies from Gauhati to Agartala, capital of Tripura, and airlifted refugees back in a long series of one-hour shuttle flights. Short runways in Agartala required use of the C–130s instead of larger cargo planes such as C–141s.

On June 30, the Strike Command replaced three of the four C–130s because they were due for phase inspection. The new planes came from the 513th Tactical Airlift Wing's Alpha Squadron, which included 778th Tac Alft Sq C–130s from the 464th Tac Alft Wg, on rotation in Europe. During the month-long operation, the seven C–130s transported 23,165 East Pakistani refugees from Tripura to Assam, with some planes carrying over 100 passengers. By the conclusion of Bonny Jack in mid-July, the C–130s had delivered over 2,000 tons of rice and supplies to Agartala. The cargo included one million units of cholera vaccine, 100 pounds of candy for refugee children, and 400 tarpaulins. Among the C–130 pilots were Lt. Col. Joseph R. Tollefson, Capt. Gordon E. Cochran, and Capt. Wayne G. Wiltshire.

Six MAC C–141 Starlifter aircraft participated in the operation to support the C–130 shuttle missions. They came from the 436th, 437th, and 438th Mil Alft

Wgs and the 58th Mil Alft Sq. The six planes carried 49 passengers and more than 100 tons of cargo, including spare parts, communications equipment, cargo handling matériel, water purification equipment, jeeps, tarpaulins, trailers, refrigerators, and food. The Starlifters also carried ground crews, Strike Command officers, and other personnel. Loading at MacDill AFB, Florida; Pope AFB, North Carolina; Robins AFB, Georgia; and Little Rock AFB, Arkansas, most of the cargo craft flew to Gauhati via Torrejon AB, Spain, and New Delhi, India. Two other planes transported 10 Japanese Red Cross jeep ambulances from Yokota AB, Japan, to India for refugee relief.

There were a few problems during the month-long operation. Monsoon rains delayed some flights. Morale suffered when Indians complained that the United States, despite its aid for the East Pakistani refugees, continued to provide military aid to West Pakistan. Intensive use of the C–130s required many spare parts.

During Bonny Jack, 13 Air Force cargo planes airlifted over 2,100 tons of relief cargo and more than 23,000 refugees. Ambassador Keating praised the airlift as a demonstration of U.S. humanitarian concern for the welfare of East Pakistani refugees.

41.
Name: Pleiku Evacuation.
Location: South Vietnam.
Date(s): Late April 1972.
Emergency: A North Vietnamese invasion of South Vietnam forced thousands of refugees to flee southward.
Air Force Organization(s) Involved: 4th and 53d Mil Alft Sqs.
Airlifted: 782 South Vietnamese refugees.
Aircraft Employed: C–141 (two).
Operations: At the end of March, North Vietnamese forces launched a full-scale invasion of South Vietnam. Using tanks and heavy artillery, the communist offensive threatened South Vietnam's northern provinces and central highlands. As many as 350,000 refugees, mostly women and children, fled southward. When enemy forces threatened Kontum, about 240 miles north of Saigon, refugees poured into neighboring Pleiku in the central highlands. Communist troops also gathered around Pleiku and cut its main highway to the coastal cities. A swelling refugee population feared encirclement.

U.S. cargo planes, including C–130s, C–141s, and C–5s, airlifted weapons and ammunition to South Vietnam during the offensive. C–141s unloading arms at Pleiku airlifted some refugees to Saigon. Two evacuation flights were especially noteworthy. On April 29, a 4th Mil Alft Sq C–141 flew 394 South Vietnamese refugees from Pleiku to Tan Son Nhut AB in Saigon. Never had so many passengers flown on a Starlifter, which normally carried only 90 passengers. A seven-man crew led by Capt. Richard Semingson flew the mission. The refugees sat on the floor of the cargo compartment holding onto tie-down straps.

At about the same time, another C–141 transported 388 South Vietnamese refugees from Pleiku to Saigon. Flown by Capt. Erik Jensen of the 53d Mil Alft Sq, the Starlifter had delivered Howitzer shells to Pleiku. Aware that enemy mortar shells might begin falling on the airfield, requiring an emergency departure, Jensen and his crew loaded the passengers with the plane's engines running. Boarding took an hour and a half, and fumes from the four jet engines became a nuisance.

Personnel of the 616th Military Airlift Support Squadron helped the refugees off the Starlifters when they landed at Tan Son Nhut. Local Vietnamese Scouts helped evacuees find temporary shelter with families in Saigon. By May, friendly troops had reopened the highway connecting Pleiku with the coastal cities, reducing the need for airlift.

42.
Name: Han River Flood.
Location: South Korea.
Date(s): August 19–20, 1972.
Emergency: Torrential rain flooded the Han River valley in the Seoul area.
Air Force Organization(s) Involved: Detachment 1, 33d Aerosp RR Sq.
Airlifted: 748 flood victims and 1,100 pounds of food.
Aircraft Employed: HH–3 (two) and HH–43 (one).
Operations: Torrential rain drenched South Korea in mid-August. On August 19 and 20, the Han River flooded Seoul. Swelling to as wide as six miles, the river flowed as fast as 30 mph and put parts of the city under more than six feet of water. Thousands of people were stranded on roof tops, telephone poles, or floating debris. The worst flood in Korea in 65 years left 398 people dead, 130 missing, 405 injured, and hundreds of thousands homeless.

Detachment 1 of the 33d Aerosp RR Sq at nearby Osan AB responded to emergency calls with rescue helicopters. Using two HH–3 Jolly Green Giant craft and a smaller HH–43 Huskie, the detachment rescued 748 people in two days. The crews hoisted stranded people from flooded areas, taking the injured, sick, and elderly to Osan AB. One of the larger helicopters shuttled 70 people from a disappearing island in the river to a school yard three miles away. Most helicopter flights proceeded despite continued heavy rain. The crews flew medical workers and 1,100 pounds of food to stranded refugees.

43.
Name: Cambodian Rice Airlift.
Location: Cambodia.
Date(s): October–December 1973.
Emergency: Fighting around Phnom Penh cut overland supply routes to the Cambodian capital, producing a food shortage.
Air Force Organization(s) Involved: 374th Tac Alft Wg.

Airlifted: 3,000 tons of rice.
Aircraft Employed: C–130 (number unknown).
Operations: The Cambodian government of Premier Lon Nol fought Khmer Rouge rebels in 1973. Fighting reduced the country's food supply and impeded food distribution, and by autumn serious food shortages affected Phnom Penh as insurgent forces interdicted supply routes to the capital.

Although the Air Force had halted bombing missions in Cambodia, U.S. C–130 cargo planes from the 374th Tac Alft Wg continued to fly military supplies from Thailand to Lon Nol's forces. The U.S. embassy in Phnom Penh requested an emergency airlift of rice in addition to ammunition already being flown to the city. In October, C–130s began hauling rice from Battambang, an area of Cambodia where rice was still plentiful, to Pochentong Airfield near Phnom Penh. Between October 2 and 12, the planes hauled 847 tons of rice to the capital. By Christmas, they had delivered 3,000 tons.

The food airlift faced hazards. On October 8, Khmer Rouge forces fired a Strella SA–7 surface-to-air missile at a C–130 as it departed Pochentong. Although the missile did not hit the plane, the incident halted the rice airlift for two days. Monsoon rains also delayed operations.

Despite such problems, the rice airlift succeeded in temporarily ending the food shortage in the Cambodian capital. Opening of land routes to Phnom Penh and boat deliveries up the Mekong River from South Vietnam increased rice stocks and made further food deliveries by air unnecessary.

44.
Name: Bangladeshi Flood and Famine.
Location: Bangladesh.
Date(s): August and December 1974.
Emergency: Heavy rain flooded rivers in Bangladesh, inundating over half the country and displacing millions of people. Epidemics and famine followed.
Air Force Organization(s) Involved: 63d Mil Alft Wg and 374th Tac Alft Wg.
Airlifted: 1,050 tons of food, tents, blankets, tarpaulins, and water containers.
Aircraft Employed: C–141 (two) and C–130 (one).
Operations: Heavy rain flooded the Brahmaputra and Ganges River valleys of Bangladesh during the summer. By early August, 30,000 square miles—more than half the country—were inundated. The flooding, combined with a cholera epidemic, killed more than 800 people and displaced as many as five million. Beset also by an economic crisis, Bangladesh appealed for international aid.

In August, MAC flew 50 tons of tents, blankets, tarpaulins, and water containers to Dacca, the capital of Bangladesh. Three 63d Mil Alft Wg C–141 Starlifter cargo planes departed Andersen AFB, Guam, for the operation, but one Starlifter remained at a staging base at U Tapao, Thailand, due to engine trouble. One C–141 returned to U Tapao to retrieve the disabled plane's load.

The airport at Dacca lacked adequate mechanized equipment, so each aircraft was unloaded by hand, a task which took almost four hours per plane. The cargo included 600 six-man tents and 15,000 blankets. Lt. Douglas H. Poppe and Lt. Michael S. Venturino served as aircraft commanders, and crews came from the 63d Military Airlift Wing's 14th and 15th Mil Alft Sqs.

Despite the airlift and other international aid, Bangladesh continued to suffer from the effects of the flood. The food shortage threatened Rangpur, Mymensingh, and other cities in the northern part of the country. At the end of October, Secretary of State Henry Kissinger flew to Dacca to discuss further U.S. aid with the prime minister of Bangladesh, Sheik Mujibur Rahman.

At the end of the year, the Air Force flew another airlift to Bangladesh, this time to deliver food. Extensive preparations preceded the operation. The Agency for International Development, which funded the project, shipped large stocks of food from surplus U.S. civil defense stocks to Chittagong in southeastern Bangladesh. The 374th Tac Alft Wg used a C–130 from Clark AB in the Philippines to shuttle the food from Chittagong to the famine area. At the end of November, the cargo plane flew to Bangladesh, staging through U Tapao.

Between December 3 and 18, the C–130 flew 110 sorties between Chittagong and old World War II airfields in northern Bangladesh, carrying 1,000 tons of food. The plane flew to Dacca periodically for maintenance. Lt. Col. Herbie C. Tillett served as mission commander. A Norwegian C–130 also airlifted food to Bangladesh in December. On December 19, the U.S. C–130 returned to Clark AB, its mission accomplished.

45.
Name: Burmese Flood.
Location: Burma.
Date(s): August 26–27, 1974.
Emergency: The Irrawaddy River flooded large parts of Burma, driving hundreds of thousands of people from their homes.
Air Force Organization(s) Involved: Twenty-second Air Force, 63d Mil Alft Wg, and 53d Mil Alft Sq.
Airlifted: More than 34 tons of medical supplies.
Aircraft Employed: C–141 (two).
Operations: During August, monsoon rains in Burma flooded the Irrawaddy River valley, inundating more than 1,800 villages along its banks. By August 20, 12 people had died and 500,000 had been driven from their homes. The Burmese government asked the United States for an airlift of medical supplies.

On August 26 and 27, two Twenty-second Air Force C–141 Starlifter aircraft transported more than 34 tons of medical relief cargo from Clark AB in the Philippines to Rangoon, capital of Burma. The Agency for International Development, an arm of the State Department, provided the supplies. A six-man crew from the 53d Mil Alft Sq of the 63d Mil Alft Wg flew one of the planes. Commanded by 1st Lt. Thomas Grove, the C–141 was diverted from a routine mission to Kadena AB, Okinawa, Japan. After flying 10 pallets of medical supplies from Clark to Rangoon, the plane returned to Kadena.

46.
Name: Thai Flood.
Location: Thailand.
Date(s): January 12–27, 1975.
Emergency: Heavy rains flooded the provinces of southern Thailand. High water cut roads and contributed to a cholera epidemic.
Air Force Organization(s) Involved: 56th Sp Ops Wg and 374th Tac Alft Wg.
Airlifted: More than 350 tons of food, clothing, medical supplies, boats, and fuel.
Aircraft Employed: C–130 (two+), CH–53 (two), and UH–1 (two).
Operations: Torrential rain flooded the southern provinces of Thailand in January, killing more than 200 people and driving over 15,000 from their homes. The flood cut highways and railroads, inhibiting the distribution of food. It also spawned a minor cholera epidemic. On January 11, King Bhumibol Adulyadej asked William R. Kintner, U.S. ambassador to Thailand, for an airlift to relieve the flood victims. The king donated most of the supplies to be airlifted.

Between January 12 and 25, C–130s from the 374th Tac Alft Wg transported more than 350 tons of rice, milk, medical supplies, clothing, boats, and fuel from Don Muang Royal Thai AFB to Trang and Hat Yai in the disaster area. The four-engine cargo planes flew 24 sorties during two weeks, with Capt. Donald M. Dessert, Jr., commanding the first C–130. Princess Vitawadi of Thailand rode on a subsequent flight to represent the royal family.

Most of the cargo consisted of 222-pound sacks of rice. Each C–130 load averaged between 10 and 15 tons, and the cargo piled up at the Trang and Hat Yai airfields. To help distribute the rice, the 56th Sp Ops Wg used a pair of CH–53 helicopters. They flew 39 missions between January 19 and 27. Two smaller UH–1 helicopters also helped distribute relief cargo in the disaster area until roads reopened.

There were some problems during the airlift. A C–130 bogged down in mud at Trang and another experienced a starter malfunction. Poor distribution planning allowed too much food to pile up at air terminals while people in remote flooded regions went hungry. But, overall, the relief operation was successful. After U.S. cargo planes and helicopters returned to their home bases, Thai military forces continued to distribute relief supplies to flood victims in southern Thailand.

47.
Name: Singaporean Oil Spill.
Location: Strait of Malacca.
Date(s): January 14–16, 1975.
Emergency: A Japanese supertanker carrying 237,000 tons of crude oil ran aground near Singapore and began spilling oil into the Strait of Malacca.

Humanitarian Airlift Operations

Air Force Organization(s) Involved: 437th Mil Alft Wg.
Airlifted: A 12-member Coast Guard team and 18 tons of pumping equipment.
Aircraft Employed: C–141 (one).
Operations: On January 6, the Japanese supertanker *Showa Maru*, carrying 237,000 tons of oil, ran aground about eight miles from Singapore. The ruptured ship spilled one million gallons of light crude oil into the Strait of Malacca. Leaders of Singapore, Malaysia, and Indonesia threatened to close the strait to supertankers. President Ford, anxious to reassure the governments of U.S. support as communist forces threatened to take over all of Indochina, authorized cleanup assistance.

Between January 14 and 16, a 437th Mil Alft Wg C–141 Starlifter from Charleston AFB, South Carolina, flew a 12-member Coast Guard team and 18 tons of pumping equipment to Singapore. The cargo included four systems capable of pumping 1,000 gallons of oil a minute. Flying 11,000 miles, the plane staged at Hickam AFB, Hawaii; Andersen AFB, Guam; and Clark AB in the Philippines.

48.

Name: Vietnamese Evacuation (Babylift, New Life, Frequent Wind, and New Arrivals).
Location: South Vietnam, Thailand, Philippines, Guam, and Wake.
Date(s): April 4–September 16, 1975.
Emergency: As communist forces took over South Vietnam, more than 130,000 refugees fled by sea and air.
Air Force Organization(s) Involved: 60th, 62d, 63d, 436th, 437th, 438th, and 446th Mil Alft Wgs; 514th Mil Alft Wg (Associate); 314th and 374th Tac Alft Wgs; 56th Sp Ops Wg; 21st Sp Ops Sq; 9th Aeromedical Evacuation Group (Aeromed Evac Gp); and 40th Aerosp RR Sq.
Airlifted: At least 50,000 refugees; more than 5,000 relief workers; and 8,556 tons of supplies, including food, bedding, and shelters.
Aircraft Employed: C–141 (number unknown), C–130 (31+), CH–53 (7), HH–53 (2), and C–9 (number unknown).
Operations: In April 1975, communist forces took over South Vietnam and Cambodia (Kampuchea). Khmer Rouge troops entered Phnom Penh in the middle of the month, just after Marine Corps helicopters evacuated the last U.S. citizens in an operation called Eagle Pull. As North Vietnamese and Viet Cong forces closed in on Saigon and the South Vietnamese government began to collapse, tens of thousands of refugees sought to escape the country. Thousands fled by sea, riding in small boats to Navy ships in the South China Sea or in ships to the Philippines and beyond. Thousands more escaped by air.

The Vietnamese refugee airlift, the largest aerial evacuation in history, encompassed a series of overlapping operations that are difficult to separate: Babylift, New Life, Frequent Wind, and New Arrivals. In these operations, the Air

432

Force, working with the Navy and private contractors, flew more than 50,000 refugees from southeast Asia to islands in the Pacific Ocean and eventually to new homes in the United States.

President Ford announced Operation Babylift on April 3 at a news conference in San Diego, California. U.S. cargo planes would transport hundreds of Vietnamese and Cambodian orphans from southeast Asia to the United States. The president of World Airways, Ed Daly, originated the idea, and the U.S. ambassador in Saigon, Graham Martin, advocated the use of Air Force aircraft in addition to commercial contract airliners. The Agency for International Development and private adoption agencies helped to sponsor the airlift.

Operation Babylift began with tragedy. On April 4, a C–5 Galaxy from the 60th Mil Alft Wg, which had just delivered howitzers to Tan Son Nhut AB in Saigon, loaded more than 300 passengers—including at least 230 orphans—for a flight to the Philippines. About 14 minutes into the flight, as the plane climbed to 23,000 feet, an explosive decompression blew out the rear cargo doors and damaged flight controls to the tail. Capt. Dennis Traynor tried to fly the disabled plane back to Saigon. Unable to steer precisely, he was forced to crash-land in rice fields about five miles from Tan Son Nhut. Miraculously, more than half of the passengers survived, including 149 orphans. The Air Force grounded the C–5s, but continued the operation with other cargo planes.

Operation Babylift lasted from April 4 through May 6. Participating organizations included the 60th, 62d, and 63d Mil Alft Wgs and the 514th Mil Alft Wg (Associate), which flew C–141 Starlifters; the 374th Tac Alft Wg, which flew C–130 Hercules airplanes; and the 9th Aeromed Evac Gp, which used C–9s to airlift some of the C–5 crash victims to safety. Air Force cargo planes carried 949 Vietnamese orphans from Saigon and Cambodian orphans from U Tapao, Thailand, to U.S. bases in the Philippines and Guam. They later flew through Hickam AFB, Hawaii; McChord AFB, Washington; and Norton and Travis AFBs, California, to reception centers in California, Washington, and Georgia.

The Military Airlift Command airlifted 1,794 Babylift passengers. Another 884 orphans flew out of South Vietnam on private planes not under military contract. Most of the more than 2,500 refugee children found homes in the United States.

Closely related to Operation Babylift was Operation New Life, which evacuated Vietnamese from South Vietnam just before the government's collapse. The Thirteenth Air Force helped to coordinate Air Force airlift efforts under a single theater airlift manager, Brig. Gen. Richard T. Drury. Air Force cargo planes airlifted more than 50,000 passengers from Saigon in 375 Operation New Life flights. Between April 4 and 28, C–141 Starlifters from the 60th, 62d, 63d, 437th, and 438th Mil Alft Wgs airlifted refugees out by day, while C–130s from the 374th and 314th Tac Alft Wgs evacuated Vietnamese by night. There were 161 New Life C–130 missions, which transported 20,834 passengers from Saigon to the Philippines the last week in April. At first, the cargo planes flew the refugees

Humanitarian Airlift Operations

to U.S. bases in the Philippines, but when President Ferdinand Marcos set limits on the number of refugees in his country, the Air Force flew the evacuees on to Guam and Wake, where they were processed for further travel to the United States.

Babylift and New Life overlapped. A 514th Mil Alft Wg (Associate) C–141 flown by Maj. Wayne DeLawter carried 189 orphans from Saigon to Clark AB in the Philippines. Immediately after unloading the passengers, the Starlifter boarded 250 other Vietnamese refugees for a flight from Clark to Guam. The mission lasted 19 hours.

During April, the Navy set up 13 Vietnamese camps on Guam. Refugees also found temporary shelter at Andersen AFB. By air and sea, almost 112,000 refugees traveled through Guam on their way to the United States, with at least 70,000 arriving by air. The island sheltered as many as 50,430 at a time. When Guam filled with refugees, a newer processing camp on Wake Island went into operation.

Many Vietnamese who fled from Saigon had worked for U.S. agencies or belonged to families of those who did and feared that the new government would threaten their lives. Others sought to escape because they did not want to live under a communist system. Still others were wives or children of U.S. citizens who had served in South Vietnam, either in the military or as civilians.

At the end of April, Operation New Life faced increasing dangers as enemy forces approached closer to the center of the South Vietnamese capital. On April 24, gunfire damaged a C–130 as it flew over the Saigon area. Two days later, both a C–130 and a C–141 were hit by bullets near Tan Son Nhut AB. On April 27, the C–141 flights out of Saigon ceased. When communist artillery hit and set on fire a C–130 on the ground at Tan Son Nhut on April 28, Hercules flights out of Saigon also ended.

When Operation New Life concluded, it had compiled a record of 201 C–141 flights and 174 C–130 sorties. Two C–130 missions evacuated Vietnamese refugees from Vung Tau on the coast, but other flights took escapees out of Saigon.

On the last two days of the Saigon siege, April 29 and 30, helicopters offered the only air escape route from South Vietnam. Navy and Marine Corps CH–46 and CH–53 helicopters carried out most remaining U.S. and Vietnamese refugees, but nine Air Force helicopters—seven CH–53s from the 56th Sp Ops Wg and two HH–53s of the 40th Aerosp RR Sq—took part in Operation Frequent Wind.

The U.S. helicopters airlifted more than 6,000 passengers out of Saigon on April 29 and 30, including over 5,000 Vietnamese. Of 662 helicopter sorties, the Air Force flew 82. The helicopters shuttled between the besieged capital and U.S. ships in the South China Sea, including the aircraft carrier USS *Midway*. The 21st Sp Ops Sq, a unit of the 56th Sp Ops Wg, carried 1,831 evacuees to the carrier. When the *Midway* became overcrowded, the squadron also moved 804 refugees from the carrier to other Navy ships in the flotilla.

More than 73,000 evacuees fled by boat from South Vietnam to the Philippines in April. Between April 29 and May 9, MAC C–141s and C–130s transported more than 31,000 Vietnamese refugees from the Philippines to Guam. The 196 flights comprised 61 by C–141s and 135 by C–130s. Between April 30 and May 14, C–130s carried 21,570 refugees from the Philippines to Guam. The 374th Tac Alft Wg flew most C–130 missions, supported by a squadron rotating from the 314th Tac Alft Wg, based in Arkansas. Air Force refugee airlift flights to Guam, at times suspended because of overcrowding, concluded on May 17.

The temporary refugee camps in the Philippines, Guam, and Wake demanded tremendous quantities of relief supplies to feed and shelter the thousands of Vietnamese who fled to them, not only by Air Force airlift but also by U.S. Navy vessels and commercial airliners under MAC contract. During the spring of 1975, MAC transported 8,556 tons of cargo to the camps, including beds, mattresses, blankets, tents, rations, evaporated milk, baby food, and insecticides. Delivered primarily by C–141s of the 437th and 438th Mil Alft Wgs, most cargo went to the main refugee camps on Guam and Wake. Riding aboard many of the 414 Air Force flights were thousands of relief workers, including medical personnel, cooks, bakers, and engineers.

The last Vietnamese evacuation airlift operation, New Arrivals, transported tens of thousands of refugees from temporary camps on Pacific Ocean islands to the United States. The 60th, 62d, 63d, 436th, 437th, and 438th Mil Alft Wgs and the 314th Tac Alft Wg employed C–141s, C–130s, and C–5s to airlift refugees from the Philippines, Guam, and Wake through Hickam, Norton, Travis, and McChord AFBs to processing centers at Eglin AFB, Florida; Fort Chaffee, Arkansas; Camp Pendleton, California; and Fort Indiantown Gap, Pennsylvania. Between April 29 and September 16, the Air Force flew 251 military missions in support of the New Arrivals operation. Commercial planes under contract to MAC flew 349 other flights for the operation.

Fort Chaffee lacked adequate runways for the Arkansas-bound refugees, so they landed at nearby Fort Smith and rode buses to the Fort Chaffee processing center. In 15 days in May, 73 commercial and 123 military flights transported 24,560 passengers to Fort Smith. Some Vietnamese riding on Boeing 747s landed at Little Rock AFB and transferred to smaller military aircraft that could land at Fort Smith.

More than 130,000 Vietnamese refugees traveled from the Pacific island camps to the United States in the spring and summer of 1975. How many rode aboard Air Force planes is not certain, but there were probably more than 50,000, as many as had flown from Southeast Asia to the Pacific islands in Operation New Life.

The Vietnamese evacuation airlift operations demonstrated the utility of a single theater airlift manager, the effectiveness of integrating strategic and tactical airlift resources, and above all, the critical contribution of ground support personnel to mission success. The airlift operations also exposed weaknesses in emergency airlift evacuation procedures, aircraft structures, and diplomatic relations.

Airlift could not transport all of the refugees who sought to escape as communist forces took over South Vietnam in the desperate spring of 1975. Thousands of people who sought escape were left behind, but the airlift did carry tens of thousands to freedom.

49.
Name: Sri Lankan Cyclone.
Location: Sri Lanka.
Date(s): November 27–29, 1978.
Emergency: A cyclone hit Sri Lanka, leaving more than 200 people dead and as many as 150,000 homeless.
Air Force Organization(s) Involved: 60th and 63d Mil Alft Wgs.
Airlifted: 66 tons of tents, blankets, and tools; and a 20-man disaster assistance team.
Aircraft Employed: C–141 (five).
Operations: On November 25 and 26, a cyclone struck the island of Sri Lanka just southeast of the southern tip of India. High winds and rain left more than 200 people dead and 150,000 homeless. The government appealed for U.S. aid through the United States embassy in Colombo, the capital. The State Department decided to sponsor relief through the Agency for International Development's Office of Foreign Disaster Assistance.

Working with the State Department, the JCS directed MAC and its Twenty-second Air Force to organize and execute an emergency airlift to Sri Lanka. The Pacific Airlift Center at Hickam AFB, Hawaii, coordinated the operation.

Between November 27 and 29, five C–141 Starlifters carried a 20-man disaster area survey team from Hickam AFB and 66 tons of tents, blankets, and tools—including saws, shovels, axes, and machetes—from Andersen AFB, Guam, and Clark AFB in the Philippines to Colombo's Katunayake International Airport. Three of the C–141s came from the 60th Mil Alft Wg, based at Travis AFB, California; the other two came from the 63d Mil Alft Wg at Norton AFB, also in California. The disaster area survey team completed its mission on December 13 and returned to Hickam on a Twenty-second Air Force C–141.

50.
Name: Cambodian Famine Relief.
Location: Airlift to Singapore.
Date(s): December 3–9, 1979.
Emergency: Civil war and a Vietnamese invasion contributed to famine in Cambodia. The UN and the International Committee of the Red Cross sought an airlift of equipment to distribute food and medical supplies.
Air Force Organization(s) Involved: 60th Mil Alft Wg.

436

Airlifted: 145 tons of trucks and cranes.

Aircraft Employed: C–5 (two).

Operations: In the late 1970s, civil war in Cambodia and a Vietnamese invasion contributed to a famine that threatened the people with mass starvation. The United Nations International Children's Emergency Fund (UNICEF) and the International Committee of the Red Cross shipped food and medical supplies to Phnom Penh, the capital of Cambodia, but relief workers lacked sufficient equipment to unload and distribute the cargo. In late 1979, officials from the relief agencies purchased 10 cargo trucks and nine truck-mounted cranes in Japan and requested U.S. assistance to airlift the equipment to Phnom Penh.

The State Department relayed the request to the Defense Department, which assigned the mission to MAC. To accommodate the massive cargo, the Air Force used what was then the largest aircraft in the world, the C–5 Galaxy. On December 3 and 4, the 60th Mil Alft Wg from Travis AFB, California, flew two Galaxies to Yokota AB, Japan, to pick up the 19 vehicles, which weighed about 145 tons. The airplanes flew to Clark AB in the Philippines for refueling and crew rest and awaited diplomatic clearance to land at Phnom Penh.

Failing to secure such a clearance, the State Department arranged for the C–5s to take their cargo to Singapore, where the equipment was transferred to ships for sealift to Cambodia. The C–5s completed delivery to Singapore's Tengah AB on December 9.

51.

Name: Korean Flood.

Location: South Korea.

Date(s): September 2, 1984.

Emergency: The Han River, swollen by heavy rain, flooded its valley, stranding over 100 Koreans.

Air Force Organization(s) Involved: 38th Aerosp RR Sq.

Airlifted: At least 96 flood victims.

Aircraft Employed: CH–3 (one) and HH–3 (two).

Operations: In early September, the rain-swollen Han River in the northern part of South Korea spilled over its banks, killing at least 81 people, driving 100,000 from their homes, and stranding more than 100 in the Seoul area.

The Western Pacific Rescue Coordination Center dispatched helicopters to rescue flood victims. On September 2, the 38th Aerosp RR Sq used two HH–3s and a CH–3 to lift more than 96 flood victims to higher ground. One helicopter was forced to land because of an engine fire, but there were no injuries. An Army HH–60 helicopter also participated in the emergency missions. The four aircraft rescued 136 flood victims in 15 sorties that day.

52.
Name: Korean Shipwreck.
Location: Off the coast of South Korea.
Date(s): January 28, 1985.
Emergency: A fishing vessel with a 10-man crew aboard ran aground in high winds, waves, and freezing temperatures.
Air Force Organization(s) Involved: 38th Aerosp RR Sq.
Airlifted: 10 shipwreck victims.
Aircraft Employed: H–3 (two).
Operations: On January 28, the Korean fishing vessel *Sung Bock Ho* lost power near Songju Island and began drifting in the Yellow Sea about 50 miles from Kunsan harbor, South Korea. The Korean Combined Rescue Coordination Center reported the ship's distress signal to the 38th Aerosp RR Sq at Osan AB, and the squadron sent a pair of H–3 Jolly Green Giant helicopters on a search and rescue mission.

By the time the helicopters reached the *Sung Bock Ho*, it had run aground on large rocks. Thirty-knot winds and waves up to nine feet high lashed the vessel, while freezing temperatures coated the deck with ice. Eight of the 10-man crew huddled on the bow of the boat as its stern began to sink. The remaining two crew members clung to the top of the pilot's tower.

One of the helicopters, flown by Capt. John B. Bond, hovered high overhead to serve as a communications link and to drop smoke markers for the other helicopter, commanded by Capt. Mark C. Noyes. Noyes lowered two pararescue men to the deck of the sinking vessel to assess the condition of the boat's crew. They reported that the men were suffering from exposure and needed immediate evacuation. Carefully avoiding the rocks and guide wires around the pilot's tower, Noyes and his crew hoisted the 10 fishermen and two pararescue men onto the helicopter and flew the shipwreck victims to a Kunsan hospital. The 38th Aerosp RR Sq earned the Jolly Green Giant Association "Rescue Mission of the Year" award for 1985 for their work.

53.
Name: Osan Fire.
Location: South Korea.
Date(s): April 5–6, 1986.
Emergency: A fire at a jet fuel tank lasted for several hours and threatened to spread.
Air Force Organization(s) Involved: 63d Mil Alft Wg and 38th Aerosp RR Sq.
Airlifted: Fire-suppressant foam and burn victims.
Aircraft Employed: C–141 (four) and H–3 (one).
Operations: On April 5, a 700,000-gallon tank of jet fuel exploded and burned at Osan AB in South Korea. The inferno killed 16 people and injured 11. Strong winds and a fuel pipeline feeding the ruptured tank kept the fire burning for more

than 12 hours. Firefighters began to exhaust their supplies of foam in their efforts to control and extinguish the fire.

In response to the emergency, four C–141 Starlifter aircraft from the 63d Mil Alft Wg delivered fire-suppressant foam to Osan AB. A 38th Aerosp RR Sq H–3 helicopter flew some burn victims from Osan to a hospital in Seoul for medical treatment. The airlifts supplemented joint military efforts on the ground, which prevented the fire from spreading and limited the loss of life.

54.
Name: Bangladeshi Flood.
Location: Bangladesh.
Date(s): September 10–15, 1988.
Emergency: A flood killed 1,200 people and left as many as 28 million homeless.
Air Force Organization(s) Involved: 60th, 62d, 63d, and 436th Mil Alft Wgs.
Airlifted: At least 100 tons of plastic sheeting, water containers, water purification units, boats, tents, blankets, and a field hospital.
Aircraft Employed: C–5 (one) and C–141 (one).
Operations: During the summer, the heaviest monsoon rains in decades descended on the Brahmaputra River valley in northeastern India and Bangladesh. By September, more than three-quarters of Bangladesh and most of the capital city of Dacca were inundated. At least 1,200 people perished in the flooding and 28 million of a total population of 110 million were forced from their homes. The government appealed to the United States for aid.

The State Department's Agency for International Development and Office of Foreign Disaster Assistance coordinated relief efforts with the Defense Department's Office of Humanitarian Assistance. In response to their requests, MAC conducted two airlift flights to the disaster area.

A 436th Mil Alft Wg C–5 Galaxy left Dover AFB in Delaware on September 10 for the first Bangladesh relief mission. It flew to Andrews AFB in Maryland, where it picked up 80 tons of supplies. The cargo filled 34 pallets and included 62 rolls of plastic sheeting for shelter, which could cover more than 2.2 million square feet. It also included 10,000 five-gallon water containers, two water purification units, and water storage tanks. Jay F. Morris, the acting director of AID, rode aboard the C–5 as it took off from Andrews.

The Galaxy developed mechanical trouble over western North America that prevented in-flight refueling and forced it to divert to Elmendorf AFB, Alaska, for repairs. After maintenance and a crew change, the C–5 continued to Yokota AB in Japan, where it changed crews again before proceeding on to Bangladesh. After two in-flight refuelings between Japan and Bangladesh, the aircraft landed at Dacca on September 11.

A 62d Mil Alft Wg C–141 from McChord AFB, Washington, flew the second Bangladesh relief mission. It picked up boats, tents, and blankets from an

Humanitarian Airlift Operations

Office of Foreign Disaster Assistance stockpile at Howard AFB in Panama. From there it flew via Norton AFB in California, Hickam AFB in Hawaii, and Wake Island in the Pacific to Kadena AB in Okinawa, Japan. There it loaded a field hospital before continuing on to Bangladesh, where it landed on September 15. Like the C–5, the C–141 also changed crews on the long trip to southern Asia.

The two airlift flights delivered more than 100 tons of equipment and supplies to Bangladesh, helping flood victims to recover. After the operation, Dr. Robert K. Wolthuis, the DoD director of humanitarian assistance, praised MAC for its support of U.S. foreign policy objectives in southern Asia.

55.
Name: Sea Angel.
Location: Bangladesh.
Date(s): May 10–June 13, 1991.
Emergency: A typhoon with winds of 150 mph and a 20-foot tidal wave swept across the densely populated coast of Bangladesh.
Air Force Organization(s) Involved: Twenty-second Air Force; 834th Alft Div; 60th, 349th, 436th, and 438th Mil Alft Wgs; 374th Tac Alft Wg; 353d Sp Ops Wg; 17th Sp Ops Sq; and 18th, 22d, and 312th Mil Alft Sqs.
Airlifted: More than 3,000 tons of relief equipment and supplies, including helicopters, water purification equipment, food, medicine, clothing, cots, batteries, and water bottles; and 510 passengers, including military personnel to distribute supplies.
Aircraft Employed: C–5 (6), C–141 (13), C–130 (2), and HC–130 (2).
Operations: On the night of April 29–30, Cyclone Marion struck the low-lying coast of Bangladesh. Winds as high as 150 mph tore homes apart and drove a 20-foot tidal wave across densely populated islands in the Bay of Bengal west of Chittagong. Torrential rains contributed to coastal flooding. As many as 139,000 people died and millions were left homeless. Aware of shortages of food, shelter, potable water, and medicine, Prime Minister Khaleda Zia asked the United States for humanitarian assistance. President Bush responded with an operation whose original name, Productive Effort, was later changed to Sea Angel.

Marine Corps Maj. Gen. Henry C. Stackpole III commanded a 7,000-man joint task force for Operation Sea Angel. Many troops and cargo moved by ship from the Persian Gulf, where they were deployed for Desert Storm, and some reached Bangladesh by air. The 834th Airlift Division's Col. Edward G. Hoffman served as airlift commander under Stackpole.

Six C–5 and 13 C–141 missions transported more than 600 tons of equipment and supplies from Saudi Arabia, Thailand, Hawaii, Japan, the Philippines, and Guam to Bangladesh beginning on May 10. Flown by crews from Twenty-second Air Force military airlift wings and the 438th Mil Alft Wg, the four-engine jet transports carried helicopters, water purification equipment, food, medicine, clothing, cots, batteries, and water bottles. They also transported 510 passengers,

440

mostly military personnel to distribute relief supplies in the flooded disaster area. Many troops came from the Persian Gulf, but some deployed from a training exercise in Thailand. The C–5s and C–141s unloaded at Dacca, the capital of Bangladesh.

Two HC–130s from the 353d Sp Ops Wg and two C–130s from the 374th Tac Alft Wg transported relief supplies from Dacca to Chittagong in Bangladesh's devastated coastal region. Within the country, the four-engine prop-jets distributed over 2,400 tons of relief supplies, some of which had been sealifted to Bangladesh. To move the airlifted cargo from Chittagong to the flooded areas, the joint task force used Army, Navy, and Marine Corps helicopters and landing craft.

One of the most outstanding Air Force missions transported five Army Blackhawk helicopters and crews from Hawaii to Dacca on May 13. A 60th Mil Alft Wg C–5 flown by a 312th Mil Alft Sq crew carried out the mission. On May 19, another 60th Mil Alft Wg C–5, flown by Capt. Dan Tank and his crew, delivered 60 marines and 24 water purification units from Japan to Dacca.

Sea Angel demonstrated the ability of U.S. armed forces to respond to two simultaneous crises. While joint forces delivered thousands of tons of relief equipment and supplies to Bangladesh, U.S. military units continued to send aid to thousands of Kurdish refugees in northern Iraq and eastern Turkey.

56.
Name: Mongolian Medical Mission.
Location: Mongolia.
Date(s): July 22, 1991.
Emergency: Mongolia suffered shortages of medical supplies.
Air Force Organization(s) Involved: 445th Mil Alft Wg and 730th Mil Alft Sq.
Airlifted: Almost 20 tons of medical supplies.
Aircraft Employed: C–141 (one).
Operations: Inspired by reforms in Eastern Europe and in the Soviet Union, Mongolia removed the Communist Party's monopoly on power and in 1990 held its first multiparty elections. At the same time, the country moved away from socialism and toward a free market economy. Joseph Lake, U.S. ambassador to Mongolia, was anxious to encourage Mongolia's drift toward democracy and economic freedom and aware of the country's dire need for medical supplies. He therefore arranged in 1991 with Robert Wolthuis and Gregory Touma of the Department of Defense to airlift excess DoD medical supplies from an Army warehouse in Okinawa, Japan.

On July 22, a C–141 Starlifter, piloted by Lt. Col. John Dorris, AF Res, carried almost 20 tons of medical supplies from Kadena AB in Okinawa to Ulan Bator, capital of Mongolia. Dorris led an eight-man crew from the 730th Mil Alft Sq of the 445th Mil Alft Wg, based at Norton AFB in California. The 2,000-mile flight crossed over China in an area never before reached by a U.S. military aircraft. About 100 Mongolian volunteers unloaded the Starlifter in four hours. The cargo included 39,000 pounds of bandages, sutures, catheters, forceps, stethoscopes, and other medical supplies. Dorris allowed the Mongolians to tour his aircraft after the delivery. The airlift reduced the medical supply shortage and improved the relationship between the United States and Mongolia—a relationship that was nonexistent during the Cold War.

57.
Name: Chinese Flood Relief.
Location: China.
Date(s): August 6–9, 1991.
Emergency: Heavy rain flooded central and eastern China, killing more than 1,000 people and leaving hundreds of thousands homeless.
Air Force Organization(s) Involved: 60th Mil Alft Wg and 75th Mil Alft Sq.
Airlifted: 75 tons of blankets and medical supplies.
Aircraft Employed: C–5 (one).
Operations: Extremely heavy rain descended on central and eastern China in late July and early August. At least 18 of China's 30 provinces were flooded, leaving 1,400 people dead and driving hundreds of thousands from their homes. When China requested U.S. humanitarian assistance through diplomatic channels, the Department of State contacted DoD for a humanitarian airlift of relief supplies.

Between August 6 and 9, a C–5 Galaxy piloted by Lt. Col. Robert A. Sutley and a crew from the 75th Mil Alft Sq flew blankets and medical supplies from Travis AFB in California to Shanghai, China. Its 32-pallet cargo weighed 75 tons. The airlift demonstrated that the United States would provide humanitarian relief to the Chinese people, despite the government's 1989 suppression of pro-democracy demonstrators in Beijing.

58.
Name: Mongolian Medical Airlift.
Location: Mongolia.
Date(s): October 2, 1991.
Emergency: Mongolia suffered medical shortages when communism collapsed there.
Air Force Organization(s) Involved: 834th Alft Div.
Airlifted: Eight ambulances and 15 pallets of medical supplies.
Aircraft Employed: C–5 (one).
Operations: When Joseph Lake, the U.S. ambassador to Mongolia, reported continued serious medical supply shortages in the wake of the collapse of the communist economy, the State Department arranged with the Defense Department to airlift excess medical supplies similar to an operation flown in July (see Mongolian Medical Mission, July 1991).

On October 2, a C–5 Galaxy aircraft under the direction of the 834th Alft Div flew eight ambulances and 15 pallets of medical supplies from Kadena AB in

Okinawa, Japan, to Ulan Bator, capital of Mongolia. The ambulances came from Army units in Korea and the medical supplies were excess DoD property. Dr. Anthony Gray, representing the Defense Department's Office of Global Affairs, accompanied the ambulances and medical pallets to Ulan Bator.

On October 5, Dr. Gray and Ambassador Lake formally presented the ambulances and medical supplies to the Mongolian minister of health, P. Nyamdawa, who expressed gratitude for the cargo.

59.
Name: Mongolian Medical Relief.
Location: Mongolia.
Date(s): January 20–25 and September 13–17, 1992.
Emergency: Mongolia continued to suffer medical shortages in the wake of the failure of its socialist economy and the collapse of its benefactor, the Soviet Union.
Air Force Organization(s) Involved: 60th Alft Wg, 349th Mil Alft Wg, 22d Alft Sq, and 312th Mil Alft Sq.
Airlifted: More than 60 tons of medicine, hospital equipment, and medical supplies.
Aircraft Employed: C–5 (two).
Operations: The United States continued to airlift medical supplies to Mongolia and the Air Force flew two missions to the capital, Ulan Bator, in 1992, one in January, and another in September. The flights were in response to requests from the State Department, which tried to support the health services of Mongolia as its economy struggled to recover from the failure of socialism.

On January 20, a 60th Alft Wg C–5, flown by a crew composed mostly of Air Force reservists from the 349th Military Airlift Wing's 312th Mil Alft Sq, flew from Travis AFB in California to Kadena AB, Okinawa, Japan. There it loaded 56 tons of medicine, hospital equipment, and medical supplies, some privately donated and some from DoD. The cargo filled 36 pallets. On January 25, the Galaxy flew over China to Ulan Bator, where about 100 Mongolians unloaded the aircraft by hand in subfreezing weather. U.S. embassy staff in Ulan Bator signed over the medical cargo to Mongolian health officials.

The 60th Alft Wg flew a similar mission to Mongolia in September. Another C–5 Galaxy, flown by a 22d Alft Sq crew, journeyed to Kadena on September 13, where it loaded medical relief supplies from a stockpile in Okinawa. Four days later, the airplane crew delivered its cargo to the Mongolian capital.

60.
Name: Nepalese Flood.
Location: Nepal.
Date(s): August 11–15, 1993.
Emergency: Flooding in Nepal near Kathmandu washed out bridges.

Air Force Organization(s) Involved: 436th Alft Wg.
Airlifted: At least 190 tons of bridge components.
Aircraft Employed: C–5 (three).
Operations: Rain and melting snow flooded central Nepal during early August, washing out bridges near Kathmandu, the capital. Responding to a diplomatic request for assistance, the United States and the United Kingdom joined efforts to bring relief to the Nepalese.

The British gathered 190 tons of Bailey Bridge components at RAF Mildenhall, England. Between August 11 and 15, three C–5 Galaxies from the 436th Alft Wg at Dover AFB, Delaware, airlifted the bridge sections from Mildenhall to Kathmandu, with each flight lasting about 27 hours. Engineers used the airlifted components to replace two of the lost bridges in Nepal.

61.
Name: Indian Earthquake.
Location: India.
Date(s): October 2–4, 1993.
Emergency: An earthquake in central India left at least 10,000 people dead and many more thousands homeless.
Air Force Organization(s) Involved: 60th and 436th Alft Wgs.
Airlifted: 1,000 rolls of plastic sheeting, 950 tents, and 18,550 five-gallon water containers; and 22 pallets of blankets, litters, shelter halves, and medical supplies.
Aircraft Employed: C–5 (two).
Operations: On September 29, a series of earthquake tremors, one registering 6.4 on the Richter scale, struck the state of Maharashtra in central India. The quakes leveled thousands of mud-brick homes in 30 villages, leaving at least 10,000 people dead and thousands homeless. It was the worst earthquake to hit India in more than 50 years.

After the Indian government agreed to accept an offer of U.S. disaster relief, the State and Defense Departments organized an airlift. In early October, two AMC C–5 Galaxies—one from the 60th Alft Wg at Travis AFB, California, and the other from the 436th Alft Wg at Dover AFB, Delaware—flew the airlift to Bombay, capital of Maharashtra. The cargo included 1,000 rolls of plastic sheeting, 950 tents, and 18,550 five-gallon water containers from the Office of Foreign Disaster Assistance; and 22 pallets of blankets, litters, shelter halves, and medical supplies from the Department of Defense's Office of Humanitarian and Refugee Affairs. Ambassador Raymond L. Flynn rode aboard one of the C–5s as a personal envoy of President Clinton.

62.
Name: Indian Airlift.
Location: India.
Date(s): Early May 1994.

Emergency: A leper colony in Calcutta needed medical supplies.
Air Force Organization(s) Involved: 910th Alft Gp.
Airlifted: Medical supplies.
Aircraft Employed: C–130 (number unknown).
Operations: Early in the 1990s, a Youngstown, Ohio, heart specialist named Dr. Paul Wright, who periodically traveled to India as a medical missionary, learned of a leper colony in Calcutta that needed medical supplies. He collected donations in the Youngstown area and arranged with Col. Bernard Pieczynski, the commander of the local 910th Alft Gp, to airlift the supplies to India aboard a C–130 aircraft scheduled to fly to Thailand for a training exercise. The Denton Amendment authorized such a delivery.

In early May 1994, the AF Res group delivered the medical supplies to Calcutta on its way to Thailand, as planned. The C–130s, which would have flown empty, were able to relieve the suffering of some of Calcutta's leprosy victims.

63.
Name: Siberian Flood.
Location: Russia.
Date(s): October 30, 1994.
Emergency: A flood northeast of Vladivostok left hundreds of people homeless and created shortages of medical supplies.
Air Force Organization(s) Involved: 62d Alft Wg.
Airlifted: 20 tons of medical supplies, blankets, and tarpaulins.
Aircraft Employed: C–141 (one).
Operations: Heavy rain produced extensive flooding in eastern Siberia northeast of Vladivostok in late October. The floods left 11 people dead and hundreds homeless. The United States, already sending aid to Russia to encourage the country's movement toward democracy and a free market economy, offered $2 million in disaster relief, which helped to help pay for a humanitarian airlift of relief supplies to area hospitals.

On October 30, an AMC C–141 Starlifter transported 20 tons of medical supplies, blankets, and tarpaulins from Kadena AB, Okinawa, Japan, to Vladivostok. Ground vehicles delivered relief supplies to four area hospitals the next day. The airlift reinforced a closer relationship between Russia and the United States.

Chapter 7
The Pacific and Australia

This chapter describes humanitarian airlifts in the Pacific Ocean region, including the East Indies and Hawaii, and Australia.

During World War II, the Japanese attacked U.S. islands in the Pacific, including Hawaii, the Philippines, Guam, the Aleutian Islands, American Samoa, Wake Island, and Midway. While driving the Japanese from the Pacific, U.S. forces left the world's largest ocean an American lake. At the end of the war, several island groups, formerly under Japanese control, fell under trusteeship of the United States. After the Philippines gained its independence in 1946, it remained a U.S. ally. In 1959, Hawaii and Alaska, including the Aleutians, gained statehood.

Through the mid-1990s, the United States maintained many air bases in the Pacific region, which were used to support Cold War military operations and exercises and protect shipping routes to Japan. These bases contributed to U.S. missions in the Korean and Vietnam conflicts and facilitated humanitarian airlifts.

The number of U.S. air bases on Pacific islands declined as the Cold War ended. In 1970, the Air Force operated 11 regional bases, including Itazuke, Misawa, Tachikawa, and Yokota in Japan; Kadena and Naha in Okinawa; Clark in the Philippines; Andersen in Guam; Ching Chuan Kang in Taiwan; Hickam in Hawaii; and Johnston in the central Pacific. By 1994, the bases at Itazuke, Tachikawa, Naha, Clark, Ching Chuan Kang, and Johnston had been closed.

More humanitarian airlifts went to the Pacific islands than any other region of the eastern hemisphere, and only North America and Latin America received more relief airlifts. The Air Force flew about 100 humanitarian operations in the Pacific between 1947 and 1994.

Japan and the Philippines might be called the natural disaster centers of the world. Heavily populated, these islands are subject to intermittent volcanic eruptions and are situated along one of the world's most active earthquake belts. They also lie astride the path of frequent typhoons that develop over the earth's largest ocean. Almost half of the Pacific humanitarian airlift operations went to either Japan or the Philippines.

Twenty Air Force humanitarian airlifts in the Pacific flew 100 or more tons of relief cargo, and six delivered at least 1,000 tons. Three of the largest airlifts relieved typhoon victims in Guam. In Fiery Vigil, the Air Force evacuated more than 14,000 U.S. nationals from the Philippines after the spectacular eruption of Mount Pinatubo in June 1991, which permanently closed Clark AB. Half of the six largest Pacific relief operations took place during the administration of President George Bush, from 1989 to 1992.

Humanitarian Airlift Operations

Statistics: Pacific and Australian Airlifts

Number of humanitarian airlifts: 101.

Most common emergencies: typhoons and tropical storms (39), shipwrecks (16), floods (14), and earthquakes (8).

Most frequent recipients: Japan and the Ryukyu Islands (29), Philippines (20), and Marianas and Guam (6).

Three largest operations, in chronological order: Typhoon Pamela, 1976 (2,650 tons); Fiery Vigil, 1991 (14,000 evacuees); and Typhoon Iniki, 1992 (almost 7,000 tons and 12,000 passengers).

Chronological Listing: Pacific and Australian Airlifts

1. Camiguin Island Volcano	Dec. 1951
2. Operation Warm Clothes	Mar. 1952
3. Operation Ricelift	Mar. 1952
4. Typhoon Olive	Sept. 1952
5. Japanese Shipwreck	Mar. 1953
6. Kyushu Flood	July 1953
7. Wakayama Flood	July 1953
8. Chinese Shipwreck	May 1954
9. Cathay Pacific Airliner Crash	July 1954
10. Nagoya Fire	Oct. 1954
11. Mindanao Earthquake	Apr. 1955
12. Hiroshima Maidens	May 1955
13. Shizunai Flood	July 1955
14. Hokkaido Pestilence	July–Aug. 1955
15. Typhoon Louise	Sept.–Oct. 1955
16. *Tanada Maru* Shipwreck	Dec. 1955
17. Project Gohan	Dec. 1956
18. Kyushu Flood	July–Aug. 1957
19. Hirosaki Flood	Aug. 1958
20. Typhoon Ida	Sept.–Oct. 1958
21. Typhoon Vera	Sept. 1959–Feb. 1960
22. Hawaiian Tsunami	May 1960
23. Yamanashi Relief	June and Dec. 1960
24. Hokkaido Polio Epidemic	Aug. 1960
25. Luzon Flood	Sept. 1960
26. Niigata Blizzard	Jan. 1961
27. Mindanao Flood	Feb. 1962
28. Taiwanese Cholera Epidemic	Aug. 1962
29. Marcus Island Typhoon	Oct. 1962
30. Typhoon Karen	Nov. 1962
31. Japanese Blizzard	Feb. 1963
32. Indonesian Flood	Feb. 1963
33. Indonesian Food Airlift	Apr. 1963
34. *Midori Maru* Disaster	Aug. 1963
35. Typhoon Gloria	Sept. and Oct. 1963
36. Niigata Earthquake	June 1964
37. Muroran Ship Fire	May 1965
38. Ryukyus Rescue	May 1965
39. Typhoon Lucy	Aug. 1965
40. Leper Airlift	Aug. 1965
41. Anthrax Epidemic	Aug. 1965

42. Taal Eruption	Oct. 1965
43. Misawa Fire	Jan. 1966
44. Samoan Typhoon	Feb. 1966
45. Typhoon Sarah	Sept. 1967
46. Typhoon Jean	Apr. 1968
47. Philippine Shipwreck	Apr. 1968
48. Tokachi-Oki Earthquake	May 1968
49. Manila Earthquake	Aug. 1968
50. Minami Daito Airlift	Sept. 1968
51. Typhoon Della	Sept. 1968
52. Manila Floods	Aug.–Sept. 1970
53. Batan Island Earthquake	Oct. 1970
54. Typhoons Joan and Kate	Oct. 1970
55. *Tong Lam* Shipwreck	Oct. 1970
56. Typhoon Patsy	Nov. 1970
57. Typhoon Yolling	Mar. 1971
58. *Kee Lung* Shipwreck	Oct. 1971
59. Scarborough Shoal Shipwrecks	Nov. 1971
60. *Yakal* Shipwreck	Nov.–Dec. 1971
61. Operation Saklolo	July–Aug. 1972
62. Typhoon Celeste	Aug. 1972
63. Capiz Province Flood	Oct. 1973
64. Australian Flood	Feb.–Mar. 1974
65. Cyclone Tracy	Dec. 1974–Jan. 1975
66. Dengue Vector Control	May–June 1975
67. Typhoon Olga	May 1976
68. Typhoon Pamela	May–June 1976
69. Balinese Earthquake	July 1976
70. Eniwetok Evacuation	Dec. 1977
71. Tropical Storm Alice	Jan. 1979
72. *Ta Lai* Shipwreck	Mar. 1979
73. Typhoon Meli	Apr. 1979
74. Project Valentine Assist	Dec. 1979
75. Philippine Shipwreck	Sept. 1981
76. Typhoon Iwa	Nov. 1982
77. KAL Flight 007	Sept. 1983
78. Typhoon Keli	Aug. 1984
79. Pines Hotel Fire	Oct. 1984
80. Typhoon Eric	Jan. 1985
81. *Sung Bock Oh* Sinking	Jan. 1985
82. *Marcos Faberes* Shipwreck	Oct. 1985
83. *Asunción Cinco* Shipwreck	Dec. 1985
84. Guadalcanal Typhoon	May 1986

85. Philippine Airlift — Sept. 1986
86. Typhoon Kim — Dec. 1986
87. Typhoon Uma — Feb. 1987
88. Typhoon Nina — Dec. 1987–Jan. 1988
89. Philippine Medical Airlift — Jan. 1988
90. Typhoon Roy — Feb. 1988
91. Typhoon Ruby — Oct. 1988
92. *Selina* Shipwreck — Dec. 1988
93. Typhoon Ofa — Feb.–Mar. 1990
94. Philippine Earthquake — July–Aug. 1990
95. Panamanian Shipwreck — Dec. 1990
96. Fiery Vigil — June–July 1991
97. Tropical Storm Zelda — Dec. 1991
98. Typhoon Val — Dec. 1991 and Jan. 1992
99. Typhoon Omar — Aug.–Sept. 1992
100. Typhoon Iniki — Sept.–Oct. 1992
101. Provide Refuge — Feb.–Mar. 1993

Humanitarian Airlift Operations

Operations: Pacific and Australian Airlifts

1.
Name: Camiguin Island Volcano.
Location: Republic of the Philippines.
Date(s): Early December 1951.
Emergency: A volcanic eruption buried homes in ash and produced lava flows that drove thousands of people from their homes.
Air Force Organization(s) Involved: Flight B, 2d Air Rscu Sq.
Airlifted: 15 Philippine medical personnel and 4.4 tons of rice and Red Cross medical supplies, including blood plasma and drugs.
Aircraft Employed: Unknown.
Operations: On December 4, the volcano Hibokhibok erupted on Camiguin Island in the southern Philippines. A blast of hot poisonous gases, raining ash, and lava flows killed more than 200 people and left 20,000 homeless in seven villages. As Philippine boats and ships evacuated hundreds of people to Mindanao, a larger island just south of Camiguin, government leaders appealed to the United States to help deliver food and medicine to the volcano victims. U.S. Army, Navy, and Air Force units stationed in the Philippines responded.

Flight B of the 2d Air Rscu Sq, based at Clark AB near Manila, airlifted more than four tons of rice and medical supplies—including blood plasma and morphine—to Camiguin. The flight covered more than 400 miles. The unit also transported 15 Philippine medical personnel to the disaster area. Other U.S. and Philippine military organizations shuttled relief cargo from Manila to Camiguin and Mindanao by air and sea, despite heavy rain from a nearby typhoon. The relief missions helped to sustain the homeless victims until the crisis was over.

2.
Name: Operation Warm Clothes.
Location: Japan.
Date(s): March 1952.
Emergency: An earthquake, tidal waves, and landslides struck northern Japan, leaving thousands of people homeless.
Air Force Organization(s) Involved: 374th Trp Carr Wg.
Airlifted: Hundreds of pounds of clothing, blankets, medicine, and food.
Aircraft Employed: C–54 (one).
Operations: In early March, the heaviest earthquake to hit northern Japan in 50 years struck eastern Hokkaido and northern Honshu. Tidal waves and landslides compounded the destruction, which left 2,800 people homeless in eastern Hokkaido. The Japanese Red Cross collected hundreds of pounds of clothing, blankets, medical supplies, and food and asked the Combat Cargo Command for transportation from the Tokyo area to Hokkaido.

Using a C–54 transport airplane, the 374th Trp Carr Wg at Tachikawa AB near Tokyo airlifted the relief supplies to Camp Chitose, an Army installation in southern Hokkaido. From there, surface vehicles delivered the cargo to Red Cross workers at Kiritappu in the disaster area.

Designated Operation Warm Clothes, the Hokkaido airlift was the first of many U.S. humanitarian airlifts that assisted the Japanese after World War II and it reinforced friendly relations between the United States and Japan. The Korean War, raging just across the Sea of Japan, increased the number of U.S. military aircraft available in Japan for such missions.

3.
Name: Operation Ricelift.
Location: Japan.
Date(s): March 27–28, 1952.
Emergency: Floods isolated villagers in northern Japan, depriving them of adequate food supplies.
Air Force Organization(s) Involved: 3d Air Rscu Sq.
Airlifted: Two tons of rice.
Aircraft Employed: H–5 (one).
Operations: In late March, rapidly thawing snow flooded villages such as Fudai-cho and Hiranamisawa at the base of mountains in northern Honshu, Japan. The flooding isolated about 1,400 villagers, cutting off food supplies. Inhabitants of the town of Kuji collected two tons of rice for their neighbors, but lacked the ability to deliver it. Japanese officials requested a U.S. airlift.

The Air Rscu Svc responded with Operation Ricelift. Flying an H–5 helicopter, Lt. Robert L. Dunlap of the 3d Air Rscu Sq delivered the rice from Kuji to the Fudai-cho area in a series of shuttle flights on March 27 and 28. Each flight carried an average of 400 pounds of rice. The airlift helped to sustain the Honshu flood victims until roads reopened for normal food deliveries. For this mercy mission, the prefecture governor expressed profound thanks.

4.
Name: Typhoon Olive.
Location: Wake Island.
Date(s): September 1952.
Emergency: A typhoon hit Wake Island, forcing hundreds of people to evacuate.
Air Force Organization(s) Involved: Pacific Division, MATS.
Airlifted: Fresh water, food, blankets, and medical supplies.
Aircraft Employed: C–97 (one).
Operations: On September 15, Typhoon Olive struck Wake Island in the mid-Pacific Ocean. The powerful tropical storm destroyed many buildings, depriving people of adequate shelter, potable water, food, bedding, and medical supplies. Since Wake was an important staging base supporting Korean War military operations, the Air Force was quick to respond to the emergency.

Humanitarian Airlift Operations

As soon as the winds abated, the Pacific Division of MATS flew a C–97 Stratofreighter from Kwajalein in the Marshall Islands to Wake Island. The large four-engine aircraft carried a cargo of fresh water, food, blankets, and medical supplies. The C–97 was soon joined by other aircraft, including a Civil Aeronautics Administration C–54, a Coast Guard B–17, and a Pan American Airways Stratocruiser.

Together, the aircraft evacuated 464 passengers from Wake to Hawaii and Guam, returning to Wake with 200 pounds of medical supplies, 8,100 pounds of food, 5,600 gallons of fresh water, 500 cots, 500 blankets, 7,250 rations, and tents to shelter 350 people.

5.
Name: Japanese Shipwreck.
Location: Tori Shima.
Date(s): March 18, 1953.
Emergency: A ship ran aground on rocks in heavy seas.
Air Force Organization(s) Involved: 33d Air Rscu Sq.
Airlifted: 31 shipwreck victims and food, water, and medical supplies.
Aircraft Employed: H–19 (two) and SA–16 (one).
Operations: Before dawn on March 18, the 130-ton Japanese ship *Ryosho Maru*, with 38 crew members aboard, ran aground in heavy seas. It rested on rocks near the coast of Tori Shima, a small island west of Okinawa used by U.S. forces as an aircraft target range. After dawn, a U.S. F–80 from Okinawa spotted the wreckage and contacted Air Rscu Svc units at Kadena AB.

Within an hour, an SA–16 flying boat from the 33d Air Rscu Sq dropped food, water, and first aid supplies to the shipwreck survivors on the island. An Army ship moved to the site, but found the seas too rough for a boat rescue. A 33d Air Rscu Sq H–19 helicopter carried most victims from Tori Shima by hoist to the deck of the Army ship, despite rough seas and high winds, which made the transfer extremely difficult. The small helicopter evacuated a few injured to Mercy Hospital in Okinawa. When hydraulic problems grounded the helicopter, a second H–19 evacuated the remaining survivors to Kadena. The 33d Air Rscu Sq evacuated 31 of 38 *Ryosho Maru* shipwreck victims. One crew member died and the remaining six were presumed drowned.

6.
Name: Kyushu Flood.
Location: Japan.
Date(s): July 1953.
Emergency: Torrential rain produced flooding in Kyushu that killed more than 600 people and drove over one million from their homes.
Air Force Organization(s) Involved: 315th Air Div, 315th and 483d Trp Carr Wgs, 39th Air Rscu Sq, and 43d Trp Carr Sq.

Airlifted: More than 60 tons of water purification equipment, generators, blankets, medical supplies, clothing, food, life rafts, tents, and water cans; unknown numbers of Red Cross and medical personnel; and insecticide.

Aircraft Employed: C–119 (33+), C–46 (3+), C–47 (2+), and H–19 (2+).

Operations: Typhoon season brought torrential rainfall to Japan in June and July, producing the worst flooding in Japanese history. More than 34 inches fell in June, the heaviest rain in 61 years. Floods in northern Kyushu left more than 600 people dead, 1,000 injured, and over one million homeless. High waters closed the undersea tunnel between Kyushu and Honshu for the first time since it opened in 1937, cutting the only railroad link between Japan's most important islands. Several rivers, such as the Chikugo, Onga, and Nishi, spilled over their banks, inundating towns such as Ongagawa and Nakama in Fukuoka prefecture. Japanese authorities requested U.S. assistance, and Maj. Gen. Roy H. Lynn, commander of Japan Air Defense Force, ordered relief operations.

The U.S. bases in the area responded immediately. Itazuke AB sent surface vehicles with relief workers and supplies, while Ashiya AB issued more than 129,000 sandbags. Air Force personnel at bases across Japan contributed to disaster relief funds. The Japanese Red Cross, the American Joint Relief Committee, and U.S. military organizations in Japan collected relief supplies for the flood victims, while the 315th Air Div organized an airlift.

Between July 2 and 13, the 483d Trp Carr Wg used a fleet of C–119 Flying Boxcars to transport at least 33 loads of relief equipment and supplies from Tachikawa AB in the Tokyo area to Kyushu. Each of 12 flights carried a five-ton water purification machine. Five other flights delivered electric generators. Eight C–119s transported food, shoes, and clothing, while six airlifted medical supplies. Other Flying Boxcar flights delivered blankets, water cans, tents, and life rafts. The wing used regularly scheduled and routine training flights from Honshu to Kyushu as well as newly generated flights to transport the emergency cargo to such cities and towns as Moji, Kurume, Kokura, and Kumamoto. Some missions also delivered supplies to Ashiya and Itazuke ABs in the disaster area.

C–119s were not the only U.S. aircraft involved in the relief flights. The 315th Trp Carr Wg used C–46s to transport relief workers, a Danish Red Cross team, and blankets to the flooded island. Air Rescue Service C–47s and helicopters, some from the 39th Air Rscu Sq, also participated in the mercy missions. The C–46s and C–47s sometimes dropped food and water to people marooned in flooded areas where landings were impossible. Some C–46s also sprayed DDT insecticide over communities in Kyushu after Japanese authorities requested these missions, fearing a rise in pestilence and disease in the wake of the floods.

By late July, the torrential rains had moved eastward over Honshu. To express his gratitude for the airlift, Katsuji Sugimoto, governor of Fukuoka prefecture, sent a letter of appreciation to Col. Maurice F. Casey, commander of the 483d Trp Carr Wg.

7.
Name: Wakayama Flood.
Location: Japan.
Date(s): July 1953.
Emergency: Heavy rain caused flash flooding that destroyed several villages in the mountain valleys near Wakayama.
Air Force Organization(s) Involved: 315th Air Div; 315th, 374th, and 483d Trp Carr Wgs; and 3d Air Rscu Sq.
Airlifted: More than 100 tons of food, clothing, medical supplies, and blankets.
Aircraft Employed: C–119 (one), C–47 (one), and C–46 (two+).
Operations: The same kind of torrential rain that had recently flooded Kyushu (see Kyushu Flood, July 1953) produced flash floods in parts of southern Honshu at the end of July. Flooding was especially destructive in villages located in narrow mountain valleys near Wakayama, south of Osaka. Cascading logs smashed buildings in Gobo and a landslide buried Hashimoto. Officials in the prefectures of Wakayama and Nara appealed for help, and the Japanese Red Cross asked the 315th Air Div to airlift relief supplies to isolated flood victims.

During six days at the end of July, Air Force cargo planes operating from Itami AB delivered more than 100 tons of food, medical supplies, blankets, and clothing to the flood victims. Most cargo was dropped from the planes because flooding or rough terrain made landings impossible. In three days, a 483d Trp Carr Sq C–119 Flying Boxcar airdropped 17 tons of food and medical supplies to survivors stranded on high ground in the flood region. Smaller airplanes, such as C–47s and C–46s from the 315th and 374th Trp Carr Wgs and the 3d Air Rscu Sq, also dropped relief supplies. The planes sprinkled leaflets asking isolated flood victims to mark areas where they wished the cargo to land. In some cases, U.S. military personnel double-bagged 100-pound sacks of grain so they could be dropped at low altitudes without parachutes to isolated villagers. Among the food items delivered were wheat, rice, barley, sugar, and C rations.

As they had been during the Kyushu flood airlift, Japanese officials were quick to express appreciation for U.S. help. Mr. Takaguta Shikado, president of the Japanese Red Cross, thanked Maj. Gen. Chester E. McCarty of the 315th Air Div for assistance during the crisis. Humanitarian airlifts such as the Wakayama flood relief operation strengthened the growing friendship between the United States and Japan.

8.
Name: Chinese Shipwreck.
Location: Triton Island, South China Sea.
Date(s): May 16, 1954.
Emergency: A typhoon sank a Chinese fishing vessel.
Air Force Organization(s) Involved: 31st Air Rscu Sq.
Airlifted: Seven shipwreck survivors.

Aircraft Employed: SA–16 (one).

Operations: On May 16, a 31st Air Rscu Sq SA–16 seaplane crew from Clark AB in the Philippines, searching the South China Sea for two Japanese ships missing since a recent typhoon, spotted seven shipwreck survivors on the small, barren island of Triton. Capt. D. R. Baker landed the SA–16 on the sea near the island and two crew members rowed life rafts over to pick up the survivors.

The seven survivors were Chinese fishermen whose boat had sunk in the typhoon. Nine crewmen had perished in the storm, and the survivors had been marooned on the tiny island for eight days without food or fresh water. As the SA–16 returned to Clark AB, its crew gave flight lunches and first aid treatment to the shipwreck survivors. At Clark AB, medical personnel treated the survivors for dehydration, malnutrition, and minor lacerations. One doctor estimated that the seven fishermen might have died after two more days on the island.

9.

Name: Cathay Pacific Airliner Crash.

Location: South China Sea.

Date(s): July 23, 1954.

Emergency: Chinese fighters shot down a British airliner with 18 people aboard over the South China Sea.

Air Force Organization(s) Involved: 31st Air Rscu Sq.

Airlifted: Nine crash survivors.

Aircraft Employed: SA–16 (one).

Operations: On July 23, a British airliner carrying 18 passengers, including six U.S. citizens, was flying a routine route from Bangkok, Thailand, to Hong Kong. Although the Cathay Pacific Airways DC–4 was clearly marked, a pair of Chinese fighter pilots shot it down near Hainan, an island in the South China Sea. Before the plane crashed, its pilot radioed a distress signal. Nine people, including three U.S. nationals, survived the bullets and crash into the sea. The survivors climbed into a large yellow life raft and hoped for rescue.

The distress call was heard by a civilian rescue control center in the Philippines, which contacted the 31st Air Rscu Sq at Clark AB. There a SA–16 amphibious rescue aircraft was preparing to take off on a training flight. Capt. Jack T. Woodyard flew the SA–16 with five crew members to search for the downed airliner. After a four-hour flight from the Philippines, he located the survivors with the help of British and French airplanes that could not land on the heavy seas.

Using a small island to block the heavy waves, Woodyard landed on the South China Sea and taxied over two miles to the survivors' raft. Despite the threat of more Chinese aerial attacks, he and his crew loaded the nine survivors into the SA–16 and taxied again behind the small island for takeoff. To help his overloaded airplane into the sky, Woodyard used JATO (jet-assisted takeoff) equipment. One survivor, a young Chinese girl, died on the way to Hong Kong, but the other eight recovered after hospitalization.

Humanitarian Airlift Operations

Facing intense international criticism for shooting down a civilian airliner over international waters, the Chinese Communist government admitted mistaking the aircraft for a Chinese Nationalist plane and apologized. Aircraft from two U.S. aircraft carriers vainly searched the crash site for more survivors. For their work in the rescue mission, Captain Woodyard earned the Distinguished Flying Cross and his crew earned Air Medals.

10.
Name: Nagoya Fire.
Location: Japan.
Date(s): October 16, 1954.
Emergency: An oil storage fire raged out of control.
Air Force Organization(s) Involved: 315th Air Div and 374th Trp Carr Wg.
Airlifted: 14.5 tons of foamite.
Aircraft Employed: C–124 (one).
Operations: On October 16, an oil storage fire broke out in Nagoya, one of Japan's largest cities. The fire spread out of control, prompting the Fifth Air Force, headquartered in Nagoya, to ask the 315th Air Div for an emergency airlift of firefighting materials.

On the same day, a 374th Trp Carr Wg crew, flying a C–124 Globemaster II aircraft, transported 14.5 tons of liquid and powdered foamite, a fire-fighting chemical, from Tachikawa AB to Komaki AB, near Nagoya. Firefighters used the airlifted foamite to contain the raging fire.

11.
Name: Mindanao Earthquake.
Location: Republic of the Philippines.
Date(s): April 3, 1955.
Emergency: An earthquake produced a tidal wave in Lake Lanao that devastated a lakeside village.
Air Force Organization(s) Involved: 31st Air Rscu Sq.
Airlifted: Two planeloads of medical supplies.
Aircraft Employed: SA–16 (two).
Operations: On April 1, an earthquake struck the Lake Lanao area of Mindanao in the southern Philippines. The tremor produced a tidal wave on the lake that devastated the shoreline village of Dansalan, leaving 400 people dead and scores homeless. President Ramon Magsaysay of the Philippines traveled to the disaster site and requested Air Rscu Svc aid through the Thirteenth Air Force. The 2d Air Rscu Gp assigned the mission to the 31st Air Rscu Sq, stationed at Clark AB.

On April 2, after a survey flight determined that medical personnel at the disaster scene urgently needed medical supplies, the 31st Air Rscu Sq dispatched two SA–16 Albatross amphibious aircraft. Flown by crews under Capt. Jack T. Woodyard and Capt. W. L. Warren, the two rescue planes flew medical supplies, including tetanus and gangrene antitoxin, from Clark AB to the disaster scene. After the planes landed on Lake Lanao near Dansalan, local boatmen transferred the medicine to medical personnel in the village.

The mission served a two-fold purpose. It helped doctors save some disaster victims and it enhanced Philippine-American relations. President Magsaysay praised the Air Rscu Svc for its help, and the Philippine press publicized the humanitarian flights, demonstrating the advantages of a U.S. military presence in the islands.

12.

Name: Hiroshima Maidens.

Location: Japan.

Date(s): May 5–8, 1955.

Emergency: Young Japanese women disfigured by the atomic bomb attack on Hiroshima sought advanced plastic surgery.

Air Force Organization(s) Involved: 21st Trp Carr Sq.

Airlifted: 25 burn victims.

Aircraft Employed: C–54 (one).

Operations: When the atomic bomb exploded over Hiroshima on August 6, 1945, it killed more than 70,000 people and injured thousands more. Japanese medical personnel treated many burn victims, but, for some, the scars kept coming back. In 1952, about two dozen young women, shunned by society because of their disfigurement, sought help from Reverend Kiyoshi Tanimoto of the Nagaragawa Methodist Church. Reverend Tanimoto called them the "Hiroshima Maidens."

U.S. visitors to Japan, including *Saturday Review* editor Norman Cousins, learned of the plight of the young women and brought it to the attention of charitable organizations in the United States. They agreed to sponsor the Hiroshima Maidens on a journey to the United States for the most advanced plastic surgery available. Medical doctors at Mount Sinai Hospital in New York, including Dr. Arthur J. Barsky, offered their services and the hospital agreed to cover treatment expenses. Two doctors flew to Hiroshima to screen the patients, and U.S. families offered to share their homes while the young women underwent treatment.

When he became aware that the Hiroshima Maidens needed transportation to New York, Kiyoshi Togasaki, president of the *Nippon Times*, requested an Air Force airlift through the 315th Air Div, which operated U.S. troop carrier organizations in Japan.

The 374th Troop Carrier Wing's 21st Trp Carr Sq used a C–54 Skymaster cargo airplane for the mission. Under the command of Capt. Fred J. Ryan, Jr., the aircraft left Iwakuni AB on May 5, with 25 Hiroshima Maidens, two doctors, and a 10-man crew aboard. Ryan stopped at Hickam AFB in Hawaii and Travis AFB in California before landing at Mitchell AFB in New York on May 9. From there, the young women were taken by ground vehicles to Mount Sinai Hospital in Manhattan.

Extensive treatment, involving several operations on some of the patients, produced dramatic improvements in their appearance and physical ability. At the end of 1956, *Time* magazine published before and after pictures of the most disfigured young woman. With additional treatments for her hands and arms, she was able to pursue a career as a nurse.

13.
Name: Shizunai Flood.
Location: Japan.
Date(s): July 4–5, 1955.
Emergency: A flash flood cut off the town of Shizunai and forced its residents onto roof tops.
Air Force Organization(s) Involved: 38th Air Rscu Sq.
Airlifted: 60 flood victims and blankets, food, and drinking water.
Aircraft Employed: SH–19 (three).
Operations: In early July, heavy rains caused flash flooding in Hidaki prefecture, in south central Hokkaido. The town of Shizunai was particularly hard hit. Floodwaters cut it off from other communities by washing away roads and railroad lines and forced residents onto the roofs of their homes.

Before long, news of the town's distress reached Chitose AB, about 35 miles away, where the 38th Air Rscu Sq maintained a detachment of SH–19 rescue helicopters. Canceling a scheduled July 4 celebration at Misawa AB in northern Honshu, the squadron dispatched an SH–19 to Shizunai. The helicopter discovered scores of villagers clinging to the tops of buildings or small islands in the midst of floodwaters. On July 4, the SH–19, piloted by 1st Lt. Stanley E. Wright and 1st Lt. Kenneth H. Bowen, began to evacuate flood victims, hoisting many from roofs. When the helicopter experienced mechanical problems, the 38th Air Rscu Sq dispatched another SH–19 to deliver spare parts and to join in the rescue flights. By the end of the day, the two helicopters had evacuated about 60 people to dry land.

On July 5, a third SH–19 helicopter joined in the operation, delivering blankets, food, and drinking water to the evacuees and to Japanese cut off from normal supply channels. During the two-day operation, a 38th Air Rscu Sq SA–16 float plane flew over the helicopters, providing communications assistance and searching for survivors, but was unable to land on the water because of floating debris.

The helicopter airlifts of evacuees and relief supplies to Shizunai contributed to friendly relations between the Japanese and U.S. military forces stationed in Japan. In a letter of gratitude to the commander of Misawa AB, Col. John P. Randolph, Governor Toshifumi Tanaka of Hokkaido commended the 38th Air Rscu Sq for its flood relief missions.

14.
Name: Hokkaido Pestilence.
Location: Japan.
Date(s): July 21–August 13, 1955.
Emergency: Insects multiplied out of control in the Japanese national forests of Hokkaido.
Air Force Organization(s) Involved: 483d Trp Carr Wg.
Airlifted: 328 tons of insecticide.
Aircraft Employed: C–119 (three).
Operations: Rapidly multiplying insects alarmed Japanese forestry officials in Hokkaido, northernmost of Japan's major islands, during midsummer. Aware that Air Force organizations in Japan maintained aircraft capable of aerial spraying, the Japanese government requested special extermination missions over the Hokkaido forests.

Between July 21 and August 13, the 483d Trp Carr Wg used three C–119 Flying Boxcars for the special mission. The Japanese provided insecticide and labor to load the airplanes. In just over three weeks, the wing aircraft sprayed 328 tons of insecticide over vast stretches of forest marked by Japanese officials. Some of the 79 flights carried 1,000 gallons of insecticide at a time.

The spraying operation demonstrated the versatility of U.S. airlift resources in the Far East while contributing to friendly relations between the United States and Japan.

15.
Name: Typhoon Louise.
Location: Iwo Jima.
Date(s): September 26–October 1, 1955.
Emergency: A typhoon with 170–knot winds devastated Iwo Jima.
Air Force Organization(s) Involved: 374th and 483d Trp Carr Wgs.
Airlifted: An engineer aviation battalion and more than 30 tons of relief equipment and supplies.
Aircraft Employed: C–124 (10), C–119 (3), and C–54 (1).
Operations: On September 25, Typhoon Louise struck Iwo Jima, a small island in the western Pacific about 650 miles southeast of Japan. Winds of 170 knots destroyed many buildings at Central AB, home of the 6415th Air Base Squadron. The storm also interrupted communications between Iwo Jima and Japan.

To survey the damage, restore communications, and deliver relief supplies, the 374th Trp Carr Wg at Tachikawa AB, Japan, dispatched a C–54 Skymaster to Iwo Jima on September 26. It carried medical supplies, medical personnel, and communications workers.

On September 27–29, the 374th Trp Carr Wg flew eight C–124 Globemaster II airplanes from Japan to the devastated island. Two of these aircraft carried 30 tons of emergency equipment and supplies, including a truck with a communications van trailer, two electric generators, tents, shelter materials, and additional medical supplies. The other six C–124s transported the 919th Engineer Aviation Battalion from Itazuke AB, Kyushu, to Iwo Jima to rebuild facilities there.

In the same three-day period, a C–119 Flying Boxcar from the 483d Trp Carr Wg also delivered emergency supplies from Japan to Iwo Jima. Four more cargo planes—two 374th Trp Carr Wg C–124s and two 483d Trp Carr Wg C–119s—airlifted equipment and supplies from Tachikawa and Ashiya ABs to Iwo Jima on October 1.

In less than one week, the 315th Air Div, under which the two wings operated, airlifted 14 planeloads of emergency workers and relief cargo from Japan to Iwo Jima. The flights helped to restore the island's essential infrastructure, allowing Central AB to resume its mission of providing emergency landing and refueling services for aircraft flying long Pacific routes.

16.
Name: *Tanada Maru* Shipwreck.
Location: Japan.
Date(s): December 27, 1955.
Emergency: After a ship ran aground off the coast of Japan, it began to break up and sink.
Air Force Organization(s) Involved: 38th Air Rscu Sq.
Airlifted: 14 seamen.
Aircraft Employed: SH–19 (one).
Operations: On December 27, the *Tanada Maru*, a Japanese freighter, foundered on rocks about 300 yards from shore near Hachinohe in northern Honshu, Japan. Twelve-foot waves broke up the vessel and threatened to drown the 28 crew members.

In response to the ship's distress call, the 38th Air Rscu Sq, stationed at nearby Misawa AB, dispatched an SH–19 helicopter piloted by Capt. Harry Hedges and 1st Lt. Herbert G. Gates. In less than an hour, the helicopter crew hoisted 14 crew members from the ship to the shore. Squadron fixed-wing airplanes, including an SC–47 and an SA–16, searched for survivors. In addition to the 14 airlifted survivors, seven Japanese seamen made their way to shore without the help of the helicopter. Seven more could not be found.

17.
Name: Project Gohan.
Location: Japan.
Date(s): December 22, 1956.
Emergency: An unusually severe winter led to crop failures and famine in Hokkaido.
Air Force Organization(s) Involved: 315th Air Div, 374th and 483d Trp Carr Wgs, and 6485th Ops Sq.

Airlifted: 21 tons of rice.

Aircraft Employed: C–119 (two) and C–54 (one).

Operations: A terrible winter produced crop failures and famine in Japan's north-ernmost major island of Hokkaido. Mr. Shintaro Fukushima, president of the *Japan Times* newspaper, organized a campaign called Rice for Hokkaido that caught the attention of Maj. Gen. Russell L. Waldron, commander of the 315th Air Div, stationed at Tachikawa AB in Honshu.

General Waldron sponsored an airlift of rice from Honshu to Hokkaido. Dubbed Project Gohan (gohan is the Japanese word for rice), the operation involved three 315th Air Div aircraft: two twin-engine C–119 Flying Boxcars and one four-engine C–54 Skymaster. Waldron piloted the C–54, which he borrowed from the 6485th Ops Sq. Col. Leroy M. Stanton, commander of the 483d Trp Carr Wg, and Col. Francis W. Williams, commander of the 374th Trp Carr Wg, flew the C–119s. The three airplanes transported 21 tons of rice from Tachikawa AB to Chitose AB in Hokkaido. Greeting the planes as they landed was Toshifumi Tanaka, the governor of Hokkaido, who thanked the Americans for their help. Japanese trucks distributed the rice from Chitose to villages farther north.

Personnel of the 315th Air Div also contributed 360,000 yen (about $1,000) to buy more rice for the people of Hokkaido, and General Waldron presented a check to Mr. Fukushima, leader of the Rice for Hokkaido campaign. The money was enough to furnish the people of Hokkaido with two boxcars of rice.

The humanitarian airlift inspired others. In January, a Royal Thai Air Force detachment stationed with the 374th Trp Carr Wg at Tachikawa AB flew about two tons of rice from their own food supplies to Chitose AB on a Thai C–47.

18.

Name: Kyushu Flood.

Location: Japan.

Date(s): July 28–August 4, 1957.

Emergency: Floods devastated Kyushu around the communities of Isahaya and Omura.

Air Force Organization(s) Involved: 315th Air Div; 483d Trp Carr Wg; Detachment 3, 24th Helicopter Squadron; and 8th AB Gp.

Airlifted: More than 88 tons of blankets, mattresses, tents, and food.

Aircraft Employed: C–119 (seven), H–19 (three), C–47 (two), H–21 (two), and L–20 (number unknown).

Operations: Heavy rain caused floods in western Kyushu, Japan, at the end of July, creating the need for bedding, shelter, and food in communities such as Omura and Isahaya in Nagasaki prefecture. After Japan requested U.S. help, Air Force organizations in Japan such as the 315th Air Div and the Fifth Air Force participated in a relief operation called Operation Angel.

In 11 days, Air Force cargo aircraft and helicopters airlifted 88 tons of emergency supplies from Ashiya, Tachikawa, and Itazuke ABs to the disaster area.

Among the planes were seven C–119 Flying Boxcars from Ashiya's 483d Trp Carr Wg, which delivered 45 tons of blankets, mattresses, and tents to the disaster area on July 28. Wing Commander Col. Leroy M. Stanton flew the lead airplane. The 8th AB Gp at Itazuke AB, flying C–47s and L–20s on eight relief sorties, flew one ton of chlorine and medical supplies to the disaster zone between July 28 and 30.

Supplementing these deliveries, the 24th Helicopter Squadron's Detachment 3 flew H–21 helicopters to the disaster scene. From July 25 through August 4, the squadron delivered 42 tons of emergency supplies to flood victims and transported 118 passengers. Five Air Force helicopters—three H–19s from Ashiya and Itazuke ABs and two H–21s from Itazuke AB—participated in relief flights for the Kyushu flood victims.

Aid came from other sources as well. The Itazuke AB chapel collected 320,000 yen for the flood survivors. Northwest Airlines airlifted 30 tons of relief supplies, including food, clothing, and medical supplies, from Honshu to Itazuke AB near the disaster zone. From there, Japanese trucks distributed the relief cargo to disaster victims. Together with the U.S. military airlifts, the assistance reinforced friendly relations between the United States and Japan.

19.
Name: Hirosaki Flood.
Location: Japan.
Date(s): August 11–12, 1958.
Emergency: Heavy rain caused flash flooding of the Iwaki-Gawa River and the city of Hirosaki.
Air Force Organization(s) Involved: 6139th AB Gp.
Airlifted: 133 passengers.
Aircraft Employed: H–19 (one), C–47 (one), and L–20 (one).
Operations: Torrential rain over the mountains of northern Honshu, Japan, spilled the Iwaki-Gawa River over its banks and flooded the city of Hirosaki on August 11. Fierce currents prevented the use of rescue boats, so city officials asked Misawa Air Base's 6139th AB Gp, stationed about 80 miles to the east, for help with a helicopter.

On the same day, Lt. Roger Anderson flew a rescue team of six people, including a Japanese interpreter, to the flooded city in an H–19 helicopter. Hirosaki's police and fire chiefs briefed crew members on locations and numbers of stranded survivors. Using a school yard as a base, the helicopter crew lifted 15 persons to safety that evening, including 11 rescued from an island in the middle of the swollen river that was rising at a rate of one foot every 20 minutes.

Before sunrise on August 12, the 6139th AB Gp helicopter was back in the air, lifting stranded flood victims by cable from roofs, bridges, vehicles, trees, and islands of higher ground and transporting them to relief centers at local schools. Two other Misawa-based aircraft, a C–47 and an L–20, supported the helicopter by spotting victims and delivering fuel and parts. In a series of shuttle flights, the H–19 crew rescued 118 persons that day, averaging five adults or seven children per flight.

As darkness approached and the river began to recede, Lieutenant Anderson's crew returned to Misawa AB. In two days they had rescued 133 flood victims at Hirosaki. The superintendent of police, Mr. Ozaki Koichi, awarded certificates of appreciation to the helicopter crews for their outstanding lifesaving efforts.

20.
Name: Typhoon Ida.
Location: Japan.
Date(s): September 27–October 4, 1958.
Emergency: A typhoon struck Tokyo and the Izu peninsula of Japan, causing flash flooding.
Air Force Organization(s) Involved: 24th Helicopter Squadron.
Airlifted: More than one ton of medical supplies, clothing, food, blankets, and life rafts.
Aircraft Employed: H–21B (three).
Operations: On September 26, Typhoon Ida struck Japan with winds up to 100 mph. More than 22 inches of rain fell over the Izu peninsula southwest of Tokyo, causing flash flooding that killed 175 people along the Kano River valley. The storm caused landslides and washed away bridges throughout the peninsula, closing roads and isolating villages. The next day, Typhoon Ida continued moving northward, lashing Tokyo with 80 mph winds before moving on to Hokkaido. In a message to Premier Nobosuki Kishi, U.S. Ambassador to Japan Douglas MacArthur, Jr., pledged assistance.

Between September 27 and October 4, the 24th Helicopter Squadron, operating under the 315th Air Div, flew a series of relief flights to airlift supplies to storm victims, drop life rafts, survey damage, and rescue stranded people. Flying H–21B helicopters, the squadron flew three Japanese doctors and 500 pounds of medical supplies from Fuchu AS to scattered villages on the Izu peninsula on September 28.

On October 3, the helicopters carried 900 pounds of clothing, food, and blankets from Showa AS to Yugashima and its environs. The squadron carried half a ton of clothing from Tachikawa AB to the Izu Red Cross hospital near Shuzenji on October 4. Other helicopter flights to the Izu peninsula and around Tokyo surveyed damage, located victims, and delivered relief supplies and funds contributed by religious organizations and U.S. military personnel in Japan. By October 4, floodwaters had receded and roads were reopened, making further emergency helicopter operations unnecessary.

Humanitarian Airlift Operations

21.
Name: Typhoon Vera.
Location: Japan.
Date(s): September 1959–February 1960.
Emergency: A typhoon with 115 mph winds flooded central Japan, leaving thousands of people dead, injured, and homeless.
Air Force Organization(s) Involved: 315th Air Div, 1503d Air Trpt Wg, 483d Trp Carr Wg, and 24th Helicopter Squadron.
Airlifted: 413 tons of food, clothing, medicine, blankets, and other relief supplies.
Aircraft Employed: C–124 (11), C–130 (5+), and H–21 (1).
Operations: On the night of September 26, Typhoon Vera struck the Nagoya area of central Japan with 115 mph winds and heavy rain. It quickly became the worst storm in Japanese history, breaking dikes and flooding vast areas. The typhoon drove more than 380,000 people from their homes and left 4,000 dead, 900 missing, and 12,000 injured. The Japanese requested help from U.S. military forces stationed in Japan, including an emergency airlift by the 315th Air Div.

The division responded with a massive relief operation that delivered over 413 tons of emergency supplies from Tachikawa, Chitose, and Ashiya ABs in other parts of Japan to Komaki AB near Nagoya in the disaster area. The cargo included food, clothing, blankets, and medical supplies. Among the participating organizations were the 1503d Air Trpt Wg, the 483d Trp Carr Wg, and the 24th Helicopter Squadron.

In October, the 1503d Air Trpt Wg flew 11 C–124 Globemasters to transport 220 tons of relief cargo to typhoon victims. In five days of airlift, the four-engine Globemasters delivered blankets, clothing, food, and equipment from Tachikawa and Chitose ABs to Komaki AB.

Meanwhile, the 483d Trp Carr Wg at Ashiya AB flew C–130s to the disaster area loaded with tons of clothing and bedding. The C–130s also delivered rescue workers, medical personnel, and cash donated by U.S. citizens stationed in Japan.

People in the United States also donated supplies to the typhoon victims, and five C–130s on routine flights from the United States to Japan transported 19 tons of this type of cargo between December 1959 and February 1960. For example, in December, three C–130s delivered over 10 tons of relief cargo collected by Japanese-American residents of Denver.

Helicopters supplemented the work of the large cargo-carrying aircraft. First Lt. Carl H. Murray and his five-man crew flew a 24th Helicopter Squadron twin-rotor H–21 helicopter to evacuate 137 people from flooded areas in seven days. Murray and his crew also transported 150 officials, relief workers, and medical personnel to the disaster area and delivered more than two tons of food, mostly rice and powdered milk.

The victims of Typhoon Vera took months to recover from the disaster, but were grateful for the help they received. On March 17, the minister of agriculture and forestry, Mr. Takeo Fukuda, sent a letter of appreciation to the 315th Air Div

466

for the emergency airlift, which delivered 88 percent of all cargo sent to the disaster area by military units in the Far East. The operation contributed to Japan's continuing economic development and growing partnership with the United States.

22.
Name: Hawaiian Tsunami.
Location: Hawaii.
Date(s): May 1960.
Emergency: Four seismic sea waves devastated the eastern shore of Hawaii.
Air Force Organization(s) Involved: 1502d Air Trpt Wg and 50th Air Trpt Sq.
Airlifted: More than 12 tons of equipment and supplies, including a generator, refrigerator vans, clothing, and food.
Aircraft Employed: C–124 (number unknown).
Operations: On May 21 and 22, tremendous earthquakes in Chile (see Chapter 2, Amigos Airlift, May–June 1960) produced seismic sea waves that raced westward across the Pacific Ocean at a speed of more than 400 mph. Sixteen hours later, four waves, magnified by the sloping sea floor, pounded the eastern coast of the island of Hawaii, 6,800 miles away from the epicenter of the Chilean earthquake. Although the Hawaiians had ample warning, more than 50 people died at Hilo and hundreds were left homeless. Hawaii, which had become a state the previous year, declared a state of emergency and requested federal assistance.

Before the end of the month, the 1502d Air Trpt Wg, from Hickam AFB on the island of Oahu, airlifted more than 12 tons of emergency equipment and supplies to Hilo. The wing's 50th Air Trpt Sq flew C–124 Globemaster II airplanes for the relief operation, delivering an electric generator, refrigerator, vans, clothing, and food to the disaster victims.

23.
Name: Yamanashi Relief.
Location: Japan.
Date(s): June and December 1960.
Emergency: After a typhoon struck central Japan, floods killed livestock, reducing agricultural production.
Air Force Organization(s) Involved: 315th Air Div.
Airlifted: 36 hogs and 14 cows.
Aircraft Employed: C–130 (two).
Operations: When a typhoon hit central Japan near Nagoya in September 1959, it flooded agricultural lands in the Yamanashi area, killing many livestock (see Typhoon Vera, September 1959–February 1960). Under President Eisenhower's People to People program, citizens of Iowa contributed swine and cattle for the farmers of central Japan.

In June, the 315th Air Div transported 36 hogs aboard a C–130 Hercules cargo aircraft returning to Japan after modification in the United States. Although one hog died on the long flight across the Pacific, the other 35 survived to become breeding stock for Japanese farmers.

The division flew a similar mission in December, moving 14 Jersey dairy cows from the United States to Japan aboard another C–130, also returning to Japan after modification in the United States. The cows were a gift from the American Jersey Cattle Club of Iowa for the Kiyosato Educational Experiment Program of Yamanashi prefecture's breeding farm near Kofu, Japan.

24.
Name: Hokkaido Polio Epidemic.
Location: Japan.
Date(s): August 21–28, 1960.
Emergency: A polio epidemic struck more than 600 people, threatening the lives of those whose paralysis affected their lungs.
Air Force Organization(s) Involved: 315th Air Div and 1501st Air Trpt Wg.
Airlifted: Eight iron lungs and 12 chest respirators.
Aircraft Employed: C–130 (one), C–133 (one), and C–124 (one).
Operations: In August, a severe polio epidemic in Hokkaido, Japan's northern-most main island, struck more than 600 people. Fifty died, many from paralysis of the lungs. On August 20, the Japanese government requested U.S. assistance, and President Eisenhower authorized an airlift of iron lungs and chest respirators from the United States to Japan.

The National Polio Foundation immediately offered some of its iron lungs for the Japanese polio victims, but they had to be flown from Los Angeles, California. A MATS C–124 Globemaster II delivered four iron lungs to Travis AFB, California, where they were transferred to a C–133 Cargomaster of the 1501st Air Trpt Wg for the flight across the Pacific. The C–133 landed at Tachikawa AB on Honshu, where the medical equipment was transferred again to a 315th Air Div C–130 Hercules for the flight to Hokkaido.

Within a week, the Air Force delivered another four iron lungs and 12 chest respirators, purchased by the Japanese government, from California to Japan. This time a 315th Air Div C–130 made the Pacific crossing. The plane had been mod-ified in the United States and was returning to Japan, so it carried the medical equipment instead of flying empty. It also carried Mark Bortman, director of President Eisenhower's People to People program. The C–130 landed in Hokkaido on August 28, after a stop at Tachikawa AB.

From August 21 to 28, the Air Force delivered eight iron lungs and 12 chest respirators from the United States to Japan. An elderly Japanese man, grateful for the relief of the polio victims, donated a pair of Japanese dolls in a display case to the People to People organization. The dolls arrived on another C–130 destined for modification in the United States.

25.
Name: Luzon Flood.
Location: Republic of the Philippines.
Date(s): September 1960.
Emergency: Heavy rains caused floods that contaminated drinking water.
Air Force Organization(s) Involved: 1501st and 1502d Air Trpt Wgs.
Airlifted: Three water purification machines weighing more than eight tons.
Aircraft Employed: C–124 (two).
Operations: In late August, heavy rains produced floods in five provinces of central Luzon, the most important island in the Philippines. The floods contaminated drinking water in 80 towns, prompting the government to ask the United States for water purification equipment. To airlift the equipment, the State Department depended on MATS.

In September, the West Trpt AF flew two C–124s to airlift three water purification machines, weighing 8.4 tons, to the Philippines. One of the C–124s, from the 1501st Air Trpt Wg, flew the three machines from Dover AFB, Delaware, to Travis AFB in California. Another C–124, operated by the 1502d Air Trpt Wg, carried the equipment across the Pacific to Manila. The Globemaster II stopped in Hawaii, Wake, and Guam on the way, and arrived at Manila International Airport within 10 minutes of the announced arrival time.

26.
Name: Niigata Blizzard.
Location: Japan.
Date(s): January 1961.
Emergency: Heavy snow cut railroad lines to Niigata, causing a food shortage.
Air Force Organization(s) Involved: 315th Air Div and 815th Trp Carr Sq.
Airlifted: 2.5 tons of food.
Aircraft Employed: C–130 (one).
Operations: In January, heavy snow blocked railroad lines to Niigata, a city in northern Honshu, Japan, depriving the city of some food deliveries. Among those affected were detachments of U.S. Air Force and Coast Guard personnel. The 315th Air Div responded with an airlift.

One C–130 Hercules airplane, commanded by Lt. Russell R. Young, transported 5,000 pounds of food to Niigata from Tachikawa AB near Tokyo. Crew members airdropped the cargo on eight passes over the snowbound airport at an altitude of 800 feet. The airlift contributed to the relief of Niigata until rail lines reopened and provided the 815th Trp Carr Sq with training in airdrop techniques. Only one food bundle was damaged on impact.

27.
Name: Mindanao Flood.
Location: Republic of the Philippines.
Date(s): February 8–23, 1962.
Emergency: Torrential rains caused flooding that isolated the city of Butuan from food supplies.
Air Force Organization(s) Involved: 315th Air Div, 21st and 22d Trp Carr Sqs, and Thirteenth Air Force.
Airlifted: 39 tons of rice, sugar, medicine, medical personnel, and equipment, including two H–19 helicopters.
Aircraft Employed: C–124 (two), C–130 (two), C–123 (one), and H–19 (two).
Operations: In early February, torrential rains in Mindanao, the southernmost of the major Philippine islands, produced flooding. High water cut roads, isolating Butuan and neighboring towns from adequate food supplies. The Philippine government in Manila contacted U.S. Air Force officers at nearby Clark AB for an airlift to Mindanao of food from warehouses in Luzon.

The Pacific Air Forces assigned the relief operation to the 315th Air Div, which had just completed a training exercise in the Philippines. Col. L. J. Mantoux, vice commander of the division, assumed direction of the relief airlift at Clark AB. He tapped crews and aircraft of the 21st and 22d Trp Carr Sqs for the emergency.

On February 8, two C–124s from the 22d Trp Carr Sq airlifted nearly 10 tons of cargo—including two H–19 helicopters, medical supplies and personnel, and food—from Clark AB to Davao City in Mindanao. Crew commanders included Maj. Odith K. Spurrier and Capt. Carroll P. Eppley. Soon after the C–124 deliveries, the two helicopters began flying over the inundated areas to locate stranded populations.

Between February 17 and 23, the 21st Trp Carr Sq joined in the relief operation. Two C–130s loaded with rice and sugar from government warehouses near Clark AB attempted to fly to Cagayan de Oro, a large airfield near the flooded area of Mindanao, but turned back three times because of bad weather. On the fourth flight, one C–130, accompanied by a Thirteenth Air Force C–123, finally reached Cagayan de Oro after a stop at Cebu City. The crews learned that floods had cut roads between Cagayan de Oro and Butuan, so flights would have to go directly to Butuan's Ben Cosi Airport. The small airport's 3,200-foot runway was not sufficient for a fully loaded C–130 to land.

One C–130 left the Philippines, but the other remained with the C–123 to shuttle loads from Davao City to Butuan. In a few days, the two planes delivered 13 tons of rice and sugar to the hungry community. The C–123 soon dropped out of the operation because of engine trouble, leaving the remaining C–130, under command of Maj. James E. Webster, to carry on alone.

When the excess food supplies at Davao were depleted, Webster and his crew returned to Clark AB for 16 more tons of rice and sugar. At Davao, Webster divided the cargo into two eight-ton loads and delivered them in two flights to Butuan. Capitalizing on the C–130's short landing ability with a limited load, Webster was able to complete the food deliveries to the small airport on February 23. By then, the Air Force had airlifted 39 tons of food, medicine, medical personnel, and equipment to Mindanao flood victims.

28.
Name: Taiwanese Cholera Epidemic.
Location: Republic of China (Taiwan).
Date(s): August 8–15, 1962.
Emergency: Almost 200 Taiwanese developed cholera and 11 died.
Air Force Organization(s) Involved: 315th Air Div and 817th Trp Carr Sq.
Airlifted: Three planeloads of cholera vaccine and saline solution.
Aircraft Employed: C–130 (three).
Operations: A cholera epidemic broke out in Taiwan in mid-July. By August 5, 199 cases and 11 deaths had been reported. The disease threatened the people of the island and other nations whose ships docked in Taiwan. Several Japanese merchant seamen came down with cholera after visiting Taiwan.

Between August 8 and 15, the 315th Air Div airlifted cholera vaccine and saline solution from Thailand to Taiwan. The 817th Trp Carr Sq, based at Naha AB, Okinawa, conducted the operation with three C–130 flights from Bangkok to Taipei on August 8, 9, and 15.

29.
Name: Marcus Island Typhoon.
Location: Pacific Ocean.
Date(s): October 15, 1962.
Emergency: A typhoon ravaged the island with high winds and heavy rain.
Air Force Organization(s) Involved: 315th Air Div and 815th Trp Carr Sq.
Airlifted: Two tons of food.
Aircraft Employed: C–130 (one).
Operations: A typhoon struck tiny Marcus Island in the western Pacific Ocean during the first half of October, devastating a weather station and depriving its personnel of adequate food supplies.

Notified of the need for an emergency airlift, the 315th Air Div in Japan dispatched a C–130 Hercules transport from the 815th Trp Carr Sq, stationed at Tachikawa AB. On October 15, the C–130 airdropped 3,500 pounds of food to the island, helping sustain the weather team until food stocks could be replenished by sea.

30.
Name: Typhoon Karen.
Location: Guam.
Date(s): November 1962.

Humanitarian Airlift Operations

Emergency: A typhoon with 175 mph winds severely damaged 90 percent of Guam's buildings and left 45,000 people homeless.

Air Force Organization(s) Involved: 315th Air Div; 21st, 22d, 345th, 815th, and 817th Trp Carr Sqs; West Trpt AF; 1501st, 1502d, and 1503d Air Trpt Wgs; East Trpt AF; and 1607th and 1611th Air Trpt Wgs.

Airlifted: Over 1,000 tons of equipment and supplies, including tents, food, medicine, blankets, clothing, generators, communications equipment, tools, and spare parts; and more than 700 passengers, including evacuees, Red Cross workers, troops, technicians, and medical and maintenance personnel.

Aircraft Employed: C–118, C–124, C–130, C–133, and C–135 (more than 50 total).

Operations: For a small island in the western Pacific Ocean, Sunday, November 11, was a tragic day. On that Veterans Day, Typhoon Karen struck Guam with winds of 175 mph. High seas and heavy rain compounded the blow. The storm damaged 90 percent of the island's buildings beyond repair and tore the roofs from four of five homes. Officials estimated property destruction at $100 million, but the human costs were even more tragic. At least six people died, hundreds were injured, and 45,000 were left homeless. The acting governor, Manuel Guerrero, immediately requested emergency federal assistance. Two of the Defense Department's most important Pacific bases, Andersen AFB and Agana NAS, shared Guam's devastation.

The Air Force's PACAF and MATS joined efforts to bring relief to the people of Guam. Among the organizations involved were the Pacific Air Force's 315th Air Div and its 21st, 22d, 345th, 815th, and 817th Trp Carr Sqs, which flew C–130 Hercules transports. For MATS, the Eastern Transport Air Force's 1607th and 1611th Air Trpt Wgs, and the Western Transport Air Force's 1501st, 1502d, and 1503d Air Trpt Wgs employed C–118 Liftmasters, C–124 Globemaster IIs, C–133 Cargomasters, and C–135 Stratolifters. About 50 Air Force cargo aircraft participated in relief operations to and from Guam after Typhoon Karen.

Most airlift flights flew homeless victims to the United States or other Pacific islands such as Wake or Oahu. Many planes flew military personnel and dependents from Andersen AFB or Agana NAS to Travis AFB in California. At the same time, the aircraft transported Red Cross workers, technicians, maintenance personnel, and troops to Guam to restore the island's facilities. Emergency flights carried more than 700 passengers to and from Guam in November.

In addition to passengers, Air Force transports delivered more than 1,000 tons of equipment and supplies to Guam for disaster relief, including tents, food, medicine, blankets, and clothing. To restore Guam's military facilities, the aircraft also delivered electrical and liquid oxygen generators, communications equipment, aircraft spare parts, tools, and a field kitchen. Sources of the airlifted supplies included Clark AB in the Philippines, Tachikawa AB in Japan, Naha AB in Okinawa, Hickam AFB in Hawaii, March and Travis AFBs in California, Lockbourne AFB in Ohio, and Forbes AFB in Kansas.

By the end of November, Guam was on its way to recovery for both military and civilians. The 50 Air Force planes had moved more than 700 passengers and 1,000 tons of cargo in response to the greatest disaster in the island's history.

31.
Name: Japanese Blizzard.
Location: Japan.
Date(s): February 3, 1963.
Emergency: Heavy snow cut off Japanese cities from fresh food supplies.
Air Force Organization(s) Involved: 315th Air Div and 815th Trp Carr Sq.
Airlifted: Four tons of food.
Aircraft Employed: C–130 (one).
Operations: When heavy snow blocked highways, railroads, and airport runways in western Honshu, Japan, during late January, residents of isolated communities such as Kanazawa, Toyama, and Niigata went without fresh food for more than a week. Learning of the plight of their countrymen, the people of Ibaragi prefecture, a farming region in central Honshu, gathered more than four tons of fresh vegetables for the snowbound communities. On February 1, Japanese government officials asked the 315th Air Div, which operated U.S. military transport planes in Japan, to deliver the food to the disaster area.

On February 3, an 815th Trp Carr Sq C–130 crew under the command of Lt. Col. William H. Lewis airlifted the food from Tachikawa AB near Tokyo to Komatsu. Flying slowly at an altitude of 800 feet, the crew dropped bundles of vegetables over Komatsu's airport. As the food descended, about 60 Japanese officials and workers lined the snow-covered runways waiting to retrieve it for delivery to the snowbound communities.

32.
Name: Indonesian Flood.
Location: Indonesia.
Date(s): February 7–17, 1963.
Emergency: A flood struck the Indonesian capital, producing a threat of disease.
Air Force Organization(s) Involved: 41st Air Trpt Sq and 1608th Air Trpt Wg.
Airlifted: Eight tons of medical supplies.
Aircraft Employed: C–130 (one).
Operations: In early February, floods brought an increased threat of disease to Djakarta, capital of Indonesia. Indonesian authorities requested U.S. aid, and President Kennedy authorized a MATS airlift of medical supplies from the United States to Indonesia.

On February 7, a C–130 from the 1608th Air Transport Wing's 41st Air Trpt Sq took off from Charleston AFB, South Carolina, on a mission that would take it and eight tons of medical supplies halfway around the world. On the way to

Djakarta, the Hercules cargo plane stopped at Travis AFB, California; Hickam AFB, Hawaii; Wake Island; and Clark AB in the Philippines.

The airlift relieved the flood victims and reinforced U.S. ties with Indonesia at a time when that country was drifting away from the West toward a closer relationship with the Soviet Union and Communist China.

33.
Name: Indonesian Food Airlift.
Location: Biak.
Date(s): April 1963.
Emergency: Hunger threatened children in West Irian.
Air Force Organization(s) Involved: 315th Air Div.
Airlifted: Over three tons of canned food.
Aircraft Employed: C–130 (one).
Operations: In the early 1960s, the UN sent troops to Indonesia to ease the transition from Dutch to Indonesian rule in western New Guinea, which became West Irian. In April 1963, Christian missionaries sought food for malnourished children in West Irian. After U.S. Air Force and Canadian personnel stationed with UN forces on the nearby island of Biak learned of the need, they contributed to a food fund and purchased 3.6 tons of canned goods from Clark AB in the Philippines. The food was available and inexpensive because of damaged cans and labels.

A January 1963 Air Force directive authorized and encouraged PACAF to transport personnel and cargo for People to People projects such as this one. The 315th Air Div, then flying a series of missions to airlift UN supplies to Indonesia, allowed one of its C–130s to carry the canned food to Biak. From there, a missionary ferried the food by private plane to West Irian children.

34.
Name: *Midori Maru* Disaster.
Location: Ryukyu Islands.
Date(s): August 17–20, 1963.
Emergency: A passenger ship with 256 people aboard capsized and sank.
Air Force Organization(s) Involved: 313th Air Div, 33d Air Rscu Sq, and 51st AB Gp.
Airlifted: Shipwreck survivors.
Aircraft Employed: HH–19 (four) and HU–16 (three).
Operations: On August 17, the *Midori Maru* passenger ship, operating as a ferry between islands in the Ryukyu chain near Okinawa, encountered high winds and heavy seas. Overloaded with 256 passengers and top heavy, the ship rolled over and sank before it had time to send an SOS. Some passengers clung to telephone poles that had been part of the ship's deck cargo, but many were trapped below deck, where they had gone to try to escape the rain.

Hours after the disaster, the rescue center at Naha AB in Okinawa learned of the disaster. Lt. Col. Robert P. Ash, commander of the 33d Air Rscu Sq, launched a search with HU–16 Albatross aircraft, while boats and ships in the area moved in to rescue survivors. The 313th Air Div, which had operational control of the aerial part of the operation, employed four USAF HH–19 helicopters, two from the 33d Air Rscu Sq and two from the 51st AB Gp at Naha. Eight U.S. Army, Navy, and Marine Corps helicopters joined the search and rescue operation. The Navy and Marine Corps used four UH–34 helicopters, while the Army flew a UH–1A and three large 20-passenger CH–21s from Okinawa's Hamby Air Field.

The smaller helicopters plucked survivors from the sea and carried them to the small island of Nagannu Shima, about two miles away. Paramedics treated the worst injury cases. The larger CH–21 helicopters shuttled survivors from Nagannu Shima to Naha AB. Three HU–16 Albatross aircraft from the 33d Air Rscu Sq circled over the disaster area to search for survivors, coordinate the movements of the helicopters and rescue boats, and illuminate the scene with flares when darkness set in.

The operation ended on August 20. Of the 256 people on board the *Midori Maru* when it capsized, 144 were rescued. Most traveled to Okinawa by boat, but helicopters saved 38. At Naha AB, they received medical treatment, food, and shelter until they were well enough to return home.

35.
Name: Typhoon Gloria.
Location: Republic of China (Taiwan).
Date(s): September 20 and October 20–24, 1963.
Emergency: A typhoon flooded Taiwan, leaving hundreds of people in need of food, clothing, and bedding.
Air Force Organization(s) Involved: 315th Air Div and 21st and 304th Trp Carr Sqs.
Airlifted: 20 tons of food, blankets, and clothing.
Aircraft Employed: C–130 (one) and C–124 (one).
Operations: Typhoon Gloria hit northern Taiwan in mid-September, bringing high winds, tides, and heavy rain to Taipei, the capital. The storm produced shortages of food, bedding, and clothing. Officials estimated damage at over $11 million.

On September 20, Air Force Brig. Gen. Frederick J. Sutterlin, the chief of staff of the Taiwan Defense Command, asked the 315th Air Div to transport food to Taipei. Within 24 hours, the division responded with a humanitarian airlift led by Capt. David M. Baird and a five-man crew in a 21st Trp Carr Sq C–130 that delivered 10 tons of baby food and canned meat from military stocks at Naha AB in Okinawa to Taipei International Airport.

Victims of Typhoon Gloria continued to suffer from food, clothing, and bedding shortages into October. Between October 20 and 24, a C–124 from the 442d

Troop Carrier Wing's 304th Trp Carr Sq, stationed at Richards-Gebaur AFB, Missouri, airlifted 10 tons of relief supplies for the storm victims of Taiwan. The cargo consisted of wheat, blankets, and clothing donated by the Christian Reformed World Relief Committee. Maj. Robert J. Shippee led a nine-man crew on the flight, which stopped in California, Hawaii, Wake Island, and Tachikawa AB in Japan.

The humanitarian airlift flights in September and October delivered 20 tons of food, blankets, and clothing to victims in Taiwan. Besides bringing relief to the storm victims, the airlifts reinforced U.S. ties with the Republic of China at a time of heightened Cold War tension in southeastern Asia.

36.
Name: Niigata Earthquake.
Location: Japan.
Date(s): June 16–19, 1964.
Emergency: An earthquake struck Niigata, collapsing structures and causing flooding and oil fires.
Air Force Organization(s) Involved: 315th Air Div and 36th Air Rscu Sq.
Airlifted: 106 tons of relief equipment and supplies, including 90 tons of fire-fighting foam, 12 tons of fuel for rescue helicopters, and 4 tons of food and clothing.
Aircraft Employed: HH–43 (two), HC–54 (one), and C–130 (number unknown).
Operations: In mid-June, an earthquake registering 7.7 on the Richter scale devastated Niigata, a coastal city of 326,000 people in western Honshu. The initial tremor and more than 50 aftershocks destroyed thousands of structures, including apartment buildings, homes, and bridges. The violent vibrations produced a tidal wave in Niigata and temporarily reversed the flow of the Shinano River, flooding large sections of the city. Scores of oil tanks on the outskirts of the city burst into flames, sending columns of black smoke 20,000 feet into the air.

Japanese officials asked for help from the 36th Air Rscu Sq at Tachikawa AB near Tokyo. Lt. Col. Robert R. Dyberg immediately dispatched two HH–43 helicopters and an HC–54 to Niigata. The small helicopters refueled at Utsunomiya, 75 miles north of their home base, on the way to the disaster zone. Dyberg set up an on-scene command post at Niigata and began using helicopters to evacuate people to safer areas. He quickly learned of the need for more helicopter fuel and for fire-fighting foam to battle the huge oil tank fires.

The 315th Air Div, also based at Tachikawa, employed a small fleet of C–130s to deliver the foam and fuel. In four days of mercy missions, the C–130s airlifted 12 tons of aviation fuel and 90 tons of fire-fighting foam to Niigata. They also transported four tons of food and clothing to the area for Niigata's refugees.

Although the helicopters effectively evacuated many Japanese to safety and distributed food and clothing to them, using fuel delivered by the 315th Air Div C–130s, the big cargo planes had little success airdropping foam over the oil tank fires. Flames defied the foam and an army of firefighters on the ground for four days. But despite earthquake, flood, and fire, Niigata suffered only 27 residents dead and 403 injured.

37.
Name: Muroran Ship Fire.
Location: Japan.
Date(s): May 24–25, 1965.
Emergency: An oil tanker caught fire.
Air Force Organization(s) Involved: 315th Air Div and 815th Trp Carr Sq.
Airlifted: More than 30 tons of fire-suppressant chemical.
Aircraft Employed: C–130 (three).
Operations: When the Norwegian oil tanker *Heimvard* struck a pier at Muroran on Hokkaido in northern Japan on May 23, it generated a huge oil fire. Hard-pressed to control the dangerous fire, which threatened other parts of the port, Japanese officials asked the 315th Air Div to transport a fire suppressant to Hokkaido.

On May 24 and 25, the 315th Air Division's 815th Trp Carr Sq airlifted more than 30 tons of bromochloromethane, a chemical fire suppressant, from Tachikawa AB near Tokyo to Chitose AB in Hokkaido near Muroran. The squadron flew three C–130 cargo airplanes, piloted by Capt. James E. Heldt, Capt. Daniel Harmon, Jr., and Maj. Richard J. McGlynn. Japanese Self Defense Force trucks transported the fire-suppressant chemical to Muroran, where it was used by local helicopters to spray the fire. Firefighters eventually extinguished the blaze.

38.
Name: Ryukyus Rescue.
Location: Ryukyu Islands.
Date(s): May 26, 1965.
Emergency: A typhoon approached a small island with low elevation and inade-quate shelter.
Air Force Organization(s) Involved: 33d Air Rscu Sq.
Airlifted: 12 Japanese workmen.
Aircraft Employed: HH–43 (one).
Operations: A typhoon approached the Ryukyu Islands in late May. Twelve Japanese workmen on one of the smaller islands needed to be evacuated because the island was only 10 feet above sea level and lacked shelter able to withstand strong winds, waves, or heavy rain. Notified by Japanese officials of the emer-gency, the 313th Air Div asked the 33d Air Rscu Sq at Naha AB in Okinawa to airlift the workmen to safety.

On May 26, the 33d Air Rscu Sq used an HH–43B helicopter to evacuate the 12 workmen to a larger island that had an adequate typhoon shelter. One of the squadron's HU–16B amphibious aircraft flew top cover for the helicopter during the mission. Without the airlift, the workmen would have risked drowning.

39.
Name: Typhoon Lucy.
Location: Ryukyu Islands.
Date(s): August 26, 1965.
Emergency: A typhoon deprived the people of Yonaguni Island of adequate food supplies.
Air Force Organization(s) Involved: 315th Air Div and 464th Trp Carr Wg.
Airlifted: More than three tons of food.
Aircraft Employed: C–130 (one).
Operations: In late August, Typhoon Lucy struck Japan and the Ryukyu Islands, producing flooding and landslides and sinking ships. When the 315th Air Div learned that the storm had left the people of the tiny island of Yonaguni at the end of the Ryukyu archipelago without adequate food supplies, it organized an emergency airlift.

The division used a C–130 on rotational duty in the western Pacific from the 464th Trp Carr Wg for the operation. On August 26, the Hercules cargo aircraft airlifted 6,500 pounds of dried food from Kadena AB in Okinawa to Yonaguni for the typhoon victims.

40.
Name: Leper Airlift.
Location: Okinawa, Japan, and Taiwan.
Date(s): August 1965.
Emergency: Lepers in colonies in the Far East needed dental treatment.
Air Force Organization(s) Involved: Fifth Air Force.
Airlifted: 25 dental personnel and about two tons of dental equipment and supplies.
Aircraft Employed: C–54 (one).
Operations: In the 1960s, the Social Welfare Fund of Mainichi Newspapers in Japan sponsored annual dental treatments for lepers in the Far East. In 1965, 13 professors and 12 students from Osaka Dental College gave up their summer vacations to participate in the program.

To transport them from Osaka to the leper colonies, the Fifth Air Force furnished a C–54 aircraft and crew. In August, the Skymaster airlifted the 25 dental personnel and 3,500 pounds of their equipment and supplies to three leper colonies in Japan, Okinawa, and Taiwan. The dentists and students treated over 1,000 patients that month.

41.
Name: Anthrax Epidemic.
Location: Japan.
Date(s): August 1965.
Emergency: An anthrax epidemic struck 320 people.
Air Force Organization(s) Involved: 36th Air Recovery Squadron.
Airlifted: Anthrax medicine and two doctors.
Aircraft Employed: HH–43 (one).
Operations: In late August, 320 Japanese villagers around Nishine Town contracted anthrax from eating infected beef. Dr. Kunihiko Tsuchiya, the local physician, began searching for the proper medication. The 439th Air Force Hospital at nearby Misawa AB obtained the medicine for Dr. Tsuchiya from the Tokyo area.

From Misawa AB, a 36th Air Recovery Squadron HH–43B helicopter crew airlifted the medicine and two Air Force doctors to Nishine Town. The treatment worked. A week after the mission, Dr. Tsuchiya reported that all patients were recovering well.

42.
Name: Taal Eruption.
Location: Republic of the Philippines.
Date(s): October 1965.
Emergency: A volcano erupted violently, destroying two villages, killing hundreds of people, and forcing thousands to flee.
Air Force Organization(s) Involved: 315th Air Div, 1502d Air Trpt Wg, and 6485th Ops Sq.
Airlifted: 10 tons of food, clothing, and utensils.
Aircraft Employed: C–124 (two) and C–118 (two).
Operations: On September 28, the volcano Taal in southern Luzon, about 40 miles from Manila, erupted violently. The volcano, which was surrounded by a lake, had been dormant since 1911. When it erupted, it destroyed two of four area villages with a combination of blast, lava flow, flood, and poison gas. Hundreds of people died and tens of thousands fled the region.

When residents of Hawaii learned of the disaster, they collected 10 tons of relief supplies, including food, clothing, and utensils. A pair of 1502d Air Trpt Wg C–124s from MATS transported the cargo from Hilo to Hickam AFB on Oahu. From there, the Pacific Air Forces' 315th Air Div airlifted the relief cargo to Clark AB near Manila, flying two C–118s on October 3 and 6. The 6485th Ops Sq provided the crews for the Liftmasters.

Trucks carried the supplies from Clark to the disaster area. Other Air Force units in the Philippines donated truckloads of food, clothing, medicine, and cots to the victims of the volcano, supplementing the airlift from Hawaii.

43.

Name: Misawa Fire.
Location: Japan.
Date(s): January 11–12, 1966.
Emergency: A large urban fire consumed much of downtown Misawa.
Air Force Organization(s) Involved: 315th Air Div and 815th Trp Carr Sq.
Airlifted: 10,000 blankets.
Aircraft Employed: C–130 (two).
Operations: Ignited by a mishandled gas heater, a fire spread through downtown Misawa in northern Japan on January 11. Helping local firefighters battle the blaze were almost 1,000 Air Force personnel from nearby Misawa AB, which was untouched by the fire. Fanned by high winds and a water shortage, the fire destroyed 434 buildings and left homeless 5,583 of the city's 37,480 residents.

The 815th Trp Carr Sq, a component of the 315th Air Div in Japan, flew two C–130 planeloads of relief supplies from Yokota AB to Misawa on January 11 and 12. The cargo included 10,000 blankets for the homeless fire victims who found temporary refuge at Misawa AB.

44.

Name: Samoan Typhoon.
Location: American Samoa.
Date(s): February 1–3, 1966.
Emergency: A typhoon devastated the island of Tutuila, leaving 90 people dead.
Air Force Organization(s) Involved: 61st Mil Alft Wg.
Airlifted: More than 13 tons of equipment and supplies, including electrical and construction equipment, tools, and rice.
Aircraft Employed: C–124 (three).
Operations: At the end of January, a strong typhoon hit American Samoa, devastating the capital city of Pago Pago on Tutuila Island. The storm left 90 people dead and hundreds without adequate shelter or electricity. Federal officials asked MAC to transport emergency equipment and supplies from Hawaii to Samoa.

Between February 1 and 3, the 61st Mil Alft Wg, stationed at Hickam AFB near Honolulu, flew over 13 tons of relief cargo to Pago Pago, 2,300 miles away. The wing flew three huge C–124 Globemaster IIs, which carried an electrical generator, half a ton of wire, 10 tons of construction tools and matériel, and 2.2 tons of rice. Engineers used the airlifted construction and electrical equipment to restore shelter and services in Pago Pago, while relief workers distributed the rice to storm survivors.

45.

Name: Typhoon Sarah.
Location: Wake Island.
Date(s): September 17–26, 1967.

Emergency: A typhoon with 140 mph winds destroyed housing, communications, and electrical facilities on Wake Island.
Air Force Organization(s) Involved: Twenty-second Air Force and 60th, 61st, 62d, 63d, and 437th Mil Alft Wgs.
Airlifted: More than 500 evacuees and 260 tons of equipment and supplies, including communications material, lumber, generators, and cots.
Aircraft Employed: C–124, C–141, C–133, and C–130 (21 total).
Operations: On September 16, Typhoon Sarah struck Wake Island in the central Pacific Ocean with 140 mph winds, heavy rain, and high waves. Although the storm caused only two injuries, it crippled the island's communications and electrical facilities and left hundreds of people homeless. The Federal Aviation Administration asked MAC for an emergency operation to restore the utilities on Wake, an important air link in the ongoing airlift of military personnel and supplies to Southeast Asia during the Vietnam War.

The Military Airlift Command, in association with the FAA and the Coast Guard, initiated an emergency airlift on September 17. In the first two days, 10 aircraft evacuated more than 500 residents of Wake Island, mostly service members and dependents, to Hawaii. The airplanes included three Air Force C–124s and five C–141s, one FAA C–135, and one Coast Guard C–130.

By September 26, 23 flights had transported 260 tons of equipment and supplies to Wake to aid reconstruction efforts. Among the aircraft were C–124s, C–141s, C–133s, and C–130s. Cargo included a mobile communications tower airlifted from Alaska, thousands of board feet of lumber, 20 generators, and more than 100 cots.

The Twenty-first Air Force's 437th Mil Alft Wg and the Twenty-second Air Force's 60th, 61st, 62d, and 63d Mil Alft Wgs participated in the operation. After the airlift, FAA chief William F. McKee thanked Gen. Howell M. Estes, commander of MAC, for helping to repair Wake Island's facilities. The emergency flights helped to restore housing on Wake so that evacuated military families could return.

46.
Name: Typhoon Jean.
Location: Mariana Islands.
Date(s): April 1968.
Emergency: A typhoon with 190 mph winds devastated Saipan, Tinian, and Rota, leaving homeless most of the islands' inhabitants.
Air Force Organization(s) Involved: 315th Air Div; 314th Tac Alft Wg; 6100th Ops Sq; and 38th, 776th, 777th, and 815th Tac Alft Sqs.
Airlifted: 351 tons of food, kitchen equipment, bedding, and other relief cargo; and at least 25 relief workers.
Aircraft Employed: C–130 (six+) and C–54 (one).
Operations: In early April, Typhoon Jean developed in the Pacific Ocean south-

east of the Mariana Islands and headed northwest. Strategic Air Command units at Andersen AFB in Guam, with the help of MAC, evacuated aircraft and personnel to Okinawa, Thailand, and Hawaii, but the storm narrowly missed the island. On April 11, the typhoon struck Saipan, Tinian, and Rota, other islands in the Marianas chain north of Guam. The storm packed 190 mph winds that destroyed or damaged 98 percent of the buildings on the three islands and left almost all of the 12,000 inhabitants homeless.

The Pacific Air Forces' 315th Air Div responded almost immediately with a humanitarian airlift. Within 17 hours, six division C–130s were on the way from Tachikawa AB in Japan. Along with a 6100th Ops Sq C–54, they carried 27 tons of kitchen equipment and 25 food service personnel. In 11 days, 56 C–130 sorties transported 351 tons of relief cargo, mostly food and bedding, from Japan and Taiwan to the Marianas. Some aircraft delivered relief cargo to Guam, while others shuttled it between Guam and Saipan, over 100 miles away.

Among the organizations participating in the emergency airlift were the 314th Tac Alft Wg, stationed in Taiwan, and the 38th, 777th, and 815th Tac Alft Sqs, stationed at Tachikawa AB in Japan. Two of these, the 38th and the 777th, were on rotation to the 315th Air Div of PACAF.

47.
Name: Philippine Shipwreck.
Location: Republic of the Philippines.
Date(s): April 10, 1968.
Emergency: Heavy seas capsized two fishing boats with 31 people aboard.
Air Force Organization(s) Involved: 31st Aerosp RR Sq.
Airlifted: Two rafts and two pararescuemen.
Aircraft Employed: HC–130 (one).
Operations: On April 10, two Philippine fishing boats capsized in heavy seas about five miles west of one of the Batan Islands north of Luzon in the Philippines, spilling 31 fishermen into the sea. A distress call alerted the 31st Aerosp RR Sq at Clark AFB near Manila.

The squadron immediately launched an HC–130 four-engine rescue aircraft with a nine-man crew under the command of Maj. Robert T. Dobson. Dobson flew 400 miles to the shipwreck site to locate survivors, some of whom had swum to shore. About 15 remained in the water. Dobson's crew dropped a pair of life rafts, but the shipwreck victims were unable to climb aboard them. The HC–130 crew then dropped two pararescuemen, who helped the fishermen climb aboard the rafts. At dusk, three Philippine patrol boats arrived to pick up the survivors. The 31st Aerospace Rescue and Recovery Squadron's emergency mission saved 15 fishermen.

48.
Name: Tokachi-Oki Earthquake.
Location: Japan.
Date(s): May 16–20, 1968.
Emergency: An earthquake registering 7.8 on the Richter scale struck northern Japan.
Air Force Organization(s) Involved: 315th Air Div; 6100th Ops Sq; 22d Mil Alft Sq; 36th Aerosp RR Sq; and Detachment 7, Pacific Aerospace Rescue and Recovery Center.
Airlifted: 128 tons of equipment and supplies, including electrical generators, water purification units, water trailers, food, blankets, trucks, pipe, ditch diggers, and paper plates and cups; and 25 civil engineering personnel.
Aircraft Employed: C–124 (eight), C–130 (two), HH–43 (two), HC–130 (one), and C–54 (one).
Operations: The largest earthquake to hit Japan since 1923 struck on May 16. Although its epicenter was beneath the strait between the islands of Hokkaido and Honshu near Tokachi-Oki, the quake wreaked havoc in northern Honshu around the city of Misawa, killing at least 44 people, injuring 246, and leaving 1,200 homeless. Fires broke out in the city, and Air Force firefighters from nearby Misawa AB, home of the 475th Tac Ftr Wg, lent assistance. When they became aware of a need for potable water in the disaster area, base officials asked the Fifth Air Force for an airlift of water purification equipment. Although the earthquake had damaged buildings at Misawa AB, the runways were still usable, allowing the emergency airlift to start immediately.

Within hours, Air Force units in Japan were responding to the disaster. An HC–130 of the 36th Aerosp RR Sq flew over the Misawa area to survey the damage. Soon afterwards, a 6100th Ops Sq C–54 flew from Tachikawa AB to Misawa with 25 civil engineering personnel to help with reconstruction.

Local Japanese police asked Misawa AB for help when they learned about a train stranded between Misawa and Aomori with 200 hungry children aboard. In response, two HH–43 helicopters from Detachment 7 of the Pacific Aerospace Rescue and Recovery Center at Misawa delivered 240 food rations to the train passengers.

Eight C–124s from the 22d Mil Alft Sq, under operational control of the 315th Air Div, and two division C–130s flew equipment and supplies from Tachikawa AB to Misawa within five days of the earthquake. The cargo included electrical generators, water purification equipment, water trailers, construction equipment, 4,000 loaves of bread, 1,200 packages of hamburger rolls, 3,200 cases of soft drinks, paper plates and cups, and blankets. Most of the food and blankets were donated by Japanese citizens from Tachikawa. By May 20, 14 Air Force planes had airlifted 128 tons of relief cargo to the earthquake victims of the Misawa area.

49.

Name: Manila Earthquake.

Location: Republic of the Philippines.

Date(s): August 4–12, 1968.

Emergency: An earthquake registering 6.0 on the Richter scale caused a large apartment building in central Manila to collapse.

Air Force Organization(s) Involved: 6200th AB Wg.

Airlifted: Rescue workers.

Aircraft Employed: C–54 (one).

Operations: Before dawn on August 2, a major earthquake registering 6.0 on the Richter scale shook downtown Manila, capital of the Philippines. The Ruby Towers Apartments, a six-story, block-size building with more than 500 residents, collapsed in a huge pile of concrete rubble. The government of President Ferdinand E. Marcos quickly asked the U.S. ambassador, G. Mennen Williams, for help while Maj. Gen. Gaudencio Tobias of the Philippine army organized a task force. In response to the ambassador's summons, RADM Draper L. Kaufman took charge of military forces assigned to the rescue effort.

Most U.S. rescue workers were Marine Corps and Navy personnel from Sangley Point Naval Station near Manila. But Clark AB, under the command of Air Force Col. Ernest W. Pate, also sent rescue personnel, including civil engineers and volunteers. Most rescue personnel rode to Manila on trucks and buses. In addition to the workers, Clark AB provided water containers, C rations, oxygen bottles, jackhammers, cement saws, hard hats, flashlights, gloves, shovels, picks, crowbars, and medical supplies.

Because of ruined bridges on the highway, rotating the rescue teams the 60 miles between Clark AB and Manila every day became a problem, whereupon the 6200th AB Wg established an air link. A 6200th AB Wg C–54 aircraft shuttled twice daily between Clark and Nichols Field, a Philippine air force station on the outskirts of Manila. Buses provided by the U.S. embassy completed the transportation of workers between Nichols Field and downtown Manila. The airlift lasted from August 4 to 12.

The operation exposed poor communications linking U.S. forces in the Philippines. But it was also beneficial in many ways. It helped to save 235 of 549 people trapped in the collapsed apartment building. U.S. military assistance improved relations between the Philippines and the United States when they were strained by the Vietnam War. The relief operation reduced leftist pressure on the Marcos government to expel U.S. forces from the Philippines. U.S. military personnel who participated in the disaster relief operation earned the Philippine Presidential Humanitarian Award.

50.
Name: Minami Daito Airlift.
Location: About 200 miles east of Okinawa.
Date(s): September 6, 1968.
Emergency: Typhoons approaching the Ryukyu Islands forced postponement of area shipping to Minami Daito.
Air Force Organization(s) Involved: 315th Air Div and 374th Tac Alft Wg.
Airlifted: 15 tons of food, including wheat, rice, flour, powdered milk, and salad oil.
Aircraft Employed: C–130 (one).
Operations: In early September, two typhoons in the western Pacific Ocean created heavy seas that forced postponement of regular food shipments to Minami Daito, an island about 200 miles east of Okinawa. Notified of food shortages on the island, the 315th Air Div of PACAF undertook a relief airlift.

One 374th Tac Alft Wg C–130 Hercules aircraft and crew, based in Okinawa, delivered 15 tons of food to Minami Daito on September 6. The cargo included rice, flour, wheat, powdered milk, and salad oil. The airlift helped to sustain the people of Minami Daito until shipping to the island resumed.

51.
Name: Typhoon Della.
Location: Ryukyu Islands.
Date(s): September 25, 1968.
Emergency: A typhoon devastated two islands in the Ryukyus, leaving residents in need of supplies.
Air Force Organization(s) Involved: 315th Air Div, 314th Tac Alft Wg, and 776th Tac Alft Sq.
Airlifted: Emergency equipment and supplies.
Aircraft Employed: C–130 (four).
Operations: During September, Typhoon Della struck the Ryukyu Islands southwest of the Japanese main islands. The 315th Air Div responded with an emergency airlift of relief equipment and supplies to the two hardest hit islands, Kume Shima and Miyako Jima. The division postponed some of its regularly scheduled flights to allow the emergency mission to proceed.

On September 25, the division's 314th Tac Alft Wg launched four C–130 cargo airplanes from Ching Chuan Kang AB in Taiwan for the operation. They transported relief supplies from Clark AB in the Philippines and Naha AB in Okinawa to Kume Shima and Miyako Jima. Lt. Col. Carl H. Holt of the 776th Tac Alft Sq served as one of the pilots. The 7th Aerial Port Squadron provided ground crews to unload the aircraft after they landed on the devastated islands.

Humanitarian Airlift Operations

52.
Name: Manila Floods.
Location: Republic of the Philippines.
Date(s): August 30–September 7, 1970.
Emergency: A typhoon dropped almost 22 inches of rain on the Manila area in six days, forcing 30,000 people from their homes.
Air Force Organization(s) Involved: 6200th AB Wg, 463d Tac Alft Wg, and 31st Aerosp RR Sq.
Airlifted: Over six tons of food, clothing, and medical supplies.
Aircraft Employed: HH–3 (two), C–130 (one), C–47 (one), and H–19 (one).
Operations: When Typhoon Meding approached Luzon in the northern Philippines in late August, almost 22 inches of rain fell in Manila. Floods inundated large areas around the city and extensive areas of Pampanga province, home of Clark AB. In parts of Manila, floodwaters reached six feet and an estimated 30,000 people were forced to leave their homes. President Ferdinand Marcos declared Manila and its suburbs a disaster area.

Philippine officials requested U.S. assistance through the U.S. ambassador, Henry A. Byroade. Both Byroade and Mr. Virgilio Sanchez, president of the mayors' league of Pampanga province, asked Clark AB for airlift support. The base, under the command of Col. Averill F. Holman, responded quickly. By August 30, the base's 31st Aerosp RR Sq had launched a pair of HH–3E Jolly Green Giant helicopters to conduct an aerial survey. These two aircraft also airlifted stranded people to safety and delivered food and medicine to flood victims, flying 16 sorties during a week of emergency operations.

The 463d Tac Alft Wg participated in relief operations as well. On September 5, it flew a C–130 Hercules cargo plane with 6.5 tons of food and clothing from Clark AB to Manila. The cargo was distributed at Camp Aguinaldo, a social welfare center in the Manila area. Clark AB's 6200th AB Wg joined in the emergency airlift. In early September, a C–47 Skytrain delivered 50 cases of C rations to Nichols Field in Manila, where Philippine air force personnel distributed them to flood victims. A 6200th AB Wg H–19 helicopter distributed relief supplies in early September.

U.S. personnel at Clark AB donated about 66,000 pounds of relief supplies, most of which was distributed by land to the flood victims. A base chapel served as a collection facility for money, food, clothing, medicine, blankets, and pots and pans, while the Disaster Preparedness Office on base coordinated relief efforts. U.S. Army and Navy units in the Philippines also sent aid to flood victims, and Navy helicopters from Cubi Point distributed relief supplies to Luzon.

The disaster relief operations helped to counteract anti-American feeling engendered by the increasingly unpopular Vietnam war, a communist insurgency in the Philippines, U.S. support for Malaysia—with which the Philippines had a territorial dispute—and disturbing incidents between U.S. military personnel and Philippine civilians.

53.
Name: Batan Island Earthquake.
Location: About 150 miles north of the Philippines.
Date(s): October 8, 1970.
Emergency: An earthquake deprived the people of Batan Island of adequate food supplies.
Air Force Organization(s) Involved: 463d Tac Alft Wg and 772d and 773d Tac Alft Sqs.
Airlifted: Three tons of rice and milk.
Aircraft Employed: C–130 (one).
Operations: In early October, an earthquake struck Batan Island, about 150 miles north of Luzon in the Philippines. The earthquake, in conjunction with tropical storms, disrupted communications and transportation links between the island and Luzon, creating a food shortage. The U.S. embassy in the Philippines asked the Thirteenth Air Force for an emergency food airlift to Batan.

The 463d Tac Alft Wg at Clark AB undertook the mission, flying a C–130 Hercules cargo airplane. On October 8, it flew to Manila, where it was loaded with 6,500 pounds of rice and condensed milk. From there it flew to Batan, a small island without an airstrip suitable for the C–130 to land. The crew, composed of personnel from the 772d and 773d Tac Alft Sqs, airdropped the food in parachuted containers to the earthquake victims. The emergency food airlift helped to sustain the population of the tiny island until regular shipping resumed.

54.
Name: Typhoons Joan and Kate.
Location: Republic of the Philippines.
Date(s): October 19–27, 1970.
Emergency: Two typhoons hit the Philippines, one in Luzon and the other in Mindanao.
Air Force Organization(s) Involved: 314th and 463d Tac Alft Wgs; 6200th AB Wg; 50th, 772d, 773d, and 774th Tac Alft Sqs; 9th Aeromed Evac Gp; and 20th Ops Sq.
Airlifted: Over 300 tons of food and medical supplies and more than 400 injured evacuees.
Aircraft Employed: C–130 (12), C–47 (1), C–54 (1), and C–118 (number unknown).
Operations: Typhoon Joan, also called Typhoon Sening, hit southern Luzon in the northern Philippines on October 13, bringing strong winds, heavy rain, and high tides. Two towns suffering particularly heavy damage were Virac on Catanduanes Island and Naga in Camines Sur Province, about 200 miles southeast of Clark AB. The storm left about 600 people dead and at least 80,000 homeless.

Humanitarian Airlift Operations

Less than a week later, another storm, Typhoon Kate, hit Mindanao in the southern Philippines, devastating Davao and Cotabato City and leaving 583 people dead.

More than 1,000 people perished in the two storms, and 90,000 were left homeless. President Ferdinand Marcos of the Philippines asked the U.S. embassy in Manila for aid, and Ambassador Henry A. Byroade contacted U.S. military forces in the Philippines. The Thirteenth Air Force, headquartered at Clark AB in Luzon, channeled the tasks to Air Force organizations in the Philippines.

The 463d Tac Alft Wg, also headquartered at Clark AB, played a leading role in disaster relief operations after the two storms. The wing flew a dozen C–130 Hercules four-engine cargo aircraft in the emergency operations, flying more than 250 tons of food—including AID milk, flour, and wheat, and medical supplies—from Nichols Field near Manila to Virac and Naga between October 19 and 27. The wing airlifted injured Filipinos from Virac and Naga to medical facilities in Manila. During the same week, a 463d Tac Alft Wg C–130 crew transported a team of Philippine officials and more than seven tons of food and medical supplies to Davao in Mindanao.

The 50th Tac Alft Sq of the 314th Tac Alft Wg, based at Ching Chuan Kang in Taiwan, also participated in disaster relief operations in the Philippines. Like the 463d Tac Alft Wg, it used C–130s to fly food and medical supplies from Manila to Virac and Naga and to carry injured Filipinos to Manila for medical treatment.

Other Air Force organizations in the Philippines joined the emergency operations. Using a four-engine C–54 and a twin-engine C–47, the 6200th AB Wg at Clark AB airlifted an additional six tons of relief supplies from Manila to Naga and Virac during mid-October. The 9th Aeromed Evac Gp also lent a hand. Flying in 20th Ops Sq C–118s, it evacuated injured from the disaster zone to Manila.

All U.S. armed services in the Philippines responded to the emergency. The Navy anchored an aircraft carrier off the coast of Catanduanes Island near Virac and flew Navy and Marine Corps helicopters to the devastated cities, delivering food and medical personnel and supplies.

The Philippine government expressed appreciation to the United States for the emergency relief missions. Mrs. Imelda R. Marcos, wife of the president, met and thanked air crews, and her husband authorized a Philippines presidential unit citation to participating units.

55.
Name: *Tong Lam* Shipwreck.
Location: Republic of the Philippines.
Date(s): October 27–28, 1970.
Emergency: A merchant ship ran aground in rough seas, forcing crew members to abandon ship.
Air Force Organization(s) Involved: 31st Aerosp RR Sq.

Airlifted: 39 shipwreck survivors.

Aircraft Employed: HC–130 (one) and HH–3E (three).

Operations: On October 27, rough seas forced the merchant ship *Tong Lam* aground about 200 miles west of Luzon in the Philippines. When it learned of the emergency, the Thirteenth Air Force's Joint Rescue Coordination Center notified the 31st Aerosp RR Sq at Clark AB near Manila. The squadron dispatched an HC–130 to look for survivors. When crew members of the four-engine aircraft spotted the sinking ship, they circled overhead to drop life rafts to survivors. The rafts helped many of the merchant ship's crew to survive during the hours of darkness.

By the light of the next day, three HH–3E helicopters of the 31st Aerosp RR Sq flew to the disaster scene. The Jolly Green Giant helicopters hoisted 39 ship-wreck survivors to safety and flew them to Cubi Point NAS on Luzon for shelter and treatment.

56.

Name: Typhoon Patsy.

Location: Republic of the Philippines.

Date(s): November 21 and 24, 1970.

Emergency: A typhoon caused power failures and food shortages on Luzon and neighboring islands.

Air Force Organization(s) Involved: 463d Tac Alft Wg.

Airlifted: 14 tons of food and electrical generators.

Aircraft Employed: C–130 (two).

Operations: The third typhoon to hit the Philippines in a month struck Luzon and neighboring islands on November 19. Typhoon Patsy brought winds of 124 mph, heavy rain, and high seas, depriving Manila of electrical power and leading to food shortages on the island of Polillo, about 90 miles east of Manila in the Philippine Sea. The Philippines asked the Thirteenth Air Force at Clark AB for assistance.

Air Force units at Clark AB immediately dispatched convoys of trucks to Manila to deliver generators and relief supplies. On November 20, the Air Force delivered an emergency generator from Clark AB to a Manila hospital. Emergency airlift operations had to wait until the Clark aircraft, evacuated in anticipation of the storm, returned to the base.

On November 21, a C–130 crew from the 463d Tac Alft Wg delivered two generators weighing 6.7 tons from Clark AB to Manila. Three days later, another 463d Tac Alft Wg C–130 delivered at least 7.5 tons of bread buns from Clark AB and Nichols Field to Polillo Island. Passing over a soccer field in the center of Polillo town, the aircraft made 24 passes in one hour, dropping at least 25,000 buns in 220-pound bundles from an altitude of about 150 feet. The food sustained the people of Polillo Island until regular shipments by sea resumed. The two flights delivered just over 14 tons of emergency equipment and supplies to the victims of Typhoon Patsy.

Humanitarian Airlift Operations

57.
Name: Typhoon Yolling.
Location: Ryukyu Islands.
Date(s): March 4–5, 1971.
Emergency: A tropical storm from the Pacific Ocean struck Okinawa.
Air Force Organization(s) Involved: 60th and 437th Mil Alft Wgs.
Airlifted: 41 tons of relief equipment, including trucks, trailers, and ambulances.
Aircraft Employed: C–5 (one) and C–141 (one).
Operations: In early March, Typhoon Yolling, a tropical storm from the Pacific Ocean, struck Okinawa in the Ryukyu Islands. The Air Force, then using Kadena AB on the island in a training exercise involving the airlift of paratroopers from North Carolina to Korea, launched an immediate relief airlift.

On March 4 and 5, two MAC cargo planes delivered 41 tons of equipment from Clark AB in the Philippines to Kadena AB. The cargo included nine trucks, nine trailers, and an ambulance. A huge C–5 Galaxy, then the largest cargo airplane in the world, carried 26 tons of equipment to Kadena from the 437th Mil Alft Wg of Charleston, South Carolina. A 60th Mil Alft Wg C–141 Starlifter from Travis AFB, California, flew the other 15 tons from Clark to Kadena.

In 1972, the United States and Japan signed a treaty transferring Okinawa and the Ryukyu Islands from the United States to Japan, with the condition that U.S. military bases remain.

58.
Name: *Kee Lung* Shipwreck.
Location: Republic of the Philippines.
Date(s): October 7, 1971.
Emergency: The high winds of Typhoon Elaine created 25-foot waves that swamped a merchant ship, causing it to begin to sink.
Air Force Organization(s) Involved: 31st Aerosp RR Sq.
Airlifted: 25 merchant seamen.
Aircraft Employed: HH–3 (two) and HC–130 (two).
Operations: On the evening of October 6, Typhoon Elaine swept across the western Pacific Ocean near Luzon, packing 70-knot winds that caused 25-foot waves. The waves swamped the Panamanian-registered merchant ship *Kee Lung*, en route from Bangkok, Thailand, to Taiwan with a Chinese crew. When the ship began to sink, the crew radioed a distress signal that was received by the Thirteenth Air Force's Joint Rescue Coordination Center in the Philippines. In response, the 31st Aerosp RR Sq at Clark AB in the Philippines dispatched two HC–130s just after midnight to search for the stricken ship. With the aid of another merchant ship, they located the sinking *Kee Lung*. Heavy seas made a ship-to-ship recovery impossible, so the HC–130s summoned two HH–3 Jolly Green Giant helicopters, also from the 31st Aerosp RR Sq, for an air rescue.

When the helicopters arrived, one lowered a pararescueman to the sinking ship to help with a hoist harness. In less than two hours, one of the helicopters lifted 16 shipwreck survivors and the other rescued nine. After refueling from one of the HC–130s, the HH–3s flew the *Kee Lung* crew to Manila for shelter and medical treatment.

59.
Name: Scarborough Shoal Shipwrecks.
Location: South China Sea.
Date(s): November 30, 1971.
Emergency: Four fishing boats ran aground on a shoal about 150 miles from land in the South China Sea.
Air Force Organization(s) Involved: 31st Aerosp RR Sq.
Airlifted: 30 shipwreck survivors.
Aircraft Employed: HH–3 (two) and HC–130 (one).
Operations: At the end of November, the Thirteenth Air Force's Joint Rescue Coordination Center learned that four fishing boats had run aground on Scarborough Shoal, about 150 miles west of Luzon in the South China Sea. The Thirteenth Air Force directed the 31st Aerosp RR Sq at Clark AB in the Philippines to respond.

A 31st Aerosp RR Sq HC–130 aircraft located the survivors on wreckage in the water and vectored two HH–3 helicopters to the disaster area. One helicopter rescued 16 shipwreck survivors, while the other hoisted seven more to safety. One of the HH–3s retrieved seven more survivors from the USS *Oklahoma*, where they had been flown by Navy helicopters. The two Jolly Green Giants transported 30 shipwreck victims to Manila for medical treatment and shelter.

60.
Name: *Yakal* Shipwreck.
Location: Pacific Ocean.
Date(s): November 30–December 2, 1971.
Emergency: A merchant ship with 41 persons aboard sank hundreds of miles from land.
Air Force Organization(s) Involved: 41st Aerosp RR Wg and 33d and 36th Aerosp RR Sqs.
Airlifted: 10 survivors and life rafts with survival kits.
Aircraft Employed: HC–130 (two) and HH–3 (two).
Operations: On November 30, the Philippine merchant vessel *Yakal* sank in heavy seas in the western Pacific Ocean about 275 miles southeast of Okinawa. Some of the 41 persons aboard managed to cling to floating debris from the sunken ship. News of the disaster reached units of the 41st Aerosp RR Wg based in Okinawa and Japan, and they were tasked with an emergency rescue mission.

The same day as the tragedy, the 36th Aerosp RR Sq at Yokota AB, Japan, launched a four-engine HC–130 to search for survivors. After locating them, the plane dropped life rafts and survival kits and radioed coordinates to ships in the area. Running low on fuel, the HC–130 landed at Kadena AB in Okinawa.

The plane returned to the disaster site the next day, joined by another 36th Aerosp RR Sq HC–130 that served as an airborne command post for rescue craft in the area. This aircraft refueled two HH–3 helicopters from the 33d Aerosp RR Sq that flew from Kadena and Naha ABs in Okinawa. One of the helicopters lowered pararescueman SSgt. Richard D. Hindman into the Pacific. With his help, the HH–3 crew lifted eight shipwreck survivors to safety, despite the threat of sharks in the vicinity. The other helicopter lowered Sgt. William J. Preble into the sea at the disaster site. He and his crew hoisted two more survivors to safety aboard the helicopter. The helicopters rescued 10 *Yakal* passengers on December 1 and 2.

The Air Force was not alone in this rescue operation. Navy P–3 aircraft and local surface ships also participated, rescuing three shipwreck survivors and recovering five bodies between November 30 and December 2. Unfortunately, 12 of those aboard the *Yakal* were never found.

61.
Name: Operation Saklolo.
Location: Republic of the Philippines.
Date(s): July 21–August 15, 1972.
Emergency: Weeks of torrential rain flooded northern and central Luzon, killing more than 300 people and isolating 700,000.
Air Force Organization(s) Involved: 374th Tac Alft Wg; 36th, 774th, and 776th Tac Alft Sqs; and 31st Aerosp RR Sq.
Airlifted: More than 2,000 tons of food, medical supplies, clothing, fuel, and other relief supplies; and at least 1,533 passengers, including Army disaster assistance relief teams and medical evacuees.
Aircraft Employed: C–130, HC–130, H–3, and H–43 (numbers unknown).
Operations: The approach of a series of typhoons and tropical storms brought weeks of torrential rain to the island of Luzon in the northern Philippines during July and early August. In July, more than 77 inches of rain fell over central and northern Luzon, putting some highways under three feet of water. Over 300 people died and 700,000 were isolated and in need of food. By August 4, about 100,000 flood evacuees had crowded into 40 shelters in the Manila area. This was the worst disaster in the Philippines since World War II.

The Philippine government sought relief from the United States, whose Agency for International Development sponsored a humanitarian operation called Operation Saklolo. U.S. military organizations from the Army, Navy, Marine Corps, and Air Force participated in the operation under direction of RADM John H. Dick. To feed the isolated flood victims, bakers in Manila prepared thousands of nutribuns, high protein bread rolls, from AID flour. Relief officials set up a

Philippine regional disaster relief coordination center at Clark AB in Luzon. Admiral Dick organized an airlift to transport the nutribuns from Manila to Clark and distribute them from Clark around Luzon.

During Operation Saklolo, Air Force C–130 Hercules cargo airplanes transported 2,000 tons of relief supplies in Luzon, including food, medical supplies, clothing, and fuel. The aircraft were flown by the 36th and 774th Tac Alft Sqs, on rotational duty in the western Pacific, and the 776th Tac Alft Sq of the 374th Tac Alft Wg, based at Ching Chuan Kang AB in Taiwan. Most of the C–130s delivered nutribuns from Nichols Field near Manila to Clark AB, where they were distributed to flood victims by trucks, helicopters, and boats. Each C–130 delivered an average of 75 tons of cargo per day, flying in poor weather that included low ceilings, poor visibility, and heavy rain. Three C–130s shuttled daily between Manila, Clark, and the U.S. naval base at Subic Bay during the operation.

At least one Hercules flew relief supplies from Davao in the southern Philippines to Manila for flood victims in Luzon. Clark AB's 31st Aerosp RR Sq also employed HC–130s to deliver food among key points on Luzon during the emergency.

To distribute food and other supplies accumulating at the Clark AB relief center, Admiral Dick relied on Air Force helicopters at the base and Navy and Marine Corps helicopters from nearby Cubi Point NAS. Air Force H–3s and H–43s from the 31st Aerosp RR Sq transported hundreds of bags of nutribuns to flood victims, some by landing on small areas of high ground surrounded by floodwaters and some by airdropping in regions without landing zones.

Crowds of hungry people flocked to each helicopter as it landed or descended, hoping to get some of the food. The 31st Aerosp RR Sq distributed 50 tons of food, medical supplies, and clothing from Clark AB to villages in central and northern Luzon cut off from normal transportation routes. Small H–43s transported Army disaster assistance relief teams around the island, where they gave over 305,000 cholera and typhoid inoculations. Larger H–3 helicopters flew medical supplies and food, including rice and nutribuns, from Clark AB to villages around Luzon. The Jolly Green Giants evacuated medical patients to hospitals in the Manila area. Among the Air Force helicopter pilots were Capt. Loran Rodway and Capt. Richard P. O'Dell. Captain O'Dell represented the 31st Aerosp RR Sq at an awards ceremony in Manila at the conclusion of Operation Saklolo.

At that ceremony, President Ferdinand Marcos awarded the Philippine Republic Presidential Unit Citation to 30 U.S. military organizations participating in the flood disaster relief operations. The operation reinforced friendly relations between the United States and the Republic of the Philippines during a crucial stage in the Vietnam War and proved that the two nations could work together in a common cause. It also demonstrated that U.S. military organizations from several services could carry out joint operational goals.

62.
Name: Typhoon Celeste.
Location: Johnston Island.
Date(s): August 17–18 and 23–29, 1972.
Emergency: Typhoon Celeste threatened Johnston Island with winds more than 100 knots in velocity and 45-foot waves.
Air Force Organization(s) Involved: 63d and 436th Mil Alft Wgs.
Airlifted: 524 passengers and 48 tons of supplies, mostly food.
Aircraft Employed: C–141 (three).
Operations: In the middle of August, Typhoon Celeste approached tiny Johnston Island in the mid-Pacific Ocean, threatening the inhabitants with 100-knot winds and 45-foot waves. The United States, which administered the island, decided to evacuate the more than 500 inhabitants to Hickam AFB, Oahu, several hundred miles to the northeast. Most inhabitants were military personnel.

On August 17 and 18, two MAC C–141s from the 63d and 436th Mil Alft Wgs transported 381 of Johnston Island's residents to Hickam AFB in four flights. A Saturn Airlines commercial airliner, chartered by MAC, transported another 143 passengers from Johnston to Oahu in two more flights. The three aircraft evacuated 524 passengers to Hawaii in two days.

Just after the last evacuation flight, Typhoon Celeste struck Johnston Island, destroying many of the island's facilities. Immediately after the storm's departure, the Navy sent a 20-man team by sea to Johnston to clear debris and reopen the runway.

A 63d Mil Alft Wg C–141 returned Johnston Island's residents from Hickam AFB from August 23 to 29. The Starlifter made eight flights, moving more than 500 passengers and 48 tons of food and other supplies to sustain the population during the island's reconstruction. The airlift saved lives and provided relief supplies to typhoon victims returning to Johnston Island.

63.
Name: Capiz Province Flood.
Location: Republic of the Philippines.
Date(s): October 1973.
Emergency: A tropical depression flooded the central Philippines, cutting off food supplies.
Air Force Organization(s) Involved: 31st Aerosp RR Sq.
Airlifted: 11 tons of bread.
Aircraft Employed: HC–130 (one).
Operations: In October, a tropical depression produced torrential rain that flooded the island of Panay in the central Philippines. The storm left three dozen people dead and more than 15,000 homeless. Governor Cornelio L. Villareal, Jr., of Capiz province, aware that food supply routes had been temporarily blocked, requested aid from government officials in Manila, where bread was stockpiled.

The Philippine government asked U.S. military officials for an airlift of nutribuns (see Operation Saklolo, July–August 1972) from Manila to Roxas in the disaster area.

The 31st Aerosp RR Sq at Clark AB on Luzon accepted the assignment. At the start of the mission, Maj. Norman Golden led an eight-man crew in an HC–130 from Clark to Manila International Airport to pick up 70,000 high protein nutribuns. Philippine air force personnel helped to load the aircraft. Later that day, Golden landed his four-engine plane at Roxas, where Philippine air force personnel and volunteers unloaded 11 tons of bread. Relief officials on the ground supervised food distribution to the flood victims.

The airlift provided a subsistence diet for 10,000 people for a week. By then, the waters had receded enough to allow normal food deliveries on Panay.

64.
Name: Australian Flood.
Location: Australia.
Date(s): February–March 1974.
Emergency: Floods blocked highways and railroads linking Alice Springs to other parts of Australia.
Air Force Organization(s) Involved: 63d Mil Alft Wg.
Airlifted: 76,369 gallons of fuel.
Aircraft Employed: C–141 (one).
Operations: In early February, heavy rain descended on central Australia, flooding highways and railroads that linked Alice Springs with other parts of the country. Aware of fuel shortages in the community and learning that the United States possessed an aerial bulk fuel delivery system, the Australian government asked the United States for an emergency airlift.

A 63d Mil Alft Wg C–141 Starlifter crew, led by Capt. Larry R. Jamison, flew the mission. They carried the fuel delivery system, which consisted of three pillow-type fuel bladders on a 20-foot modular platform, from MacDill AFB in Florida halfway around the world to Australia. The system had a fuel capacity of almost 9,000 gallons. Accompanying the fuel bladders were pump specialists.

Between February 15 and March 14, the C–141 crew transported 76,369 gallons of fuel in 10 missions from a Royal Australian Air Force airfield at Edinburg to a airfield at Alice Springs. From March 14 through 23, the crew returned the fuel bladder system and pump operators to MacDill.

65.
Name: Cyclone Tracy.
Location: Australia.
Date(s): December 26, 1974–January 3, 1975.
Emergency: A cyclone devastated Darwin, leaving thousands of people homeless.

Air Force Organization(s) Involved: 60th and 63d Mil Alft Wgs; and 7th, 14th, and 53d Mil Alft Sqs.

Airlifted: 301 tons of water purification equipment, electrical generators, building materials, food, and medical supplies; and 1,122 evacuees.

Aircraft Employed: C–141 (three).

Operations: On Christmas Day in 1974, Cyclone Tracy struck Darwin on the northern coast of Australia. High winds destroyed or tore the roofs off most buildings, leaving many of the town's 40,000 residents homeless. Australia asked the United States for assistance to airlift relief supplies to Darwin and to transport homeless refugees to other parts of Australia.

The Military Airlift Command responded with a humanitarian operation, flying two C–141 Starlifters from the 63d Mil Alft Wg and one C–141 from the 60th Mil Alft Wg. Capt. Jon R. Johnson and a 14th Mil Alft Sq crew flew one of the Starlifters, diverted from a routine mission in Australia. A 53d Mil Alft Sq crew under Lt. Steven Burkholder flew another C–141 from the 63d Military Airlift Wing's home at Norton AFB, California, across the Pacific to Australia. The aircraft from California carried water purification equipment, electrical generators, and provisions to Darwin and evacuated more than 700 homeless refugees to Sydney, a large city in southeastern Australia. Most of the evacuees were women and children, who sat on blankets in the aircraft cargo holds, strapped down for safety. One C–141 flight flew 320 evacuees from Darwin to Sydney.

The third C–141 in the airlift came from the 60th Mil Alft Wg at Travis AFB, California. On December 28, Maj. Lewis W. Like and his 7th Mil Alft Sq crew flew to Brisbane, Australia, stopping in Hawaii to pick up an Airlift Control Element team. In Australia, Like's crew shuttled generators and building materials from Amberley Royal Australian Air Force Station in Brisbane to Darwin. On return flights, the C–141 evacuated homeless storm victims from Darwin to Brisbane.

By January 3, the three Starlifters had flown more than 300 tons of relief equipment and supplies to Darwin to assist in the town's reconstruction. The cargo included four water purification trucks, four large electric generators weighing more than seven tons each, building materials, food, and medical supplies. The relief airlift evacuated over 1,000 homeless storm victims to shelters in Sydney and Brisbane.

In the nine-day operation, the Air Force conducted ten C–141 flights. After the airlift, Air Commodore L. H. Williamson of the Royal Australian Air Force commended MAC for its part in the Darwin disaster relief.

66.
Name: Dengue Vector Control.
Location: Guam.
Date(s): May 13–June 1975.
Emergency: Mosquitoes threatened to spread disease in epidemic proportions among crowded Vietnamese refugees in Guam.

Air Force Organization(s) Involved: 302d Tac Alft Wg and 906th, 907th, and 911th Tac Alft Gps.
Airlifted: Insecticide to spray 45,000 acres four times.
Aircraft Employed: UC–123 (two).
Operations: About 47,000 Vietnamese refugees filled camps on the Pacific island of Guam in late spring and early summer. Fleeing South Vietnam, they hoped to settle in the United States (see Chapter 6, Vietnamese Evacuation, April–September 1975). Public health officials feared mosquitoes would spread diseases such as dengue fever in the crowded population on the tiny island, so they asked DoD for an insecticide spraying operation. The Joint Chiefs of Staff turned to the Air Force's 302d Tac Alft Wg, the only organization equipped and trained to carry out the mission. The wing possessed UC–123K aircraft with spraying apparatus to spray thousands of acres at a time. The operation, initiated on May 13, was called Operation New Life—Dengue Vector Control.

Crews from the 302d Tactical Airlift Wing's 906th, 907th, and 911th Tac Alft Gps ferried two UC–123s from Rickenbacker AFB, Ohio, to Andersen AFB in Guam. They stopped on the way at McChord AFB, Washington; Elmendorf AFB, Alaska; Adak in the Aleutian Islands; Midway Island; Kwajalein in the Marshall Islands; and Wake Island. The journey covered 7,700 nautical miles. One of the UC–123s arrived in Guam on May 15, but the other was delayed by maintenance problems and did not arrive until May 21.

The actual spraying began on May 23 and continued through the end of June. Maj. George Rowcliffe, chief of the 302d Tactical Airlift Wing's spray branch, led a 22-man task force during the operation. The task force included two entomologists, Lt. Col. Len Trager and Capt. Al Bullard, who prepared the insecticide. The two UC–123 crews sprayed 45,000 acres four times in one-week intervals. Crews flew 18 hours during aerial spraying and came to call themselves the Skeeter Squirters. The operation succeeded in suppressing the mosquito population on Guam, preventing the outbreak of an epidemic.

67.
Name: Typhoon Olga.
Location: Republic of the Philippines.
Date(s): May 26–31, 1976.
Emergency: A typhoon struck Luzon with winds of more than 100 mph and heavy rain that flooded lowlands, washed away bridges, and produced mud slides.
Air Force Organization(s) Involved: Detachment 1, 41st Rescue and Weather Reconnaissance Wing.
Airlifted: 60 tons of oats, milk, bread, and other relief supplies; and 734 evacuees.
Aircraft Employed: H–3 (four).
Operations: On May 24, Typhoon Olga—also called Typhoon Didang in the Philippines—struck Luzon in the northern Philippines, bringing winds of more than 100 mph and torrential rain. Floods and mud slides killed more than 200

people and drove one million from their homes. Typhoon Olga flooded seven provinces in the worst disaster to hit the country since the floods of 1972 (see Operation Saklolo, July–August 1972).

The Philippine government appealed for international help while the country's national disaster center in Manila coordinated relief and rescue efforts. At least seven nations sent aid, including the United States. U.S. military units based on Luzon, in cooperation with the State Department, responded quickly.

Detachment 1 of the 41st Rescue and Weather Reconnaissance Wing, based at Clark AB on Luzon, participated in disaster relief operations from May 26 through 31. Under Lt. Col. Chuck Wicker, the detachment flew four H–3 Jolly Green Giant helicopters to deliver food and other relief supplies to flood victims or evacuate them from danger. Helicopter crews used a staging base at Basa made available by the Philippine air force.

After surveying flood damage and locating victims, the detachment delivered 60 tons of relief supplies, mostly food, in 74 flights over six days. Adapting deliveries to conditions in the disaster area, helicopter crews airdropped some loads and landed others on islands of higher ground. The Agency for International Development contributed much of the airlifted food, including rolled oats, powdered milk, and nutribuns.

Besides delivering food and other relief supplies, the Air Force H–3 helicopters evacuated hundreds of stranded flood victims from inundated or isolated areas to safety. Most were trapped by landslides or washed-out roads along a 20-mile stretch of Highway 5 in the Cagayan Valley of the Sierra Madre near Dalton Pass, about 110 miles north of Manila. In scores of stranded cars, trucks, and buses, 1,000 people suffered without food or potable water. Two detachment helicopters shuttled 734 people to safety in 62 flights, carrying most to the nearby village of San Jose, where a school yard was converted into a temporary helicopter landing pad. Some evacuees had not eaten in four days.

Other helicopters, from U.S. naval units in the Philippines and from the Philippine air force, evacuated stranded flood victims and airlifted food. U.S. aircraft delivered 185 tons of food, medicine, and fuel and rescued 1,977 persons after Typhoon Olga. At the same time, trucks from Clark AB delivered tons of donated food, clothing, shoes, and medicines to flood victims.

68.
Name: Typhoon Pamela.
Location: Guam.
Date(s): May 23–June 9, 1976.
Emergency: A typhoon with winds as high as 150 mph and torrential rain devastated the island of Guam.
Air Force Organization(s) Involved: Twenty–second Air Force; 60th, 62d, and 63d Mil Alft Wgs; and 374th Tac Alft Wg.
Airlifted: 2,652 tons of equipment and supplies, including construction equip-

ment, building materials, electrical generators, food, water, telephone equipment, bedding, and medical supplies; and at least 99 civil engineering and communications personnel.

Aircraft Employed: C–141 (seven), C–5 (six), and C–130 (one).

Operations: When Typhoon Pamela hit Guam the night of May 20–21, residents of the island were ready. Aircraft from the 54th Weather Reconnaissance Squadron, based at Guam's Andersen AFB, had flown several times to the storm as it approached the tiny Pacific island. Forecasters knew the direction and intensity of the storm and advised evacuation of the aircraft at the base.

Despite preparations for the typhoon, the people of Guam did not expect the destruction they faced. Wind gusts of more than 150 mph and 27 inches of rain in a 24-hour period flooded the island and tore apart most buildings. Typhoon Pamela killed at least five people, injured 500, and deprived thousands of homes. Officials measured the damage in hundreds of millions of dollars.

Andersen AFB suffered the same level of destruction as the civilian community. For 14 hours the base could not communicate with the outside world. Its runways, flooded and buried under scattered debris, were closed. President Ford declared Guam a disaster area and DoD authorized Army, Navy, and Air Force units in the area to render assistance to both the military and civilian communities.

The Military Airlift Command initiated a relief airlift on May 23, as soon as runways at Anderson AFB were clear of debris. Until June 9, MAC supervised the airlift of more than 2,652 tons of cargo to Guam by air. At least seven C–141s, five C–5s, and one C–130 transported the cargo, which consisted of construction equipment and materials, generators, telephone and communications equipment, food, medical supplies, bedding, air conditioners, water pumps, freezers, and trucks. Most of the material came from Hickam AFB in Hawaii and Clark AB in the Philippines. The Military Airlift Command flew 111 flights for Guam's disaster relief. Besides equipment and supplies, the flights carried Air Force civil engineers for construction projects and telephone workers to restore communications.

Three Twenty-second Air Force military airlift wings participated in the humanitarian airlift that followed Typhoon Pamela: the 60th from Travis AFB, California; the 62d from McChord AFB, Washington; and the 63d from Norton AFB, California. The 374th Tac Alft Wg, stationed at Clark AB, also participated.

The four wings used three types of cargo airplanes in the relief operation. C–141 Starlifter crews flew 83 missions. A 63d Mil Alft Wg C–141 diverted from a mission in the Pacific was the first airplane to land on Guam after Typhoon Pamela. All three military airlift wings flew Starlifters. The 60th Mil Alft Wg also flew C–5s, on a total of 24 relief missions. One Galaxy, flown by Lt. Col. Donald Fremming, carried electrical generators and navigational landing equipment at the beginning of the airlift from Clark AB to Guam to restore the tower facilities at Andersen AFB knocked out by the typhoon. Other 60th Mil Alft Wg Galaxy pilots participating in Typhoon Pamela relief flights were Capt. Alan R. James and Capt. Darrell D. Green. The third type of cargo aircraft used in the emergency was the C–130, flown by the 374th Tac Alft Wg on three missions. A civilian airliner under contract flew one airlift mission for Guam after Typhoon Pamela.

Navy and Army organizations in the Pacific also delivered equipment and supplies to Guam after the storm or supplied workers to restore buildings, telephones, and electricity.

In June, the legislature of Guam passed a resolution to express gratitude for the aid supplied by the United States during disaster relief, aid which stimulated reconstruction of the island.

69.
Name: Balinese Earthquake.
Location: Indonesia.
Date(s): July 21–22 and 25–26, 1976.
Emergency: A powerful earthquake struck the island of Bali, injuring thousands of people and leaving tens of thousands homeless.
Air Force Organization(s) Involved: 374th Tac Alft Wg and 62d Mil Alft Wg.
Airlifted: More than 47 tons of tents, cots, and blankets.
Aircraft Employed: C–130 (two) and C–141 (one).
Operations: During the middle of June, a strong earthquake struck the small island of Bali, just east of Java, in Indonesia. The temblor injured thousands of people and left 100,000 homeless. Indonesia requested U.S. assistance, and the Department of State, in cooperation with DoD, organized an airlift of bedding and tents.

On July 21 and 22, two C–130 cargo airplanes from the 374th Tac Alft Wg from Clark AB in the Philippines transported 20 tons of tents, cots, and blankets from Andersen AFB in Guam to Sentani Airport in Indonesia. Some supplies had been used for Typhoon Pamela victims on Guam (see Typhoon Pamela, May–June 1976).

Four days later, on July 25 and 26, MAC diverted a 62d Mil Alft Wg C–141 Starlifter from a mission at Clark AB for Indonesian earthquake relief. Lt. Gregg Maxwell and his 8th Mil Alft Sq crew flew the Starlifter to Tengah Royal Singapore AB to pick up 27 tons of blankets, 310 cots, and 570 six-man tents donated by C.A.R.E. Workmen loaded the palletized blankets and cots on the plane, but placing the tents on the floor of the aircraft took hours. Once loaded, the C–141 flew to Bali International Airport in the disaster area.

The airlifted relief supplies provided temporary bedding and shelter for thousands of earthquake victims. The operation also contributed to friendly U.S.-Indonesian relations.

70.
Name: Eniwetok Evacuation.
Location: Marshall Islands.
Date(s): December 26–29, 1977.

Emergency: A typhoon with wind gusts over 100 mph threatened the people of Eniwetok Atoll.
Air Force Organization(s) Involved: 62th, 63d, and 446th Mil Alft Wgs.
Airlifted: 830 evacuees.
Aircraft Employed: C–141 (four).
Operations: Typhoon Mary developed near Wake Island in the Pacific Ocean on December 23. By Christmas Day, it packed wind gusts exceeding 100 mph and was approaching Eniwetok, an atoll barely above sea level in the Marshall Islands.

Although Eniwetok had been the site of atomic bomb testing in the early 1950s, many of its residents had since returned. In 1977, hundreds of U.S. nationals were working in a federal cleanup project to rid the atoll of the remnants of its radioactive debris. In December, about 850 people crowded the tiny island chain. Typhoon Mary interrupted the cleanup project and persuaded Eniwetok residents and visiting workers to evacuate.

On December 26 and 27, four MAC C–141 Starlifters evacuated 830 people, including residents and federal workers, from Eniwetok to Andersen AFB in Guam. The air crews and aircraft came from the 62d, 63d, and 446th Mil Alft Wgs, based at McChord AFB in Washington and Norton AFB in California, on rotational duty in the Pacific with the Far East Intratheater pool at Yokota AB, Japan. Capt. Stewart Palmer of the 4th Mil Alft Sq piloted one of the C–141s, which carried 230 people from the atoll to Guam. Almost 50 of these were natives of the Marshall Islands, including the chief of Eniwetok. They found temporary shelter on Guam while the typhoon swept past their homes.

Typhoon Mary did not hit Eniwetok directly, but came close enough to bring 60-knot winds to the island group. The C–141s returned the evacuees to Eniwetok between December 27 and 29, after the storm passed.

71.
Name: Tropical Storm Alice.
Location: Marshall Islands.
Date(s): January 1979.
Emergency: A tropical storm with winds gusting to 75 knots destroyed structures on Namorik Atoll.
Air Force Organization(s) Involved: 63d Mil Alft Wg and 15th and 53d Mil Alft Sqs.
Airlifted: 75 tons of building materials.
Aircraft Employed: C–141 (three).
Operations: On January 5, Tropical Storm Alice struck the Marshall Islands, then a trust territory of the United States. Wind gusts up to 75 knots destroyed homes and other buildings on Namorik Atoll. Responding to a request for emergency assistance from the administrators of the islands, the Federal Disaster Assistance Agency office in Honolulu asked for a military airlift of building materials to the Marshalls.

The Military Airlift Command responded, flying three 63d Mil Alft Wg C–141 Starlifters laden with 75 tons of building materials from Norton AFB, California, to the Marshall Islands. The three crews—two from the 15th Mil Alft Sq and one from the 53d Mil Alft Sq—landed at Majuro, administrative capital of the islands, because Namorik Atoll lacked an adequate airstrip for the huge cargo aircraft. Ships transported the construction materials from Majuro to Namorik.

72.
Name: *Ta Lai* Shipwreck.
Location: Yellow Sea.
Date(s): March 30–31, 1979.
Emergency: A 3,000-ton freighter ran aground in heavy seas and began to sink.
Air Force Organization(s) Involved: Detachment 13, 33d Aerosp RR Sq.
Airlifted: 28 Taiwanese seamen.
Aircraft Employed: H–3 (one).
Operations: On the late afternoon of March 30, the 160-foot-long Taiwanese freighter *Ta Lai* encountered a strong storm in the Yellow Sea west of the Korean peninsula. The heavy seas broke the ship's anchor chain, setting the 3,000-ton vessel adrift. About dusk, the ship struck submerged rocks and ran aground. Before long, the hull began leaking and the ship began to sink, endangering its 28-man Taiwanese crew. The *Ta Lai* broadcast a distress signal.

When the 314th Air Div Rescue Center at Osan AB in South Korea heard the SOS, it dispatched an H–3 Jolly Green Giant rescue helicopter from Detachment 13, 33d Aerosp RR Sq. Although they had been on duty since noon, Maj. James E. McArdle, Jr., and his four-man crew accepted the mission.

Assisted by a South Korean C–123, the H–3, dubbed Rescue 709, located the *Ta Lai* in the Yellow Sea about 35 miles west of the Korean mainland. McArdle's crew found that the ship's superstructure reached more than 50 feet above the deck, forcing the helicopter to hover far above the endangered seamen. To illuminate the scene, the helicopter dropped parachute flares. It also dropped excess fuel to compensate for the weight of the rescued seamen. Waves of 12 to 15 feet and winds in excess of 15 knots challenged the helicopter crew as it lowered pararescueman Sgt. Mark Zitzow by cable to the shifting deck of the *Ta Lai*. With the help of his crewmen, Zitzow hoisted 11 Taiwanese seamen to the helicopter. Rescue 709 flew the men to Kwang-Ju AB on the Korean peninsula, where it refueled for another mission.

McArdle's helicopter returned two more times to the *Ta Lai*, hoisting another 11 seamen to safety on the second flight, and the final six on a third sortie. By that time, the H–3 rescuers were fighting not only wind and waves but also fatigue. McArdle's copilot, 1st Lt. Van J. Leffler, had to take over at times during the intense operation.

Each of the three flights delivered rescued *Ta Lai* crewmen to Kwang-Ju AB. By the time the rescue mission concluded at 4:15 a.m., all 28 Taiwanese seamen were safe. For his heroic part in the rescue operation, Major McArdle earned the 1979 MacKay Trophy, awarded by the Air Force chief of staff, Gen. Lew Allen, Jr., for the most meritorious flight of the year.

73.
Name: Typhoon Meli.
Location: Republic of Fiji.
Date(s): April 3–6, 1979.
Emergency: A typhoon hit the southern and eastern Fiji Islands, leaving hundreds of people homeless.
Air Force Organization(s) Involved: 438th Mil Alft Wg and 18th Mil Alft Sq.
Airlifted: 21 tons of relief supplies, including cots, blankets, tents, and water containers.
Aircraft Employed: C–141 (two).
Operations: On March 28, Typhoon Meli hit the southeastern islands of the Republic of Fiji in the southwestern Pacific Ocean. The storm brought extremely strong winds, high waves, and heavy rain that destroyed hundreds of homes and left 30 islanders dead. The Fiji government requested emergency assistance from the United States, and the State Department contacted DoD on April 3 for an airlift of relief supplies to Fiji.

Between April 3 and 6, MAC flew 21 tons of bedding, tents, and water containers from AID and Office of Foreign Disaster Assistance stockpiles in the Canal Zone and Guam to Nandi International Airport in Fiji.

The Military Airlift Command used two C–141 Starlifters for the operation. The first arrived on April 5 from Howard AFB in the Canal Zone to deliver 300 tents and tent flies and 1,890 portable water containers. The second arrived on April 6 and delivered 400 double-decker cots, 600 cotton blankets, and 760 water containers from Andersen AFB in Guam. Capt. Kermit Rufsvold of the 18th Mil Alft Sq, 438th Mil Alft Wg, piloted the second Starlifter, which was diverted from an exercise in the Pacific. The airlift helped to shelter and sustain homeless Fijians until they could rebuild their shattered homes.

74.
Name: Project Valentine Assist.
Location: Marshall Islands.
Date(s): December 2–28, 1979.
Emergency: A typhoon in the Marshall Islands brought 15- to 20-foot waves to Majuro Atoll, which had a maximum elevation of 6 feet above sea level.
Air Force Organization(s) Involved: Twenty-second Air Force and 60th, 62d, and 63d Mil Alft Wgs.
Airlifted: 650 tons of food, water purification equipment, an Army field kitchen, Red Cross supplies, communications and power generation equipment, trucks, and other relief cargo; and 250 support personnel.

Aircraft Employed: C–141 (35) and C–130 (five).

Operations: In late November, Typhoon Abby approached Majuro Atoll, a coral reef island in the Marshall Islands, a trust territory of the United States. High winds drove 15- to 20-foot waves over the small coral reef island, which had a maximum elevation of only 6 feet above sea level. Flooding destroyed homes, contaminated food and water supplies, and disrupted communications and power generation. On December 1, President Carter declared the atoll a major disaster area and ordered MAC to undertake a relief airlift.

Between December 2 and 28, the Twenty-second Air Force flew 40 cargo planes to Marshall Islands International Airport on Majuro Atoll in an emergency airlift called Project Valentine Assist. They transported 650 tons of relief equipment and supplies from Hickam AFB, Hawaii; Andersen AFB, Guam; Wright-Patterson AFB, Ohio; and other locations in the continental United States. The cargo included food, water purification equipment, an Army field kitchen, medical supplies, communications and power generation equipment, 20 trucks, a forklift, cots, tents, blankets, cooking and eating utensils, lumber, and tools. The planes also carried 250 support personnel to help rebuild the island's infrastructure, most from the 125th U.S. Infantry Division, stationed in Hawaii.

The air fleet included 35 C–141s and five C–130s from the 60th, 62d, and 63d Mil Alft Wgs, based in California and Washington. Many crews were diverted from regularly scheduled Pacific flights to assist in the emergency operation, which helped the people of the Marshall Islands reconstruct their capital.

75.

Name: Philippine Shipwreck.

Location: Calayan Island.

Date(s): September 22, 1981.

Emergency: A Philippine warship with 97 crewmen aboard ran aground in a typhoon, leaving 79 people dead or missing and 18 injured.

Air Force Organization(s) Involved: 31st and 33d Aerosp RR Sqs.

Airlifted: 16 pararescuemen and seven evacuees.

Aircraft Employed: H–3 (two) and HC–130 (one).

Operations: On September 21, Typhoon Clara swept along the northern Philippines, bearing 115 mph winds that endangered a Republic of the Philippines destroyer escort called the *Datu Kalantiaw*. The 200-foot-long ship, carrying a 97-man crew, headed for a cove at Calayan Island, about 90 miles north of Luzon, where it anchored. Rough seas and high winds snapped the anchor chain, and the ship ran aground on rocks and capsized.

Learning of the disaster from sources in the Philippines, the Western Pacific Rescue Coordination Center at Kadena AB in Japan alerted U.S. units at Clark AB and Cubi Point NAS on Luzon for a search and rescue operation. On September 22, a Navy P–3 aircraft located the wreckage and several injured crewmen on a nearby beach. Three Air Force aircraft arrived on the scene, an

HC–130 Hercules from Kadena and two H–3 helicopters that flew 285 miles from Clark AB.

The HC–130, piloted by Maj. Marshall A. Eto, served as an aerial refueling platform for the helicopters, directing them to survivors. The helicopters were flown by Capt. Steven Roark and 1st Lt. David Pribyla, each leading a five-man crew. The helicopters left four pararescue specialists in the school yard of Calayan Island's central village, where they set up an emergency treatment center. The pararescuemen treated 18 injured seamen, releasing 4 and preparing 14 for medical evacuation flights to Laoag AB, 90 miles away in Luzon. An Air Force helicopter and a Navy helicopter conducted the evacuation. The other Air Force H–3, after refueling from the HC–130, continued to search for more shipwreck survivors. Navy aircraft also searched, covering an area of 30 square miles. They found only dead bodies.

The same day, the USS *Mount Hood* arrived with a 12-man Navy recovery team. Pribyla and his crew ferried the team from the deck of the *Mount Hood* to the *Datu Kalantiaw*, then resting on its side on offshore rocks, to search the sinking ship for more survivors. Again, all they found were bodies. Of the 97-man crew of the sinking ship, only 18 survived, leaving 79 dead or missing.

After September 22, the Philippine navy took over the search and recovery mission. The Philippine minister of defense, Juan Ponce Enrile, praised the U.S. efforts as representative of the bond between the nations. With this operation, the Aerospace Rescue and Recovery Service recorded its 20,000th saved life since 1946.

76.
Name: Typhoon Iwa.
Location: Hawaii.
Date(s): November 25–28, 1982.
Emergency: A typhoon knocked out electrical generation facilities on the island of Kauai.
Air Force Organization(s) Involved: 60th Mil Alft Wg and 22d, 75th, and 86th Mil Alft Sqs.
Airlifted: 77 tons of power generation equipment, including three large generators and one power substation.
Aircraft Employed: C–5 (two) and C–141 (one).
Operations: On the evening of November 23, Typhoon Iwa hit the northern islands of Hawaii, including Kauai, Oahu, and Niihau. The worst storm to hit the Hawaiian archipelago since 1959, Typhoon Iwa injured 700 people. Winds of more than 100 mph winds devastated Kauai, destroying its power plants and forcing 6,000 people from their homes.

Responding to a call from Washington, D.C., for an emergency airlift, the 60th Mil Alft Wg at Travis AFB in California transported almost 77 tons of power generation equipment to Hawaii between November 25 and 28. The cargo included three 750-kilowatt gas turbine generators and one power substation from Point Mugu NAS in California. Two huge C–5 Galaxy cargo aircraft and one C–141 Starlifter performed the mission, flown by crews from the 22d, 75th, and 86th Mil Alft Sqs. They landed at Hickam AFB on Oahu.

Civilian barges ferried the generators and substation from Oahu to Kauai, where members of the Hawaiian National Guard and the Army's 25th Infantry Division set them up and operated them until regular electrical service was restored.

The Typhoon Iwa airlift, flown by the Air Force and carrying Navy equipment set up and operated by Army and National Guard personnel, demonstrated the effectiveness of a joint U.S. military response to an emergency.

77.
Name: KAL Flight 007.
Location: Sea of Japan.
Date(s): September 1983.
Emergency: A Soviet fighter shot down a South Korean airliner with 269 people aboard.
Air Force Organization(s) Involved: Twenty-second Air Force, 834th Alft Div, 60th Mil Alft Wg, and 33d Aerosp RR Sq.
Airlifted: 36 tons of search and salvage equipment and supplies and 36 search and salvage specialists.
Aircraft Employed: HC–130 (three), C–141 (four), and C–5 (one).
Operations: On August 31, Korean Air Lines Flight 007, a gigantic Boeing 747 airliner, left New York en route to Seoul. After refueling in Anchorage, Alaska, the jumbo jet headed across the Pacific Ocean and strayed over Soviet territory, including the Kamchatka peninsula and southern Sakhalin Island. Before dawn on September 1, a Soviet SU–15 interceptor shot down the airliner as it was about to reenter international airspace. KAL Flight 007 disappeared over the Sea of Japan with 269 people aboard, including many U.S. citizens. Among them was Congressman Larry McDonald from Georgia.

While Soviet officials originally refused to admit what had happened and later rationalized the shootdown as a defense of their airspace, U.S. military forces in the Pacific, in cooperation with the Japanese Self Defense Forces, launched an intensive search of the Sea of Japan near Sakhalin. They did not expect to find survivors, but they did hope to find the aircraft's flight recorder to reveal more about the tragedy.

Three HC–130 aircraft from the 33d Aerosp RR Sq at Kadena AB in Japan deployed at Yokota AB for the search. An HC–130, flown by Capt. Mark Leuthold and his crew, was the first U.S. aircraft over the search area. It was joined by a Navy P–3 aircraft and surface vessels.

To support the search and salvage operations, MAC flew at least 36 tons of equipment and supplies and 36 search and salvage specialists from the United States and from Ramstein AB in West Germany to Hakodate on Japan's northern island of Hokkaido. The Military Airlift Command used four C–141s and one C–5, the latter from the 60th Mil Alft Wg at Travis AFB in California. Despite these efforts, searchers found no survivors and never found the flight recorder from KAL 007.

78.
Name: Typhoon Keli.
Location: Johnston Island.
Date(s): August 19–20, 1984.
Emergency: A storm with winds in excess of 115 mph approached Johnston Island, threatening its more than 300 residents.
Air Force Organization(s) Involved: Twenty-second Air Force, 62d Mil Alft Wg, and 4th Mil Alft Sq.
Airlifted: 382 U.S. military and civilian personnel.
Aircraft Employed: C–141 (two).
Operations: In mid-August, Typhoon Keli approached Johnston Island, a small coral atoll in the Pacific Ocean about 715 miles southwest of Honolulu. Most of the island's residents worked at an Army weapons facility. They faced winds greater than 100 mph, torrential rain, and waves more than 40 feet high. When another typhoon had threatened the same island in 1972 (see Typhoon Celeste, August 1972), MAC evacuated the residents. The Pacific Command asked for a repeat performance.

The Twenty-second Air Force used two C–141 Starlifters for the operation. One was flown by Capt. Russell Wiley and a 4th Mil Alft Sq crew from the 62d Mil Alft Wg and carried 261 evacuees on the floor of the huge aircraft. The two C–141s transported 382 passengers from Johnston Island to Hickam AFB on Oahu, a journey of 715 miles, on August 19 and 20. Twelve hours after the evacuation, Typhoon Keli struck Johnston Island.

79.
Name: Pines Hotel Fire.
Location: Republic of the Philippines.
Date(s): October 23–24, 1984.
Emergency: A hotel fire killed 17 people and injured 61.
Air Force Organization(s) Involved: 31st Aerosp RR Sq and 374th Tac Alft Wg.
Airlifted: 58 evacuees.
Aircraft Employed: H–3 (one) and C–130 (one).
Operations: On October 23, the resort Pines Hotel in Baguio, Republic of the Philippines, caught fire. Among the guests at the eight-story hotel were about 200 U.S. World War II veterans visiting the Philippines to celebrate the fortieth anniversary of Gen. Douglas MacArthur's Leyte landing with the Sixth Army in October 1944. Many guests escaped from the ground floor, but nine were forced by flames and smoke to the rooftop.

Humanitarian Airlift Operations

The 31st Aerosp RR Sq, responding to calls from the Thirteenth Air Force Command Center and the Western Pacific Rescue Coordination Center, scrambled two H–3 Jolly Green Giant helicopters. One helicopter aborted its mission because of maintenance trouble, but the other, flown by 1st Lt. Carl Binford and a four-man crew, hovered over the burning hotel to rescue the guests on the roof. After lowering a rescue harness and hoisting four hotel guests to safety, Binford's crew returned to the burning hotel. The advance of smoke and flames toward the trapped guests forced rescuers to abandon the slow hoisting procedure. Binford hovered his craft a few inches from the hotel roof while the remaining five guests climbed aboard.

The same helicopter later flew eight injured guests from Baguio Airport to Clark AB for medical treatment. On October 24, a 374th Tac Alft Wg C–130 transported 41 more injured fire victims—13 who were on stretchers and 28 who were ambulatory—from Baguio Airport to the Clark AB hospital. On the aircraft, the 9th Aeromed Evac Sq treated and cared for the patients.

In two days, the Air Force saved nine lives and transported another 49 people to Clark AB for medical treatment. Despite these heroic efforts, 17 people perished in the blaze.

80.
Name: Typhoon Eric.
Location: Fiji.
Date(s): January 19–21, 1985.
Emergency: Typhoon Eric devastated the island of Viti Levu, leaving 3,000 people homeless.
Air Force Organization(s) Involved: 60th and 349th Mil Alft Wgs; and 7th, 75th, and 312th Mil Alft Sqs.
Airlifted: 186 tons of relief supplies, including 2,400 tents, tarpaulins, plastic sheeting, and water trailers.
Aircraft Employed: C–5 (two) and C–141 (one).
Operations: In mid-January, Typhoon Eric hit Viti Levu, the largest island in the Fiji group north of New Zealand. The storm destroyed hundreds of dwellings, leaving at least 3,000 people homeless. After the government of Fiji asked the United States for relief, the State Department contacted MAC for an emergency airlift of supplies.

On January 19, MAC diverted three 60th Mil Alft Wg cargo aircraft from Pacific missions for the humanitarian operation. Two of these were C–5 Galaxies, flown by Maj. John Drexler and Maj. Richard Martenson, with crews from the 75th and 312th Mil Alft Sqs, the latter representing the Air Force Reserve's 349th Mil Alft Wg. The two C–5s transported 160 tons of tents, tarpaulins, plastic sheeting, and water trailers from Andersen AFB, Guam, to Nandi International Airport on Viti Levu. Never before had C–5s landed in Fiji. Damaged cargo-handling equipment at Nandi required the crews, aided by Fijian soldiers, to unload the

C–5s by hand, a task which took about four hours per plane.

The third 60th Mil Alft Wg aircraft taking part in the operation was a C–141 Starlifter, flown by Maj. Allan M. Dickson and a crew from the 7th Mil Alft Sq. Dickson and his crew transported 26 tons of relief supplies, including 400 tents, from Hickam AFB, Hawaii, to Nandi. Again, Fijian soldiers did most of the work in unloading the plane by hand.

Between January 19 and 21, MAC flew 186 tons of cargo from Hawaii and Guam to Fiji on three of the largest cargo aircraft in the world. The relief supplies helped to shelter the homeless of Viti Levu until their homes could be rebuilt.

81.
Name: *Sung Boch Oh* Sinking.
Location: Yellow Sea.
Date(s): January 28, 1985.
Emergency: A South Korean fishing vessel with 10 crewmen aboard was sinking rapidly.
Air Force Organization(s) Involved: 38th Aerosp RR Sq.
Airlifted: 10 shipwreck survivors.
Aircraft Employed: H–3 (two).
Operations: On January 28, Korean authorities notified the Western Pacific Rescue Coordination Center that a South Korean fishing vessel called the *Sung Boch Oh* was sinking in the Yellow Sea. The 38th Aerosp RR Sq immediately launched two H–3 Jolly Green Giant helicopters, directed to the distress signal by an Airborne Warning and Control System (AWACS) aircraft.

One of the H–3 helicopters, piloted by Capt. Mark C. Noyes, hoisted aboard all 10 survivors of the sinking ship and took them to Kunsan AB in southwestern South Korea for medical treatment. The other helicopter stood by to assist if necessary. The helicopters then returned to their home base at Osan AB, South Korea, to prepare for the next emergency.

82.
Name: *Marcos Faberes* Shipwreck.
Location: Pacific Ocean.
Date(s): October 16, 1985.
Emergency: After its load shifted, a ship with more than 90 people aboard sank in the Pacific Ocean north of Luzon in the Philippines.
Air Force Organization(s) Involved: 31st, 33d, and 41st Aerosp RR Sqs.
Airlifted: 33 shipwreck survivors.
Aircraft Employed: H–3 (two) and HC–130s (two).
Operations: On October 15, the load of the Philippine ship *Marcos Faberes* suddenly shifted, forcing the stern downward into the sea. In four minutes, the ship sank in the western Pacific Ocean. About 50 of the more than 90 passengers clung to floating debris. A passing Japanese vessel, the *Keranji*, reported to Hong

Kong that it had recovered 34 survivors of the sunken vessel, but about 60 more were missing.

Notified by Hong Kong and Guam of the disaster, the Western Pacific Rescue Coordination Center diverted crews and aircraft from a Cope Thunder search and rescue exercise in the area to rescue other survivors. A Navy P–3 aircraft from Cubi Point NAS in the Philippines located the shipwreck about 60 miles north of Luzon. Another passing ship, the tanker *Japan Violet*, recovered 16 survivors.

On October 16, two H–3 Jolly Green Giant helicopters, piloted by Capt. Page A. Wagner and Capt. Barry E. Gottshall of the 31st and 33d Aerosp RR Sqs, flew to the shipwreck scene. The five-man crews hoisted 17 survivors to safety aboard the hovering helicopters. To help the weak victims hold the rescue harness, a pararescueman rode along for each lift. The pararescuemen included SSgt. David Vogele and SSgt. Dale Lackey, SrA. Max Montgomery, and Amn. Jack Vanlue.

The helicopters flew these 17 survivors to Calayan Island, about 20 miles from the disaster site. One helicopter hovered over the *Japan Violet*, hoisted aboard the 16 survivors the ship had recovered, and flew them to Calayan Island as well. To provide first aid for the 33 shipwreck victims on the island, a 33d Aerosp RR Sq HC–130 dropped two pararescuemen by parachute.

After the *Marcos Faberes* survivors received treatment and some rest, the two H–3 helicopters transported them from Calayan Island to a hospital at Laoag in the Philippines, about 70 miles away. Two HC–130s, one each from the 33d and 41st Aerosp RR Sqs, refueled each helicopter four times during the flights among the disaster site, the Japanese ship, Calayan Island, and Laoag. The HC–130s searched the area for other survivors, but none were found.

83.
Name: *Asunción Cinco* Shipwreck.
Location: South China Sea.
Date(s): December 18–20, 1985.
Emergency: A ship with 177 people aboard sank many miles from the nearest land.
Air Force Organization(s) Involved: 31st Aerosp RR Sq.
Airlifted: 13 shipwreck survivors and a four-man medical team.
Aircraft Employed: H–3 (two).
Operations: On December 18, the Philippine interisland ship *Asunción Cinco*, carrying 150 passengers and 27 crew members, sank about 95 miles southwest of Manila in the South China Sea. Philippine authorities notified the Western Pacific Rescue Coordination Center, which dispatched Navy and Air Force search and rescue units from Cubi Point NAS and Clark AB. A Navy P–3 aircraft spotted some survivors and dropped life rafts to them, while the USS *Overseas Alice* diverted to the scene.

Two 31st Aerosp RR Sq H–3 helicopters, flown by Capt. Page Wagner and Capt. Barry Gottshall (see *Marcos Faberes* Shipwreck, October 1985), participated in the emergency operation. On December 19, they hoisted 13 survivors from the sea and flew them to Cubi Point for medical treatment. One helicopter suffered a winch hoist failure, so the five-man crew had to use a rope ladder instead. Each helicopter lowered a pararescueman to the water to help survivors climb onto the rescue harness or rope ladder.

Navy helicopters also lifted shipwreck survivors from the sea, taking 14 of them to Cubi Point and 48 to the *Overseas Alice*. On December 20, an Air Force helicopter transported a four-man medical team from Cubi Point to the ship to treat the victims. Navy and Air Force crews rescued 75 people from the *Asunción Cinco*, but more than 100 passengers and crew were still missing when the search and rescue operation ended.

84.
Name: Guadalcanal Typhoon.
Location: Solomon Islands.
Date(s): May 1986.
Emergency: A typhoon with winds up to 140 mph devastated the Solomon Islands.
Air Force Organization(s) Involved: 374th Tac Alft Wg, 316th Tac Alft Gp, and 21st and 345th Tac Alft Sqs.
Airlifted: 40 tons of emergency supplies, including communications equipment, canned meat, plastic sheeting, water tanks, medicine, and batteries.
Aircraft Employed: C–130 (four).
Operations: In May, a typhoon struck Guadalcanal in the Solomon Islands east of New Guinea, bringing 140 mph winds and torrential rain that killed almost 100 people and left more than 90,000 homeless. Swollen streams and mud slides washed away villages, bridges, and roads. The government of the Solomon Islands requested U.S. assistance, and the Department of State's Office of Foreign Disaster Assistance authorized a humanitarian airlift.

Flooding of the Lunga River damaged the runway at Henderson Field, Guadalcanal, and prevented commercial aircraft from landing. The commander of the Pacific Command, ADM Ronald J. Hays, turned to Air Force C–130 units based in the Pacific to accomplish the mission.

During the last week in May, four MAC C–130 Hercules airplanes from the 374th Tac Alft Wg at Clark AB in the Philippines and the 316th Tac Alft Gp at Yokota AB in Japan delivered 40 tons of relief cargo to Guadalcanal. Two of the C–130s flew 24 tons of plastic sheeting from an AID stockpile at Andersen AFB, Guam, to Henderson Field. A third C–130 delivered three tons of radios, batteries, and communications technicians from Okinawa. A fourth C–130 flew over 13 tons of canned meat from Port Moresby, Papua New Guinea. These four aircraft also delivered water tanks and medicine to the island.

The airlifters overcame some difficult problems. Adverse weather challenged the skills of the pilots and Henderson Field's damaged runway could barely accommodate the large C–130s. The field's compressed air refueling equipment, designed for small aircraft, had to be recharged frequently for the larger planes, delaying flights.

Despite the difficulties, the airlift brought enough relief equipment and supplies to the Solomon Islands to sustain the storm victims during reconstruction. At the conclusion of the operation, Admiral Hays congratulated all units on a job well done.

85.
Name: Philippine Airlift.
Location: Republic of the Philippines.
Date(s): September 18–23, 1986.
Emergency: Shortly after Mrs. Corazon Aquino replaced Ferdinand Marcos as president of the Philippines, she traveled to the United States seeking aid.
Air Force Organization(s) Involved: 436th Mil Alft Wg.
Airlifted: 93 tons of medical supplies and food.
Aircraft Employed: C–5 (two).
Operations: In August, the Americares Foundation, a private international relief organization, applied to the U.S. government for shipment of $10 million in medical supplies to the Philippines under terms of the Denton Amendment to the Foreign Assistance Act. The amendment permitted DoD to transport humanitarian relief supplies to foreign countries on a space-available basis, at no charge to donors or consignees. The Americares Foundation timed the request to coincide with a September visit to the United States of the new president of the Philippines, Mrs. Corazon Aquino, who was seeking U.S. assistance for her new regime.

In response to the request and President Aquino's visit, President Reagan authorized a humanitarian airlift to Manila to deliver the medical supplies on C–5 training flights across the Pacific. One C–5 would stop on the way at Hickam AFB, Hawaii, to pick up additional medical supplies from Tripler Army Medical Center.

On September 18, the 436th Mil Alft Wg at Dover AFB, Delaware, flew two C–5 Galaxy cargo aircraft to Andrews AFB in Maryland, where personnel from the 93d Aerial Port Squadron palletized and loaded 93 tons of medical supplies and food. Cargo for one airplane came from DoD, while the other C–5 was filled with Americares Foundation supplies. President Aquino personally accepted the gift on the Andrews AFB flight line on September 19.

One C–5, flown by a 9th Mil Alft Sq crew and loaded with 24 tons of supplies, landed at Manila International Airport on September 23 after stopping on the way at Travis AFB, California; Hickam AFB; Wake Island; and Andersen AFB, Guam. The other Galaxy, loaded with 69 tons of supplies and flown by a 3d Mil Alft Sq crew, flew direct from Travis AFB to Clark AB in the Philippines.

In Manila, Vice President Salvador H. Laurel of the Philippines greeted the aircraft and expressed thanks on behalf of his people. Personnel of the 374th Tac

Alft Wg at Clark AB unloaded the two C–5s, taking less than two hours per plane. The airlift assisted the new government of President Aquino and strengthened the historically close relationship between the United States and the Philippines.

86.
Name: Typhoon Kim.
Location: Mariana Islands.
Date(s): December 7, 1986.
Emergency: A typhoon with winds as high as 193 mph devastated the island of Saipan.
Air Force Organization(s) Involved: 54th Weather Reconnaissance Squadron.
Airlifted: Seven tons of food, clothing, gas lanterns, flashlights, candles, batteries, books, and toys.
Aircraft Employed: WC–130 (one).
Operations: Typhoon Kim, one of the most powerful typhoons ever to threaten the islands of the western Pacific, approached the Marianas in early December, packing winds up to 193 mph. The typhoon came close enough to Guam to force the evacuation of B–52s and KC–135s stationed there, but narrowly bypassed the island. Saipan was not so lucky. On the night of December 3, the storm brought strong winds, torrential rain, and high waves to the island, knocking out electricity and destroying over half of the houses in the village of Tanapag in northern Saipan.

When news of the disaster reached the 54th Weather Reconnaissance Squadron on Guam, the organization was ready. It had a tradition of dropping gift packages to islands around Guam every December in a project called Christmas Drop. Using the Christmas Drop organization and collection system already in place, the people of Guam donated seven tons of relief supplies to the typhoon victims of Saipan. The Andersen AFB First Sergeants Association provided $1,100 in candles, flashlights, and batteries, and the Christmas Drop committee contributed over $750 in food, including hundreds of pounds of rice and 30 cases of vegetables. Other donated supplies included gas lanterns, clothing, books, and toys.

On December 7, Maj. Robert C. Copenhafer, Jr., and his 54th Weather Reconnaissance Squadron crew transported the seven tons of relief cargo from Guam to Saipan aboard a WC–130 aircraft. The trip covered about 118 miles. After Bishop Tomas Camacho of Saipan and local government officials accepted the goods with gratitude, a convoy of vans and trucks transported the supplies to Mount Carmel High School for distribution to the needy.

87.
Name: Typhoon Uma.
Location: Vanuatu (formerly New Hebrides).
Date(s): February 13–15, 1987.

Humanitarian Airlift Operations

Emergency: A typhoon hit the central islands of Vanuatu, leaving hundreds of people homeless.
Air Force Organization(s) Involved: 60th and 62d Mil Alft Wgs and 374th Tac Alft Wg.
Airlifted: At least 64 tons of tents and plastic sheeting.
Aircraft Employed: C–141 (two) and C–130 (two).
Operations: In early February, Typhoon Uma hit the central islands of Vanuatu, a South Pacific nation east of Australia. Through diplomatic channels, Vanuatu asked the United States for help in sheltering its hundreds of citizens left homeless by the storm. Responding to a State Department request, the JCS authorized a MAC humanitarian airlift.

Four MAC aircraft—two C–141 Starlifters from the 60th and 62d Mil Alft Wgs and two C–130 Hercules from the 374th Tac Alft Wg—took part in the subsequent emergency operation. Lt. Col. Roger Baskett and Maj. Timothy Spellman served as mission commanders. Because the larger C–141 jet cargo aircraft could not land easily on the small airfield at Port-Vila, Vanuatu, Baskett and Spellman planned to have the Starlifters deliver their cargoes to Port Moresby, Papua New Guinea. The C–130s would then shuttle the cargo from Port Moresby to Port-Vila.

One C–141 flew 500 tents weighing 38 tons from Andersen AFB in Guam to Port Moresby, while the other delivered 200 rolls of plastic sheeting, weighing 26 tons, from Singapore. The two C–130s made six trips between February 13 and 15 to transport 64 tons of tents and sheeting from New Guinea to Vanuatu, a distance of about 1,500 miles. The 374th Tac Alft Wg aircraft also transported 26 Navy Seabees to Port-Vila to repair a school that had been damaged by the storm. After delivering their cargo, the C–130s flew around the islands of Vanuatu searching for shipwrecked survivors of Typhoon Uma. They refueled in New Caledonia.

After the operation, the U.S. ambassador at Port Moresby, Everett E. Bierman, thanked the Air Force crews for their efforts. The airlift provided temporary shelter for Vanuatu's storm victims and reinforced friendly relations between the United States and the South Pacific island nation.

88.
Name: Typhoon Nina.
Location: Philippines and Federated States of Micronesia.
Date(s): December 5, 1987–January 1988.
Emergency: A typhoon devastated islands in the western Pacific.
Air Force Organization(s) Involved: 374th Tac Alft Wg.
Airlifted: At least 34 tons of relief supplies, including rice and clothing.
Aircraft Employed: C–130 (six).
Operations: At the end of November, Typhoon Nina swept across the western Pacific, devastating the Truk Islands in the Federated States of Micronesia and southern Luzon in the Philippines. After the affected governments requested U.S.

514

assistance through diplomatic channels of the State Department, the Defense Department organized humanitarian relief. The Military Airlift Command's 374th Tac Alft Wg at Clark AB in the Philippines used six C–130s for the emergency.

Between December 5 and early January, two 374th Tac Alft Wg C–130s and Navy and Marine Corps helicopters flew more than 80 tons of relief supplies to Legazpi City on the southern tip of Luzon. The C–130s, flown by crews from the 21st Mil Alft Sq, carried pallets of rice and fuel for the helicopters from Clark AB.

In December, four more 374th Tac Alft Wg C–130s shuttled relief supplies daily from Andersen AFB in Guam to Moen, largest of the Truk Islands in Micronesia. The crews came from the 21st and 345th Tac Alft Sqs. Two crews alternated typhoon relief missions with Christmas Drop operations, which the 374th Tac Alft Wg had taken over from the 54th Weather Reconnaissance Squadron when the squadron inactivated at the end of September 1987 (see Typhoon Kim, December 1986). Christmas Drop delivered parachuted Christmas packages from Guam to neighboring islands. On December 18, the C–130s transported more than seven tons of toys, clothing, and supplies to Truk for the typhoon victims.

89.
Name: Philippines Medical Airlift.
Location: Republic of the Philippines.
Date(s): January 25–28, 1988.
Emergency: The Philippine government requested medical supplies.
Air Force Organization(s) Involved: 60th Mil Alft Wg.
Airlifted: 102 tons of medical supplies.
Aircraft Employed: C–5 (two).
Operations: In early 1988, the government of the Philippines requested U.S. medical supplies through diplomatic channels. The United States had provided similar aid less than two years earlier (see Philippine Airlift, September 1986). The Americares Foundation, a private relief organization dedicated to filling emergency medical needs worldwide, offered antibiotics, bandages, nutritional supplements, needles, syringes, vaccines, crutches, wheelchairs, and other medical supplies donated by pharmaceutical companies and hospital suppliers in the United States. Under the McCollum Act, which allowed shipment of excess, nonlethal DoD supplies, the State Department asked DoD to airlift the cargo to the Philippines.

The Twenty-second Air Force's 60th Mil Alft Wg at Travis AFB in California used a pair of C–5 Galaxies for the operation. Between January 25 and 28, the aircraft delivered 102 tons of medical supplies to Manila, stopping on the way at Hickam AFB, Hawaii, and Andersen AFB, Guam. Personnel from the 374th Tac Alft Wg at Clark AB helped to unload the C–5s.

Raul Manglapus, the Philippine foreign affairs secretary, thanked the United States for its assistance in a ceremony in Manila attended by the U.S. ambassador,

Nicholas Platt. The airlift helped to satisfy medical needs and demonstrated the commitment of the United States to the welfare of the Philippines.

90.
Name: Typhoon Roy.
Location: Marshall Islands.
Date(s): February 19–22, 1988.
Emergency: A typhoon devastated the Marshall Islands, destroying homes and knocking out electrical power.
Air Force Organization(s) Involved: 60th Mil Alft Wg and 86th Mil Alft Sq.
Airlifted: 50 tons of construction material and transformers.
Aircraft Employed: C–141 (one).
Operations: Typhoon Roy, an unusual winter typhoon, struck the Marshall Islands in February. The storm's powerful winds, torrential rain, and monstrous waves knocked out electrical facilities and destroyed hundreds of homes on the low coral Pacific islands. The Pacific Air Forces contacted MAC for a special assignment airlift mission to airlift construction materials to rebuild housing on the islands.

On February 19–22, the 60th Mil Alft Wg flew 50 tons of construction material and electrical equipment from Travis AFB in California through Hickam AFB in Hawaii to Kwajalein, one of the largest of the Marshall Islands, which had an airstrip large enough to accommodate C–141 aircraft. Flown by an 86th Mil Alft Sq crew, the Starlifter carried five pallets of plywood, 168 residential-type doors, and two transformers. The airlift helped to jump-start reconstruction efforts in the Marshall Islands, which had gained independence from the United States only two years earlier.

91.
Name: Typhoon Ruby.
Location: Republic of the Philippines.
Date(s): October 25, 1988.
Emergency: The wind and heavy rains of a typhoon flooded parts of Manila, stranding many residents.
Air Force Organization(s) Involved: 31st Aerosp RR Sq.
Airlifted: 27 flood victims.
Aircraft Employed: HH–3 (two).
Operations: During the last week of October, Typhoon Ruby hit Luzon in the Philippines with high winds and torrential rain. Floods following the storm stranded many residents of Marikina, a suburb of Manila. The Western Pacific Rescue Coordination Center, through its liaison at Thirteenth Air Force, directed the 31st Aerosp RR Sq at nearby Clark AB to respond.

On October 25, two of the squadron's HH–3 helicopters flew to Marikina. Using rope ladders and hoists, they lifted 27 stranded residents to safety. The mission required more than eight hours of flying time.

92.
Name: *Selina* Shipwreck.
Location: Pacific Ocean.
Date(s): December 12, 1988.
Emergency: A ship with a 20-man crew aboard sank in heavy seas.
Air Force Organization(s) Involved: 33d Aerosp RR Sq.
Airlifted: 11 shipwreck survivors.
Aircraft Employed: HC–130 (two) and HH–3 (one).
Operations: On December 12, winds gusting to 50 knots and 25-foot waves swamped and sank the Panamanian ship *Selina* 450 miles south-southwest of Okinawa. The Japan Maritime Safety Agency notified the Western Pacific Rescue Coordination Center, which diverted three aircraft from the 33d Aerosp RR Sq to the scene.

The aircraft included one HH–3 helicopter piloted by Capt. William A. Mozzo and a four-man crew. Diverted from a training flight from Japan to the Philippines, Mozzo's crew reached the survivors after flying seven hours. The helicopter was refueled on the way from a pair of 33d Aerosp RR Sq HC–130s and a Marine Corps KC–130. At the disaster site, the aircraft rendezvoused with a pair of Japanese aircraft that located the 20-man crew of the *Selina* in a pair of life rafts.

As darkness approached, Mozzo hovered over one of the life rafts and hoisted all 11 passengers aboard, fighting heavy seas and strong winds. The nine remaining *Selina* survivors in the other life raft were rescued by a Japanese fishing vessel. Still refueling from the HC–130s, the HH–3 carried the 11 shipwreck survivors to Clark AB in the Philippines. On the way it had to ascend to 9,000 feet to fly over the Sierra Madre of northeastern Luzon. The helicopter successfully completed its mission after flying more than 11 hours.

93.
Name: Typhoon Ofa.
Location: Western Samoa and American Samoa.
Date(s): February–March 1990.
Emergency: A typhoon with winds in excess of 100 mph devastated Samoa.
Air Force Organization(s) Involved: 60th and 63d Mil Alft Wgs.
Airlifted: 410 tons of cargo, including helicopters and construction equipment, and 149 passengers.
Aircraft Employed: C–5 (three) and C–141 (three).
Operations: On February 4, Typhoon Ofa struck Samoa, about 1,600 miles northeast of New Zealand. The storm packed winds of more than 100 mph that demolished many island structures. The Agency for International Development's Office of Foreign Disaster Assistance sponsored a military airlift to Western Samoa, while FEMA directed a similar airlift to American Samoa, a U.S. territory.

On February 6, a 60th Mil Alft Wg C–5 Galaxy diverted from Hickam AFB in Hawaii to Western Samoa, carrying two UH–60 helicopters, six trailers, a fuel bladder, and construction equipment. The next day, a 63d Mil Alft Wg C–141 Starlifter from Norton AFB, California, landed in Western Samoa with more construction equipment.

The Military Airlift Command airlifted more than 500 rolls of plastic sheeting, tools, and construction workers from Guam to Western Samoa and American Samoa. When the Typhoon Ofa relief operation ended, three C–5s and two C–141s had airlifted 149 passengers and 410 tons of cargo to the stricken islands.

94.
Name: Philippine Earthquake.
Location: Republic of the Philippines.
Date(s): July 17–August 1, 1990.
Emergency: An earthquake registering 7.7 on the Richter scale destroyed many buildings in Baguio, killing or injuring more than 3,200 people and leaving thousands homeless.
Air Force Organization(s) Involved: 60th, 62d, and 438th Mil Alft Wgs; and 374th Tac Alft Wg.
Airlifted: 582 tons of tents, plastic sheeting, blankets, medical supplies, hard hats, picks, shovels, and food; and 2,475 passengers, including search and rescue teams, medical personnel, and relief officials.
Aircraft Employed: C–141 (two) and C–130 (five).
Operations: On the morning of July 16, an earthquake measuring 7.7 on the Richter scale struck Luzon in the northern Philippines. The area around Baguio, a mountain resort city north of Manila, suffered the most damage when many of its large buildings, including hotels and schools, collapsed. The earthquake killed more than 600 people, injured 2,600, and left thousands homeless.

The Philippine government immediately requested U.S. assistance. Clark AB was only 45 miles from the quake epicenter. Not heavily damaged by the earthquake, Clark served as a relief cargo terminal for the humanitarian airlift sponsored by the Office of Foreign Disaster Assistance.

On July 17, two MAC C–141 Starlifters flew 41 tons of relief equipment and supplies from the United States and Guam to Clark AB. One C–141, from the 438th Mil Alft Wg at McGuire AFB, New Jersey, loaded 24 search and rescue team members, dogs trained to find trapped victims, five Office of Foreign Disaster Assistance officials, and 13 tons of rescue equipment and supplies at Andrews AFB, Maryland.

The rescue workers, some of whom had had experience helping earthquake victims in Armenia in 1988 and 1989, came from the fire departments in Fairfax County, Virginia, and Dade County, Florida. The cargo included generators, power tools, water, food, and radios. The C–141 flew first to Travis AFB, California, where a 60th Mil Alft Wg crew took over for the 17-hour flight across the Pacific Ocean to Clark AB. The 7,200-mile journey required two aerial refuelings from SAC KC–135s.

The second C–141, flown by a 62d Mil Alft Wg crew, diverted from a mission at Hickam AFB, Hawaii, for the earthquake relief operation. It transported over 28 tons of relief supplies from Andersen AFB, Guam, to Clark AB. The cargo included tents, plastic sheeting, blankets, medical supplies, hard hats, picks, and shovels.

Five 374th Tac Alft Wg C–130s, stationed at Clark AB for training at the time of the earthquake, participated in the subsequent relief operation. The earthquake closed the main road between Manila and Baguio, making airlift especially critical. Between July 17 and August 1, the C–130s transported 541 tons of relief equipment and supplies and 2,446 passengers from Clark to the disaster area. The cargo consisted primarily of food, medical supplies, and tents.

The airplanes could not fly to Baguio directly until July 20, when the city's runway was repaired enough to tolerate C–130 landings. For three days the planes dropped off their cargo at San Fernando. Marine Corps helicopters ferried the cargo from San Fernando to Baguio, where a golf course was turned into a temporary helicopter landing zone. From July 20 through August 1, the C–130s delivered relief supplies directly from Clark AB to Baguio.

When the earthquake relief airlift ended at the beginning of August, seven MAC aircraft had delivered 582 tons of relief freight and 2,475 passengers. U.S. military personnel on the ground assisted the people of Luzon in their efforts to recover from the worst earthquake to hit the area in more than a decade. Little did they realize that an even worse catastrophe would strike the island less than a year later.

95.
Name: Panamanian Shipwreck.
Location: Yellow Sea.
Date(s): December 1–2, 1990.
Emergency: A ship with 22 crew members aboard ran aground on rocks.
Air Force Organization(s) Involved: 38th Air Rscu Sq.
Airlifted: 22 shipwrecked seamen.
Aircraft Employed: MH–60 (two).
Operations: On December 1, a blizzard in the Yellow Sea forced a Panamanian ship to run aground on rocks about six miles west of Kunsan, South Korea. Responding to a distress call, the 38th Air Rscu Sq at Osan AB launched two MH–60G Pave Hawk helicopters. The aircraft discovered the grounded ship and her crew of 22 aboard, but heavy snow and gigantic waves prevented an immediate rescue.

On December 2, when the wind and waves subsided, the helicopters returned to the shipwreck site. One hoisted all 22 seamen from the vessel and ferried them to a small island nearby. Both helicopters then transported the shipwreck victims to Kunsan AB for medical treatment.

96.
Name: Fiery Vigil.
Location: Republic of the Philippines.
Date(s): June 8–July 2, 1991.
Emergency: The eruption of Mount Pinatubo in the Philippines forced the evacuation of more than 18,000 people from U.S. military bases on Luzon.
Air Force Organization(s) Involved: Twenty-first Air Force; Twenty-second Air Force; 834th Alft Div; 60th, 62d, 63d, 437th, 438th, 445th, and 446th Mil Alft Wgs; 374th Tac Alft Wg; 624th Military Airlift Support Group; and 729th and 730th Mil Alft Sqs.
Airlifted: More than 15,000 passengers and over 2,000 tons of cargo.
Aircraft Employed: C–5 (12 missions), C–141 (195 missions), C–130 (38 missions), and C–9 (1 mission).
Operations: In June, Mount Pinatubo erupted on Luzon in the northern Philippines with a magnitude over seven times that of Mount Saint Helens in 1980. An estimated seven billion tons of ash spewed out of the volcano and a series of earthquakes shook the area. On June 15, the day of the worst eruption, Typhoon Yunya passed near Mount Pinatubo, dumping torrential rain that mixed with huge clouds of ash and descended like wet concrete on three U.S. military bases in the area: Clark AB, Subic Bay Naval Base, and Cubi Point NAS. The weight of the ash accumulating on roofs collapsed many structures. To evacuate U.S. military personnel and their families from the Luzon bases, the Navy and Air Force executed an operation called Fiery Vigil.

Earth tremors around the volcano a few days before the eruption had warned personnel at Clark AB, about 10 miles west of Mount Pinatubo. The Pacific Air Forces began evacuating aircraft from Clark AB on June 8. That same day, a 374th Tac Alft Wg C–9A evacuated premature babies, their mothers, and medical attendants from the base hospital to Kadena AB in Japan. Most Clark AB personnel evacuated by land to Subic Bay, about 30 miles to the southwest, before the first violent eruption on June 12. Remaining personnel left for the naval base on June 15.

The continuing eruption rained ash on Subic Bay and Cubi Point NAS as well as Clark AB. Clouds of abrasive ash in the atmosphere forced cancellation of aircraft flights at the military installations and at Manila's international airport. As living conditions worsened at Subic Bay, the Navy began on June 16 to evacuate thousands of U.S. military personnel and their dependents by ship to Mactan International Airport on Cebu Island, 350 miles away from the volcano in the southern Philippines. From there, Air Force and commercial aircraft flew evacuees to Andersen AFB in Guam as the first stage in their return to the United States.

Lt. Col. David L. Spracher, director of operations for the 374th Tac Alft Wg, directed the airlift from Mactan. For a time, the Navy ships, including two aircraft carriers, delivered evacuees to Mactan faster than aircraft could take them away, but an increase in air missions eventually shortened waiting times on Cebu. More than 100 C–141 flights and six C–5 flights airlifted more than 14,000 passengers from Mactan to Andersen AFB in June. A pair of C–141s transported hospital patients from Mactan to Kadena AB for later flights to Hickam AFB in Hawaii. Commercial airliners transported additional thousands of evacuees from the Philippines to Guam.

After the ash rain decreased at Cubi Point NAS on Luzon at the end of June, engineers cleared a runway, and the 374th Tac Alft Wg began transporting U.S. citizens from there to Mactan and Andersen AFB. The wing's C–130s evacuated more than 1,400 passengers from Cubi Point to Guam.

Fifty-nine flights—57 by C–141s and two by C–5s—airlifted more than 7,900 passengers from Andersen AFB to the United States in the next stage of Fiery Vigil. The evacuees traveled by way of Hickam AFB, or Yokota AB in Japan and Elmendorf AFB in Alaska. The Military Airlift Command's 834th Alft Div coordinated the trans-Pacific flights. Commercial aircraft transported about 11,000 additional passengers from Guam to the United States. The evacuees landed at one of three Air Force bases in the United States designated as repatriation centers: McChord in Washington and Travis and Norton in California. Over half of the evacuees went to McChord.

Fiery Vigil was the largest evacuation operation to the United States since the fall of South Vietnam in 1975. It transported more than 18,000 U.S. citizens, including 14,646 civilian dependents of military personnel, almost halfway around the world. Fiery Vigil demonstrated the ability of different branches of the armed forces and commercial airline companies to work together and reduced the suffering of thousands of people.

Americans were not the only beneficiaries of Air Force airlift missions responding to the eruption of Mount Pinatubo. When conditions in Luzon improved enough for them to land, two MAC C–5 Galaxies also transported 34 pallets of excess Desert Storm rations from Dhahran, Saudi Arabia, to the Philippines to help feed the thousands of local people who were forced from their homes by the eruption.

Mount Pinatubo closed the oldest and largest U.S. overseas air base. On July 17, 1991, the United States announced that Clark AB would not reopen. The cost of rehabilitating the field exceeded the anticipated benefits as the Cold War drew to a close. But U.S. naval facilities on Luzon, however, were expected to remain in operation a little longer.

97.
Name: Tropical Storm Zelda.
Location: Marshall Islands.
Date(s): December 1991.
Emergency: A tropical storm devastated Kwajalein Atoll in the Marshall Islands with high winds, waves, and rain.

Air Force Organization(s) Involved: Twenty-second Air Force and 834th Alft Div.

Airlifted: The equivalent of six C–130 loads.

Aircraft Employed: Unspecified.

Operations: On November 28, Tropical Storm Zelda struck Kwajalein Atoll in the Marshall Islands, damaging or destroying much property with high winds, waves, and rain. After President Bush declared the region a major disaster area on December 6, FEMA supervised relief activities. The Defense Department supported the effort, providing debris removal, utility repair, food, water, and shelter through the Pacific Command.

Twenty-second Air Force cargo aircraft flew two special assignment airlift missions for the Marshall Islands relief operation. They transported to Kwajalein the equivalent of six C–130 loads of humanitarian supplies from Andersen AFB, Guam, and Hickam AFB, Hawaii. To help distribute the supplies arriving by air and sea, the Army flew two UH–60 Blackhawk helicopters. The military delivery and distribution of food, medical supplies, and construction supplies to storm victims hastened their recovery.

98.

Name: Typhoon Val.

Location: American Samoa and Western Samoa.

Date(s): December 1991 and January 1992.

Emergency: A typhoon hit Samoa, destroying or damaging hundreds of homes and depriving people of electricity, running water, and communications.

Air Force Organization(s) Involved: Twenty-second Air Force, 834th Alft Div, 436th Alft Wg, 709th Alft Sq, and 60th Alft Wg.

Airlifted: 36 tons of food and medical supplies; plastic sheeting, 5,000 cots, 2,500 water cans, and 15 generators; and 118 support personnel.

Aircraft Employed: C–5 and C–141 (at least 12 missions).

Operations: In early December, Typhoon Val hit Samoa in the southwestern Pacific Ocean. The storm's strong winds deprived the islands of electricity, clean running water, and communications. The typhoon also destroyed or damaged hundreds of homes.

The United States administered the territory of American Samoa, the eastern islands in the group. Not long after the governor appealed for U.S. emergency assistance, President Bush declared the islands a major disaster area, setting in motion a relief operation under the control of FEMA. Western Samoa, an independent nation comprising the larger islands in the Samoan group, also appealed to the United States for disaster relief, which was coordinated by the Office of Foreign Disaster Assistance. The Defense Department's joint Pacific Command supported both relief organizations in the emergency.

The Pacific Command depended on MAC for airlift support. The Twenty-second Air Force, which conducted routine channel missions across the Pacific

Ocean, diverted at least nine C–5 Galaxies and three C–141 Starlifter jet transport aircraft to assist both American Samoa and Western Samoa during December. The 834th Alft Div of the Twenty-second Air Force also participated in the airlift, as did the 60th Alft Wg. Sixteen missions transported relief supplies from bases around the Pacific, including Hickam AFB in Hawaii, Andersen AFB in Guam, Osan AB in South Korea, and Yokota AB in Japan. Aircraft loading in Korea staged in Japan on the way to Samoa. One C–5 flight originated at Andrews AFB, Maryland, stopping in California on the way to Pago Pago, administrative capital of American Samoa. Most flights went to Pago Pago, but at least one C–5 unloaded at Apia, capital of Western Samoa. Cargoes included huge rolls of plastic sheeting, 5,000 cots, 2,500 water cans, 15 electric generators, and 118 support personnel.

The relief effort extended into early 1992. On January 5, a 436th Alft Wg C–5, flown by a 709th Alft Sq crew, transported 36 tons of food and medical supplies to Pago Pago.

99.
Name: Typhoon Omar.
Location: Guam.
Date(s): August 29–September 25, 1992.
Emergency: A typhoon, bringing winds up to 150 mph and 16 inches of rain, hit Guam, leaving 5,000 people homeless and many more without electricity or running water.
Air Force Organization(s) Involved: 60th, 62d, 63d, 349th, 374th, and 445th Alft Wgs; and 15th, 21st, 22d, 53d, and 730th Alft Sqs.
Airlifted: Almost 2,000 tons of food, medical supplies, construction equipment, generators, charcoal, and other relief supplies; and 793 passengers, mostly military engineering personnel and relief workers.
Aircraft Employed: C–5 (21 missions), C–141 (27 missions), and C–130 (9 missions).
Operations: On the evening of August 27, Typhoon Omar hit Guam in the Mariana Islands of the western Pacific, bringing winds as high as 150 mph and 16 inches of rain. The storm destroyed or damaged thousands of houses, leaving 5,000 people homeless and thousands more without electricity or running water. Omar was the worst typhoon to hit Guam since 1976 (see Typhoon Pamela, May–June 1976). President Bush declared the island a federal disaster area.

To direct and coordinate military disaster relief for Guam, the Pacific Command activated the Joint Task Force Marianas under RADM Edward K. Kristensen. He relied on units of AMC, PACAF, and the AF Res for airlift missions. These included the Twenty-second Air Force's 60th, 62d, and 63d Alft Wgs from California and Washington; the Air Force Reserve's 445th Alft Wg from California; and the Pacific Air Forces 374th Alft Wg from Yokota AB, Japan. The Air Mobility Command's Twenty-first Air Force could not support the operation because it was flying relief missions in response to Hurricane Andrew, which hit southern Florida at about the same time that Typhoon Omar hit Guam (see Chapter 1, Hurricane Andrew, August–October 1992).

The airlift began on August 29, as soon as the runway at Andersen AFB was cleared of debris and declared safe. By mid-September, the Air Force had flown 57 relief flights to Guam: 21 were flown by C–5 Galaxies, 27 by C–141 Starlifters, and 9 by C–130 Hercules aircraft. The transports delivered 1,998 tons of cargo and 793 passengers, most of whom were relief workers and military construction personnel, from U.S. bases around the Pacific and from the United States. Cargo included heavy construction equipment, generators, food, medical supplies, and charcoal. Some of the flights were Twenty-second Air Force channel flights that stopped at Guam on previously scheduled trans-Pacific missions, but most were special assignment airlift missions to Guam. For example, on September 1, a C–5 transported 62 tons of relief supplies from Yokota AB to Guam. Some AMC aircraft participating in Typhoon Omar relief operations depended on the Tanker Airlift Control Center at Scott AFB, Illinois, for scheduling.

The Joint Task Force Marianas concluded Typhoon Omar relief operations on September 19, but Air Force aircraft continued to deliver relief supplies to Andersen AFB until at least September 25. The airlift, in conjunction with sealift operations by the Navy and ground support from Navy and Air Force organizations stationed on the island, helped thousands of people in Guam recover from one of the worst storms ever to hit the Marianas.

100.
Name: Typhoon Iniki.
Location: Hawaii.
Date(s): September 12–about October 18, 1992.
Emergency: A typhoon hit Kauai with sustained winds of 130 mph, leaving at least 7,000 people homeless.
Air Force Organization(s) Involved: 60th, 62d, 63d, 137th, 146th, 349th, 374th, 436th, 445th, 463d, and 512th Alft Wgs; 154th, 162d, and 176th Comp Gps; 15th, 25th, 53d, 75th, 326th, 517th, 710th, and 729th Alft Sqs; and 168th Air Refueling Squadron.
Airlifted: 6,888 tons of generators, plastic sheeting, food, cots, mobile showers, mobile kitchens, blankets, tents, construction equipment, medical supplies, utility trucks, and other relief equipment and supplies; and more than 12,000 passengers, including military and civilian relief workers and evacuating tourists and residents.
Aircraft Employed: C–5 (37 missions), C–141 (77 missions), C–130 (464 missions), and KC–135 (number unspecified).
Operations: Typhoon Iniki hit Kauai, Hawaii, on September 11, less than a month after Hurricane Andrew devastated southern Florida (see Chapter 1, Hurricane Andrew, August–October 1992) and Typhoon Omar hit Guam (see

Typhoon Omar, August–September 1992). With wind gusts as high as 160 mph, Typhoon Iniki destroyed or heavily damaged thousands of homes, leaving at least 7,000 people homeless. The governor of Hawaii, John Waihee, asked for federal assistance, and President Bush declared Kauai a disaster area. The Federal Emergency Management Agency called on other federal agencies to participate in the third major relief effort for U.S. storm victims in a month.

The Defense Department organized a joint task force consisting of Army, Navy, Air Force, Marine Corps, and Coast Guard elements. Col. Robert E. Hammond and Col. Earl Harrington supervised the airlift portion of the relief operation, which involved aircraft and crews from AMC, PACAF, the AF Res, and the ANG. At least 11 airlift wings and three composite groups eventually took part in the relief airlift. Among the participating airlift wings were the 60th, 62d, 63d, 436th, and 463d of AMC; the 349th, 445th, and 512th Alft Wgs of the AF Res; the 137th and 146th Alft Wgs of the ANG; and the 374th Alft Wg of PACAF.

Between September 12 and mid-October, the Air Force conducted at least 578 missions to or from Kauai in the relief operation, including 464 C–130 flights, 77 C–141 flights, and 37 C–5 missions. Some KC–135s from AMC took part as cargo carriers beyond their normal air refueling duties. In just over a month, the air fleet delivered 6,888 tons of equipment and supplies, including generators, construction equipment, electrical utility trucks, medical supplies, plastic sheeting, tents, cots, blankets, food, mobile showers and kitchens, and other relief cargo.

Military transport aircraft also moved more than 12,000 passengers during the operation, including almost 1,500 Kauai tourists and residents to hotels on neighboring Oahu for temporary shelter and nearly 4,500 military workers to Kauai for a secondary cleanup operation called Clean Sweep. Thousands of Red Cross and civilian workers rode aboard the Air Force transports.

In the first week, 53 flights transported 1,500 tons of cargo and 1,316 passengers from the continental United States to the disaster area. Most of the flights were special assignment airlift missions, but some trans-Pacific channel flights of the Twenty-second Air Force also transported relief supplies to Hawaii. At first, the larger C–5s and C–141s dropped their cargoes on Oahu for delivery to Kauai by smaller C–130s, but after Kauai's runway at Lihue was repaired, the Galaxies and Starlifters flew directly to Kauai.

The relief operation demonstrated the ability of the services to work together in a joint task force, reinforcing the total force concept. By October 19, ANG aircraft alone transported 8,282 passengers and 2,713 tons of cargo to and from Kauai. The operation also proved the ability of DoD to conduct three large relief efforts simultaneously.

Humanitarian Airlift Operations

101.
Name: Provide Refuge.
Location: Marshall Islands.
Date(s): February 13–March 9, 1993.
Emergency: 535 Chinese refugees from a disabled freighter needed food and other relief supplies.
Air Force Organization(s) Involved: Twenty-second Air Force and 60th and 62d Alft Wgs.
Airlifted: At least 18 tons of relief supplies and hundreds of passengers.
Aircraft Employed: C–5 (one) and C–141 (five).
Operations: In early February, a freighter heading for the United States carrying 535 Chinese refugees suffered engine failure. As food and water aboard the ship ran low, the crew broadcast distress signals. A Coast Guard ship responded, towing the ship to nearby Kwajalein Atoll in the Marshall Islands.

Between February 13 and March 9, the Twenty-second Air Force airlifted 18 tons of food and other relief supplies from Hawaii to Kwajalein to sustain the refugees. A C–5 and a C–141 participated in the operation, which was called Provide Refuge. The two aircraft also transported 118 passengers. Subsequently, four AMC C–141s and three commercial contract aircraft carried the refugees to Hawaii, where immigration officials would determine whether they would be admitted to the United States.

Glossary

and

Note on Sources

Glossary

AAF	Army Air Forces
AB	Air Base
AB Gp	Air Base Group
AB Wg	Air Base Wing
Aeromed Alft Sq	Aeromedical Airlift Squadron
Aeromed Alft Wg	Aeromedical Airlift Wing
Aeromed Evac Gp	Aeromedical Evacuation Group
Aeromed Evac Sq	Aeromedical Evacuation Squadron
Aerosp RR Gp	Aerospace Rescue and Recovery Group
Aerosp RR Sq	Aerospace Rescue and Recovery Squadron
Aerosp RR Wg	Aerospace Rescue and Recovery Wing
AFB	Air Force Base
AF Res	Air Force Reserve
AID	Agency for International Development
Air Comdo Sq	Air Commando Squadron
Air Comdo Wg	Air Commando Wing
Air Div	Air Division
Air Rscu Cen	Air Rescue Center
Air Rscu Gp	Air Rescue Group
Air Rscu Sq	Air Rescue Squadron
Air Rscu Svc	Air Rescue Service
Air Trpt Gp	Air Transport Group
Air Trpt Sq	Air Transport Squadron
Air Trpt Wg	Air Transport Wing
Alft Div	Airlift Division
Alft Gp	Airlift Group
Alft Sq	Airlift Squadron
Alft Wg	Airlift Wing
AMC	Air Mobility Command
ANG	Air National Guard
AS	Air Station
B–17	Flying Fortress, four-engine propeller heavy bomber (in World War II)
B–25	Mitchell, twin-engine propeller medium bomber
B–26	Marauder, twin-engine propeller medium bomber

B–29	Superfortress, four-engine propeller very heavy bomber (in World War II)
BIFC	Boise Interagency Fire Center
C–5	Galaxy, four-engine jet transport
C–7	Caribou, twin-engine propeller transport
C–9	Nightingale, twin-engine jet transport
C–12	Huron, small twin-engine propeller utility aircraft
C–21	Small twin-engine jet transport
C–45	Expediter, twin-engine propeller transport
C–46	Commando, twin-engine propeller transport
C–47	Skytrain, twin-engine propeller transport
C–54	Skymaster, four-engine propeller transport
C–74	Globemaster I, four-engine propeller transport
C–82	Packet, twin-engine propeller transport
C–97	Stratofreighter, four-engine propeller transport
C–118	Liftmaster, four-engine propeller transport
C–119	Flying Boxcar, twin-engine propeller transport
C–121	Super Constellation, four-engine propeller transport
C–123	Provider, twin-engine propeller transport
C–124	Globemaster II, four-engine propeller transport
C–130	Hercules, four-engine turboprop transport
C–131	Samaritan, twin-engine propeller transport
C–133	Cargomaster, four-engine propeller transport
C–135	Stratolifter, four-engine jet transport
C–137	Stratoliner, modified Boeing 707, four-engine jet transport
C–141	Starlifter, four-engine jet transport
CH–3	H–3 modified for cargo
CH–21	H–21 modified for cargo
CH–43	H–43 modified for cargo
CH–47	H–47 modified for cargo
CH–53	H–53 modified for cargo
C.A.R.E.	Cooperative for American Remittances Everywhere

CIS	Commonwealth of Independent States
Comp Gp	Composite Group
Comp Wg	Composite Wing
CONAC	Continental Air Command
DoD	Department of Defense
East Trpt AF	Eastern Transport Air Force
EEE	Eastern Equine Encephalomyelitis
F–51	(P–51) Mustang, small single-engine propeller fighter
F–80	Shooting Star, jet fighter
F–82	(P–82) Twin Mustang, twin-engine propeller fighter
F–84	Thunderjet, jet fighter
FAA	Federal Aviation Administration
FEMA	Federal Emergency Management Agency
Ftr Gp	Fighter Group
Ftr Wg	Fighter Wing
Ftr Wpns Wg	Fighter Weapons Wing
H–1	Iroquois, small helicopter
H–3	Sea King, large helicopter
H–5	Small utility and rescue helicopter
H–13	Sioux, small utility and rescue helicopter
H–16	Very large helicopter prototype
H–19	Chickasaw, rescue and utility helicopter
H–21	Workhorse (Bent Banana), large helicopter
H–21B	A model of H–21
H–34	Choctaw, large rescue helicopter
H–43	Huskie (Pedro), small rescue helicopter
H–47	Chinook, large helicopter
H–53	Sea Stallion, large helicopter
H–60	Pave Hawk, large helicopter
HC–54	C–54 modified for search and rescue
HC–97	C–97 modified for search and rescue
HC–130	C–130 modified for search and rescue
HH–1	H–1 modified for search and rescue
HH–3	Jolly Green Giant, H–3 modified for search and rescue
HH–19	H–19 modified for search and rescue

HH–19B	A model of H–19 modified for search and rescue
HH–34	H–34 modified for search and rescue
HH–43	H–43 modified for search and rescue
HH–43B	A model of H–43 modified for search and rescue
HH–53	Super Jolly Green Giant, H–53 modified for search and rescue
HH–60	H–60 modified for search and rescue
HU–16	Albatross, amphibious twin-engine propeller transport
HU–16B	A model of HU–16
JCS	Joint Chiefs of Staff
KC–10	Three-engine jet refueler/transport, tanker version of DC–10 airliner
KC–97	C–97 modified as a refueling tanker
KC–135	Stratotanker, C–135 modified as a refueling tanker
L–4	Piper Cub, small single-engine airplane
L–5	Sentinel, small single-engine airplane
L–20	Beaver, single-engine sea plane
MH–53	H–53 modified for special operations
MH–60	H–60 modified for special operations
MAC	Military Airlift Command
MAFFS	Modular Airborne Fire-Fighting System
MATS	Military Air Transport Service
Mil Alft Gp	Military Airlift Group
Mil Alft Sq	Military Airlift Squadron
Mil Alft Wg	Military Airlift Wing
mph	Miles per hour
NAS	Naval Air Station
NATO	North Atlantic Treaty Organization
O–2	Small twin-engine observation airplane
OIRSA	Organismo International Regional de Sanidad Agropecuaria (International Regional Organization for Agricultural Health)

Ops Gp	Operations Group
Ops Sq	Operations Squadron
PACAF	Pacific Air Forces
R6D	Liftmaster, U.S. Navy version of C–118 (in MATS)
RB–26	B–26 modified for reconnaissance
RC–130	C–130 modified for reconnaissance
RF–51	F–51 modified for reconnaissance
RF–80	F–80 modified for reconnaissance
RF–84	F–84 modified for reconnaissance
RAF	Royal Air Force
Rscu Sq	Rescue Squadron
Rscu Un	Rescue Unit
SA–16	HU–16 modified for search and rescue
SB–17	B–17 modified for search and rescue
SB–29	B–29 modified for search and rescue
SC–54	C–54 modified for search and rescue
SH–19	H–19 modified for search and rescue
SR–71	Blackbird, twin-jet supersonic reconnaissance aircraft
SAC	Strategic Air Command
Sp Ops Gp	Special Operations Group
Sp Ops Sq	Special Operations Squadron
Sp Ops Wg	Special Operations Wing
T–6	Texan, single-engine propeller trainer
T–7	Navigator, twin-engine propeller trainer
T–11	Kansan, twin-engine propeller trainer
T–29	Convair-Liner, twin-engine propeller trainer, similar to C–131
T–33	T-Bird, single-engine jet trainer
T–39	Sabreliner, twin-engine jet trainer
TAC	Tactical Air Command
Tac Alft Gp	Tactical Airlift Group
Tac Alft Sq	Tactical Airlift Squadron
Tac Alft Wg	Tactical Airlift Wing
Tac Ftr Gp	Tactical Fighter Group
Tac Ftr Wg	Tactical Fighter Wing
Trp Carr Gp	Troop Carrier Group
Trp Carr Sq	Troop Carrier Squadron

Trp Carr Wg	Troop Carrier Wing
TUSLOG	The United States Logistic Group
U–6	Beaver, single-engine propeller light cargo airplane
U–10	Courier, single-engine propeller utility airplane
UC–123	Modified C–123
UC–123K	A model of UC–123
UH–1	Utility helicopter, see H–1
UH–1N	Utility helicopter, a model of H–1
UH–3A	Utility helicopter, a model of H–3
UH–16	Utility helicopter, see H–16
UH–19	Utility helicopter, see H–19
UH–60	Utility helicopter, see H–60
UH–60G	Utility helicopter, a model of UH–60
UN	United Nations
UNICEF	United Nations International Children's Emergency Fund
U.S. South Comd	United States Southern Command
USAF	United States Air Force
USAF South Air Div	USAF Southern Air Division
USAF South Comd	USAF Southern Command
USAFE	United States Air Forces in Europe
USEUCOM	United States European Command
USSR	Union of Soviet Socialist Republics
VC–137	C–137 modified for transporting VIPs, sometimes used as Air Force One
VEE	Venezuelan Equine Encephalomyelitis
VT–29	Modified T–29
WC–130	C–130 modified for weather reconnaissance
West Trpt AF	Western Transport Air Force
YC–97	Experimental version of C–97
YC–124	Experimental version of C–124
YH–13	Experimental version of H–13

Note on Sources

Most of the information for this book comes from three general sets of sources: the document collection of the Air Force Historical Research Agency at Maxwell AFB, Alabama; the books and periodicals of the neighboring Air University Library; and, for the most recent operations, notes and documents from Air Force command history offices, because organizational histories and published works were not yet available.

I relied primarily on organizational histories. Among them were command histories, such as those of the Military Air Transport Service, the Military Airlift Command, the Air Mobility Command, the Caribbean Air Command, the Southern Air Command, the United States Air Forces in Europe, the Pacific Air Forces, and the Tactical Air Command. Monographs produced in command history offices were also invaluable. Histories of the Air Force Reserve; the Aerospace Rescue and Recovery Service; the Twenty-first and Twenty-second Air Forces; the 315th, 322d, and 834th Air Divisions; and a host of wings and squadrons provided most of the primary source information.

For information on the disasters or emergencies, I depended heavily on newspapers and periodicals such as the *New York Times*, *Washington Post*, *Time*, *Life*, *Newsweek*, and *U.S. News and World Report*. Important details came from periodicals by or about the Air Force, such as *Air Force Times*, *Airman*, *Air Reservist*, *Citizen Airman*, and *Air Force Magazine*.

Joseph P. Tustin's *USAFE Humanitarian Missions, 1945-1962* and Timothy A. Fuhrman's *Humanitarian Airlift: U.S. Response to Natural Calamity, 1960-1974* were valuable sources.

www.ingramcontent.com/pod-product-compliance
Lightning Source LLC
Chambersburg PA
CBHW050925150426
42812CB00051B/2315